A National Newspaper Foundation Project

The Newspaper

Everything You Need to Know to Make It in the Newspaper Business

D. Earl Newsom
and 28 Media Experts for the National Newspaper Foundation

Introduction by Walter W. Grunfeld

A SPECTRUM BOOK

PRENTICE-HALL, INC., Englewood Cliffs, New Jersey 07632

Library of Congress Cataloging in Publication Data

NEWSOM, D. EARL.
  The newspaper.

  Bibliography: p.
  Includes index.
  1. Journalism. 2. Advertising, Newspaper.
3. Newspaper publishing—United States. I. National
Newspaper Foundation (U.S.) II. Title.
PN4775.N44   070.5   81–1003
ISBN 0–13–616045–X   AACR2
ISBN 0–13–616037–9 (pbk.)

Editorial/production supervision by Louise M. Marcewicz
Interior design by Christine Gehring Wolf
Cover design by Graphikann
Manufacturing buyer: Cathie Lenard

© 1981 by Prentice-Hall, Inc., Englewood Cliffs, New Jersey 07632

A SPECTRUM BOOK

10   9   8   7   6   5   4   3   2   1

Printed in the United States of America

This Spectrum Book can be made available
to businesses and organizations at a special discount
when ordered in large quantities. For more
information, contact:

    Prentice-Hall, Inc.
    General Book Marketing
    Special Sales Division
    Englewood Cliffs, New Jersey 07632

Prentice-Hall International, Inc., *London*
Prentice-Hall of Australia Pty. Limited, *Sydney*
Prentice-Hall of Canada, Ltd., *Toronto*
Prentice-Hall of India Private Limited, *New Delhi*
Prentice-Hall of Japan, Inc., *Tokyo*
Prentice-Hall of Southeast Asia Pte. Ltd., *Singapore*
Whitehall Books Limited, *Wellington, New Zealand*

Contents

INTRODUCTION
by Walter W. Grunfeld

page xi

ACKNOWLEDGMENTS
by D. Earl Newsom

page xii

Chapter 1
A Nation of Hometown Newspapers
by Neale Copple

page 1

Chapter 2
Covering the News
by Kenneth R. Byerly

page 7

Chapter 3
The Basics
of Good News Writing
by René J. (Jack) Cappon

page 15

Chapter 4
News Headline Writing—
As Art and Craft
by Richard D. Smyser

page 22

Chapter 5
The Editorial Page
by Paul Greenberg

page 27

Chapter 6
Handling News Pictures
by Kenneth Blum

page 33

Chapter 7
Using Readership Research
by Maxwell E. McCombs

page 44

Chapter 8
Newspaper Page Design
by Kenneth C. Bronson

page 55

Chapter 9
Newspaper Production
by Robert E. Schweitz

page 71

Chapter 10
The Retail Advertising Budget
by Stephen J. Van Osten

page 79

Chapter 11
**Market Data—
The Basis of Advertising Sales**
by John L. Fournier, Jr.

page 95

Chapter 12

**Approaches
to Selling Advertising**

by Morley L. Piper

page 100

Chapter 13

**Advertising Gimmicks
and Special Promotions**

by James S. Steele

page 108

Chapter 14

**Cooperative Advertising—
A Neglected Source of Revenue**

by C. Randall Choate

page 116

Chapter 15

Creating Display Advertisements

by Roy Paul Nelson

page 123

Chapter 16

Classified Advertising

by Cal Tremblay

page 133

Chapter 17

The Business of Journalism

by Gene Chamberlin

page 143

Chapter 18

Marketing the Newspaper

by George W. Trotter

page 151

Chapter 19

**The Shopper—
Friend or Foe?**
by William E. Branen

page 162

Chapter 20

Managing Personnel
by Candi Van Meter

page 170

Chapter 21

The Minority Press
by Carolyn A. Stroman and Paula M. Poindexter

page 183

Chapter 22

**Labor Relations
in the Newspaper Industry**
by John B. Jaske

page 188

Chapter 23

**Public Notices,
Postal Laws, and Other Legal Issues**
by William A. Bray

page 203

Chapter 24

Libel and Invasion of Privacy
by David L. Hill

page 210

Chapter 25
Antitrust Law
and the Newspaper Industry
by Robert L. Ballow

page 219

Chapter 26
Evaluating Newspaper Properties
by Gerald L. Grotta

page 229

Chapter 27
The Newspaper Associations
by Irvan J. Kummerfeldt

page 234

Chapter 28
Things to Remember—
for Today and Tomorrow
by D. Earl Newsom

page 240

GLOSSARY

page 245

BIBLIOGRAPHY

page 247

INDEX

page 251

Introduction

by Walter W. Grunfeld

Close contact with fellow editors and publishers of community newspapers during my tour of the United States a number of years ago as president of the National Newspaper Association (NNA) convinced me that I had a number of allies who strongly believe that (1) community journalism should receive greater attention in the nation's journalism schools and (2) these schools are in serious need of a text which would be helpful in giving adequate exposure to the subject.

Those of us in the field are fully aware that young journalism students graduating today are basically unfamiliar with the numerous positive aspects of our profession. Most of us enjoy our work tremendously and find it totally fulfilling, but all too often we have difficulty projecting our thoughts and our true feelings on community journalism.

The more I talked to people on my tours, which eventually covered close to 60,000 miles in thirty-eight states and two foreign countries, the more I was convinced that the time had come to promote the publication of a new text. The last book (by Kenneth Byerly) appeared almost twenty years ago.

The idea was presented to my colleagues at the NNA, who gave it their immediate endorsement and thought it would be a perfect project, with the National Newspaper Foundation (NNF) to act as a clearinghouse for raising the necessary funds.

Initially, contact was made with key publishers who saw merit in the text, other press associations, and other foundations which shared the opinion that time was now at hand for a new book.

While much correspondence and many personal calls followed, raising funds was not the most difficult project I have ever handled. I received almost instant cooperation and interest from several of our own weekly publishers, the American Newspaper Publishers Association, the Gannett Foundation, and several deans of journalism schools, as well as two publishing concerns.

After the necessary funds were obtained, a committee was established by the NNA on which donors and key publishers were invited to serve as an editorial opinion and content forum. Its basic responsibility was to advertise for and later interview candidates to act as text editor. All of us on the committee were delighted and honored by the unanimous selection of D. Earl Newsom, a well-qualified and prominent journalism educator and former newspaperman with a national reputation and following.

Since his selection as editor, Earl has had contact with key people whose expertise on various subjects in our profession is well known and well accepted. Consequently, we have been able to attract top talent to act as authors and contributors, who, as a team, have made this entire effort possible.

Shortly after the selection of the editor, as we began to focus on basic newspaper problems, our efforts underwent a significant change of course. As the saying goes, a funny thing happened on our way to a community journalism book. The more we talked with publishers and employees, and the more we probed specific problems, the more we came to realize that the information we were gathering could be used to help *all* newspapers, not just community newspapers. We saw that most of the problems of newspapers, regardless of size, are basically the same. There may be differences in magnitude, but not in substance.

Libel and antitrust laws and personnel and postal problems apply to all newspapers, community and metropolitan. So do problems of advertising, circulation, readership research, clear writing, and competition from free papers ("shoppers"). At the request of those concerned beyond the community field, we broadened the scope of our volume to serve the entire newspaper field. Our title, originally *Community Journalism,* became *The Newspaper.* Our book, we believe, will serve

WALTER W. GRUNFELD

Mr. Grunfeld is editor and publisher of The Independent Newspapers, Marathon, New York. He is a recipient of the Amos Award, the highest award given to a community journalism publisher in the United States. He is president of the National Newspaper Foundation and former president of the National Newspaper Association and of the New York Press Association. He conceived the idea that led to this journalism text.

"We saw that most of the problems of newspapers, regardless of size, are basically the same. There may be differences in magnitude, but not in substance."

as a valuable guide to any publisher or employee of any size newspaper and as an unusual text for a variety of journalism courses. It gives a total picture of the newspaper.

As you study these chapters, you will still find a strong community-journalism flavor that fulfills the original purpose. Our chapter on reporting, for instance, has been prepared primarily for community staffs, yet those on larger newspapers will find it helpful, too. This broadened scope makes the book a contribution to the entire field.

Helping to make this textbook possible has been a source of great pride to me personally, and I am grateful for the outstanding support I have had from so many throughout the country in this endeavor.

Most of all, however, I feel that the book will help our young people to succeed in our chosen field. Likewise, it will serve as a valuable reference text to those of us who struggle daily with knotty problems and always appreciate knowing how our colleagues find the right solution. It is to these ends and for the benefit of the newspapers of America that we have prepared this book.

Acknowledgments

by D. Earl Newsom

Putting together a volume of this magnitude has required the generous help of many individuals in the professional and academic fields. The editor and the National Newspaper Foundation are sincerely grateful to all those who gave time and effort because they wanted to help the cause described by Walter Grunfeld in the Introduction.

The editor is grateful to Walter and also to William G. Mullen, past executive vice president of the National Newspaper Association, and his staff, especially Margaret Walsh, who gave daily help and encouragement to the project, and to Peter A. Dragon, who headed the NNF textbook advisory committee during the early stages of the project.

Several authors rendered valuable help in addition to their chapter contributions. These included Dean Neale Copple, William E. Branen, Gene Chamberlin, Ken Byerly, Bill Bray, Dr. Maxwell E. McCombs, Morley Piper, and Professor Roy Paul Nelson.

Many National Newspaper Association members responded to the call for assistance. Some served as technical advisers and others as reviewers of chapters. These included Harold Hudson, Perryton (Texas) *Herald;* Eugene D. Johnson, White Bear Lake (Minnesota) *Press;* Fred Wulfkuhler, Paragould (Arkansas) *Daily Press;* John and Jackie Lou McMaster, Ayer (Massachusetts) *Public Spirit;* George Measer, Williamsville (New York) Bee Newspapers; Jim Pate, Madill (Oklahoma) *Record,* who helped untangle several chapters; and Robert M. White II, Mexico (Missouri) *Ledger,* whom we tried to coax into being a chapter author.

A special thanks must go to the entire staff of the Stillwater (Oklahoma) *Daily News-Press.* The facilities and resources of the newspaper were made available daily to help on this project. Special technical help was rendered by James R. Bellatti and Lawrence F. Bellatti, copublishers; Lee Bell, managing editor; Ken Light, advertising manager; Sam Viney, national advertising manager; Rick Bellatti, director of photography; Roland Treat, circulation manager; Leo Tunnell, production superintendent; and Dale Van Deventer, chief camera technician. Dale was responsible for handling some of the difficult art reproductions.

Among those in the academic field who made special contributions were Dr. Michael J. Petrick, Central Michigan University; Dr. Richard Lee, South Dakota State University; Dr. Harry Heath, Oklahoma State University; and Dr. Ronald Farrar, University of Kentucky.

Others rendered help on chapters or in special ways. Thomas D. Jones, president of Tazewell Publications, Morton, Illinois, and Edward W. Mehrer of Peat, Marwick, Mitchell & Co., Kansas City, aided in the chapter, "The Business of Journalism," Calvin Mayne of the Gannett Foundation was more than a member of the advisory committee: He suggested authors and offered valuable counsel. Jeffrey Colin Van, former editor of *Publishers' Auxiliary,* served as counselor and reviewer, and John Beddow, then of the Baltimore *Sun* advertising staff, provided valuable assistance on the chapter on advertising.

Reed Sarratt, executive director of the Southern Newspaper Publishers Association, always found time to respond to requests for information and assistance; Marion Krehbiel gave valuable help on the newspaper evaluation chapter. Terry Maguire, American Newspaper Publishers Association vice president for legal and government affairs, served as reviewer and counselor on several chapters; John Fournier's staff joined in gathering information for the market data chapter and this included Alva Thornbrugh, Jr., Peter Beer, Larry Hill, and Don Smith.

Marcia Wellwood, graduate assistant at Northern Illinois University, helped assemble information for the chapter on newspaper associations. Penny E. Homer of ANPA's public affairs department, was kind enough to locate material for the chapter, "The Business of Journalism."

The chapter on antitrust law was particularly tedious, and the editor is especially thankful for the special help rendered by Dean E. Westman, and later by Daniel C. Kaufman, both of the King & Ballow organization. Bill Boykin, executive director of the Inland Daily Press Association, was helpful in the section dealing with costs, and Shirley Dean, classified manager of Paddock Publications, Illinois, aided in providing perspective in the chapter on classified advertising. James D. Stuckey of the Newspaper Production and Research Center, Oklahoma City, helped prepare illustrative material for the chapter on news headlines, and A. E. P. Wall, editor of the Chicago *Catholic,* was a source of encouragement throughout the preparation of the manuscript. An expression of gratitude is certainly due Chandra Davis whose typing, retyping, and help on clerical chores made it possible to get twenty-eight chapters completed by deadline.

A final thanks to the people at Prentice-Hall who believed in the merit of this project and saw it through to completion, particularly Mary Kennan, Louise Marcewicz, Jeannette Jacobs, and Christine Gehring Wolf.

During the past two years, the editor has been in contact with scores of individuals, and undoubtedly some names have been overlooked. To these people, the editor apologizes. The omissions do not reflect lack of appreciation, only the fact that some names may have been lost in the stacks of information and paper.

Chapter 1

A Nation of Hometown Newspapers

by Neale Copple

As journalism moves into the last decades of the twentieth century, there is the distinct possibility that specialization may have gone too far. From a pool of specialists, how do you pick the future managers? Among the smaller newspapers—the overwhelming majority in this country—where do you find or how do you train generalists in a world of specialists?

Neither of those questions is hypothetical. Many of the profession's leaders have been asking such questions as, Why should my news staff members be ignorant of my newspaper's economy? Or, on the other hand, Why should my business staff members be uneducated in the basic news functions of this newspaper?

In one sense, that is what this book is all about. In part, it was written with the assumption that there is no excuse for ignorance among specialists about the total newspaper. It was written with the assumption that there is no excuse for the same kind of blissful ignorance among journalism students, whether majoring in news, advertising, photography, or one of the other facets of the business. There is another very practical reason for the "total newspaper" concept. That reason requires an understanding of the American newspaper business itself.

American journalists are often aghast when they go abroad or when they play host to foreign journalists.

Almost without exception they run into what one might call the *national newspaper concept*. That concept is simply the supposition that there must be in this country a handful of newspapers that are national newspapers which serve and influence most of the people of the United States.

It is easy to trace the national newspaper syndrome to its source. In most countries of the world there are national newspapers. In many places, such as Great Britain, national newspapers serve millions of readers over a relatively small geographical area. In other places, such as Russia, national newspapers serve millions of readers over a relatively large geographical area. And, at least in the case of Russia, the national newspapers carry the governmental line.

In foreign nations where there are national newspapers, there also exists a provincial press. Obviously, that refers to the smaller, regional newspapers out in the provinces. Thus, to some the word *provincial* is not exactly flattering. In many countries it indicates a lack of sophistication and something less than cosmopolitanism. Not so in the United States. One of the reasons foreign journalists and foreign governmental leaders do not understand the American press is that they do not understand that it is a press composed *entirely* of provincial newspapers.

NEALE COPPLE

The author is dean of journalism at the University of Nebraska, a former newspaperman, and author of journalism texts.

"The vast majority of the American press is made up of small and medium-sized newspapers. While there is and needs to be specialization on those newspapers, their very size and mission require knowledge about the total newspaper."

Hometown Newspapers Dominate

Some journalists don't like the word *provincial,* either, and there is a better word: *hometown.* We are a nation of hometown newspapers.

1

Oh, American journalism does have its great metropolitan newspapers. The one most often mentioned first by foreign journalists in the New York *Times.* Or foreign business persons may pick our great business newspaper, the *Wall Street Journal.* And certainly there are other great metropolitan giants. But all together they are but a handful compared with the rest of the nation's newspapers. Even the metropolitan newspapers, with their huge circulations, serve only a minority of the nation's readers.

For example, among the nation's smallest newspapers—those dailies and weeklies with circulations of 10,000 or less—there are some 9,000 publications. That group of small newspapers alone has an estimated circulation of 38 million to 150 million readers. Those are the smaller newspapers. What about the larger ones?

The American Newspaper Publishers Association (ANPA) statistics for 1980 showed 1,576 daily newspapers. That list combined morning and evening papers in many instances. Of those 1,576 papers, only 124 exceeded 100,000 in circulation. That is only 7.8 percent of all the daily newspapers in the country. The clincher, however, came with the location of the median newspaper, the one in the very middle of the size range: the Barre-Montpelier (Vermont) *Times-Argus,* with a circulation of 12,054. These statistics speak with some finality to those who might doubt that America is a country of hometown newspapers.

The logic becomes rather obvious. The vast majority of the American press is made up of small and medium-sized newspapers. While there is and needs to be specialization on those newspapers, their very size and mission require knowledge about the total newspaper.

This book becomes, then, a kind of handbook for the general practitioner of journalism. It is not a challenge to the metropolitan newspapers, for there is much here that can help them, too. It is, instead, an effort to put the nation's hometown newspapers into perspective at a time when they are more vigorous and their opportunities are greater than ever before in history.

METROS, SMALL WEEKLIES

Countless publishers and editors have tried to emphasize the uniqueness of their newspaper. They have done it in their mastheads and as part of their nameplates. Their favorite proclamation is something like "The only newspaper in the world that gives a damn about our town."

That slogan may be a touch oversimplified, but it does focus on the basic strength of the newspaper. Both the metros and the smaller newspapers publish for the public. Both have a sense of community service. However, the giant newspaper has no choice but to scatter its shot. The editors of the metropolitan newspaper cannot assume that they publish everything for all their readers. They can and do hope that most of their readers at least see a few major stories. But they must assume—and the readership surveys back that assumption—that they publish for a whole variety of publics or communities.

Indeed, some large newspapers have zoned editions for communities outside their city but within their trade areas. However, aside from the zoned news, the readers still divide themselves into groups. Given groups concentrate primarily on sports, or markets, or editorials, or any one of the other areas into which news is departmentalized in large dailies. Smart editors of large newspapers accept those patterns and design their news publications for those groups, or *subcommunities,* if you please.

The problems of editors below the metropolitan class are sometimes totally different. To take a close look at those, it is easiest to examine the microcosm of the newspaper world—the small weekly newspaper.

For example, it is not too difficult to find weekly newspaper subscribers who read every word—news, editorial, and advertising—in the paper every week. That may sound like a very nice problem and normally it is. However, that kind of intense readership is an indication of the intimate relationship between a small newspaper and the community it serves. To publish in that kind of intimate environment requires a special sensitivity that is not nearly so apparent on a larger newspaper. And intimacy, with all its warmth and joy, is accompanied by added responsibilities.

Just for a moment, put yourself in the shoes of the publisher of a small weekly newspaper. Walk the main street with that publisher. Talk to the merchants about their advertising problems. Sell them and take next week's ads back to your newspaper.

With that part of the day's work over, go to the town council meeting as a reporter for your paper. Take a look at the council members about whom you are going to write, perhaps, the lead story for your newspaper. Among those council members will be many of the same people to whom you sold ads earlier in the day. And now, a little later in the week, as deadline pressures begin to build, sit down at your typewriter and produce an editorial that may very well be critical of some action taken by the council, which happens to also have a majority of members who are your advertisers.

READERS FEEL CLOSER

Now put yourself in the shoes of a subscriber to the same small weekly. Your family has taken the paper faithfully for three, even four, generations. The paper has not just reported the births, marriages, and deaths in your family, but it has also recorded most of the major activities in your life. You are not just a reader, you are a faithful reader. Since the paper reports on the activities and people you have known most of your life, you read almost every word. You use the advertisements as a shopping list. You know the newspaper so well, and it, in turn, knows you so well, that you have developed a "prepublication sense." That sense tells you in advance how your newspaper will probably react to some news event or to some news issue. And when you pick up the paper, your prepublication sense usually is right. You're even a bit annoyed if the paper has not reacted as you expected.

Now add one more aspect to this rather typical profile of a weekly newspaper reader. Your paper, like many small hometown papers, makes a special event of high school graduation each spring. Merchants buy congratulatory advertising and the pictures and names of every graduate are run in a special layout. You, a third-generation reader of this paper, have a daughter in the graduating class. By accident, her picture and name are dropped from the layout and nobody notices until after the press run.

Of course, this simply could not happen on a large-city newspaper. The very most that could be dropped from a routine graduation story on one of several high schools might be the daughter's name, listed in an agate column. But on a small weekly paper, this easily understandable accident would create embarrassment, chagrin, and possibly gossip for at least a week before the newspaper could make a correction.

You would have to explain perhaps a hundred times that your daughter had not dropped out of school, had not been kicked out, had not gotten into any number of fanciful scrapes. The high school principal would explain almost as many times that he had submitted her name and picture to the paper. The local publisher and editor would apologize to you and your spouse, your relatives, your daughter herself, the principal, close family friends, and some not-so-close friends.

The point is rather obvious, or should be by now. No one says there is no sensitivity, no compassion among the journalists in the metropolitan press. The point is that the intertwined relationship of a small newspaper with its community multiplies the sensitivity and possibly the need for compassion several times over. Successful hometown editors and publishers understand that difference and correctly feel a need to dwell upon it.

Leadership and Courage

Keep the need for sensitivity in mind.

Now add a measure of courageous leadership. What is that last ingredient? It is what every successful publisher has to display sooner or later. The nature of the business demands it. It can happen in any number of ways.

To begin with, journalistic ethics are, like any workable codes, neither black nor white. Our ethics do not say, "Thou shalt be fair, come hell or high water." In practice they say, "Thou shalt try like hell to be fair under the current and local circumstances." The problem may be that it is less personally painful to be fair in the relative anonymity of a large city than in the intimacy of a small community. But it always requires leadership.

Robert M. White II, editor of the Mexico (Missouri) *Ledger,* has his way of making the point. He first describes an incident involving the New York *Times.*

A part of greatness is not necessarily cosmic decisions on cosmic issues. The small decisions also set the tone for greatness. I remember when Arthur Ochs Sulzberger, the father of the present publisher of the New York Times, *told an API [American Press Institutional] group of which I was a member the following: "We have changed our policy recently on suicides. I got a call a few nights ago about a death story we were working on. The call was from the wife of the man who died. She explained that he had jumped out of the window of the top floor of the hospital, thereby killing himself. She asked that the story point out that he had terminal cancer and he chose that way out. So in the lead instead of calling the death suicide, we pointed out that he died, how he died, and that he had terminal cancer. We didn't use the word suicide."*

I think that kind of policy sets a tone of compassion to a paper and still takes away none of the vital but often trying necessity of objective, accurate coverage.

It would be interesting to know, for example, how many newspapers, if there are any newspapers, who have not at one time or another been boycotted by some advertiser. Of course, every experienced executive on every newspaper knows advertisers do not advertise to

control editorial policy. They advertise for a more important and vital reason to themselves—to sell more goods and services and make more profit. That is why advertisers advertise. However, now and then, in piques of anger or because the advertiser happens to be a lesser man, advertisers may attempt to boycott a newspaper.

I remember when the late Henry Bradley was a publisher in New England and the late Russ Stewart was a cub reporter working for him doing movie reviews. He wrote a review that was unfavorable. The theater owner marched in and announced to Henry Bradley he was not going to run any more advertising in the newspaper until the reviewer, Russ Stewart, was fired. Henry Bradley took the owner of the theater into the newsroom to Russ and told the owner to repeat what he had said. The theater owner did. And then Henry Bradley said, "No, you are not going to cancel your advertising. I'm not going to let you advertise again in the paper until you understand that we are not changing our theater reviews—they are our honest opinion."

Russ Stewart always said from that moment on he knew he was in love with this business. And, of course, he was for the rest of his distinguished career, including being the executive vice president of the Chicago Sun-Times *and chairman of the ANPA [American Newspaper Publishers Association] Advertising Bureau.*

White, a third-generation publisher in a famous journalism family, is concerned about great newspaper leadership on any newspaper, no matter what its size. And there are certainly common qualities for greatness on any newspaper. Indeed, although the general public often views the Pulitzer Prizes as awards to large newspapers, the record among the community press belies that notion.

Another White in the neighboring state of Kansas, William Allen White, made the Emporia *Gazette* famous when he won the Pulitzer Prize for editorial writing in 1923. In an editorial concerning fear and freedom, White produced a journalistic masterpiece that may be more applicable today than when he wrote it. He wrote it first as a personal letter to a friend and then decided to publish it under the title "To an Anxious Friend" as an answer to others who had protested his views.

July 27th, 1922.   You tell me that law is above freedom of utterance. And I reply that you can have no wise laws nor free enforcement of wise laws unless there is free expression of the wisdom of the people—and, alas, their folly with it. But if there is freedom, folly will die of its own poison, and the wisdom will survive. That is the history of the race. It is proof of man's kinship with God. You say that freedom of utterance is not for time of stress, and I reply with the sad truth that only in time of stress is freedom of utterance in danger. No one questions it in calm days, because it is not needed. And the reverse is true also; only when free utterance is suppressed is it needed, and when it is needed, it is most vital to justice.

Peace is good. But if you are interested in peace through force and without free discussion—that is to say, free utterance decently and in order—your interest in justice is slight. And peace without justice is tyranny, no matter how you may sugar-coat it with expedience. This state today is in more danger from suppression than from violence, because, in the end, suppression leads to violence. Violence, indeed, is the child of suppression. Whoever pleads for justice helps to keep the peace; and whoever tramples on the plea for justice temperately made in the name of peace only outrages peace and kills something fine in the heart of man which God put there when we got our manhood. When that is killed, brute meets brute on each side of the line.

So, dear friend, put fear out of your heart. This nation will survive, this state will prosper, the orderly business of life will go forward if only men can speak in whatever way given them to utter what their hearts hold—by voice, by posted card, by letter, or by press. Reason has never failed men. Only force and repression have made the wrecks in the world.

And community journalists have a documented record for courage. In fact, it may take more courage when an editorial campaign may literally anger all of the small-town journalist's

immediate neighbors. In Columbus, Georgia, Julian La Rose Harris led the *Inquirer-Sun* in a crusade in 1926. It was directed against the Ku Klux Klan at a time when the Klan had the power to destroy a newspaper. The crusade won a Pulitzer Prize.

Two North Carolina papers, the semiweekly Whiteville *News Reporter* and the weekly Tabor City *Tribune*, shared the service award in 1953. This, too, dealt with Klan violence, and the battle went on for three years.

The Columbus *Inquirer-Sun* won again in 1955 for its attack on the corruption in nearby Phenix City, Alabama.

Perhaps in response to those who doubt the seriousness with which community editors take their editorial duties, a series of small newspapers have won the Pulitzer Prize for editorial writing. In 1946, 1950, 1957, 1963, and 1964, small Southern newspapers, four of them from the state of Mississippi, won the highest award the profession can give for editorial excellence and courage. The Southeast did not have a monopoly, however. Small newspapers in Anchorage, Alaska, Lufkin, Texas, and Omaha, Nebraska, have won Pulitzers. The award-winning Omaha *Sun Newspapers* demonstrated the journalistic excellence of which the so-called suburban press is

capable. Led by its editor, the late Paul Williams, its publisher, Stan Lipsey, and chairman of the board, Warren Buffet, the *Sun* risked religious and community disfavor in an examination of the financial affluence of Boys Town.

New Technology Makes Waves

Remember, however, in the midst of this concern for editorial excellence, journalistic courage, and exemplary leadership, that this book is about the total newspaper. Yet another change in the latter half of the twentieth century has emphasized the need for knowledge of the total newspaper. That change involved one of the first technological advances in the business since the invention of the linotype at the start of the century. Offset, one of the oldest forms of printing, came to the newspaper. Sleek, relatively quiet offset presses began to replace the Goliaths of the industry. Phototypesetters replaced the once beloved but accursed clattering linotypes. The whole makeup process, which had involved

FIGURE 1–1 Advances in offset printing and photocomposition made it possible for Mrs. Margaret Taylor (standing near window) and a staff of three to continue operating the Davis (Oklahoma) *News* after the death of her husband. The *News* is published at a central plant. *Photo by Rick Bellatti, Stillwater (Oklahoma)* News-Press.

the complicated placement of metal type, was exchanged for scissors, paper, and paste or wax.

On the smaller papers the staff members were no longer slaves to the cantankerous linotype or its equally unpredictable companion, the flatbed press. In fact, many of the nation's weeklies no longer had an in-house press run. The paper was pasted up and taken to a nearby central offset plant for the rapid press run. Of course, some of the larger weeklies and small dailies became the central plants. Their fast offset presses could produce their own newspaper, sometimes in a matter of minutes. That left hours of free press time for other newspapers in the area that did not have their own press.

This same technological change hastened a trend that was already underway: group ownership of smaller newspapers. The offset revolution encouraged central plant publishers to acquire ownership of the newspapers in their area. The same trend created new management opportunities. It became possible for a journalism student to become resident publisher and editor of a weekly newspaper within a very few years after graduation.

The refinement of the offset process had its effect upon the larger papers, too. That was particularly true among the small and medium-sized dailies in the 1970s. They also shifted to offset in varying degrees. Some went all the way to new offset presses. Others adapted their rotary presses to take plates made from pasted-up pages of photoset type. Obviously, the shift to offset had its effect upon the total newspaper. The American printer, a historic and sometimes romanticized figure, either changed jobs or began to disappear from the American newspaper scene. The economic effects of that change are apparent. The effects upon the remainder of the newspaper's staff may not be quite as apparent. As the back shop process became simpler, the responsibilities for those who produce the news and advertising became greater. And, to belabor the obvious, the need to know the total newspaper became proportionately greater. Furthermore, after having slept or at least dozed for more than half a century, the Rip Van Winkle of technology—newspaper technology—was just beginning to stir.

There were other profound changes, however, apart from technology. The "shopper" or "penny saver," distributed free and claiming total market coverage, made inroads in many cities and towns, forcing traditional paid-circulation newspapers to change their methods of operation and marketing. Terms like *antitrust* and *labor relations* were once concerns of only the metropolitan press. Even before the 1980s they began to cause anxiety among community publishers. Many of the latter consider the shopper the greatest menace to the well-being of the hometown newspaper.

The severe competition, including shoppers, that followed the new technology caused more antitrust legislation involving even smaller newspapers. Unions showed increased interest in community newspapers to offset membership losses elsewhere, forcing publishers to give more attention to employee attitudes and needs.

The Rise and Fall of Typography

Meanwhile, not back at the ranch but back on the university campuses, there were stirrings and strainings in journalism education. In the post–World War II decades, new schools of journalism were established and the older schools grew. They grew in enrollment. They were housed in news buildings. They added professors. They added masters programs and doctoral programs. They grew in every way but one—the training of journalism's generalists.

The story may be best told through a course that was virtually eradicated from the journalism curriculum: typography. It was a course mostly about printing. More than that, it was a course in printing. The students learned in varying degrees to practice the printer's craft. And it was in the curriculum because most of the early schools of journalism were preparing people to go into the weekly field—which was most of the nation's press.

However, to the master typography professor, the course was much more than going through the steps that ended up putting black letters on white paper. Those master professors considered it sound education to put a student in front of a California job case, type stick in hand, composing, slowly and usually painfully, words, sentences, and paragraphs, one metal letter at a time. It was discipline, and it was something else. It was a personal connection to history.

The skillful and talented typography professor made that connection from the students back through generations of printers all the way to Gutenberg. In the process, the student discovered that journalists were in at the beginnings of the movement. Many of those colonial journalists fostered the revolution, put basic freedoms into words, and were instrumental in the adoption of the Bill of Rights.

PIONEERS IN RECORDED HISTORY

That lesson, through typography, led to another. As white civilization crept across this country, there was a definable progression of steps. First came the traders, the trappers, the mountain men, the explorers, and, yes, the adventurers. Then came the settlers with their plows. And soon after the plows came the presses. For the West Coast the presses often were shipped on the stormy voyage around the Horn. But for the Midwest, the presses bumped their way in wagons. And each time one arrived, a journalist set up shop.

Those pioneer journalists were, of course, always printers. But they were more. With them came a reminder of the democratic experiment and the freedoms and responsibilities thereof. The interpretations were sometimes strange and their view of freedoms were sometimes somewhat limited. But in their writings you can find the early mental struggle with freedom as a practical human concept.

Those early journalists were other things, too. By today's standards they seem opinionated in most of what they wrote, no matter where it was in their newspapers. Their early political coverage sometimes read like Revelations or Dante's *Inferno*. And they tended to be a trifle partisan. Take the following coverage by a Democratic paper of a Republican rally: "The Republican Party presented its platform last night. It was sparkling and clean. But before the week is out it will be filthy and covered with slime. . . ." Now this from a Republican paper covering a Democratic rally: "The Democratic candidate in a fine white shirt pranced the planks last night. He pranced in glee—probably because he was the only man present in a clean shirt. . . ."

Yes, the earliest journalists practiced freedom with opinion. Often they were also poets. Usually they were essayists, because that was the literary form of the day. And they were always contemporary historians. Their newspapers are the only good source to trace the development of their communities. Usually, if you could determine the character of the newspaper, you could also discover the character of the community.

That was another lesson taught by the master professor of typography. And there was one more, one that may eventually have led to the demise of the course.

The master professor of typography taught the art and romance of type and the forms it could take on the printed page. It was important that the student know, by the force of examination if necessary, the lineage of a typeface. What was its family? Who was the artist who created it? Was it clean? Was it dirty? Was it blatant? Was it beautiful? Could it be read? Could it talk? Could it sell?

THE NEW APPROACH

Sometime along about the middle of the twentieth century, journalism educators and journalists from larger newspapers began to question the legitimacy of typography as a course. Does it belong in a college curriculum? they asked. Are we training printers or journalists? Production has moved to the back shop; printers, usually members of the union, do that.

As a result, typography and many classes in community journalism gradually faded from the academic scene. So, possibly, did much of the sentimental history of American journalism. Certainly, many journalism educators and journalists chose to phase out one of the tools of the profession's general practitioners.

The typography course is only an example in this case. It is an example that shows that journalism schools, like the industry itself, have shifted and turned in an effort to find an up-to-date base from which to educate. Some schools have turned toward badly needed research. Other schools have turned toward basic professional curricula. And some schools have sought a middle ground with a mixture of both. In some cases there has been emphasis on specialists. And in other cases there has been an extreme-generalist approach in which broadcasting, news-editorial, advertising, and a number of other kinds of students have all taken the same basic curriculum with only a small effort at specialization. However, most journalism educators would admit that they are thus far finding it difficult to teach the total newspaper concept that would produce journalists with a broad understanding of the profession into which they intend to go.

The "Total" Newspaper in the Computer Age

Where those students will go will also be a different world. Once started, the technological revolution grew in the closing decades of the twentieth century. The shift to offset and phototypesetting was just a start. By 1980 almost every newsroom of every daily newspaper in the country and a good many of the weeklies had entered the computer age. The computer era was not confined to the newsroom. It, with its classic symbol, the *video display tube* (VDT), could be found in advertising and a number of other offices of the newspaper.

As the linotype disappeared from the back shop, the typewriters were disappearing from the up-front areas of the newspapers. Reporters were learning to write stories on the VDT and editors were learning to edit on it. But that was not the end; computerized technology swept throughout the newspaper. By 1980 a good many newspapers could arrange and display a full quarter page on the tube. And pagination, a full page, was already a research fact and was soon to become a newspaper reality.

Once again a technological change added emphasis to the need for the knowledge of the total newspaper. Decisions that had been made in the back shop through the printer were being made up front where the news and advertising originated. It was taking away the time-honored excuse for a mistake—"The printers did it"—by placing the responsibility upon those who originated the content.

By the 1980s the newspaper business had become a more demanding, more satisfying, more professional place that insisted upon journalists with a greater understanding of what this book is all about—the total newspaper and what an individual needs to know to make it in the newspaper business.

Chapter 2

Covering the News

by Kenneth R. Byerly

This chapter focuses on reporting the news for weekly, semiweekly, and small daily newspapers. Since many other books emphasize reporting for the larger metropolitan papers, this chapter fills a gap for the reporter or editor whose efforts will likely center on events in a local environment.

What basic principles should community newspapers—weeklies, semiweeklies, and smaller dailies in nonmetropolitan and suburban areas— follow in news writing and content? How should they differ from those of metropolitan dailies?

An answer to these questions was given recently by the women's page editor of a large daily in a fast-growing city that had been a big country town not many years ago.

"What is your biggest problem?" she was asked.

Her reply: "Getting people to realize that we are a big city now. They can't understand that we no longer have space for stories on every tea, bridge club, and child's birthday."

But weeklies, semiweeklies, and nonmetropolitan dailies do have room for the folksy, local news that means so much to people. This is a great strength in competing with the big-city dailies that burst in upon their communities.

This does not mean that community papers should report drivel, but they can cover the home front in their communities and areas in a detail and a style that the metropolitan dailies

can't even begin to touch.

Take religion, for example. The prize-winning editor of a metropolitan daily once said, "Religion, whether it is Baptist, Catholic, Presbyterian, Jewish, Mormon, or any faith, touches as many lives as any other thing. Even those who oppose it want to read about it."

The newspapers we consider in this chapter can do a much better job of covering religion on a local level. They can and should do this too in other important fields such as local and regional government, courts and crime, school news, sports, local business activities, features, pictures, and many others.

Are there pitfalls that weeklies, semiweeklies, and smaller dailies should avoid in obtaining such local and area news?

And how can these newspapers get and keep the cooperation and respect that are so important in dealing with the local people, organizations, institutions, government, and other news sources while at the same time covering the unpleasant news that must be reported?

What methods should such newspapers use when keeping the best interests of their readers and communities in mind?

These are questions this chapter seeks to answer, laying special stress on local news, the rendering of service, and the kindliness that are so important to good community newspapers.

KENNETH R. BYERLY

The author is publisher of the Lewistown (Mont.) *News-Argus,* author of *Community Journalism,* and professor emeritus in journalism at the University of North Carolina.

"A community newspaper should share in the hopes, heartaches, laughs, sorrows, accomplishments, disappointments, and joys of its readers. There are times, though, when an editor must be a watchdog, take his gloves off, and report harmful things as they are."

Treat the Suburbs Special

All the above factors are vital to the suburban press and rural or small-city newspapers alike. But there are differences, too. In pointing them out, it is important to understand that the suburban field is a very fast-growing one in which there are many new and outstanding opportunities.

These differences and similarities are described by Don J. Smith, executive editor and director of the Fournier Newspapers, an excellent suburban group in the Seattle area, and Mary Durkin, now an instructor in the Mass Communication Department at the University of Wisconsin at La Crosse. Durkin has also been managing editor of three excellent suburban newspapers in the Chicago area that run the gamut in readership from the highly educated, high-income North Shore to the blue-collar western suburbs.

Suburbanites seek two things, Durkin says, The "good life" with homes in the "rustic, open, wholesome rural areas in which to bring up their children," and making sure that their financial investment in the suburban area and their ties to the urban center where they often work are sound.

A suburban newspaper "must understand the unique mentality of suburbanites and their governments," Durkin says. "They must promote the favorable aspects of the area and protect suburbanites from the very real potential for harm in the form of both innocently ignorant and maliciously corrupt politicians."

BASIC NEEDS SIMILAR

This sometimes means tougher and more detailed investigative reporting than is usually needed in a small town newspaper, but, as Don J. Smith stresses, most of the basic needs of the community and suburban press remain much the same otherwise.

"The community paper helps its people live in that community by telling them about local politics, local schools, local history, and the opportunities available to residents," says Smith.

"The suburban paper helps residents of (the) community to survive (there) by telling them about local politics, local schools, local history, and the opportunities available to them as residents."

Smith's experience has been that "the community paper demands a great deal of very personal news . . . names, names, names."

PERSONAL NEWS A MUST

The suburban paper demands personal news too, Smith says, but because of its larger audience, personal news becomes news about people with whom readers can identify, news about familiar people, places, and things.

"In the suburbs," he explains, "competition is fierce because the stakes are high. In some instances, when we've slipped from our role as a 'community' newspaper, smaller weeklies have risen to remind us there still is need for news about little things and about people on a local level."

The suburban paper is caught in the middle between the metro daily and the community weekly, Smith feels.

"A suburban paper must operate as its community paper, and must also cover the same breaking news events as the metro daily whenever they occur within the suburban paper's circulation area," he emphasizes, adding that the paper must provide "depth and insight into local news of major importance even when the metros, radio, or television get the story first."

Suburban and rural community weeklies and small dailies alike, however, must place their major stress on local news, community service, and kindliness. These are essential, and they are keynotes in this chapter.

They obviously won't have the staff, money, or space to compete with a paper like the *Milwaukee Journal,* for example, in covering federal government in Washington or state government in Madison, nor should they try.

On the other hand, the *Milwaukee Journal* cannot possibly give detailed coverage of Wisconsin's seventy-one county governments, or the several hundred smaller cities, towns, and villages that are served by more than 230 community and suburban weeklies and dailies in that state.

In other words, the federal government is watched by hundreds of newspapers and radio and television stations. Scores of them are concerned with state government in most states.

But most small city, town, and county governments get primary attention from no papers except the one or two hometown ones in their area. So community newspapers should concentrate on thorough coverage of local government and give this high priority over news of state and federal government.

This applies also to other phases of community news. After all, a chuckhole in a main street often causes greater local concern than, say, a revolution in Bolivia. A community paper should cash in on such local interests.

Stories on local government can be classified under several heads. Here are some major ones.

COUNCIL AND COMMISSION MEETINGS. Actions by county commissioners, town or city councilmen, and other local elected officials are as important in their communities as decisions of Congress are to the nation, sometimes even more so. They are often more newsworthy locally, too.

Citizens of one small city said little when the Congress raised their Social Security taxes sharply, but hit the ceiling when their city council raised the tax on female dogs from one to five dollars a year. The measure was fought for weeks. Letters to the editor poured in to the local newspaper.

Coverage of municipal council and county commissioners' meetings is a must.

OFFICIALS. Elected and appointed officials—the town clerk, sheriff, county attorney, assessor, city attorney, county clerk, and others—conduct or supervise much of the work of local government. They are news sources that should be checked regularly.

Thoughtful questions often elicit interesting and important stories.

The problems are many. Take the mayor of a small North Carolina town, for example, who was asked by the local paper to name some of his problems. Here are several he cited:

- "Citizens must cease and desist from cutting into meter boxes after service has been cut off for nonpayment of bills. There'll be a twenty-five-dollar fine for violations."

- "Some youngsters are using street light bulbs for air rifle targets . . . three hundred bulbs in the past seven months. If the practice doesn't stop, some areas will be in the dark for a time."

- "Citizens must stop using heavy fifty-five gallon oil drums for garbage cans."

These things sound petty, but you can be sure there was plenty of discussion—and some action—on the problems reported in the local paper.

DEPARTMENTS. Water, fire, roads, health, welfare, streets, parks—these are some of the many departments of government on a local level. Their work concerns many or most citizens. Much of it is routine, so little attention is paid to them unless something goes wrong. Their activities are then very much in the news and there is often an uproar.

ANNOUNCEMENTS AND WARNINGS. City fathers usually prefer compliance to arrests, so they often warn motorists of a drive against speeders or tell residents they will be fined if sprinklers are allowed to spray streets or sidewalks.

They want citizens to know of inconveniences and deadlines and will want to tell them ahead of time if water is to be cut off from 2 to 4 P.M. Tuesday or the deadline for registering to vote in the next election is 5 P.M. Friday.

Newspapers should run such stories. They are important to readers.

CAMPAIGNS. The way to win elective office is to be elected. The way to stay in elective office is to be reelected. This sounds trite, but professional politicians never forget it.

These elected officials play key roles in determining tax levies, services made available, paper work, and inconveniences to citizens.

This means community newspapers should cover election campaigns

with care and fairness. By far the greatest stress, of course, should be on the local and regional candidates.

This does not mean that state and federal campaigns should be ignored by community newspapers. Much attention should be given to them when issues have local angles or candidates campaign or speak in a newspaper's area.

SOME FINAL THOUGHTS ON REPORTING LOCAL GOVERNMENT. A community newspaper should try to avoid sarcasm or spitefulness in political reporting and editorials. Officials, candidates, and their supporters may forget columns of full and fair news coverage but will bitterly resent and forever remember any sarcastic word or comment. A newspaper that practices such methods is usually less effective.

Some editors are careful not to print angry remarks made by public officials when they know they "didn't mean them." There is merit in this policy.

Government is important business. Good government is everyone's business, especially a newspaper's. Local officials often work more effectively if they know that their newspaper will treat them fairly and that it is eager to improve the community. On the other hand, a community newspaper should also serve as a watchdog, but a friendly, fair, and firm watchdog. "Do it the gentlemanly way," is one community publisher's creed. It is a good one.

It is a community newspaper's job to get "close to local government, but not get in bed with it." It should report its activities so that people will "feel and understand it."

School News Inspires Pride

Our children are near and dear to us. They are in school five to six hours a day, eight to ten months a year. Teachers mold them and their future. And schools take a big bite out of our local

tax dollar, often more than half of it.

So schools are important. Where there are schools, there is news.

Well-reported school news does more than inform readers. It inspires pride in students and teachers, recognizes accomplishments, and stimulates desire by administrators to spend tax dollars wisely.

It is particularly important, therefore, that a community newspaper take a positive, helpful approach to school news, but this does not mean that it should report only the good and overlook the bad.

There is less chance of incompetence, indifference, or even dishonesty creeping into our schools if a newspaper is willing to act as an alert watchdog that will bark when danger appears.

A community newspaper should champion new construction, better salaries, needed equipment, and other improvements, but only when convinced this is in the best interest of the children and the community.

There are many facets that should be covered in school news:

- Student Activities: Grades, attendance, special activities, and projects, unusual accomplishments, etc.

- Teachers: Their background, problems, achievements, special activities beyond the call of duty, etc.

- Administration: Hot lunches, disciplinary problems and accomplishments, bus routes, curriculum, etc.

- School Board: Costs, policies, problems, construction and equipment needs, etc.

- Parent-Teacher and Other Community Groups: Programs, issues, meeting reports, etc.

A community newspaper can liven things up when needed interest in schools is lacking, and tone them down when tempers flare.

It should report school news calmly and stress issues rather than personalities as much as possible in editorials. This is sometimes difficult, but school fights can leave lasting scars, so a community editor needs judgment, patience, and restraint.

What is best in the long run for a community and its schools should be a key factor in reporting school news. Pious self-righteousness has no place in such coverage.

Business Is News

Many reporters, especially younger ones, sometimes think of all business news as advertising and consequently resist writing about it. Some are even antagonistic toward it.

They're right, of course, if the so-called news is advertising that should be paid for and run as such.

But there is much in business that is of communitywide interest; this is news and should be reported. Here are seven general headings:

1. *Main Street.* Parking meters, citywide shopping promotions, holiday closings, the sale of a business or the opening of a new one, an established firm that's going out of business, and others.
2. *Industrial.* It's important news when a new industry locates in a newspaper's area, or an old one comes out with a new product that will mean a sharp increase in employment. Layoffs or new markets that mean more jobs can also be newsworthy.
3. *Construction and Real Estate.* New construction is a long-term investment that indicates faith by the investor in the community's future. It is news, for example, when someone builds a new store or shopping center, an apartment complex, sometimes even just a house. Paving of parking lots, new sidewalks and curbs, and other such improvements can also be news in a community newspaper.
4. *Public Utilities and Transportation.* A truck line sets up new routes to additional communities, a second power line assures better service in times of emergency, railroad grain shipments rise sharply, electricity rates go up. . . . Events like these

affect a community. They are news and should be reported.
5. *Business Conditions and Prospects.* Tourists bring many new dollars to a community. So restaurant, motel, and filling station operators—merchants and others, too—will be interested if the local Chamber of Commerce is getting more travel inquiries than usual.

A banker returning from a state meeting has been told by other bankers that they expect business conditions to be much better in the months ahead, or worse. A story on this can be important.

Job placements at the local employment office are up sharply.

Such stories will have high readership.
6. *Business Organizations.* What's happening at meetings of the Chamber of Commerce, Rotary, labor unions, Business and Professional Women, Kiwanis, Soroptomist, Junior Chamber of Commerce, Lions, and others?

Many of these meetings are routine with little news value, but actions taken can often be important and newsworthy.
7. *People in Business.* Here is a chance for many fine feature stories and pictures.

A local truck driver logs 250,000 miles without a scratched fender, a woman who has clerked in a store for fifty years retires, a well-known waitress figures that she has now served 100,000 meals, a displaced Vietnamese person starts a local business. . . .

Such stories have high interest. They afford many opportunities for quotes, memories, happy or discouraging incidents, humor, and other angles.

Report Religion, Don't Preach

The Communists tried to ban religion when they took over Poland, but the Catholic Church survived there, grew stronger, and eventually a Pole become the pope. This is just one example of

the great importance and strength of religion to many no matter what the denomination.

Suppers, youth rallies, church construction, revivals, special speakers and programs, holidays, new preachers or priests, entertainments, and anniversaries are a few of the scores of subjects on which news stories about religion may be written. Pictures can be used often and will be much appreciated.

The humdrum need not be reported, as much happens in churches and religious groups that is lively and interesting. All such events should be covered.

The following are a few points to remember in reporting news of religion.

DON'T PREACH. The reporter should remember that he is a reporter and not a preacher. Reporting religion is not a way of proclaiming the gospel. It is a way of informing those who do proclaim it, or are interested in it.

MEN OF INFLUENCE. Most preachers are men of influence. It is important to understand them and their problems and to work with them as much as possible.

GOOD AND BAD. Don't be surprised if some preachers want a newspaper to print only good news of churches. But remember, the Bible reports both good and bad news. A newspaper too at times should report bad news, but handle it with great care.

DENOMINATIONS. Each denomination has its own beliefs, traditions, and customs, so stories written on their activities should contain correct terminology and doctrine.

CHURCH FIGHTS. Don't let your paper become involved in church fights unless it is absolutely necessary. Such fights can become bitter and divide a congregation and community. Wounds heal slowly. Scars show for years. Sometimes there is legal or other newsworthy action that should be reported, but much of the squabbling and recrimination in such fights should be ignored by newspapers.

WORTHINESS. If a newspaper is

to do a satisfactory job of covering church news, the publisher, editor, and reporters must recognize religion as the significant and worthwhile source of solid news that it is. They must have a sincere interest in it and feel that religion is worth covering.

Crime News: Beware!

We all want able, honest police protection, but few of us really understand the many problems policemen have. We seldom do anything to make their task easier.

Every community editor, for example, has heard this complaint: "It wasn't the ticket that made me mad. It was the way the policeman gave it to me." But how can a police officer give someone a ticket in a way that will please him?

Facing death or injury is a police officer's job. There are frustrations, too. Some members of the force may be incompetent, arrogant, or even dishonest, but the vast majority are courteous, hard-working, honest, and dedicated. They seldom get credit for it, but most of them do their jobs faithfully and well. So police officers need and usually deserve the sympathetic understanding of newspaper people. With it they can do a better job of protecting the public.

However, reporters should not permit friendship to be a screen behind which some police officers may hide incompetence, indifference, or dishonesty.

Crime stories can be "dynamite" if not handled discreetly, especially in community newspapers that are close to their readers. Here are some things to remember in reporting crime stories:

1. Libel suits are a grave danger for newspapers that are careless in reporting crime stories.
2. Innocent people may be humiliated by errors in names and facts.
3. Sensational reporting on criminals may create public fear that is not justified by facts. However, people should be informed if there is real danger.

4. Records should be checked and the officials responsible consulted and quoted.
5. Details must be checked carefully.
6. Rumor, if reported, should be designated as such so that readers won't confuse it with fact.

Courts vary greatly by types and in importance, so each should be identified. Civil courts act on private controversies; criminal courts deal with offenses against the state. State courts, on an ascending scale, can include justice of the peace courts, local municipal or police courts, county and district courts, and appellate or supreme courts. There is also a nationwide system of federal courts.

There are many special problems in reporting news of crime and courts that must be handled with care and tact.

"DON'T USE MY NAME." Every editor is familiar with the person who is convicted for drunken driving or shoplifting and who then says something like, "Don't use it in the paper because my mother is sick. If she sees it, it will kill her."

The editor could get indignant and say, "We don't make the news. We just print it. You should have thought of that before you drove your car while drinking."

But this reaction just irritates and "rubs it in." It is better to explain patiently, "We have to treat everyone alike. The conviction is a matter of court record. We have no choice but to use it."

WHY PRINT IT? Some community newspapers run no court news unless it is of major importance.

This is a mistake in community newspapers, according to the chief justice of a state supreme court who told an editor: "Many people fear publicity more than a fine, so it is very important that you report arrests and court actions in such things as traffic violations, drunken driving, shoplifting, and disturbing the peace. Newspapers are often a greater deterrent in this way than are the police or the courts. A big story isn't needed. Just a few lines anywhere in your newspaper will be seen by readers and have the desired effect."

TELL IT RIGHT. Many editors are asked by the one involved in a conviction to withhold the story or his name. A tactful editor who has had good success with such reporting explains, "You can't keep things like this secret in a small community. People are going to talk, and the more they talk the bigger it will get. It will get worse and worse. So it is far better to run the story correctly now."

This is generally true.

EXCEPTIONS? Are there times when a conviction should be left out of the paper?

Perhaps, but they are very rare, and the decision to do so must be based on unusual and proven facts.

"Every time my name appears in the paper my business picks up," a Kentucky moonshiner told the local editor after an arrest. In this case it might pay to cut off his free advertising.

Another weekly editor stopped printing names of a local factory's employees who were arrested for drinking or disorderly conduct. "Many were family men," he explained, "and they were fired even if it was their first offense." Was the editor right or wrong? It is a moot question.

INFORMED PUBLIC. Many editors feel that an informed public assures greater justice in the courts and has a wholesome effect on police officials, so insist on reporting court cases. Their argument is sound.

FAIRNESS IN REPORTING. When some west Texas cowboys were going to lynch a horse thief in the 1880s, the legendary Judge Roy Bean, who held court in saloons, is reported to have said, "Wait a minute, boys. We're going to give this man a fair trial before we hang him."

Reporters should not "hang" a man in the newspaper when he is arrested or before the jury reaches a verdict. The news must be reported, but the details should be presented in a manner that will not influence the public unduly or unfairly.

ACCURACY IN QUOTES. You can't unscramble eggs.

This adage applies also to the reporter who misquotes or quotes out of context. The result is misinformation for the reader, and serious damage can be done to the person who is misquoted.

A correction later seldom undoes the damage, as the first impression is often the lasting one.

Hence, a reporter must be extremely careful when quoting. If there is reason for doubt in the mind of the reporter on a quote to be used, it should be checked first with the person quoted or with others who are reliable and were on hand when the statement was made.

The importance of this cannot be overemphasized.

REPORTING ASSISTANCE.
Keeping informed on court and police action need not be a time-killer. It is not possible for a community paper to have a reporter at all court sessions, but lawyers, clerks, and judges can keep reporters informed. Staying on good terms with such people is helpful, but reporters should be careful that officials do not use this friendship and cooperation to suppress or slant information.

GOOD TASTE. Consideration for others is of extreme importance in reporting crime and court news, as is judgment in reporting lurid details.

The privacy of relatives and friends should not be invaded unwarrantedly in reporting crime news. If the president of a town bank is arrested on an embezzling charge, there is seldom any need to name his grown sons and daughters in the story unless they are involved. They will suffer enough from their father's arrest.

GLORIFYING CRIMINALS. Care should be taken that news stories do not glorify criminals as was done in the days of Jesse James. When kids play "cops and robbers" nowadays most of them want to be the "good guys." This wasn't always so years ago when newspapers, radio, television, and other news media often made heroes of bandits and killers.

JUVENILES. Should the names of juvenile lawbreakers be published in newspapers? Is this a deterrent to delinquency? Experts disagree on the an-

swers to these questions.

The best policy? If your state's law forbids or limits printing the names of juvenile offenders, comply with it, of course. If it does not, judgment should be used in each case based on the circumstances. The name of a juvenile who commits a capital crime should probably be used in most cases, some argue, if the law permits, even if it is a first offense. In minor crimes, it may sometimes be more appropriate to ignore the first offense, but perhaps report subsequent convictions if there is no law against it.

Fairness, the greatest general good, the opinions of others who are well informed—all should be considered in reaching decisions on what to print regarding juvenile offenses.

NO JOY. No editor or reporter should get joy out of reporting the troubles of others. "If you do," one editor tells his reporters, "don't work for me. It will reflect in your writing. You will get yourself and the paper in trouble."

The Rest of the News

There are many other facets of local life that should be covered in community newspapers and that add to readership. The basic principles are much the same as those already discussed.

Here are some of these areas, with brief comments.

SPORTS

Some people have no interest in sports. Others are fanatics. Some go to games only when their team is winning. Others never miss. Some care little for spectator sports like football and basketball, but love participation sports such as golf, fishing, tennis, or bowling.

Big dailies almost never run scores of sporting events in smaller communities, if at all. So weeklies and small dailies can give their readers something here that the metros can't—personalized reporting, photos of

hometown and area sporting events, and local sports features. Such coverage pays off big in circulation and readership among young and old alike.

WOMEN'S PAGE

Watch a woman when she picks up a newspaper. She often turns first to the women's page. Men may scoff at such news, but many read it when it concerns them—a son's engagement, the marriage of a friend's daughter, and even such things as recipes, a novel plan for a new house, someone's flower garden, or new decor for a living room or kitchen if contemplating remodeling.

This coverage offers many picture opportunities. The page can have such appeal that many newspapers designate it a family page rather than a women's page.

How should news and features be covered here? Horace V. Wells, Jr., veteran publisher of the successful Clinton (Tennessee) *Courier-News,* says, "It's been one of our strong points. We try to cover it just like any other news—plan ahead, have regular contacts, pound a beat by telephone, and follow up on leads. We work at it. This is the whole secret."

PERSONAL ITEMS

Names make news, but not names alone. Names should be used often, but only when there is something newsworthy about the person or persons named. One should dig for added details.

Here is an example of how a bad item can become good simply by asking a few more questions:

BAD: *Mr. and Mrs. George Sanders of Jonesboro spent Sunday here visiting Mr. and Mrs. Jack Wade.*

GOOD: *World War II days were recalled here Sunday when Mr. and Mrs. George Sanders of Jonesboro spent the day with Mr. and Mrs. Jack Wade. The two men were in the first wave that hit Omaha Beach on D-Day when the Allies invaded France in 1944.*

The same names are used in both examples, but the second has zest and life. The mention of Omaha Beach and D-Day will recall many memories to readers who were in the service and to others at home who prayed for the safety of their loved ones and friends overseas. It will cause comment by friends when they meet Jack Wade on the street.

Community newspapers can build solid circulation too by having good correspondents in the nearby areas that they serve, or could serve if developed properly.

These correspondents can cover hard news, look for smaller items, write features, and tip editors on important breaking stories that may require added help to cover.

FARM NEWS

Baseball players like to talk baseball, musicians music, and politicians politics.

It's the same with farmers. They want to talk and read about farming, as do their wives, yet many community newspapers in rural areas run little if anything about farming. This is a mistake.

"We feel," said a Nebraska weekly editor, "that farming in our trade area should be covered with lively stories and pictures. This means prowling the back roads in search of unusual feeding operations, new barns and other storage structures, irrigation, and seasonal pictures of plowing, grasshopper poisoning, or storm damage.

"When nothing else is going on I fill the gaps by writing about prominent farmers and the ideas that make them money. Our farm page also carries the County Extension and Home Extension Agent columns which I edit down to a nub, and any releases from the University of Nebraska Extension Service that pertain to local conditions, persons, or crops. We try to use two or more farm pictures a week and receive much impact from them."

Some of the many facets of newsworthy farm stories include new or better crops and animals, farm improvements and methods, crops prospects and yields, rainfall or other weather news, farm organizations, government farm programs and regulations, fairs, farm sales, outstanding farmers, and farm oddities.

Don't write down to farmers. They are intelligent, thoughtful, and well-informed. They are intensely interested in what they and others around them are doing. A newspaper that gives such newsworthy farm information to farmers will gain in circulation and readership.

Many farm and ranch stories merit coverage on page 1.

FEATURE STORIES

Dig a little and you'll find a feature story in every person and in many things. Local and area features have high readership and make friends. They give a community newspaper another big advantage over the metro dailies that come into their area.

Features can be written about people, animals, weather, anniversaries and seasons, history and landmarks, organizations and institutions, hobbies, oddities, humor, and a host of other things. Features need not be long. They should often be illustrated with a picture or pictures.

PICTURES

Old-time community editors can remember when they were proud if they had a local picture or two in their papers.

Those days are gone since the coming of offset. Every newspaper today can and should run many local and area pictures. The possibilities in hard news, sports, features, and human interest stories are endless.

But poor pictures hurt rather than help. Good camera work and planning are important. So is proper cropping.

It has been said that a picture is worth a thousand words. Not so. But a good picture plus twenty-five well chosen words can be worth far more than an in-depth article. Cutlines (captions) are important. They should be written with care.

HEALTH NEWS

People talk constantly about their health and that of others. What they talk about, they want to read about. So sensible and tactful reporting about the sick and injured is important.

Hospital, health department, and other health agency news can mean much to many.

There is sometimes conflict between doctors and reporters. This has lessened somewhat in recent years, and there is often increasing understanding by both sides of the others' problems.

A reporter should understand that a doctor's first responsibility is to his patient. Doctors should realize too that newspapers have responsibilities to their readers. Courtesy and consideration by a reporter can often accomplish much with doctors and others in the healing professions.

Sensible coverage of health news can be and often is a solid help to those in the healing professions as well as the public. So it is important that newspapers and those in health work together with understanding and harmony as much as possible.

OBITUARIES

An obituary is the final page in a person's life. It is often clipped and kept in the family Bible for years, even generations. It is exceedingly important.

There are basic things to keep in mind when gathering information for an obituary and in writing it. These principles also apply to the broader questions asked in the first paragraphs of this chapter, namely: What basic principles should community newspapers—weeklies, semiweeklies, and smaller dailies in nonmetropolitan and suburban areas—follow in news writing and content? How should they differ from those of metropolitan dailies?

A curt, discourteous young reporter for a community newspaper in Montana considered himself a newspaper expert. His concerned publisher told him, "Obituaries mean much to relatives and friends. So use what they request, within reason. And never forget that they have just lost a loved one. They are upset and under great strain. Above all, be kindly and understanding."

Three days later a respected, long-time resident died. Some relatives said that a four-line poem written by the deceased reflected his philosophy on life and asked if it could be included in the obituary.

"We're a newspaper," the young reporter said sarcastically. "We can't print that kind of stuff."

The relatives were insulted and hurt. "That was years ago," the publisher recalled, "but no member of that family has spoken to me since. They hold me responsible even though that reporter disregarded my instructions. And somehow I can't blame them too much. Our reporter's attitude was inexcusable, and particularly so in a smaller community such as ours."

MISTAKES CAN HURT. Mistakes or omissions in an obituary in any newspaper greatly disturb relatives and friends of the deceased. The community editor must be more acutely aware of this because of closeness to his readers.

For example, a community editor was told, "My brother had a big family and I forgot to include the name of one of his sons when I gave you material for the obituary. We want to send copies to many relatives and friends. Would you be willing to run the entire story over again with the forgotten son's name included?" Such things put a community editor in a difficult position. But it would be difficult to find a community publisher who has not received such a request, and perhaps difficult to find one who has not found a way to grant it at one time or another.

CONSIDER EACH PERSON. No man lives his life without doing something different. This should be reflected in his obituary.

Horace V. Wells, Jr., publisher of the Clinton (Tennessee) *Courier-News,* stressed this when he said, "In a small town every man is an individual, a human being with some friends. This isn't always true in the city. No one dies who does not deserve some recognition, but this varies with how widely he was known, and how much he had contributed to others."

So don't follow a script on obituaries. Give each person the traits and characteristics that marked his personality, even if he just loved dogs or planted trees. If he helped organize the Sweet Home Baptist Church and donated the land on which it was built, say so. Few readers will remember that far back, but most will know the church.

These attitudes toward obituaries stress the great importance of the human touch in the community newspaper, be it a weekly or a small daily, in the city or out of town.

Conclusion

A community newspaper should share in the hopes, heartaches, laughs, sorrows, accomplishments, disappointments, and joys of its readers.

It should report these things with care, accuracy, and kindliness. There are times though when an editor must be a watchdog, take his gloves off, and report hurtful things as they are.

The community newspaper must work constantly to improve the area, and to serve the best interests of its readers, their organizations and institutions.

Summing up, the role of a community newspaper can perhaps be described vividly by referring to a country preacher who was alert to local happenings and worked constantly for the betterment of his community and its people. This was back in 1957 when the Reverend Samuel (Sam) Neil Varnell, Jr., was named Tennessee's Rural Minister of the Year. He was then pastor of five small churches of the Piney Flats Methodist parish in the cattle, corn, and tobacco country of eastern Tennessee. The Reverend Varnell had preached half of his thirty-eight years while serving twenty-five little churches at one time or another in the hill country of Virginia and Tennessee.

The minister's story was told then in the now-superseded weekly *Saturday Evening Post.* He was keenly aware of the local angle that community newspapers should stress, as the following quote from the article makes evident.

At the end of his visit, he always asks if the family would like him to say a word or prayer. He throws back his head, squinches his eyes tight, and speaks to the Lord as directly and simply as if He were in the room.

The Reverend Varnell takes note of the family's blessings—the new roof on the house, the tobacco barn full, the son just returned from Army service— and gives thanks for these things. He asks God's mercy upon the sick, or family members far from home, or prays for rain in time of drought. . . .

The Reverend Varnell was also a community leader. His role, which should be that of a community newspaper too, was described colorfully and well in the same article.

It is no longer enough for a country parson to be a more-or-less enlightened and effective preacher of the Word. If he is to fulfill his duty to the rural community, he must be a pastor in the ancient sense—a shepherd leading his flock to a better life on earth . . . he must understand his community in a sociological sense, and lead it in every good fight—against soil erosion and the pollution of streams and the destruction of forests; for community health centers and better schools, good roads and honest government . . .

The Reverend Varnell was a country preacher who spent his life back in the hills, but he loved and understood his people. He worked constantly for their well-being.

Community newspapers aren't preachers and they shouldn't try to be. But the role played by the Reverend Varnell in working for the well-being of his people is similar in many ways to the one that community newspapers should embrace, whether they be weekly, semiweekly, or daily, in rural or suburban areas.

Chapter 3

The Basics of Good News Writing

by René J. (Jack) Cappon

New technology has transformed plant and process in much of the newspaper industry, but no technology teaches the newspaper's simple product, the written word. That remains a nontransferable human skill.

It is also the point on which the reader's allegiance turns—a truism worth restating in times when allegiance can no longer be taken for granted. Changing life patterns and social arrangements, inroads by electronic media, plain demographics, and educational trends stressing audio-visual communication over print have all weakened the bonds between newspaper and reader.

Lee Hills, chairman of the Knight-Ridder group, took note of the challenge a few years ago. "Never before has the quality of the product loomed so important," he said. "News-editorial quality—which I interpret as all those things which make a good newspaper indispensable—also builds prestige and is the most important factor in attracting talent, not only editorial talent but business-side talent as well."

And he added: "Editorial excellence is not a goal to be sought and one day achieved and then retired to the trophy case. It is an ambition which must be pursued anew each day—never ending, never totally achieved."

This applies with special force to writing, which is to editorial excellence what sunshine is to a plant. The most

inviting makeup and graphics, the most painstaking coverage of the news will not be ultimately decisive unless the copy is clear and lively. Today's impatient, preoccupied reader cannot be asked to plow through superfluous verbiage, grope through murky jargon, stumble over convoluted sentences, or puzzle out meanings.

Ironically, newspaper people themselves sometimes underestimate the harm loose writing can do. They are, after all, professional readers. The practiced journalist has little trouble guessing the sense of an awkward passage and mentally reordering jumbled syntax as he reads. Most ordinary citizens, including well-educated ones, don't usually have the same facility with print, and those who do will still appreciate lucid, straightforward prose.

Good news writing, then, is clear, precise, and succinct, qualities attainable only by close attention to the workings of words and sentences.

RENÉ J. (JACK) CAPPON

The author is general news editor of the Associated Press. He has published numerous articles on news writing and has conducted writing clinics and seminars for newspaper staffs and professional groups around the country.

"The most inviting makeup and graphics, the most painstaking coverage of the news will not be ultimately decisive unless the copy is clear and lively."

Wordiness Dulls Writing

The first requirement is that each word perform honest labor, even in a brief phrase. In "on a monthly basis," for

example, only *monthly* does work, and it is sufficient: The paper appeared monthly.

Wordiness is perhaps the most common flaw of news writing. It reduces readability, blunts the news element, and slows the pace. Many sources contribute to wordiness: overuse of the passive form, circumlocution, officialese, jargon, abstraction, devotion to adjectives and adverbs, and others.

Verbosity is not the same as length. A 2,000-word article can be succinct, a 200-word short grossly overwritten. The following sentence, from a story about one of California's perennial brush fires, seems succinct enough:

Five rescue ambulances stood by to rush the injured to nearby hospitals.

But eight of these twelve words are unemployed. Ambulances usually rescue, they don't dawdle, they carry the injured rather than the healthy, and they seldom hunt for remoter hospitals. "Five ambulances stood by" was all the writer needed.

More frequently, pruning entails some rewording, but the small labor is well worth it:

King told the meeting the matter should be studied further and that in the interim, there should be a freeze in the issuance of new liquor licenses in the state.

This can be sharpened to read:

. . . and that meantime no new liquor licenses should be issued.

Twelve words are saved, along with other benefits: The pompous "in the interim" becomes "meantime," and the awkward passive form is straightened out with the introduction of an active verb—an operation that usually improves a sentence or a clause. (Most sentences beginning with "there is" and "there was" should be suspect.)

Pruning must never go to the point where it imperils clarity, but neither should writers insult their readers' intelligence by belaboring something that is obvious in the context. Two examples are "controversial" and "financially troubled," both threadbare in journalistic usage.

WASHINGTON—After three months of bitter debate, Congress passed a controversial aid-to-education measure. . . .

If Congress has bitterly debated that long, controversy can be taken for granted.

Similarly, "financially troubled" is overkill in the lead which reports that XYZ Company has just fired its work force and filed for bankruptcy.

USING ADVERBS AND PREPOSITIONS

Some writers seem unable to use certain adjectives, such as *few, many, short,* without an adverbial dressing gown, for example, *relatively, comparatively, unduly.*

Relatively few senators were willing to go on record on this provision of the energy bill.

The Green Bay Packers rebuilt in a comparatively short time.

The government stressed that the descent of the Soviet nuclear satellite should cause no undue alarm.

Relative to what? Compared to whom? And what's "due" alarm? Comparatives are wasted words unless an actual comparison is offered in the story. Here they are meaningless modifiers that should be stricken.

It is poor practice, too, to convert plain, specific words into longer, more abstract phrases: Bad weather becomes "unfavorable weather conditions," showers become "shower activity," and a hurt economy becomes "an economy adversely affected"—or even one "suffering a negative impact." Writers should avoid this thickening of language, as they should avoid jargon phrases like "viable alternative." A man looking for an alternative is obviously looking for one that works.

Wordy, circumlocutory prepositions likewise waste time and space—expressions such as *in the field of, with reference to, in the case of,* and the faddish *in terms of.* The wounds they strike may be small, but the cumulative hemorrhage can be substantial. Some examples:

POOR: *Dr. DeBakey is an undisputed leader* in the field of *medicine.*
BETTER: *Dr. DeBakey is an undisputed leader in medicine.*

POOR: *The St. Louis Cardinals had no change* as far as *their game plan*
was concerned.
BETTER: *The St. Louis Cardinals had no change in their game plan.*
BEST: *didn't change their game plan.*

POOR: *Smith said he was seeking clarification* concerning the *governor's attitude* in relation *to the tax ceiling.*
BETTER: *Smith said he was seeking clarification of the governor's attitude toward the tax ceiling.*

POOR: *Mr. Morgan complained that the sanitation department was starved* in terms of *funds and personnel.*
BETTER: *Mr. Morgan complained that the sanitation department was starved of money and personnel.*

POOR: *It was not clear what actions the new pope would take* with respect to *the large issues facing the Church. But changes are expected* in the case of *the Vatican curia.*
BETTER: *It was not clear what actions the new pope would take on the large issues facing the Church. But changes are expected in the Vatican curia.*

POOR: *Chief Johnson, questioned* with reference to *detention of the three juveniles, said he could make no exception* in the case *of such offenders.*
BETTER: *Chief Johnson, questioned about the detention of the three juveniles, said he could make no exception for such offenders.*

REDUCING WORDY PHRASES

Many automatic phrases like the following offer a chance to economize on words. The one-word version is usually better:

- in the majority of cases (mostly)

- in the near future (soon)

- in spite of the fact that (despite)

- ahead of schedule (early)

- take into custody (arrest)

- give consideration to (consider)

- in the direction of (toward)

- in the event of (if)

- few in number (few)

- take action (act)

- a large proportion of (many)

- will be the speaker at (will speak at)

- with the exception of (except, except for)

- a considerable number (many)

- at the present time (now)

- at this point in time (now)

More entertaining, though no more desirable, are the redundancies that sneak into copy while everybody is looking the other way:

High-speed *chase*, organic *life*, farm *crops*, loud *shout*, continue to *exist*, mutual *collaboration*, *attach* together, awkward *predicament*, close *proximity*, completely *destroyed*, absolute *perfection*, *depreciate* in value, *consensus* of opinion, predawn *darkness*, midair *collision*, gainfully *employed*, *never* at any time, period of *time*, past *history*, true *facts*, regular *annual conventions*, temporary *reprieve*, total *extinction*, new *record*, serious *danger*, major *breakthrough*, *whether* or not, *may* possibly, root *cause*, *smile* on her face, advance *planning*, and so on down a long list.

PARAPHRASE VERBOSE QUOTES

Direct quotes enliven a story, but when the statement is repetitious and verbose, a crisp paraphrase moves the story along more effectively. Sometimes, of course, the source or the circumstances dictate a verbatim quote. But that isn't the case in the following examples:

The senator said, "During this period of time, which covers *six years, this subcommittee held* a total of *only six days of hearings."*

The non-italicized words in this gaseous sentence are superfluous. The writer cannot tamper with the direct quote, but he can paraphrase: The sen-

ator said the subcommittee held only six days of hearings in six years.

A humble California deputy sheriff went the senator many times better. He too was dutifully quoted in full:

"Right now, we are optimistic that our investigative leads are developing toward positive information that we think will take us to a suspect."

This is a prize example of what H. L. Mencken called "bow-wow language"—the stilted pomposity wrapping a penny idea into $10 worth of cotton wool. All the writer need have said was this:

The deputy sheriff said investigators thought they were getting closer.

Much space could be saved in newspapers every day by bearing down on such padding. Nowhere is the case against wasteful words better put than in Strunk and White's *Elements of Style:*

Vigorous writing is concise. A sentence should contain no unnecessary words, a paragraph no unnecessary sentences, for the same reason that a drawing should have no unnecessary lines and a machine no unnecessary parts. This requires not that the writer make all his sentences short, or that he avoid all detail and treat his subjects only in outline, but that every word tell.

ABSTRACTIONS CREATE FOG

If long-winded prose taxes readers, large doses of abstract writing will keep them from getting interested enough to be taxed. A fog descends between writer and reader when copy deals largely in generalities, vague approximations, and indefinite concepts rather than specifics, sharp detail, and images. Sentences should be "picturable," full of people and objects. Here's an example of the opposite:

Research has shown that accidents are proportionately more prevalent with motorcycle use and are of a more violent nature.

This shows the worst characteristics of abstract writing. Nothing acts on anything. The sentence is static. The only verb is the feeble *has shown.* There's no suggestion that the sentence has something to do with people. Accidents that are more prevalent hurt no one, even if they are of a more violent nature. Here's a translation:

Research has shown that motorcyclists have more accidents proportionately than other drivers and are more often killed or seriously injured.

Another example:

POOR: *Officials are also seriously concerned about the higher costs but say that* it is difficult to measure or quantify the impact of the energy crisis in terms of job losses or plant closings.

BETTER: *Officials are also worried over the high costs but say it's hard to tell how many workers have been thrown out of jobs or how many plants have shut down because of the energy crisis.*

Again, the rewrite substitutes people for the abstraction, and the sentence is stronger.

The improved version is shorter in the first example but two words longer than the original in the second. Important as brevity is, if it takes a few extra words to make a sentence more readable and comprehensible, they are worth it: "She contended that many women have been socialized against quantitative studies" is briefer but indigestible compared with, "She contended that many women have been discouraged from studying math and the exact sciences."

Lavish use of abstract nouns like *issue, question, purpose, nature, character,* and *problem* creates a pall. People live in slums, not "in slum conditions." They cross a dangerous intersection, not "an intersection of a dangerous nature." They worry about traffic, not "traffic questions." They spend money for housing, not for "housing purposes."

A "health problem" can be anything from an ingrown toenail to terminal cancer, a "financial problem" from bankruptcy to difficulty in collecting outstanding payments, "prison facilities" from a steam table for the kitchen to a new dormitory wing. It is impossible to avoid all abstract words, and there are stories that must be told largely in abstractions. But good writers will sprinkle them with particulars, concrete examples, and illustrations:

The FBI, U.S. attorneys, and grand juries in several cities are looking into alleged corruption in the General Services Administration, which serves as the federal government's builder, landlord, and supply house.

A hundred years ago Herbert Spencer, the philosopher and social scientist, showed in his *Philosophy of Style* what happens when particulars replace bloodless generalities:

GENERAL: *In proportion as the manners, customs, and amusements of a nation are cruel and barbarous, the regulations of its penal code will be severe.*

SPECIFIC: *In proportion as men delight in battles, bullfights, and combats of gladiators, will they punish by hanging, burning, and the rack.*

SIMPLIFY BUREAUCRATESE

The chief manufacturers of abstract verbiage are officials and bureaucrats at all levels and in all institutions, public and private. Too much of their jargon, gobbledygook, bureaucratese, or pudder—a British word for it—seeps into the news columns. The reporter's job is to translate the dialect into plain English.

Here's vintage bureaucratese:

The agency announced plans today to maximize its outreach among the underprivileged by more efficient utilization of funding resources.

This means no more than an effort to reach more of the poor by spending money more wisely, and that's how it should have been written.

Principal Smith may well *say* that in the future his school will provide for "increased parental input into the curricular decisionmaking process." In news language, this should be converted into the statement that parents will be given a greater voice in shaping the curriculum.

Wordiness, abstraction, and pomposity are staples of bureaucratese, and certain words—only a few of which can be listed here—are symptoms: *utilize, viability, prioritize, maximize, optimize, finalize, target* (as a verb), *capability, remuneration, methodology, restructure, interact, relate to, approximately.* Plainer, shorter words should be used for all these.

Look what happens when bureaucratese slips into leads:

POOR: *A state civil service examination to fill uniformed court officer jobs* had a grossly disproportionate impact on blacks and Hispanics as compared to whites, *it was charged in a federal suit filed Wednesday.*

BETTER: *A state civil service examination to fill uniformed court officer jobs was unfair to blacks and Hispanics, it was charged in a suit filed in federal court Wednesday.*

One word, *unfair*, takes care of the quoted jargon in the original version.

POOR: *Utilities were under mandate Wednesday not to cut off service during the winter months to* dwellings housing individuals whose health might thus be endangered.

BETTER: *Utilities were under orders Wednesday not to cut off service during winter to the elderly and seriously ill.*

School jargon is especially oppressive in that it fuzzes a subject that is close to many readers and needs to be written about in the clearest way. In this dialect a library has become a resources center, and you teach English skills rather than English. Is little Jane shy and having trouble making friends? She doesn't "socialize adequately" or "fails to relate to her peers." Does little John throw paper balls at teacher? He "lacks adequate motivation to adapt to behavioral norms." If they try hard enough, and are sure of their facts, news writers should be able to transcribe this language into plain English.

This discussion so far has centered on the use of words in ways that give copy clarity, precision, and life. It can be summed up with advice formulated fifty years ago by Henry

Fowler, author of the classic *Dictionary of Modern English Usage:*

Prefer the familiar word to the far-fetched.
Prefer the concrete word to the abstract.
Prefer the single word to the circumlocution.
Prefer the short word to the long.

Fowler's directions overlap somewhat, and they are not meant as absolutes. Sometimes the longer, less familiar word fits the meaning better than the short. But the prescription, intelligently applied to news writing, will go far to restrain looseness, verbosity, and abstraction. And it's an antidote to jargon as well.

KEEP SENTENCES SHORT

Choosing precise words is vital to readability. So is their proper arrangement in the sentence. A short sentence is more likely to be clear than a long one. A strong admixture of short sentences in copy greatly furthers reading ease. Readability is endangered when the length of the average sentence exceeds twenty words. Note that an average is called for; that allows for plenty of variation of short and longer sentences.

It's helpful to limit sentences to one idea or to a range of closely related ones. When a sentence goes much more than thirty words, consider breaking it into two. Here's an overloaded one:

The records show that the recruiter made calls from his Austin, Texas, office to the police department and the Angelina County district attorney's office in Lufkin on November 12, 1975, according to the Marines, who also said that a third call was made to the county sheriff's office but there is no telephone record to prove it.

The relative clause of the tail end is a common malpractice. The full stop is a great aid to sanity; in the above passage it should come after *Marines*, followed by a new sentence ("They also said . . .").

The following example shows how much more readable copy becomes when sentence length is held in check:

POOR: *Hemple thinks the Dobles probably were the most expensive cars ever built, estimating that in an era when a good mechanic went for $12 a day, it cost over $55,000 to produce each chassis, with the bodies costing extra.*

The makers, who apparently thought a lot of the product, offered an unconditional three-year, 100,000-mile warranty.

BETTER: *Hemple thinks the Dobles probably were the most expensive cars ever built. He estimates that in an era when a good mechanic went for $12 a day, it cost $55,000 to produce each Doble chassis, with the bodies costing extra.*

The makers apparently thought a lot of the product. They offered an unconditional three-year, 100,000-mile warranty.

Sentences should have pace and movement. They should not struggle along with an accumulation of relative, dependent, and parenthetical clauses. A long subordinate clause at the start of a sentence, marching ahead of the main idea, is especially cumbersome in leads, where it usually buries the news element:

Saying that the long controversy should be ended in the public interest, Sen. Joseph Cranshaw (D-Asbury) Tuesday withdrew his amendment that has delayed passage of the public housing bill.

This needs to be turned around (and is best split into two sentences):

Sen. Joseph Cranshaw (D-Asbury) Tuesday withdrew his amendment that has delayed passage of the public housing bill. He said the long controversy should be ended in the public interest.

Clarity suffers when related ideas aren't kept together. Even a short sentence derails under such circumstances:

POOR: *The pictures were shown to the church's governing 12-man synod, of which Stylianos was a member, last week.*

BETTER: *The pictures were shown last week to the church's 12-man governing synod, of which Stylianos was a member.*

KEEP MODIFIERS IN PLACE

Modifiers must be kept close to the words modified, or inadvertent humor results:

The couple left for a motor trip amid confetti and tiny snowballs traveling in casual clothes.

The dangling modifier is a common disaster:

POOR: *Like diabetes, cancer, and heart trouble, convent walls can't keep out her disease.*

BETTER: *Convent walls cannot keep out her disease (alcoholism) any more than they can cancer, diabetes, or heart trouble.*

A sentence should *assert.* Readers are interested in what is, not in what is not. Negative statements can often be framed in a positive way.

NEGATIVE: *Department officials insist that employees usually do not come to work late.*

POSITIVE: *Department officials insist that employees usually are on time.*

NEGATIVE: *The company decided not to go through with the restoration project.*

POSITIVE: *The company abandoned the restoration project.*

Verbs Make Writing Vivid

Many writers believe that adjectives and adverbs, freely laid on, give copy its color, but the secret of vivid sentences is the verb. It is the verb that makes sentences move. Craftsmen write with verbs and nouns. They use adjectives and adverbs sparingly, only when they lend definition and economy to the subject, not merely for adornment or emphasis.

Sports writers are prone to violate this principle: "The amazing Blue Devils, in a spectacular show of strength, mercilessly crushed the outclassed . . ."

Tedious reading. If something is amusing, tragic, dramatic, or spectacular, the story should *show* the readers rather than tell them.

Too many writers are fond of noun-adjective combinations:

The survivors experienced extreme hunger and cold in their mountain hideout.

This sentence limps along with a weak verb, two abstract nouns, and an adjective; it could march briskly on two strong verbs:

The survivors starved and froze in their mountain hideout.

The right verb makes for brevity as well as vigor:

POOR: *The economy showed a quick revival.*

BETTER: *The economy rebounded.*

POOR: *"I don't know," the witness said in a barely audible voice.*

BETTER: *"I don't know," the witness whispered.*

Verbs like *experience, move, issue* (an order), and *take* (action to) are inherently weak. So is *to be* in all its forms; "George bowls well" is better than "George is a good bowler," which is wordier and less direct.

Strong action verbs are especially important in leads:

POOR: *A federal judge issued an order Thursday barring a municipal union from going through with a contract ratification vote.*

BETTER: *A federal judge Thursday blocked a contract ratification vote by a municipal union.*

In the following lead, verb and verb complement merely mumble about what went on:

POOR: *An Allegheny Airlines plane with 23 passengers aboard was forced to take evasive action to avoid collision with a small plane . . .*

BETTER: *An Allegheny Airlines plane with 23 passengers aboard had to dive out of the path of a small plane . . .*

Don't Overload Leads

Leads of course fail for reasons other than a puny verb. The most common error is overloading with secondary detail. The opposite mistake is to provide too little specific detail, leaving the lead vague. The precise middle ground isn't always easy to discover. What's certain is that no one should try to cram all the five W's—who, what, when, where, why—into the opening sentence.

Here's an example of overload:

The St. Claire's Hospital Board of Supervisors has voted unanimously not to appeal a New Jersey Supreme Court ruling that allows Karen Anne Quinlan's father to have her life-support system disconnected, a spokesman said today.

Unnecessary detail apart, this lead illustrates another frequent failing—too much emphasis on the organization, place, event, or person that creates the news and too little emphasis on the news itself.

A more readable version:

The New Jersey hospital where Karen Anne Quinlan has lain in a coma for nearly a year will not challenge a court decision granting her the right to "death with dignity."

In the lead below, the writer attempts too much—a chronology that should be left for later elaboration. Assuredly the firemen didn't pause in battling the fire to look for more bodies:

POOR: *Surprised firemen came across ten bodies—and then began looking for more—as they battled a blaze in a Des Moines department store Sunday after officials said everyone had left the building safely.*

BETTER: *Firemen unexpectedly came across ten bodies in a burning Des Moines department store Sunday after company officials told them everyone had safely left the building.*

Typical of many poor leads, the first version below starts with the source rather than the news, even though the source is of secondary importance:

POOR: *Director Jerry Griffin of the Boswell Correctional Center said a 50-year-old inmate walked away from his work-release job.*

BETTER: *A 50-year-old inmate walked away from his work-release job at the Boswell Correctional Center, director Jerry Griffin said today.*

And this lead is too vague to lure the reader to go on:

Democrat Bruce King and Republican Richard Skeen disagreed again on what should be done about the liquor problem in New Mexico.

What is the problem? What did they disagree about?

Few readers, on the other hand, would resist the following leads, simple, direct, and containing just the right specifics:

Linda Henderson told a judge she spent $14,000 in six weeks on a car, stereo, television, whirlpool bath, a $239 clock, and assorted furniture so she could get back on welfare. And she did.

Bill Cashman, a fireman, says he didn't mind posing nude for a centerfold in a magazine for women who like men. But he has a $2 million objection to use of the picture by a magazine for men who like men.

In leads as in other sentences, the active voice is preferable: "Police arrested Jones" is shorter and more direct than "Jones was arrested by police." A significant exception in news writing is when the subject's prominence requires emphasis: If it's Mayor Jones who was arrested, it's "Mayor Tom Jones arrested by police."

Clichés should be avoided for the simple reason that they are boring. On occasion, however, a cliché seems to fit the sense more smoothly than anything else at hand. Then it's better to use it than reach for an outlandish figure of speech. One caution about a cliché, if one must be used: don't tamper with it (for example, throwing out the baby with the *dish*water), and don't set it off in quotation marks, which merely call attention to the poverty of the phrase.

Use Neutral Words

If baseball, in its own hallowed cliché, is a game of inches, writing is a game of nuances. Good writers know that words, even synonyms, are not interchangeable. An ear deaf to connotations—those subtle clusters of associations that sound along with the word's explicit meaning—can lead to trouble.

Such words can carry editorial and judgmental overtones that don't belong in an objective news story. *Admit* is a good example. The verb implies yielding information reluctantly, under some pressure. "The auto firm's chairman admitted that more cars had to be recalled this year" therefore has implications absent from the neutral *conceded* or *said.*

Refute is an ancient trap—it means demolishing an argument and clearly suggests a judgment. The neutral word is *rebut.*

Claim is not a synonym for *assert, say,* or *insist.* One claims a disputed right; the subject of a claim is always under some doubt. To write that "the policeman claimed he saw the gun" suggests he may not be telling the truth. If that's what's intended, fine; but the neutral verb would be *insisted* or *said.*

Reform is another loaded word. It means "to make better by removing faults or defects." It connotes improvement, something no one in his senses would argue against. But one man's reform can be another man's disaster, so the word should not be used in designating controversial actions—"Abortion law reforms" for abortion law changes, for example.

Bureaucrat is pejorative and should not be used for officials, state employees, or civil servants.

Warn implies genuine danger and, used loosely, lends unwitting credence to political exaggeration. For example: "The candidate warned that a Republican victory would bring disaster to millions of senior citizens."

Even seemingly neutral words like *emphasize* or *point out* need to be used with some care. They create a certain prejudgment in favor of the matter under discussion: "The officials emphasized that no further harm can come from asbestos insulation" suggests that the point is settled; the reader mentally supplies "the fact that" after *emphasized.* If the point isn't settled, *said* would be the better choice.

And the little word *only* has obvious editorial overtones in some contexts: "Only three government programs were started" implies a judgment. It's best to let the figures speak for themselves.

Chapter 4

News Headline Writing– As Art and Craft

by Richard D. Smyser

A headline should invite, maybe even intrigue. A headline should attract the reader most who likely wants—or needs—to read the news story over which it appears. A headline might occasionally, when appropriate and in good taste, startle or amuse. But most of all, a headline should be accurate.

Headlines are more than makeup tools and gimmicks. They are, to the reader, a news story in miniature. Readers expect headlines to give information correctly and fairly. When the reader feels that the headline distorts or is unfair, he feels as cheated as when he sees unfairness, distortion, or inaccuracy in the body type.

Readers don't know about problems of deadlines, space, and word counts. They want only a headline that tells them something, that directs them properly.

A 1969 report on newspaper credibility by the Associated Press Managing Editors Association (APME) listed four reasons for public distrust of newspapers, one of which was "too succinct, imprecise, misleading, or inaccurate headlines."

The following year, in a more extensive APME survey of 625 newspaper readers across the country, only 17 percent said they would rate headlines in their newspaper "accurate and fair."

Qualifiers May Mislead

The 1970 study concluded that the most serious problem with headlines is with "qualifiers"—the subtleties of meaning that too often are lost in the effort to be brief. Some examples:

The story said: *"The Baltimore Orioles' two southpaw aces appeared destined for holdout status."*

The headlines said: *"Baltimore's Pitching Strength Holding Out for More Money"* and *"O's Hurlers Holding Out."*

The heads should have said: *"McNally, Cuellar May Become Holdouts Soon."*

The story said: *"A Soviet nuclear attack submarine has surfaced in Cuban waters, the Pentagon announced Wednesday. . . . This was the first U.S. disclosure that a submarine was among Russian naval vessels making a new series of port calls and visits to Cuba."*

The headlines said: *"Russian Nuclear Sub Surfaces in Cuban Port"* and *"Soviet Attack Sub Visits Cuba."*

The heads should have said: *"Soviet Sub Surfaces Near Cuba."*

RICHARD D. SMYSER

The author is editor of the Oak Ridge (Tennessee) *Oak Ridger* and is widely known as a lecturer to journalism students and professional organizations.

"Readers expect headlines to give information correctly and fairly. When the reader feels that the headline distorts or is unfair, he feels as cheated as when he sees unfairness, distortion, or inaccuracy in the body type."

The story said: *"Senators trying to make it easier to choke off filibusters conceded defeat in their first test today, but they say they'll do better in a second try."*

The headline said: *"Filibuster Stoppage is Doomed."*

Time and Space Problems

Major causes of headline weaknesses are two primarily technological problems of the news business: lack of time and lack of space.

Many headlines are written under press of time. But we should not use this as an excuse for a poor head any more than an auto company should excuse faulty auto parts on the grounds that it was hurrying to make a shipment.

Many headline writing ills could be corrected if all headline writers would read each story in full. This is especially necessary now that writers write in other than the old fashioned pyramid style (all the "five w's" in the first paragraph).

Whenever possible, a headline writer should let the reporter who wrote the story see the headline before it is used and agree that it is a fair representation of the sense of the story.

Headline writers and reporters can be mutually protective. They can help each other avoid what neither wants to give: a wrong impression. On smaller newspapers a reporter may write his own headlines, but these should be checked by someone before they appear in print.

The problem of space is less easy to solve, especially since the trend is toward more innovative makeup. But headline writers should insist on sufficient room to write a good headline. Large type and white space are great, but if there is slavish devotion to them, meaning often takes second place—and so does credibility.

If there is not enough space to write a sensible headline, the headline writer should ask the editor if he can spread the story over another column, make room for another line, or choose a smaller type size.

Frank M. Williams, news editor of the Fort Myers (Florida) *News-Press,* advises in Gannett's *Editorially Speaking:* "You can't play the reader for a fool. The most attractive layout in the world will bring him to the page, but the best written story won't get read unless the headline forces him into the body type."

Some Basic Rules

Editors and copy readers are prima donnas about headlines as often as they are about layout. Many have pet likes, dislikes, nevers, and don'ts.

Many of these are of value, like this of Robert Bentley, then editor of the Fort Myers *News-Press,* in *Editorially Speaking:* "Don't undersell a bright story with a drab headline; but by the same token, don't try to brighten up a serious, factual story with a flippant headline." And some rules, of course, are necessary. Here is a good list of headline do's and don'ts:

- Do be specific.

- Don't generalize.

- Do be clear.

- Do be accurate.

- Don't overwork headline words such as rip, nip, set, etc.

- Don't split the lines of your head improperly. Headlines should be easy to read.

- Don't pad your heads.

- Do try to fill at least two thirds of the space on each line, however.

- Don't say something that needs attribution without using the attribution in the headline.

- Don't parrot the lead.

- Don't use headlines that have a dual meaning.

- Don't use too many modifiers.

- Don't editorialize (watch headlines with question marks).

- Don't use quotes in headline with colon or dash. These are signs of a lazy headline writer.

- Don't use initials. They tend to be confusing.

- Do allow enough space to write a good head.

But generally there have been too many headline rules, fads, and fetishes

FIGURE 4–1 Breaking news headlines improperly at the ends of lines can create wrong impressions.

Penneys, T.G.&Y. To Close Out Main Street Stores

Senator Lies
In State
At Capitol

Jones Criticizes LEAA

MIA Issue Draws Ire Of VFW

FIGURE 4–2 Studies show readers often do not understand initials in headlines and many resent them.

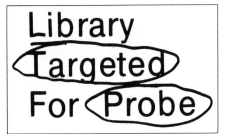

FIGURE 4–3 "Headlinese" may dull a headline.

and too little emphasis on the most important aspect of all: that headlines convey information accurately. And there may be times when the best way to convey information accurately is to end a line with a preposition or to break a verb from its object. If such is the case, then rules are best put aside in the interest of clarity.

Beware of "Headlinese"

As the APME report said, "Headline writing is art as much as craft. It can be taught. It needs to be taught in journalism schools, in newspaper training sessions. It should *not* be taught by emphasizing don'ts, rules, head count." Rather it should be taught emphasizing plain, simple English. And that means avoidance of "headlinese." This is the language peculiar to headlines and

headline writing which developed because of the technological expediencies mentioned above—lack of time and lack of space.

But as surely as there are many good, useful short words (see list), there are abominations.

For example, it is neither fair nor even accurate to say that one politician "hit" another when indeed all he did was criticize him. Some editors refuse to accept such words as *probe, parley, hike, OK,* and *eye.* And who besides another headline writer ever heard of a *solon?* A good rule of the thumb is this: If you can read your headline aloud before a reasonably intelligent group of people without embarrassment or explanation, it is probably all right.

The Key Word

A useful tool in headline writing is the key word principle. Read the story and then ask, What is the one word that absolutely *must* be in this headline?

Sometimes it is obvious. If an item is about the President, either the word *President* or the President's name is essential. Is it about a city or a town? The town name should be in the head to catch the attention of readers there.

But key words can be more than persons, places, or times. They might be words like *believes, claims,* or *reports,* to alert the reader that what he is about to read is not hard fact.

The Long and the Short of Headline Writing

Short words are, of course, a necessity in headline writing. Here are some widely used substitutions of short words for longer ones.

Accident—mishap, wreck, crash
Accumulate—mass
Acquire—gain, get, take
Acquit—clear, free
Agreement—accord, OK, win
Apprehend—nab
Approve—favor, OK
Attempt—try, bid
Belittle—slur
Confront—face
Damage—ruin, mar, wreck, spoil
Decision—rule
Decline—wane, ebb, fall, dip
Discussion—talk, study, confer, weigh
Encourage—spark, spur, urge, stir
Fight—assail, ban, vie
Flight—hop

Former—ex
Honor—hail
Inaugurate—set, begin, start
Inform—tell
Imitate—mock
Inquiry—quiz, probe, study
Journey—trek, trip
Mutual—joint
Prevent—bar, foil, halt
Promise—vow, swear
Refuse—deny
Schedule—slate, list
Silent—mum
Steal—loot, rob
Terminate—close, stop, end
Tremble—jar, jolt
Wrangle—row

How to Count Headlines

The use of video display terminals has made headline counting unnecessary in many instances. When heads are written on VDTs, the writer knows immediately whether they will fit and can make necessary adjustments. Nevertheless, there are still many handwritten or typewritten headlines, and anyone in print media needs to know the basics of head counting.

Although there are variations, the following method is usually considered standard for counting news headlines:

All capital letters are counted as 1½ units, except *M* and *W*, which are counted as 2, and *I*, which is counted as 1.

All lowercase letters are counted as 1 unit, except *m* and *w*, which are counted as 1½, and *f, i, j, l,* and *t*, which are counted as ½ unit because they are so narrow.

Numbers are counted as 1½ units, except the number *1*, which is counted as ½ unit.

Punctuation marks are counted as ½ unit each, except the question mark, which is wide enough to be counted as 1.

Spaces between words are counted as 1 unit by some newspapers and as ½ unit by others.

This method is applied as follows:

Headline and unit counts	Total Count
1½ 1 1 1½ 1 ½ 1 1 ½ 1 1½ ½ ½ 1 1 D r u m r i g h t C i t e d	14½
1½ 1 1½ 1½ 1 1 ½ 1 1½ 1 1½ 1 ½ A s ‘B e s t T o w n’	14½
1½ 1 1½ 1 1 1 1 1 1½ 1 1 1 C o w b o y s R o p e	13½
1½ 1 1 1 1 1½ 1 1 ½ 1 1½ 1½ ½ ½ 1½ J a y h a w k s, 3 0 – 1 0	16

Because typefaces vary in width of letters, the newsroom employee will find it helpful to paste up an example of each headline font in use, from the smallest to the largest point size, and write the size and head count beside each head. This schedule can serve as a guide to accurate counting, especially for beginners.

Headline rule makers often condemn simple label headlines. But, as the APME study states, "There is something to be said for labels—verbless heads—on some subjects. The label at least tells the reader the topic, and if it is a hot readership subject, you can turn him on."

A label is always preferable to what might be a misleading headline. There are circumstances when "City Council Meets Tonight" is better than a headline that, although containing more lively words, might give a totally distorted impression of the nature of the business before the Council.

Headlines Can Libel

Headlines should not be libelous. And headlines can be libelous even though they are atop a story that is utterly without libel.

The most obvious, if also the most frequently occurring example, is the headline on the routine crime report. The story says that the driver of the car in the fatal crash was charged with drunken driving. But the headline says "Drunk Driver Kills Two." The headline has closed the case . . . and possibly opened another.

Young reporters are often particularly insensitive to the legal dangers of headlines and need to be reminded and reminded again.

A reporter should not slough off responsibility for a bad headline on his story by saying he didn't write it, the copy reader or the editor did. At the very least it is the responsibility of the writer to complain, to make the headline writer aware of the misimpression his headline has created.

Involve the Staff

There is a place for the intriguing, the humorous, the witty, even the "cute" headline. Indeed, there are stories that cry out for this type of head. A good headline writer spots them instinctively. Such stories have certain elements with the potential for a twist, a pun, a double entendre, a fascinating visual play. If only you can think of it! Always try to.

Here is where time is so important. Here also is where shared ideas can be the key, where the "chemistry of ideas" can be put to use, where bad ideas, horrible puns, tasteless shadings can often be harnessed for peaceful purposes.

So when time allows, make the supreme effort for the perfect head. Encourage a sort of stream-of-conscious brainstorming among the staff. Encourage all to blurt out their very worst ideas—ideas that you would never think of using. They just might nudge some cog in some other mind which might then nudge yet another cog in another mind which might then produce the perfect headline.

It is a contradiction that there should be pressures on headline writers. Theirs is one of the most important tasks in the business of communication. And yet sometimes they know precisely what the headline should say to attract attention, to evoke interest, to lead the proper readers to the story, all in fairness and accuracy, but the space isn't right.

The technology that revolutionized newsroom production in the 1960s and 1970s should be used to the maximum to lessen the problems of the headline writer—to make it possible for the ideal headline to get into print more often.

Readable, interest-provoking, attention-directing, and, most of all, accurate headlines are very much a part of newspaper readability and credibility. Writing them is indeed, as the APME report says, art as much as craft.

Chapter 5

The Editorial Page

by Paul Greenberg

Editorials are the heart and soul of a newspaper. A newspaper without editorials is like a day without sunshine, or a gentle shower, or a thunderstorm, or an avalanche—depending on the nature of the editorials. Editorials give a newspaper a character of its own apart from the news it reports. They allow the paper to establish a relationship between itself and the community it serves, sometimes by saying what only a friend and neighbor can. Cut out editorials, or offer only a poor excuse for them, and readers will notice.

Take a Line

Remember that what makes the editorial page different is opinion. It is as important to keep editorial opinion from being replaced by news as it is to keep editorializing out of the news columns. Take a word of advice from H. L. Mencken: "An editorial, to have any rationale at all, should say something. It should take a line." Preferably a distinctive line consistent with the paper's character, even conscience. That's one reason I would not recommend signing editorials, which ought to be the opinion of the newspaper as an institution rather than of an individual. Over the years, that institution should develop a personality as distinctive and interesting as that of a ship or country. It will be a good sign when

people begin referring to newspapers by the feminine pronoun.

Please, as few as possible of those pseudoeditorials that are tactfully described as "balanced" and "objective," terms that serve as polite synonyms for "vague" and "dead." Absent a clear opinion, don't try to fuzz. It will show. Either drop the subject or stop and think long enough to acquire an opinion. You will do the reader a service either way. Avoid printing any editorial that can be summed up by the phrase, "This is a most serious question that deserves study."

Editorials should not be limited to political subjects. A piece promoting walnut trees or good manners, or even some quality still plentiful in our society, might be more interesting and beneficial than one more piece of punditry. Don't confine humor to the other pages. Then again, beware the humorous editorial; it can turn out most solemn of all. Humor generally makes a better appetizer, or seasoning, than an elaborately served main course.

Take everything that can be called news analysis, background, and so on and stick it somewhere in the paper other than the editorial column. Let the editorial reflect its original, honest meaning: the opinion of the editor. Better a shorter editorial column than an adulterated one. News and information may be useful, even essential, to back up an opinion. But do not use them as a substitute for it. News items, like beams, may remain exposed in a handsomely constructed edifice; they should not be confused with the

PAUL GREENBERG

The author is editorial page editor of the Pine Bluff (Arkansas) *Commercial,* a nationally syndicated columnist, and winner of a Pulitzer Prize for editorial writing.

"Don't set out to write an editorial, but to say something about something. . . . Don't let time or pride of authorship seduce you into printing anything you haven't thought and felt through."

whole structure. As a general rule, try to express an opinion early in an editorial, preferably in the first sentence or two. That gives the reader fair notice. It may even hold his attention, by getting him to wonder how the paper is going to uphold so improbable an assertion.

It is so common to find strong editorial opinion on matters far removed from the interests of advertisers and subscribers that there is a word for it: Afghanistanism. But the closer to home, the greater an editorial's im-

Light in December

'His name is Christmas," he said.

"His name is what?" one said.

"Christmas."

"Is he a foreigner?"

"Did you ever hear of a white man named Christmas?"...

"I never heard of nobody a-tall named it," the other said.

And that was the first time Byron remembered that he had ever thought how a man's name, which is supposed to be just the sound for who he is, can be somehow an augur of what he will do, if other men can only read the meaning in time. It seemed to him that none of them had looked especially at the stranger until they heard his name. But as soon as they heard it, it was as though there was something in the sound of it that was trying to tell them what to expect; that he carried with him his own inescapable warning, like a flower its scent or a rattlesnake its rattle. Only none of them had sense enough to recognise it. They just thought that he was a foreigner...

— William Faulkner, *Light in August*

In Pine Bluff, his name was Joe Telles, and he arrived, as best anyone could tell, some time in the morning of December 21st, 1967, four days before Christmas, and the last day of his life. Not that anyone could have known that on one of those busy days just before the holiday arrived. He was another complication of the season, down on his luck and sick, needing help. Maybe that is the essence of being a Joe Telles, being an unknown for others, and a complication. There are forms and groups and deputies to take care of such matters. It probably didn't occur to anyone to take especial notice of his name, that is, until it could no longer avail him, or us, in this life.

He died that night on the floor of the county jail. Not because he belonged there, but because he didn't seem to belong anywhere else, having been deposited there after a long day of being passed from station to station in his way through Pine Bluff; his body was shipped out promptly. Later, when the newspaper began asking questions and trying to piece together his movements that last suffering day, it was assured that he had been "taken care of." And somebody else wanted to know why the paper was interested at all, an item already having been printed. Because it was a story, of course, maybe the oldest story, and part of the Good News.

Maybe that is why, on December 21st in Pine Bluff, one is drawn back to ask after Joe Telles, and wonder what was in his name, and why it was more than just the sound for who he was, but somehow an augur of what he would come to mean, like Faulkner said. Maybe he stopped at this siding to tell us, if we would hear. Not that one had a right to expect any answers from him; he probably had questions enough of his own to ask, to judge from his brief annals of poverty and trouble. No, the answers have to come from ourselves. But the Joe Telleses can raise the questions. "The basic questions,' to quote Paul Tillich, "to which the Christian symbols are the answer." That is sufficient, more than sufficient to those who would summon the courage to look, and ask.

Again it is four days before Christmas, and the lists of things to do grow longer, more consuming. They are lists of things to do — not of things to think, or question, or contemplate. But things to be got out of the way. The terror and awe and immediacy of life are not likely to be listed there. And when the time comes for contemplation, or worship, or just pause, that time too may find its way onto the lists, duly assigned to the professionals in these matters, and carried out on schedule and in a body. That is not bad, or necessarily good. It is like a responsive reading — just what the congregation makes of it. But it is not done alone, the way Faulkner is read, or the way Joe Christmas came, and went, in *Light in August*. Or in the solitary way Joe Telles passed through Pine Bluff, and this world, on that single day in December that must have seemed an eternity. Or with the directness that the simple words in the Gospel always have: "Inasmuch as ye have done it unto one of the least of these my brethren, ye have done it unto me."

One hesitates to make the wish, but somewhere on the bulging schedules and lists, this fourth day before Christ Mass, let space be made for eternity, for the soul strength to confront the questions Joe Telles raised.

pact. And the greater the paper's responsibility.

One of the better if perhaps apocryphal mottos for a small newspaper is supposed to have adorned one in Beckley, West Virginia, years ago: "The Only Newspaper in the World That Gives a Damn about Beckley." That kind of identification with the community, however phrased, is a great responsibility and should be strengthened by frequent exercise.

Speak Up

Thomas Hobbes, who would have made a dandy country editor, once observed that only "Such truth as opposeth no man's profit, nor pleasure, is to all men welcome." And to all men tedious reading. Surely it is better to encourage a strong exchange of opinions in the community than to print platitudes in the guise of editorials. Such an exchange whets people's appetite for more, increases tolerance for the differences that should mark a diverse society, and in general invigorates the democratic process. For the editor, it offers a great opportunity to be magnanimous in victory or graceful in defeat or error.

Editorials need not be infallible to be valuable. Even if they only get people talking or perhaps even thinking, or educate the editor by the reaction they prompt, they will have been worthwhile. Exposing one's views is a bit like participating more fully in life. It usually results in getting to know one's neighbors better, maybe even liking them more. It keeps the critical faculties, the editor's and others', from atrophying. In short, it's interesting. You go to bat every issue.

As Archy once told Mehitabel, or maybe the other way around, "If you make people think they're thinking, they'll love you; but if you really

FIGURE 5–1 Editorials need not always be on political subjects. On December 21, 1967, a transient passing through Pine Bluff died on the floor of the county jail. Every year since then, the *Commercial* has commemorated the event with this editorial on the meaning of Christmas. *Reprinted courtesy of the Pine Bluff (Arkansas)* Commercial.

make them think, they'll hate you." That's too hard on people. The ruffled feelings may prove only transient. The satisfactions last. So does the reader's interest, if only to see what the editor is going to say next. To be effective, an editorial must reflect the shared values of the community and at the same time raise them. It's a neat trick, but about the only one worth trying with an editorial policy.

Ideas Are Everywhere

Where do you get ideas for editorials? Everybody has ideas for editorials. Breathes there the editor with soul so dead who never to himself has said, "This, this, is the solution"? Attend meetings, develop local sources (some to be taken with a carton of salt), live in the community, and draw from personal experience. *Read the newspaper.* And the ideas will probably come more rapidly than one can think them out. Beware suggestions from outside the paper. Not because they're necessarily bad but because others' ideas are not as readily, clearly, and personally expressible. And think a lot. There's no substitute for it. The process has saved many a good editorial, and prevented many a bad one from appearing in print and embarrassing the whole newspaper.

How to Write Editorials

Don't set out to write an editorial, but to say something about something. The style that comes most naturally and

FIGURE 5–2 A municipal budget hearing can be a monumentally dull exercise. This editorial goes beyond the figures to point out a contrast between sums being lavished on what the newspaper regarded as frills and the less-than-adequate amounts devoted to basic services and human needs. It personalizes what could have been columns of dull figures. *Reprinted courtesy of the Pine Bluff (Arkansas)* Commercial.

Time to Speak Up

Tuesday night, it was time for a public hearing on Pine Bluff's city budget for 1979. And the pleas heard made a good deal more sense than the mayor's request earlier for a 25 per cent pay increase for himself and the city attorney.

For example, Police Chief Bobby Norman asked for a 10 per cent raise for the department's employees not in uniform, and submitted a salary schedule that he said would bring the pay of police in Pine Bluff up to salary levels in Little Rock. He mentioned that this year the force had lost nine qualified people to better offers and that the Civil Service examinations that once might attract a hundred applicants now get only a quarter as many. It's "pitiful," said Chief Norman, when a city this size has only three or four policemen out on the streets at night, and that in emergencies the department has to be "saved" by calling in volunteers — Specials who are only part-time cops and have a good deal less training.

If anything, Chief Norman may have been understating the case for better police salaries. This situation — "it's like being in quicksand," he said — has been allowed to develop through year after year of neglect. Now it's to the point where, by the time one officer is properly trained, the department may lose two to other police departments. This is asking for trouble and scandal — some of which already has occurred. And not just in the city police department. The county needs to improve its services, too. The most vile behavior and abuse of prisoners has just been reported at the county jail.

The need to start concentrating on the basics was driven home again and again during the public hearing Monday night. Fire Chief Ray Jacks told Pine Bluff's City Council that the monthly starting salary for a fireman has increased only $60 over the past three inflation-ridden years.

The director of the Jenkins Memorial Childrens Center,

"What does it say about a community, or a society, when its policemen, firemen, and teachers are among the lowest paid of its professionals, but hundreds of thousands of dollars can be found every year to support a convention center? It says that, in our order of priorities, physical safety, good law enforcement, and the minds of our children come down the list."

would hurry and generate some more income for basic services, or at least stop sopping up the tax revenue needed to maintain them decently.

A budget says something more about government than how much money comes in and how much goes out. It points to where people's priorities are — not just the priorities they pay lip service to, but those they are willing to pay for with their tax dollars. What does it say about a community, or a society, when its policemen, firemen, and teachers are among the lowest paid of its professionals, but hundreds of thousands of dollars can be found every year to support a convention center? It says that, in our order of priorities, physical safety, good law enforcement, and the minds of our children come down the list. And it shows a sorry society in the making if priorities are not changed, and quickly.

Unless there is a pot of gold at the end of Barraque Street, the citizens of Pine Bluff would seem to have a painful choice at budget time: We can aim to be a replica in miniature of those great cities that go all out to attract out-of-towners and build impressive public monuments that look good on postcards, while conditions deteriorate for those who must live there, particularly if they are the poor, elderly, or troubled. Or we can stop playing this game of empty prestige and begin turning the budget around to emphasize basic services again. We can aim for a community where cops are looked to with respect and assurance, a community where

We're Thankful For...

Home and family and friends, for health and holiday seasons and the memory of celebrations past.

For Thanksgiving dinners that look like Norman Rockwell pictures. For everything on the traditional Thanksgiving menu, whether one cares for it or not. For the colors of it. It all *looks* so good. For nuts and cheeses and wines in all their variety. For hearty breakfasts and orange marmalade. For pancakes. Oatmeal. Mexican food. Baklava. For greens, grits and cornbread. And for the taste of water on a warm day.

For civility among strangers. For country talk and country ways. And country ham. For the smell of coffee on cold mornings and familiar sights seen after long absence. For family reunions and the generations past. For people who still enjoy their work. For workers and artisans, servants and professionals who hold to the old-time standards, even if they use modern tools. For the chance to watch somebody who really knows what he's doing, like a veteran at it carving the turkey.

For the change of seasons and the serenity of an overcast day in the woods, and how a dark blue sky brings out the greens in a landscape. For mountains and beaches, for rolling hills and red-rock deserts. For the sound of rain on the roof. For the crackle of wood in the fireplace and the savor of the first fire of the season. For frosty mornings and the first snow of winter. For the first signs of spring, and autumn. For the feel of a football, and of bicycling through fallen leaves. And for the clean sting of a tennis ball hitting the sweet spot of the racket.

For familiar faces. For Father John O'Donnell at St. Joseph's. And Brother Ed Matthews at Lakeside Methodist. For Mr. Jimmy McGaughy and Earl Chadick Sr. For old clothes that finally have been broken in just right. For Pine Bluff's tireless Sunbeam girl, ever swinging at Main and Harding. For old movies and reprints of anything by Rebecca West, Janet Flanner or Mary McCarthy. For the feel of a good book, and the anticipation it stirs. For bookstores. For the first lesson in a foreign language and the sense it gives of a whole new world opening up. For all-night coffee shops, and the smell of leather in shoe-repair shops. For old furnitures stores and Army surplus stores. For new ideas, new friends, new alternatives, new hopes and crinkly new dollar bills.

For good company and solitude. For the presence of a friend when no words need pass. For music. Mozart and Vivaldi. Dixieland jazz and patriotic marches, barber shop quartets and the Happy Goodman Family. For the King James Version. For good teachers and the kind of good cop who couldn't be, wouldn't want to be, anything else. For the armed forces of the United States of America. For firemen. For Ann Lightsey at the public library in Pine Bluff, the kind of children's librarian who has a smile for everybody, even adults. For small towns and the look of their main street at Christmastime, or in the heat of a July afternoon. For America, and the look of it in an Edward Hopper painting. For El Greco and Breughel. And butterflies.

For the feel of a freshly sharpened No. 2 pencil. For the unquestioning love of a child. And for how Halloween and Thanksgiving are still celebrated the same way in school. For trick-or-treaters and cut-out Pilgrims, their clothes dutifully colored black. And for the new ways in school of learning old lessons.

For the critics who keep us humble, and for those who don't. For glimpses of peace in the headlines, for the unaccountable good things, the grace of the world. For America, the very sound of the word. And for that most American of holidays, the one set aside for a people who take so much for granted the rest of the year. Thanksgiving....

How's your list coming?

simply is best. It may require a lot of rewriting. If nothing comes naturally, remember the old maxims of good writing: Be clear, simple, and straightforward except on those rare occasions when the rules were made to be broken. Try writing editorials as though they were addressed to a single individual—a public official, a retired gentleman on Main Street, your Aunt Matilda, an angry young man. Reread and rewrite and, if necessary, forget it. Don't let time or pride of authorship seduce you into printing anything you haven't thought and felt through.

Edit, edit, edit. Then have the piece edited, or at least read, by someone else. The general sign of good editing is that the piece becomes shorter, not longer. An editorial writer who edits his own stuff is in the same predicament as the lawyer who represents himself. Sometimes it helps to put an editorial aside for a day and then look at it fresh. And it may be better to write out a projected editorial before criticizing it than to talk the idea over first with an editor or reporter. Many a good editorial has been talked away. Make the editorial sound good. Trust your ear.

Write with feeling and edit with care, so that the sharp edge of the writing will remain, perhaps even be honed. Don't be afraid of the unorthodox, the whimsical, the singular, either in style or content. Few good editorials are predictable. Try to go that one step beyond some immediate issue in the news to examine the attitude, philosophy, or morality behind it.

One of the more popular ways to organize an editorial might be called the Neo-Classical Cycle: Offer an opinion, document it, play around with its ramifications, then restate it at the end. Then there is the presentation of a problem and the working out of the preferred solution. My favorite is the Sure-Fire System. Write about what interests you most, what you know best and feel strongest about. Store up information, quotes, telling analogies on the subject. As in the case of the fellow

FIGURE 5–3 The style that comes naturally and simply is best for editorials, written as though they were addressed to a single individual. *Reprinted courtesy of the Pine Bluff (Arkansas)* Commercial.

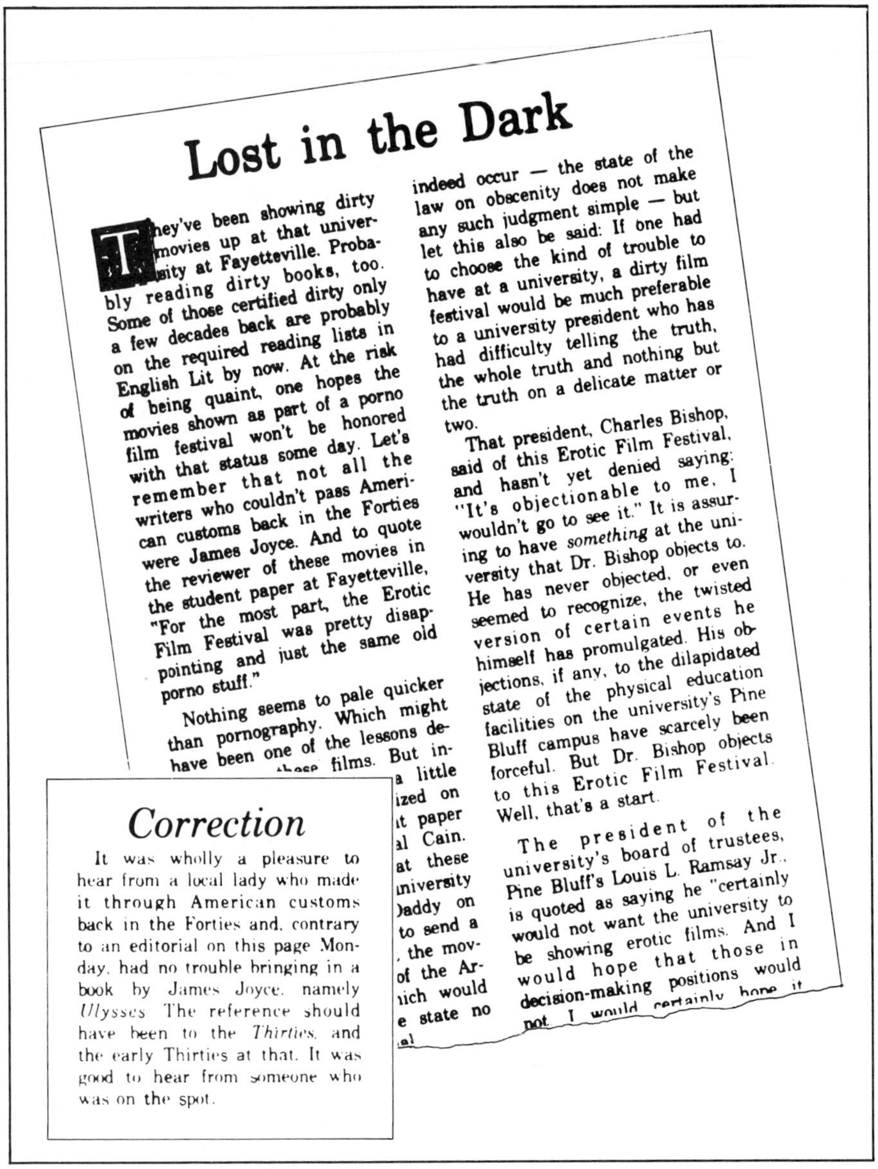

Lost in the Dark

They've been showing dirty movies up at that university at Fayetteville. Probably reading dirty books, too. Some of those certified dirty only a few decades back are probably on the required reading lists in English Lit by now. At the risk of being quaint, one hopes the movies shown as part of a porno film festival won't be honored with that status some day. Let's remember that not all the writers who couldn't pass American customs back in the Forties were James Joyce. And to quote the reviewer of these movies in the student paper at Fayetteville, "For the most part, the Erotic Film Festival was pretty disappointing and just the same old porno stuff."

Nothing seems to pale quicker than pornography. Which might have been one of the lessons de-... those films. But in... a little ... ized on ... it paper ... al Cain. ... at these ... iniversity ... Daddy on ... to send a ... the mov- ... of the Ar- ... nich would ... e state no ... al

indeed occur — the state of the law on obscenity does not make any such judgment simple — but let this also be said: If one had to choose the kind of trouble to have at a university, a dirty film festival would be much preferable to a university president who has had difficulty telling the truth, the whole truth and nothing but the truth on a delicate matter or two.

That president, Charles Bishop, said of this Erotic Film Festival, and hasn't yet denied saying: "It's objectionable to me, I wouldn't go to see it." It is assuring to have something at the university that Dr. Bishop objects to. He has never objected, or even seemed to recognize, the twisted version of certain events he himself has promulgated. His objections, if any, to the dilapidated state of the physical education facilities on the university's Pine Bluff campus have scarcely been forceful. But Dr. Bishop objects to this Erotic Film Festival. Well, that's a start.

The president of the university's board of trustees, Pine Bluff's Louis L. Ramsay Jr., is quoted as saying he "certainly would not want the university to be showing erotic films. And I would hope that those in decision-making positions would not I would certainly hope it...

Correction

It was wholly a pleasure to hear from a local lady who made it through American customs back in the Forties and, contrary to an editorial on this page Monday, had no trouble bringing in a book by James Joyce, namely *Ulysses* The reference should have been to the *Thirties*, and the early Thirties at that. It was good to hear from someone who was on the spot.

FIGURE 5–4 Print corrections on the editorial page when warranted or even partially warranted. In this editorial on pornography and "dirty books," an alert reader noted an error in a reference to James Joyce. *Reprinted courtesy of the Pine Bluff (Arkansas)* Commercial.

who shoots first and only then draws the target around his bullet hole, people will wonder how the writer manages to hit the bull's-eye so frequently. The more things one develops an interest in, the better the system works.

Assorted Caveats

Beware conflicts of interest or the appearance thereof. The smaller the town, the more difficult it may be for the editor to avoid getting drawn into causes that seem to conflict with editorial independence. Remember how to say no.

And remember that editorials can praise, too. Don't make the editorial column a standing litany of complaints. Editorials may have to be left for last in the case of a small newspaper with a limited staff, but don't let them become hasty afterthoughts or space fillers. While considering the news of the day, consider your opinions about it, too. Perhaps even map them out mentally. Cushion the editorial writing with some time for reflection. (This is such good advice that I myself fully intend to follow it some day.) But don't

let the need for "research" become a substitute for editorial writing.

Be honest, even in the heat of rhetoric. Be the harshest critic of the editorial product before it appears in print and rewrite accordingly. You'll be glad you did. Never fudge even in the best of causes. Art is short, conscience long in this business. Attack the strongest part of the opposition's case and not the weakest. The reader one most wants to influence will know the difference. It's not sporting, or really much fun, to go after straw men. Don't save your mightiest blows for some defenseless civil servant while never disagreeing with the local bank president or chamber of commerce. Readers understand how that goes, too.

Be personal in style, allusions, and impact, but not in argumentation. Be hard on ideas, not people. Revive the lost art of strong but civil disagreement. Print corrections when warranted or even only partially warranted. Print them at least as prominently as the original mistake. And do print them under their proper name ("Corrections") and not "Clarifications" or "Amplifications" or "Further Ado." It only hurts for a little while.

The Rest of the Page

Good editorials are the prerequisite of a good editorial page, but there is more to it. Like headline writing. Make the heads active. Avoid the ubiquitous and deadly label head ("The Courthouse Location"). Instead, use verbs, idiom, questions ("Anyplace but There!"). Dignity need not be dull.

Unless a newspaper is convinced that it has a monopoly on the truth, its editorials should be balanced with articles advocating other opinions. Give the reader a balanced diet of opinions from other sources—columns, cartoons, guest pieces. The more local, the better. A good local cartoonist is a great asset. The object is to make all the page appealing and useful to the reader. To quote Robert M. White II of the Mexico, Missouri, *Ledger,* the editorial page should be "respectful not only in content but also in appearance. And to be respectful to the reader is, among other things, to try to attract and hold him." But don't let the more technical side of the job (graphics, makeup, writing headlines, and editing columns) entice you away from the essential function of the editorial page: to present sound opinion, particularly the newspaper's, expressed particularly well.

Special attention should be paid to the Letters column. A good, abundant Letters column is the surest indication that the rest of the page, particularly its editorials, say something to someone. The care and feeding of letter writers is a job that should not be neglected. They too serve the public and attract readers—and invigorate the democratic process. And the more letters you print, the more you may get.

Recommended Reading

Other people's editorials. Books strong on ideas. *The Masthead,* which is the journal of the National Conference of Editorial Writers, P.O. Box 34928, Washington, D. C. 20034. The NCEW is a group dedicated to fellowship and improving the quality of the American editorial page, two admirable and much needed activities. Its annual meetings, which feature working sessions during which editors criticize each others' editorial pages, are worth attending.

Chapter 6

Handling News Pictures

by Kenneth Blum

This should be the golden age of photojournalism in newspapers. The continuing development of the 35mm single-lens reflex camera, with its speed, versatility, and almost unlimited variety of lenses, has made taking pictures easier than ever before. The popularity of photography is booming, and beginning photographers find a wealth of information in courses (some offered for college credit) and magazines to help them become proficient. There's an abundance of talent for hire. Offset printing has made page production simple and reproduction near perfect.

But while the use of pictures in newspapers has improved, there are still too many editors around who are skilled "word men" but pathetically lacking in the editing techniques needed to handle pictures effectively. Likewise, there are too many photographers whose pictures are wooden and meaningless.

The dull, trite pictures—the check-passers, the handshakers, the police lineups—are still with us. So is the page with twenty-five washed out two-column by three-inch pictures of county fair ribbon winners. So is the excellent picture that has been ruined by being buried in two columns on page 27.

Progress has been a slow, tedious process. Technical improvements in camera and printing equipment have advanced much faster than the basic skills of the people who use them. In general, pictures in today's hometown newspapers still tend to record events unimaginatively.

What Is A Good Picture?

But just what is a good picture? A precise definition is difficult because we're dealing with the unique emotional and intellectual responses of human beings. It's just as hard to define a good novel or a good movie.

Still there are common characteristics of good newspaper pictures. Good newspaper pictures draw attention immediately. Their quality is determined by their emotional impact upon the reader. They draw responses like "Wow, that's John Brown!" and not "That's certainly a nice picture of John Brown."

Good newspaper pictures tell the truth.

And, most important, good newspaper pictures tell a story.

The editor may be able to improve a picture through bold cropping, proper sizing, or a snappy catchline, but first he must have a good picture with which to work.

The Editor-Photographer

The most important factor in the development of a visually effective newspa-

KENNETH BLUM

The author is general manager of the Orrville (Ohio) *Courier-Crescent,* an award winning photographer, and a writer of numerous articles appearing in professional publications.

"Good newspaper pictures draw attention immediately. Their quality is determined by their emotional impact on the reader. And, most important, good newspaper pictures tell a story."

per lies in the professional relationship between the editor and the photographer. The editor is only as good as the photographer who shoots the pictures he uses. The photographer is only as good as the editor who assigns and handles his pictures.

It's up to the editor—the coordinator of the product, the boss—to take the lead.

The editor must know a good picture when he sees one, as he knows a good story when he reads one. He must throw out bad pictures, as he throws out poorly written news stories. He must seek out ideas for good pictures as vigorously as he seeks out leads and tips for news and feature articles. He must praise the good picture as he praises the good news story. He must encourage, even discipline, the photographer who isn't performing up to his capabilities, as he would the apathetic reporter. He must establish ground rules and policy for use of pictures, as well as editorial content. He must demand truth and accuracy from both writers and photographers.

In short, it's not an editor's function to show partiality to either words or pictures. He deals with both, and it's his responsibility to develop the technical and managerial skills to handle both effectively.

Pictures are "reporting" as much as the written story is. They should be treated with the same respect—no more, no less.

In this vein, the photographer must view himself as a "visual reporter."

Like the writer, he may specialize or be a jack-of-all-trades. At a fire, he functions as a spot news reporter. At a school picnic, he functions as a feature reporter. In more involved assignments—for instance, the plight of the elderly—he serves as an investigative reporter.

The important thing is that he must remember that first and foremost he is a journalist on an equal footing with the writer. The only difference is that he communicates visually instead of verbally.

The Posed Picture

The first and perhaps most important step in handling pictures begins with the picture assignment. For many newspapers, this give rise to an inevitable, heated debate concerning the posed, cliché picture—club officers, award winners, gavel passings, etc. On the metro daily, the vast scope of the paper's circulation eliminates any possibility of using this type of picture. But for the weekly and small daily, where content is more personal, the ar-

gument lingers on.

In one corner, editors insist that since local names and faces are news in a community newspaper, readers enjoy and demand posed pictures, and it's up to the newspaper to provide what readers want.

In the other corner, editors claim that the posed picture is a visual wasteland, the result of "picture politics" and pressures put on the editor by well-meaning but aggressive people intent on getting their picture in the paper and publicity for their organizations. By eliminating posed pictures, they claim that more emphasis can be placed on pictures with genuine visual impact.

Perhaps one of the best arguments against the posed picture was presented by Randy West, editor of the Corydon (Indiana) *Democrat,* in an editorial to his readers:

This newspaper gets a lot of requests for photographs.

We're happy about that because we want to be told about news events and good picture possibilities. However, we sometimes have to turn down some requests for a variety of reasons. Occasionally, there's not enough time for a photographer to get to the scene. Sometimes a story would be more informative to the reader than a photograph.

But most of the requests we turn down have to do with posed pictures.

As a rule, we don't want to take posed pictures for that reason: they're posed. Usually a posed picture is a bad one. It looks posed. It's unreal, artificial, phony. When people "pose" for a picture, they usually cease to be themselves and assume a toothy attitude they think the photographer wants them to assume. Unfortunately, this is a carryover from the days when people had to stand still and 'hold it' while the photographer made the exposure with a big, clumsy camera with a slow shutter speed.

Things have changed. Camera equipment is much more sophisticated and pictures can be taken faster and better. It's now possible to take pictures of people as they really are, not as they think they should be for a photo.

Newspapers have changed, too, many of them that is. This newspaper does not want to pose a picture situation any more than we would want to pose

a news situation. We don't ask people to do something so that we can write a news story about it; we don't ask people to do something for a photographer so he or she can take a picture.

Consequently we try hard to avoid traditional posed pictures, like the trophy or check presentation, the ribbon cutting, the congratulatory handshake and other visual clichés that people have grown accustomed to over the years, thanks mainly to lazy photographers, politicians, public relations people and those who want their picture in the paper.

Of course, there are exceptions to the rule. We still use engagement, wedding and other kinds of posed pictures that people send in. And advertisers can use almost any picture they want in their ads.

For the past several years, this newspaper has tried to eliminate posed news and feature pictures. We have concentrated on trying to show what Harrison County and its people are like. We try to be realistic and honest. We think subscribers who buy our newspaper appreciate our attempts. Some of our pictures have won awards. They weren't posed.

We live in a fascinating, colorful pleasant place with very interesting and fascinating people, and we try to show Harrison County and its people like they are.

West said there have been no complaints about his paper's policy.

While there may be a period of adjustment, most editors who have adopted similar policies receive little if any flak from readers. Communicating with and educating the public, as West did, is a big step toward heading off any problems.

The Compromise

For the community editor who still insists that there is a demand for posed pictures and a legitimate place for them in his newspaper, there is a compromise.

The editor must always remember that he is running pictures because they are good pictures, because they are pictures that earn readership, because they tell a story. Therefore, if posed pictures are deemed worthwhile, the editor must insist that the photographer challenge himself to bring back a good, original picture no matter how seemingly dull the assignment.

To accomplish this, the photographer must be given free creative rein and develop skills in informal portraiture.

Here are some guidelines:

- Never allow more than five persons in the picture.

- Tactfully take charge at an assignment. Experiment with ways to help people look natural. A professional but personal attitude helps people relax, and that increases the odds for good results.

- Take plenty of frames. Film is the cheapest part of the photo budget. More pictures increase the chance of getting a good picture. But don't use the film just because it's available. Make every shot an all-out attempt for quality.

- At all costs, avoid the "police lineup" picture (people against a blank wall staring at the camera).

- Use background to add interest and information to the picture (for example, if a citizens' committee has been appointed to study overcrowding of schools, take a picture of them in an overcrowded classroom).

- For added interest, shoot from a high or low angle.

- Use props when appropriate (for instance, city councilmen studying an architect's rendering of a new fire station).

- Use natural lighting or a bounce flash whenever possible. Avoid a straight-on flash.

- Try to show a news situation whenever possible (a group of Boy Scouts planting trees, firemen actually using a new aerial ladder truck, etc.).

Still, although some posed pictures are admittedly better than others, more and more successful newspaper editors are finding that they aren't as popular with readers as they are with the groups and organizations that have become accustomed to their appearance.

Local faces do have enormous appeal in a newspaper. But it's much better to show those faces in a natural environment, in a situation that definitely and honestly tells a story.

In this context, great picture assignments evolve from the editor and photographer constantly "thinking pictures." Ideas may come from their ingenuity or from outside sources—readers, other newspapers and magazines, etc.—or from a combination of both. The editor and photographer who constantly seek out good picture ideas will find them. This planning can eliminate most of the problems that may come up at the assignment and can multiply the chances that a great picture will result.

One word of caution is needed. The editor should never give "do this, do that" instructions. After briefing the photographer on the nature of the assignment, the editor must give the photographer creative leeway and, in turn, expect competent results.

Picture Policy

Whether the newspaper is for or against posed pictures, it's vitally important to develop a written picture policy for the benefit of the staff and for sound public relations. Everyone on the staff should have a copy, understand it, and be able to verbalize it to the public.

There are three good reasons for this "camera constitution." First, it acts as a check against an editor's making an assignment based on outside pressure or the mood he happens to be in. Second, it helps clear up any misunderstandings with the public. Third, it establishes a foundation upon which a visually effective newpaper can be built.

The policy could include the following.

- How long a photographer can wait at an assignment (assuming the paper assigns posed pictures). A ten-minute time limit is a good idea. Otherwise the photographer can waste hours. Once this rule is enforced a few times, the procrastinators will get the message.

- Under what circumstances the newspaper will or will not assign a photographer.

- Exactly what type of picture the newspaper wants and why. If posed pictures are permitted, the policy should explain what types of posed pictures are used. If they are not taken, the policy should explain why not and what types of picture assignment ideas are preferred.

- How many people may appear in a posed picture.

- How to treat wedding, engagement, and anniversary pictures.

- How to approach sports and team pictures.

The more specific the policy the better. It is critically important that it be consistent. It must treat the important and the unimportant, the meek and the overbearing alike.

The policy will support the editor who must say no tactfully to a person who has a bad picture idea. However, he must constantly watch for bad picture requests that can be changed into good visual possibilities.

For instance, an administrator at an institution for the mentally retarded asks the editor to assign a photographer to take a picture of seven residents who have earned certificates for completing an art course. According to the picture policy, the request would be turned down. But an alert editor would immediately sense the visual possibilities. He would assign a photographer, not to take a cliché picture of seven people with certificates but, perhaps, a series of pictures of the residents lovingly at work on their masterpieces.

Before giving a final no, the editor must use this picture "possibility thinking" to be sure a golden visual opportunity doesn't slip away.

Once a commitment has been made to assign a photographer, that promise must be kept. This is vital for sound public relations. The editor must answer requests for assignments with a definite yes or no; a maybe is usually defined as a yes by the caller, and the newspaper will be in for a dose of bitter criticism if a photographer doesn't show up.

Editing the Picture

There's little if anything even a competent editor can do to improve an inferior picture. He can rewrite a sloppily prepared news story, but he can't magically create drama and detail in an underexposed picture of ten persons lined up against a wall. He best serves his newspaper and his readers by tossing it in the nearest wastebasket.

But there are a variety of editing skills that he can use to make a good picture even better. Cropping, sizing, effective cutlines, and page layout can all contribute toward giving the good picture the optimum visual impact it deserves.

Many of these skills are intuitive and improve as the editor develops a "feeling for pictures," knowledge of his readership, and common sense.

In any case, every picture must be handled with care, individually. The editor must concentrate his efforts on quality, not quantity.

PROOF SHEETS

Picture editing begins with the proof sheet, which contains small trial prints of all the photos taken.

The photographer knows that, film costs being low, taking plenty of frames while striving for quality increases the odds for a great picture. But glancing at the resultant chain of negatives isn't enough to determine their visual potential. A proof sheet must be studied carefully with a magnifying glass. The frames to be printed full size are then marked with a grease pencil.

At times, this still isn't enough for an intelligent final choice. When the merits of two or three frames are competing with each other, it's best to go ahead and make full-size prints of all of them and then make a decision.

By the way, if pictures on a proof sheet seem unclear or out of focus, examine the frame numbers. If the numbers are fuzzy, a bad proof sheet was made. If the numbers are clear, the pictures are at fault.

CROPPING

Once the editor has the full-size print in his hands, he edits it the same way he does news copy—by cutting out the nonessentials. Everything that doesn't communicate or that distracts from the visual message of the picture is eliminated through cropping with a grease pencil.

Cropping a picture can also change its proportion, and a strong vertical or horizontal picture can do wonders for a page layout. As much as possible, it is wise to avoid the standard eight-by-ten print.

But while the axiom "crop ruthlessly" is a good one, the skilled editor knows when to be conservative. Cropping can make a great picture, but it can also ruin a great picture.

Actually, the skilled photographer learns to do most of the cropping with his camera. Moving as close as possible to his subject, he eliminates as much nonessential material as possible while getting the largest possible image, and thus maximum detail, on the negative. Even before he takes the picture, he learns to visualize what the final print will look like.

He also crops in the enlarger, only using the portion of the negative that is visually relevant.

But it's still important that the photographer leave some room for the editor to exercise judgment.

SIZING

After the picture has been properly cropped, it must be given plenty of space to achieve its potential to communicate. It is much easier for the reader to put himself into the picture when it is large.

FIGURE 6–1 The object of effective cropping is to get rid of all nonessentials, of anything that distracts from the visual message of the picture. Also, cropping can change the proportion of a picture; a strong vertical or horizontal print can do wonders for a page layout. *Photo courtesy of Kenneth Blum.*

This principle does not apply to the weak picture. Oversizing will only draw twice as much attention to its weaknesses. The best solution is to not use a weak picture at all.

In general, it's a good idea to play a picture one column wider than the

FIGURE 6–2 A large photo has tremendous impact, but the picture, like this one, must be good. A bad picture played large will only look twice as bad. *Reprinted courtesy of* The Times *of Kettering, Ohio. Photos by Dave Alton and Larry Lambert.*

Would you believe this lofty parachute is an information booth for the upcoming River Festival? DeDe McConnaughey tie-dyed it in her bathtub...   Photo by Dave Aton

River rebirth

Festival aims to celebrate benefits of Great Miami

BY PEGGY MAGILL
Staff Writer

Colorful balloons and brightly painted banners will hang, and a great fish, the talisman of the Great Miami River Festival, will fly above the many festivities.

"We want to capture the audience before they get on the island," said Joey Bellamy of Centerville, theme and decorations chairman of the third annual event. "We've tried to put all of the color and excitement we could think of into this," she added.

What better way to celebrate the rebirth of a river? All this effort to make ready for the 1978 festival to be held Saturday and Sunday, June 10 and 11, at Dayton's Island Park. A project of the river corridor committee of the Dayton Area Chamber of Commerce, its purpose is to bring people back to the river to enjoy its scenic and recreational value.

MORE THAN 40,000 people are expected to attend the festival this year, according to DeDe McConnaughey, task force chairman. Mrs. McConnaughey has also gotten into

the decorating act in preparation for the festival, having tie-dyed huge parachutes in the bathtub of her Kettering home. The colorful, voluminous 'chutes will be used to form a gazebo which will be the information center on the island.

The two south of town women are committed to the county-wide project because the whole community will benefit from the river now and in the future.

"Basically, I'm working on this because the river festival is a way for the entire community to know what our river corridor plan is all about," said Mrs. McConnaughey, member of the river corridor committee. "The river doesn't just offer recreation — it is rich with cultural activities — the Wegerzen Garden Center, Dayton Art Institute, the Indian site to be restored, Riverbend Art Center and the Museum of Natural History are all along the river — so many things families can do for little money."

From an economic standpoint, there is a potential of

new housing along the river and the existing housing needs improvement, she said.

"THE SUBURBS need a healthy downtown," Mrs. McConnaughey continued. "The river belongs to the whole area, so we have involved people from the whole area to work on this festival."

Joey Bellamy, former fashion art director for Rike's, said this is her first experience working on a community project, and that she is becoming much more aware of what's going on. She, as head of decorations, said most of the food and game concessions will be operated by churches, neighborhood groups and civic clubs.

The island will be decorated to recreate the area somewhat as it was at the turn of the century, following this year's theme, "Down by the Riverside," she said. Free rides for children, continuous entertainment in the bandshell, cultural displays and exhibits and many water events, including the first festival boat parade, will all be offered for the admission price of $1 for those over 12, and free for those under 12 who are accompanied by an adult.

"We've tried to get a lot of the civic organizations to decorate their stands and as an incentive are offering a $250 prize for the best one. Everyone involved is also to wear a costume," she said.

THE TICKET booths are designed in the shape of miniature river boats with paddle wheels, and the ticket takers will be dressed in old-fashioned swimming suits.

Students from the Dayton schools, under the direction of Armand Martino, have made the brightly colored batik panels which will hang from streetlights on the bridge going over to and on the island. The large, open-ended "wind sock" fish kite, imported from Japan, is more than 20 feet long. Smaller versions will hang from strategic points. Volunteers from all of the groups involved have agreed to get together Friday to paint the street and prepare for the big weekend.

"People are working together from all over town," said Mrs. McConnaughey. "When this is over, these people won't forget they know each other. That's how things get done in this town," she added.

For C'ville Ox Roast
'Weatherman' assures fine skies

BY LAURI LEACH
Staff Writer

Centerville area residents can expect sunny weather for the 33rd annual Lions Club Ox Roast, which is scheduled for June 15-17.

Just ask George McClish. He just put in an order for three weeks of sunny weather.

Mr. McClish, 81 and a member of the Centerville Lions Club, is in charge of the weather during the Ox Roast for the third year.

"OUR VICE president said, 'McClish, you'd better order fine weather,'" Mr. McClish related. "So I've got it in order. I hope I can deliver.

"I ordered three weeks of nice weather in June, so they'd have nice weather for setting up and taking down," he added.

Mr. McClish will be easy to recognize at the Ox Roast. He'll be wearing his white weather hat. He also has a weather chart with three "Smile" buttons symbolizing three good days of weather during the Ox Roast.

"I don't know if I'll do it after this year," Mr. McClish said. "Controlling the weather really gets to be a strain."

TWO YEARS ago, when Mr. McClish began his job as weather chairman, he managed to bring good weather to the community for the entire Ox Roast weekend. Last year he wasn't as fortunate. The Ox Roast was hit with a half hour shower Friday night.

"If there's rain at the Ox Roast, then people aren't out there spending their money," Mr. McClish said. "We probably lost a couple hundred dollars during the

time it rained last year. I've got good weather on order. I don't know what else I can do."

In addition to controlling the weather, Mr. McClish will also be a member of the committee that will dispense prizes to different booths.

"I've worked on that every year since I've been a Centerville Lions Club member," he said. "The Cat Rack — where you throw three baseballs at a wooden beam to knock it over — is the biggest attraction. I guess it's a challenge."

MR. McCLISH has been a member of the Centerville Lions Club for six years, but he is a charter member of the Mad River Lions Club and still attends meetings in Mad River at least twice a year.

"As far as I'm concerned, the Lions is one of the best groups around," Mr. McClish said. "The group does so much for community service.

"The Lions, for example, have taken blind and handicapped children horseback riding," he added. "That may seem tame to us, but it's a real thrill for those children. Seeing things like that make me proud to be a Lion."

Proceeds from each year's Ox Roast also go to community service. This year, 25 per cent of the proceeds will be earmarked for acquiring an emergency heart defibrillator monitor for the Centerville-Washington Twp. Fire Dept. Funds will also be used toward a jogging and hiking trail in Archer

Park.

LAST YEAR, funds went to senior citizens and to the Developmental Center for Handicapped Children. The Lions have raised $192,000 from the Ox Roast since its conception.

The Lions are not the only organization involved in the Ox Roast, though. Boy Scout Troop 516 has set up for the event and cleaned up the grounds afterwards for several years. The Centerville High School soccer team and Coach Gary Avedikian will be in charge of parking.

The Centerville Coeds will help the Lions distribute tickets. The Rotary Club will provide rides for handicapped youngsters on Saturday morning of the Ox Roast.

"Everyone in the community participates," Lion Ted Baker said. "Our wives, families, neighbors and friends will help. It takes about 400 volunteers to put on an Ox Roast."

SOME OX ROAST events have already begun. Posters by middle school artists advertising the event were judged Thursday night by Centerville Mayor Vic Greene, Washington Twp. fire Chief Randall Staley and Mary Sikora of the Dayton Newspapers.

First prize, a $10 gift certificate for an album at Dingleberry's, went to Dawn West of Magsig Middle School, Kristelle Erickson of Hadley Watts Middle School, Dave Krufar of Tower Heights Middle School and Richie Remski of Hithergreen Middle School.

(Continued on page 2b)

George McClish has fine weather on order...   Photo by Larry Lambert

editor first thinks. With experience, however, he'll learn to sense the size that will produce optimum visual impact.

Again, there is the question of quality versus quantity. It's much better to run fewer pictures and give them the display they need to communicate than to run too many pictures and squeeze them beyond recognition. Even pictures in a "highly acceptable" category must yield to the great, relevant picture that needs space to achieve dramatic impact.

If possible, the editor should provide prints that are the exact size of reproduction. Actual size is best. Oversize is next best. Undersize is worst.

Words with Pictures

It's a rare picture that can stand on its own without words to explain why it's being printed. Virtually all pictures are either meaningless or, at best, confusing unless they're accompanied by short, explanatory cutlines (captions).

CUTLINES

Writing cutlines is a delicate art. If the picture accompanies a story, too much information can draw the reader's attention away from the text. The function of the cutlines is to draw attention to the text, not to take its place or repeat it.

If the picture stands on its own without a story, the key is to provide all essential information in an extremely brief text. The cutlines should state concisely what is happening in the picture, identify the people, and give any relevant details the reader might otherwise miss. They should never point out what is obvious in the photo.

This doesn't mean that cutlines have to be dull writing. Snappy, clever cutlines can help a picture—depending of course on the subject—but the basics must still be followed.

Unless common sense dictates otherwise, cutlines are written in the

present tense ("the police chief accepts" and not "the police chief accepted") and start with an interesting and relevant point. Two or more unrelated facts should never be included in a single sentence. Cutlines should never begin with a name. And phrases such as "is pictured here," "shown above," "pictured above" should be avoided.

Some examples:

BAD: *"Quarterback Alan Miller is pictured above handing off the ball to running back John Wilson, who was immediately greeted by an opposing tackler."*
BETTER: *"Rushing for 185 yards in Orrville's win over Wadsworth, fullback John Wilson is finally nailed for a two-yard loss in the fourth quarter."*

BAD: *"Jim Snyder, who owns Snyder's Auto Parts and Machine Shop at the corner of High and Main Streets in Marshallville, shows off his replica of a 1939 Ferrari he built from a special kit and the frame of a 1973 Volkswagen, at the Wayne County Fair."*
BETTER: *How do you make a bug beetle-u-tiful? Jim Snyder has the answer. Using a special kit and the frame of a 1973 Volkswagen, he built this replica of a 1939 Ferrari. The car is on display at the Wayne County Fair.*

CATCHLINES

Studies show that "catchlines"—lines of display type between a picture and its cutlines—can increase readership of cuts and stories under the pictures by as much as 25 percent. (A variation of the catchline is the sideline, which runs at the side of the cutlines and which is just as effective.)

Their value is undeniable as long as they are used effectively. To be potent, they must draw attention; they must be "catchy." They never should be considered "little headlines."

For instance, let's assume there is a five-column picture of local doctors' wives taking over jobs at a hospital so the staff can have a brief Christmas party in the cafeteria. A dull catchline would read: "Wives fill in at hospital." A snappy catchline would read: "Wives give staff-a-caucus."

Usually there are no holds barred

when it comes to writing a snappy catchline but, again, sometimes the subject of the picture dictates how creative an editor can get. It would be in poor taste, of course, to use a pun under a picture of a fatal accident.

CREDIT LINES

Picture credit lines usually serve as a photographer's reward for a great picture. Even more important, they help to personalize the paper, acquainting the reader with a human being who is doing a good job.

In general, newspapers should use more bylines on stories and pictures. The more the public recognizes the newspaper as a people-oriented product the better.

In rare instances, the picture credit line can be used to shake up a lackadaisical photographer. The editor can take a bland picture, run it, and attach a credit line. While he may not like running the picture at all, under the right circumstances it can be used to encourage improved results.

Layout of Photos

The worst mistake an editor can make is to prepare a pretty layout and chop pictures to fit. It is far better to take a good, hard look at the picture and determine what size it requires to achieve its visual potential.

There are numerous ways to bend and wrap headlines and body type and still come up with an effective layout. A picture, if it is to achieve visual impact, doesn't enjoy the same flexibility.

This doesn't mean that there aren't rules for coordinating pictures with type. For instance, a picture and a related story should never be run on separate pages. Keep them together. Unrelated pictures should never be so close to each other as to compete for the reader's attention. Pictures should face into the page. A picture should never be run below a story headline and above its text acting as a barrier between the headline and text. Headlines under pictures should be exactly the same width, exactly under the caption. Even if the picture is unrelated to the story, it is most effective when it is exactly the same width as the headline. Only this time, the two would be separated with a cutoff.

Picture Pages

The most rewarding and challenging project the editor and photographer can pursue as a team is the single-theme picture page. The project involves a graduation from single-picture thinking to multiple-picture coordination.

But first, it's necessary to distinguish among four types of picture pages.

A *picture story* sets out to accomplish what its name implies: to tell a story. It has definite visual continuity.

A *picture essay* revolves around a central point or theme. It may have a problem to analyze or a point to make.

A *picture group* is a collection of pictures on the same subject, but the page doesn't have the cohesiveness or sense of purpose of the story or essay. There are examples of effective picture groups, but generally they are relatively ineffective.

Last and least is the outmoded *picture group* of miscellaneous pictures on varying subjects patched together on a page. The page may be titled something like "The Week in Pictures" and feature everything from a tennis match to an auto accident. While the page may attract reasonable readership, the pictures would be used more effectively if they were run throughout the newspaper.

Half the battle in producing a great picture page is in the planning stage.

First, a visually relevant subject must be found. Then the specific story, theme, or angle must be studied and outlined. Without this "homework," the photographer might overlook pictures needed to communicate the purpose of the page effectively. It increases the possibility of good pictures and makes shooting in the field easier.

It must be firmly established that the page isn't designed as a showcase for the photographer's creativity. If a picture isn't consistent with the theme or doesn't contribute to the telling of the story, it must be discarded even if it is a "pretty" picture.

Neither the editor nor photographer can be hurried. The photographer needs plenty of time to concentrate and probe. The editor needs plenty of time to study which pictures will provide variety, impact, and continuity. A rush job, especially in the case of a picture story or essay, will yield only shoddy, inconclusive results.

The layout itself usually uses a "hen and chicks" approach. A dominant picture (the hen) is played perhaps 50 percent larger than the smaller (chicks) pictures. Often, the large picture contains an overall view to orient the reader. Other pictures are varied in size, shape, and content. But while the pictures provide variety, they still maintain continuity and consistency with the story or theme to fulfill the purpose of the layout. This unified whole must leave no unbridged gaps and be easy for the reader to understand.

In general, four to seven pictures are ideal for a broadsheet page layout. Eight or nine are almost always too many. The barrage of ten to fifteen pictures is certain to ruin the layout's effectiveness.

It is also important to remember that typographic gimmicks like spot colors, squiggly tapes, and cookie cutter shapes are useless and hinder the picture page. Good pictures with good cutlines will speak for themselves.

Pictures in Sections

Pictures used in the society and sports sections of community newspapers tend to get into a visual rut.

On society or family news pages, 80 percent of the pictures are often studio portraits of brides, brides-to-be, or couples observing their silver or golden wedding anniversaries. While these events warrant pictures, there is no reason why they can't be more interesting.

First, it's hard to understand why wedding and engagement pictures are always just of the woman. Both the man and woman are engaged or married, so why not show them both? Better yet, why not show them in a more natural setting?

Anniversary pictures, which always show the couple, also suffer from the studio photographer's rigidity. Cosmetically they look good, but good newspaper pictures should tell a story. It would be much better to show the couple in a natural environment—together at home, at work in their garden, or inspecting a family heirloom.

The only way to change these picture traditions is for the newspaper to educate the public and to remind studio photographers repeatedly that other approaches are acceptable.

Aside from wedding, engagement, and anniversary pictures, people-oriented feature pictures can add impact to society pages. Opportunities are endless and again involve the editor and photographer in creatively "thinking pictures." Possibilities range from a costume party at a nursery school to a 100th birthday party at a nursing home. The key is to get into the habit of planning effective assignments for the page every week.

Sports pictures also tend to follow a rigid pattern. Week after week, dozens of so-called "action shots" show the same old thing—the fullback running for a three-yard gain, the center shooting a basket.

The best sports pictures are different. They show the cheerleader crying after a bitter defeat, the coach being carried off the field, an argument with

Following pages:

FIGURE 6–3 (page 40) This layout uses the "hen and chicks" approach. The picture of Billy Graham is played perhaps 50 percent larger than the other pictures. Notice how the horizontal shape of the Graham picture adds impact. *Reprinted courtesy of* The Times *of Kettering, Ohio. Photos by Larry Lambert.*

FIGURE 6–4 (page 41) Anywhere from four to seven pictures are sufficient for a single-theme picture page layout. Eight or nine are almost always too many. *Reprinted with permission from the Corydon (Indiana)* Democrat. *Story and photos by Randy West.*

Billy Graham: 'Nowhere in the Bible are we promised a tomorrow'...

Billy Graham ignites

'Trying to run a space age on a horse and buggy spiritual condition'

BY LAURI LEACH
Staff Writer

Special guest Myrtle Hall...

"It's pouring outside tonight, but thousands of you came anyway. You came because this is the time for you to accept Christ in your heart as your Savior."

This is the time. Time is the theme of Billy Graham's message at the halfway point of his Tri-State Crusade in Cincinnati. The man whose charisma has drawn 16,521 people to Riverfront Coliseum on a rainy, foggy Tuesday night says that now is the accepted time to come forward.

And thousands of those people come forward as they have come in crusades before or as they have seen others do on televised crusades. They come down to the same words they have heard before on televised crusades.

"If you came on a bus or with friends, they'll wait," Billy Graham says predictably. "Even if you're sitting on the top row, it will only take 30 seconds to come down. Now is the time to give your heart to Jesus."

To stress the theme of time in the crusade, a soft organ and piano prelude starts promptly at 7:30. The working press is seated on the floor, pens poised in right hands, left index fingers ready to push the "record" button on tape recorders.

The audience has stretched its collective necks in vain for a glimpse of Dr. Graham. The luckier ones catch sight of the "voice of the crusade," the almost-as-famous George Beverly Shea. Another famous crusade figure, Cliff Barrows, steps up to the lecturn on the platform.

"The choir is going to sing through 'He is My Reason for Living,' twice, and then we want you out there to stand up and sing it with the choir," Mr. Barrows orders.

The choir, volunteers from 900 tri-state churches, fills an entire side of the coliseum. Choir voices fill the entire coliseum.

"He is my reason for living,
He is my joy and my song;
He is my rock, my salvation,
I'll praise Him the whole day long.

"Now, everybody!" Cliff Barrows shouts and lifts the audience up with a swooping gesture.

The press stands, too. Reporters eye each other speculatively. "Is he going to sing? Should I sing?" Furtively, the press murmurs the words along with the audience and joins the audience in the next two hymns.

Mr. Barrows introduces the first guest, Myrtle Hall, who sings Mozart's "Hallelujah" and a second song, "No One Ever Cared for Me Like Jesus." And Bev Shea sings the hymn he is most famous for: "How Great Thou Art."

John Roush, a Kettering native now coaching football at Miami University, is the second special guest. His wife, parents and many members of Kettering's Christ Methodist Church, are there to hear him give testimony and sing.

Tape recorder buttons click as Billy Graham stands alone at the podium. This is the man the audience has been waiting for. Many of the lights are turned off, and the audience is silent.

The photographers have received the word from Dr. Graham's public relations director, Don Bailey. No shots of Dr. Graham during his message.

Having captured the attention of nearly everyone in the crowd, Dr. Graham begins his talk on time with a text from I Kings 18:21. It is the story of the prophet Elijah and the dual between his God and the idols Baal and Ashtoreth.

"I think Elijah is the most dramatic person in the entire Bible, excluding Jesus," Dr. Graham says. "He challenged the people of Judah to a dual. They had a choice between their selfish appetites and desires or the true and living God.

"Elijah said, 'How long halt ye between two opinions?'" he continues. " 'If the Lord be God, follow him: but if Baal, then follow him.' He gave the people a choice but said there was little time to make the decision."

Dr. Graham says time is moving rapidly. Armageddon, he says, is "staring us in the face."

"Unfortunately, we are trying to run a space age on a horse and buggy moral and spiritual condition," Dr. Graham continues. "But you can change. Only one power in the world can change human nature, and that is Jesus Christ. You can be born again."

Time is brief, though, Dr. Graham says. The last thing the late Bing Crosby wrote was, "We have each been given the same amount of time in a day: 1,440 minutes per day, 168 hours per week." Life is a vapor.

Time is urgent and tyrannical. At this point, a small boy, who doesn't know about photographer's rules, slowly approaches the platform with an instamatic camera. Immediately, four ushers converge on him, but slowly, to give him a chance to get one picture.

But time works against him. He fumbles with the flash cube in his haste. An usher walks up to the boy, places an arm around his shoulders and guides him off the floor. Time is urgent and tyrannical.

Dr. Graham tells of a man who has tithed his time to the church. If everyone did this, Dr. Graham says, the country could be changed.

"Nowhere in the Bible are we promised that there will be a tomorrow," the evangelist says. "Every time you hear the (Continued on page 17)

Volunteers from 900 tri-state churches formed the choir...

'It's time to accept Christ in your heart'...

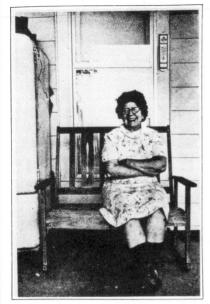

CECIL CONRAD holds milk pails for his pride and joy, twin calves, on his farm in Helltown. His wife, Edna Lucille, at left, takes a break from household duties on their back porch rocker.

STORY AND PHOTOGRAPHS BY RANDY WEST

Welcome to Helltown

A NOT-SO-FEARSOME DOG keeps an eye on strangers from the shady yard of a stately old farmhouse.

The road to Helltown isn't paved with good intentions, but it is paved.

Helltown, Ind., a heavenly little community, can be found in Franklin Township about 4½ miles northwest of Lanesville and the same distance southeast of Crandall.

You can hear the muffled sounds of trains on the Southern Railway nearby, and in the winter you can catch a glimpse of cars in the distance on I-64.

But you can't find Helltown on any map.

It isn't a town and never has been. And no one is certain — or they're not saying — how Helltown got its unflattering and misleading name.

Even without the name, Helltown is the kind of place city people make jokes about. You know, "If you blink, you'll miss it." It's just a hilly county road leading through a gentle valley with rich farmland, a number of very well-kept old farmhouses, a few new ranch-style residences, and a 20-lot subdivision with seven homes under construction.

Russel Crone, who was 78 on Saturday, moved to Helltown on March 12, 1900. "I can just hear my mother tell it. It was the happiest day of her life because they got to live by theirselves," Russel recalled one hot, steamy morning recently while he sat on a cistern at his extraordinarily neat 80-acre farm.

Russel and his two sisters, Mildred, 71, and Nellie, 69 (another sister, Hazel, died three years ago), live near the road that links Crandall and the Lanesville interchange on I-64.

"It's a wonderful place," Russel says. He

(Continued on page 16)

THERE ARE NO TRAFFIC JAMS on the hilly road to Helltown, located between Lanesville and Crandall. At right, Russel Crone relaxes outside his farmhouse. He moved to Helltown on March 12, 1900.

an official, an impassioned speech at half time in the locker room.

These "different" pictures are all around the photographer. Capturing them requires imagination, experience, and persistence.

Editorial Page Pictures

Pictures can be used on editorial pages to dramatize a point, but newspapers that use this resource are few and far between. A "commentary" picture can equal or excel the impact of a local editorial cartoon.

A street full of chuckholes, a railroad crossing in need of flasher warning signals, a fire hazard, a cemetery overrun with weeds are just a few of an unlimited number of opportunities to use this form of visual persuasion to improve the community.

The pictures can run on their own or above a written editorial. The editor will find that they can be enormously persuasive.

Pictures in Ads

If pictures can add impact to news pages, why can't they do the same for display advertising?

One look at any good magazine is proof that strong pictures in ads can create a positive image and sell merchandise. Newspapers haven't even begun to use this resource.

But, like the news or feature picture, if a picture is used in an ad it must be an effective picture. Poor quality not only defeats the purpose of the ad but, even worse, creates a negative rather than a positive image.

On the other hand, a technically good picture that tells a sales story can build an advertiser's image and business and, in turn, build the newspaper's ad linage.

Pictures in ads can either be used to sell merchandise in commercial ads or to build a positive image in institutional advertising.

For the former, photos don't work well for small items (a toothbrush, a scouring pad); line art reproduces far better. But for items such as used cars or real estate, pictures can add realism and interest.

Some products can be illustrated effectively by showing a local customer with an accompanying testimonial—for instance, Joe Smith using a snowblower purchased at a local hardware store. In the text, he may tell about how easy it is to use the machine and the great deal he got at the hardware store.

A before-and-after series can be extremely effective. The ad can show a local home before and after it was remodeled; or a lawn before and after it was landscaped. Add a testimonial from the owners and you have an unbeatable combination.

Pictures can work similar wonders when the goal of the ad is to build a favorable business image.

Is there a car dealer who stresses a clean, efficient service department? Demonstrate this by using strong pictures of the service areas in an attractive ad layout.

Is there a department store that stresses services such as gift wrapping, credit plans, installation, etc.? These can all be shown effectively in a single ad or series of ads.

Does a bank like to emphasize friendly service? A series of ads with accompanying employee biographies can get the point across.

Ideas are unlimited, and this time involve the ad director and photographer in constantly "thinking pictures." Again, the necessity of running good pictures and handling them with skill can't be overemphasized.

The Picture Morgue

Any picture that could possibly be used at some future time should be filed in a neat, well-organized picture morgue or library.

Actually there should be at least two files, one for individuals and the other for events and subjects. Many newspapers file negatives chronologically. Whatever system is used, someone on the staff must assume the important responsibility of keeping the files organized and up-to-date.

If there are any slip-ups—no picture is available of an accident victim whose photo was used in the paper just a month earlier—the person in charge of the morgue should be disciplined accordingly.

To build a file of good, usable pictures of individuals, here is another tip: Whenever a news photo contains a good image of a face, it should be cropped out and filed. In many cases, the more natural expression will work better than a studio portrait.

The Small Newspaper

Many editors of small-circulation weekly newspapers say their operations simply can't afford the time and expense to produce good pictures and to use them effectively. In all but a few cases, this line of reasoning is not justifiable. There's no reason why writing, layout, and photography can't be just as sharp in a twelve-page newspaper as a sixty-page newspaper. There are examples of large dailies with terrible pictures. There are also examples of twelve-page weeklies with exceptional pictures.

It all depends on the emphasis on quality, whether the staff consists of two employees or twenty. Cameras and darkroom equipment aren't that expensive relative to other production equipment. Besides, 90 percent of the job of producing a visually effective newspaper lies in the development of the personal skills of the editors and photographers.

For newspapers that need outside help, there are several sources. Freelancers and correspondents can contribute good local pictures at a reasonable cost.

Photography is one of the most popular hobbies in the world, and there are amateurs in every community who would love to have their work displayed.

First, the editor must find them. This may involve running an ad or simply contacting a local photography club.

Once a prospect has been found, the newspaper can provide and process the film and print the usable pictures. A flat fee can be paid for each picture used, along with the all-important credit line. A print of the picture and the negatives (unless they are needed in the morgue) should also be provided to the photographer.

Correspondents who double as writers and photographers can also be used to contribute pictures. However, since photography probably isn't their speciality, they should be brought into the office and shown how to take good pictures. A copy of the paper's picture policy should also be given to them.

The free-lancer and the correspondent must both understand that a picture will not be used if it is not a good one.

If a picture is not used, the contributor should be told why. Feedback is vitally important if the proportion of good pictures from outside sources is to remain high.

Chapter 7

MAXWELL E. McCOMBS

Dr. McCombs is John Ben Snow Professor of Newspaper Research at Syracuse University, director of the Syracuse University Communications Research Center, and director of newspaper readership research for the American Newspaper Publishers Association.

"In-newspaper questionnaires or coupons, interviews in shopping centers . . . and other catch-as-catch-can methods of obtaining feedback do not provide a representative picture of how the entire community is responding to the newspaper. With a scientifically selected probability sample, a small number of interviews can provide a precise and representative picture of the entire community."

and the focus and flow of the conversation constantly shift in order to maintain the involvement of both parties. For the good conversationalist, just like the good classroom teacher, there is constant attention and reaction to the feedback provided by the audience before them. But editors and reporters are remote from their audience much of the time, so this feedback must be systematically organized and used. This is what readership research is all about. Readership research is a planned, systematic look at the audience's reactions to the messages being produced by their community newspaper.

Scientific Sampling Required

The two key words in that last sentence are *planned* and *systematic*. They are the keys both to this chapter and to useful readership research. The basic purpose of this chapter is to present an overview of readership research, to explain the kinds of questions it can answer and the kinds of information it can provide. In other words, its purpose is to show the newspaper editor or publisher how to plan readership research. But the best possible planning is of little value if the execution of the plan is not systematic.

In terms of readership research and audience surveys, *systematic* means the use of probability samples of the audience, scientifically selected to represent the entire audience. In-newspaper questionnaires or coupons,

Using Readership Research

by Maxwell E. McCombs

A political orator haranguing an empty square is not communicating. An actor with a spellbound audience is communicating superbly. Both examples underscore the point that communication requires the involvement of two parties—a communicator and an audience. Most newspaper editors and reporters desire to be like the actor with his spellbound audience eagerly awaiting the next line. But many times, unfortunately, journalists are more like

the orator with his empty square.

The basic problem which journalists and all other mass communicators face is how to obtain sufficient *feedback* to maintain a steady flow of real communication. For some communicators the two-way nature of communication is easy to maintain because it is simple to assess the audience's reaction. In a typical conversation between two persons, for example, there is a steady stream of feedback, interviews in shopping centers or on street corners, and other catch-as-catch-can methods of obtaining audience feedback do not provide a representative picture of how the entire community is responding to the newspaper. With a scientifically selected probability sample, a small number of interviews can provide a precise and representative picture of the entire community. Since the methodological techniques for drawing probability samples are well explained in many research texts, these details will not be repeated here. But this chapter will assume that such precision samples will be used to obtain feedback from the community.

Research Provides Feedback

Readership research programs can provide two basic types of feedback to journalists. Research can monitor the ongoing interests and attitudes of the audience and determine the extent to which the day-by-day efforts of the hometown newspaper match them. This can be done both for the ever-changing flow of daily and weekly news as well as for the various standing features which appear regularly. This is the steady flow of feedback which any communicator needs to maintain effective contact with his audience.

Readership research also can provide vital feedback on those special occasions when major changes or innovations are planned for the newspaper—anything from the introduction of a new feature or specialized news service to a major revamping of the newspaper's format or a totally new section or magazine.

In all such instances, readership research is the means used to guarantee feedback to editors and their staff on how the audience is responding to the newspaper's current efforts. Publishing a newspaper requires a high degree of disciplined creativity. Research is not a substitute for this creativity. It does

not reduce the editor and his or her staff to automatons. Rather it ensures disciplined creativity, journalistic efforts which communicate effectively to its audience, instead of art for art's sake.

Readership research provides editors with documented evidence—empirical facts not really unlike those collected by reporters—on the extent to which an audience reads their material, finds it understandable or interesting, and accepts it. This does not imply that the editor who uses readership research must pander to the audience. A negative reaction to current efforts does not necessarily mean that the approach should be abandoned for something more popular. It does mean that, in areas where current efforts are not communicating well, refinements are needed.

If the negative reaction is to a comic strip or a typeface, the best option may be to change those features. One's professional values are not compromised by dropping a comic strip or changing a typeface. Even the financial cost of the latter may be more than offset by the popularity of the replacement. But if the negative reaction is to city council or school board stories, dropping these items from the newspaper is not a viable option. Nor is this what the research implies.

A Response, Not a Command

Remember that readership research is systematically organized feedback from the audience to the newspaper. It is a response, not a command! If the response is negative, some change should be made to try to make it more positive. This means approaching the topic in a different way. After all, covering city council or school board meetings by writing a journalistic set of minutes—ranking items on the agenda from most to least important rather than listing them chronologically—is not the only way to cover gov-

ernment and communicate its activities to local residents. Different styles of writing, more effort to personalize formal meetings and show their pertinence to residents' daily lives, even different types of stories can all be used to communicate the workings of local government.

Here again, research does not substitute for the creative efforts of the editor. Rather it calls them forth to solve a communication problem which exists in the community. Research documents the presence or absence of communication problems and the viability of proposed solutions. Research per se does not solve problems. Editors do that, using research as a tool to pinpoint where the problem is and to provide some guidance on how to go about overcoming the problem.

The Focus of Research

To this point, research has been defined as systematically organized feedback from the audience to the newspaper. While some simple examples have been cited, nothing has been said in detail about the *focus* of this feedback. In practice, this feedback covers innumerable details of the newspaper and the audience. It is this welter of information, encompassing many categories and based on many different techniques of research and observation, which confuses the newcomer to readership research. It also tends to dilute the effectiveness of most research efforts. Individual studies also often lack a clear focus.

In order to know where to look and what kinds of feedback to obtain, an editor and his researcher need a definition of feedback which includes the actual focus of attention, describing precisely what feedback is desired.

To define this focus, two aspects will be discussed in some detail. First, what thing, what literal object, does the editor want to look at, and what does he want the audience to look at? Second, once they are looking, which characteristics or attributes are to be commented on? Of course, in both situations one should ask why these specifics were selected in the first place.

The choices in the first stage of focusing the research are quite simple:

- Specific items (or types of items) in the newspaper

- Entire pages or sections in the newspaper

- The entire newspaper

SPECIFIC ITEMS

More research has been done on individual news stories, editorials, or features, than on any other feedback target. There are several reasons for this. Most importantly, these are the items under the direct control of the editor. If the feedback is negative on a story in yesterday's newspaper, the editor has several options for direct action. He can exhort the reporter to do better. He can assign someone else to that type of story next time. He can suggest a different way of writing the story, or a different way of displaying the story in the newspaper.

In the case of a syndicated feature, his options are more limited, but he still has full control of the situation. In short, research on specific items in the newspaper often is directly actionable. An editor has to make numerous decisions each day on many specific items. Research can be a valuable input to this decision making.

Another reason why so much research has focused on specific items in the newspaper is that this is one of the easier types of research to do. It is both easier for the person being interviewed to answer about a specific item in the newspaper—responses even can be enhanced by showing the item—and easier for the researcher who has to frame the questions. This type of research is also easy to interpret.

But the ease of organizing, executing, and interpreting research on specific items in the newspaper is deceptive because the usefulness of this kind of research is severely restricted. Research represents an investment of time and other resources, and the dividends from this type of research are quite limited. Unlike the producer of other consumer goods—and newspapers *are* consumer goods—an editor has a new inventory every issue.

Research on yesterday's front page, or any other news page, is not directly applicable to tomorrow's product. At best, one can make inferences, or the research can guide intuitions about what to do in the new situation. But the feedback provided is neither direct nor specific. In contrast, producers of other consumer goods can obtain direct and specific feedback through research focused on specific items because the same item is produced over a lengthy period of time.

The same types of news, however, do recur over time, so some readership research focuses on such general categories as local news, sports, government news, etc. Striving for broader applicability, these efforts have given up the specificity of the individual item—most often without achieving the goal of direct applicability. What is local news to one editor doesn't qualify as local news according to another editor's definition. And, unfortunately, neither editor's definition may be accepted by the local audience.

One of the major tasks of news researchers at present is to define such traditional categories as local news and sports in ways which take into account both journalistic values and audience interests and behavior. This kind of readership research provides empirically based guidelines about the specific stories which an editor must handle each day.

NEWSPAPER SECTIONS

The editor's job is more than handling a host of individual stories each day. These stories must be assembled into the pages of a newspaper; and more and more there is an emphasis in North American journalism on special types of pages. Sports, editorial, business, and family pages have been newspaper mainstays for a long time. Some readership research makes these special sections the focus of attention.

Examination of several newspapers' sports pages in recent years has found the size of the audience to be substantially smaller than was generally assumed—and perhaps less than would justify sport's share of the newshole (percent of space allotted to news content). Other research on the sports pages has distinguished between the readership of national college and professional sports on the one hand and local high school sports on the other. While national sports draw a heavier audience of young people and high-income people, predominantly men, local sports have high appeal among older persons and especially among women.

More recently, research has been used to pretest ideas for new kinds of special pages (everything from CB radio to haute cuisine and fashion) and to monitor audience acceptance once these new pages have made their debut.

Research which focuses on a special page or section of the newspaper can tell the editor how many readers this material reaches, what kinds of people they are, and how they respond to the page. It enables an editor to shape some very specific goals for these pages. If the goal is to reach a particular audience segment, such as young marrieds, housewives, or businessmen, this kind of research indicates whether the goal is being achieved. If not, the research can help identify where action needs to be taken.

THE ENTIRE NEWSPAPER

Just as research can obtain audience reactions to an entire page or section of the newspaper, it also can measure audience reactions to the newspaper taken as a whole. People do have opinions and feelings about their community newspaper as a newspaper, not just about its specific sections and items. These opinions and feelings about such things as the overall performance of the local newspaper, the adequacy of its coverage, and the accuracy of its stories influence how frequently people actually read the newspaper.

For example, in a study of three weekly newspapers serving adjacent towns in upstate New York, respondents were asked: "If a friend of yours moved to this area, would you advise him to subscribe to the local newspaper?" Overall, about 36 percent replied "Definitely yes," but there was considerable discrepancy in the proportion of positive replies for each of the weeklies. While one weekly received a strong endorsement from 43 percent of its readers, another got high ratings from only 26 percent.

These kinds of summary attitudes and feelings about the newspaper are among the factors explaining why some people are regular newspaper readers and others are not. People also have feelings about how much a newspaper should cost, how it compares to other newspapers available to them, and how it compares with its broadcasting competitors.

To sum up, there are three possible areas of focus for readership research: specific items, special pages, and the entire newspaper. Which of these is the appropriate focus for a particular newspaper and its research? The answer depends on the editor's goals and the plan he has developed.

One editor's goals may revolve around the specific content of the newspaper. His research is assigned the task of providing the feedback necessary for the fine tuning of the ways in which these items are written and displayed. Another editor's goal may involve major changes in the newspaper, new layouts, new sections, and organizational changes in the staff. Other editors may be concerned with the overall acceptance and evaluation of their newspapers in the local community.

These goals, whatever they are, are the heart of an effective research plan. The more explicitly they are framed and the more explicitly they can be stated in researchable terms, the more effectively the plan can guide the newspaper's research effort.

What to Look At

Having a plan is important because it

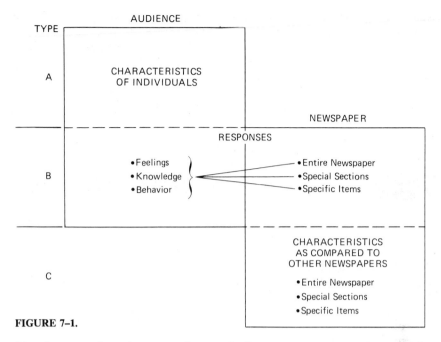

FIGURE 7–1.

guides the research to the proper focus so it can produce actionable feedback. The three broad areas of focus just discussed tell the researcher *where* to look. But they do not specify *what* to look at. Since there is perhaps an infinite number of things to look at, an overview is needed for the editor who wants to devise an effective research plan.

This overview is outlined in Fig. 7–1, which catalogues the three major types of data readership projects consider. Note that types B and C can cover any of the three focal points just discussed.

PERSONAL CHARACTERISTICS

One type of data frequently encountered in readership research consists of details on the personal characteristics of newspaper audiences (Type A). Usually this constitutes a demographic profile of people in the local community, according to sex, level of formal education, income, and age. A review of readership research conducted over the past twenty-five years, reported in the ANPA *News Research Report* No. 3, found that demographic descriptions of the newspaper audience were by far the most common research perspective. Typical of this research are such

findings about community weeklies and dailies as:

- Newspaper readership increases with age, usually peaking in the forties or fifties and then declining somewhat in the sixties and seventies.

- Nonreaders are disproportionately found in the low-income and low-education groups in the community.

- Sports and government news is read more by men than women.

But there are many other personal characteristics which can be related to newspaper readership. People also can be described in terms of their life styles, their involvement in civic and political affairs, the number of friends and relatives they have in a community, and many other criteria. The creative analyst of the newspaper audience can think of many personal characteristics which are potential explanations for an individual's attitude toward the community newspaper.

RESPONSES TO THE NEWSPAPER

Responses to the newspaper constitute the second type of information which can be determined through research. Typical are questions about people's reading behavior, ranging from "Did you read yesterday's newspaper?" to "How frequently do you work the crossword puzzle appearing in the newspaper?" Also falling into this category are the attitude questions developed by Chilton Bush and widely used by Syracuse University's Communication Research Center. Survey respondents are asked their opinions about such things as the completeness of their community newspaper's coverage of various topics, its fairness, its freedom from pressure, its morality, and its overall performance.

Other questions in this category are designed to determine the reasons why people read the local paper. They might elicit such responses as "to keep up with events," "to have something to talk about with others," and "to help me in my daily life."

For the most part, these questions are valid for all three areas of focus. They can be applied to the entire newspaper, some of its pages, or specific items, as indicated in Fig. 7–1. Three general types of responses can be distinguished among readers: their feelings toward the newspaper, their knowledge of its contents, and their behavior as readers.

The attitude and motivational questions just cited represent the audience's feelings about the newspaper (or some portion of it). If, as in one of the previous examples, a newspaper is being compared with its competitors, data on these audience feelings is paramount. On the other hand, if the goal of the research is to evaluate the effectiveness of the newspaper in communicating specific information about the community, then the data collected should concentrate on knowledge.

In other instances, the response of interest is actual behavior, or at least self-reports by the audience of their reading behavior. How many members of the audience actually read the latest issue of the newspaper? How frequently do they read the special sections? How many persons actually read each item in the newspaper?

It is possible to study other types of behavior as well. How many persons buy a newspaper on the street? How

does an individual read the newspaper? From front to back scanning all items? Or do some go directly to the special sections of interest to them, ignoring all else? Again, the goals of the research help specify which responses should be studied.

NEWSPAPER CHARACTERISTICS

Audience responses to the newspaper are not the only kinds of data which can be explored in readership research. Just as a Type A study determines characteristics of the audience, a Type C study can determine the characteristics of the newspaper, its various pages and sections, and individual stories. For example, in ANPA *News Research Report* No. 2, "Content, Appearance, and Circulation," dozens of a daily newspaper's *content characteristics* (such as number of local editorials, presence or absence of New York Stock Exchange listings, and number of front-page news pictures) and *format characteristics* (such as use of spot color, serif type in headlines, and column width) are related to the circulation penetration of newspapers.

Organizing Readership Research

Fig. 7–1 provides a convenient framework for cataloguing the hundreds of pieces of readership research which are available in the scientific literature. It also provides a guide for seeing where a proposed new piece of research fits into the overall picture of newspaper readership research. Since almost all scientific research on newspaper readership is a combination or comparison of information of all three types outlined in Fig. 7–1, organizing this overview is an easier task than it might appear to be. Only three basic comparisons or combinations exist! Using the labels A, B, and C to designate these

three basic types of readership research, these comparisons can be described as A–B, B–C, and B–B.

The first type, A–B, represents a comparison of personal characteristics and responses to the newspaper. The next, B–C, a comparison of responses to the newspaper with characteristics of the newspaper, and the third, B–B, the comparison of two different sets of responses to the newspaper. A few examples of each type will serve as illustration; creative editors and researchers can, of course, think of hundreds of specific examples of these basic types.

TYPE A–B: DEMOGRAPHIC ANALYSIS

The most common example of the first type, A–B, is demographic analysis of newspaper readership, the most popular type of readership research analysis.

Table 7–1 presents an example in which responses to three different kinds of newspapers (dailies, paid weeklies, and free newspapers) are compared among different demographic groups. These data are from a national survey conducted by the Newspaper Advertising Bureau. For daily newspapers, we see little difference in the readership levels of men and women, but among all the other demographic categories, there are sizable differences in the percentage of persons who read a daily newspaper the previous day. This is less true for the readership of paid weeklies. Table 7–1 shows only small differences among various demographic groups in their readership of weekly newspapers. Finally, the demographic analysis of the readership of free newspapers again reveals significant differences for nearly all these personal characteristics.

Table 7–2 presents another example of demographic analysis, a comparison of readers and nonreaders at various income levels. In this survey conducted in upstate New York, nonreaders are persons who read *neither* a daily *nor* a weekly newspaper with any regularity. Just as in Table 7–1, newspaper readership increases as in-

TABLE 7–1: READERSHIP OF DAILY NEWSPAPERS, PAID WEEKLIES, AND FREE PAPERS

	Read Daily Newspaper Yesterday	*Read Past 7 Days:* Paid Weekly	*Read Past 7 Days:* Free Paper
Total Adults (N = 3,048)	69%	34%	34%
By sex:			
Male	70%	34%	31%
Female	67%	34%	36%
By age:			
18–24	64%	33%	38%
25–34	60%	33%	34%
35–54	71%	37%	34%
55–64	76%	34%	35%
65 or older	74%	30%	26%
By education:			
Some high school or less	60%	31%	28%
High school graduate	67%	34%	36%
Some college	77%	36%	37%
College graduate	80%	38%	36%
By family income:			
Under $8,000	61%	31%	28%
$8,000–$9,999	65%	36%	31%
$10,000–$14,999	69%	36%	39%
$15,000–$24,999	77%	34%	38%
$25,000 & over	77%	37%	44%
By mobility:			
Resident four years or less	61%	34%	43%
Resident five years or more	70%	34%	32%

Adult Readership of Weekly Newspapers and Shoppers, March 1978; Newspaper Advertising Bureau, Newspaper Readership Project.

TABLE 7–2: NEWSPAPER NONREADERS AND INCOME

	Income Under $5,000 (N = 187)	$5,000– $10,000 (N = 244)	$10,000– $15,000 (N = 229)	Over $15,000 (N = 398)
Newspaper Nonreaders	13%	10%	4%	3%
Newspaper Readers	87%	90%	96%	97%

Reprinted courtesy of Ottaway Newspapers, Inc.

come increases, while the proportion of nonreaders in each category steadily declines.

Actual behavior is not the only audience response which readership studies can measure. Fig. 7–1 also lists feelings and knowledge, so Table 7–3 reports data on one type of feeling, people's opinions about the accuracy of their newspaper's headlines. Again this is type A–B research, a comparison of feelings about one aspect of the entire newspaper among groups with different personal characteristics. In Table 7–3 the personal characteristics used are some of the same demographic characteristics used in the previous analyses.

While there is little or no difference in men's and women's opinions about the accuracy of headlines, there are significant differences among the age and income groups. Older persons, especially those age 56 and older, are most trusting of the community newspaper's headlines. Among the income groups, the perceived accuracy of the headlines tends to decline with increased income. Most trusting are those with annual incomes of less than $5,000. Least trusting are those in the highest income group.

Table 7–4 presents data on a very different kind of opinion—whether the newspaper usually presents both sides of important issues. Yet the basic patterns are quite similar to those in Table 7–3. There is little difference among men and women, although women show a slight tendency to be more trusting. Among the age groups, again it is the older respondents who are most trusting and the highest income groups who are the most skeptical. The data in Tables 7–3 and 7–4 (see page 50) also came from an upstate New York study.

These four examples of A–B readership research are all demographic analyses of some response to the entire newspaper. Of course, responses to specific sections or specific items in the newspaper could also be analyzed demographically. Or any kind of response to the entire newspaper, its sections, or specific contents could be analyzed in terms of other personal characteristics, such as membership in various civic organizations, favorite hobbies and sports, or even abstract psychological characteristics. Creative and intelligent use of research can generate dozens of other parameters.

TYPE B–C: READERSHIP FACTORS

While A–B research, especially demographic analysis, is exceedingly common, the second type of basic readership research, B–C, is just the opposite. It is rarely seen. One example is Maxwell McCombs' and John Mauro's study, "Predicting Newspaper Readership from Content Characteristics," which appeared in the Spring 1977 issue of *Journalism Quarterly*. While this was a study of a large daily newspaper, the same kind of analysis shown in Table 7–5 could be applied to small dailies and to weeklies. The table lists the six most important predictors of readership in that particular study. The number to the right of each is a beta weight, a statistical score which tells us how important that variable is in the prediction of how many people read most of the item. Comparing the scores determines the relative importance of the factors. In this study, the page on which an item appears, its form (news story, feature, listing, etc.), and the amount of space devoted to the text of the item are, in order, the most significant predictors of readership. It also should be noted that four of these scores have minus signs, indicating that a low page number (for example, page

1) and a small amount of text are associated with higher readership.

TYPE B–B: ATTITUDES AND BEHAVIOR

The third basic type of readership research, B–B, is a comparison of responses. There are numerous possibilities. Figure 7–1 showed three types of responses (feelings, knowledge, and behavior) directed at three targets (the entire newspaper, specific sections, particular items), so there are nine subtypes of B–B research. There are, of course, numerous specific examples of each.

For the flavor of these kinds of readership analysis, consider Tables 7–6 through 7–10. In the first, Table 7–6, two behaviors are being compared, readership of a daily newspaper vs. readership of a weekly. These data, taken from a Newspaper Advertising Bureau national survey, indicate that the reader of a local weekly is more likely also to read a daily than is a nonreader of a weekly.

Table 7–6 also indicates that this

TABLE 7–5: STANDARDIZED BETA WEIGHTS FOR CONTENT CHARACTERISTICS USED TO PREDICT READERSHIP OF ALL NEWSHOLE ITEMS

	Read Most		Read Most
Page	−0.275	Geographic Significance	+0.196
Form	+0.246	Topic	−0.173
Size of text	−0.214	Source	−0.057

Reprinted courtesy of *Journalism Quarterly*

TABLE 7–3: ACCURACY OF HEADLINES

Survey Question: "In your experience, do headlines in the *(name of newspaper)* give you an accurate idea of what really happened?"

| | Sex | | Age | | | | | | Income | | | |
	Women	Men	18–25	26–35	36–45	46–55	56–65	Over 65	Under $5,000	$5,000– 10,000	$10,000– 15,000	$15,000– 25,000+
Usually	75%	74%	73%	70%	73%	72%	79%	80%	79%	79%	77%	70%
Sometimes	21%	21%	22%	25%	22%	22%	17%	18%	18%	18%	20%	24%
Usually not	4%	5%	5%	5%	5%	6%	4%	2%	3%	3%	3%	6%

Reprinted courtesy of Ottaway Newspapers, Inc.

TABLE 7–4: OBJECTIVITY OF REPORTING

Survey Question: "Does the *(name of newspaper)* usually present both sides of important issues?"

| | Sex | | Age | | | | | | Income | | | |
	Women	Men	18–25	26–35	36–45	46–55	56–65	Over 65	Under $5,000	$5,000– 10,000	$10,000– 15,000	$15,000– 25,000+
Usually	60%	57%	53%	52%	55%	56%	62%	69%	67%	63%	58%	54%
Sometimes	32%	31%	33%	36%	34%	32%	29%	25%	26%	29%	33%	33%
Usually Not	8%	12%	14%	12%	11%	12%	9%	6%	7%	8%	9%	13%

Reprinted courtesy of Ottaway Newspapers, Inc.

TABLE 7–6: READERSHIP OF DAILIES VS. WEEKLIES

	Local Paid Weekly		Local Free Weekly	
	Reader	Nonreader	Reader	Nonreader
Read daily 4 or 5 days in past week	72%	64%	69%	65%
Read daily 3 days or less	28%	36%	31%	35%

Adult Readership of Weekly Newspapers and Shoppers, March 1978; Newspaper Advertising Bureau, Newspaper Readership Project.

is considerably less true for the reader of a free newspaper ("shopper"). Readers and nonreaders of free newspapers show very little difference in regular reading of a daily.

Tables 7–7 and 7–8 provide further illustration of B–B research. In each of these tables, readers' attitudes toward their weekly newspaper are examined according to their reading behavior, that is, those who read only a weekly versus those who read both a weekly and a daily newspaper. In both cases these reading behavior patterns make a considerable difference in readers' evaluations of the weekly. Exposure to a daily newspaper reduces positive feelings toward the weekly. These tables illustrate only two of the dozens of attitude questions which have been used in recent readership research.

So far the illustrations of B–B research have used combinations of actual behavior and attitudes. Tables 7–9 and 7–10 (see page 52) add another kind of response to the mix, readers' motivations for reading a newspaper. In Table 7–9, four psychological motives are examined to see how well they predict use of a daily newspaper. In Table 7–10, the same four motives are examined as predictors of weekly newspaper readership. In all five parameters there is a strong association between the strength of the motive and the likelihood of being a regular newspaper reader.

For example, persons who are high on "feeling up-to-date" are twice as likely to be everyday readers of a daily newspaper than are persons who score low on this item. They are also more likely to be regular readers of a weekly. All of these pieces of information help explain differences between regular and occasional readers. Each

of these B—B studies helps to fill out the picture of newspaper readership.

Using Readership Research

As an editor grows more comfortable with readership data and more accustomed to marshaling it for key editorial decisions, the complexity and sophistication of the data used will increase. Early in their use of readership research, most editors and their staff members feel comfortable with simple A–B type results: for example, demographic analysis of who reads specific types of news and specific standing features in the newspaper. As familiarity with readership data and techniques grows, journalists typically become more interested in learning how entire groups of variables—such as the readership scores for a large number of stories—are related to some criterion such as the frequency of reading the newspaper. In short, the questions posed for readership research become increasingly complex.

This is more than a matter of increasing intellectual curiosity. It is a matter of deepening insight into how the community newspaper serves its audience. Or, put another way, editors will ask increasingly specific and penetrating questions about the mass communication process which links the

TABLE 7–7: IN YOUR EXPERIENCE, DO HEADLINES IN THE (NAME OF NEWSPAPER) GIVE YOU AN ACCURATE IDEA OF WHAT REALLY HAPPENED?

	Reads Weekly Only (N = 82)	Reads Weekly & Daily (N = 239)
Usually accurate	64.6%	51.0%
Sometimes inaccurate	28.0%	38.5%
Usually inaccurate	7.3%	10.5%

Reprinted courtesy Communications Center, Syracuse University.

TABLE 7–8: IF THE PRESSES AT THE (NAME OF NEWSPAPER) BROKE DOWN AND THE PAPER COULDN'T BE PRINTED AGAIN FOR TWO OR THREE DAYS, HOW MUCH WOULD YOU MISS THE PAPER?

	Reads Weekly Only (N = 84)	Reads Weekly & Daily (N = 242)
A great deal	27.4%	19.8%
Some	34.5%	34.3%
Very little	25.0%	22.7%
Not at all	13.1%	23.1%

Reprinted courtesy Communications Center, Syracuse University.

hometown newspaper and its audience. This also means that these questions will yield more practical and actionable answers. This question of practicality brings us back to an earlier point, the importance of having a research plan, a systematic guide to the kinds of questions which will guide key editorial decisions.

Too many readership projects are organized without any plan in mind. They do little more than satisfy passing curiosity. Too many research planning sessions begin with such remarks as "Wouldn't it be interesting to know. . . ." Why would it be interesting to know? What would you do with that information once you had it? A good research plan begins with specific goals and specific questions relevant to those goals. Once these are specified, the design of the research is easy. An explicit research plan makes it clear whether the appropriate focus is the entire newspaper, certain sections of the newspaper, or specific items within the newspaper. It also makes it clear whether any characteristics of the audience or the content need to be studied and it guides the research planner through the mass of audience responses which could be included. In short, an explicit research plan defines the type of research needed and makes readership research practical.

Organizing a Research Program

Once a research plan has been devised and decisions have been made about the actual, specific types of readership research which are needed, it is time for the projects to get underway. The details of how research is actually conducted and training in the specific techniques of drawing samples from the audience, designing a questionnaire, conducting interviews, analyzing newspaper content, and analyzing audience and newspaper data are far beyond the scope of this chapter. They are the subject matter of entire books. They are the technical areas of expertise for which an editor turns to his researcher. But there are two essentially nontechnical aspects of organizing a research program which do need to be emphasized here: drawing on previous research and selecting a researcher.

DRAWING ON PREVIOUS RESEARCH

Every new research project conceived by a community newspaper need not begin *de novo*. The idea and the research question may seem totally new to a particular newspaper and its executives, but most likely some previous research pertinent to this question has been reported in the readership research literature. In short, prior to investing any substantial sum of time and money in gathering new data, check to see how much is already known.

In some cases, the answer to a question posed by the community newspaper has been reported in someone else's research. Occasionally, the circumstances of the prior research allow one to accept the answer without any need for further verification or testing in the local situation. More commonly, prior research overlaps the new

TABLE 7–9: FREQUENCY OF DAILY NEWSPAPER READING BY STRENGTH OF MOTIVE FOR READING NEWSPAPER

	Feel up-to-date			Read for Information			Read for Fun		
	High	Medium	Low	High	Medium	Low	High	Medium	Low
Every day	65.9%	57.8%	30.4%	69.7%	63.3%	59.5%	63.7%	49.3%	34.5%
Less than every day	34.1%	48.2%	69.6%	30.3%	36.7%	40.5%	36.3%	50.7%	65.6%

Reprinted courtesy Communications Center, Syracuse University.

TABLE 7–10: FREQUENCY OF WEEKLY NEWSPAPER READING BY STRENGTH OF MOTIVE FOR READING NEWSPAPER

	Feel Up-to-date			Read for Information			Read for Fun		
	High	Medium	Low	High	Medium	Low	High	Medium	Low
Every week	76.2%	63.3%	48.1%	83.1%	68.7%	57.8%	73.5%	62.9%	51.2%
Less than every week	23.8%	36.7%	51.9%	16.9%	31.3%	42.2%	26.5%	37.1%	48.8%

Reprinted courtesy Communications Center, Syracuse University.

research question or suggests additional factors to be considered, but it does not yield an exact, immediately actionable answer. Here the value of checking the research literature lies in the enhancement and fine tuning of the new research. Questions can be more precisely framed, and more sophisticated analyses of the data can be planned.

Good research is cumulative, building on prior knowledge of the subject. Good research also means prudent investment of time and money on well-specified, unexplored targets rather than aimless wandering over ill-defined or previously explored targets.

Where can the reports of this previous research be found? While a thorough exploitation of college research library resources and personal contacts in the newspaper industry would yield a lengthy list of sources, two major and readily available sources will be described here. One is an industry source, the other an academic source.

The industry source is the News Research Center of the American Newspaper Publishers Association. The principal publication of the center is *ANPA News Research Reports,* an ongoing series of reports summarizing new research findings in a variety of areas. Perhaps most valuable in this series to date is Report No. 3, which presents an overview of 469 research findings on newspaper readership and circulation completed between 1950 and 1976. All of these findings have been placed in a computerized bibliography which can be indexed in a variety of ways. This allows an editor or researcher maximum flexibility in exploring the types of studies already available. Details on how to gain access to these findings and how to obtain both a bibliography and abstracts of those which are pertinent to any particular interest are presented in Report No. 3. (Although this computerized bibliography initially extended only to 1976, work is underway to add materials from recent years.)

A second major source of information about previous research on many aspects of journalism and mass communication is *Journalism Quarterly.* In each issue of this research quarterly is a section titled "Articles on Mass Communication in U.S. and Foreign Journals." Analogous to the *Readers' Guide To Periodical Literature,* this bibliographic listing in *Journalism Quarterly* covers periodicals ranging from *Editor & Publisher* and *Newsweek* to the *Stanford Law Review* and the *Indian Journal of Communications Arts.* To facilitate a search for articles on a particular subject, listings are organized under approximately twenty broad categories, such as "Audience and Communicator Analysis" and "Community Journalism." The listings are not cumulated, so it is necessary to examine each issue of the journal.

Journalists or researchers who spend some time with these or other information sources prior to embarking on new research will find the quality of their investment in new research greatly enhanced.

SELECTING A RESEARCHER

More and more newspapers are creating their own research staff or at least designating a single individual as research manager with the responsibility of coordinating and facilitating research efforts within the organization. However, this is still beyond the needs or financial ability of most community newspapers. For these newspapers there are two useful sources of research expertise: commercial research firms and mass communication researchers in university schools and departments of journalism. The community newspaper seriously interested in readership research should carefully explore these alternatives locally and select the researcher who can best provide the specific kinds of information needed about newspaper readership at a reasonable cost.

In all cases, the executives of the community newspaper should take the lead in designating the questions on which the research is to focus. In other words, the best research results are obtained when the local newspaper has carefully formulated an explicit set of goals and carefully devised a research plan to provide information pertinent to those goals. Researchers can be useful partners in shaping these plans, but too often the entire job of framing a research plan is left to the researcher alone.

Even though it generally is not the case, the community newspaper and its researcher also can be partners in the actual execution of the research plan. Obviously, the researcher is the technical expert on how to do the research. But there are many specific jobs which are essentially clerical that can be carried out by the community newspaper staff. There are several advantages in this involvement if it is properly supervised by the researcher. First, even such simple involvement as reproducing the questionnaire or assisting with the arrangements for interviewer training brings a newspaper staff psychologically closer to the project and enhances their interest in its findings. Second, use of the staff for these tasks can reduce the costs of the research. A staff member's time contributed to a research project does not have to be charged for. When outsiders are brought in to do the job, it is necessary to add their salaries and expenses to the cost of the project. A third advantage is that this involvement in a research project brings greater understanding, and perhaps even some research expertise, to the community newspaper.

Summing Up

Readership research involves five basic steps. The first step is the determination of the newspaper's goals. Why does it want to do readership research? In the process of framing an explicit answer to this question, the hometown newspaper will identify the primary focus of the research to be done—the entire newspaper, special sections of the newspaper, or specific items within the newspaper.

The second step in framing a research plan is to specify which characteristics of, or responses to, the focal objects are to be studied. These range from such responses to the entire newspaper as opinions and frequency of use to such characteristics of specific items as length and topic. This brings into sharper focus exactly what the research is to examine.

The third step specifies the exact combination of information desired. What type of research is needed? Type A–B, B–B, or B–C? Once this general strategy has been decided, what specific kinds of information are desired? This step must explicitly identify the analysis to be performed on the data.

The fourth step involves fine-tuning the research plan by carefully examining past research on the topics designated in the research plan. This can maximize the usefulness of new research, avoiding questions which already have been answered and framing new questions which advance understanding and insights about newspaper readership.

The final step is selecting a researcher and actually doing the research. With the careful planning outlined in the previous four steps, this step—which always looks so formidable and complex to journalists—will turn out to be the most straightforward step of all. The final result of these five steps will be practical, actionable information to guide the daily and long-range decisions of the daily or weekly newspaper.

Chapter 8

Newspaper Page Design

by Kenneth C. Bronson

The design of a newspaper has four basic functions: to make the newspaper attractive and interesting; to make the newspaper as easy to read and understand as possible; to grade the news for the reader; and to maintain a style of continuity throughout the newspaper.

Design begins with a "show window" front page and established, easy-to-read inside pages that follow a pattern of continuity in the placement of news and advertising.

Research into readership as it relates to design is sadly lacking, but some data support the contention that people do try to tell a newspaper by its front page—contradicting the cliché about not telling a book by its cover.

Two studies conducted by J. W. Click and Guido H. Stempel III for the American Newspaper Publishers Association demonstrated what had been assumed in the 1960s and 1970s: that the front-page format is the newspaper's personality. The studies found people do read a great deal into the first impression that the front page provides.

emphasis on wider columns, large graphics, and more horizontal than vertical makeup of body type on the page.

But good design is more than modular makeup and wide columns. Another element emerged in the mid-1970s when newspapers began embracing the concept of producing a product to fulfill the needs of its own market. This marketing concept for newspapers had a profound impact on newspaper design.

"Design the newspaper for the market it serves: Understand the readers—their reading habits, preferences, life styles—and design accordingly," was the advice of Richard A. Curtis, design editor of the Miami *News* at a special American Press Institute seminar on design in the summer of 1978.

Simplicity of design probably is the single most important thread weaving through the concepts of graphic designers. Viewed in its most elementary terms, design is simple in that it involves just four elements: art, type, white space, and color.

KENNETH C. BRONSON

The author is vice president of Stauffer Communications, Inc., a nationally known lecturer on newspaper design, and a former newspaper editor.

"The total newspaper planning method has been a boon to newspaper design improvement. . . . Systematic placement of both advertising and news content can contribute to the formation of a well-designed product that proclaims a personality style."

Design for the Market

Those studies also concluded that readers prefer modern front-page formats to traditional formats. Modern, in this case, referred to modular design, with

Consider Photographs Foremost

As the public became more visually aware through the influence of television, newspapers in the late 1970s

turned to the art element, through good photography and graphics, as its primary design vehicle, even though type continued to constitute the major portion of the newspaper product.

For most newspapers, photographs represent the only art element.

The Examiner

Vol. 75, No. 262   48 Pages —3 Sections   Independence, Mo.   Saturday, March 29, 1980   15¢

The weather

Chance of rain again today; highs in the 50s; lows in the 40s.

Kennedy leaves before speaking to audience

When Sen. Edward Kennedy hit downtown Kansas City Friday night, he made two stops. But he didn't say much at either one.

The first was at his 11th floor hotel room at the Radisson Muehlebach. His entrance to the hotel lobby was short and swift. Hesitating to sign autographs for fans and surrounded by a host of Secret Service men, who outnumbered the press, he entered the elevator and disappeared.

An hour later, the senator came downstairs to attend the Martin Luther King Memorial Hospital Dinner. He sat at the head table and listened for more than an hour to a series of ceremonial presentations and speeches, then left without speaking.

According to Secret Service personnel, Kennedy was to have spoken at the dinner, which was attended by about 1,200 persons. The Secret Service men registered some surprise that Kennedy chose to leave before the program ended.

The Rev. John W. Williams, who gave the dinner's keynote address, indicated when he came to the podium that he would cut his presentation short, so the audience could hear remarks from the senator. But Kennedy said he wanted to hear Williams' speech.

Williams, however, spoke for almost 45 minutes during which time Kennedy made little effort to conceal his boredom. When the speaker concluded his talk in which he mentioned the presidential hopeful's presence several times, Kennedy exited swiftly.

Leaving the ballroom, he returned to the mezzanine level of the hotel and once again disappeared into the hotel elevator, speaking to no one.

Today the senator is scheduled to visit the Eisenhower Recreational Center in Kansas City, Kan., and to lead the March of Dimes Walk-a-thon. Later he is to appear at the Kansas City, Kan., City Hall, then return to the Radisson Muehlebach for a closed meeting with labor leaders followed by press interviews and a meeting in the afternoon with Jewish community leaders — another closed meeting.

The senator is scheduled to leave Kansas City from Municipal Airport at 2:30 p.m. and head for Wichita, where he is scheduled to give the Eisenhower Lecture at Wichita State University.

While Sen. Kennedy took a sentimental campaign journey Friday to West Virginia — the scene of his brother John's big 1960 primary victory — John Anderson took on Ronald Reagan's farm policy in Wisconsin.

President Carter stayed at home in the White House, but his manager Rober Strauss hinted the president may soon end the Rose Garden strategy and set out on a limited travel schedule to counter the surge Kennedy apparently has made.

While Reagan went home to California for a couple of days of rest, Anderson attacked Reagan's farm policy as he campaigned on a Wisconsin pig farm. Anderson said he had been involved in farm legislation for most of his 20 years as a congressman unlike "Mr. Reagan who scratched his head about parity."

Examiner Photo by Leighton Mark

Sen. Edward Kennedy's face tells the story. The Democratic presidential nomination candidate was in Kansas City Friday night on a one-night stop before going to Wichita, Kan. While in Kansas City he was to be a speaker at a dinner for the Martin Luther King Memorial Hospital. Kennedy, however, did not make his scheduled speech.

Snyder spends most money

By Lola Butcher
Of The Examiner

Fourth District City Council candidate Bill Snyder has spent more money campaigning than any of the seven other council candidates, according to campaign finance disclosure reports filed with the Jackson County Election Board.

According to the reports, which must be filed at least seven days and no more than 12 days prior to the Tuesday election, Snyder has spent $5,656.06 in his campaign. He has received $5,781.06 in contributions.

By comparison, Snyder's opponent, Charles Franklin III, has spent $2,588.66. He has received $2,769.36 in contributions.

Other candidates receipts and disbursements follow:

1st District: John Carnes received $3,587.80 and spent $1,705.90; Carl Mesle received $1,065.76 and spent $75.

2nd District: Marilyn Wright received $5,221.09 and spent $2,189.34; Phil Middleton received $1,832.46 and spent $17.84.

3rd District: Merideth Francis received $3,297.15 and spent $3,136.56; Mike Martin received $5,229.31 and spent $2,385.57.

The Good Government League endorsed and contributed $1,702.34 to Mesle; $1,814.62 to Middleton; $1,854.62 to Francis; and $1,653.62 to Franklin.

The United Eastern Democrats endorsed and contributed $4,222.57 to Carnes; $5,456.99 to Martin; $5,861.47 to Schmidt; and $2,427.18 to Snyder.

Not all the candidates filled out their campaign finance disclosure forms the same way. For some, the amount of contributions received does not include the "in-kind," or non-monetary contributions of supplies or man-hours the candidate may have received from campaign workers or others.

For example, according to the finance disclosure forms, Carnes's total receipts do not equal the amount the UED claims it gave him. Likewise, Mesle's total receipts are less than the GGL contribution to Mesle.

But Middleton's total receipts apparently includes the entire amount the GGL contributed to his campaign.

The GGL has had receipts of $15,572.59 in the election period; the club's expenses and contributions to candidates have amounted to $12,158.08.

The biggest GGL fund raiser was a Feb. 22 dinner in honor of GGL founders, at which the club cleared $1,199.02. The club's single biggest contributor was C.W. Jones, 2919 Lee's Summit Road, who gave $1,000.

The United Eastern Democrats received $15,051 in the election period. Expenses have been $7,630.70, not including its contributions to candidates.

The club's most successful fund raiser was a showing of "And Justice For All," at which $7,221 was taken in. There were no expenses recorded for the event.

The club's biggest contributors are J.R. Stewart, who gave $3,000, and Lu Vaughn, who gave $2,115.

Will Palmer, inset left, and Harold Card, part-owners of the state's richest coal reserves, claim to be in a vicious business. Card said a private investigating firm has found a competitor planted rumors about them that led to their expected loss of a 15-year contract to supply coal for Independence. On the average day, 30 truckloads bearing 20 tons of coal each leave Bronaugh destined for the Independence Power and Light Department.

Examiner Photos by Leighton Mark

Repeal of contract leaves future uncertain for coal firm

By Lola Butcher
Of The Examiner

NEVADA — Will Palmer glanced around his shoulder as if trying to see beyond the next hill.

"If some coal doesn't come out of that pit in a minute or two here, we're going down to see why," he told his visitor. But before the 60 seconds were up, a 20-ton truck was lumbering around the bend, laden with coal.

The truck dumped its load and returned to the pit for another. A crane lifted the coal into a processer for cleaning and, within the hour, the coal began its 120-mile trip north from Bronaugh to Independence.

For the last two years, that process has been repeated 30 times a day to keep Independence homes and businesses warm in the winter, cool in the summer and lit-up day and night.

Until recently, Palmer, president of Midwestern Mining and Reclamation Inc., and Independence city officials, and two firms of "middle men" hoped this relationship would continue for another 15 years.

But Monday night the Independence City Council is expected to repeal the contract that would have kept Midwestern coal fueling the City of Independence in the future.

The current contract with Midwestern will run its course by the middle of next week; the city hopes to buy another 75,000 tons of the coal on a short-term contract. Beyond that, where Independence will buy its coal and where Midwestern will sell its coal is uncertain.

Related story, page 12

Duane Simpson, director of the Independence Power and Light Department, has long recognized the need for a long-term coal contract.

"Like everything else, the price of coal is going up almost every month," he said this week. Since Independence two years ago converted its Blue Valley Power Plant from natural gas to coal consumption and recently acquired the coal-burning Missouri City Power Plant, the rising coal costs bite hard in Independence.

The long-term coal contract would give the city security of knowing where the next load of coal would be coming from and that the price-per-ton would be no higher tomorrow than today.

Such a contract would also give security to the small coal producer because he could rely on a fixed production level and income flow. Each year the freight rate and labor rate could be re-negotiated.

The day Doug Klusmeyer, whose Associated Producers Inc. is a "middle man" between the city and the mining company, submitted a bid for the long-term coal contract, it was the same day that contract began to fall through.

Associated Producers won the contract, but allegations were made that Klusmeyer's friendship with Phillip Hanson, production manager at the Independence power plant, might have compromised Hanson's integrity.

Two city investigations concluded the friendship was above board, but the City Council decided to void the contract — partly because "a cloud of suspicion" was hanging over it, partly

because Associated Producers hadn't been able to meet the performance bond requirements.

The city is to seek bids for a second time, and Associated Producers will be allowed to bid again.

Klusmeyer and Midwestern Mining and Reclamation hired a private investigator to discover the source of the allegations. Harold Card, Midwestern's general manager, claims a competitor planted the rumors.

Simpson said the coal business is just vicious enough for that to happen.

"This is nothing new," he said. "Any number of cities have gone through the same agony — Columbia, Springfield. It's just too bad."

For Midwestern, the ordeal may mean closing the mines temporarily until another buyer is found, but Card isn't worried.

"There will always be a market for our coal," he said.

For Independence, the loss of the contract may be more costly.

Simpson estimates the market value of coal has risen 10 percent since the bids were submitted last summer. That means that each ton of

the 600 tons of coal that comes to Independence each day may cost about $24 instead of $22.05, the price quoted in the Associated Producers contract.

Independence burns between 20,000 and 25,000 tons of coal a month; the new contract could cost the city more than $40,000 a month.

"In my point of view, the contract was all the city could have wanted," Simpson said.

The city wanted a performance bond of nearly $1 million, one element Associated Producers couldn't come up with. Simpson said he thinks the city will have to re-evaluate that requirement when it seeks bids a second time.

"The coal performance bond is so large. It has become an industrywide problem," Simpson said.

Associated Producers has indicated it will bid again, but whether the supplier will be Midwestern Mining and Reclamation and what the price will be is unknown.

"That is the best coal in the state of Missouri," Simpson said. "We had the opportunity to buy it at a good price."

It's countdown time for the sesquicentennial celebration of the RLDS World Conference April 6 through 13. All sorts of preparations are under way to ensure the Auditorium is in tip-top shape. William A. Gregson (center), supervisor for engineering services for the RLDS Auditorium, discusses plans for the construction of an on-stage rainbow with Independence artists Judith and Robert McWilliams.

Examiner Photo by Leighton Mark

RLDS seeks housing for conference visitors

By Susan Shepherd
Of The Examiner

While final preparations are being made in the RLDS Auditorium to ready for the sesquicentennial observance of the RLDS church founding, a last minute scamper is also being made to house out-of-town visitors who are not yet accommodated.

About 75 persons are without a place to sleep during the RLDS Conference April 6 to 13, according to Pam Maybee, secretary of the housing committee.

"As far as housing goes, most of the people need to be within walking distance of the Auditorium. These are the people who are flying or busing in," Maybee said. "That's where the critical need is."

The housing committee provides this temporary home-finding service for out-of-towners before each biennial World Conference. Although it makes no actual arrangements for the guests, it acts as a liaison between those who need accommodations and those offering them.

"This is a service we provide every World Conference," Maybee said. "They call us to notify us they need a place to stay."

She said the housing committee then sends out word to housing representatives in each congregation. Most housing needs are usually taken care of, she said, attributing the increased need this year to the 150th year celebration.

More than 150 persons have been directed to about 100 homes in Independence through the housing committee already, Maybee said. But with less than two weeks left before the founding day activities begin, the word on housing isn't encouraging.

"We are strongly recommending now that people try to make their own arrangements," she said. "We aren't having much luck finding any more homes."

What visitors are in need of is a place to sleep, Maybee said. Meals can be obtained at local restaurants, at the Laurel Club Dining Room in the RLDS Auditorium, or at the RLDS Stone Church cafeteria. While guests are expected to pay for their rooms, that isn't necessarily the rule.

"Most people aren't asking for payment, some are," she said. "I'd hate to say a given amount, it just depends.

"If a hostess has one (a price) in mind, she can tell us, and we'll relay it to the visitor," she said.

Besides home-finding, another service of the housing committee is to send out hotel information to out-of-town members when requested.

"One man called and said he tried to get in three hotels before he finally found one," Maybee said.

Not only is the sesquicentennial World Conference attendance exhausting residential housing and area hotels and motels, but campsites are also becoming scarce because of the estimated 12,000 people expected at the conference, she said.

"The Campus is full," Maybee said. "The last space was given out today (Monday) in fact." About 220 campers will be set up on the Campus, Pleasant and Pacific, and more than 200 of those will use complete hook-ups.

Because most of the normal alternatives for boarding have been taken, people are resorting to other methods. Maybee said people are offering their campers and driveways as places to anchor for the week, and others have cleared their attics to house visitors.

FIGURE 8–2 Photographs that illustrate a story should be packaged with the type block in such a manner that the reader will move from the photo into the story. *Reprinted with permission of Stauffer Communications, Inc.*

And since readership studies indicate a reader will see a photograph on the page before anything else, the use of this art element must be considered foremost.

Photographs generally need to be anchored: to the top or bottom of a page, under a squared-off copy block, or to a headline. Photographs that illustrate a story should be packaged with the type block in such a manner that the reader will move from the photograph into the story. Readership studies have shown this is best accom-

FIGURE 8–1 The front-page format is the newspaper's personality. People read a great deal into the first impression this page makes. *Reprinted with permission of Stauffer Communications, Inc. Art reproductions in this chapter by Dale Van Deventer, Stillwater (Oklahoma) News-Press.*

plished when the story is directly below the photograph with a headline the same width as the photo. The reader's eyes naturally flow from the photograph into the story.

UNUSUAL SIZING HELPS

Most designers agree that the unusual sizing of a photograph will create additional reader interest, regardless of its placement in relation to the story (although all agree that the story and picture should be integrated in some manner).

Cropping, or the elimination of some elements of the original photograph, often can produce such an unusual size. Cropping also should be uti-

lized to remove conflicting focal points from the picture and to heighten visual impact.

Because it does present such a visual impact, the photograph should represent a key point of the news or feature story. And while size is important in this respect, perhaps the most important feature of the photograph is the story it tells.

Peter Masters, director of graphics for the General Services Administration in Washington, D.C., explained this point in a 1978 speech on design at the American Press Institute: "The picture will say different things depending on what you do with it. For example, if you have a picture of a man walking down the road, and you show the man walking out of the picture, you are saying: 'He's come a long way.' If you have the man walking into the picture, you are saying: 'He has a long way to go.' And if you show the man walking in the middle of the picture, you are saying: 'He's come a ways, but he still has a way to go.' "

CAPTION LINES IMPORTANT

Caption lines, sometimes called cutlines, are another important element of the visual. If the eye is first drawn to the photograph on the page, then the reader will also want some questions answered: Who is in in the picture? Why is the picture used? These questions call for at least two requirements of every caption: identification and justification.

It is very unusual for a photograph to be so forceful and telegraphic that a caption is not needed. More often, captions are imperative to complete the story the photograph starts to tell. Because of this, cutline writing must be good writing—brief, but complete and factual.

Two other common-sense guidelines for photographic presentations should be remembered: When using a series of photographs, group them into a logical block and attempt to get the action to lead the reader into the next photo or copy block; and, when using thumbnails (small illustrations placed in the copy), frame them with about a half-pica of white space and be careful not to break the reader's natural eye movement through the copy block.

GRAPHICS AID COMMUNICATION

While photographs are the most common art element in newspaper design, other graphic devices also are utilized to present the reader with whatever visual presentation is best for maximum communication.

Sometimes, only a graphic can effectively complete this channeling of information from the encoder (editor or reporter) to the decoder (reader).

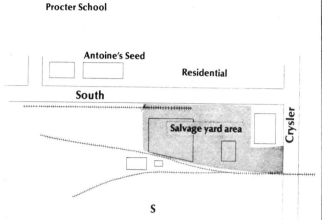

PROBLEM OF THE WEEK

Junk yard upsetting neighbors

By Paul Spencer
Of The Examiner

The city's plans to relocate a salvage yard have generated a storm of criticism from residents, businessmen and the Independence Board of Education.

The city long has intended to purchase the A. Markus and Son salvage yard, Truman and Main, either through negotiations or condemnation proceedings, using funds from a federal community development block grant.

If the city buys the property, however, part of the grant must be used to pay the costs of relocating the salvage yard to a site chosen by Milton Markus, the owner.

And therein lies the problem—Markus plans to relocate to a property he owns at Crysler and South Street, which he currently uses to load scrap onto trains. Many local residents don't like the appearance of the present salvage yard, which has been there about 20 years, and they think it would get worse if the salvage yard were expanded.

The school board also is upset about the relocation because Procter Elementary School is just a block north and the board plans a $575,000 expansion on the school building.

The school board Tuesday sent a letter to the City Council saying the expanded salvage yard would create a hazard for children walking to school, increase the noise level in the area and perhaps create a rodent problem.

"The potential nuisance of an enterprise such as a salvage yard could prove deleterious to the neighborhood and Procter School," the board wrote.

The presidents of the Procter Parent-Teacher Association and Procter Neighborhood Council No. 10

also sent a letter to members of that Neighborhood Council, warning residents the city's plans would result in a "huge, unsightly junk yard." The letter also said the salvage yard would decrease property values in the area.

The Neighborhood Council plans to ask the U.S. Department of Housing and Urban Development, which administers the federal grant, for an environmental impact statement, in hopes it would delay the relocation.

In addition, two petitions have been signed by about 200 residents protesting the relocation. And John Carnes, 1st District city councilman, told Neighborhood Council members the relocation would mean "your tax money is being used to downgrade your own neighborhood."

The city's hands are tied, however, on where the salvage yard would be

relocated because if the city buys the Truman and Main property, it has no say about where the salvage yard is relocated. The new site is zoned M-1, light industrial, which permits use for a salvage yard.

Under the zoning ordinance, Markus would be required to build a fence to screen the salvage from view within 2,500 feet. The city's Planning Department determined, however, Markus would have to build a fence about 20 or 30 feet high to meet that requirement.

Markus requested a variance from the screening requirement, and the city Board of Adjustment granted the variance in October, allowing Markus to build a 10-foot-high fence. Board Chairman Jim Gamble said he voted to grant the variance because such a tall fence would be at least as unsightly as the salvage yard with a

shorter fence.

The school board and at least one local resident feel they were not given adequate notice of the board's meeting. Attorney Norman Humphrey said because the zoning ordinance required the salvage not be visible within 2,500 feet, residents in that radius should have been notified of the hearing.

Gamble said the board more than fulfilled the legal requirements of notifying nearby residents. State law requires only that a legal notice be published between five and 15 days before a hearing.

Humphrey said mailing notices only to owners within 185 feet sets a double standard because the zoning variance would affect property within a 2,500-foot radius. "It think the notification requirements are a farce," he said.

FIGURE 8–3 Sometimes only a drawing can communicate effectively to the reader. *Reprinted with permission of Stauffer Communications, Inc.*

As Harold Evans, editor of the London *Sunday Times* and author of several books on typography said at the American Press Institute (API) in 1978: "How can you tell the story headlined 'Rescuers dig for miners trapped by rising waters' without a graphic illustration? Only through a drawing showing the relationship of the miners, the water, and the rescuers can you communicate this story to the reader."

Graphics generally fall into two categories, fact and flavor (sometimes termed "feature").

Fact graphics are devices such as charts, pie graphs, bar graphs, maps, floor plans, diagrams of the movement of people in a crime scene, simplified representations such as that for Evans' story of the trapped miners or to explain a production line or a space flight, etc.

Fact graphics present information to the reader that is more easily understood visually than it is verbally. In selecting the graphic device, the editor or artist should ask himself, As a

reader, what do I want to know from this story?

Flavor, or feature, graphics are more decorative than informational, although they should convey the central theme of the story. As Gus Hartoonian, art director of the *Chicago Tribune*, stated at the API seminar: "Every graphic depends on teamwork among writer, headline writer, and artist. The graphic must carry out the central theme of the writer and have a strong relationship with the headline."

Most flavor graphics utilize recognizable elements put together in a striking, unexpected manner—such as a bandage covering up a tear in a dollar bill to reflect the problem of the American dollar on the world market.

But graphics also can be pen or pencil drawings, watercolor art, oil paintings, or combinations of several mediums. Some of this art is produced directly for the page and some of it is photographically reproduced. Three-dimensional art, such as sculpture, obviously has to be photographed for newspaper use.

Photo illustrations—combining a photograph with art and/or type—sometimes are needed to communicate effectively with the reader. Diagramming, using an arrow to point out a prime element in the photo, using type blocks within the photo, etc., can be helpful to the reader but should be used only when the photograph does not stand on its own merits.

Since maps are the most widely used graphic device, a word of caution is merited: Keep the map simple and reproduce it large enough so that it is easily understood. Every newspaper should maintain a source file of maps, including road maps, U.S. Geological Survey topographical maps, state geological survey maps, and atlases. Simple color overlays can simplify map design and increase reader interest in maps.

FIGURE 8–4 Combining art with a photograph can often communicate best. Photo by Rich Clarkson. *Reprinted with permission of Stauffer Communications, Inc.*

Art Attracts, Type Repels

It is the capturing of reader interest which presents the greatest problem in the second design element: Type. Whereas art immediately achieves reader interest by attracting the eye, the grayness of type in any large mass tends to repel, rather than impel, the reading of the story. The treatment of type, therefore, becomes of utmost importance.

While few research findings make strong cases for either serif or sans serif type, most typographers believe serifs do aid in the perception of individual letters and words. Most body copy, therefore, is set in serif. Headlines, where fewer characters are involved, often are set in sans serif for both contrast and a more contemporary "look." Sans serif usually is used also for classified advertising and other smaller type. The rationale for this use is that numerals without serifs are easier to read. Therefore, where numerals are important, as in classified adversiting, sports box scores, stock market tables, etc., sans serif is the better typeface for readability.

X-HEIGHT IMPORTANT

Legibility and readability are also affected by two lesser-known measurements of type: brightness contrast and *x*-height.

Since newsprint is not white but about 10 percent gray, and since newspaper printing achieves only about 70 percent blackness in its transfer of ink to paper, the need for a type-face for newspapers somewhat heavier than book type is evident.

The *x*-height—the height of a lowercase letter without an ascender or descender, of which the letter *x* is an example—is most important in de-

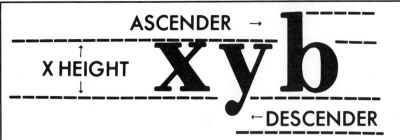

FIGURE 8–5 The *x*-height of type is important in determining legibility. Research also shows that all-capital letters are hard to read.

termining legibility. While a taller *x*-height increases legibility, it also often condenses the individual letters. A taller *x*-height allows the use of a smaller size of type whereas a shorter *x*-height calls for the use of larger typefaces.

Since words are perceived by outline shape, the relationship of the *x*-height to readability can easily be understood, as can the importance of capital and lowercase letters. One of the strongest findings in readability research is that words in all-capital letters are hard to read. To the eye, every word has a particular outline shape when set in lowercase letters. But words in all-capital letters have a uniform shape, therefore requiring more eye fixations. All-capital letters also require about 30 percent more space and slow reading speed by about 13 percent.

TYPE TRICKS RETARD READING

Another research finding is that reverse type is difficult to read. It retards reading speed by at least 15 percent if it does not totally repel readership. Placing a screen background behind type also inhibits readership since it reduces

the brightness contrast drastically.

A third conclusion drawn by typographers through readership research is that italic type is more difficult to read and has lower reader appeal. Italic type, therefore, should be used only in small amounts. And since italic is often used for emphasis, typographers suggest that a semibold type be used instead. Semibold causes less eye fatigue and does not have a negative effect on legibility.

FIGURE 8–6a and **b** (below and top of page 61)
Reverse type is difficult to read and to reproduce.
Placing a screen background behind type also reduces readability.
Reprinted with permission of Stauffer Communications, Inc.

LENGTH AFFECTS LEGIBILITY

The length of a line of type also has a profound influence on legibility and readability. Edmund C. Arnold, probably America's best-known typographer since the 1950s, called the length of the line "the most important single variable in determining readability."

"The *optimum line length* is the only typographical factor that can be determined by mathematics," Arnold stated in his book, *Modern Newspaper Design*. "This optimum is one-and-a-half times longer than the lowercase alphabet length."

Other typographers caution against such a restrictive formula for line length. They do, however, agree that short lines hamper readability since the eye can't make maximum use of horizontal perception. A secondary problem of the short line is the number of hyphenations at the ends of lines and the word spacing within the line. They would agree, too, that a long line length is also hard to read and that a 20- to 24-pica line probably is the maximum.

This interest in line length and its effect on readability reached its zenith in the early 1970s when many newspapers chose narrower web widths to offset the rising cost of newsprint. Because of this, columns were widened from the former 11-pica

e Examiner

16 Pages   Independence, Mo.   Friday, March 21, 1980   15¢

The weather

Not so cool tonight with clear to partly cloudy skies; low in the upper 30s. Sunny and mild Saturday with a high in the 60s.

grees with some faults in Antonio's audit

interest to be redeemed over a 25-year period.

Antonio, who is not a lawyer and has no power to enforce his recommendations, said the Municipal Building Authority Inc. is "apparently being used to avoid the restrictions" of a section of the Missouri Constitution regarding city indebtedness. He recommended an outside legal opinion be sought.

The city apparently doesn't plan to do so.

"This recommendation appears irrelevant since the City Council has already arranged for and obtained this opinion from two firms of nationally recognized bond counsel," the city responded in a two-page statement.

The city's financial advisors, Stern Brothers and Co., determined the total refinancing of the project by creation of a building authority was the least expensive of three financing plans suggested.

This was the only city response to which Antonio had a rebuttal: "We again recommend that outside legal counsel provide an opinion, that the opinion be in writing, and that it be specifically on the question of the compliance of the lease agreement with the Missouri Constitution and applicable statutes. To date, the city has not provided us with such an opinion."

On another issue, Antonio said the use of Power and Light money for two city parking lots apparently violates the City Charter. The city has spent $259,522 of Power and Light Fund money to buy two parcels of land.

In 1974, Power and Light Fund money paid for a public parking lot. The fund has not received any of the revenue earned from the public parking lot, Antonio said.

Antonio recommended the council decide whether it will build a power and light drive-in payment booth on some land purchased in 1972 for that purpose. The lot was paved in 1976 and is currently being used for a Police Department parking lot.

He said the city should decide if the land is to be used for power and light functions, and if not, it should repay the Power and Light Fund the original purchase price of the land plus a reasonable amount of interest for the years the city has been using the land.

The city responded by saying, "There has been no legislative expression to indicate a lack of further interest in constructing a power and light drive-in faciltiy. Neither do records indicate legislative intent with regard to use, at the time of purchase of the second property, for any purpose other than a public parking lot."

It went on to say the city will review its current plans for use of the property as Antonio suggested.

When the audience jeered at the city's response, Antonio laughed.

(See AUDIT, Page 16)

Auditor: review city attorney's role

By Lola Butcher
Of The Examiner

City officials apparently do not agree with the opinion of State Auditor James Antonio, who said at a Thursday night meeting he thinks City Attorney Sam Cottingham may be violating Missouri state law. However, the audience at the meeting seemed to agree.

At a public meeting called to release findings of an audit of Independence's books, Antonio's opinion was met with agreement. The city's response to Antonio's opinion was met with anger.

"I can't believe you astute gentlemen would let something like that pass," John Cogswell, 417 N. Main, told Antonio when he delivered his opinion and the city's response to a crowd of about 50 persons.

Antonio said, "I don't have the authority to throw anybody off anything."

Cottingham, who is paid $25,788 annually by the city, serves on the board of directors of Chrisman-Sawyer Bank, the city's official depository. The city's contract with Chrisman-Sawyer Bank was awarded under competitive bidding.

Members of the audience contended Chrisman-Sawyer was not the low bidder the first time bank bids were sought. However, when the city decided to change its bid requirements, Chrisman-Sawyer became the low bidder.

According to Antonio's assistants, the city then decided to re-solicit bids. In the meantime, Chrisman-Sawyer had raised its interest rate on savings; and by the time of the second bid, Chrisman-Sawyer was clearly the lowest bidder.

Antonio's report said Cottingham apparently did not have a role in the city's award of the contract. Cottingham also serves as the bank's general counsel.

"We did not observe anything wrong that seemed to have been done because Mr. Cottingham was a member of the board," Antonio said.

"By virtue of being on the board of directors of Chrisman-Sawyer Bank and serving as its general counsel, he would appear to be directly or indirectly interested in the contract between the city and the bank," the report said. Antonio recommended the city review Cottingham's relationship with Chrisman-Sawyer Bank and take any action deemed appropriate.

The city said no action is necessary.

"Interest would imply the exercise of judgment by the counselor which would be injurious to the city.... Due to the fact that he had no part in the drawing of, solicitation for, evaluation or awarding of the contract no such exercise of judgment was possible or necessary."

Cottingham has said he will not resign from the position while allegations of conflict of interest are being made because it looks like an admission of guilt.

"It doesn't matter to a hill of beans (his compensation for being a director of the bank), but I don't feel I have done anything wrong," Cottingham said.

"We (board of directors) approve all loans, authorize various officers to approve loans, things like that," Cottingham said. "City funds don't ever come up."

Cottingham said he believes if he was a city councilmember and a bank director, he would be in conflict of interest because the council selects the bank.

---

standard to 13 or 14 picas, with the number of columns on the page reduced from eight to six or even five, in some cases. Typographers generally applauded this move because of the improved readability.

With wider columns generally the established format among American newspapers in the late 1970s, typographers began turning their attention to the finer details of legibility and readability. Word spacing, or the lack of consistency thereof, became the new battle cry—and became the subject of much debate over whether or not type is easier read when it is justified or unjustified on the line.

Should Lines Be Justified?

Rolf F. Rehe, assistant professor of typography at the Herron School of Art, Indiana/Purdue University, emerged as one of the stronger proponents of unjustified newspaper lines.

"I prefer an unjustified typesetting style in which the lines are of fairly equal width," Rehe wrote in *Technical Communication*. "In addition to reducing or eliminating end-of-line hyphens, we realize another important gain in legibility: All the word spacing is equal. In justified typesetting we have to either reduce or increase word spaces to block out the lines. Often we end up with an assortment of very narrow or very wide word spaces. In unjustified typesetting, that process is not necessary. With no doubt, the eye is more comfortable reading text that has uniform word spacing than it is reading text having varying word spaces."

Rehe admitted that a number of studies have found little significant difference in legibility between the justified and unjustified typesetting styles, but he predicted that "within the next decade unjustified typesetting will be the style of the day."

So while it appears as if the style of the line makes little difference, research does show that the modular, or copy block, approach in handling type masses does enhance readership of the type. A column of type running the length of the long newspaper page is a formidable challenge for the reader. Taking that type and arranging it in a two-column block half the length of the page will increase readership dramatically. This increase will continue as the type is placed in wider, and thus shorter, copy blocks.

Copy Blocks Grade Content

The editor or designer should attempt to deal in copy blocks that are sized to be pleasing to the eye, keeping in mind that the size of the copy block very probably grades the content for the reader. A large copy block most certainly communicates a sense of importance to the reader.

It would seem logical, therefore, that the larger copy blocks should be at the top of the page with smaller ones further down. Generally, it is better not to mix and match copy block sizes down the page, but rather to reduce width size as you descend the page.

Arnold's influence on American newspaper typography might best be seen in this "grading" technique, especially on the front page. Arnold contended that the newspaper's best "attention compeller" should be in the upper left corner of the page, or in what he termed the *primary optical area.* Until this time, most newspapers used the upper right corner (and many still do) for the top story of the day. Arnold contended this was a holdover from the past when newspapers used a banner headline at the top of the page each issue and the story just naturally fell out of the headline on the right side of the page. He contended this placement of the top story was like asking the reader to read the page backwards, from right to left.

Guide the Reader

With modular page layouts and more emphasis on the horizontal, typographers today believe the size of the copy block, the placement of art (photo or graphic), and the use of the other two design elements—white space and color—can influence the reader's starting point on the page as much as the upper left or upper right location factor.

On inside pages, the copy block should be visualized as complementary to, rather than in competition with, the advertising on the page. Generally speaking, strong copy blocks at the top of the page will provide an excellent framework for the advertising on the page. Chicago designer Hayward R. Blake contends: "Design is bringing order and providing organization to the entire product, not just to the front page." And Louis Silverstein, assistant managing editor and designer of the New York *Times,* adds: "Advertisements are held in place by the typography around them. Create simple strong visual units that arbitrarily divide the inside pages above and beside the ads."

Of course, there are times when the story content dictates long copy blocks. When this happens, the editor

Tempo Entertainment

At 76, Arrau is at the top—and rising

John VonRhein
Music critic

THE PIANO RECITAL As High Art will never enter the list of endangered species so long as the best pianists of the present generation carry the grand tradition into *their* old age as nobly as Claudio Arrau is carrying it into his.

Of course, old age as it is commonly conceived seems blissfully irrelevant in the case of Arrau. Now 76, the great pianist continues to play with a brilliance, poetry, indefatigability, and authority that defy the laws of nature. Arrau has attained as high a standing among pianists as it is possible to attain, and the almost eerie thing about it is that he continues to surpass himself.

Sunday afternoon brought us yet another long and demanding Orchestra Hall recital of the sort Arrau invariably tackles with as much external fuss as he would expend tying his gray silk cravat. The program held

> "Arrau has attained as high a standard among pianists as it is possible to attain, and he continues to surpass himself."

standard Romantic works that turn up time and again in lesser hands, but few greater. Arrau put them all in a fresh, mellow perspective that was at once true to the printed page and wondrously free of its limitations. There were no encores, nothing to break that phenomenal concentration of pianism and expressive communication. And the revelations were prime Arrau.

HE OPENED with a double dose of Beethoven sonatas, the D Major (Op. 10, No.

3) and the "Appassionata," Op. 57, projecting thoughtful, emotionally contained statements of both. His was a far less impetuous, restless "Appassionata" than one usually hears, but it didn't lack drama or purity of conception.

Debussy is not a composer one automatically associates with Arrau, but the three "Images," Book One, proved him an impressionist of Gieseking stature. His "Reflets dans l'eau" were as full of coloristic detail, and not too much pedal, as his other piece of water music, Liszt's "Jeux d'eau a la Villa d'Este." But the high point for this listener was Liszt's Ballade in B minor, a veritable symphonic poem transferred to the keyboard. Arrau's playing was a miracle of virile, yet refined, romanticism.

Finally, Arrau turned to Chopin's Ballade in A-flat (Op. 47) and Scherzo in B minor (Op. 20), treating them neither showily nor with exaggerated rubato, but rather in a warm, rhythmically supple manner that always tempered bravura with impeccable taste.

I WISH I COULD report that the K&K Experimentalstudio and Pupodrom, two multimedia ensembles from Vienna who made their local debut Friday night in

Thorne Hall on Northwestern University's Chicago campus, did to theater of the ridiculous what Arrau does to Chopin, but such was not the case. In fact, the only encouraging thing I have to report from the whole dull evening was that the event opened Contemporary Concerts' 23d season with a larger audience—nearly 400 intrepid listeners—than this important series has ever enjoyed.

"Pupofon," the groups' joint, eveninglong effort, attempted to illustrate modern man's self-dehumanization through artifacts of his switched-on technology, using puppets, actors, projections, and a sometimes raucously amplified *musique-concrete* soundtrack by Dieter Kaufmann. It opened with a bearded chap in tutu and swim fins and a zombielike woman in formal tails waltzing around the stage, joining electric plugs, and shouting multilingual endearments while the stage overflowed with balloons. The audience had fun batting them around.

There were other nonliberal nonhappenings involving a 10-foot Messiah-figure who arises from under a crazy-quilt of bodies wearing a crown of Christmas-tree lights, and a near-nude woman struggling to break free of wires and electrodes.

THE TROUBLE with "Pupofon," besides its dull, smug pretentiousness, was that most of its visual and aural images weren't clever enough to be genuinely bizarre, witty enough to constitute good satire, or hard-edged enough to point up the inherent socio-cultural ironies. Most of them were simply tedious.

It's no longer enough to fill the stage with absurdities to remind us that we live in absurd times. We get enough of that in real life.

FIGURE 8–7 Some typographers prefer unjustified type because it permits uniform spacing between words. *Copyrighted © Chicago Tribune. All rights reserved. Reprinted with permission.*

or designer may use subheads, initial letters, photos, graphics, and quotation blocks to break up the grayness and increase reader interest in the copy block. If subheads are used, take care that they not make the story appear as if it is disjointed or a series of small stories. Art elements and quotation blocks also should not be used where they create a physical barrier for the eye.

There are times, too, when several paragraphs of statistical data can be presented in just a few lines of tabular type. Not only is this generally easier to read, but it also adds a pleasant change of pace for the reader who is trying to plow through the copy block.

Captions and Headlines Provide Contrast

This change of pace also is necessary in headlines and photo captions, which constitute two additional uses of type

in designing a newspaper.

Caption lines should be used in a typeface that offers a contrast to the body type, but is complementary to it. For most newspapers, this means setting the caption lines in a boldface type matching the body type.

A "grabber," "kicker," or "catchline" is sometimes used to entice the reader into the caption, especially if the photograph stands alone without an accompanying story. The style for usage of such elements should conform to the newspaper style for other headlines.

It is this continuity throughout the newspaper that makes the use of headlines doubly important. While the primary function of the headline is to entice the reader into the body copy, the headline also should conform to the overall design of the newspaper.

Generally, this is best done by restricting headline type to one family, or two at the most. With modern phototypesetting, one family of type can be "massaged" into at least a dozen variations—some good and some not so good!

Since it has already been established that all-capital letters and italic type are hard to read, headlines using these faces should be restricted and not overused. Generally, the size and boldness of the headline should be related to the story's importance to the reader. This grading of the news by the size of the headline most often follows the step-down principle—heads becoming smaller in size as the reader travels down the page.

Typographers are wont to debate the importance of type size in headlines. Evans, the British expert, noted that "headlines in American newspapers are too big, waste too much space, and the extra condensing of typefaces in headline type is very bad typographically." Other typographers contend that, ideally, all headlines should count the same, regardless of the size of type. To these experts, the ideal would be 22 to 25 characters per line.

DEVICES CAUSE CONTROVERSY

Typographical agreement is reached concerning downstyle headlines, in which only the first letter of the headline and all proper nouns are capitalized. The use of devices such as kickers, "hammers," hoods, decks, and others, however, still engenders controversy.

Opponents of such devices say they are not functional, that their function evaporated when offset printing replaced letterpress or when cold type replaced hot type. It is true that many typographical devices, such as kickers, were developed in letterpress days to achieve more white space around headlines. Decks accomplished much the same.

Proponents of such devices say their use should not be eliminated just because the printing process has changed. Rather, they contend, their use should be governed by the effect the designer wishes to achieve with the total package, regardless of whether that package is a single story or a full page.

For the untrained typographer or designer, some guidelines are in order for the use of these devices. Kickers generally should be no longer than one third the length of the main headline and no more than one half the type size of the main headline.

Hammers are the opposite of kickers, generally being twice the size of the main headline but still no longer than about one third of the main headline on the copy block.

The main headline under both kickers and hammers should be indented slightly to give additional impact to the kicker. Centered kickers usually appear to be floating in space and therefore fail to achieve the impact desired for such devices.

The hood, or boxed head, does not eliminate the confusion the reader must feel when confronted with two headlines side by side. Yet it is in this manner that the hood is most often used. It is usually better to separate headlines by illustrations, body copy, or white space.

FIGURE 8–8 The hammer is the opposite counterpart of a kicker, and is usually twice the size of the head underneath.
Headlines under both hammers and kickers gain even greater impact when indented slightly.
Reprinted with permission of Stauffer Communications, Inc.

AUTOMOTIVE

Shine
A good one can protect your car

With the cost of even economy cars skyrocketing, the family automobile is no longer a means of transportation so much as it is a necessary investment.

Protecting that investment is becoming a science in itself with a variety of ways to make sure the paint shines longer and the upholstery doesn't stain.

Which is best, which has the best price and which has the best warranty is often difficult to determine.

Like any industry, it's difficult to get something for nothing, so beware of the do-it-yourself "wonder" chemicals that do the job with almost no work and no money. They sometimes can cause more damage than good.

When such a protective coating is applied so that it allows a breakdown of the bond between the coating and the paint, it will only hold in newly deposited pollutants that enter through any breach in that film, preventing pollutants from being washed away. This, plus moisture, will have the effect of protecting, to great degree, those substances rotting away the paint film itself.

Guarantees for wonder products most often include only a replacement bottle of the product or a money refund to cover the cost of the product — without any consideration for potential damage to the automobile.

The logic boils down to: Why take a chance on a $10,000 automobile just to save $10?

Get Guaranteed Protection

The next step is to select a paint protection process. Make sure that not only the product, but also the application of a paint protection treatment is guaranteed. There are also guarantees that descend in value over a period of years a certain percentage each year. Look for some type of maintenance program for the process. It only makes sense that with continued build-up of pollution and weathering of the protection treatment, that the treatment itself will need some sort of yearly maintenance. Find out how much that will cost.

In the case of many professionally-applied protection processes, the process is guaranteed for as long as the customer owns the car, along with inexpensive annual resealants for the compound that literally penetrate paint, seal it and leave it with a high-gloss shine.

This is a triple-acting formula that's essential for real protection against natural elements and pollutants. The guarantee encompasses not only the product, but customer satisfaction that the process fulfills all claims. The process is applied by car appearance and maintenance specialists located at associate dealerships or at new car dealers offering appearance maintenance services.

Protect Interiors, Too

In addition to paint protection, it's important to consider the interior of the car as well. A clean-looking interior provides added value at trade-in time and increased pride of ownership.

This can usually be done by new car dealers, or by a car appearance maintenance specialist. Again, look for a guarantee that lasts for as long as the customer owns the car. Also make sure that the protection to the applied will not change the texture of the interior fabric and make it stiff. There are treatments available that won't change the soft and supple texture of even the lushest velours.

By planning a complete car appearance maintenance program, it is possible to keep the family car new-looking until trade-in time again — when a better appearance means hundreds of dollars more.

While it may be a popular pasttime for car buffs, rubbing several layers of wax onto one's car to get a mirror-like shine is a lengthy and involved process. Having a paint-protective treatment applied is one alternative. (Examiner photo by Kerwin Plevka)

WHITE SPACE HELPS

White space also plays an important role in the use of side headlines to bring order out of what might otherwise be chaos for the reader. Generally, the reader will be drawn into the body type more easily if the side head (usually placed to the left of the copy block) is set flush right, uneven left, with about a pica of space between the headline and type. This allows the white space to frame the uneven left lines of the head. A side head set flush left, uneven right, often leaves a sea of white space separating the headline and body type. This is not conducive to easy transition between headline and body type.

Because of the importance of white space to the side head, its use should be limited to the top or bottom of the newspaper page. To use it in the middle of the page, or on top of advertising, requires very careful treatment.

The white space problem in side heads is just one of many connected with its use. White space probably poses more problems for the average newspaper editor or designer than any of the other four design elements. Often, editors and designers are not even aware of the pitfalls in utilizing white space effectively.

White space can lead readers into a copy block or into a visual trap. For example, wrapping four columns of type in six columns may make the gutters more of a hindrance than a help to easy reading. The same is true for the space between headline and body copy, the frame around a copy block, the space around a photograph or graphic, and the white space between rules and type.

Generally, white space is best used as a frame around a copy block, much the same as a ruled box would be used. To get maximum effect, about a pica of white space should separate heads and copy, about a pica and a half should separate a headline from the story above it, and about a pica

should be used for gutters between columns of type.

LIMIT BOXES AND RULES

Maximum effectiveness can be achieved with white space when cutoffs and rules are avoided and the use of boxes is limited on the page. Rules, or black lines, often are hurdles or roadblocks for the reader. And boxes can actually repel readership if the rule is too black.

Some graphic designers contend, however, that rules and boxes are necessary to give form and to create visual units on the page. To achieve this, it usually is better to use a light, clean border and leave a frame of white space between the border and the visual unit being framed. In this manner, you get the white space working with the rule, rather than the rule disrupting the white space.

The rapidly changing design of newspapers from the late 1960s through the 1970s evolved around a wider type measure and the elimination of column rules. It is interesting to note, therefore, renewed interest in column rules a few short years after they disappeared. Typographical purists would claim the return of the column rule is one of the "fads" that apparently have influenced many newspaper editors during this period.

Some designers claim, again, that the column rule brings order to a design in much the same manner as boxes. The debate on this subject probably will linger for years.

One or two words are needed about rules, borders, and boxes. They tend to become art objects on the printed page and therefore their placement next to other art objects should be studiously analyzed. Also, rules are not needed around a screen background (even though readership is low, some newspapers still produce standing heads that are screened and often reversed). The box used in this manner is certainly not functional.

Make Color Functional

Functionalism also is important in the use of the fourth design element, color.

While studies have shown that headlines in color seldom increase readership and in fact may repel readership, some newspaper editors continue to fly in the face of solid evidence, daubing color on headlines without any thought as to its effect on the reader. Only in the rarest of circumstances should color be used in a headline.

Color can be overwhelming, especially in photography. A full-color photograph will completely dominate the average page. Care must be used in these cases not to lose readership from the remainder of the page.

Color photography most often is used in sufficient size to ensure its dominance. Readership studies show that color photographs in small size, especially if there are several small color photos on the page, are often no more effective than black-and-white photographs.

Duotones are also attention compellers. Expert use of the various screens available, such as crossline, mezzotint, straight line, etching, wavy line, steel engraving, spiral, and contour, can provide some pleasing, and eye-opening one-color illustrations.

Aside from photography, graphics such as maps and bar graphs obviously lend themselves to spot color treatment. Color, in these cases, often helps to define information contained in the graphic and makes it easier for the reader to comprehend. Naturally, when color is used in a graphic, a color key must be used.

Whereas using color in headlines or body copy does not gain readership, using color in tint blocks and rules sometimes can be very effective in spotlighting attention on a particular copy block. The brightness contrast factor, however, should be considered and the tint block restricted to no more than a 10 or 20 percent screen if type is to

FIGURE 8–9 Effective use of large art, color, and strong "reefer" heads give impact to this tabloid page. Nameplate, heavy border around art, and some of the type were in green. *Reprinted courtesy of the* Illinois Times, *Springfield.*

Illinois Times

April 20-26, 1979   25¢

DOWNSTATE ILLINOIS' WEEKLY NEWSPAPER

THE STATE NEGLECTS THE OLD
LOOKING FOR THE CHEAPEST WAY OUT
P. 4

A NEW BOOK OF ILLINOIS FISH STORIES
P. 8

IN SEARCH OF A NUCLEAR DISASTER PLAN
P. 11

NEW LIFE IN AN OLD CASTLE
P. 14

How enlightened linguists tackle the him/her problem
P. 16

Arnie Weissmann

VOLUME 4 NUMBER 30   Because of the adult day care center at St. John's Hospital North in Springfield, Charles Sharp does not have to live in a nursing home.

be printed over the block. When using color on a rule, the rule can be heavier than normal to give the color added impact.

Design to Communicate

In all discussion of newspaper design, simplicity is the key. It is best to have one or two strong, simple, easy-to-understand patterns on a page. And it is these patterns that have helped develop the latest newspaper design technique, packaging the news.

It is in the packaging that the newspaper achieves continuity throughout its product. It is this continuity that carries out the style of design.

Since it is the business of the newspaper to communicate, the fulfillment of this function should be the design goal. The design, then, should be organic in that it must grow from its content but maintain the continuity that allows the reader to exclaim with every issue: "This is my paper!"

It would be foolish, of course, to emphasize the package without regard to the content. A can of oil is packaged differently than a box of breakfast cereal. Eggs are packaged differently than cabbage. For each product there is a distinctively different package. And newspapers are no exception.

This is where marketing research plays a critical role in the design process. Newspaper markets vary from community to community. As Blake, the well-known Chicago designer, stated after designing his first newspaper: "Research kept me from going on an ego trip."

This marketing concept goes deeper than just the design of a newspaper. It may even determine the size of the product—broadsheet, tabloid, magazine, or half-tabloid.

Tabloids Are Popular

Since the tabloid size is popular in many markets, it is often assumed that its design should somehow be "different" from that of the broadsheets.

This is true to some degree, again depending on the market. A tabloid relying on street sales would certainly need a different front page design from that of a product which is primarily home-delivered.

The use of large graphics on the front page of a tabloid, perhaps imitating its magazine counterparts, is quite commonplace. Whether the remainder of the page should contain copy blocks or headline teasers for stories on inside pages depends on the news content of each issue.

Perhaps it is the packaging of a tabloid that clearly separates it from a broadsheet newspaper. Since sectionalizing is difficult, if not impossible, most tabloids adhere to the "strong beginning, strong middle, strong ending" concept, placing several open pages in these locations for dramatic news displays. Many tabloids even expect the reader to read from the back page forward for certain departmental news such as sports.

SOME POINTERS ON TABLOID DESIGN

A design "road map" for the reader to travel through a tabloid is most important. It is harder to anchor features and page packages without the benefit of sections. Therefore, indexes and "reefer lines," display lines that refer to material on other pages, in the first part of the product are doubly important.

And while it is difficult to sectionalize a tabloid product, it is easier to devote entire pages to departmentalization. The reader, therefore, can be advised that entire pages contain related information and news stories.

On inside pages containing ads, tabloids often find type blocks—especially strong horizontal displays at the top of the page—more effective than trying to mix art with the dominant advertising display. Since few if any stories appear on the front page of tabloids, readers may actually give more attention to inside pages than they would if they were reading broadsheet pages.

Because of the size of the page, editors of tabloids could well consider using a slightly smaller body type, as well as smaller headline faces. It should be noted, too, that a "cleaner," lighter typeface on the inside pages will provide better contrast to the heavier typefaces and bolder display of the advertisements.

The art element of designing a tabloid page must be considered the most critical, primarily again due to the size of the page. Graphics, including photographs, should be smaller in size unless dominance of the page is desired. Unusual sizing again is best, as it is with the larger broadsheet.

Since the division of the tabloid page into visual units for quick reader comprehension should be a goal, type modules boxed with a light rule may be helpful, especially on those pages containing several advertisements.

Packaging for Easy Reading

Effective communication with the reader cannot be overemphasized. Since newspaper design provides the channel for direct communication from reporter and editor to reader, this consideration must determine how each individual issue will be packaged. The story on an American walking on the moon will obviously have to be presented in a different package from one on a sandstorm in the Sahara.

The philosophy of newspaper packaging, from the front page to the last, is to make the newspaper as inviting and as easy to read as possible. The average reader spends only fifteen to twenty minutes with his or her copy of the newspaper. Readership surveys also show that people are creatures of habit—they read their newspaper the same way every day.

Attaining effective communication, then, requires us to (1) package the news content for easy reading, and

FIGURE 8–10 The importance of such devices as an easy-to-read index cannot be overemphasized. *Reprinted with permission of Stauffer Communications, Inc.*

THE SHAWNEE NEWS-STAR

(USPS 492-180) Shawnee, Okla VOL. 85—NO. 299 SUNDAY, MARCH 30, 1980 64 Pages in Four Sections DAILY 15¢—SUNDAY 25¢

Conventions give edge to Carter

By JERRY SCARBROUGH
Associated Press Writer

President Carter assured himself of at least 34 of Oklahoma's 42 national convention delegates Saturday by soundly whipping Sen. Edward Kennedy at the party county conventions.

Carter won 723 of the 932 delegates who will go to the district and state conventions while Kennedy had only 88 delegates and 120 went uncommitted.

One favored Oklahoma Sen. David Boren.

Carter got 78 percent of all the delegates selected, compared to 9 percent for Kennedy and 13 percent uncommitted.

Carter's strong showing at Saturday's conventions assures him of 24 of the 29 national delegates who will be chosen at the April 19 district meetings and at least 10 of the 13 who will be elected at the state convention May 3-4.

Kennedy was assured of only two delegates at the district level — one in the 1st District which is dominated by Tulsa, and one in the 5th District which is made up primarily of Oklahoma City.

Since he had only 9 percent of the total number of delegates, Kennedy will need a substantial number of unvommitted delegates to join his foreces at the state convention or he will face a shutout there.

By congressional district, the delegate totals and the number of national delegates those figures assure are:

—1st District: Carter 72, Kennedy 31, uncommitted 31, which means Carter will get two national delegates to one each for Kennedy and uncommitted.

—2nd District: Carter 158, Kennedy 2, uncommitted 24, which means Carter will win all six national delegates.

—3rd District: Carter 183, Ken-

Carter, Page 3A

County vote is 15 of 19 for Carter

By DAVID ALEXANDER

Delegates to the Pottawatomie County Democratic Convention gave President Carter 15 of the 19 delegates to the district and state conventions in a marathon four-hour session Saturday.

Four of the delegates to the two conventions remained uncommitted.

Ninty-eight Carter delegates, 18 uncommitted delegates and eight Kennedy delegates were present at the convention. County Democrats elected 147 delegates Mar. 11. There were 124 present at the convention.

Delegates to the district and state conventions are alloted proportionately to candidates who have at least 15 percent of the delegates attending the convention.

Kennedy failed to receive the required 15 percent and Kennedy delegates were forced to realign with the uncommitted delegates or the Carter delegates. Uncommitted delegates are free to align

County, Page 3A

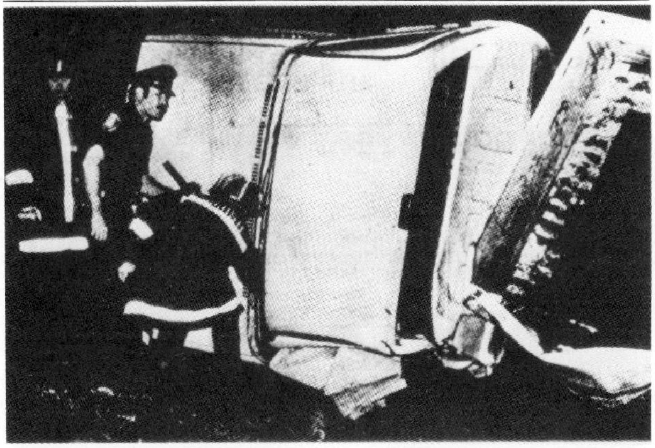

Shawnee policemen and firemen examine a pickup following a collision at Highway 177 and Leo late Friday. Forty-year-old Howard D. Richards, Tecumseh, was killed in the collision. According to police reports, Richards attempted to cross Highway 177 at Leo and pulled in front of a southbound tractor trailer. Richards' pickup spun around once after impact and went onto its side on the center median. The tractor trailer jumped the center median and stopped blocking both northbound lanes of 177. Ervin Lee Blanchard, Tecumseh, a passenger in the Richards vehicle, was also injured. The driver of the tractor trailer escaped injury. Damage to the two vehicles was estimated at $7,500. (Photo by Tracy Farley)

Shah's condition satisfactory after surgery

CAIRO, Egypt (AP) — The former shah of Iran was in very satisfactory condition Saturday after removal of his enlarged and possibly cancerous spleen, said the American surgeon who performed the operation.

Dr. Michael DeBakey of Houston told a news conference that Shah Mohammad Reza Pahlavi's spleen was bloated to 10 times its normal size and "was threatening his life."

He said the deposed ruler was in very good spirits, could leave the Maadi Military Hospital in 10 days and "should be able to lead a perfectly normal life."

The shah's wife, Farah, and their four children watched the 90-minute operation Friday night on closed-circuit television. Spokesmen said the shah was convalescing in his second floor suite, which commands a clear view of the Nile River and the Pyramids of Giza.

DeBakey, head of the Egyptian and American surgical team, said laboratory workers were examining samples from the shah's spleen, liver, and bone marrow for signs of malignancy. He could not confirm that the spleen was cancerous.

Asked if the shah's life was in danger without the surgery, DeBakey said, "Yes." He said the lymphatic cancer diagnosed earlier "is not threatening his life at this time. With the proper treatment that has been used before to which he has responded well ... It's possible for him to go on for an indefinite period of time."

"He should be able to lead a perfectly normal life physically and in every other way." DeBakey said. "He should be able to ... be physically active like he was. He can play tennis and things like that."

Armored cars lined the riverbank near the hospital and soldiers armed with automatic weapons ringed the building. Egyptian President Anwar Sadat has granted the former monarch permanent sanctuary.

The shah left Panama last Sunday, after a 100-day residence, the day before Iranian lawyers

Shah, Page 3A

City election voting set Tuesday

Shawnee voters will elect a mayor and two commissioners and decide the fate of six city charter revisions in the upcoming election Tuesday.

Candidates for mayor are Jerry Ozeretny, 4325 N. Kickapoo, and Arnold Davis Jr., 2 Navajo Circle.

Ozeretny has served on the city commission for two years. He is a supervisory program controller at Tinker Air Force Base and is section chief of the Policy and Systems Section, Directorate of Materiel Management at the Oklahoma City Air Logistics Center at Tinker.

Ozeretny emphasizes the need to work with the Department of Transportation and the highway commissioner to come up with a road improvement program for upgrading city streets.

Ozeretny is also concerned with the vitality of the downtown business district. "We need to be concerned about the vitality of the downtown area, so the city doesn't become sectionalized because of shopping centers.

"This all goes to keep our tax base up and provide the city with necessary operating revenues"

Ozeretny is also concerned about the possibility of establishing an internal transportation system within Shawnee. "The feasibility of an internal transportation within the city needs to be explored especially in our current situation of needing to conserve energy."

Ozeretny helped get the city financial advisory board organized. The board is made of financial experts from local banking and savings and loan institutions who assist the city government with large financial packages for municipal projects.

Davis is running for mayor after having served on the city commission for six years. Davis said he feels the direction the city

City, Page 3A

Railroad given okay to serve RI customers

OKLAHOMA CITY (AP) — The Interstate Commerce Commission has granted the Missouri-Kansas-Texas railroad permission to serve Rock Island customers from McAlester to Oklahoma City from April 1 through May 31.

The ICC in Washington D.C. Friday gave the Katy railroad authority to serve the Rock Island stretch temporarily but did not provide subsidies to fund the operation.

When cleanup operations on the Rock Island's Oklahoma line begin Tuesday, the only parts of the track to be served by other railroads will be the McAlester-Oklahoma City segment, the Enid-Kansas state line segment to be operated by the St. Louis-San Francisco, and a segment in the Panahandle to be operated by the St. Louis-Southwestern.

The Katy already had rights to use the Rock Island lines from McAlester to Oklahoma City, K.R. Ziebarth, Katy executive vice president, said.

White House denies Iran report

By The Associated Press

Iranian state radio reported Saturday that President Carter sent a personal letter to Ayatollah Ruhollah Khomeini admitting past mistakes in U.S. foreign policy and calling for an international commission to settle the U.S.-Iran crisis. The White House categorically denied the report.

"The president sent no message to Khomeini," White House press secretary Jody Powell told reporters.

The radio report, monitored in London, also quoted Carter as saying, "I can quite understand that the occupation of our embassy in Tehran could have been an acceptable reaction for Iranian youths" to the U.S. decision to allow the ousted shah into the United States last October for medical treatment.

Militants took over the U.S. Embassy on Nov. 4, and hold 50 Americans hostage for the return of the shah for trial on murder and corruption charges. The militants said they would allow religious services on Easter Sunday, April 6, for the hostages who spent their 147th day as captives Saturday.

Iran radio said Khomeini's office released the purported Carter letter, and quoted the author as saying he had not been involved in the shah's flight from Panama to Egypt last Sunday and had vetoed his possible return to this country for further treatment.

Doctors who removed the shah's dangerously enlarged spleen in Cairo, Egypt, said the former monarch was in good spirits and satisfactory health. Dr. Michael DeBakey of Houston, who directed the surgery, said the spleen had

Report, Page 3A

News-Star rainfall report

(Rainfall reporting sites showed the following measurements for rain that began early Saturday and ended about 10:30 a.m.:)

17 Juel Drive	.45	Twin Lakes	.70
1216 N. Louisa	.33	South Rock Creek	.40
9 Birdie Ln.	.42	North Rock Creek	1.20
141 S. Eden	.42	St. Gregory's	.42
Tecumseh		Earlsboro	.50
East of City	.20	Stroud	1.00
407 Guilliams Road	.43		

Good Morning!

Home

Family builds dream home — Not everybody can build their own dream home, but the J. Floyd Jacksons–Floyd, Jane, and sons, Johnny and Mike–did just that. The home and its residents are featured on Page 1C.

Local

Tuesday's voting places listed — Voting places for Tuesday's Shawnee city commission and mayorial elections are listed by ward and precinct on Page 2A.

State

Peace meeting — A better handle on the prospective adjournment date of the 1980 Oklahoma Legislature could be the only benefit from Sunday's peace meeting at the Governor's Mansion. Page 5A.

Girl Scout murder case, year later — A year ago Sunday, grim jurors filed into a stifling courtroom to announce the fate of a man charged in a case that had stunned the nation, the bludgeoning deaths of three Girl Scouts. Page 5A.

National

New York threatened again — Fourteen years ago, bus and subway workers paralyzed New York City with a 12-day strike. A series of walkouts threatened for this week — by virtually every aspect of transportation in the city — could make the 1966 strike seem tame. Page 2A.

Karen Ann turns 26 — Four years ago, the New Jersey Supreme Court gave Karen Ann Quinlan's parents permission to have her life-supporting respirator removed. Doctors predicted she would die, yet Miss Quinlan, who was 26 on Saturday, continues to breathe on her own. Page 15A.

House seats change with census — Census officials say the 1980 tally will boost the political power of the West and the South, with as many as 14 House seats moved from other states. Page 6A.

Man holds shakey ground — Eighty-four-year-old Harry Truman won't leave his lodge on the slopes of erupting Mount St. Helens despite the urgings of a team of scientist who fled a monstrous roaring sound. Page 11A.

Political roundup — Sen. Edward M. Kennedy, believing New York and Connecticut exposed President Carter's political vulnerability, seeks to hand the incumbent another double-loss in the approaching Wisconsin and Kansas primaries. Page 6A.

World

Norway calls off search — **Hope is all but gone for the 85 men missing in the North Sea's icy waters since their oil rig hotel capsized, and officials say they are calling off the massive air-sea search for survivors. Page 11A.**

Farm

Leasing farm implements not popular here — Leasing farm equipment as opposed to purchasing has been receiving press in agricultural publications but it's not popular here, points out Mike Nichols in his farm column. Page 16A.

Sports

Will Staubach retire? — Dallas Cowboys' quarterback Roger Staubach will announce Monday whether he retires after 11 years in the National Football League. Page 1B.

Weather

Decreasing cloudiness statewide — Decreasing cloudiness with rain ending northeast Sunday, high in the 50s. Fair Sunday night, low in upper 20s to upper 30s. Partly cloudy Monday, high in low to mid 60s. Sunrise today at 6:22 a.m. Sunset at 6:49 p.m. SATURDAY: High 46. Low 36. Details on Page 3.

Other features

Bridge	10C	Men in uniform	10A
Classified	9-16B	Obituaries	2A
Comics	14C	Oklahoma	5A
Daily Crossword	14C	Records	8A
Dear Abby	6C	School menus	15-16A
Editorial	6A	Society	1-7C
Entertainments	Escort	Sports	1-8B
Horescope	14C	Worry Clinic	7C

Starology

Young boys and girls between the ages 4 and under, and 6 to 16 and over interested in racing tricycles and bicycles are invited to attend a meeting at the new Shawnee International Raceway 1 p.m. April 5. The facility is located just west of the Heart of Exposition Center. Track regulations, rules, procedures and scheduling will be discussed. Parents of the youngsters are also welcome.

Gordon Cooper Vo-Tech School will hold its annual open house today from 1:30 to 4 p.m. Superintendent Dr. John Bruton invited the public to attend and view the 19 secondary programs plus the adult diesel, secretarial and practical nursing programs.

A test of the emergency capabilities of Shawnee Cablevision will be undertaken at noon Monday. Shawnee Civil Defense director Ron McCalip will use his special hook-up to the cable for a test of the emergency broadcasting capabilities. All cable-supplied channels will be interrupted for the brief test.

Jon Kulp, Oklahoma City kennel owner and dog trainer, will present a free seminar here Monday. The seminar will be held at the Gordon Cooper Vo-Tech School seminar center and is a preview of upcoming dog obedience courses. However the seminar is open to everyone, not just those enrolled in the class. It's promised to be very entertaining and is scheduled to start at 7 p.m.

Despite the weather, Eileen Woodcock couldn't miss the coronation of her grandchild, Jennifer Woodcock, as senior class queen at Bristow High School Thursday night. Jennifer's dad, Riley, drove over for Mrs. Woodcock.

(2) anchor certain features and pages so that the habitual reader knows where to find them day after day or week after week.

The elements of packaging can be stated simply: Heads and copy go together, so that when the reader finishes the headline, the eye is in a position to move directly into the copy. The same is true of photographs and stories, especially if the story is placed under the photograph with a headline as wide as the photograph.

Stories and photos of like nature should be packaged together for the reader's convenience. Newspapers began doing this with the picture page long before doing so with body copy.

If headlines and stories go together, if photos and stories go together, if like stories and like photos go together, then it follows that complete pages of similar news should achieve the goal of making the news convenient for the reader—especially if we announce to the reader what kind of news that page contains. This can be done through the use of a distinctive page logo.

This is not a particularly new concept; newspapers have been doing it for years with sports news, women's news, the editorial page, comic page, classified advertising, and the financial pages. It has only been recently, however, that newspapers have added general news packaging to their products, a format the national news magazines have been using for many years.

This packaging approach can also include several packages on the same page, with each unit conveniently labeled to tell the reader what is there. Newspapers are using multiple packaging within a page with such things as public record items; weather forecasts and temperature readings; news briefs from around the world, the nation, the state, and the region; columnists; entertainment; syndicated features; and other items.

Keep Labels Similar

The labeling of these columns, features, and pages provides the newspaper with another opportunity for continuity of style. The style element in this case may repeat a portion of the newspaper's front page flag, or it could be as simple as a horizontal line across the top of each page carrying the newspaper's name, the date, and the page

FIGURE 8–11 Labels on columns, features, and pages should be similar in design and integrated into the page layout in a consistent manner. *Reprinted with permission of Stauffer Communications, Inc.*

number. In all instances, these labels should be similar in design and should be integrated into the page layout in a consistent manner.

Consistency is also carried out by anchoring certain news packages on the same page of every issue of the newspaper; that is the second part of the packaging function. This requires a solid commitment from management that space will be provided for the package on an every-issue basis.

Since the product varies considerably in the number of pages from issue to issue, it is easiest to achieve anchoring when the paper is sectionalized. This is one of the main advantages of broadsheets over tabloids. Within sections, the anchored elements can appear in the same relationship to the

section every day, regardless of the number of pages in the section. For example, the last two pages of the second section of every issue might contain the financial pages—stock market data listed in exactly the same manner in every issue, for example, so that the reader will know precisely where on the page to look for his or her favorite stock.

On another scale, a community newspaper may have news reports from various neighborhoods in its coverage area located in the same position within the newspaper in every issue.

All this is accomplished, of course, through the "dummy"—the scaled-down layout of every page in the newspaper. Traditionally, page dummies have been produced by the

advertising department. However, due primarily to the influence of the marketing concept, newspapers have moved more and more into total newspaper product (TNP) planning. This method brings all departments of the newspaper together in planning each issue.

TNP Planning Improves Design

The TNP planning method has been a boon to newspaper design. For the first time, it gives the editor or news

FIGURE 8–12 Total Newspaper Product design would have prevented this problem of news picture and ad picture side by side. *Reprinted with permission of Stauffer Communications, Inc.*

designer a voice in determining product size and overall format.

Hopefully, TNP has eliminated the days when newspapers poured advertising and news into the inside pages in much the same manner as one pours molten metal into a form. TNP has helped newspaper editors and publishers realize that, once the metal is cast, it is the form that determines its shape. It is readily apparent that the form must be carefully planned and designed.

Planning the total newspaper product, therefore, can eliminate haphazard form. Systematic placement of both advertising and news content can contribute to the formation of a well-designed product with personality and style. Too often in the past, newspaper editors did not realize the reader was buying the product for the advertising content as well as the news content. Once editors realized this, it became obvious that both news and advertising need to be treated as a single entity, with thought and design.

Generally, it is better to place advertising in a consistent manner on each page—either on the left, on the right, or on both sides of the page with the "well" in the middle. Most designers prefer as much news space at the top of the page as possible, especially in the upper left of each page. They would prefer, too, that advertising be placed across the bottom of the page instead of being stacked vertically up the sides. This is most important because when advertising is placed in the upper half of the page, it fulfills most of the graphic needs of that page, thereby diminishing the effect of visual news treatment.

The Ultimate Goal of Design

Once the product is carefully planned—with the sections or pages anchored from issue to issue, with the pages neatly packaged with modular and graphic units and attractively labeled, with a style of standing heads, column heads, and page logos giving the product cohesion and continuity, and with the content determining the design not only on the front page show window but throughout the newspaper—once all this has been accomplished, the newspaper will be achieving its goal of communicating effectively with the reader.

It is attractive and interesting.

It is easy to read and understand.

It grades the news for the reader.

It has a style of continuity throughout.

With these design functions achieved, readability is improved. Almost as important, efficiency in the production of the newspaper is improved. Everyone working on the paper will know precisely the guidelines for producing each edition.

And, in the final analysis, the reader will be tempted to describe his or her newspaper not only in terms of its looks but also in terms of its content—which is the ultimate goal of the newspaper design function.

Chapter 9

Newspaper Production

by Robert E. Schweitz

For more than four hundred years, the craft of printing from type did not advance much beyond the way Johann Gutenberg practiced it in the fifteenth century. Metal type was cast in molds and then stored in trays until assembled to make words and lines of reading matter. The type was inked, paper placed on it, and pressure applied so that the ink would transfer to the paper.

About a century ago, Ottmar Mergenthaler was able to set whole lines of metal type, to precise lengths, on his linotype machine. This greatly speeded the setting of type and the composition of pages. The linotype and machines like it were universally used by newspapers in this country for setting type until the 1960s, when the computer typesetting revolution got into full swing.

About the same time, the offset method of printing newspapers began to grow in popularity. An outgrowth of lithography, a graphic arts discovery of the eighteenth century, offset has now become the dominant process for printing both small and large newspapers.

Consequently, the whole process of manufacturing newspapers changed dramatically in the second half of the twentieth century. The old systems of hot metal and letterpress (printing from raised type surfaces) have virtually disappeared.

The Dinosaur Age of Typesetting

In the hot metal days, every story coming from the editorial department had to be retyped on the linotype or on a perforating machine which produced tape to drive the linotype machines.

The metal slugs of lines of type were then locked into a metal frame, or "chase," on a wheeled table. The table was then rolled to a machine which pressed a papier-maché matrix, or mat, over the type. The mat, when removed, had an image of the page impressed in it. Then the mat was put into a half-cylindrical mold into which molten metal was poured. When the metal was cooled and removed it, too, was half cyclindrical and was called a stereo plate. The plates, each weighing about forty pounds, were clamped on the press and as the press ran ink was rolled onto the plates and paper pressed against them to print the newspapers. Some plants used plastic plates rather than metal ones.

The system was cumbersome and slow. Linotype machines could set only five or six newspaper lines a minute, compared to modern computer-run typesetters producing more than a thousand lines a minute.

ROBERT E. SCHWEITZ

The author is vice president and editorial director of the Army Times Publishing Co., Washington, D.C.

"The time will come when newspapers will no longer have composition or platemaking departments. Editorial and advertising people will perform, through computers, all of the so-called back shop operations with the exception of running the presses."

Today, Reporters Set Type

The old hot metal and letterpress methods also created a sharp division between the editorial and mechanical departments. That line has disappeared. Today, reporters and editors routinely set their own type, thanks to the revolution in the manufacturing of newspapers: Type is set every time they type on their keyboards. Even the complex job of arranging all the type and pictures on the page can be done by editorial people through the use of computers and video display screens.

The new systems also cut down on labor costs and, in the smallest community newspapers, make it possible for fewer than a dozen employees to do everything from covering the news to running the press.

Production Now a Cooperative Effort

There is a trend, too, toward the centralization of production facilities. Newspaper plants are being situated to serve the mechanical needs of several newspapers. This is particularly true in the suburban newspaper business.

Some smaller newspapers buy their typesetting or printing from commercial printers or other newspapers. In general, smaller newspapers have been quicker to modernize than some of the larger metropolitan dailies. This is true because the bigger papers have huge investments in their present equipment and are mindful of the consequences for their union member employees when new equipment eliminates jobs. Community newspapers have not been highly organized by the printing trade unions.

In many areas, community newspaper publishers also do commercial printing for additional revenue. Sometimes the printing revenue is financially as important to the publisher as that generated by the newspaper.

Whatever system is used, the manufacturing of newspapers still involves three broad functions: getting the reporters' and editors' words into type, printing the papers, and getting them to the readers.

Converting Copy to Type

The first step beyond the editorial room, of course, is entering the text, headlines, and pictures into the manufacturing system. Modern newspapers, even small ones, generally use some kind of computerized photographic or electronic typesetting system.

Actually there is no real "type"

in these systems, if one uses Webster's definition of the word: "A rectangular block typically of metal or wood bearing a relief character from which an inked print is made."

These new "cold type" systems essentially produce images on photographic paper or film through either electronic or photographic processes.

Some newspapers send their editorial and advertising copy to persons who operate tape-perforating machines. Just as for the linotype operation described earlier, these perforators produce paper tape which indicates au-

FIGURE 9–1 The operator inserts copy into the scanner. *All photos in this chapter courtesy of Army Times Publishing Co.*

tomatically to the typesetting machines the letters to set, the size and style of type desired, and line length. The main problem with the tape system is that every keystroke on the typewriter made by the reporter has to be repeated by the person operating the tape perforator. In addition, the paper tape has imperfections which cause mistakes. Sometimes a piece of bark in the paper or a grease spot will produce a different letter in the text than the one intended.

Replacing the paper tape in some instances has been the diskette, which resembles a phonograph record. As the operator punches the perforator keyboard, the news copy is coded electronically on the diskette. Diskettes can activate the typesetting machines in the same manner as tape. On some smaller newspapers, reporters write their stories directly on the perforating machines.

Many newspapers use copy scanners (optical character-reading devices, or OCRs) and video display terminals (VDTs). These can also produce tape that would then be fed to typesetting machines, but more and more newspapers have gone "on line" from their copy-entry system (OCR or VDT) to their computers. This means the VDTs and scanners send their signals along wires directly to their computers rather than relying on the transfer of tape from one machine to the other.

The scanners, which have declined in use on newspapers since the introduction of VDTs, are really reading machines. Reporters type their copy on typewriters that have a typeface the machines can read. The editor makes his changes on the copy with a pen whose ink is a color to which the machines are blind, usually blue or red. The editor's inked changes are typed between the lines either by a desk person, a correction typist, the reporter, or a production person.

The editorial and ad copy is fed, sheet by sheet, into the scanner, which "reads" the copy either with television cameras or fiber optic devices. Because each letter and number has a different configuration, the scanner can recognize it.

After reading the copy, the scanner either makes a paper tape, which is fed to a computer, or transmits its information "on line" to the computer where the text is stored, justified, and hyphenated in the proper places. There is no rekeyboarding of the reporters' copy as there is with some tape-perforation operations.

The same is true of the video display terminals. The VDTs are an electronic step even more advanced than the scanners used for setting news stories and headlines.

There is no paper, no typewriter. Instead, the reporter or editor has before him a screen much like the one on a television set. In front of and below the screen is a keyboard. As he types on the keyboard the text is displayed on the screen. It is also stored in the VDT's computer memory or in the memory of another computer.

There are even portable VDTs that allow reporters to send stories by phone wire from press boxes, press rooms, or other remote sites, directly to the copy desk.

Electronic Editing

The editor can call a story up on his own screen by punching a code into the system and edits the story using his own keyboard. He can insert letters, words, or paragraphs. He can change the wording of a story merely by "typing" new letters over the old. The old ones may disappear. Several versions of a story may be stored in the computer memory.

VDTs, informally called "tubes," give the editor information about the length the story will be when it is set in type and whether the headline he is writing is too long, too short, or just right.

VDTs can perform other newsroom functions as well, depending upon how they are programmed. Editors need logs of what stories have been written so they can call them up and work on them. The VDTs can log the stories already in the system by writer, subject, slug, or all three.

In addition, some systems can be used to ask questions of the reporters. An editor may, for example, want to ask a reporter for the middle initial of someone named in a story. He can get the reporter's attention by transmitting a signal to the reporter's own tube, then ask the question electronically and get a reply the same way.

In the future is an even more advanced system which may or may not be used in newsrooms. Electronic devices now can "hear" the spoken word and transmit the signals to a computer to be set in type. No keyboarding is necessary.

Typesetting with Light

As words are entered into the system, by whatever method, they must be translated into printlike images on photographic paper or film by some kind of typesetting device. The impulses which drive the typesetters come directly from perforated or magnetic tape or from computers which have received earlier impulses from scanners, VDTs, or tape.

Once the material is keyboarded, a signal is sent to a computer which stores the text on tape or disc. The lines are justified and words hyphenated at the ends of lines where necessary.

The computer, in turn, drives the typesetter. Most phototypesetters work in approximately the same way. They contain film strips, discs, drums, or grids which have on them negatives of the letters, numbers, and other characters. As the typesetter gets its signals, each character called for is momentarily placed before a light source. The light flashes through the negative, sending a light ray in the shape of the type character to a mirror and then through a lens, and implants a latent image of the type character on photosensitized paper or film.

In some typesetters the lens can be regulated so that the image on the paper can be adjusted to the size called

FIGURE 9–2 Video display terminal operator corrects a story stored in the computer.

New Approaches to Proofreading

After the type is set it is usually proof-read. In some highly automated operations using VDTs, the editor proof-reads the stories on his screen before he sends them to be set, but proofreading from the type is still the best insurance against typographical errors.

Various systems are in use; just a few are described here.

The most common method is to send the developed photosensitized paper galley in column form to proof-readers who either compare it with the original copy (in scanner operations) or read it for errors (in VDT operations). The proofreader marks the galley where changes need to be made. Corrections can then be made (actually cut in) when the galley is glued to the pasteup sheet.

Many cold-type plants use a combination of systems, for example, VDTs and scanners. In one system, reporters and editors produce all their copy for the scanners. The scanners read the copy and signal the computers to provide printouts of each story and

for by the editor or the ad department. Thus a wide range of sizes, from the small agate type used for classified ads to large front-page headline type, is available.

The lens is similar to a zoom lens on a slide projector in that it stays in one place but projects a variety of sizes of images.

In some typesetters a number of lenses on a rotating turret provide various sizes of type. The drums, film strips, discs, and grids can be changed automatically to provide a wide variety of typefaces. Some contain more than one face.

Once all the latent images are implanted on the paper or film, the photosensitive material is developed in an automatic developing machine by much the same process as is used by photo finishers. Long rolls of "type" complete with headlines, bylines, and other type devices are scrolled out of the developing machine and cut apart by story or column.

Second-generation phototypesetters are even more advanced than the earlier photocomposition machines. Many do not use discs or any form of negative. The images of the letters are formed on a cathode ray tube (CRT) and then beamed onto the photosensitive material.

The CRT phototypesetters are much faster than their predecessors and will eventually be capable of setting several thousand newspaper lines per minute. A full-sized newspaper page, if it were set solid with text, would contain about one thousand lines of type.

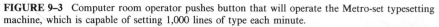

FIGURE 9–3 Computer room operator pushes button that will operate the Metro-set typesetting machine, which is capable of setting 1,000 lines of type each minute.

FIGURE 9–4 Galley is rolled out of automatic processor.

on them go from ad scheduling to the editorial department, where desk people draw in where the pictures and stories should go. They also indicate the headlines and slug lines for picture captions. They indicate special rules or boxes if they wish them to appear on the printed page. They are, in effect, drawing a map for the composition department to follow when the page is made up.

The dummies go from the editorial department to the composing room. The columns of news stories and ads are matched with the dummies of the pages on which they are to be pasted down.

While most newspaper composition is done by production people, on some smaller papers editorial workers do the pasting up.

The Pasteup

When all columns of type (and, in some systems, prints of the pictures) are assembled with the dummy, the dummy then goes to a pasteup artist, who stands at a board similar to a draftsman's table. The surface can be of wood or of plastic, the back of the latter

advertisement. The printouts are compared to the original copy and corrections noted on the printout, which then goes to a VDT operator who uses his keyboard to enter the corrections.

In other combination operations, the hand-edited copy, once scanned, goes to a VDT operator whose responsibility includes inserting changes called for by the editor (indicated in colored ink on the copy), proofreading on the VDT screen, and making corrections via the VDT.

The Pages Take Form

Once all the type has been set and proofread it must be put into page form.

Each page of a newspaper has to be designed by someone. Often it is a combination of work by the ad schedulers and the editors. The front page, or other pages without advertising, are dummied by the editor.

The ad department has a list of all the ads sold for every edition of the newspaper. The ad department draws the outlines of every advertisement on a dummy, which is a sheet

of paper the same shape as the newspaper page, but usually one-quarter the size. It has lines on it setting off the columns of type to appear on the page. It also carries bottom-to-top numbering which permits easy calculation of the number of lines and/or inches in a column.

Editorial pages with advertising

FIGURE 9–5 Pasteup artist follows the dummy (upper left) as she lays type and pictures onto the "flat."

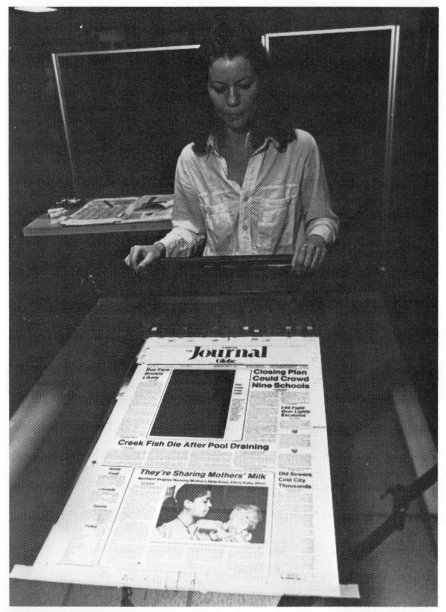

FIGURE 9–6 Pasteup is placed in easel prior to being photographed.

camera or plate department. There is no pasteup step under such a system. It is a very complex and very expensive system and probably will not be in wide use on most community papers for some time.

Processing Pictures

Up to this point we have discussed mostly how words get into type. But newspapers make substantial use of photographs and drawings, too. Before platemaking processes are described it would be well to explain how pictures are processed for newspapers.

There are generally two kinds of art used in newspapers—photographs and line drawings.

Black-and-white photographs are considered "continuous tone" art. Photos have gradations of tone from black to white flowing into one another. This differs from line art in that the latter is made up of lines.

If one examines closely a photograph reproduced in a newspaper, it becomes apparent that the picture is made up of little dots. Under magnification one can see that in the light areas the dots are smaller and farther apart than they are in the dark areas. The newspaper reader's eye sees the picture, not the dots, unless he looks very closely. Dots bunched together make their area of the picture darker.

The dot effect is produced by photographing the picture through a screen and attaching the resulting negative or print either to a negative of the page or, in the case of the screened print, directly to the flat. Continuous tone photos reproduced with the use of a screen are called halftones.

Line drawings require no screen because the art has distinct black and white areas. They can therefore be pasted up and photographed at the same time as the headlines and text.

All of the above applies to black-and-white reproduction only. Color is produced in a similar way except that, instead of a single-screened negative, four must be made, one for each color of ink. When overlaid one on the other, these will reproduce color art with continuous tone.

lit much like a light table.

The artist places a pasteup sheet, or "flat," on his board. The flat is a lined, page-size sheet of heavy paper on which the type and pictures are to be pasted down.

The type sheets and photos are run through a machine that puts a wax coating on their undersides. The artist then lays each piece of text, headline, and picture on the flat, exactly as called for on the dummy. For lines, rules, and borders, the pasteup person applies cellophane tape which has the desired rules and designs printed on it.

In some shops this is the step during which the corrections are put in.

After the proofreader notes errors, the lines and paragraphs which need to be reset are run through the typesetting system. The corrected portions are then pasted in the proper places on the flats. The pasteups are now ready for the camera or platemaking department.

The entire composition process will soon be superseded by a new electronic pagination process. Editors will be able to make up pages on CRTs, photos and all. When the elements of each page are as the editor likes them on his screen, he presses a key and the page is composed on photosensitized material which is then ready for the

Getting Pictures onto Pages

There are two general methods of getting the pictures into the pages. The pasteups, or flats, described earlier will be photographed, and a negative produced during that process used to make a plate.

In some plants during pasteup a "window" is put onto the flat where the picture is to go. The window is a piece of material (either ruby colored or black) which is cut to the same size and shape as the picture, placed in the exact position intended for the picture. When the negative is made, that space becomes a clear area, hence the name "window." A screened negative of the picture is then stripped into the page negative where the window appears.

In other operations, screened positive prints (photomechanical prints called "screened PMTs") are placed directly on the flat during pasteup.

Once completed, the pasteup goes to the camera department where each page is photographed.

A negative is produced for each page. The negative is opaqued (that is, unwanted clear dots are covered so they will not show up as black dots on the finished paper). These negatives are used to make offset plates.

Offset Platemaking

There are two main methods of making offset plates. The conventional system involves exposing light-sensitive plates, through a negative, to arc or xenon lights. The newer method employs laser beams.

The page negative comes from the camera department to the plate-making department. The negative is placed over a chemically coated, thin metal sheet. An arc light or pulsed xenon light is turned on and the latent image is "burned" into the plate. This is similar to printing on photographic paper in a darkroom. The image is developed and coated.

The laser platemakers "read" the flats and implant the image on the plate material. Some even produce a negative for each page as well as a plate.

The laser system has the advantage of eliminating the camera step, the plate exposure procedure, and the development step. It is also faster. In either system the product is a thin, metal sheet surfaced with a smooth image of a newspaper page.

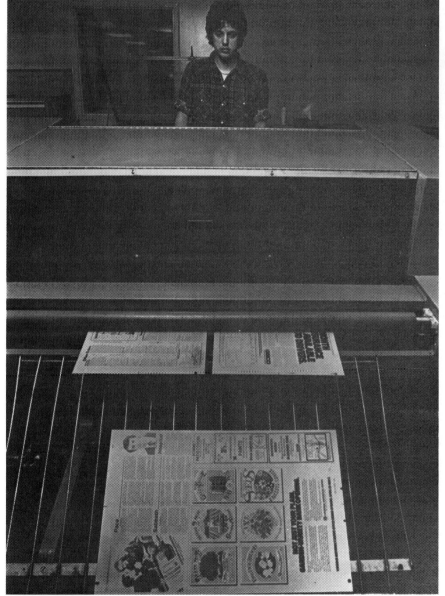

FIGURE 9–7   Plate emerges from automatic plate processing machine.

Preparing the Presses

Once the plates are finished they go into the pressroom. Newspaper pressrooms are generally the most exciting and dramatic of all the production areas. Visitors to newspaper plants often ask to watch the giant presses roll.

But before the presses start, a great amount of "make ready" must be done. Huge rolls of newsprint must be put onto reels. These heavy rolls are transported from the paper storage areas on small trolley-like trucks which can be rolled on tracks that lead di-

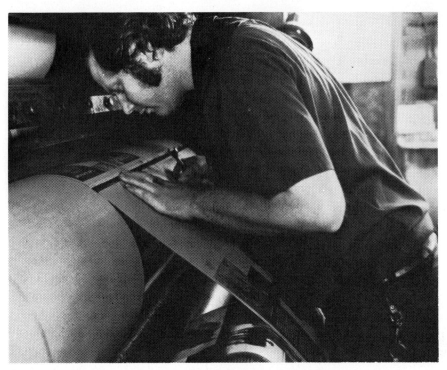

FIGURE 9–8 Pressman attaches thin metal offset plate to press roller.

rectly to the press reels.

The paper then must be webbed over and under many cylinders and metal bars and into the folder where the papers will come off the press. The path the paper takes through the press may change for every press run. Much depends upon the number of pages and sections to be printed. Color printing adds new complications as each color requires another plate to transfer its ink to the paper.

In offset printing, adjustments have to be made to get the proper mixtures of water and ink. When color printing is done, the positioning of the plates becomes even more critical.

Tensions for the paper web must be very exact, and the humidity and temperature in the pressroom will determine how the run will go.

But once the preparations are all made, bells are rung to signal a press start and the huge machines begin to hum. The level of noise increases as speed picks up until proper running speed is achieved.

In a web-fed rotary press, the huge webs of paper called "newsprint" are fed into the machinery past the plate cylinders and then to a folder which cuts the pages to proper size, folds them, and spews out individual newspapers at high speeds.

How Offset Works

Offset printing is really lithography and is based on the fact that oil and water do not mix.

The image on the offset plate is made up of an oillike chemical which attracts ink. Printer's ink is oil-based. The nonimage portion of the plate is metal. This attracts water which repels the ink.

The thin metal plates are mounted on the press. As the press turns, an ink roller and a water roller put a proper mixture of both substances on the plate. The ink adheres to the image portions of the plate. Then the plate transfers the ink onto a rubber "blanket" or cylinder. The blanket "offsets" or transfers the ink to the paper as it is fed through the press.

Newer developments in presses forecast plateless presses. In these highly computerized processes, ink "jets" will spray the letters and pictures on the paper at high speed. Even address labels for mail subscribers can be jetted onto the papers while they are still in the press.

As the papers come off the press,

they are carried or sent by conveyor to the mailroom. There the papers are counted either automatically or by hand into bundles for carrier or mail delivery.

Preparing for Delivery

Many community newspapers are highly mail-oriented but other newspapers are delivered to readers by carrier boys and girls. However, before the newspapers leave the plant for the carriers or for the post office some other processes have to take place.

Often newspapers carry inserts. These can include sections of the newspaper, advertising matter, or special supplements. In small newspapers (and even in some large dailies), much of the inserting is still done by hand. However, more and more inserting is being mechanized.

For mail operations, the papers then go to a labeling machine which carries all of the subscribers names and addresses on little labels. One label is pasted on each paper as it goes through the machine. In many cases the label is "stamped" on the paper from small metal plates that imprint the name and address.

In more sophisticated operations, the labels are printed by computer and arranged in such order that the papers arrive at the post office presorted for the mailman in just the way he walks his route. In carrier-delivered operations, the papers are generally sorted by the number of subscribers in each carrier's route.

Once the papers leave the mailroom, they come under control of the circulation department, whose job it is to service the newsracks, carriers, and post offices.

Chapter 10

STEPHEN J. VAN OSTEN

The author is vice president for retail sales programs for the Newspaper Advertising Bureau, New York, and a director of seminars for newspaper personnel on retail advertising budgets.

"You are in a perfect position to be of greater service to your accounts than you may have realized—and your accounts often need and want your help. One of the areas in which retailers most need help is advertising budgeting."

The Retail Advertising Budget

by Stephen J. Van Osten

To some businesses, advertising is seen merely as an expense of doing business, with no thought of helping to create or build a market, introducing a new product or service, announcing a store opening, or telling the public about a new credit policy. Sometimes "advertising" is considered a place to put a son-in-law until he can learn something about the business. Or it may be the first step of a newspaper "executive training program." The fact is that advertising has a much more important place in the scheme of things for the newspaper and for the advertiser.

For example, most retailers realize and admit that just one ad in the newspaper reaches far more people than all of their sales staff can on any given day. And most advertisers certainly agree that they would rather have a sales person accidentally quote a wrong price than have a price error in an ad. And yet there is a lot of head scratching by local merchants regarding the need for advertising. Some justify advertising by saying that they need it to "keep our name before the public." Others might say, "Oh, I run an ad every Christmas, even if I don't need it." Still others say, "When my competition advertises, I advertise." All of these reasons may seem somewhat tenuous, but actually each is a good reason to advertise. But, the best reasons to advertise are to increase store traffic, to generate more sales, and to increase profits.

How Advertising Works

For any given product or service on any given day, there is only a very small or "thin" market. For example, according to a recent survey conducted by Response Analysis Corporation, only 20 out of 1,000 women will buy any lingerie today, only 5 out of 1,000 women will buy a small appliance today, and only 3 of 1,000 will buy any floor covering today. That's what is meant by a "thin" market. No matter how good the merchandise is, no matter how low the price is, there are only a very few people in any market who will buy. And it is for this reason that the smart advertiser conducts a continuing advertising program designed to reach as many people as possible with the complete sales story.

Advertisers often wonder about the virtues of the various advertising media available to them, and often advertisers are very hard pressed to come up with a solid, factual answer. Questions range from Can I do better advertising in the newspaper or on the radio?

to How good is direct mail . . . or ball point pens . . . or calendars . . . or whatever? To answer these questions, the advertiser must determine what the objective of the advertising program really is.

The objective of most advertising programs is to reach the greatest number of prospects in the target audience at the lowest possible cost within the shortest amount of time. These three elements—people, dollars, and time—must be included in any examination of available media. Outdoor posters, for example, tend to reach only people riding in motor vehicles, and reach them going only one way. Ball point pens seem to wind up in the pockets of employees or in the desks of competitors. And when one is in need of a particular product, there does not seem to be much reason for looking at a calendar to find out about price, availability, styles, colors, etc.

However, there is just such a place an estimated 136 million people turn to every day: newspapers. The fact of the matter is that advertising is one of their major reasons for reading a newspaper. Radio and television reach many people, but generally at great expense and only after multiple exposures to a selling message or commercial. In addition to this problem, the local advertiser must also face the problem of multiple radio and television stations—"fragmentation of the market" is the term used by marketing people. In other words, when using broadcast, the advertiser must use all of the stations and channels to reach even a small portion of the target audience. But newspapers give massive coverage of virtually every market, because virtually everyone reads and responds to newspapers.

Timing for the Biggest Market

Most every merchant has heard—and considered—the analogy between duck hunting and advertising. The theory is that the smart duck hunter sets out more decoy ducks when the ducks are flying than when the ducks are not flying. Same thing with advertising: place more ads in the newspaper when more people are reading the ads; that is when more people are in the market for those products or services the advertiser is offering. In the retailing business this situation is referred to as *timing*.

Timing is probably the single most important element in advertising effectiveness, perhaps even more important than the total amount of dollars spent on advertising. There is, in fact, a right time and an "unright" (although not "wrong") time to advertise everything. For example, the best time to sell window-mount air conditioners is just prior to and during the hot weather months of May, June, July, and August. Approximately 75 percent of all air conditioners are sold during this season. Reason would suggest that if three-quarters of the sales are being made during this four-month period, most of the advertising should be run before and during this period. During the other eight months, when only about 25 percent of the sales are made, advertising should be greatly curtailed, because very few people are buying air conditioners at that time. The really smart, aggressive merchant probably would put his entire annual air conditioner budget into the four-month period when sales were hottest, plus run a clearance sale in September. Conversely, when people are ready to buy skiing equipment, that is the time the smart merchant advertises skis, boots, poles, etc.

Because *buying patterns* repeat themselves year after year after year, the wise merchant uses his past sales records to predict accurately how people will buy in his store this year. To draw a sales pattern, the merchant totals his monthly sales (in dollars) and then divides each month's sales by the annual total. The figure he gets for each month will be the month's sales expressed as a percentage of the annual sales. For example, a jeweler checks his records for last year and makes a list of the actual sales for each month. Then he divides the annual sales into each of the monthly sales figures and gets the percentage of the annual sales contributed during each month, as we have done in the sample (Table 10–1).

Table 10–1: Jewelry Sales Last Year		
Month	$	%
January	7,500	6
February	6,250	5
March	7,500	6
April	7,500	6
May	10,000	8
June	11,250	9
July	7,500	6
August	8,750	7
September	8,750	7
October	10,000	8
November	11,250	9
December	28,750	23
TOTALS	$125,000	100%

With these percentages, the advertiser can chart his own sales pattern (Figure 10–1).

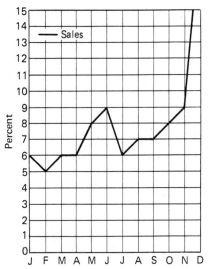

FIGURE 10–1

With the knowledge that buying patterns repeat themselves, the smart retailer can use last year's sales information to predict how people are likely to buy from his business this year. Last year's pattern is actually a guide to how an advertiser can plot his advertising plan this year, keeping in mind, of course, that as selling opportunities go up, the amount of advertising pressure also should go up. "When there are more ducks flying (customers shopping), put out more decoys on the pond (more ads in the newspaper)."

FOLLOW TRENDS

Advertising timing should attempt to capitalize on rising sales trends and aid the advertiser in preventing the wasting of advertising dollars during slow selling periods. Generally speaking, the advertising budget should help the advertiser to "fill in the valleys and cut down on the peaks." Another look at our jewelry store sales pattern will help to explain this analogy. Figure 10–2 now shows the "typical" or average sales (buying) pattern for a retail jeweler. Added to the chart is an advertising pattern for a jeweler. Notice how the advertising curve seems to have little or no relation to the sales pattern.

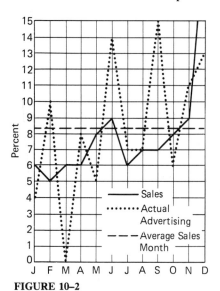

FIGURE 10–2

Note that there has been added a third set of data, a straight line which runs all the way across the chart at 8.3 percent. This represents the "average" sales month; that is, what the sales pattern would look like if sales were the same every month of the year. The peaks and valleys referred to earlier are shown by the actual sales pattern in relation to the sales pattern for the "average" month. For instance, there are valleys in January, February, March, April, July, August, and September. There are peaks in June, November, and December. The wise retailer will chart these three patterns to determine (1) where his sales peaks and valleys are during the year, and (2) if he has been taking advantage of

the way people buy in his store, that is, if he has been setting out most of those decoys when most of those ducks are flying.

In the case of this jeweler, the answer is obviously no. For example, in January there is a valley—6 percent actual sales. But even though this is a slow sales month, the jeweler actually underadvertised by spending only 4 percent of his annual advertising budget. In effect, instead of trying to fill in the valley, he was digging a deeper hole. A similar situation, although even more exaggerated, exists in March. This retailer is missing selling opportunities.

But, there is an even worse way to squander advertising dollars. In September there was a slight sales valley— 7 percent—but the jeweler plowed in too many ad dollars to help fill the valley. He overadvertised by using 15 percent of his annual ad budget for promotion during a month when he could expect to do only about 7 percent of his annual business. It must be pointed out here that overspending and underspending are *both* wrong and costly. Overspending means using too many ad dollars for a particular period, which will cause a shortage of ad dollars during another period (compare the advertising expenditures of September and March).

The way to maximize the effectiveness of each dollar invested in advertising is to overadvertise slightly during weak sales months and underadvertise slightly during strong sales months. In Figure 10–3, a recommended advertising pattern has been substituted for the actual advertising pattern for this particular jeweler.

This kind of direct relationship between sales and advertising can be accomplished simply by listing in one column the percentage of sales expected to be done for each month, and in the adjacent column list a figure which is about halfway between the sales percentage and the "average" month's sales figure of 8.3 percent. For example, in January the halfway figure would be about 7.1 percent for advertising; for February, about 6.6 percent; for December, about 15.7 percent.

By looking more closely at the last chart, it can be seen that we are attempting to "fill in the valleys and

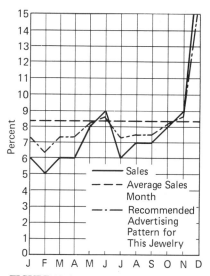

FIGURE 10–3

cut down on the peaks." The advertiser is still putting out more decoys during December (because there are so many more customers spending so much more money), but he is also "borrowing" some December advertising dollars to give needed support to the weak sales month during the rest of the year.

Why Budget?

Many smaller businesses consider their advertising program (if indeed there really is a "program") to be flexible to the point of discontinuance when cash grows short. The biggest problem with this rationale is that there is no advertising just when a program of promotion is most needed. And there is a long-range problem in cutting back on advertising: loss of identity in the market place. Every time an ad is *not* run, a portion of the prospects for the store's merchandise or services may forget about that business and buy elsewhere, probably from a nearby store that did advertise. Still another problem is the great mobility of the family unit. In the United States, for instance, about 20 percent of the population moves every year. Families move out of a market and other families move into that market, but the only way to tell these new families in town about where to buy is with a consistent advertising program.

An important concept to keep in mind when establishing an advertising budget is that the advertising program should not be designed to save money, but rather to increase traffic into the store. Cutting corners by saving five dollars on an ad one week might very well result in the loss of a fifty-dollar sale. The objective of every advertising budget should be to get the selling message to as many of the prime prospects as possible, using the least amount of money. This would be described as making the advertising dollars work hard, that is, getting one hundred cents' worth out of every dollar invested in the newspaper.

One sure way of letting advertising dollars slip away is to miss out on using cooperative advertising dollars which have accrued for an account. A thorough understanding and appreciation of Chapter 14 "Cooperative Advertising," will go a long way toward preventing the loss of ad dollars and making every ad dollar work harder for the advertiser.

Many local businessmen, whether dealing with the general public or not, find themselves continually pressed for "no-interest ad dollars." These are dollars not used strictly for advertising purposes, but which are donated to local civic and social groups such as charity balls, fraternal picnics, and yearbooks. In some instances these donations are worthwhile for the merchant, but not as advertising—their value is limited to that of public relations and should be considered in that manner. Paying the printing expense for the tickets for the junior prom is a nice, public-spirited gesture, but this should not be counted on to sell much merchandise.

The typical consumer does not buy from a retailer because he is a nice person, but because he offers good values, low prices, credit, free parking, extensive stock, fast delivery, or some other consumer benefit. Be sure that your local businesses understand that advertising is designed to sell merchandise, while public relations is designed to make the business seem like a good citizen. Be sure your advertisers know the difference; it could mean a change in the way they budget their advertising dollars.

Methods of Budgeting for Advertising

There are many ways to budget monies for advertising, and each has its advantages and disadvantages. Several kinds of budgeting techniques will be discussed, but the budget as a percentage of projected sales is generally recommended and will be covered in depth.

"What's Needed versus What's Left." Some businesses look at how many dollars are left in the sugar bowl after determining all costs for manufacturing, shipping, salaries, and so forth. If there are any pennies or dollars in the bottom of the bowl, they are allocated to advertising. The business may be able to buy only one tiny ad in a trade publication, or it may be able to make a huge multimedia buy in every market in the country. The problem, of course, is that the need has not been determined first. This is analogous to a doctor prescribing medication, hospitalization, and an operation without first examining the patient. At the local or retail level of business, the proper procedure is first to examine the "patient" to determine the problem, then estimate the cost for a solution. This method is referred to as the "what's needed" technique. By deciding beforehand on a proper solution, we have a far better chance of not wasting advertising dollars.

Project Budget. This technique should be considered when a special opportunity or problem comes along, such as the opening of a new branch store, a change of ownership, the creation of a new department, etc. A certain amount of money is budgeted for the situation, and when the project is launched or completed, the ad dollars are gone, and the project no longer has a special budget. If it is a continuing project, its support will come from the general advertising budget rather than a special fund.

Zero-Base Budget. This is a shibboleth of government budgeteers designed to reassure the taxpayer that a close eye is being kept on all programs.

Theoretically, each year every budget is reduced to zero, and is only reestablished if there is a need for the particular program. This technique should only be used at the local or retail level if the business is deciding every year if it intends to continue in business.

Departmental and Merchandise-Line Budget. Advertising budgets can be expressed in two ways: dollars and space. A discussion of the departmental or merchandise-line budget will be handled in the section "Allocating the Space."

Special Task Budget. This kind of budget is similar to the project budget described above, but it is usually used when referring to a very limited job, such as announcing a change in telephone number or store hours or the acceptance of another bank credit card. A special fund is established, and when the dollars are gone, the task supposedly is completed.

Public Relations Budget. Any business, large or small, has many publics to be considered: government, customers, vendors, employees, neighbors, and others. Programs designed to communicate a message to any of these groups *while not trying to sell a product or service* are to be considered public relations, not advertising. Therefore, the costs for programs not designed to sell merchandise or services should not be borne by the advertising budget, but rather by a separate public relations budget. This can be labeled "public relations," "charity," "good will," "gift," but not "advertising."

Basic Advertising Budgeting

The advertising budgeting method used by almost all businesses involved in consumer goods, whether manufacturer, wholesaler, or retailer, is based on a percentage of potential sales. For example, a retailer expecting to do $100,000 in sales this year might budget three percent for advertising, or

$3,000 for the year. Although it is not an especially good idea, some retailers use a percentage based on last year's sales. The problem with this method is that when a business has had a bad sales year, the following year's promotional budget will be reduced (rather than increased), almost assuring another bad year.

Table 10–2 shows the average percentages of sales designated for advertising by various kinds of retail businesses. When referring to these figures it should be kept in mind that they represent averages, and therefore, should not necessarily be considered absolutely correct for any business. After all, what business is "average" in terms of location, size, personnel, lines of merchandise, credit policies, competition, selling area, etc.?

TABLE 10–2: AVERAGE ADVERTISING INVESTMENTS

Kind of Business	Average		Kind of Business	Average	
APPLIANCE, RADIO, TV DEALERS[1]	2.3%		$300,000–$400,000		1.2
under $500,000		2.2%	$400,000 and over		1.4
over $500,000		2.3	DRY CLEANING SHOPS[2]		
$1,000,000 and over		2.3	under $50,000		1.7
AUTO ACCESSORIES AND PARTS STORES[2]			$50,000 and over		1.7
$50,000–$200,000		0.9	FLORISTS[2]	2.1	
AUTO DEALERS (NEW CAR/ FRANCHISED)[3]	0.8		FOOD CHAINS[9]	1.1	
			FURNITURE STORES[12]	5.0	
AUTO PARKING AND REPAIR SERVICES[4]	0.9		under $500,000		5.0
			$500,000–$1,000,000		6.2
BAKERIES[2]	0.7		$1,000,000–$2,000,000		5.0
BANKS (COMMERCIAL)[4]	1.3		$2,000,000–$5,000,000		4.8
BEAUTY SHOPS[5]	2.0		$5,000,000 and over		4.6
BOOK STORES[6]	1.7		GASOLINE AND SERVICE STATIONS[4]	0.8	
CAMERA STORES[7]			GIFT AND NOVELTY STORES[2]		
under $100,000		0.8	$25,000–$50,000		1.4
$100,000–$250,000		0.8	HARDWARE STORES[13]	1.6	
$250,000–$500,000		0.8	HOME CENTERS[13]	1.3	
$500,000 and over		0.9	HOTELS[14]		
CHILDREN'S AND INFANTS' WEAR STORES[2]			under 300 rooms		6.7
			300–600 rooms		7.0
$25,000–$50,000		1.4	600 rooms and over		7.2
COCKTAIL LOUNGES[2]	0.9		INSURANCE AGENTS, BROKERS[4]	1.8	
CREDIT AGENCIES (PERSONAL)[4]	2.4		JEWELRY STORES[15]	4.4	
DEPARTMENT STORES[8]	2.8		LAUNDROMATS[2]		
$1,000,000–$2,000,000		2.5	under $35,000		1.3
$2,000,000–$5,000,000		2.9	$35,000 and over		1.2
$5,000,000–$10,000,000		2.8	LIQUOR STORES[2]	0.9	
$10,000,000–$20,000,000		2.8	under $50,000		0.7
$20,000,000–$50,000,000		2.7	$50,000–$100,000		0.7
$50,000,000 and over		2.4	$100,000–$200,000		1.3
DISCOUNT STORES[9]	2.4		LUMBER AND BUILDING MATERIALS DEALERS[2]		
DRUG STORES			$50,000–$100,000		0.5
Chain Drug Stores[10]	1.7		MEAT MARKETS[2]		
Independent Drug Stores[4]	1.3		$50,000–$100,000		0.6
under $70,000		1.1	MENSWEAR STORES[16]		
$70,000–$80,000		0.9	under $300,000		2.4
$80,000–$90,000		0.8	$300,000–$499,999		2.6
$90,000–$100,000		1.2	$500,000–$999,999		2.8
$100,000–$120,000		1.4	$1,000,000–$4,999,999		3.2
$120,000–$140,000		1.2	$5,000,000 and over		3.4
$140,000–$160,000		1.3	MOTELS[2]		
$160,000–$180,000		1.2	$25,000–$50,000		3.7
$180,000–$200,000		1.2	MOTION PICTURE THEATERS[4]	5.5	
$200,000–$225,000		1.3	MUSIC STORES[2]		
$225,000–$250,000		1.4	$25,000–$50,000		1.8
$250,000–$300,000		1.3			

TABLE 10–2: AVERAGE ADVERTISING INVESTMENTS *(continued)*

Kind of Business	Average		Kind of Business	Average	
OFFICE SUPPLIES DEALERS[17]			RESTAURANTS[2]	0.8	
under $100,000	1.0		under $50,000		0.6
$100,000–$250,000	1.1		$50,000–$100,000		0.9
$250,000–$500,000	0.9		$100,000–$200,000		1.7
$500,000–$1,000,000	0.7		SAVINGS BANKS (MUTUAL)[18]	1.5	
$1,000,000–$2,000,000	0.7		SAVINGS AND LOAN ASSOCIATIONS[19]	1.5	
$2,000,000–$3,000,000	0.6		SHOE STORES[2]		
$3,000,000 and over	0.6		$25,000–$50,000		1.9
PAINT, GLASS, AND WALLPAPER STORES[2]			SPECIALTY STORES[8]		
$25,000–$50,000	1.3		$1,000,000 and over		3.0
PHOTOGRAPHIC STUDIOS AND SUPPLY SHOPS[2]	2.4		SPORTING GOODS STORES[20]	3.5	
REAL ESTATE[4]			TAVERNS[2]	0.7	
Operators (except developers) and lessors of buildings	0.6		under $50,000		0.7
Subdividers, developers, and operative builders	3.1		$50,000–$100,000		0.8
Other real estate and combinations of real estate, insurance, loan, and law offices	4.0		$100,000–$200,000		0.7
			TIRE DEALERS[21]	2.2	
			TRAVEL AGENTS[22]	5.0	
			VARIETY STORES[2]	1.5	

Sources

1. National Appliance and Radio-TV Dealers Association
2. Accounting Corporation of America, Inc.
3. National Automobile Dealers Association
4. *Advertising Age*
5. *Modern Beauty Shop* Magazine
6. American Booksellers Association
7. *Modern Photography* Magazine
8. National Retail Merchants Association
9. Newspaper Advertising Bureau, Inc.
10. National Association of Chain Drug Stores
11. *Lilly Digest,* Eli Lilly and Company
12. National Home Furnishings Association
13. National Retail Hardware Association
14. Laventhol Krekstein Horwath & Horwath
15. *Jewelers' Circular-Keystone*
16. Menswear Retailers of America
17. National Office Products Association
18. National Association of Mutual Savings Banks
19. United States Savings and Loan League
20. National Sporting Goods Association
21. National Tire Dealers and Retreaders Association, Inc.
22. American Society of Travel Agents

As has been suggested in the previous sections of this chapter, just having enough advertising dollars is not enough to assure a successful advertising program. Timing is vital, too, as are the content of the ad and the selection of the correct advertising medium or media. To help ensure success, a well-designed plan must be developed and followed. In other words, plan your work and work your plan. The four-step plan that follows is one that has been used by retailers for many, many years. It is a proven method for maximizing advertising efficiency.

STEP 1: SET THE SALES GOAL

Too many retailers do not set objectives for themselves and their businesses. They have no target in sight, no standard by which to measure their performance on a daily, monthly, seasonal, or annual basis. For many local businesses, it is merely a matter of opening the front door and hoping that enough sales are made to pay the rent, the salaries, the utilities, and other costs, with a little left over for a vacation next year. Setting a sales goal is the first step toward developing a sensible, businesslike plan for success.

A sales goal should be two things: challenging and attainable. Unless the goal one sets for oneself or one's business is a challenge, there will be little or no extra effort expended toward improvement. If the goal is set too high— if it is too much of a challenge—there will be a reduction of effort when it is realized that success cannot be achieved. So, the goal must be realistic.

There are many things to be considered when setting a sales goal, such as last year's sales, competition, inventory on hand, sales personnel, cost-of-living adjustments, employment and unemployment trends, credit, and inflation, to name a few. The best way to keep current on these factors is to read the business pages of your own newspaper and at least one major daily which circulates in your area. Knowing what is going on in the marketplace is necessary in order to have the right perspective from which to view the competitive situation. When all available information has been digested, set a realistic sales goal for the period being planned. The sales goal should be at least 8 to 10 percent higher than the actual sales for the same period last year to cover the inflation factor.

Generally speaking, new and smaller businesses can grow faster than well-established businesses. Therefore, a more challenging (higher) sales goal should be set for those small businesses which have a smaller sales base. In order for an advertiser to keep greater control of his advertising program, it is recommended that the sales goal for the business be established by setting individual sales goals by department.

For Dempster Jewelers, which last year did $125,000 gross sales, we have set a sales goal for May of $11,200. This is an increase of 12 percent ($1,200) over the actual sales of $10,000 during May of last year. We arrived at this sales goal by setting individual departmental sales goals, as shown in Figure 10–4.

In setting the individual departmental sales goals, we reasoned as follows:

Diamonds: Our diamond sales last May were quite good compared to previous years. Therefore, we feel we should be able to hold this share of market again this May.

Watches: Manufacturers have been increasing their national advertising in support of digital watch sales, so we might as well take advantage of this "plus" by increasing our pressure in this merchandise line, too. (See Step 3.)

Gold Jewelry: According to stories which have appeared recently in the business pages of the newspaper, many people are buying gold jewelry for investment as a hedge against inflation as well as for fashion. This suggests an expanding market, so we are looking for an increase of about 36 percent ($504) over last May's sales. Our sales goal is set for $1,904, or 17 percent of the total store sales.

Similar decisions are made for each department or merchandise group until all of the sales goals are set. The individual sales goals are then totaled so that we have an overall sales goal for the store, in this case, $11,200 for the coming May.

(Note: This step can also be worked by estimating the percentage of the overall store sales each department will account for during the month. For example, we might figure that the gold jewelry department will increase to 17 percent of the overall store sales from last May's 14 percent, based on the expected expansion of the market referred to above.)

STEP 2: ESTABLISH THE ADVERTISING BUDGET

Consult Table 10–2 to determine how your business stands in relation to the "average" store in its classification. Dempster Jewelers calculated that last year it invested 3.8 percent of its sales for advertising. This figure is arrived at by dividing the total amount of advertising bought by the total sales volume for the store last year:

$$\$4,750 \div \$125,000 = .038 = 3.8\%$$

Now we see that Dempster Jewelers is underspending compared to the national average figure of 4.4% for advertising. By using the technique illustrated in Fig. 10–5, any local business can determine the right amount of advertising needed because the budget is based directly on the sales goal. The example has been completed for the particular situation facing Dempster Jewelers.

FIGURE 10–4

1. set a sales goal

Next month is MAY

Department or merchandise group	Month's sales last year		Month's sales goal this year	
DIAMONDS	$ 3,000	(30%)	$ 3,360	(30%)
WATCHES	$ 1,800	(18%)	$ 2,240	(20%)
GOLD JEWELRY	$ 1,400	(14%)	$ 1,904	(17%)
REPAIR	$ 1,100	(11%)	$ 1,120	(10%)
STERLING FLATWARE	$ 900	(9%)	$ 896	(8%)
STERLING JEWELRY	$ 800	(8%)	$ 560	(5%)
OTHERS	$ 1,000	(10%)	$ 1,120	(10%)
TOTALS	$ 10,000	(100%)	$ 11,200	(100%)

2. decide how much advertising

Next month is _____MAY_____

1. % of sales invested overall _____3.8_____

MONTH'S ADVERTISING LAST YEAR

2. Dollars _____$237.50_____

3. Linage _____79" @ $3.00_____

MONTH'S PLANNED ADVERTISING THIS YEAR

4. Sales Goal _ _ _ _ _ _ _ _ $_____11,200.00_____

5. % for advertising _ _ _ _ _ _ _ X _____4.2_____%

6. Advertising Budget _ _ _ _ _ _ $_____470.00_____

7. Linage

$3.00

Earned rate per column inch
or agate line

157"

470.00

$ Budgeted

- Line 1. Percentage of sales invested in advertising last year overall.

- Line 2. Dollars spent for advertising in May of last year.

- Line 3. Number of column inches (or agate lines or column centimeters) of space used in May of last year.

- Line 4. Sales goal for May of this year.

- Line 5. Percentage of sales to be invested in advertising this May.

- Line 6. Advertising budget for this May (multiply Line 4 by Line 5).

- Line 7. Advertising space available this May (advertising dollars divided by the earned rate).

FIGURE 10–5

Notice that because Dempster Jewelers has been below average in terms of advertising investment (3.8 percent compared to 4.4 percent nationally), an increase in promotional pressure has been effected by raising the percentage for advertising to 4.2 percent. This is still below the national average, but it puts Dempster Jewelers in a much better competitive position. In a few months, we can increase the percentage again until we find the precise amount of investment needed.

A Word on Budget Reserves. Many larger retailers set aside a monthly reserve fund or advertising kitty which can be used to boost sales in slow departments or to take advantage of a department's unexpectedly "hot" sales. These kinds of opportunities do not always come along, but when they do, it is reassuring to have some "extra" advertising dollars to help sales and profits along. When a reserve fund is established, it is generally about 10 percent of the total monthly budget. The only problem is that smaller advertisers like to set aside the 10 percent kitty, and then when the end of the month rolls around, they say something like, "Well, we had a pretty good sales month, so I really don't need to spend that extra 10 percent on advertising." This, of course, destroys the four-step plan which has been worked out in such a meticulous manner.

The whole basis of the planned advertising program is to determine where we want to go in sales, and then apply the proper amount of advertising pressure in the market place to do the job. If we drop off 10 percent of that pressure, we should not expect to reach our sales goal. It is strongly recommended that none but the largest retailers consider setting aside dollars for a reserve fund, because all other retailers need every cent allocated for advertising . . . and usually more.

STEP 3: ALLOCATE THE SPACE

One of the pitfalls in retail advertising is the misallocation of advertising space to departments or merchandise lines. Some departments get more space than they should have, some get much less. The retailer may feel that, since he is using the right amount of advertising, it does not matter how the space is divided between departments. A closer look at this incorrect theory reveals the pitfall. By overpromoting some departments and underpromoting others, the advertising will actually be losing readership. For example, the repairs department at Dempster Jewelers is expected to do only 10 percent of the business ($1,120) during May, and so it might be decided not to advertise that department at all.

This is where a knowledge of the

newspaper reader comes in handy. It has long been a truism that the reader shops the newspaper before shopping the store. But what about the newspaper reader who is seeking information on where to get that beautiful pocket watch repaired? If Dempster Jewelers does not advertise the repairs department, the reader will seek out the information in competitive ads in the newspaper. That means a loss of certain readers of Dempster Jewelers advertising, which will mean a loss of traffic into the store, which will almost certainly mean a loss of sales and profits. That is the pitfall caused by underadvertising key departments.

To avoid this common problem, it is recommended that the amount of advertising space be allocated roughly according to the sales potential of the department. For example, in Fig. 10–6 we see that during May the diamonds department is expected to account for about 30 percent of the sales volume (this information is transferred from Step 1); therefore, the diamonds department should get about 30 percent of the advertising budget. Watches are expected to do about 20 percent of the store's business, so it should get about 20 percent of the ad budget.

This method of advertising space allocation may seem to be rather mechanical, automatic, and inflexible, and it is. At this point we suggest that the retailer put his expertise, his managerial skills, to work. This is where the true "merchant" can shine. For example, the diamonds department is expected to contribute about 30 percent of the sales this month, but it might be expected to contribute about 45 percent of the profits. Therefore, the "merchant" would want to slightly overpromote this department and give it, say, perhaps 35 percent of the ad space.

Other things to be considered here are expanding or new departments, departments which produce extra traffic, and so forth. Remember, any deviation from the ratio percentage of month's sales to percentage of month's advertising must, of course, be slight to avoid underadvertising key departments and therefore losing certain readers of the ad. The newspaper advertising representative probably does not have this kind of detailed information about the account's business, so the allocation recommendation should be based on sales potential as originally stated.

When the percentage of the total available space has been decided for each department, simply multiply the percent by the space available for the month to get the actual space per department. For example, diamonds will get 35 percent of the space or 55 column inches (.35 $\times$ 157").

STEP 4: DEVELOP A SCHEDULE

There is no such thing as an advertising schedule until it is in writing, and the more detail in it the better. If an advertiser has been running one ad per week on, say, Wednesday, for the past fifteen years, that is not an advertising schedule, it is a habit. Times are changing, markets are changing, retailing is changing. Wednesday may no longer be the best day to run that retailer's ad. Maybe there should be more than one ad per week. Maybe there should be more than one newspaper used by the advertiser. These questions must be pondered jointly by the newspaper advertising representative and the account. Both have important input needed to find the best solution.

FIGURE 10–6

3. decide what to promote

Department or merchandise group	% of month's sales	% of month's advertising	Linage
DIAMONDS	30 %	35 %	55"
WATCHES	20 %	20 %	31"
GOLD JEWELRY	17 %	20 %	31"
REPAIR	10 %	10 %	16"
STERLING FLATWARE	8 %	6 %	10"
STERLING JEWELRY	5 %	5 %	8"
OTHERS	10 %	4 %	6"
Totals	100%	100%	157"

SUNDAY	MONDAY	TUESDAY	WEDNESDAY	THURSDAY	FRIDAY	SATURDAY
1	2 14 Col. in. ad Watches 7″ Gold 3″ Repairs 4″	3 Night Opening	4	5 15 Col. in. ad Diamonds 5″ Sterling Flatwear 10″	6 Night Opening	7
8	9 14 Col. in. ad Watches 10″ Repairs 4″	10 Night Opening	11	PAYROLL DAY 12 30 Col. in. ad Diamonds 20″ Gold 10″	13 City Wide Dollar Days Night Opening	14
MOTHER'S DAY 15	16 10 Col. in. ad Watches 7″ Gold 3″	17 Night Opening	18	19 15 Col. in. ad Diamonds 5″ Others 6″ Repairs 4″	20 Night Opening	21
22	VICTORIA DAY 23 (CANADA) 14 Col. in. ad Gold 10″ Repairs 4″	24 Night Opening	25	PAYROLL DAY 26 15 Col. in. ad Diamonds 8″ Watches 7″	27 Night Opening	28
29	MEMORIAL DAY 30 2 - Day "End of Month" Sale 30 Col. in. ad Diamonds 22″ Sterling Jewelry 8″	31 Night Opening				

FIGURE 10–7

When developing an advertising schedule, many factors must be considered, such as days of the week when retail traffic is heaviest, local night openings, special local and national merchandising opportunities, major payroll days for workers in the area. (In some instances, payroll information is available from local chambers of commerce or state government offices.) The more information the decision makers have, the more solid the decision can be.

Fig. 10–7 shows the advertising schedule for May for Dempster Jewelers.

This schedule attempts to take advantage of Mother's Day by promoting the diamonds and gold jewelry departments the weekend prior to the event. Notice that the repairs department is mentioned four different times during the month, using just four column inches of space each time. For added frequency, the space for repairs could be reduced to just two column inches each time, but doubling the messages to eight. Larger-than-normal ads are run to promote City-Wide Dollar Days which lead into Mother's Day, and the big two-day "End of Month" Sale. The advertising representative and the advertiser should keep track of how well the ads pulled, so that the schedule can be changed to provide any needed improvement during the following months.

Many retailers keep a scrapbook of ads which have run, indicating pertinent data such as date and day of week, weather conditions, actual sales of the advertised items, total store sales for the day, and so forth. By keeping this kind of merchandising diary, the advertiser can more easily spot and capitalize on "hot" items or departments. If an item is selling very well, promote it more heavily than previously planned, on the theory that the ad will develop more store traffic, and even more related items can be sold to the additional customers in the store.

Typical Retailer Sales Patterns

If an advertiser does not have sales figures for the previous year, the sales patterns shown in Fig. 10–8 can be of help in getting the account started on a planned advertising program of his own. If the kind of business you are working with is not included in those shown here, the "All Retail Stores" pattern should be used.

If there is one thing we should all learn from this discussion of budget-

Total retail sales by types of stores

Percent of the year's total sales done each month.

Source: U.S. Department of Commerce 1979

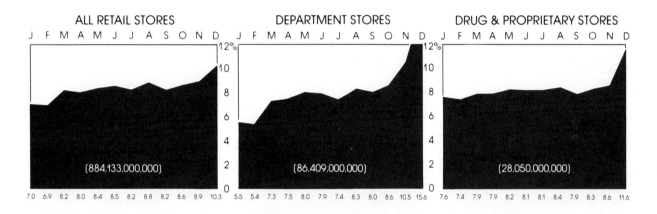

ALL RETAIL STORES
(884,133,000,000)

7.0 6.9 8.2 8.0 8.4 8.5 8.2 8.8 8.2 8.6 8.9 10.3

DEPARTMENT STORES
(86,409,000,000)

5.5 5.4 7.3 7.5 8.0 7.9 7.4 8.3 8.0 8.6 10.5 15.6

DRUG & PROPRIETARY STORES
(28,050,000,000)

7.6 7.4 7.9 7.9 8.2 8.1 8.1 8.4 7.9 8.3 8.6 11.6

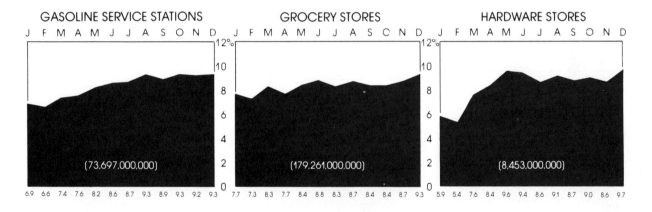

GASOLINE SERVICE STATIONS
(73,697,000,000)

6.9 6.6 7.4 7.6 8.2 8.6 8.7 9.3 8.9 9.3 9.2 9.3

GROCERY STORES
(179,261,000,000)

7.7 7.3 8.3 7.7 8.4 8.8 8.3 8.7 8.4 8.4 8.7 9.3

HARDWARE STORES
(8,453,000,000)

5.9 5.4 7.6 8.4 9.6 9.4 8.6 9.1 8.7 9.0 8.6 9.7

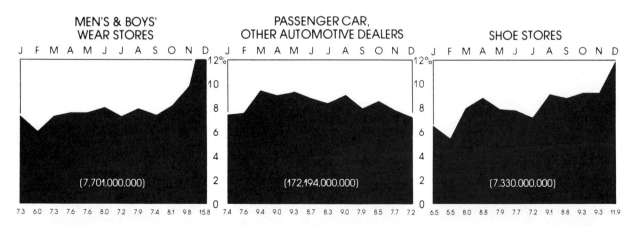

MEN'S & BOYS' WEAR STORES
(7,701,000,000)

7.3 6.0 7.3 7.6 7.6 8.0 7.2 7.9 7.4 8.1 9.8 15.8

PASSENGER CAR, OTHER AUTOMOTIVE DEALERS
(172,194,000,000)

7.4 7.6 9.4 9.0 9.3 8.7 8.3 9.0 7.9 8.5 7.7 7.2

SHOE STORES
(7,330,000,000)

6.5 5.5 8.0 8.8 7.9 7.7 7.2 9.1 8.8 9.3 9.3 11.9

FIGURE 10–8

FIGURE 10–8 (continued)

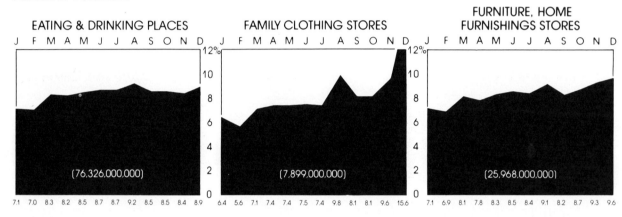

EATING & DRINKING PLACES

J F M A M J J A S O N D

(76,326,000,000)

7.1 7.0 8.3 8.2 8.5 8.7 8.7 9.2 8.5 8.5 8.4 8.9

FAMILY CLOTHING STORES

J F M A M J J A S O N D

(7,899,000,000)

6.4 5.6 7.1 7.4 7.4 7.5 7.4 9.8 8.1 8.1 9.6 15.6

FURNITURE, HOME FURNISHINGS STORES

J F M A M J J A S O N D

(25,968,000,000)

7.1 6.9 8.1 7.8 8.3 8.5 8.4 9.1 8.2 8.7 9.3 9.6

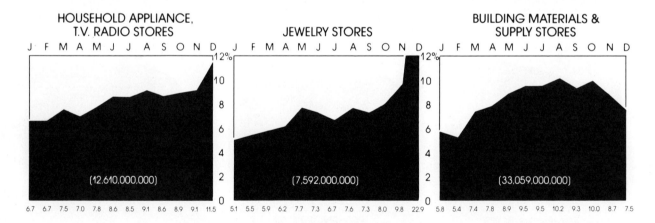

HOUSEHOLD APPLIANCE, T.V. RADIO STORES

J F M A M J J A S O N D

(12,610,000,000)

6.7 6.7 7.5 7.0 7.8 8.6 8.5 9.1 8.6 8.9 9.1 11.5

JEWELRY STORES

J F M A M J J A S O N D

(7,592,000,000)

5.1 5.5 5.9 6.2 7.7 7.3 6.7 7.6 7.3 8.0 9.8 22.9

BUILDING MATERIALS & SUPPLY STORES

J F M A M J J A S O N D

(33,059,000,000)

5.8 5.4 7.4 7.8 8.9 9.5 9.5 10.2 9.3 10.0 8.7 7.5

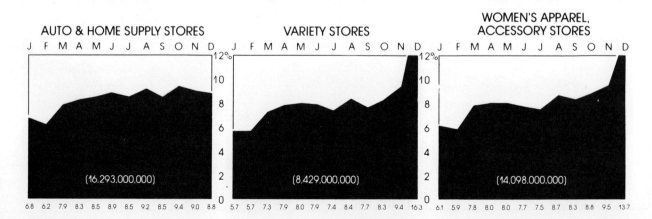

AUTO & HOME SUPPLY STORES

J F M A M J J A S O N D

(16,293,000,000)

6.8 6.2 7.9 8.3 8.5 8.9 8.5 9.2 8.5 9.4 9.0 8.8

VARIETY STORES

J F M A M J J A S O N D

(8,429,000,000)

5.7 5.7 7.3 7.9 8.0 7.9 7.4 8.4 7.7 8.3 9.4 16.3

WOMEN'S APPAREL, ACCESSORY STORES

J F M A M J J A S O N D

(14,098,000,000)

6.1 5.9 7.8 8.0 8.0 7.7 7.5 8.7 8.3 8.8 9.5 13.7

FIGURE 10–9

1. set a sales goal

Write down the sales figures for next month last year — for the whole store and for each department.

Then, in view of this performance and your own knowledge and judgment of this year's picture, rough in sales goals for next month.

Use the profit pointers at right as a reminder of the factors to be considered in making your sales goal realistic but challenging.

PROFIT POINTERS
- Your sales last year
- Population, income, employment levels
- New and expanded departments
- Tie-ins with merchandising events
- Current prices and stock on hand
- What competitors are doing, getting
- More aggressive selling and advertising

Next month is _____

Department or merchandise group	Month's sales last year	Month's sales goal this year
_____	$ _____ (%)	$ _____ (%)
_____	$ _____ (%)	$ _____ (%)
_____	$ _____ (%)	$ _____ (%)
_____	$ _____ (%)	$ _____ (%)
_____	$ _____ (%)	$ _____ (%)
_____	$ _____ (%)	$ _____ (%)
_____	$ _____ (%)	$ _____ (%)
_____	$ _____ (%)	$ _____ (%)
_____	$ _____ (%)	$ _____ (%)
_____	$ _____ (%)	$ _____ (%)
_____	$ _____ (%)	$ _____ (%)
_____	$ _____ (%)	$ _____ (%)
_____	$ _____ (%)	$ _____ (%)
TOTALS	$ _____ (100%)	$ _____ (100%)

FIGURE 10-10

2. decide how much advertising

Before working out your budget, consider these Profit Pointers:

- Stores in less favorable locations use more advertising
- So do those that are new and expanding
- Strong competition raises the size of the budget needed
- Stores stressing price appeal usually promote more heavily
- Special dates and events offer additional sales opportunities
- Added sales produced by increased advertising are more profitable...more money can be invested to get them
- Investigate valuable co-op dollar support available from almost all of your suppliers

Follow these instructions for working out your ad budget:

1. Write down the percent of sales you invested in advertising last year.
2. Write in your dollar investment in advertising during next month last year.
3. Write in amount of linage this brought.
4. Write in your sales goal for the coming month.
5. Multiply it by the percent you plan to invest in advertising.
6. This gives you your ad budget.
7. Dividing your budget by the newspaper's space rate will give you the amount of linage you have to promote your store next month.

Next month is _____

1. % of sales invested overall _____

MONTH'S ADVERTISING LAST YEAR

2. Dollars _____

3. Linage _____

MONTH'S PLANNED ADVERTISING THIS YEAR

4. Sales Goal _ _ _ _ _ _ _ _ _ _ _ _ _$_____

5. % for advertising _ _ _ _ _ _ _ _ _ _ _X_____%

6. Advertising Budget_ _ _ _ _ _ _ _ _$_____

7. Linage

_____) _____
Earned rate per column inch $ Budgeted
or agate line

FIGURE 10–11

3. decide what to promote

List your store's departments and the percentage of your month's total sales which each department traditionally contributes. Plan your advertising so that you allot each department the promotional pressure which it earns.

For instance, if the sales goal of Department A is 9% of the total store sales goal this month, then earmark for it something like 9% of the month's planned advertising space.

Don't be strait-jacketed by this outline. Let your business experience guide you in weighting the advertising you will invest in each of your departments. Check the profit pointers at right for additional factors to consider.

PROFIT POINTERS

- Check month's heavy traffic pullers
- Look for departments where seasonal curves drop next month . . . must be cleared now
- Dig for "sleepers," currently hot, but which don't show up in last year's figures
- Promote newly expanded departments harder
- Calculate and integrate co-op support available for each line of merchandise

Department or merchandise group	% of month's sales	% of month's advertising	Linage
_____	_____%	_____%	_____
_____	_____%	_____%	_____
_____	_____%	_____%	_____
_____	_____%	_____%	_____
_____	_____%	_____%	_____
_____	_____%	_____%	_____
_____	_____%	_____%	_____
_____	_____%	_____%	_____
_____	_____%	_____%	_____
_____	_____%	_____%	_____
_____	_____%	_____%	_____
_____	_____%	_____%	_____
_____	_____%	_____%	_____
_____	_____%	_____%	_____
Totals	_____100%	_____100%	_____

ing, it is that there are no absolutes in advertising. All we can really hope for is to digest a summary of the best thinking on the subject and review the methods most often used by most advertisers, and then properly apply this learning while we keep looking for ways to improve. By following the recommendations and procedures outlined here, at least we will not have to repeat the errors of all the newspaper advertising sales people who came before us.

Help Them Get It on Paper

If certain of your accounts do not yet have a formal advertising plan, the three forms (Figs. 10–9, 10–10, and 10–11) will come in very handy. You may photocopy them for local use without obtaining permission from the Newspaper Advertising Bureau. Use them, along with a blank calendar page, to help your advertisers get more for each dollar they invest in your newspaper.

Chapter 11

Market Data–The Basis of Advertising Sales

by John L. Fournier, Jr.

Today's advertiser is better educated and better informed than ever before. This means that even the smallest newspaper must have accurate primary and secondary market information available, even if only on a mimeographed sheet. We must remember that even a town with only one hardware store is still supplied by a wholesaler with a large marketing department that needs to know about that community and that must be able to help the hardware owner merchandise it properly. The local newspaper usually is the only source for the collection of this specific data.

The gathering of information about a newspaper's market, and using that information to promote advertising sales, involves these three basic steps:

- Gathering facts and figures about people in the newspaper's circulation area, sometimes called its "universe."

- Translating the raw information into objective, refined sales material.

- Putting the refined data to work in various ways to promote the sale of advertising.

Marketing Representative Needed

It is important that each newspaper, large or small, daily or weekly, have someone designated as its marketing representative to head a strong marketing program. The marketing program is as important to a newspaper as it is to any other manufacturer. The marketing representative's duty is to provide the advertising sales force with the aids it needs to deal with any sales situation that may come up in the field. Today's sales people must be armed with marketing material that can help them plan advertising programs for any size retailer, from the small independent to the largest chain.

On some smaller newspapers, the manager of the advertising department may be the marketing representative. On weeklies, the publisher or advertising manager may have the marketing responsibility. In still other instances, a professional research organization may be employed to gather data needed for the advertising promotion effort. Sometimes the information gathering

JOHN L. FOURNIER, JR.

The author is president of Fournier Newspapers in Kent, Washington, an organization widely known for its gathering and use of advertising market data.

"Today's sales people must be armed with marketing material that can help them plan advertising programs for any size retailer, from the small independent to the largest chain."

will be a joint effort by the newspaper and a professional organization. The latter may have specialized talent and skills in gathering and refining market data, and the newspaper may be wise to utilize such services when they are available.

The search process in the newspaper's marketing thrust is a never-ending one. The newspaper must constantly search and re-search, define and redefine its universe. This is especially true in a rapidly changing and growing area. Failure to keep abreast of these changes can make an advertising sales force much less effective.

Two Types of Data

The newspaper is concerned with two types of data for its advertising promotion: *primary* data and *secondary* data. Primary data are gathered by the newspaper about itself and its circulation area. Secondary data are collected largely from standard reference sources or gathered by external professional organizations.

PRIMARY DATA

The primary data search begins with questions that define the newspaper's marketplace. What is the marketplace? What is the ADI (area of dominant influence) or circulation universe? What are outstanding characteristics of the newspaper itself that can be used effectively in advertising promotion? The newspaper's marketing material must state clearly both demographic and psychographic information. The former deals with statistics about people and the latter is concerned with how people behave as consumers.

A way to begin answering these questions is through an analysis of the circulation itself. For advertising promotion purposes, a newspaper should have at hand information that gives these five basic facts about its circulation:

- The total circulation

- The area it covers

- A breakdown of the circulation by sectors showing coverage in each sector

- Growth of the circulation over a period of years

- Comparison of circulation coverage with that of competing media

There are numerous ways of using this information in promotion. The simplest of these would be a map showing the newspaper's area of dominant influence and its circulation growth.

Other helpful primary information can be gathered from the newspaper's representatives. The classified advertising people can gather a file of success stories on want ads. The circulation manager can contribute information on housing, and carriers can obtain information on nonsubscribers. Display advertising representatives can gather testimonials on the effectiveness of the newspaper's advertising. The publisher or advertising manager can obtain helpful information through a questionnaire for advertisers that may define their needs and attitudes.

Valuable primary data can be obtained through the use of a professional research organization. Periodic readership surveys can show how widely read the newspaper is in its circulation area and give the newspaper specific figures to use in promoting its outstanding features. The organization can also obtain information on shopping habits and consumer preferences of people in the local area.

SECONDARY DATA

In determining whether to buy advertising space in a newspaper, an advertiser may be more concerned with secondary data. This will include information on such subjects as population, housing, retail outlets, industry, payrolls, and education. A look at advertising promotion material from many newspapers indicates a need for the following types of data in planning advertising promotional material:

POPULATION. Total population, rural and urban, by sectors, sex, age, family size, and ethnic group, as well as statistics on births and deaths.

HOUSING. Total number of dwelling units, single-family and multi-family units, new units with annual average, owned and rental units, appliances and equipment, length of occupancy of owned homes.

RETAIL MARKET INFORMATION. Total retail sales; retail sales by major types of stores showing growth figures; list of major retail chains, department stores, and discount stores; number of retail outlets by types of stores, total dollars spent for food, etc.

EMPLOYMENT. Total number of adults employed, total payroll estimate of the area, a breakdown showing numbers of employees and percentages by category (professional, laborer, farm, clerical, sales, etc.).

INDUSTRIAL. A list of manufacturing and industrial plants in the circulation area, with description, annual volume, payroll (if available), and total number of employees.

EDUCATION. Educational level of the area by sex, and enrollment of any local institution of higher learning.

The amount of information available is so vast and can be subdivided in so many ways that a newspaper should plan its advertising promotion as far in advance as possible and ascertain what types of information will be needed for its purposes. Gathering information is expensive and there is little point in collecting data that cannot be put to use.

Where to Get Information

For the smaller newspaper with limited resources, the problem may be where to find market information it needs for its advertising promotion. One of the major objectives of this chapter is to provide a list of sources for this purpose. The following should provide a newspaper with more than enough material for promotional purposes. Some of these may be available at city or

FIGURE 11–1 Secondary market information is available from many sources on both state and national levels. *Reprinted courtesy of* Editor & Publisher Market Guide, Encylomedia, Sales & Marketing Management, *the Oklahoma Newspaper Advertising Bureau, and the Washington Newspaper Publishers Association.*

university libraries or at press association offices.

- *The Editor & Publisher Market Guide*. Lists data on United States and Canadian newspaper markets. (Published yearly.) 575 Lexington Avenue, New York, New York 10022

- *Sales & Marketing Management*

Survey of Buying Power. Features population, effective buying income, retail sales, and SMSA (standard metropolitan statistical area) rankings. (Published yearly.) 633 Third Avenue, New York, New York 10017

- *Standard Rate and Data Service*. A yearly publication for metro and community newspapers, this guidebook lists newspapers ad rates and circulation information, provides a competitive check point. 5201 Old Orchard Road, Skokie, Illinois 60076

- *Population and Household Trends*. Produced by the Bell Telephone System's regional marketing and forecast department. Provides information from 1975 through 1990, with a breakdown for each county served in the region. 821 Second Avenue, Seattle, Washington 98104

- U.S. Department of Interior. Population, employment, housing unit projections by state, reporting figures to 1995. Obtainable through a local or regional USDI office.

- U.S. Bureau of Census, Social & Economic Statistics Administration. U.S. Department of Commerce, Bureau of Census, Washington, D.C. 20233

- U.S. Department of Commerce. Offers publications to aid business and industry development, also retail sales figures by household. Washington, D.C. 20233.

- *Measuring Markets*. A guide to the use of federal and state statistics; available through any U.S. Department of Commerce regional office.

- Business Guides. Publishers of directories of supermarket, grocery, chain store, and department store statistics. 2 Park Avenue, New York, New York 10016.

- *Million Dollar Market* and *Middle Market*. Two directories to investigate a company's financial presence. Dun & Bradstreet, 99 Church Street, New York, New York 10007.

- *Circulation '78*. Published to show the "share of market" with other publications in the newspaper's area of dominant influence, such as *Reader's Digest, Time* Magazine, *Parade*. American Newspaper Markets, Inc., P.O. Box 182, Northfield, Illinois 60093.

- *Encyclomedia * Newspapers 1978*. A close look at competitive situations in the same newspaper market. Decisions Publications Inc., 342 Madison Avenue, New York, New York 10017.

- Local Chamber of Commerce Offices. Often offer up-to-date facts on commercial growth as well as industrialization, zone changes, population shifts, and new business in the community.

- State Newspaper Associations. For example:
  - Washington Newspaper Publishing Association. For weekly newspapers, offering facts and figures related to circulation, trade area, mechanical requirements for newspaper advertising, billing services for national advertising orders, and many sales promotion aids. 3838 Stone Way North, Seattle, Washington 98103.
  - Oregon Newspaper Publishers Association, Inc. Publishes a book for daily and weekly newspapers with sections dealing with secondary research data such as readership of newspaper, special survey assistances, and clinics for advertisers to better understand the advertising market and the newspaper's place in this market. 2130 S.W. 5th, Suite 2, Portland, Oregon 97201.
  - Oklahoma Newspaper Advertising Bureau. This special bureau of the Oklahoma Press Association produces focus surveys for its member newspapers including market data and readership studies especially for the small daily and weekly newspaper market. 3601 North Lincoln Boulevard, Oklahoma City, Oklahoma 73105.

- State Department of Revenue. The State Tax Commission has retail sales tax figures by county, where applicable, to provide reports on spending power for the preceding year.

- U.S. Post Offices. Current house counts which can be applied to your circulation numbers and result in "point of penetration" facts for advertising sales effectiveness. See your local postmaster.

- Colleges and Universities. The marketing, communications, and research departments can often provide research survey findings for the newspaper's market.

- Organizations for Planning and Development. Many local groups offer forecasts on growth patterns based on employment trends and economic factors. Seek contacts from your Chamber of Commerce.

- Industrial Associations. Such organizations as the Wyoming Mining Association (in Casper) offer activity reports that will have a direct bearing on the area's economy, which affects all other factors in the marketplace. Ask your Chamber of Commerce for names of such groups in your area.

- Other Media. Local radio, television, and direct mail operations have many competitive statistics that can aid newspaper advertising sales. They have sales aids to share with newspapers such as youth market life style studies from both their national advertising bureaus (RAB and TVAB) plus local surveys that help them compete with other electronic media. Direct mail houses can offer information that can help you reach an income group you may want to isolate for a special mailing.

- Newspaper Advertising Bureau. Provides for its members market studies, advertising sales aids, slide presentations, and other helpful material. 485 Lexington Avenue, New York, New York 10017.

- Suburban Newspapers of America Advertising Bureau. Provides its members with many inexpensive do-it-yourself surveys for the smaller newspapers. 111 East Wacker Drive, Chicago, Illinois 60601.

- International Newspaper Promotion Association. An association of newspapers, both dailies and weeklies, that exchange data and ideas on selling, marketing, and research. P.O. Box 17422, Dulles International Airport, Washington, D.C. 20041.

Putting the Data to Work

Once the newspaper has gathered the primary and secondary information, it then moves on to the next step in the procedure, which is to prepare promotional material for use in advertising sales. Assuming that a meaningful amount of research data has been gathered, the newspaper begins the sorting and refining process. The marketing manager will be wise to conduct interviews with key advertisers in the

FIGURE 11–2 Whether for a community newspaper or a large daily, promotional material can be created from market data that will help advertising sales, and much of it is relatively inexpensive. *Reprinted courtesy of the Vancouver (Washington)* Columbian *and Fournier Publications.*

community to find out what factors influence them most in making their advertising investments. Their answers, plus information gathered by the advertising sales staff from national advertisers and chains, will help determine what data will be most effective in advertising promotion. The newspaper will also gain by studying promotional efforts of other newspapers.

Whether for a community newspaper with little or no budget for survey work or electronic visual presentations, or for a large daily with thousands to spend, promotional material can be developed that will aid advertising sales. Most of the information listed in secondary sources is free. Using this material, the newspaper can print either a brochure or a single promotion sheet that can be very effective yet low in cost. Such pieces can be printed on newsprint or on special paper stock.

There are many other sales promotion pieces that have proved effective in stimulating advertising sales. A few of these are:

- *Circulation maps:* Show related coverage of the newspaper in the marketplace.

- *Circulation numbers:* Show how many households receive the newspaper published in the area of dominant influence. Print these figures in color and the percent of penetration in black on the same sheet.

- *Advertising rates and contracts:* Use a simple rate card for clear understanding; prepare an advertising agreement on a separate sheet.

- *Competitive information:* Keep an active file on the competition's activities, whether radio, television, or another newspaper in your market. Present comparisons in a printed graph showing your strengths as related to theirs.

- *In-paper ads:* Promote a sales event and the newspaper itself.

- *Envelopes:* Use large size for tear sheets. An excellent idea is to print a selling message on the outside, as they pass from hand to hand in delivery and do a selling job even while unopened.

- *Business cards:* Publish the ad rates on the back side of the salesperson's card for quick reference.

- *Letterhead stationery:* Use a continuous message or the newspaper's slogan.

- *Truck signs:* Carry a newspaper slogan all over town on vans that drop bundles to carriers.

- *File folders:* Specially print on all four sides; these can serve as a sales kit to the advertising salesperson. The kit should contain market promotion material.

Conclusion

You can see how research, marketing, and promotion are linked together in the sale of advertising. Keep in mind that newspapers are print media, so it is best to present the newspaper's primary marketing messages in print. Branch out as the budget permits. Always communicate with the sales force about new material that becomes available for use in advertising promotion. With a good sales organization and the proper use of marketing information, newspapers have a chance to open the doors of most media space buyers and make the sale.

Chapter 12

MORLEY L. PIPER

The author is director of the New England Newspapers Advertising Bureau, and author of *Positive Impressions,* a manual on sales development and sales training for newspaper people. He has conducted clinics in advertising selling for many professional groups.

"Selling time is the sales person's most valuable asset. . . . The basic principle in its simplest form is to identify the misuses of time, and then try to develop procedures, a regimen, to correct these misuses."

Approaches to Selling Advertising

by Morley L. Piper

Newspaper advertising is interesting, exciting, challenging, stimulating, satisfying, and rewarding. And, like any other worthwhile endeavor, it can have its moments of frustration, irritation, and even discouragement.

One reason that selling newspaper advertising is interesting is that no two clients are exactly alike. They may have similar stores, they may perform the same services, they may have products that are nearly alike, but their marketing and sales problems are different. One may have an image of quality, one may appeal to younger people, and another may be selling seconds. One may appeal only to one neighborhood, or one segment of your circulation, while another needs all your circulation and perhaps more. Each client has a different problem, a different sales goal.

The newspaper advertising salesman becomes acquainted with these problems and goals and demonstrates how his newspaper can contribute to the advertiser's needs. He presents his newspaper as the number one medium for the advertiser and backs it up with facts. The competitive salesman approaches every account ready to use all resources available to influence the advertiser positively towards newspapers. As he discovers sales approaches that will produce excellent results, he is encouraged to greater and greater efforts which eventually lead to more linage, higher levels of earnings, and wider opportunities for personal promotion. The challenge to succeed and to excel is present in the newspaper advertising business everywhere.

Criteria for Success

There are three criteria for successful newspaper sales people:

- Ambition, drive, desire. The outstanding sales people in this business always seem to have the kind of drive and desire that help to create a positive selling attitude.

- Selling effort. There's nothing to replace just plain hard work. Everyone knows this, but not everyone does it.

- Dedication. The amount of time you are willing to spend as a student of the newspaper business is directly proportional to the degree of success you can achieve.

Professional sales people are constantly striving to improve their proficiency in the newspaper selling process. If you will concentrate on just these several essentials to selling newspaper advertising, greater sales will certainly result:

- Know the newspaper and the market it serves.

- Know the accounts and their problems well.

- Know the competition.

- Know yourselves as sales people.

- Plan your selling.

- Make a sufficient number of good, sound sales calls.

- Be persistent.

- Ask for the order.

- Keep reselling and asking for the reorder.

- Provide creative service to the accounts.

Plan the Sales Effort

Planning is essential in order to make possible more selling calls per day. Selling newspaper advertising is, for the most part, a game of percentages, just like selling in any other industry. The more effective calls a sales representative makes on the advertising decision makers, the more sales will result.

Selling time is the sales person's most valuable asset. The more efficient he becomes in using it, the greater success he will have. Preparation for the call, thus, is essential.

Effective selling is organized selling. It is the organization of many things—thoughts, words, sales materials. It's also organized use of time. As a general rule, less than 50 percent of a street sales representative's time is spent in actual person-to-person contact; that time must be utilized productively.

TIME MANAGEMENT: THE FIRST ESSENTIAL

Admittedly, time organization is difficult, but it is a basic discipline that a space sales person needs to be effective in this business. There are numerous books and courses at the university level on time management. Some of the theories become quite complex. In reality, though, the basic principle of time management is quite simple, deceptively so. The basic principle in its simplest form is to identify the misuses of time, and then try to develop procedures, a regimen, to help correct these misuses.

In newspaper advertising, there are about five time leaks most frequently mentioned as the biggest wastes of sales time. They are all familiar to anyone associated with newspaper advertising but, elementary as they are, it is surprising how often even experienced newspaper people fall into these time traps:

- Poor territory routing.

- Wasting waiting time.

- Nonproductive habits and routines.

- Haphazard telephoning.

- Poorly prepared sales calls.

Here is a checklist to assist in avoiding these time traps:

- *Organize.* Organization is a key word. First, organize material for your calls. Then organize each day of each week in order to make as many calls as possible.

- *Prepare.* Making a sales call when not fully prepared to present the newspaper's story in the most effective possible way is worse than making no call at all. A poor call will injure the impression the prospect has of your newspaper—and damage your own image as well.

- *Be considerate.* In most communities, even the smallest, the pace in advertising and in retailing is hectic. Time is at a premium. A casual call—just "dropping in because I happened to be in the neighborhood"—is often unwelcome. Avoid calls of this type when possible, even with close business friends.

- *Add dignity.* When the call is of special importance and will take a considerable amount of time, it should be dignified by a telephone call first for an appointment. Calling beforehand will tell the advertising prospect several things about you, things that will have an important psychological effect on the prospect. First, it will relate to him that you have something of substance to tell him; second, it will tell him you are considerate, that you do not expect to walk in and take a lot of time without notice; and third, it will prove that you are organized.

- *Handle refusals properly.* When you telephone for an appointment, be prepared for a no. To counter this, have another date ready. Few people will refuse an appointment when offered a choice of two or three dates and times.

- *Utilize the entire day.* While it may be difficult to schedule early morning or late afternoon calls, added calls can often be picked up by knowing personal preferences. Use the early morning to organize your selling day and the later afternoon for disposing of questions raised during the day and for processing ads that have been sold.

- *Group geographically.* Confine calls to a limited geographic area to reduce time wasted in moving from one call to the next.

- *Concentrate on selling.* Do not consume valuable time with conversation that has no bearing on business. It is seldom possible to plunge headlong into business, but exchange pleasantries without overdoing them and then get to work.

- *Design material for repeat use.* In the interest of time saving, prepare a basic set of sales materials covering the salient points of the newspaper. Design it so that it may be personalized by the addition of data that may bear directly on each prospect's business. It takes time to develop sales kits but once assembled, they will save valuable time.

- *Schedule carefully.* While the

emphasis here has been on compressing as many calls into a day as possible, beware of overdoing. Do not schedule the day too tightly. Leave sufficient time to move from one call to the next. Tardiness on a call reflects on your ability to organize and schedule valuable time.

ORGANIZATION AND THOUGHT BOOST SALES

Again *organize* is the key word for anyone in this business. By organizing and planning your selling day and week, you can make better sales calls on regular advertisers and carve out time for the vital purposes of prospecting for new business.

SEEK NEW BUSINESS

You must continue to develop new business. Advertisers come and go. They increase space; they decrease space. They drop the paper from their plans. They move into town; they move away. The retail business is changing constantly, and those changes affect newspaper advertising. Thus, new business is necessary to sustain the volume necessary for the newspaper's support and future growth.

Sales people should develop a list of nonadvertisers. There are many sources from which to do this: the Yellow Pages; competing dailies, weeklies, and shoppers; lists of users of direct mail, radio, TV, and outdoor; city directories; etc. Using the Yellow Pages, in fact, is an excellent exercise. If you have never done so, go through the Yellow Pages and list advertisers who are not in the newspaper but logically could be prospects. It will be a real eye-opener to discover just how many businesses could or should be advertising in your classified and run-of-paper (ROP) newspaper columns.

In organizing your work to increase space sales, don't overlook present advertisers who should be using heavier ad schedules. Every sales person has accounts who don't advertise frequently enough or who do not use

enough space to realize the full potential of their businesses. For these, it is important that you prepare carefully an advertising plan—a schedule and budget—for the advertiser to consider. If you think carefully enough about an advertiser's program which is inadequate, you can very often lead the advertiser into a planned and budgeted program which will produce more space sales for the newspaper and more business for the account.

It usually takes many calls to sell an account, so persistence in selling is needed. If you are persistent and can keep the pressure on gently without irritating the advertiser and creating a hostile attitude, you will sell many new accounts and increase the space of some of your present advertisers.

The Approach is All-Important

The prospect falls into one of three categories. He either wants to run advertising in the newspaper, he does not want to, or he is indifferent.

The goal of the sales person is either to confirm his thinking, to try to change his mind, or to create a desire to buy. Your approach, then, is vital to the success of your call. Your primary purpose is to gain immediate, undivided attention. In any kind of selling, what happens in the critical opening minutes represents about 80% of the chances for the sale.

The approach is an exercise in creative salesmanship. Good sales tools and skill in employing them are needed to gain immediate attention. Having an objective for each call and making sure something specific is taken to show the account are the surest ways to make an effective approach.

Sales Tools You Need

You do not need to learn a magic formula for super salesmanship (if such exists) nearly as much as you need to

become an authority about your newspaper and the market it serves. Remember that first on the list of essentials for selling newspaper advertising is "know the newspaper and the market it serves." If you do not know these two elements well, it is doubtful that you can sell advertising very successfully. You should know the newspaper and the market better than any other media sales person making calls in the area.

There are other things your prospects will need to know about the newspaper to make a decision. This knowledge usually falls into just a handful of areas:

- The market: geography, economics, demographics

- The newspaper's coverage of the market: penetration of households

- Editorial content of the newspaper

- Readership data: related to editorial and advertising content

- Response to advertising success stories

- Advertising volume: linage figures

- Technical data: rates, deadlines, contracts, policies

- Services offered: copy/layout, type setting, production, tear sheets

This is only the beginning. As an advertising space sales person you must discover the best method of presentation by considering the individual advertiser's problem. Thus, some understanding of a prospect's business is necessary to speak authoritatively about its advertising needs.

When you make a sales call, have an objective for the call and be prepared to offer something specific. Never just ask if there is an ad for "this week." Have some material to show, something to tell an account, an idea to present, something to leave with the prospect.

The list of things you can take to show an account is virtually endless, but here are a few possibilities.

"SPEC" LAYOUTS. This is, as the

term implies, a "speculative" venture. It is a layout to show the advertising prospect an idea, a suggestion. It should be in rough form as opposed to finished art so changes and corrections can be easily incorporated. Such layouts are one of the most important sales tools—great for thought-provoking starters and for providing ideas. They are often salable right on the spot with little or no correction.

COLOR TISSUE OVERLAY. If your newspaper uses color, place a color tissue overlay on all spec layouts so the account will have a color version of the ad as well as the black and white. An amazing amount of color linage can be sold through this simple, effective selling device.

TEAR SHEETS. The lowly tear sheet is in the same category as the spec layout. An account is usually very interested in how other advertisers are using other newspapers and may often decide to run the same ad or a similar ad in your newspaper.

CIRCULATION FIGURES.

LINAGE FIGURES. These are always impressive to show an account. Quite often, they will convince the prospect to buy more space in the paper to outdistance or keep pace with the competition.

TESTIMONIAL LETTERS from successful advertisers.

STATISTICS on effective family buying income in the market.

EDITORIAL TEAR SHEETS of specific interest to the account.

A COPY OF THE NEWSPAPER (never be without it).

YOUR RATE CARD AND CONTRACT.

The Sales Presentation

There is an axiom in sales that the person who sells creatively does not have to sell competitively. Of course, sales people have different levels of creativity, but anyone can become more creative if willing to work at it.

The greatest opportunity for creative selling in newspaper advertising is through the sales presentation. This is where all of your preparation can pay real dividends.

A sale is made by a series of impressions on the account. Unless these presentations are positive, there will be no sale. The presentation plays a key role in these impressions.

It is in the presentation that the sales representative explains and illustrates why and how advertising in his newspaper will help the merchant. A good presentation must:

- Arouse attention

- Create desire

- Stimulate that desire

- Convince, persuade

- Promote action

USE VISUALS

It is an important key selling fact, overlooked by many, that people learn more through their eyes than they do through their ears, so a key element to success is a presentation that uses good visual material early. Many product sales people—those with tangible products—are instructed to get a sample of that product into the potential customer's hands at the earliest possible moment. In selling newspaper space, the same techniques can be used with promotion material. The lists given can provide ideas for good visuals.

It is impossible, of course, to provide detailed suggestions about presentation content because every sales situation differs from the next. Selling techniques and presentations must therefore be flexible so they can be adapted to meet the circumstances.

In any sales call, it is important to stress editorial quality. It is often overlooked, even by experienced newspaper people, but acceptance of a newspaper's editorial quality is vital to the sale of advertising. Any presentation should stimulate some positive response to the editorial performance of a newspaper.

You will find it helpful to review the 25-point checklist of general suggestions in preparing and giving newspaper sales presentations.

Closing the Sale

Without question, the weakest area in newspaper space selling is the failure to close sales. It may seem surprising, but many space sales people do not ask for the order, or attempt to get agreement on the selling points they have sought to establish. They do a splendid job up to this point, then come away empty-handed.

Why do they neglect to close the sale? Probably because they do not want to be turned down. They fear the reply will be negative or conditional or noncommittal . . . and they won't know what to do next. Many sales people appear to be uncomfortable with this phase of selling. They must realize that they will never be truly successful at selling newspaper advertising unless they learn how to ask for the order when closing the call—how and when and why.

It is necessary to go beyond the role of "service" salesman in order to close difficult sales and to open new business for the paper.

The key to success in closing sales is to develop the type of presentation that causes the prospect to want to advertise in the newspaper. This is why good sales techniques *and* a positive, correct sales attitude that will establish rapport with the prospect are so necessary in this business.

WATCH FOR SIGNALS

A sense of timing is also important in closing. The opportunity to close may occur at different stages in the sales interview, so you must be perceptive to the prospect, must recognize signals that indicate he may be ready to say yes.

General Suggestions for Preparing and Giving Sales Presentations

1. *Keep your eye on objectives.* It is a paramount rule that you understand your account's objectives before developing a presentation. You must understand the who, what, where, when, why, and how. This information should already be in your hands through previous calls. Then do your best to fit your newspaper's values to those marketing objectives.

2. *Consider your customer.* Think in terms of his needs. What does he want from his advertising? He's not interested in you unless you can show him how your paper can help his business.

3. *Look for the big truth.* Having studied your prospect's business, try to extract the single most important point about your newspaper which fits his needs. Put this single most important concept or theme in writing and leave it with him.

4. *Relate facts to concept.* Then try to relate all the facts about your paper to this single concept—editorial, circulation, audience facts, market growth. This will help you achieve consistency and impact; it will make your presentation more memorable.

5. *Keep it flexible.* Obviously you can't build a special presentation for every account you have, but you can put together basic material that can be used for all occasions and then supplement it with special data of importance to your target account. It's always a good idea to personalize it to some degree; otherwise it becomes "canned."

6. *Keep your feet on the ground.* Don't use an overblown or irrelevant approach. Chances are, you are talking with astute businessmen. Stick to basics.

7. *Schedule carefully.* Watch your timing. Tell the advertiser your basic sales story before he has set a budget for the next year or quarter.

8. *Make creative ideas relevant.* If you are going to recommend a creative idea, make sure it relates precisely to the client.

9. *Don't clutter.* Don't let the natural urge to include everything ruin your presentation by making it too cumbersome.

10. *Be brief.* Don't make your sales story too long. While there is not absolute agreement on this point, in the newspaper selling world many feel that a presentation should be no longer than 20 minutes.

11. *Avoid irrelevant gimmicks.* They will overshadow the content and give your serious effort the appearance of a sideshow.

12. *Make your presentation excel.* A presentation which is poorly planned, prepared, or delivered can reflect negatively on your paper. Make each presentation your best effort.

13. *Watch your figures.* If at all possible, keep the statistics to a minimum. Keep away from complicated charts and statistical tables. Most people won't understand them. When you do use them, validate them with the name of the source.

14. *Accent the positive.* Remember the positive approach. If you become unnecessarily competitive, you may quickly lose your prospect. He may not agree with you. You must be competitive to some extent, but you must handle your competitive data carefully. Your competition is undoubtedly making presentations, too, and your prospect will be weighing what may be conflicting claims.

15. *Be honest.* It is better to underplay than overplay your claims. If you overstate, your prospect is likely to reject your point.

16. *Give cost.* You must include cost in your sales story. But this is only one element. If your rate or cost-per-thousand is less than the competition, by all means use it, but not before you sell the quality and coverage of your paper.

17. *Defend yourself.* Be prepared to talk about your weaknesses, while stressing your strengths. Your competition has probably hammered away already at your weak spots.

18. *Anticipate questions.* After you have prepared your material, study it and anticipate any questions that may come up. These will normally concern the competitive areas which you cover. You must be ready to deal with them quickly, positively, and expertly. In fact, you should encourage questions. It is highly desirable to start a discussion.

19. *Ask penetrating questions yourself.* But don't make the mistake of asking the account if he liked your presentation. He will generally tell you his opinion on his own. Be specific. What you really want to know is, What are my chances of getting this business?

20. *Stay on the beam.* Don't wander from your original material with afterthoughts and anecdotes—you'll ruin your timing and you may start to bore your prospect. If they are important points, use them during your discussion period.

21. *Get a preview critique.* Always rehearse before your boss or other sales people and get their reaction. Then make adjustments.

22. *Don't be an actor.* Forget the dramatics. A few simple gestures are fine. Raising and lowering your voice occasionally helps; but don't make this an oratorical contest or a performance in histrionics.

23. *Watch your manners.* Don't, under any circumstances, smoke or chew gum during your sales talk.

24. *Leave references behind.* Always leave a summary or outline of what you have said behind. *And always* leave a copy of the paper and your rate card.

25. *End hard.* Have a strong, repeat strong, summary reiterating everything you have said in brief terms. And don't forget—ask for the order!

Questions like these may indicate the possibility of a closing situation:

- "What are your rates?"

- "How far in advance does copy have to be in?"

- "What is the best day of the week for my business to advertise?"

- "Could I get on the sports page?"

- "What about co-op*?"

- "Do you charge for copy or layout service?"

---

* See Chapter 14 for details on cooperative advertising.

Sometimes it is necessary to listen carefully so you won't miss the opportunity to close. When you perceive the signal, close quickly and effectively by asking for the business. Quite often you will get no positive statements or questions. In most cases, in fact, it is necessary to lead the prospect into the decision-making process.

TRY LEAD-IN QUESTIONS

One of the most effective ways to do this is to ask questions as a lead-in. "Have I covered everything to your satisfaction, Mr. Smith?" "Does this make sense to you, Mr. Smith?" "Can we schedule your first ad for next week?" "Does this fit into your plans?" "Would you like me to check out your co-op allowances on these items?" "Would you mind if we worked up a budget for you?" "Can I work up copy and layout for a series of ads?"

In effect, you are presupposing the decision will be favorable. The lead-in question asks the prospect to make a decision. Through the use of lead-in questions, you learn whether or not your sale effort has been successful. If the prospect doesn't respond favorably, he will at least uncover objections you must handle before you can possibly close the sale.

In selling advertising, each sales situation is different. Closing situations develop at different stages in the sales call. Professional space sales people must know when to build on the positive cues, how to field objections, and when to close.

The key to closing sales is to work at it, practice, experiment. If one type of close fails to work during a sales call, try another. Many sales people use only one type of close, and far too many use none and lose business that could have been won. Failure to ask for the order, or close the call, can be attributed to neglect of any number of things—not planning selling time, not knowing the prospect, not having good rapport, not being persistent, not having a proper selling attitude, lacking confidence. The end result is that the sales person creates the attitude in the prospect's mind either that he doesn't deserve the business, that it doesn't belong in his paper, or that he can be easily put off.

Once you have reached your objective, you have closed the sale or closed the call. Obviously, objectives are not always met. When you fail to meet the objective of the call, leave the door open for the future. You should not quit on the account because of a turn-down. Rebuffs in the business are frequent. Be prepared for them, and keep going back. Be persistent. It takes a lot of persistence to be successful in selling.

Handling Objections

Because of the intangibility of the newspaper business, it is vitally important to become proficient at dealing with objections. Objections can be roadblocks or building blocks. Objections have always created great difficulty for the unprepared or inexperienced sales person.

Far too many sales people get trapped in situations where objections keep them from closing business. Many make the mistake of becoming negative or defensive at the first sign of an objection.

Keep in mind, though, that many objections can be easily parried. No one, however, should be complacent about them; one must simply learn how to deal with them professionally.

These are the three ways to deal with an objection:

- *Ignore it.* Many professional sales people will override the objection and continue with their sales presentation to see if the prospect comes back to it, in which case it is a serious objection. Often, though, it will be forgotten or answered during the normal course of the sales presentation.

- *Minimize it.* Skirt around it by admitting to a minor fault, agree with the prospect, say "that couldn't be helped" or "I agree it could have been handled better" or "we're certainly sorry about that." This technique can be used mostly in dealing with superficial objections.

- *Handle it.* Answer it directly and ask questions that cast the objection in a new light, or try to turn it into a selling advantage.

Avoid arguments but don't sidestep valid objections. Don't contradict a prospect. If he objects to the idea of advertising, there is ample evidence that the advantages far outweigh the disadvantages. If the objection has something to do with advertising in the competition, exercise care about criticizing the program or the competitive media. In short, never bring the prospect's good judgment into question—the result will only be antagonism. Instead, stress the strengths of your own newspaper as an irreducible minimum for him as an advertiser.

ABOUT COSTS

An analysis of objections to advertising would reveal, no doubt, that a large share of them revolve around the question of cost. "I can't afford it." "Your rates are too high." "The budget is closed." "Business is bad right now." "I'm too small to advertise." "That ad will cost too much." Thus, if you can become proficient at handling objections about cost, you will certainly be much farther along the road to professionalism in dealing with objections.

The surest ways to combat questions about cost are to stress that advertising is not a cost but an investment; that it can help a business to grow; that it builds store sales and store traffic; that rates are based on effective circulation coverage for an advertiser; that advertising is necessary to maintain a level of business and to ward off competition; that the local newspaper is the most effective medium in the world for reaching the local market, and a local retailer should not be without it.

ABOUT EFFECTIVENESS

Another common objection is the advertiser who reports that he had "no results." The reply to this, of course, is that there are numerous advertisers, perhaps with similar businesses, who use the paper regularly with excellent results. Thus, there must be something wrong with the approach the advertiser is using. The newspaper is responsible only for the space and the coverage;

the advertiser must himself determine the proper approach to the marketplace in order to achieve maximum results.

TO POSITIONING

Position in the paper is again a contentious area and often the subject of objections and complaints. There are several studies on advertising readership, however, that emphasize that position in the paper is not nearly so important as the creative approach and execution of the ad. Further, newspapers are thoroughly read as a rule, and many of the best-read features are in the *back* sections of most papers, not in the first few pages that advertisers so often clamor to be on.

TO NEW PROPOSALS

Attracting advertisers from competitive media often gives rise to difficult objections. "We're completely satisfied with what we're doing now" is frequently heard. This is awkward because it is an affirmation the competition has done an effective selling job on the account, one that is evidently working. In this instance, emphasize the possibility of greater sales and greater profits by *adding* your newspaper to the advertising program. It is probably not possible to supplant the competition as the principal advertising vehicle right away, but it would be a step in the right direction. Bring strong selling to bear by pointing out things your newspaper can do better, or exclusively, that will offer the hope of increased sales and profits.

"We're going to skip the ad this week" is a familiar stalling device that suggests the merchant does not run an effective advertising program. The sales representative should point out that frequency in advertising is important and that a budgeted and planned program is necessary to achieve best results. In addition, if you will offer to relieve the advertiser of certain details—layouting, finding co-op allowances—it is often possible to salvage the ad. By using some imagination and

creativity, this sort of objection can usually be overcome. (Sometimes, presenting a spec layout can avoid objections like this entirely.)

"I'll think it over" is another familiar stalling objection. It frequently suggests that you have more selling to do. One technique that sometimes will force a decision or bring the real reason to the surface is to say, "You seem to have some hesitation about our paper (or this promotion). Perhaps I haven't covered all the points adequately for you. Is there anything more you need from me to make a decision?" If this does force a decision, it may or may not be favorable, but most space sales people will appreciate receiving a firm decision, even if it is negative, than to be stalled indefinitely.

ON EDITORIAL MATTERS

Many complaints in the newspaper business are about editorial material that did or did not get in the paper. The space sales person on the account takes the brunt of these complaints; perhaps he is the only person the account knows at the paper. It is a vexing area for many space sales people and there are, of course, no pat answers. But the complaint must be dealt with because it may be a real grievance in the account's mind, and it will not go away by itself.

Here are a few hints on dealing with advertisers who are angry over editorial materials or publicity: Point out that employees don't always agree with editorials or other material appearing in the paper either. The letters column is usually full of such criticism. The point is that thousands of people receive the newspaper for news. It's extremely important to them, and it just isn't possible for a newspaper to publish only material that will please everyone. A newspaper should strive for respect, not love. Its responsibility is to publish what its editors feel is important to the community and to provide accurate coverage it believes its readers want and need.

If publicity is rejected by the editorial department, you must stress that the advertising department cannot, should not, and certainly does not con-

trol the editorial content of the newspaper. Advertising sales representatives, for the most part, can only submit publicity material they receive from advertisers to management for consideration. In most instances, too, editors and publishers are willing to discuss publicity with advertisers, so a simple referral to someone else may suffice.

What it amounts to is simply this: A merchant should not advertise in a newspaper (or any other medium) because of editorial positions or news content. An advertiser does not buy an editorial position. He buys advertising space and circulation coverage of a market, and the object is to attain results from the advertising. What matters is that a complete and worthwhile newspaper is being published that can help the merchant's business.

KEEP REPLIES COOL AND COMPETENT

In handling any type of objection, keep replies short and to the point. Don't wander or get involved in lengthy, complicated explanations or arguments. Answer the objection, complaint, or question as truthfully and succinctly as possible, then quickly return to the original purpose of the call.

Generally, if your rebuttal sounds logical and professional, your prospect will hear you out. Objections are open invitations to doing more selling. Objections usually indicate that the prospect has some interest in the paper, and by voicing objections and asking questions he is giving the newspaper a chance to reply. Properly handled, objections can present good selling opportunities. Professional sales people can use them as stepping stones to closing more sales.

Creative Service: A Key to Sales

It has often been said that it is sometimes more important to service an account than to sell him. While this bromide is a generalization and only partly true, it does stress the importance of good creative service to advertisers as a means to keep and even to increase their advertising frequency and space.

Service means being helpful to an account, and sales will generally follow sincere help. There are many ways to render such service, including the following:

- Provide the account with layouts to consider between your calls.

- Make sure he receives his proofs.

- Bring him tear sheets to post in his place of business.

- Remind him to display advertised items prominently and to keep the sales clerks informed of the advertising program. Retailing is replete with stories of advertising programs that failed utterly because sales clerks were not aware of the advertising and confusion reigned when the public responded.

- Check out co-op allowances that may be available.

- Get duplicate co-op bills to the account promptly so he can get reimbursed in a reasonable time.

- Keep the account advised of promotional opportunities.

- Make budget suggestions.

- Keep him apprised of market trends in the area.

Is This for You?

Selling newspaper advertising is a rewarding profession for those who belong. Outstanding talent is hard to find, and good ad representatives are in demand in nearly every community or city where there is a newspaper. An individual can thus choose a place to live. Successful sales people are never without jobs, whether in prosperity or economic depression. Pay is often better than for editorial personnel because retail advertising brings in the largest percentage of newspaper revenue. Management seems ever conscious of that fact.

Not everyone, however, can make it in newspaper advertising sales. There are qualifications far more important than formal education. Perhaps the first is enjoying selling and finding a challenge in overcoming sales resistance. A successful sales representative is doggedly persistent and keeps making calls in the face of rejections. He knows selling is a game of percentages, and he works hard to succeed. Women have been very successful in advertising sales.

Good advertising representatives are not "desk-job" individuals. They like people and enjoy their visits with retail clients. They think positively and can influence others to do the same. They like to organize and plan their own work and even to set their own hours. They require little supervision and want little. They are proud of being "self-starters." They believe in their newspapers and exude that belief in contacts with others. They may not be flamboyant or even dynamic, but they are totally dedicated.

Without most of these important qualifications, an individual might be wise to consider another calling. With them, he or she will find newspaper advertising selling a profitable and happy life.

Chapter 13

Advertising Gimmicks and Special Promotions

by James S. Steele

Promotion is the most neglected priority in the newspaper industry today. At one time the industry ranked second only to Hollywood in promotion. It has not been many years since it was really the pacesetter, but it appears that the newspapers have now permitted the broadcast media to take the lead and dominate media promotion.

There is great concern today that newspapers are not enjoying their share of the advertising dollars that are available and being spent. Readership studies are still very shocking. Changes are occurring in the profile of the city versus the suburban territory. There

FIGURE 13–1   For newspapers the answer to "How do you spell relief?" is "C-R-E-A-T-E." *Art reproduction by Dale Van Deventer, Stillwater (Oklahoma)* News-Press.

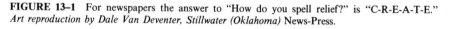

JAMES S. STEELE

The author is president of Dardanell Publications in Monroeville, Pennsylvania, and nationally known for innovation in advertising promotion and the use of gimmicks.

"These are gimmicks, but gimmick is not a bad word if it accomplishes two things: gets attention and produces results."

is no question that we are witnessing the beginning of what is called regentrification—that is, a move back into the cities.

Newspapers should keep alert to this change. Newspaper circulation and distribution will have problems, the carrier system in particular. There are developments in other areas of communications, such as satellite broadcasting, that could also become major concerns. The newspaper industry could be faced with a situation much like that of the man who jumped off a 30-story building and, as he passed the third floor, said, "I'm still OK!"

C-R-E-A-T-E

It isn't quite that drastic yet, but before the end of the century we may not recognize our industry as it exists today. Newspapers must therefore anticipate changes that will take place and prepare now to respond to these changes. A nationwide television commercial posed the question, "How do you spell relief?" The newspaper industry might well ask the same thing. But television gave the wrong answer—it spelled out the name of an antacid. The real answer for newspapers to "How do you spell relief?" is "C-R-E-A-T-E."

There is a very fine line between creation and promotion. Because when we define creativity, we're talking about a process of bringing forth something new. Creativity is simply someone's mind hard at work, putting together something that has never existed before. And maybe it's really an old idea, not a new concept. Maybe it's just a good idea from the past that needs to be dusted off and updated and implemented again. But there's no question that when this ingredient is added to promotion, two things happen—it causes attraction and response.

Harvey Firestone said, "Capital isn't so important in business. Experience isn't so important. What is important is ideas, and if you have ideas you have the main asset you need. If you have ideas, there isn't any limit to what you can do with your business and your life."

Perhaps this really adds another word in the area of promotion. But the words run parallel in pressing on toward the goal, and the three running in this race are creativity, ideas, and promotion. There is great similarity among the three.

Why We Promote

The best way to start is by defining three basic motives in the area of promotion. (And remember that "motive" is two-thirds of motivation.) The three basic motives are: we promote to communicate or introduce a new idea, we promote to increase or expand an existing or successful idea, and we promote to correct or restore a situation or an attitude.

Here are three examples, one appropriate for each of these basic motives, used by Dardanell Publications:

INTRODUCING SOMETHING NEW. Most publishers by now have been confronted with a free publication coming into their territory, a competitive publication that offers much greater saturation than their paid product. They are faced with the problem of ending up with a much lower percentage of coverage with a paid product, considering the attractiveness to advertisers of the new, market-saturated product.

How do you compete with that kind of situation via promotion? First, Dardanell came up with a new publication with a very "unnewspaper" name. No one wanted to call it another *Times, Gazette,* or *Press,* so it became the *Peachtree.* The *Peachtree* is a free publication distributed by the standard carrier system. In effect, if a carrier has fifty subscribers on his route and fifteen nonsubscribers, he delivers the regular paper to the former and the free *Peachtree* to the latter. The purpose of the *Peachtree* is to provide coverage for the advertiser. For a small additional cost, Dardanell picks up the advertising from the paid newspaper and drops it into the *Peachtree.* This satisfies the advertiser with numbers. This is an example of how promotion can communicate or introduce a new idea.

EXPANDING AN IDEA. The next step was to increase or expand this successful idea. This was done by developing appropriate features. In this case, Dardanell came up with a Miss Peach-

tree of the Week, always a young lady from within the circulation area. Many names, photographs, and profiles were submitted. Each gave additional readership value to the *Peachtree.*

We also began to feature a peach recipe every week. (We didn't realize that there were 187 different recipes that include peaches as an ingredient!) Things such as this help to stimulate even more interest in an existing idea by a promotion.

RESTORING A SITUATION. There is no question that with the end of the summer came a decline in participation in the *Peachtree.* There wasn't enough advertising interest. Possibly it was seasonal, but there was a need for a promotional idea that would stop the slide. The answer was to add to the *Peachtree* an additional advertiser service at no additional cost: we picked up the classified pages from the newspaper and published them in the *Peachtree.*

This provided the advertiser with additional numbers and coverage and made the *Peachtree* desirable once more. So here again Dardanell used a promotional principle, an idea, and promoted the idea to stimulate more advertising activity in its product.

Promotion: A New Investment

When we talk about a promotion department for the weekly or small daily newspaper we are talking about a new investment. This is probably the main reason we do not have enough promotion in the small daily or weekly operation. There is no question that you must anticipate hiring more than one person in promotion, because it is difficult to find a single individual who is able to do artwork, market research, copywriting, and all the other things that are expected of a promotion department.

In addition to a full-time promotion person you will find it necessary to start adding to the payroll part-time people needed to constitute a full-fledged effective and active promotion department. So the community publisher asks, "What is the answer to not being able to afford a promotion department?"

TRY S.T.P.

The key to the small newspaper or weekly operation that can't afford a promotion manager is S.T.P. S.T.P. stands for Spare Time Promotion. This is the alternative—the development of an in-house mobile agency. There could be many variations of this, but one approach is to have a representative of each department of the newspaper serve on a promotion committee. This can be one person from editorial, one from advertising, one from classified, one from accounting, and one from circulation. These people can devote one or two hours a month to one or two promotion meetings.

What they do is bring concerns from their respective departments, areas that are in need of promotion. At the same time, they are available to resolve and contribute answers to many problems in other departments. As an example, the person representing the editorial department can be used to write copy. If a person from circulation comes in with the problem of a loss in circulation in one of the newspapers, the committee can do collective brainstorming as a promotion committee and center on that area of circulation work. It can find ways to get circulation back on track and stimulate subscriptions.

The only way to get the committee off to a flying start—and there is something very contagious and exciting about promotion—is to be selective about who is named to participate. It must be people who have a talent or an interest in this area.

A good beginning is to form a committee, even if it's just three persons, and decide on an annual corporate promotion. This is a very basic concept and there are three parts that have to be evident in a corporate promotion. One, it must involve employees; two, there must be community exposure; and three, it must get results in the marketplace. Profit is the real goal, the motive for the whole concept.

Ideas

"EXTRA! EXTRA! COLA!"

In 1975 Dardanell Publications introduced a small bottle of soda pop. And when readers saw this small bottle of pop, they asked, "What does that have to do with publishing newspapers?" Thus, the bottle itself attracted attention. And the label on the bottle was a reproduction of a front page that read, "Extra! Extra! Cola!" The headlines said, "The powerful new drink sensation from Dardanell Publications. Providing extra coverage and extra readership to bring you extra sales." Another label at the neck of the bottle was inscribed, "The drink with the punch of a front page story. Big returns, powerful impact."

The whole thing was an advertising message—a bottle in a white box presented to advertisers as a gift. This was really the whole story being presented in the form of a bottle of soda pop.

How do employees get involved in this kind of promotion? That's where it started. In this case, each employee was given some bottles to take home and taste. With each was a questionnaire saying, "This is going to be our promotion symbol for the year 1975 and we would like for you to give it a taste test." There were perhaps a half-dozen questions on the survey, such as "Is it too sweet?" "Is it too bitter?" "Is the carbonation weak or too strong?"

The response was good. This was a special formula put together by a local bottling company, with an extra strong fizz. It certainly got employees involved. Then an ad introduced it to the community, and again the bottle of pop attracted attention. People were quite mystified that the newspaper was talking about soda pop. They couldn't immediately tie it in with the newspaper until they read the copy.

Of course, presenting the bottle of pop to advertisers when sales people made the calls was the key to getting this promotion across. Any time a salesman calls on a prospective advertiser with a gift in his hand, the door will open earlier or at least more easily

than if he made a "cold" call.

These are gimmicks but "gimmick" is not a bad word if it accomplishes two things: gets attention and produces results. One is needed with the other.

RED ARROW DAYS

In 1976, Dardanell undertook another corporate promotion. Most people recall vividly the climate at that time. We were just winding up Watergate and the Vietnam war, and the nation was trying to come out of a recession. Not just the community but the whole nation was low in spirit.

Dardanell did something to really lift the spirit of its community as well as the general apathy about the country. It started with a symbol—the vertical red arrow. The red arrow proved to be a most effective symbol of the year 1976. We started a campaign—a crusade—to lift the spirits of the people in our community and saying, "Come on, people of suburban Pittsburgh, let's climb. There's a new day, a new goal ahead."

Again Dardanell started with employees by creating Red Arrow Days. We distributed pins with a red vertical arrow on them. Any employee who wore one on Red Arrow Day was rewarded: he or she would receive a silver dollar for wearing the "up" button as evidence of his "up" attitude and support of the company's promotion.

Then the promotion moved out into the community. More than 5,000 red arrow pins were distributed to the community, and people were delighted to wear them. What the newspaper really had was 5,000 walking billboards, and when people asked, "What's the vertical red arrow for?" this was a boost for the fact that all of this was a Dardanell Publications symbol. And they were saying, "It's the 'up' promotion, the 'up' direction of 1976, and we are part of that attitude." There was great exposure, after which the campaign moved to the marketplace, hitting hard with red arrow tabloid promotions and red arrow sale days.

A newspaper should plan a corporate symbol promotion every year to kick off the new year.

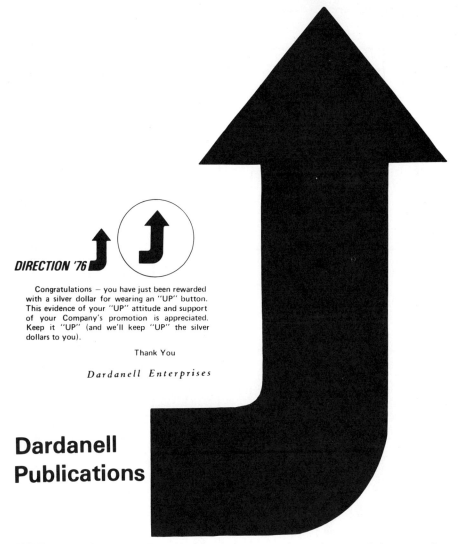

DIRECTION '76

Congratulations — you have just been rewarded with a silver dollar for wearing an "UP" button. This evidence of your "UP" attitude and support of your Company's promotion is appreciated. Keep it "UP" (and we'll keep "UP" the silver dollars to you).

Thank You

Dardanell Enterprises

Dardanell Publications

FIGURE 13–2 Red Arrow Days involved the newspaper, its employees, and the community, and brought an "up" feeling to everyone. More than 5,000 red arrow pins were distributed. *Art reproduction by Oklahoma State University Photo Services.*

CONTESTS

Another question is, What can promotion accomplish for the retail and classified areas of the small daily or weekly newspaper? Here are two contests that not only stimulated personnel in the sales area but also brought great sales results.

One of these was the DE 500 Contract Classic. This was a takeoff on the Indy 500 race, but it could have been called a number of things—a horse race, the Grand Prix, etc. The whole idea was based on new business. (All promotions should be based on new business, and bonuses and commissions should be paid on that basis.)

What was unique about this contest was that everybody participated.

Some departments often feel neglected when it comes to special sales promotions and the bonuses all go to the sales staff. There are valid arguments on both sides as to why that happens, but it certainly can't hurt to get the whole company involved in some of these promotions.

In the DE 500 Contest, each member of the sales staff became a driver—a race driver. And each driver had nine or ten members in his pit crew—these were fellow employees.

Dardanell handled this like a football draft. Each driver drew employees names from a hat until each had a full pit crew. When a sales person would win one of the heats, he would draw a number or name from his or her pit crew and that person would be awarded the very same prize.

Now what happens in a promo-

tion like this is that employees are not only involved and sharing in the bonus, but are also prodding the sales staff. There was no need for management to urge sales people to sell because each had a pit crew wanting an update on his progress. He had to win before they could win. It was fun; it was also a most successful promotion. Each newspaper can have its own format. It could be set up as a horse race.

What was most significant at Dardanell was that it was a long promotion, lasting two months, and too often it is difficult to have any kind of sales promotion that is just as exciting the last week as the first. This is one that qualified because prizes were awarded every two weeks and so, at the end of every "heat," it was a new beginning. It really maintained the momentum and interest. This is a promotion that can be used at least once a year.

THE BLITZ BONUSES

Another bonus promotion that Dardanell conducted for its advertising people was held near the end of 1977. It was called the Blitz Bonus Series, or Blitzkrieg, and every month a different bonus was offered to the sales staff. The first month it was a "Calls Blitz Bonus"—anyone who made more calls than in the two previous months would receive a compensation for each additional call that month. If he made 100 calls in October and 150 in November, he would receive fifty cents or a dollar for each additional sales call he made in November.

This accomplished several things. Not only did it encourage more sales presentations through calls, but it also provided the employer with an idea of the capacity of the staff, of how many calls they are really capable of making.

The next month it was a Unit Blitz Bonus. This time a premium or bonus was paid for increased number of units sold, regardless of the size of the ad. If there were so many additional units sold over a given period of four weeks or a month over the same period the previous year, the sales person would receive a premium or bonus on each additional unit sold.

"DE 500" RACE SPECTACULAR
THE GREAT CONTRACT CLASSIC

DRIVER	RACE CAR	FIRST HEAT (ENDS SEPT.15)	SECOND HEAT (ENDS SEPT. 29)	THIRD HEAT (ENDS OCT. 13)	FOURTH HEAT (ENDS OCT. 27)
Harry	MG				
Dave	DATSUN				
Tom	CAMARO				
Dave	JAGUAR				
Glenn	RABBIT				
Mike	FERARRI				
Irene	FASCINATION		WINNERS IRENE JERRY		
John	THUNDERBIRD				
Frank	PORSCHE				
Jean	CADILLAC	WINNERS JEAN LESTER			
Carol	MASERATI				

PIT CREWS

DRIVER Harry	DRIVER Dave	DRIVER Tom	DRIVER Dave	DRIVER Glenn	DRIVER Mike	DRIVER Irene	DRIVER John	DRIVER Frank	DRIVER Jean	DRIVER Carol
CHARLES STAUB	JUDY ROCKWELL	WILLIAM BRETZ	RICHARD GUTHRIE	SHERRY KUDRANSKI	ELIZABETH KLINE	MARY RITTER	CARMEN TOOTHMAN	DEE SORCE	KAREN ADAMS	HARRY CONNELLY
FRANK TIERNO	LISA MELL	JACK THOMPSON	ROBERT McCARTHY	JEAN THOMPSON	NANCY CLAWSON	CAROLINE DUGA	ZELLA KAMMERIDIENER	JEAN McNEMAR	WILLIAM THOMPSON	WALTER PASEWICZ
ELLA RIDGEWAY	TERESA FLATLEY	DENNIS DARDANELL	ROBERT BECKO	MARGARET MILLAR	GREGORY WILLIAMS	GEORGE HARVEY	DOMINIC PALUNOVICH	DOYLE HOUSER	ALBERT KAMINSKY	VIRGINIA PATELLA
EDITH LADICK	DORENE VENETS	GENEVIEVE LUCIDI	VIOLET TONIN	DALE LARKIN	GREGORY SMITH	MARIANNE AGNOLI	GARY THOMPSON	RALPH KATANIK	DIANNIA HOTT	KATHLEEN WOLFE
W. P. KENNEDY	MICHAEL MILLER	LINDA OWOC	HELEN COLWELL	KIMBERLY KREBS	ELEANOR ORAVEC	DORIS BAKER	PATRICIA GRESS	GLADYS BERNSTEIN	NELLIE NICOLETTI	MARK PIE'
ALICE HARPER	LYNN HALE	WILLIAM BLAIR	JEAN MADDEN	JOSEPH MARASCO	KAREN CHECK	RALPH VALERIO	JANET ASHBAUGH	ROSE THOMAS	SARAH BANDA	WILLIAM McCASLIN
CLIFF THOMPSON	RAYMOND HENRY	WILLIAM MORRIS	SHERMAN ICKES	WILLIAM OWENS	KATHERINE AGNOLI	CHARLES SWARTZEL	ALICE TOVEY	WILLIAM KESTNER	DOROTHY TITMUS	BARBARA LOHR
WILLIAM ZADARKO	EDWARD CONLEY	KEITH WATKINS	JOHN BOLAND	JOSEPH MONTE	NORMAN KOVALY	DOM DeDOMENIC	CINDY LESLIE	RITA YOUNG	GARY BELL	AUGUST LETZELTER
CLAIRE KONOP	DAVID ADAMS	PHIL LABORDA	JOHN McGUIRK	AUGUST BONDI	KARL KOSLOW	CAROL WENZEL	HENRY KARP	RICHARD MARTIN	LESTER CHURCHFIELD	EDWARD UVA
JEAN CAPOR	HELEN EBERT	JOHN JESIH			MARCIA CASTOR	JOSEPH SARNE	DENNIS McALEER			

Then there was the Bounty Blitz Bonus. This meant putting a special bounty on nonadvertisers. These bounties ranged from $100 to $1,000 per account. If, in a period of sixty days, as in the case here, a sales person was able to sell one of the bounty accounts prespecified by management, he or she would receive the full bonus, providing the advertising was run during the promotional period.

Promotion Vehicles

A newspaper needs to consider promotion vehicles, and some excellent ideas were presented in Chapter 11. Probably your own newspaper is best as a vehicle for promotion. This is the most inexpensive and one of the most effective vehicles. You may use in-house ads, or you may publish an insert about your business in your paper. Once a year you should publish some kind of insert that really promotes your business. Dardanell used an eight-page tabloid in each of its newspapers.

Most newspapers do more than advertising and publishing newspapers. There are many other divisions. Some have photo departments. Some even sell wedding invitations. But whatever services you provide, the insert is a good way of telling your community about your operations. You can include an invitation for a plant tour. You know the pluses of your business, so promote them in an insert in your newspaper at least once a year.

There are also other promotional vehicles. These include bumper stickers; billboards, which may be available for trade-out; and the broadcast media, which are available for trade for most publications. Make sure you get the best time slots that radio and TV have to offer.

Newspapers with computerized billing should print messages about future promotions right on their bills. These can be programmed into the

FIGURE 13–3 The "DE 500" Race Spectacular emphasized new advertising contracts, and involved employees in every department of the newspaper. *Art reproduction by Oklahoma State University Photo Services.*

computer. Consider all of your bills as direct-mail advertising; include success letters or some other promotion enclosure with every one.

BIG BALLOONS, NEW HORIZONS

A great promotion event for a small newspaper or a weekly chain is a balloon race. You can employ a professional balloonist, rent equipment for a reasonable cost, and challenge the local television or radio station. This brings a two-way exposure of publicity from their broadcast time as well as your newspaper space. Regardless of who wins, it creates much promotional interest.

A great service and a way of getting all your retailers to a meeting is to be host to an annual breakfast or luncheon. Early in the year is a good time to do this. The attraction is not only a free breakfast or luncheon but also the guest speaker, who could be one of your syndicated writers or a prominent retailer from a nearby town or your own. It could be someone of national importance or a leading banker with a financial forecast. A prominent enough name is well worth the cost. A forecast breakfast or luncheon is especially suitable for retailers.

Probably the best way to make a sale is to get the customer out of town, away from his business and his office, and this is exactly what Dardanell did with the Grand Tour concept. We introduced the idea in 1977 and offered each retailer and one guest a trip to Toronto. It was called "Grand Tour Toronto." Toronto is a tremendous retail mecca.

Retailers were flown to Toronto on a Friday morning and taken to a first-class hotel. A breakfast meeting was held on Saturday morning and the participants were given the itinerary for the weekend. Then they were taken by chartered buses to three shopping areas. One was the downtown shopping mall called Eaton Center, said to be the largest in the world, then to a unique suburban shopping center, and from there to an old restored shopping village with unusual specialty shops. On the buses between visits to

FIGURE 13–4 The Grand Tours provided a way to get customers out of town and away from their businesses and offices—the best way to make a sale. *Art reproduction by Oklahoma State University Photo Services.*

the centers, they were given brochures telling them what to look for and what to expect at the next stop. The concept is great because these shopping centers welcome visiting retailers from another city. Their motive is undoubtedly, "Here are some retailer prospects who may want to open a branch in our area."

This promotion was so successful that Dardanell now tries to have one Grand Tour each year, going to a different retail mecca each time. The tours represent not only a service to newspaper representatives and retailers, but also an opportunity to visit on a social level. The only commercial presentation is at the Saturday breakfast. The retailers are ready for this and expect to hear some facts about the newspapers.

Employee Promotions

Promotion is also important to your own personnel. Dardanell does a great many things promotion-wise with its employees. There is at least one annual social. This may be a river cruise, an evening on the river, or a night at the Ice Capades. Once we promoted a night at the circus for employees and their families. Many tickets for such things as these can be obtained through a trade-out.

One thing that has been popular with employees is what we call "Donuts for Doers." Two or three times a month, a large sign is placed on the employees' entrance, inscribed "Good

TALK OF THE MALL

your best advertising vehicle
because it gets results!

results results results results results

Morning, This is Donuts for Doers Day." The idea is simply to express appreciation to our employees, and we show it by giving out free doughnuts those mornings. (This can sometimes be set up as a trade-out with a local doughnut shop.) This has become a big event. It's a great way to kick off the day. It serves as a reward, too, after two or three hectic days in the shop. It causes employees to feel the company appreciates them.

It is important that every company have an anniversary or birthday and use that date to do something for employees. One year Dardanell placed 200 strawberry tarts on a table and then added an oversized birthday card that said, "You're the Berries. Happy Birthday." The employees liked this very much.

The Shopping Center

Probably the greatest national tragedy affecting the newspaper has been the shopping center. There is no reason to allow shopping centers to represent a reduction of advertising to a newspaper. There is every opportunity to turn the arrival of a new shopping center or mall into the biggest business bonanza in the history of the newspaper industry.

So often when a main street advertiser abandons his old location and moves into a shiny new shopping center or mall, he changes some advertising habits or patterns or practices or principles. Suddenly, he cuts down on advertising and becomes infected with a disease that runs rampant in shopping centers. It's called "parasitis." Parasitis is very contagious. The small, formerly active main street advertiser, now in the shopping center, decides to take advantage of the traffic the major stores bring into the center. He thinks he can ride along on the coattails of the big stores and cut back on his own advertising.

What the shopping center be-

FIGURE 13–5 Many ideas were used to promote *Talk of the Mall,* a tabloid used to respond to shopping mall advertising problems. *Art reproduction by Oklahoma State University Photo Services.*

comes then is a communal retreat for the retailer. The remedy or prescription for this problem is promotion. A newspaper must develop approaches to the shopping center. Dardanell's most successful one was for Monroeville Mall, possibly the largest mall in Pennsylvania.

Dardanell published a tabloid called the *Talk of the Mall,* on an average of twenty-two to twenty-eight times a year—about every other week—for nine years. It averaged from sixteen to twenty-four pages an issue and carried some editorial content geared to the promotional events of the center. It ran as an insert in all of our publications. The key here again was to promote the benefits of our product, not only the distribution but also the successes that participants enjoyed in this publication.

It is very important that you meet regularly with merchants in the mall. A good approach is to sponsor a luncheon and invite shopping center retailers. Select a restaurant nearby and do advance promotion that encourages them to come to the meeting. A free lunch is not always enough of an incentive, so you may need some kind of contest.

One successful effort to sell a shopping center on a tabloid promotion program used a powerful gimmick: each invitation included a silver dollar and the message that this was the first of a possible hundred dollars the merchant could win at the presentation meeting.

Whatever you do, promote vigorously and build a backlog of ideas that will inspire your community and your staff. If this takes gimmicks, use them, as long as they'll get attention and results.

Chapter 14

Cooperative Advertising: A Neglected Source of Revenue

by C. Randall Choate

As the name implies, cooperative advertising is a cooperative or joint effort between a retailer and his supplier to finance the cost of advertising a product to the consumer.

"Co-op" advertising, as it is generally called, is of extreme importance to the newspaper and the retailers in smaller communities, because it involves millions of dollars that have already been appropriated for advertising but are almost never spent. Large retailers in metropolitan areas with specialized advertising personnel usually take full advantage of co-op, and it represents a large percentage of their advertising budgets. The small independent retailer, on the other hand, is often not fully aware of what is available to him through co-op or of how to go about getting such funds. Consequently, he loses by default funds he needs desperately for his advertising budget, and the newspaper loses needed revenue.

Co-op advertising is a multibillion dollar business that involves substantial segments of the manufacturing and retailing communities. Statements in this chapter are based on generalities and circumstances that are considered predominant. Individual situations will present contradictions, exceptions, exclusions, etc., but all findings discussed here are based on a strong consensus.

The "supplier" in the co-op process can be the manufacturer of the product or, in multistage distribution arrangements, it can be the distributor or jobber or both. As an example, the manufacturer may have a co-op advertising program which goes no further than sharing advertising costs with his direct customer, the distributor-jobber. At the same time, the distributor-jobber can have his own program which shares advertising costs with his direct customer, the retailer.

The basic co-op advertising concept is very sound. It encourages all levels of the distribution process to concentrate on product advertising best suited to each one's individual needs. The manufacturer or national marketer can concentrate on national media with strong emphasis on developing product acceptance. At the same time, his co-op program encourages the distributor-jobber to tailor his media selection to that which best serves his more regional needs.

The consumer is, of course, exposed to the influence of both these advertising thrusts, but the ultimate in getting the message to the consumer is attained when the co-op arrangement reaches the retailer stage. Regardless of the total weight and thrust of adver-

C. RANDALL CHOATE

The author is vice president for sales and research for American Newspaper Representatives, Inc., an organization that represents seven thousand community newspapers.

"A newspaper should learn the precise details of every co-op program available on every item sold at retail stores in its trade area. . . . To wait for the retailer to initiate action . . . is to contribute to the mountain of unspent co-op funds."

tising, nothing happens until a cash register rings—and that happens at the retail level. The retailer's participation in the co-op process permits him to capitalize on product advertising which has been done nationally and regionally and gives him the further advantage of utilizing media best suited

116

to reach *his* consumer potential. He can effectively tie the product to *his* retail facility. His ads will feature product, of course, but they have the added attraction of being local, speaking directly to his potential customers: "Here is the product, here is where you can get it, and here is where it can be serviced."

Funding Based on Sales

There are many different methods of funding co-op advertising, but in the final analysis they will all relate in some way to the amount of product which is bought and sold.

A great many co-op programs restrict the supplier's commitment to a specific percentage of the retailer's dollar purchases of the product. Example: Supplier ABC offers to support retailer XYZ by paying for 50 percent of all retailer placed advertising of the product, up to a dollar limit of *x* percent of the retailer's purchases.

There is a variety of means of restricting co-op expenditures. It could be an exact percentage of purchases, or it could be something less specific, such as a limit on the number of ads per week or month. The retailer's past sales patterns are usually accurate enough to predict his current co-op needs.

The most frequent co-op arrangement is 50–50, in which the supplier pays 50 percent and retailer pays 50 percent. Any percentage split is, however, possible. There are many 60–40, 75–25, etc., programs. Also, there are often "specials"—attractive percentage splits designed to stimulate advertising and to clear overstocked inventories.

Special opportunities can also be created by favorable, but unpredictable, product demand developments. As an illustration, extreme weather conditions can exert a dramatic, sudden demand for certain farm-related products.

Some co-op programs are virtually unlimited. There is, of course, a built-in, automatic restraint because the retailer is not likely to invest more in advertising a product than his sales and profits would justify.

Mechanics May Vary

Co-op advertising programs can be administered in many ways, but the following outline is basic to most approaches.

The supplier establishes a budget considered appropriate to advertise the product and puts together a program designed to encourage the retailer to sponsor the cost of the advertising cooperatively.

The co-op program is very often presented in the form of a kit containing a complete description of the program: instructions, rules, regulations, restrictions, and so forth. The kit will usually also contain materials designed to assist the retailer in placing the advertising, such as reproducible material for newspaper ads, suggested scripts for radio commercials, and film clips for television spots.

The program is usually presented to the retailer by the supplier's sales force which is, of course, in periodic contact with the retailer. In some instances the supplier's salesman will assist the retailer in implementing the program. More often, the retailer is on his own.

The following is the sequence of events when a retailer decides to take advantage of a 50–50 co-op opportunity by running two newspaper ads.

- The retailer contacts the newspaper and places his order for two ad insertions, specifying dates and supplying material for reproduction.

- The newspaper runs the two ads as specified and then supplies retailer with an invoice for the full cost of the advertising, supported by the two tear sheets (actual pages of the newspaper on which the ads appeared).

- The retailer pays the invoice and receives a receipt for said payment.

- The retailer submits the receipted invoice and the supporting tear sheets to the supplier; this constitutes a request for the agreed-upon 50 percent reimbursement, as the retailer has furnished proof of both advertising and payment.

- The supplier satisfies himself that all provisions of the co-op agreement have been met and then reimburses retailer for the agreed-upon 50-percent share of cost.

Of course, there are many variations on the basic co-op theme. As one illustration, a ketchup supplier might offer a co-op program, and a retail grocery might run a full page ad containing a large number of food items of which the ketchup is but one. In this circumstance, the supplier would co-op only that portion of the page (and cost) which features the ketchup product.

It seems appropriate to note two of the more common mechanical departures from the basic format:

MEMO BILLING. In this procedure the retailer is authorized to waive furnishing the receipted media invoice and tear sheet. Instead, he is permitted to make up his own "memo bill" for advertising reimbursement. The memo bill is often based on an agreed-upon "vendor rate" which is designed to compensate the retailer for production and related costs over and above the media costs.

MERCHANDISING TRADE-OUT. Basically, this is a bookkeeping device. Instead of reimbursing the retailer with cash, the supplier ships the equivalent amount in product. The cash flow and sales benefits of such an arrangement are self-evident.

Who Uses Co-op . . . and Why?

THE MANUFACTURER

The manufacturers of goods and ser-

FIGURE 14–1 This cooperative advertising program for Snapper products shows typical requirements a newspaper must meet to qualify for co-op advertising. *Reprinted courtesy of McDonough Power Equipment Co.*

Co-operative Advertising Program for *SNAPPER Distributors and Dealers*

(Note to SNAPPER Distributors)   Please make every effort to distribute this new program to *all* of your SNAPPER dealers prior to the effective date of this program.

EFFECTIVE DATES: January 1, through December 31, 1980. McDonough Power Equipment offers this co-operative advertising program without regard to your purchases of SNAPPER products. McDonough Power Equipment reserves the right to modify this program upon 60 days written notice.

DEADLINE FOR CLAIMS: Claims must be submitted through SNAPPER Distributors within thirty (30) days after the end of the month of appearance. When claims meet the qualifications which follow, credit will be issued through SNAPPER Distributors.

APPROVED MEDIA, AMOUNT SHARED and PROOF REQUIRED:
(Note) Any claims which include agency commission must be supported by a bill from the agency.

RADIO –
SNAPPER will share in the cost of spot radio time charges up to 50°‍o of your local earned rate.
Submit for Claim:
1. Claim Form 07867.
2. Original station invoice showing date, exact time of broadcast and cost for *each* spot.
3. A fully-documented copy of each script used. (Instruct station to use *exact* documentation statement printed on SNAPPER radio scripts.)
Limitations:
• *Scripts or tapes shall be sixty (60) second spots furnished or offered by SNAPPER for the current model year (or) must be submitted for approval in advance.*

BILLBOARDS – Junior or 30 Sheet
SNAPPER will share in the cost of billboard space costs up to 50°‍o of your earned local rate.
Submit for Claim:
1. Claim Form 07867.
2. Original invoice showing exact posting dates, locations and signatures, if any, for each billboard.
3. Polaroid-type photograph of each design posted.
4. Proof of performance statement (furnished in co-op kit).
Limitations:
• *Billboard paper must be one of the designs available for the current model year (or) must be approved in advance.*
• *Space is provided for dealer name and address but the cost of printing such is not eligible for co-op.*

NEWSPAPERS –
SNAPPER will share in the cost of newspaper space up to 50°‍o of your earned local rate as long as it does not exceed the maximum rate shown on rate chart.
Providing the newspaper used has a second class mailing or controlled circulation permit *and* has been audited within the last twelve (12) months by ABC, CAC, or VAC. Any other newspaper must be submitted for approval, *through a SNAPPER Distributor.* Included with your request for approval must be a complete copy of the newspaper, a sworn circulation statement and a copy of the local rate card.
Submit for Claim:
1. Claim Form 07867.
2. Full-page tearsheet for each date and edition used.
3. Original copy of monthly statement from newspaper.
Limitations:
• *Printing material shall be <u>used as furnished</u> for SNAPPER advertising during the current model year (or) have been approved in advance.*
• *The SNAPPER advertisement must stand by itself; cannot be part of a department store-type advertisement.*
• *Space for dealer name, address, etc., cannot exceed that provided in the advertising material furnished by SNAPPER unless several dealer names are listed.*
• *SNAPPER advertising is not eligible for co-op when it appears in the Classified Section or a classified-type format.*

TELEVISION –
SNAPPER will share in the cost of television time charges up to 50% of the earned rate.
Submit for Claim:
1. Claim Form 07867.
2. Original station invoice showing date, exact time of broadcast, SNAPPER commercial number and tag, if any, used for *each* spot.
3. A fully-documented copy of each script used. (Instruct station to use *exact* documentation statement printed on SNAPPER TV scripts.)

Limitations:
* *All commercials will be the <u>complete</u> commercials offered by SNAPPER for the current model year (or) must be submitted for approval in advance.*

ADVANCE APPROVAL –
Newspaper advertisements, radio scripts or billboard designs, other than those furnished by SNAPPER, must be submitted to McDonough Power Equipment for approval through a SNAPPER Distributor *at least* 30 days in advance of their planned appearance.

MAXIMUM NEWSPAPER RATES ACCEPTABLE FOR 50/50 SNAPPER CO-OP

CIRCULATION GROUPS	Maximum Rate Per Line	Maximum Rate Per Inch
2,000,000 & OVER	$ 7.68	$ 107.52
1,500,000-1,999,999	5.81	81.34
900,000-1,499,999	5.68	79.52
800,000- 899,999	5.10	71.40
700,000- 799,999	4.47	62.58
600,000- 699,999	3.95	55.30
500,000- 599,999	3.83	53.62
400,000- 499,999	2.83	39.62
300,000- 399,999	1.79	25.06
250,000- 299,999	1.53	21.42
200,000- 249,999	1.39	19.46
150,000- 199,999	1.11	15.54
100,000- 149,999	.82	11.48
87,000- 99,999	.68	9.52
75,000- 86,999	.65	9.10
62,000- 74,999	.59	8.26
50,000- 61,999	.53	7.42
45,000- 49,999	.45	6.30
40,000- 44,999	.41	5.74
35,000- 39,999	.35	4.90
30,000- 34,999	.33	4.62
25,000- 29,999	.29	4.06
20,000- 24,999	.27	3.78
17,000- 19,999	.22	3.08
15,000- 16,999	.21	2.94
12,000- 14,999	.19	2.66
10,000- 11,999	.17	2.38
7,000- 9,999	.16	2.24
UNDER 7,000	.14	1.96

(NOTE) Newspapers with less than 8 column formats will be adjusted accordingly.

Form 08068

vices which enjoy somewhat selective distribution are the most likely candidates for a co-op advertising program. Items such as tobacco, candy, and others which are available virtually everywhere are not likely co-op candidates. The following product groups predominate in co-op advertising:

- apparel

- food

- appliances, both major and small

- proprietary drugs

- cosmetics

- jewelry store items

- automotive tires, batteries, and accessories

- hardware, paint, and housewares

- building products

- farm machinery and supplies

Among the primary reasons manufacturers use co-op are:

- It offers an opportunity to identify dealer locations. This cannot be effectively accomplished with less localized national advertising.

- It is a good vehicle for providing specific information such as price.

- It constitutes an incentive for the dealer to place emphasis on the manufacturer's product line as opposed to competitive product lines.

- It creates consumer demand and floor traffic at the point of sale.

- It permits local advertising to be in line with distribution and marketing objectives.

- The dealer's financial involvement should stimulate his interest in moving the product.

- It can be used as a sales tool by offering the dealer an attractive co-op advertising arrangement contingent upon his stocking a specific amount of the product.

- It is an excellent vehicle for advertising special promotions, special situations, etc.

- It can serve as a quickly organized defensive measure in keeping pace with competitors.

- It allows manufacturers to avoid paying national advertising rates which some national advertisers feel are predatory.

THE RETAILER

Retailers handling products in the groups listed above are the primary participants. The newspaper advertising representative should be alert for co-op opportunities in the following types of retail establishments:

- department stores

- discount stores

- apparel speciality shops

- drug stores

- jewelry stores

- appliance stores

- hardware stores

- building supplies stores

- tire and auto accessories stores

- grocery stores

- farm machinery and supplies stores

The ad rep should remind the retailer of the advantages of using co-op advertising. Some of the primary reasons are:

- It lets him stretch his promotional dollars by utilizing the manufacturer's contribution.

- It identifies his place of business with strong brand names.

- It adds the "here is where you can get it" dimension to the product identification achieved through the manufacturer's national advertising program.

- It lets the dealer focus the advertising message to his specific

trade area, where special conditions and circumstances can and do develop.

- It is well suited to creating interest (and subsequently floor traffic) in new or dramatically altered products.

- It gives the retailer more professional advertising copy, layouts, strategies, etc., than he could produce on his own. This is particularly true of the smaller retailer with a small staff and minimal advertising expertise.

- This kind of mutual involvement can strengthen the ties between the supplier and the retailer.

- It serves as a stimulant to the retailer's merchandising and promotional activity.

- It permits the supplier to place emphasis on any particular product line, for whatever reason he may deem such emphasis important. A new or increased co-op advertising allowance will create instant retailer interest and demand for the product; as the program is executed in the media, the interest and demand shift to the consumer.

- When properly utilized, it can enhance relationships between the media and both retailers and suppliers.

- It provides an ideal vehicle for getting the supplier's national advertising message into more personal media which are more specifically related to dealer trade areas, and permits stronger dealer identification.

Disadvantages of Co-op Advertising

While the basic concept of co-op advertising is generally acknowledged to be very sound, there are a great many problem areas. These problems most certainly do not manifest themselves in all instances, but they are all in sufficient evidence to cause many suppliers to eliminate co-op programs completely.

- Not as much happens as is desired. Every year millions and millions of supplier dollars allocated for co-op go unspent. Accordingly, a substantial segment of eligible retailers are either underperforming or not performing at all.

- Most co-op programs are presented to the retailer by the supplier sales force. This can and does present a variety of problems. The co-op responsibility can be considered an intrusion on valuable product-sales time. To offset this, the co-op presentation can be hurried, casual, or completely overlooked. There will be uneven involvement by the retailer, reflecting variables in individual salesmen's advertising acumen or belief in the advertising process as an important contributor to *his* sales accomplishment.

- The supplier loses a degree of control in his advertising program. There is a wide variance in this, largely dependent on the controls built into the program. But the whole concept of co-op places some decision making in the hands of the retailer.

- Advertising allowances intended for advertising can be aborted into price discounting or diverted into nonproductive advertising.

- There are substantial administrative tasks and paperwork for both the supplier and the retailer.

- In programs where the supplier furnishes complete ad layouts and copy, the advertising may be unsuited to the needs of some dealers.

- Long-term co-op programs can tie up considerable amounts of the retailer's money before he is reimbursed by the supplier.

- The dishonest and illegal practice

of double billing* exists, is an ever-present threat where it does not exist, and is quite difficult to police.

- There are very restrictive legal considerations which merit coverage in some depth.

LEGAL CONSIDERATIONS

The Robinson-Patman Act (1936) is the primary legislative control affecting cooperative advertising. The basic purpose of this act is to prevent a supplier from favoring one retailer over another *competing* retailer.

The intent of this legislation is to prevent a supplier from selling to one customer at a more attractive price than that charged a *competing* customer. It is a major factor in the policing of co-op advertising because the device of granting different co-op advertising allowances was a method of favoring certain retailers, even when identical selling prices were charged.

The word *competing* is emphasized because the restriction does not apply to noncompetitive situations. The supplier still has the option of offering different co-op arrangements in geographically unrelated markets.

It is interesting that in practice the Robinson-Patman Act protects retailers from unfair pricing practices induced by *other retailers* rather than by the supplier. Giant retailers have great influence because of the volume of business they control. They can and do request, or even demand, preferential treatment from the supplier in return for their very substantial business.

The Robinson-Patman Act is designed to protect competing retailers from the business disadvantage such special arrangements would create. Suppliers, their customers, and the media all have a responsibility to insure

---

* Double billing is the practice of paying media a specified sum for advertising but receiving a receipt for a greater amount. When the retailer presents this inflated document to the supplier, his co-op reimbursement will constitute an overpayment by the supplier and a resultant underpayment on his own part.

that co-op advertising arrangements do not violate the intent of the Robinson-Patman Act, and any of the three can be cited by the Federal Trade Commission if they are considered to be in violation.

The Small Retailer

While there is no particular design toward that end, it is a fact of business life that the huge retailers are the most prolific participants in supplier-run co-op advertising programs. There are exceptions, of course, but as a group the big retailers are more sophisticated marketers, merchandisers, and advertisers. They are better staffed with people more talented in areas which will assure maximum use of co-op opportunities.

Conversely, then, the smaller retailers, as a group, are the least active in co-op participation.

A SPECIAL OPPORTUNITY FOR COMMUNITY NEWSPAPERS?

Item: *Millions of allocated co-op advertising dollars go unspent annually.*

Item: *Smaller retailers are predominant among nonparticipants in co-op programs.*

Item: *Small retailers can be found in any size market but again, as a group, a great majority will be found in smaller markets.*

Item: *Smaller markets (suburban, nonurban, and rural) are best served by community newspapers—weeklies and small dailies.*

All of this suggests that the community newspaper is ideally positioned to capitalize on the linage growth potential offered by co-op advertising.

Every newspaper should have a sustained program of co-op advertising information. It should learn the precise details of every co-op program available on every item sold at retail stores in its trade area. Equally important, the newspaper advertising representative should initiate the effort to obtain co-op advertising dollars. Many retailers do not understand the importance of co-op advertising. Neither do they understand how to go about obtaining funds to which they are entitled. To wait for the retailer to initiate action, therefore, is to contribute to the mountain of unspent co-op funds.

The professional newspaper advertising person should act as an extension of the retailer's advertising operation. To the extent that his or her efforts do not constitute an intrusion, he or she should relieve the retailer of responsibilities in the co-op advertising process. By intensifying efforts in this area, the newspaper is ideally positioned to enhance everyone's business—its own, the retailer's, the distributor's, and the manufacturer's.

If a newspaper wants help in its co-op efforts, there are two organizations that work effectively in this area.

American Newspaper Representatives, Inc. (ANR) is a national advertising sales and service organization with a special program for co-op advertising. It represents more than seven thousand weekly newspapers. ANR's address is 2000 Industrial Building, Detroit, Michigan 48226.

Serving larger newspapers in a similar manner is the Newspaper Advertising Bureau (NAB), which provides its members with information, training aids, and other material helpful in obtaining co-op advertising. NAB's address is 485 Lexington Avenue, New York, New York 10017.

State and regional press associations may also offer information on co-op, and some conduct short courses on co-op for newspaper advertising personnel.

Chapter 15

ROY PAUL NELSON

The author is professor of journalism at the University of Oregon, author of the widely adopted university textbook *Design of Advertising,* a consultant in graphics design, and a former advertising agency copywriter.

"Too many creators of ads lose sight of the purpose of their ads while turning out clever copy and unusual layouts. Sometimes they are more interested in impressing their fellow ad makers and winning prizes in advertising competitions than in selling merchandise."

job than to read beautifully or to look elegant. Let's also admit that many poorly written and designed ads move merchandise and sell services at the local level despite their "artistic" flaws. The quality and price of the merchandise or service have a lot to do with how effective advertising is. Let the merchant pick out a desirable item and mark it down low enough, and no matter how bad the ad is—provided the reader can understand it—it will do a selling job.

But it is also possible to sell well and hard through well-written copy, pleasing typography, appealing artwork, and well-conceived design. What follows will define such advertising and suggest how it can be produced.

Creating Display Advertisements

by Roy Paul Nelson

With most of the newspaper's revenue coming from advertisers, it is imperative that the space they buy yield the results they seek. The responsibility for the success of local newspaper advertising rests mainly with the people in the newspaper's display advertising department. Few local advertisers have their own advertising departments or advertising agencies.

But small dailies and weeklies cannot afford to hire full-time writers or layout artists or illustrators. On most papers the people in the advertising department are "combination" people. They can write well enough and draw a little; they do these things

as a sideline to their main job of selling space.

Sometimes the creating goes on at the advertiser's place of business, with the ad sales person suggesting the headline and copy approach and sketching out the ad on a crumpled piece of paper. The actual copywriting and laying out take place back at the newspaper office, the sales person working from a price list given to him by the advertiser.

This chapter attempts to ready sales people for the creative aspects of advertising.

First of all, let's admit that it is more important for an ad to do a selling

Display Advertising

For a small newspaper, especially a weekly, there is not much national advertising. When it comes in at all, it comes from advertising agencies, ready for insertion. No creative work is necessary at the newspaper end. Classified advertising gets full attention in Chapter 16. A third kind of advertising is the subject of this chapter. Most newspaper people call it "display advertising," because it requires typographic and visual decisions and adequate space to be seen; but some still call it "local advertising," to distinguish it from national (or brand-name) advertising, or "retail advertising," because it is most often sponsored by retailers.

A retailer ad can do something a national ad can't do very well. It can bring competing brands together and not only compare them but give each a good sales pitch and then allow the reader to make up his own mind.

The advertising for each store or advertiser should be news-oriented, like the material in the columns surrounding the advertising. It's news when it's recent, interesting, important, nearby, and previously unknown. That a nationally advertised brand is now available at a store or that prices have been reduced could provide the needed element of news. A hardware store in an ad selling a brace-and-bit set tells the reader, "Brace yourself for a bit of news," and succeeds in labeling the ad as news and in getting in a pun at the same time.

This advertising has long-term consequences as well. It helps build and maintain a store's image. Using a consistent layout style for a given store, sticking with a certain kind of border, narrowing in on one typeface for headlines ad after ad, repeating a slogan—all of this helps establish that image. The challenge for the ad maker working for a newspaper is to move from image to image for the various advertisers.

Being associated with the display advertising department of a newspaper can also mean an involvement in various promotions to increase the paper's effectiveness as an advertising medium. Westchester–Rockland Newspapers, Inc., in the state of New York, has run a "Create-an-Ad" contest to get kids involved with one of its newspapers and with the stores who advertise in it. The contest starts out with promotional ads directed to the kids, inviting them to write an ad for their favorite store and offering to provide layout sheets and instructions. Prize money is pretty much covered by what the paper saves in production costs, because the young ad makers send in camera-ready copy. Cooperating merchants decide ahead of time what size ads they wish to sponsor.

The Purpose of the Advertising

Advertisers want maximum attention and response to their ads, and anything the creator of the ad can do to bring this about, within the bounds of good taste and fair play, can be considered good advertising practice.

It is too easy to denigrate the taste and directions of local advertisers. Their lack of respect for white space within an ad can be an annoyance to the designer just out of art school. Their devotion to reverses and other gimmicks can spell disaster to visual order. But you cannot blame advertisers for putting utility ahead of aesthetics. As Robert Pliskin of Benton & Bowles, Inc., said: "There are few things more beautiful to a businessman than the upward curve of a sales chart."

Too many creators of ads lose sight of the purpose of their ads while turning out clever copy and unusual layouts. Sometimes creators of ads are more interested in impressing their fellow ad makers and winning prizes in advertising competitions than in selling merchandise. Ads often are overdesigned. Speaking at a design conference, William Bernbach of Doyle Dane Bernbach pointed out that "the purpose of an ad is to persuade people to buy your product. The persuasion is in the idea and the words. And anything, however expert, that slickly detracts from that idea and those words is, for my money, bad design." The same could be said of copy. Any wording, however polished, that gets in the way of the message is bad copy.

The Advertising Theme

Every ad has a theme. The theme may be nothing more than a statement that a sale is going on. Or it may be more than that. It may go into the reason for the sale. It may grow into paragraphs of copy explaining the reason and urging consideration of the items on sale.

The theme can be expressed both through words and art. Sometimes a theme becomes elaborate, as when a retailer, claiming to be turning back prices to what they were in the good old days, uses breathless copy and quaint art and typography.

A danger is that the theme may become intrusive. The reader may notice the cleverness of the ad and miss the message.

Creating an ad involves not only settling on a theme but also writing copy, selecting artwork and type, and arranging all these advertising elements into a pleasing design.

Guidelines for Copywriters

Every ad needs some copy, if only a brief description of the product to set it apart from others. "When a retailer submits an ad with no copy, poor copy, or not enough copy, a good ad rep should advise him that his ad needs more power to do the selling job and tell him how to get the power," D. Earl Newsom writes in a column in *Publishers' Auxiliary.*

What the copywriter needs most is a knowledge of the advertiser and his products or services. A copywriter can be expected to take a turn at selling the product on the floor or, at the very least, to inspect it carefully or to use it himself. With a number of advertisers to take care of, the copywriter maintains files for each, with copy information and art references as well.

A copywriter also needs to know a lot about the people who read the advertising in his newspaper. Perhaps the ad will have to single out a segment of that audience. Audiences differ from paper to paper and from community to community. A question the copywriter asks himself is this: What is likely to motivate a given audience to buy this particular product at this particular time?

GET TO THE POINT

So far as the actual writing is concerned, listen to David Ogilvy: "Don't beat about the bush—go straight to the point." And, says the author of *Confessions of An Advertising Man,* "When you sit down to write your body copy, pretend that you are talking to the woman on your right at a dinner party. She has asked you, 'I am thinking of buying a new car. Which would you recommend?' Write your copy as if you were answering that question." This means that copy works best when written in an informal, unaffected, conversational style. You don't need great literary flair to be a good copywriter. You don't need to be clever. You do need to get right to the point.

"Direct writing outpulls cute writing by a big margin," says John Caples, author of several important books on advertising.

Nor does Caples put much stock in humor. "Avoid it. What's funny to one person isn't to millions of others." (Like many persons associated with advertising, Caples can be dogmatic. A light touch once in a while can make selling easier.)

Students of advertising are often advised to stress the benefits of the product rather than the product itself. Caples carries this a step further. Don't dwell only on the benefits, he advises; tell people what they'll miss if they don't buy the product.

ANSWER THE QUESTIONS

Most of the time in ads for retailers you have only small areas in which to say many things about each product they are selling. Your copy blocks consist of not much more than listings in paragraph form. You may even have to resort to abbreviations, as the writer of classified advertising does.

Even so, you try to answer all the Who? What? Where? When? Why? and How? questions likely to come up in the reader's mind. A potential buyer will want to know what it is, what it is made of, what problems it will solve, and why it is better than others.

For the sake of clarity, use subject-predicate sentences in preference to more complicated constructions. Use concrete terms instead of abstract ones. Write in the active rather than the passive voice whenever possible. Say "Morton's offers everyday low prices," not "Everyday low prices are offered by Morton's."

Parallel structure can be an important ally in your attempt to be clear. Parallel structure means that, whenever you make comparisons in your copy or accumulate selling points, you use the same phrase or sentence structure. For instance, a list should say "better tasting, faster acting, longer lasting" rather than "better tasting, faster acting, lasts longer."

Parallel structure can result in redundancy, but a little redundancy in your writing can often be desirable. To illustrate: The paragraph above, with its first two sentences beginning with "Parallel structure . . ." is clearer than it would be were the second sentence to begin with "It . . ."

KEEP SENTENCES SHORT

Keep your sentences short. Even when your copy block is long, consider using an occasional sentence fragment. Like this one. But sentence fragments. Can be. Overdone.

In a long copy block, use an occasional long sentence to bring variety to your writing. But be conscious always of the sentence's rhythm. It sometimes helps to read copy aloud to check its flow.

Rhythm helps carry the reader along. Transitions help, too. Make each sentence dependent upon the sentence before. The transition can be a matter of content. Or it can be mechanical, as when somewhere in the sentences you use transitional words and phrases like "but," "however," "yes," "of course," and "more than that." The paragraph you are now reading makes use of "too" and "or" as transitions.

To test your transitions, remove a sentence from the middle of the copy and see if the removal makes any difference to the flow. If there is no difference, it could mean your transition at that point is faulty.

Pay attention to grammar and usage. Sometimes an advertising person excuses grammatical errors by saying, "That's the way people talk." But often the error can be traced to ignorance on the part of the copywriter. The news side of the paper maintains a copy desk to catch the errors reporters make, but the advertising department typically works more informally. Perhaps on every newspaper there should be a copyeditor watching over all the display advertising.

HOW LONG SHOULD COPY BE?

Advertising copy doesn't always have to be short. Some products, some stores need lots of selling. "We've proven over and over again that an interested consumer can be persuaded to read screeds of copy—*if it is artfully composed and laid out,*" says Robert Jenkins, creative director of Ogilvy & Mather, Inc.

Ogilvy & Mather once placed in newspapers a double-page ad that carried 5,000 words. The client was U. S. Trust. The ad dealt with estate management ("How to Defend Against Bad Luck, Taxes and Family Fights Long After You Die") and brought many inquiries. The agency ran a shorter version of the ad, and it brought in as many responses, but the responses were not of the same quality as responses from the longer ad.

It seems reasonable to conclude that institutional advertising and, at the national level, automobile and major appliance advertising deserve lots of copy. Whenever a reader is to think deep thoughts or spend large sums of money, he needs convincing and reassurance. But for most local newspaper advertising, whether it is to sell a store's image or a line of merchandise, short copy should be the rule. The typical newspaper reader does not have the time to spend with advertising that a magazine reader has.

Besides, in many cases national advertising has already done the selling job for the product. It is the job of the local newspaper ad to point the reader to the store where the product can be purchased and to stress prices.

BREAK UP LONG COPY

When copy does run long, you will want to break it into "takes," using subheads, initial letters, small pieces of art, or just some extra spacing.

Use short paragraphs as much as possible, and occasionally use a single-sentence paragraph.

Or even a sentence-fragment paragraph.

HEADLINES ATTRACT READERS

"Come up with a good headline, and you're almost sure to have a good ad," says John Caples, who wrote that famous "They Laughed When I Sat Down at the Piano" ad.

As its primary job, the headline attracts the reader to the ad. It also singles out the likely prospect from the unlikely one.

Unlike the headline for a news story, the advertising headline follows no arbitrary set of rules as to length, count, tense, or grammatical construction. Anything from a mere label to a complete sentence can do the job.

The headline need not summarize the copy. It can act as the copy's first sentence. It can ask a question, although question headlines too often represent the easy way out for the copywriter.

Your ad can contain any number of headlines scattered throughout the space. In that kind of an ad, the additional headlines ordinarily would be set in a smaller size.

SINGLE LINE BEST. Where possible you will want to keep your main headline to a single line. If you must segment the headline, at least keep the lines in a single face to make the jumps easier for the reader. And pay more attention to the logic of the segments than to their length. For instance:

*Is the precut
house a bargain?*

would read better if it were arranged

*Is the precut house
a bargain?*

The tie between headline and copy or art should be obvious. Often the art dramatizes what is said in the headline. The San Francisco Convention & Visitors Bureau, in an ad directed to potential visitors, used a photograph of a busy, hilly, cable-car street. Taken with a telescopic lens, the photograph seemed to put cars and buildings right on top of cars in the foreground. The headline read: "San Francisco Isn't as Steep as It Looks." The copy listed several things a person could do for nominal fees and concluded with this line: "Now, what's so steep about that?"

The headline often serves as a slogan for the ad. As such it can be used over and over again. When the AP Parts Co. created advertising for service stations to make them more active in the muffler installation business (and to get them to sell more AP parts), it called each sponsoring station "The Original Muffler Shop," a dig at Midas and others who had cut into the market. (In 1978, when the campaign was launched, service stations accounted for less than 15 percent of the replacement-muffler business. Once they had dominated the market.)

AVOID CUTENESS. When you write your headline, pay particular attention to its rhythm. The rhythm will help the reader remember the headline. But avoid cuteness in your headline. And remember that a little alliteration goes a long way. Even puns can be overdone.

You have a number of possibilities to consider: headlines that simply tell what a product will do, headlines that take off on popular expressions or songs, headlines that make strong use of parallel structure, headlines that cause the reader to do a double take, headlines that carry double meanings. And that's just a start.

When you use a double-meaning headline, make sure both meanings are clear and appropriate to the product or store. "We Hear You Need a Muffler," says a headline for one of the ads sponsored by service stations. It is a good headline because it suggests that word has gotten around that the reader does need a muffler; and it also suggests that the noise from his car has been noticed.

Punctuation in headlines can be a problem. Copywriters and designers often leave off the question mark in a question headline. And the apostrophe is often missing, too, as in "mens clothing" for "men's clothing." "Mens" is never correct.

Advertising Clichés

Unfortunately, retail advertising wallows in clichés: sales that are "Sell-a-Brations," "Doorbusters," and "Crazy Daze," to name a few, with copy peppered by exclamation marks. What's wrong with that always-welcome word "Sale"?

Layout has its clichés, too: among them, tipped photographs, photographed faces with small cartoon bodies, letters cut out of photographs, boxes made with wavy or otherwise decorated lines, and big dots in front of each line in a list of product advantages.

Naturally, any cliché can be used to advantage occasionally. That it is a cliché suggests that it worked well enough at the beginning. But by now readers are probably tired of it.

You can't avoid some clichés. The car dealer who sells "pre-owned" rather than "used" vehicles probably won't be much moved by your suggestion that he use the more straightforward word. And what merchant would be so heartless that he would not want to "pass the savings on to you"?

Visualizing the Ad

The nature of the advertiser and his product determines the style and approach of the ad. When you make an effort to tailor each ad to the advertiser, you not only serve the advertiser better but you also avoid a sameness in your newspaper's advertising.

Ad people cannot agree as to which comes first in creating an ad, the words or the pictures. Some ads clearly are verbal; the art merely dramatizes what the copywriter says. Other ads are visual; the words help explain the art. Many retail ads belong in the latter category. Photography or drawings capture the reader's attention and tell him most of what he needs to know. All he needs to do then is hunt down the sponsor's name, which, by the way, can appear as a signature in more than one place in the ad.

Whether an ad is primarily copy or primarily art, and whether the ad is nicely designed or not, a certain amount of visualization must go on as the ad is created. What kind of art should be used? What should be the focus? Does it give strong direction? How should it be cropped?

And what about the art in context? How should all the elements in the ad be arranged?

That leads us to the subject of layout.

Levels of Layout

You have four levels of layout to consider.

At the lowest level you have the *thumbnail,* which is no more than a doodle, drawn in a size not much bigger than a postage stamp, but in proportion to the ad as it is to appear in print. The thumbnail represents a sort of shorthand to record your idea of how the ad might look. The thumbnail is for your own eyes only.

You work at first in a small size, and you work roughly, in order to save time. Perhaps you do several thumbnails. When one strikes your fancy, you resketch the ad a little more carefully, in its correct size. You are entering the rough layout stage.

The *rough layout* helps you round out your thinking and serves as a guide to the typesetter or production department. At this stage, the copy is typed on a separate piece of paper and keyed to the layout. The copy shown on the layout consists merely of ruled lines to approximate the look of copy. The layout may be shown to the client for his approval, provided he understands it is only rough and knows how to visualize it.

For fussy advertisers who need to see exactly how the ad will look, you would do a *comprehensive.* Or maybe you would do one for a potential advertiser on speculation, with the

thought of winning him over to your paper. A comprehensive requires the services of an artist with considerable ability, one who is able to duplicate typefaces accurately and render drawings that look like real photographs. Comprehensives are not much of a factor on a small paper—or even on a big paper. Deadlines are too tight and time too precious.

The highest level of layout is the *pasteup,* sometimes called the "mechanical" or "camera-ready copy." At this stage, reproductions of the type and photocopies of the art are pasted—or "waxed"—into place exactly as the material is to appear in print.

Your paper will make available to you specially gridded layout sheets for both rough layouts and pasteups. At the pasteup stage you would use a light table and a T-square and triangle as well as other pasteup tools.

Principles of Design

While advertising designers and layout artists may not be completely aware of them, principles of design dictate their decisions as to where to place the various elements in their ads. The principles apply to any activity that requires visual decisions. They work as well for architects, painters, and flower

arrangers as for persons who design printed pages and the ads upon them.

While the principles are universal, they are not easily stated. One artist's list of them might differ markedly from another's. Here is one version you might find useful in creating advertisements for your newspaper.

THE AD SHOULD LOOK BALANCED. Were you to draw a line down through the center of the ad, one side would look as heavy as the other. Every item you put into an ad has an optical weight; the idea is to adjust the placement of these weights to achieve a balance.

That is not to say that the two sides of the ad have to duplicate each other. You do not have to center everything, although that is one approach you can use. You can, instead, put most of your art on one side and most of your copy on the other. When you center everything in the ad, you achieve *formal* balance. When you pursue the second course, you achieve *informal* balance. An informally balanced ad can look just as balanced as a formally balanced ad. And it can look a good deal more lively. Most retail advertising is informally balanced.

It is not absolutely necessary that the ad look balanced. The tension created in an unbalanced ad can give the ad attention it might otherwise miss.

Anyway, new designers tend to give too much attention to balance.

FIGURE 15–1 Thumbnail sketches show formal (left) and informal balance (right).

The balance will come naturally enough as you design your ads. Of the several design principles listed here, balance is probably least important.

THE AD SHOULD CONTROL THE MOVEMENT OF THE READER'S EYE.

Items should be arranged in such a way that the reader notices them in exactly the order the ad maker wants. Ordinarily, in a printed piece, the reader starts at the top left and moves across to the top right, then down to the bottom of the ad. You can take advantage of this by putting down your ad elements one by one in the path of that travel. But if all designers took so easy a way out, all ads would look the same, and advertising design would become a sterile art.

It turns out that readers not only move from left to right and top to bottom but also from big to little, dark to light, color to noncolor, unusual shape to usual shape. So it is possible to reverse the normal left-to-right, top-to-bottom eye travel in an ad. You can start the reader off in a lower corner of the ad and move him up and to the left.

If all else fails, you can number the elements. The reader will go from your 1 to your 2 and then on to your 3 no matter where you place them in the ad.

Much of the time, especially in retail advertising, the order in which the reader takes in the items is not really important. So this principle is not overly important, either.

Now to get to four other principles, each of them vital to your ad's success.

THE AD SHOULD BE PLEASINGLY PROPORTIONED.

The items within the ad should divide the available space into units that interest the reader. Generally speaking, such units should be uneven. For instance, you would have more pleasing proportions in an ad that was mostly art or mostly copy than in an ad that was exactly half art, half copy.

A square, with its equal dimensions, is not quite as interesting as a rectangle; hence, the typical photograph in an ad is either a vertical rectangle or a horizontal rectangle, not a square. The ad itself is likely to be wider than it is deep or deeper than it is wide.

The space between art and headline should be different from the space between headline and body copy. This is not to say that you shouldn't be consistent in some of your spacing. For instance, in an ad with many headlines and blocks of copy, the space between headline and body copy should, under most circumstances, be the same throughout the ad. And spacing between lines in a block of copy would always be consistent, of course.

You take your inspiration for pleasing proportions from nature. Consider the tree and its branches. If the tree's branches matched in diameter the tree's trunk, you would have a pretty ugly specimen in your yard.

THE AD SHOULD HAVE ONE MAIN AREA OF EMPHASIS.

Put another way, there should be marked contrast between one item in the ad—probably a piece of art—and the remainder of the ad. Under most circumstances, primary emphasis should not spread to two items or more. Typically, there would be one large item in the ad, a medium-size one (or maybe several), and a small one (or maybe several). The large item, of course, would carry the emphasis.

The item being emphasized first captures the reader's attention, then presumably holds it for a while until he wanders over to the other items featured.

Many readers will see only the headline and the emphasized item. The ad should be designed to take care of those readers as well as readers who have the time to wander over to the less spectacular items and the smaller print.

THE AD SHOULD HAVE A UNIFIED FEEL.

Not only should your ad feature related items for sale; it should also use related typefaces and pieces of art to do the selling job. Instead of using many different typefaces, you would use one or two, and get your variety through different sizes and weights. Ideally, you would use only photographs or only drawings done in the same style for your illustrations.

You would have to temper the above advice with practical considerations. How big a variety of sizes and weights of typefaces does the printer

FIGURE 15–2 This 3-inch by 5½-inch ad, with its no-nonsense headline and just a few words of copy, tells enough to get people into an art supply store. Only one representative product is shown. Note that the art and headline type appear to use the same thick and thin strokes. An optical axis at the left helps unite the copy with the art. *Reprinted courtesy of Art Media, Portland, and the Portland* Oregonian. *Ad design by Michael Kelley.*

make available to you? How adequately can one source of art meet the ad's needs? For many ads, probably, you would end up using several faces; and you would gather art from ready sources, however disparate. But the idea of unity should be a starting point.

THE AD SHOULD BE SIMPLIFIED.

Unless the ad is for a discount store or a store announcing a clearance sale, you want to avoid a hodgepodge. This does not mean you must avoid crowding. A crowded look may be necessary to say "bargain." But even in a crowded ad you can simplify. You can organize items into sections and give those sections headings. You want to make things as easy as possible for the reader.

You can organize the many pieces of art in a crowded ad into, say, three main areas. The reader can deal better with three large visuals than with innumerable ones that are scattered all over the place.

You may often find reasons—good reasons—to ignore these principles. And you will probably discover that it is impossible to follow all of them in any one ad. For instance, perfect unity in an ad could destroy the emphasis you want.

But the principles are at least worth considering whenever you sit down at the drawing table. You might want to pick one of them and give it special prominence in an ad. For instance, "balance" might be the ad's theme. You would make sure the ad itself was well balanced. If your theme were "unity," you would make a special effort to see that each item in the ad worked harmoniously with the others.

FIGURE 15–3 Copy for this 4½-inch by 7-inch ad is organized into three columns separated by column rules. While the editorial side has dropped column rules, the advertising side has picked them up. Typical of many well-designed ads, this one has three visual thrusts: the headline at the top, the small illustration at the right, and the combination illustration-signature-price at the bottom. *Reprinted courtesy of the Eugene (Oregon) Register-Guard.*

Wake up, Eugene!

Big Breakfast Special, $1.45

The Big Breakfast Special is served Daily from 6:30 a.m. to 11 a.m.
Here's what you get:
1 large egg, fixed in an individual skillet just the way you like it.
2 sizzling slices of bacon.
2 of our INNcredible

Buttermilk pancakes with whipped butter and a carousel of 6 delectable syrups.

Great coffee, free refills.

At Village Inn, we leave the hot pot on your table for refills. So you get all the coffee you want, at no extra charge.

$1.45

Quick service that will get you to your desk on time and a hearty, nourishing breakfast - what a way to start your day!

Village Inn
Pancake House Restaurant

1127 Valley River Dr.

Hours: Sunday and Monday 6:30 to 10 p.m.; Tuesday through Thursday 6:30 a.m. to 12 midnight; Friday and Saturday 6:30 a.m. to 2:30 a.m.

The Ad in Place

The ad may look quite different in place in the newspaper from what it was as a rough or even a comprehensive. What surrounds the ad affects its impact.

To keep ads separate, the ad maker at the newspaper often uses line or bar borders. And the makeup person arranges the ads on a page into a sort of half triangle in order to let at least one side of every ad touch editorial matter. Advertisers seem to think this gives their ads a better chance to be read. And the smaller ads go at the tops of the pages.

Sometimes, to get better attention, advertisers ask for L-shaped ads in preference to ordinary rectangles. Or they ask for narrow, deep ads. Any of these unusual shapes requires special designing skill to keep elements together.

Typography

Not many years ago, when newspapers were mostly letterpress-printed and when type was set hot on linotype machines and through the Ludlow process, picking out a typeface for an ad was a relatively simple matter—you had perhaps no more than a dozen possibilities for headlines. Today, with phototypesetting and dry-transfer letters, you actually have thousands of typefaces to choose from.

With so many typefaces around, you have a good chance of choosing one that is entirely appropriate to the store, or to the items sold, or to the theme of the ad. You have thin, delicate faces for fashion ads and fat, heavy faces and slab serifs for ads for construction companies. Of course these considerations would apply only to the headlines. You would not necessarily try to pick an "appropriate" type for the body copy. Your only goal here is to make reading as easy as possible for the reader.

To make body copy readable, you set it as large as possible, almost never smaller than 10 points. You also put a point or two of leading between lines.

As for copy line length, you should remember that the longer the line, the harder it is to read. Don't let your copy block get any wider than 40 lowercase characters.

While you would use a great variety of types for the various ads in the paper, you would want to limit yourself to only a couple of faces within a given ad to give your ad a unified feel. Where possible, use only one face for the headline and one for the body copy in any ad, using different sizes and weights of the faces for variety.

You may be tempted to use all caps for your headlines, but often caps-and-lowercase or all lowercase works better. You can still use a large version of the type when you use all lowercase. You get all the impact of capitals, and your headline is more readable. Tests show that lowercase letters are easier to read than capitals, even in display faces. Of course, when you use an all-lowercase headline, you begin the first word—and any proper names—with a cap, just as in a regular sentence. You may drop the period in a one-sentence headline; otherwise punctuate just as you would in the body copy.

It may help to review here the several basic categories of type from the standpoint of their design.

ROMAN TYPE. While "roman" to a printer may mean any type that is upright (as opposed to italic—or slanting—faces), the term is used here to designate any type that is built of thick and thin strokes with short cross-strokes (serifs) at the terminals. Most type used on the editorial side, at least in body-copy sizes, is roman. You can subdivide roman types into old style, traditional or transitional, and modern,

customers
SALE!
FREE
Shop
ELECTRIC

FIGURE 15–4 Examples of the five basic classes of type, taken from advertising headlines in newspapers. From the top: roman, sans serif, slab serif, script, and ornamental.

but these distinctions are too complicated to go into here. (See the chapter, "Working with Type," in *The Design of Advertising*.)

SANS SERIF TYPE. Sometimes called "gothic," this type features strokes of equal thickness with no serifs at the terminals. Sans serif types are favorites with newspaper advertisers, both for headlines and body copy, because they reproduce so well, and in their bold forms they speak with such power.

SLAB SERIF TYPE. When you take a sans serif with its strong, even strokes and *add* serifs to the terminals, you have a slab serif or square serif type. Slab serif makes a good headline face because the letters are so easy to make out, even from a distance.

SCRIPTS. The script faces are designed to look like handwriting. They have only limited use in advertising, and none at all in body-copy sizes.

ORNAMENTAL TYPES. For special effects in headlines, you have all kinds of oddball faces to choose from, especially in dry-transfer letter form. You can get type that looks as though it were built out of driftwood, paper clips, icicles, and almost anything else you can think of. Obviously, these

faces, unreadable in large doses, should show up only occasionally in your advertising.

Each of these categories breaks down into various families of type. If you want further descriptions, you can consult any of the hundreds of books available on typography and letter form. And your own organization no doubt publishes a type specimen book of faces immediately available to you. To appreciate fully the variety of faces available in dry-transfer form, consult *Dry Faces,* a book published by Art Direction Book Company, New York. It catalogs one thousand typefaces available from the manufacturers of dry-transfer letters.

Some Hints on Typesetting

Whether you set your own type, as with dry-transfer letters, or have it set on hot-type or cold-type machines, you should be aware of trends in typesetting.

In headlines, you'll notice, the trend is toward tight setting, if not in newspaper advertising at least in magazine advertising. This is more than a designer's affectation. Tight setting means more words per line. It also means that the reader at a glance can take in phrases rather than only words or letters. Tight setting means closing up the space not only between letters but also between words. The space between words in a headline should be no more than the average width of a lowercase letter in that typesize.

In body copy, the trend is toward larger faces and more leading between lines. Do not crowd your body copy. Make it inviting to the reader. Do not regard a block of body copy merely as a pattern for your ad. Sometimes the whole ad can be set in a headline-size face.

It is not necessary to justify the right-hand margin of your body copy. The value of unjustified lines lies in the fact that they allow equal spacing between words. The typesetter doesn't have to crowd words together or widely space them in order to make the lines come out even at the right. And you have fewer hyphens at the ends of lines.

Photographs or Drawings?

Many retail advertising persons will tell you that the most important and difficult step in layout is choosing the illustrations. Every ad, large or small, has a better chance of attracting readers with an illustration, and the time spent finding the right art is time well spent. Ads that have the proper illustrations seem to fall into place naturally. If the art is wrong, you may never get the design you really want.

The major illustration has several functions that make it important, among them:

- It may offer the best hope of attracting attention to the ad in the midst of other ads and editorial material.

- It may carry much of the selling message if it illustrates the theme or major benefit of your ad.

- It will have strong direction and lead readers into other elements of the ad.

A large, clear illustration can sometimes make an ad successful even though other elements are weak. Offset printing makes large illustrations easy to reproduce.

Whether you use photographs or drawings depends upon costs, availability, reproduction quality, nature of the product advertised, nature of the intended audience, believability required, and other factors. The reader does tend to believe a photograph more than a drawing. With better halftone reproduction available now on offset newspapers, some big advertisers are using big photographs in preference to drawings.

In a small town, it is probably easier to get good photography for an ad than good custom artwork when your stock art is not adequate.

But a drawing can present detail more clearly than a photograph can. And it can be reproduced in line rather than in halftone, giving you more crispness. A wash drawing (which requires halftone reproduction), used in a fashion ad, has the advantage over a photograph in that the reader can imagine herself in place of the vaguely sketched model.

STOCK ART

For most newspapers, most of the time, finished art must come from the stock art services (called "mat" services when newspapers were primarily letterpress). Even the big dailies rely mostly on stock art service rather than on their own staff artists.

You have several services to choose from; *Editor & Publisher International Year Book* offers a current list. You pay for the service usually on the basis of your circulation.

Even the weeklies find that one service is not enough. The Hillsboro (Oregon) *Argus,* a 13,300-circulation semiweekly, uses three of them. The paper has an advertising staff of four full-timers and two part-timers to handle the hundred ads per issue.

Some of the services offer, in addition to art in several sizes, ads that are complete, with art, headlines, and copy in place. All you have to do is to put in the local advertiser's name at the bottom. But, time permitting, you will find your work as an ad maker more satisfying when you use such ads only as a starting point. You can quite easily move things about, crop the art, and better tailor the ad to the local advertiser's needs.

All stock art can be edited by cropping or by piecing items together. An artist on the staff can adapt the art and even change expressions on faces and other details.

Even when you have to depend on stock art, you can create a "house style" for a regular advertiser who wants to make all his ads look related. You can do this through unique arrangements of the art and through use of special borders and exclusive typefaces for headlines. A consistent style adopted for any one advertiser gives his ads a cumulative effect they would

not otherwise have. Perhaps in a period when all the other advertisers are going for big typefaces, lots of reverses, and plenty of blackness, you would work up a style for a given advertiser that depended on smaller typefaces and more white space. The contrast would make his ads stand out.

Sometimes the advertiser supplies the art, which he has received from the manufacturer. Occasionally he'll offer you a piece done by his niece or someone who, the advertiser thinks, has a certain flair for drawing.

The test of any piece of art you pick up has to be: How well will it reproduce? The trouble with most amateur artists is that they do not understand the mechanics of art reproduction. Their illustrations are often done in weak lines or tones that fade out when negatives and plates are made.

Color

Studies on the use of color in newspaper advertising show that color dramatically increases the effectiveness. One of the reasons is that color is still something of a novelty in newspaper advertising, and the contrast with plain black-and-white ads startles the reader. Another reason is that color can better define the product. And with the replacement of letterpress with offset printing, producing good color has become less of a problem.

You have available two kinds of color: process color, which gives you the full range and makes possible the reproduction of color photography; and spot or flat color, which gives you one or more solid or screened colors through mechanical means. Spot or flat color, which is cheaper than process color, usually means one color in addition to black, but it can mean several colors. The Sunday comic sections with their multiple colors make use of spot or flat color, not process color.

It is a mistake to think of color after the ad is designed. Deciding at the last minute to run one of the headlines in color and to throw a screened version of the color behind a block of copy does not make adequate use of this valuable tool. How color is to be used should be decided at the time the theme of the ad is developed.

Production

Production is the final phase of advertising preparation, where type is set, proofing is done, art is converted to a form that will reproduce, reproduction proofs are pasted into place, and plates are made for printing.

The technological revolution has hit the advertising department just as it has hit the newsroom. For instance, offset lithography has replaced letterpress as the most popular printing process. This calls for finished rather than rough pasteups at the end of the creative process; and it means cold-type rather than hot-type composition.

Before the coming of the linotype machine, it used to take a printer an hour to set 1,200 characters. Now, with computer-generated phototypesetters, it is possible to set 1,000 characters or more *per second.*

There are more recent innovations. There are now machines that compose art, text, and rules instantly on a visual display screen. Elements can be rearranged on the screen. Copy and layout can be stored for later recall.

An advantage of the new technology is that one person can assume responsibility for layout, markup, and pasteup, eliminating the possibility of errors resulting from multiple handling.

But as has been said many times, the new machinery, wherever it is used, is only as good as its operators and users make it. The established principles of clear writing and orderly presentation still apply.

Chapter 16

CAL TREMBLAY

The author is vice president of Harte-Hanks Communications, Inc., and corporate director of classified advertising for the company.

"Classified advertising, by its very nature, is the real strength of the newspaper industry. Not only is it a tremendous revenue producer, but it also creates readership greater than that found in our editorial columns. The success of classified is normally a leading indicator of the overall success of the entire operation of a newspaper."

Classified Advertising

by Cal Tremblay

Classified advertising has been called the oldest form of advertising. The use of small personal-type ads has been traced all the way back to ancient Egypt. Notices dealing with lost and found items closely resembling our modern day "want ads" have been found there on papyrus sheets. It is believed that the earliest advertisement of any kind still preserved in its original form is a notice on a papyrus sheet seeking to locate a runaway slave. It may be 3,200 years old.

In both Egypt and ancient Babylon, barkers and criers were used to shout messages of items for sale and the arrival of ships with new cargoes. Because many people could not read, the change from oral to written messages was slow.

The invention of printing from movable type by Johann Gutenberg about 1450 in Germany brought changes in all printed communication, including advertising. In 1477, a poster resembling a display advertisement appeared in London, and in 1625 the first newspaper advertisement was noted on the back page of a London newspaper. Small ads became prevalent in the 18th century.

America saw its first person-to-person ads with the appearance of the Boston *News-Letter* in 1704. The newspaper contained notices of sales or rentals of houses, farms, shops, and even vessels.

It was in the 1830's, however, that the real "want" ads made their appearance. Some publishers had considered the small ads a bother and had even refused to accept them, but Benjamin Day of the New York *Sun* gathered the ads and placed them in one section of his newspaper which he called "Wants." He charged 50 cents for each ad. James Gordon Bennett followed shortly afterward with a "Personals" column in the New York *Herald.*

The idea of want ad pages spread rapidly to other newspapers, and with this growth came a demand to have the small ads placed in classifications so they could be located more easily. Homes were listed under "Homes for Sale," and so on. Many newspapers today use more than a hundred classifications. With this development came a name change from the "Want Ads" section to the "Classified Advertising" section.

By the twentieth century, commercial advertisers had begun to take advantage of the classified section. The section had become truly the "people's marketplace," and the readership of millions of individuals who had bought and sold through classified ads became a ready-made market for business firms. Many small firms used classified ads because they could not afford larger display ads.

National Classified

Another major type of classified advertising is "national" classified. National advertising can be described in a number of ways and has different characteristics. Basically, it is advertising placed by an advertising agency and is commissionable. Fifteen percent of the cost is paid to recognized ad agencies, and some papers pay another two percent for prompt payment (ten, fifteen, or twenty days from date of invoice). The "national" rate is usually higher than the local rate because of the commission involved, although many newspapers today have one rate for all display advertising, regardless of its source.

Why are newspapers willing to pay these commissions? For one thing, copy coming from an agency is usually "camera-ready" and requires very little preparation on the part of the newspaper. What's more, agencies provide expertise. Many specialize in one certain type of advertising and its related fields. An example would be financial advertising, created for banks, savings and loan associations, brokerage houses, loan companies, financial planning consultants, leasing firms, mortgage companies, etc.

Agencies act as agents for the accounts they control. They not only place the advertising in the various media—newspaper, television, radio, magazines, outdoor—but they also plan the advertising campaigns and do all the advertising layouts, artwork, billing, and other administrative tasks. Some of the larger national and international agencies specialize in areas such as automotive, employment, or real estate advertising, while others will handle a mixture of accounts.

Organization

Classified operations may range all the way from the large metro or suburban daily with a bank of video display terminals to the small-town operation in which any individual in the front office, including the publisher, may handle want ads.

In spite of the differences that may exist in size, the classified department organization in most operations larger than a small weekly may be quite similar. Fig. 16–1 shows the functions

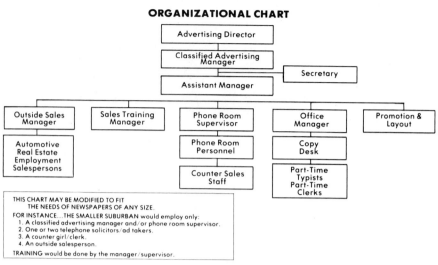

FIGURE 16–1 This personnel organization chart is flexible enough that it can be adapted to classified advertising departments of varying sizes.

of a department; the size of the newspaper usually determines the number of functions performed in the department.

Automotive advertising usually constitutes the bulk of the linage for outside sales people. In many newspapers the automotive sales division is broken away from both classified and display advertising and operates as a separate department. The automotive sales people may be permitted to place automotive advertising in the classified section or elsewhere in the newspaper, at a special automotive advertising rate. This is a wise move for the newspapers, as it eliminates duplication of sales people's efforts. It also eliminates competition between the departments. The accounts benefit, too, in that they do not have to spend time meeting with two sales people from the paper.

The three other largest areas for outside sales are employment, real estate, and merchandise for sale (mostly retailers). Outside sales representatives have assigned territories or accounts so they do not duplicate effort.

THE PHONE ROOMS

Some classified advertising departments on daily newspapers have phone rooms. Sales people sit at desks and solicit advertising by telephone. Usually a phone room is divided into two sections, voluntary sales and commercial sales. Voluntary sales personnel spend the bulk of their day taking calls (called in voluntarily) from private individuals wanting to sell small items owned by them, such as furniture, cameras, boats, cars, pets, and livestock. They must also follow up on their "expiration" or "call-back" file. The day the ad is expiring, the voluntary sales person calls the advertiser to ask if they have sold their advertised items. If so, the sales representative expresses happiness for their success; if not, the sales rep then helps the customer reword the ad or perhaps suggests a price change and then attempts to sell another run. Making call-backs is a very important procedure, as it creates satisfied customers who will call again when they have something to sell.

The commercial phone room person has assigned and contract accounts that are contacted on a regular basis—daily, three times a week, weekly, monthly, or quarterly. These business accounts place their advertising by telephone and usually change copy on a regular basis. The telephone sales person may suggest copy. Accounts are always handled by the same person, assuring them of dependable service.

The phone room supervisor must be present at all times to help with problems that crop up in the daily routine—adjustment on errors, advertising rate questions, policy questions, credit problems, and so on. The phone room supervisor must be even-tempered, intelligent, friendly, and happy if the day is to run smoothly. This supervisor is probably the most important person in your sales department.

It is important that the ad takers are kept busy, as the supervisor's performance goal bonus is usually based on the volume of advertising revenue generated by the entire team.

The smaller suburban daily or weekly newspaper (5,000 to 15,000 circulation) will, of course, have a scaled down version of this organization structure.

The daily suburban paper will usually have a classified advertising manager who reports to the advertising manager or director. Depending on the circulation of the newspaper, there will be one to four telephone ad takers. In many cases additional phone persons will work part-time on peak volume days. There will also be a full-time classified advertising clerk who will mark the expiring ads out of the paper for the composing room. This clerk will coordinate getting copy between the composing room for makeup and the accounting department for billing, do all the filing, take complaints, and do the myriad things that are required in a daily operation.

The suburban daily will very likely have one outside sales person who will create and pick up copy from accounts. The outside sales person usually works on commission, while the inside sales persons are usually paid a straight salary with perhaps an incentive for special sales promotions.

Many small weeklies have people on their staffs who wear more than one hat. The bookkeeper or the staff writers may double as ad takers. The smaller weeklies sometimes do not bill classified ads—payment is required when the ad is ordered or before it runs in the paper. Regardless of how the ads are placed, every newspaper, large and small, runs classified advertising.

Training Is Vital

Classified sales training is a vital function of a well-run department. Too often a new employee is asked to start selling without the benefit of any training. A rate card and a policy manual do not constitute a formal training program.

The person or persons responsible for the training program must hold regular classes for telephone sales and for outside sales. Sales people must be trained and retrained in many areas such as:

- How to handle objections

- The up-to-date statistics of your publication—circulation, historical development, total jobs and growth, newspaper organization, policy, production, editorial, etc.

- How to make a "cold" call

- How to write good ad copy

- Call-backs

- The benefits of multiple insertions

- Knowledge of all classified order forms used in the department and which to use when

- General knowledge of all steps of ad placement, from the original order to publication

Training sessions should not be more than an hour in length, unless it is a class of sales people who are new to classified ad sales. An hour when telephone traffic is relatively light is the best time. It is wise to involve your people in the sales training sessions—let the trainee do all the talking. Set up mock calls (telephone company will supply the equipment) and use a critique method involving each sales person.

Design a sales training program that fits your operation. You can get lots of help from the classified division of the Newspaper Advertising Bureau and from the several classified advertising services throughout the country. Change the program regularly to keep it timely. Hold meetings on a regular schedule to keep your sales people informed and fresh, and check with other newspapers to get new and different ideas. Classified advertising managers are always ready and willing to help each other.

Advanced training can be done in special groups or individually to increase verbal and written communications skills. The staffers who work with national classified accounts must be able to make professional presenta-

tions. This agency-type presentation differs widely from the presentations made to regular commercial accounts.

Training should be done on any special promotions the department is involved in. These special promotions are usually seasonal.

The counter sales staff requires people who must be carefully selected and trained, as they will represent the newspaper in daily meetings with the public. Many advertisers come personally to the office to place their advertising, and the counter staff is their only contact with the paper; thus, the image of your product is directly related to how professionally the walk-in trade is handled. The newspaper that has a good readership and shows the most interest in helping advertisers with helpful suggestions will attract the most advertisements.

Although the real job of the counter staff is to sell classified advertising, they must also be able to answer a variety of questions, sell back copies of the newspaper, mail out replies to box numbers, take complaints, and handle the many other things that the public demands. They must be very patient, professional, and helpful.

Unfortunately, training programs on the suburban daily or the small weekly newspaper are not always as well organized as they should be for best results. In many instances, training consists of sitting beside a telephone sales person and listening and watching. The sales person will teach the beginner how to use the classified forms and how to read a rate card. As there is seldom time during the day to take the ad takers away from the telephones, a breakfast or dinner meeting often is used as a training session. It is a good idea to have your advertising policies and all pertinent sales information available in written form for new personnel to read.

Many Kinds of Rates

Rate cards will vary from one publishing company to the next, but all will emphasize the multiple-insertion rate. There will be numerous types of rates:

voluntary/transient rate, national rate, bulk rate, contract rate, monthly rate, family want-ad rate, co-op rate, zoned advertising rates, and even more.

A well-structured rate schedule can encourage an advertiser to run his ad for a longer period of time. For example, for a "one-time" classified ad you might pay $1.62 a line, but if you ordered the same ad repeated seven or ten times, the "sliding scale" reduces the rate to only 84¢ a line.

The privilege of canceling when the item has been sold is always extended, and the advertiser is only billed for the advertising he has used. Thus, the advertiser uses enough advertising to sell his items, yet he earns a better rate for multiple insertions; he is happy, and the newspaper has made a profit. A "one-time" ad is not profitable, as the composing room costs of setting the ad are not earned back by the newspaper until after the second or third run. For this reason, the one-time rate is the highest rate on the voluntary card.

The contract rate card reflects the type of advertising done by a commercial firm. The advertiser may change his advertising as often as he desires, he may run several ads daily or weekly in different or identical classifications, or he may run just a "rate holder." The rate holder is a small institutional ad which fulfills the obligations of the contract he has signed and ensures that he will still get the lowest rate on the larger ads he runs at other times. The advertising linage is totaled for the month and billed at the earned rate; 500 lines total for the month would be billed at 75¢ a line for a total bill of $375.00.

Contract advertisers choose certain days of the week to run the most linage, usually weekends (Saturday and Sunday) or a day when the newspaper offers more circulation; for example, through the inclusion of a TMC (total market coverage) shopper. This creates highs and lows which are always a problem for the production department.

If a newspaper does have additional circulation on certain days of the week, or a TMC program, these additional shoppers or zoned editions are usually priced at a pickup rate which is a fraction of the advertising rate charged for the daily newspaper.

RATES LOWEST FOR INDIVIDUALS

The lowest classified ad rate on your card should be designated for the private party or "voluntary" advertiser. This advertising is generated by individuals with a special need to sell a second-hand car, used furniture, pets, whatever. This advertising creates your

FIGURE 16–2 A typical classified rate card will show a wide variety of rates. *Reprinted courtesy of the South Bay (California) Bay Breeze.*

CONTRACT RATES

Less than	DAILY BREEZE	NEWS PILOT	COMBINATION (BOTH PAPERS)	SUNDAY
250 lines, per line	59½¢	30¢	79½¢	72¢
250 lines, per line	59¢	29¢	77½¢	71¢
500 lines, per line	58¢	28¢	75½¢	68½¢
1,000 lines, per line	56¢	26¢	73½¢	66½¢
1,500 lines, per line	55¢	24½¢	72½¢	65¢
2,000 lines, per line	52½¢	21½¢	70¢	61¢
3,500 lines, per line	51½¢	20½¢	67¢	60¢
5,000 lines, per line	48½¢	18½¢	64¢	55½¢
7,500 lines, per line	46½¢	18¢	62¢	53¢
10,000 lines, per line	43¢	17½¢	57¢	51¢
15,000 lines, per line	42¢	17½¢	56¢	49¢
20,000 lines, per line	40½¢	17½¢	54½¢	48½¢
30,000 lines, per line	39½¢	17½¢	53½¢	48¢
40,000 lines, per line	39¢	17½¢	53¢	46¢

Classified contract advertiser using space as indicated above, in any one calendar month, shall be entitled to rates as set forth above. On all copy that appears in the Wednesday edition:
Add 34¢ per line for space in Wednesday Daily Breeze
Add 6¢ per line for space in Wednesday News-Pilot
Add 40¢ per line for space in Wednesday combination

NON-CONTRACT BULK SPACE RATES

	DAILY BREEZE	NEWS PILOT	COMBINATION (BOTH PAPERS)	SUNDAY
less than 25 inches	$9.94	$4.62	$12.81	$11.69
25 - 49 inches	$9.24	$4.48	$11.90	$10.85
50 - 99 inches	$8.82	$4.34	$11.27	$10.43
100 - 199 inches	$8.40	$3.64	$10.78	$10.29
200 - 299 inches	$8.19	$3.57	$10.43	$9.73
300 inches or more	$7.98	$3.50	$10.01	$9.66

Minimum space in order to qualify for above rates is 4 inches per ad. Advertiser using space as indicated above, in any one calendar month, shall be entitled to rates as set forth above.
On all copy that appears in the Wednesday editons
Add 34¢ per line for space in Wednesday Daily Breeze
Add 6¢ per line for space in Wednesday News-Pilot
Add 40¢ per line for space in Wednesday combination

COLOR RATES

R O P COLOR	DAILY BREEZE	NEWS PILOT	SUNDAY
1 color & black	$185	$85	$255
2 colors & black	$240	$125	$340
3 colors & black	$290	$175	$410

NON-CONTRACT VOLUNTARY RATES

	DAILY BREEZE	NEWS PILOT	COMBINATION (BOTH PAPERS)	SUNDAY
1 Day, Per Line Per Day	$1.10	78¢	$1.62	$1.34
2 Days, Per Line Per Day	93¢	64¢	$1.37	$1.10
3 Days, Per Line Per Day	76¢	51¢	$1.13	90¢
4 Days, Per Line Per Day	71½¢	39¢	97½¢	81½¢
7 Days, Per Line Per Day	64½¢	36¢	88½¢	77¢
10 Days, Per Line Per Day	61¢	34¢	84¢	73½¢
30 Days, Per Line Per Day	60¢	31¢	82¢	72½¢

On all copy that appears in the Wednesday editions,
Add 34¢ per line for space in Wednesday Daily Breeze
Add 6¢ per line for space in Wednesday News-Pilot
Add 40¢ per line for space in Wednesday combination

BUYERFINDER RATES (private party merchandise for sale ads only, all merchandise in ad priced, total value $150 or less)
Daily Breeze: 3 lines 3 times $3.00
Daily Breeze & News-Pilot: 3 lines 3 times $4.50

NATIONAL RATES

	DAILY BREEZE	NEWS PILOT	COMBINATION (BOTH NEWSPAPERS)	SUNDAY
Commissionable line Rate, 15% & 2%, Per Line	$1.03	$.62	$1.29	$1.20
Commissionable Bulk Space Rate, 15% & 2%, minimum 4 inches, per inch	$11.13	$8.47	$14.35	$13.58
Non-Commissionable Line Rate, Per Line	$.86	$.52	$1.07	$1.01
WEDNESDAY PICK-UP, applicable to any of above rates, add for Space placed in Wednesday paper, per line	$.34	$.06	$.40	

MISC. RATES & CHARGES

LEGAL NOTICE (3 insertions) Daily Breeze, $9.31; News-Pilot, $6.65
BOX NUMBERS, Daily Breeze $3.00; News-Pilot $1.50
PROOF CHARGES (quantities in excess of normal use) 15¢ each
TEARSHEETS (quantities in excess of normal use) 10¢ each
VELOXES, minimum charge $3.00 plus $2.50 negative charge

WEEKLY NEWSPAPERS

ZONE 1 (Reflex & Advertiser), Redondo Beach, West Torrance, 16,500
ZONE 2 (Messenger & Advertiser) Hermosa, Manhattan, Lawndale, 17,000
ZONE 3 (Gardena Breeze Advertiser) Gardena, North Torrance, 18,500
ZONE 4 (Torrance Press Herald) Torrance, Lomita, Harbor City, 19,000
ZONE 5 (Peninsula Breeze) Palos Verdes Peninsula, 13,000
ZONE 6 (Carson Star-Harbor Mail) Carson, Dominguez, 19,000
ZONE 7 (El Segundo-Hawthorne Beacon) El Segundo, Hawthorne, 14,500
ZONE 8 (Westchester-Marina Weekly Breeze) Westchester, Marina Del Rey, Playa Del Rey, 20,000
ZONE 9 (Inglewood-Ladera Breeze) Inglewood, 20,000
ZONE 10 (Harbor Mail) Wilmington, San Pedro, 15,000
ZONE 11 (Culver City Breeze) Culver City, 23,000

MECHANICAL REQUIREMENTS

Width of printed page 13⅛". Depth of printed page 21⅜". Printed column width 1 column 8.8 picas. Complete veloxes for classified-display ads may be supplied in these measurements.

Width of type page 13⅛". Depth of type page 21⅜". Column width 8.8 picas.

Columns per page, 9. Column depth 21⅜" or 299 agate lines. Full page charge 189 column inches, 2646 lines.

DEADLINES

New Copy and Cancellations, Set Solid non Classified-Display Copy.
For Tuesday through Saturday 3 p.m. Previous Day
For Monday ... Noon Friday
For Sunday ... 2 p.m. Friday
New Copy and Cancellations, Classified-Display Copy.
For Tuesday through Saturday ... 3 p.m. 2 days prior
For Monday ... 9 a.m. Friday
For Sunday ... 5 p.m. Thursday

OFFICE HOURS: Monday through Friday 8:30 a.m. to 5:30 p.m.

Sentinel
A SUN Group Newspaper

2724 Garnet in Pacific Beach
San Diego, California, 92109
P.O. Box 9008

Publication dates
Wednesday evening and Sunday morning

Classified display deadline
Wednesday edition—6 p.m., Tuesday
Sunday edition—6 p.m., Friday

Classified display deadline
Wednesday edition—12 noon Tuesday
Sunday edition—12 noon Friday
If proof is required, subtract 24 hours from the above deadline times

CLASSIFIED VOLUNTARY RATES

Open rate: $1.15 per line
Minimum 3 lines
Minimum charge $3.75

Number of Insertions	Cost per line
2 consecutive issues	1.10
3 - 5 consecutive issues	1.05
6 - 8 consecutive issues	1.00
9 consecutive issues	.95

Line - approximately 25 characters.

Copy Deadlines

Tuesday 6 p.m. for Wednesday issue.
Friday 6 p.m. for Sunday issue.

Classified Advertising

Open rate (non- commissionable)	Open rate (commissionable to recognized advertising agencies)
$1.15 per line	$1.35 per line

Minimum 3 lines
Minimum charge $3.75

Consecutive issue contracts

	per line
18 issues	.95
26 issues	.89
52 issues	.82
104 issues	.69

Volume contracts (6 consecutive months)

Lines per month	per line
100	.78
200	.74
400	.71
600	.68
800	.64

- Major account rates available for advertisers using more than 1,000 lines per month for minimum of 6 months consecutively
- For advertisers using less than 6 months add 20% to the contract rate above

Color rates

$100 per color

Office hours:	8 30 A M to 6 00 P M, Monday thru Friday Closed Saturday and Sunday
Sentinel Classified direct line:	270-1410

FIGURE 16–3 The *Sentinel* of San Diego, California, has a simpler classified rate structure. It publishes Wednesdays and Sundays. *Reprinted with permission of Harte-Hanks Communications, Inc.*

readership and it is therefore very important that you price it attractively. You will note that many papers have "family want ad rates" which are priced quite economically—"4 lines, 4 days, $4" or "7 days for $7." Some papers even offer to run your advertised item until you sell it. This is called "guaranteed results." Many different rate programs have been devised to keep the private party advertiser in the paper.

Usually the "noncontract" commercial advertiser is charged more for his advertising than private party or the contract advertiser. A number of reasons can be suggested: (1) it encourages the advertiser to sign a contract and be in the paper every day or week; (2) he is a commercial operator and should be charged more than the private party; and (3) his advertising involves the newspaper in additional composition costs, as each ad is newly set and runs only once or twice before it must be changed.

Generally, when an advertiser uses the services of an advertising agency, the newspaper bills the agency the full cost of the ad, and the agency in turn bills the advertiser the same amount. When the agency receives payment from the advertiser, it then deducts a 15 percent fee for the services it has performed and pays the difference to the newspaper. Most newspapers also give an additional 2 percent discount for prompt payment, as explained earlier in this chapter. Some agencies charge the advertiser a flat fee for creating and placing the advertising rather than using the discount method.

Contract Terms Vary

Terms of the contract vary from paper to paper, but nearly all include terms and provisions such as duration—usually a year, but some newspapers do

offer thirteen-week or six-month contracts for seasonal businesses. Usually a contract contains a "self-renewing" clause which states that the contract will renew itself automatically at the end of its term unless notified to the contrary by the advertiser.

Other provisions will include a "short rate" in case the advertiser does not complete his contract. A cancellation clause usually provides that the advertiser pay the open rate then in effect. The contract should also require that an advertiser meet the newspaper's standards of acceptance and that commercial advertisers be labeled as such.

Promotion Creates Customers

Most good newspapers have promotion departments geared to promote every department of the newspaper. The size of the promotional programs will vary with the funds available.

Circulation promotion tells the public of the benefits to be gained by subscribing to and reading the newspaper. Editorial promotion concerns itself with the informational needs satisfied by reading the paper. Display advertising and classified advertising promotion are geared to emphasizing the results derived from newspaper advertising. All promotion is aimed at the creation of customers, be they readers or advertisers.

Promotion programs should be planned a year in advance, and should have the approval of the publisher so that the space intended for the promotional campaign cannot be "bumped" by some pressing news story or last-minute ad. It should be a well-thought-out, planned program that is timely.

Classified promotion can be used to build readership. Stress the results that classified can produce. Show the advertiser how to use classified more effectively and generally create interest in classified advertising.

Promotion advertising can be designed to be run in the paper, on billboards, on radio and TV, on rack cards or truck posters, via direct mail, even using gimmicks like hot air balloons (see Chapter 13 for details). Most

DISPLAY ADVERTISING RATES

RUN OF PAPER

Rate Per Inch **$2.75** Less Discount Earned For Prompt Payment

SCHEDULE OF DISCOUNTS

The following discounts may be allowed to advertisers having no past due accounts and who pay their bills on or before the 20th day following billing date.

20% OFF on accounts over $300

15% OFF on accounts of $200 to $300

10% OFF on accounts of $100 to $200

IMPORTANT

All advertisements appearing in THE PUBLIC SPIRIT will also appear in THE FORT DEVENS SENTRY which is a weekly newspaper published on Thursday and circulated to all family housing units and military units at Fort Devens, Massachusetts.

LEGAL ADVERTISING

Citations, mortgagee's sales, etc. - $5.50 per inch (three insertions); Notices - $3.50 per inch (one insertion, $4.50 per inch (two insertions); Liquor renewals - $6.50 per renewal; New licenses (liquor, gasoline sales, etc.) - $9.50 per license.

CLASSIFIED ADVERTISING

5 Words Per Line

3 LINES:
   1 week, $2.50 - Repeat insertions 50 cents off.

4 LINES:
   1 week, $2.75 - Repeat insertions 50 cents off.

5 LINES:
   1 week, $3.00 - Repeat insertions 50 cents off.

Each additional line, 35 cents.

REPRODUCTION — The Public Spirit is printed by the photo-offset process which eliminates need for mats and engravings, provided a good proof (preferably an engraver's proof) can be supplied with the order. A clean copy of an advertisement appearing in another publication can be reproduced successfully. Ads requiring composition are produced effectively by the Public Spirit Production Department. Excessive composition will be charged extra.

SPECIFICATIONS — Width of column: 10 EMS; Length of column: 21 inches. No display advertisement accepted for less than two inches.

COPY — Advertising copy must be in the Public Spirit office by 5 p.m. on Monday, week of publication. No cancellations honored after the above deadline hour.

ADVERTISING CONTRACTS — All orders, illustrations and copy subject to approval of publisher. Forwarding of an order is construed as acceptenace of all rates and conditions under which advertising is sold at the time by the Public Spirit.

ERRORS — The Public Spirit assumes no financial responsibility for typographical errors in advertising.

TRANSIENT ADVERTISING — Cash with order.

FIGURE 16–4 The rate card of this weekly shows both its classified and display advertising rates. *Reprinted with permission of the Ayer (Massachusetts) Public Spirit.*

newspapers keep a series of promotional ads on hand to be used when circumstances make it necessary to run a filler in the newspaper.

PROMOTE MAJOR CLASSIFICATIONS

Since real estate, automotive, employment opportunities, and merchandise are the major categories in the classified section, they should get the most attention and the first consideration in all promotional efforts.

Private party advertising promotion should run constantly in the newspaper as a reminder that the classified advertising section is the least expensive, most effective way to bring in extra cash for items no longer needed. The most frequently used private party advertising promotion is the "results" story on the lower half of the front page. It usually tells how "Mrs. Jones sold her bedroom set and received thirty-five calls." This tells the reader that there is a person in town, perhaps an acquaintance, who got excellent results from her advertising, and that there are thirty-four more persons out there wanting bedroom sets.

Probably every newspaper has used contests to create readership of classified advertising. Carl R. Lehman, classified ad manager of the San Rafael (California) *Independent Journal,* suggests several contests and promotions that have been successful.

A typical one is the "Find Your Name" contest. Names are usually taken from circulation lists or the telephone book and inserted somewhere in the classified section. Those readers who find their names receive prizes. Another is a coloring contest: promotional ads feature outline art, and prizes go to the children who color them in.

Other promotions involve free "student ads,"—for summer employment opportunities—and a "Talk to Santa Claus" promotion which allows children to call a number and discuss their Christmas wants. This generates great human interest.

Others Lehman recommends include "clean-up, fix-up, paint-up" promotions in both spring and fall. Commercial gift sections at Christmas time can be combined with voluntary gift advertising to present a fine array of merchandise. Special editions on boating, travel, progress, senior citizens, or other special interests can be used to promote classified advertising and increase linage.

Plan your promotions well in advance, and let your sales people know when they will be running and what theme will be used. You will get noticeably effective results if you plan and review each promotion carefully. It is very important to the growth of the classified advertising department.

Budgets Are Necessary

Arthur G. Hodgins, former classified advertising manager of the Toronto *Telegram,* points out that although the classified ad manager is recruited for dynamic sales ability and leadership, cost awareness is also very important. Every cost must be planned and controlled, and a good place to start is with the linage projection for the following year, based on the current year. Take it a month at a time, by major classifications, to get as true a projection as possible.

Revenue can only increase if linage or rates increase. It is all based on the one source, linage. Thus, it is very important that the manager be capable of giving an accurate estimate of future linage for the budget year.

Economic conditions are an important factor, so it is basic that you research what the economists are predicting for the budget year—real estate sales, the employment situation in your area, the automotive market, and others.

As the classified advertising sections in newspapers are becoming more and more dominant, it is important to the overall newspaper budget projections that the classified advertising budget be as accurate as possible. Hod-

gins warns that a timid revenue projection can lead to a very large budget surplus, undermining good planning, and can quite possibly result in cuts in vital expenditures. Boldness and accuracy are the goals of a good classified advertising manager when budgeting linage and revenue.

Use an earned rate when converting linage to revenue. Simply take the linage you ran last year and divide it into the revenue you received. This gives you an earned rate per line. Don't forget to factor in any rate increases you are anticipating for a more accurate budget figure.

INCLUDE ALL EXPENSES

To obtain the true profit-and-loss picture, budget expenses incurred by the department in selling, handling, and promotion. The largest expenditure will be salaries. Consider base salary, bonuses and commissions, special promotions, and additions to the staff. Part-time people during seasonal peak periods must also be considered.

If there is a separate telephone number in the classified advertising department, trunk lines, WATS lines, etc., do not forget to budget these expenses.

The promotion budget includes radio, television, outdoor advertising, direct mail, brochures and printed material, and numerous other items. Ordinarily the advertising art services of the classified department are included in this promotion budget.

Stationery and supplies include all of the innumerable forms, pens, and pencils used in the day-to-day operation of the classified advertising department.

Bad debt losses can be factored in by using the yearly average percentage of bad debt losses. The amount to use will be determined by past experience and planned credit policy for the budgeted year.

Many publishers believe expenditures should not exceed *x* percent of budget and therefore need to see an analysis report. But be careful—fixed percent can mean that the classified manager ends up with money to spend that he does not need for an efficient

operation, which is wasteful, while a percentage that is too low may mean good staff and good programs suffer for lack of funds.

PLAN OBJECTIVES

Naturally, the best strategy is to keep sales costs down, but not at the expense of a well-run, well-staffed department. Too often a classified department struggles along without enough personnel because the publisher mistakenly thinks he is economizing by not hiring.

After budgeting is completed, then the tracking starts, month by month. If you find you are not making budget, you may be forced to revise your estimates. It is best to do this early in the new year.

On the smaller daily or the weekly newspaper, budgeting is usually a function of the publisher's office or the accounting department. Usually all that is asked of the classified advertising manager is a monthly linage/revenue gain over the previous year. As the manager must check with the boss before salaries can be adjusted, new personnel hired, and departmental purchases made, budgets are well controlled.

Standards of Acceptance

The desire to protect classified advertising readers dictates that standards of acceptance be adopted by newspapers. After all, there will always be the "con man" or the advertiser who tries to lure the reader into investing in a questionable scheme.

Some newspapers have written regulations dealing with standards of acceptance. Others judge each ad as it is brought in. The former policy is much better because it keeps classified personnel informed and provides them something to show advertisers.

Many questionable classified ads are related to the following classifications:

- *Business Opportunities.* Questionable ads usually describe an investment by the individual with the promise of unusually high earnings. Particularly hazardous are "opportunities" dealing with franchises and vending machines.

- *Work-at-Home Schemes.* These may involve offers of high income for addressing envelopes at home, breeding chinchillas, or sales opportunities. If an advance fee is required, the classified department should be wary. The Better Business Bureau and the Federal Trade Commission have available a great deal of material on home opportunities to help define which are legitimate and which are questionable.

- *Home Repairs.* Out-of-town promoters dealing in insulation or roofing need checking. Many communities require licensing of such firms, and the city may provide information on their reliability.

- *Help Wanted.* These may involve promises of high salaries for what are actually sales jobs that pay a commission, jobs that ask for an investment by the applicant, or offers that are training rather than true employment opportunities.

There are other categories that may seek to deceive readers. When in doubt about this type of advertisement, check with the Better Business Bureau. The BBB has information regarding advertisers who take advantage of the public. It is not necessary verbally to cite the Bureau when turning down an ad, as it is an information source only. It is best to say, "Upon advice of legal counsel, we cannot run your ad." No other explanation is necessary or advisable.

RESPECT GOVERNMENT DICTATES

The federal government has become involved in the classified advertising field through the Office of Economic Opportunity (EEOC) and through the De-

partment of Housing and Urban Development (HUD) and their fair housing guidelines.

The EEOC has made it illegal to indicate in advertising any preference as to sex, color, creed, or national origin. This dictum covers employment advertising, housing advertising, even ads for roommates.

In addition, the government, under the title of United States Employment Services, has become involved in the employment field, and their job bank computers are in direct competition with private employment agencies and newspaper "help wanted" columns.

In addition to standards of acceptance to protect consumers and to abide by government regulations, newspapers may have requirements to protect the appearance of the classified pages. These may restrict use of heavy borders, bold type, reverses, and illustrations.

Creative Selling Pays

A number of factors are involved in classified sales. A sales person must first know the benefits of classified advertising and be convinced of its worth before the prospective buyer can be convinced.

Advertising is necessary to meet competition, acquire a maximum share of the market, and achieve better results and more profit. Consistent and continuous advertising will reach the most prospects—a continuing parade of prospects every time it appears. In turn, the advertiser saves money by taking advantage of the special rates given for consecutive insertions. There is no special day or week on which to reach interested readers. Consecutive advertising is the logical way of ensuring maximum reader response.

When selling classified advertising by telephone or face to face, a sales person must have a set plan before attempting the sale. A planned presentation is the key to selling a customer.

Since it takes self-confidence, honesty, knowledge, and control to carry off a successful presentation, a

sales person must find a way of projecting these qualities in his presentation.

Sales presentations need advance planning and should include certain facts about the prospect. Keep a record for future reference and easy access. In addition to the name of the company and its key people, the following basic knowledge should be available: benefits to be offered, possible objections to be anticipated, data sheets, testimonials, and case histories. And don't forget to ask for the order!

During a person-to-person sales presentation or a telephone sales call, the prospective advertiser should be treated as courteously as possible. Give him full attention at all times, make him feel important, and attempt to keep him as an interested customer in the future.

HOW TO SELL CREATIVELY

BUILD THE CUSTOMER'S EGO. Don't challenge it. And above all, never become angry or lose control of your emotions. If you're on the defensive or you try to overwhelm your prospect, he'll become hostile and you'll lose the sale.

CREATE DESIRE. A creative sales person has to develop a healthy, optimistic mental attitude. He must create opportunities, not wait for them to happen. He must create interest and good ad copy. A good sales person will create desire. Nobody wants a classified ad—he wants only what an ad can do for him. The quickest way to make a sale is to heighten the prospect's desire for the things he wants. Stories of the successful experiences of others in filling their desires through classified advertising still constitute one of the greatest sales tools.

CREATE BUYERS. The psychology of selling reveals that it is far better to induce a person to buy than to try to sell him the article or service. Giving the prospect a chance to buy for himself results in far more sales.

The modern theory of selling states that the sales representative should engage in "buymanship." That is, he should provide the prospect with assistance in recognizing his needs and guidance in filling them to the best advantage at the least cost in time, trouble, and money. Skilled, low-pressure buymanship will result in far more business than high-pressure salesmanship. One reason is that high-pressure salesmanship often presses the prospect to the point where he begins to fight back. The creative task of today's classified sales person is to create buyers, to induce the prospects to sell themselves!

CREATE NEW BUSINESS. Creative sales people see new business possibilities all about them as they walk down the street, read through the paper, or glance over the classified columns. And "new" business can come from current advertisers—too many sales people forget there is more than one classification to sell. For example, the real estate dealer who is running "for sale" ads may also be in the property management business; he might like to have more properties to manage. If so, he is a ready-made customer for this additional classification.

CREATE ENTHUSIASM! It is sufficient for now to say that enthusiasm breeds enthusiasm. Prospects cannot be expected to become enthusiastic about classified advertising and its amazing result-getting power unless the salesperson becomes enthusiastic. In fact, lack of enthusiasm produces a negative reaction in a prospect. The creative sales person makes more sales and gets more repeat business because he is enthusiastic about his job and enthusiastic about his product or service—classified advertising.

Successful sales people have common interests with other successful, effective sales people. They set standards, they keep long-range goals, and most important, they are ambitious and they like their work. Attitude can become your real boss; it can induce you to accept bigger challenges in your profession.

Being able to work wisely by applying all these qualities is another major area that must be considered. Knowledge plus motivation equals results.

Be an achiever by doing the right things at the right time with the right people. If the right attitude, knowledge, and organization of work are combined, you'll be a successful sales person.

Copywriting

No classified staff can approach maximum productivity unless they are knowledgeable in the preparation of effective advertising copy. Good copy gets better results for the advertiser, and it enables the sales person to sell more ads and lines. The sales person who is able to offer good service to his accounts will sell more linage.

You need not be a literary giant to write good copy. Anyone who has a respectable command of the language can effectively give the reader the information he needs to be motivated into a response.

There are 5 "musts" for effective copy:

- *Attract attention.* Bear in mind that you want *favorable* attention from good buying prospects.

- *Arouse interest.* Promise the potential buyer something he wants or needs.

- *Create desire.* Appeal to the emotions, to the inner yearning for this product. Tell the prospect it will make him or her comfortable or feel good or look good.

- *Inspire confidence.* The reader must believe what you say or the ad is wasted.

- *Induce action.* Convince the reader to act *now* before anybody else does.

The steps involved in every successful sale are: take the proper approach, arouse the prospect's interest, create a desire to buy, and close the sale. Good ad copy can set this sequence in motion and give you satisfied customers.

In writing good copy, ask yourself, How do I know what the reader needs to know to be motivated? To answer this important question you must put yourself in the buyer's shoes. What would you want to know if you were reading an ad instead of writing it? The smart sales person will forget what the seller likes about the item and anticipate what the buyer would be interested in.

In preparing ads, the ability to differentiate between buying and selling points is very important. Keeping the buyer's viewpoint is a key to writing successful ads, just as it is a key to successful selling.

An incomplete ad will not motivate readers. Yet incompleteness is one of the common faults of classified ads. The advertiser wants to leave words out in order to save money. He regards the end of a line as a fence, within which his message must be confined. A classified sales person must be aware of the result-limiting effect of incomplete copy and advise the advertiser on how to change the copy so that it will include the essentials.

GOOD HEADLINES HELP

How important are headlines? Commercial advertisers feel their ad copy is more effective when a good headline is used. Getting the reader to stop for a moment, long enough to read the body of the ad, is the job of a good headline. Consider the competition—each ad is vying for attention, so your headline must be a "stopper" to grab and hold the eye and mind of the reader.

The best headline must appeal to the reader's self-interest—it must offer him something he wants. It must also induce the reader to read the rest of the ad. The length of the headline is not important; research shows that a reader will read a twelve-word headline as readily as a three-word headline.

In summary, the points you need to remember are simple and effective:

- *Keep it simple!* No need to dazzle your prospective classified reader with a lot of fancy words and flowery phrases. Tell it like it is and use words everyone understands.

- *Be specific!* Buyers want specific, useful information. Avoid vague claims. For example, "low cost" means different things to different people.

- *Be believable!* Don't make exaggerated claims, just give the facts. Facts are believable. It is important that the item you are advertising is described correctly—misleading advertising causes the reader to lose faith in the advertiser. If you want to please the public, be truthful. When you make a strong statement, be able to back it up with facts. (For further discussion of copywriting, see Chapter 15, "Creating Display Advertisements.")

Helpful Sources

Principles and Practices of Classified Advertising, a book published under the auspices of the Association of Newspaper Classified Advertising Managers, can be a helpful source for those who need more detailed information on classified operations. Each chapter is written by a specialist. Inquiries should be sent to ANCAM, Inc., P.O. Box 223, Danville, Illinois 61832. The Better Business Bureau and the Federal Trade Commission both have publications on deceptive advertising practices that can aid classified personnel.

Conclusion

Classified advertising, by its very nature, is the real strength of the newspaper industry. Not only is it a tremendous revenue producer, but it also creates readership greater than that found in our editorial columns. The success of classified is normally a leading indicator of the overall success of the entire operation of a newspaper.

Classified advertising is the number one public service of the newspaper. It has an intimate relationship with people. It is close to the lives of people, closer than any other form of advertising. Because it has an involvement in their employment, their housing, their transportation, and their family budget, it is very people-oriented. Aware publishers have recognized that the "small ads" that were once given away as a public service are now the answer to increased revenues and increased readership.

Chapter 17

The Business of Journalism

by Gene Chamberlin

News may be the name of the business, but a publisher must give as much attention to the business side of the newspaper as to the news content. It's no accident that prize-winning newspapers generally are profitable newspapers.

Quality may contribute to profit, but profit is absolutely necessary to provide for continued growth and for the improvements that make continued quality possible.

Good Records Are Indispensable

Good records are vital in managing a newspaper for quality and profit. Some publishers operate by instinct, with an eye on the checkbook balance, but generally those publishers produce neither a quality product nor a reasonable profit.

A new publisher should rely on a qualified accountant to set up a basic record-keeping system. It's wise to use an accountant who handles other newspapers and who has experience with the special information a newspaper accounting system should provide. It is also easier for a publisher to compare his operation to others if similar records are kept. It makes sense to have a system that provides figures that can easily be compared to the National Newspaper Foundation's annual cost study. It also makes sense to use a table of accounts (the list of categories in which income and expenses are grouped) based on the standard Inland Daily Press Association table or on others commonly used in the industry.

A minimum record-keeping system for the smallest newspaper should include a monthly balance sheet and operating statement. The balance sheet shows assets, liabilities, and owner's equity at a given instant. The operating statement shows income, expenses, and profit over a specific period.

These records can be prepared by someone in the newspaper office, by an outside accountant, or by an outside computer service. Records should be kept as simple as possible, since each bookkeeping procedure costs money, yet they should be complete enough to provide all the information needed to manage the business.

Pinpointing Problem Areas

Examining the balance sheet in Table

GENE CHAMBERLIN

The author is a community newspaper consultant and publisher of the Mobridge (South Dakota) *Tribune.*

"Profit is absolutely necessary to provide for continued growth and for the improvements that make continued quality possible."

17–1, for example, an experienced publisher will make some quick observations, using some fairly standard rules of thumb.

He will note that accounts receivable are too high. A rule of thumb is that a newspaper should not have more than one and a half month's business on the books at any one time. If accounts receivable grow to two months' business, it is nearly certain some of those accounts are uncollectable. Good

TABLE 17–1: SAMPLE BALANCE SHEET

ASSETS:		LIABILITIES:	
Cash	100	Payroll tax payable	1,175
Checking account	7,995	Sales tax payable	115
Accounts receivable	26,520	Accrued property tax	165
Job paper inventory	8,847		111,455
Office supplies inventory	8,847		
Current value depreciable items:		CAPITAL:	
Circulation lists	16,624	Capital stock	45,000
Bound files and morgue	7,001	Retained earnings	5,608
No-compete agreement	6,094		162,063
Printing equipment	54,050		
Real estate	31,550		
Prepaid insurance	532		
	162,063		

management includes regular attention to collecting accounts before they become a problem.

Inventory also appears to be a problem. Retail inventory, in this case office supplies, should not be more than four months' business—preferably considerably less. Job printing paper inventory normally should be less than that, generally not more than two months' consumption, though paper can be a good investment in a rising market.

Owner's equity is reflected in the "CAPITAL" entries, capital stock and retained earnings. It should be large enough to provide a hedge against a business slump and to keep debt service (payments of principal and interest) at a manageable level. There is an element of danger any time total debt exceeds owner's equity. Yet it is not unusual for debt to far exceed owner's equity in a newly purchased business.

Comparative Figures Needed

For an operating statement to be useful it is important that it contain a reference point for comparison. In group ownership, a comparative operating statement may be prepared that lists all papers in the group, making it simple to compare one with another. In single ownership, it is normal to show the same period from a year earlier in a separate column for comparison purposes. A typical operating statement such as that shown in Table 17–2 might contain four columns of figures, the first showing the current month, the second showing the entire portion of the current fiscal year completed, the third showing the same month a year earlier, and the fourth showing the same portion of the fiscal year from a year earlier.

This type of operating statement makes it simple to see how this newspaper is doing financially for the month just completed and for the portion of the fiscal year just completed and to compare those figures to a year earlier. It is possible to compare each item of income and expense listed on the operating statement.

Some operating statements add two additional columns of figures to show budget figures for the month and for the year to date. That makes it possible to compare actual performance with budget projections.

Analyzing for Opportunities

At first glance, the operating statement in Table 17–2 shows a stagnant operation in which income is standing still, expenses are being forced up by inflation, and net profit is dropping rapidly.

TABLE 17–2: SAMPLE OPERATING STATEMENT

	Month	Year To Date	Month Year Ago	To Date Year Ago
INCOME:				
Local advertising	5,840	75,397	6,766	87,675
National advertising	175	2,275	180	2,290
Classified advertising	620	6,513	490	5,021
Legal advertising	1,083	12,505	1,100	12,290
Subscriptions	1,969	24,585	1,429	18,754
Job printing	1,355	15,805	990	10,760
Merchandise sales	920	12,655	890	12,890
Total Income	11,962	149,735	11,845	149,680
EXPENSES:				
Payroll: Administrative	1,200	14,374	1,075	12,900
News and ad	2,230	26,758	1,990	23,950
Production	1,160	13,940	1,050	12,540
Job shop	460	5,482	400	4,935
Other compensation	400	4,792	360	4,295
	5,450	65,346	4,875	58,620
Printing costs	2,350	28,225	2,120	25,405
Postage	295	3,534	265	3,190
Other operating expenses	2,500	30,086	2,340	28,070
Telephone	136	1,632	122	1,465
Interest	600	7,216	530	6,390
Depreciation	757	9,090	675	8,120
Miscellaneous	200	2,396	190	2,250
Total Expenses	12,288	147,525	11,117	133,510
Net income	−326	2,210	728	16,170

It takes a close look at each of the income and expense items to find the real profit and opportunity areas.

Local advertising, the biggest part of nearly any community newspaper, appears to be dropping dangerously. We would immediately question whether rates have been raised to reflect inflation and how much linage is dropping. An analysis is in order to learn whether some major accounts have been lost or if there is a general across-the-board drop in advertising. A close look at the total advertising sales effort is in order.

Other areas of advertising seem to be keeping up with inflation—in fact, there seems to be an appreciable increase in classified advertising. It will pay to take a look at classified to see whether there is an area of strength here that is being missed in the display advertising sales effort. It may also be possible to capitalize on the strength of classified and increase business here.

There has also been an interesting rise in subscription income. This may indicate an increase in interest in the newspaper that should be used by the advertising department in selling the effectiveness of the newspaper to advertisers.

Job printing has taken a dramatic jump. Management will want to know if this is the result of a one-time job or if it represents growth that can be expected to continue.

Net profit has dropped dangerously. It has dropped to far less than could be obtained simply by taking the value of this newspaper and buying bank certificates of deposit.

On the expense side we note that payroll has increased even faster than inflation. That may be justified in a business that is expanding or in a business that has had a very low payroll, but that's not the case for this newspaper. Generally a newspaper's payroll, including administrative payroll, should not exceed 35 percent of its gross.

The increase in cost for newspaper printing doesn't jibe with advertising income. The change could be accounted for by allowing the newshole to grow to fill the unused advertising space, or it could reflect rapid inflation in central plant charges, or it could reflect a failure to increase ad rates.

These are some of the things that can be learned from this balance sheet and profit-and-loss statement, just some of the things that appear wrong with this newspaper after a cursory examination of those records. Without a monthly financial report of this nature, it is impossible for a publisher to spot many potential problems before they reach crisis proportions. The problems spotted in these basic records may lead the publisher to call for other records to provide more detailed information on specific operations.

How to Expand Your System

Generally the records kept and the information available from the bookkeeping system reflect the size of the newspaper or newspaper group. Small operations obviously can afford to invest less in record keeping than large operations.

It may be helpful for the beginning journalist to have an idea of the additional records that are available in the largest operations, simply to know how to expand a simple system if it becomes necessary to provide more detail in given areas.

Some newspapers keep a preventive maintenance form on each piece of equipment to make sure maintenance is done on schedule. Some keep a repair log to give a history of repairs made on each piece of equipment. Many keep advertising linage reports to compare column inches of advertising to the same issue or period a year earlier. Some keep weekly circulation reports to detail all circulation and circulation sales efforts and their results as well. Most have some system of aging accounts receivables, which may be as simple as making a list of past-due accounts that need attention. Some calculate cash flow and float and prepare a cash flow forecast calendar. A publisher may obtain examples of these from a newspaper accountant, fellow publishers, or possibly from a state press association.

Cost Study Can Help

One of the valuable tools for community newspaper publishers is the National Newspaper Foundation's annual cost study. It is a compilation of all income and expense data submitted by the participating weekly newspapers.

With it any newspaper publisher can compare his income and expense costs to the average and to other newspapers. The comparison can be made for each item of income, expense, and net income included in the study.

In the 1978 study summarized in Table 17–3, the 129 participating newspapers showed an average annual revenue of $416,065. Breakdowns were made for newspapers with revenues of less than $100,000, $100,000 to $250,000, $250,000 to $500,000, $500,000 to $1,000,000, and over $1,000,000. Other breakdowns were made by printing method (in-house or bought), by frequency, and by profile (suburban vs. nonsuburban, job shop vs. no job shop, competition vs. no competition).

Some caution is suggested in using these figures for comparison, however. Because they are averages, each publisher making a comparison will first want to determine how he differs from the average and what difference this will make in the various income and expense categories.

It should also be noted that the net profit figures are very low. The net income before state and federal taxes was just 8.24 percent of revenue for all newspapers included in the study. Many publishers today aim for a net income of 20 percent and start being concerned if net income drops below 15 percent. Better rates of return are frequently available on bank certificates of deposit than the 8.24 percent net for papers in this study.

Advertising and circulation play a much larger role in producing income for newspapers that purchase printing, while commercial printing is much more important for those that print in-house. This is not surprising, but it makes a big difference in how income and expenses are divided throughout the study. That makes it important for newspapers using the study to use the tables that fit their operation before making a comparison. (Data from later studies are provided for comparison purposes in Figs. 17–1 through 17–6.)

TABLE 17–3: NATIONAL NEWSPAPER FOUNDATION COST STUDY

	All Newspapers	Purchase Printing	Print In-House
Number of Questionnaires	129	101	28
Total Revenue, Average	$416,065	$309,379	$800,894
Revenue Items	Average	Average	Average
Advertising: Local	50.56 %	59.00 %	38.79 %
National	2.08 %	2.82 %	1.04 %
Classified	8.54 %	8.72 %	8.29 %
Legal Notices	2.34 %	2.96 %	1.47 %
Preprinted Inserts	3.04 %	2.81 %	3.36 %
Total Advertising Revenue	66.56 %	76.33 %	52.95 %
Circulation Revenue	10.02 %	12.05 %	7.20 %
Miscellaneous Revenue	1.36 %	1.86 %	.65 %
Total Newspaper & Shopper Revenue	77.94 %	90.24 %	60.79 %
Commercial, Web Printing	15.05 %	2.24 %	32.90 %
Commercial, Sheet Fed & Job Shop	5.82 %	6.46 %	4.93 %
Total Commercial Printing Revenue	20.87 %	8.71 %	37.83 %
All Other Income	1.19 %	1.05 %	1.38 %
Total Revenue	100.00 %	100.00 %	100.00 %
Expense Items			
Payroll: News and Editorial	7.86 %	8.77 %	6.60 %
Advertising	7.72 %	8.85 %	6.13 %
Pre-Press	6.58 %	7.07 %	5.88 %
Camera & Plate Making	1.28 %	.79 %	1.97 %
Press	1.99 %	.72 %	3.77 %
Mailing, Circulation	2.83 %	2.57 %	3.19 %
Administrative	8.18 %	8.60 %	7.59 %
Job Shop	1.51 %	1.62 %	1.36 %
Total Payroll	37.95 %	39.00 %	36.49 %
Other Compensation Costs	3.93 %	3.78 %	4.15 %
Printing Costs	21.79 %	21.37 %	22.39 %
Depreciation, Lease Payments	4.79 %	4.33 %	5.44 %
Telephone Costs	1.01 %	1.03 %	.99 %
Second Class Postage	2.15 %	3.04 %	.91 %
All Other Operating Expenses	16.96 %	16.33 %	17.83 %
Total Operating Expenses	20.11 %	20.39 %	19.73 %
Interest	1.05 %	1.35 %	.64 %
Amortization of Goodwill	.61 %	.47 %	.80 %
Miscellaneous	1.52 %	1.77 %	1.16 %
Total Expenses	91.75 %	92.45 %	90.79 %
Net Income Before State/Fed. Taxes	8.24 %	7.55 %	9.21 %
Number of Papers per Questionnaire	1	1	1
Operating Ratios-Median			
Circulation Penetration	43.67	40.91	49.74
Revenue to Retail Sales in County	.29	.25	.40
Advertising Rev. Per Broadsheet	135.13	132.96	139.92
Page, Newspaper: Tabloid	74.86	72.84	125.48
Advertising Rev. Per Broadsheet	81.61	69.01	81.61
Page, Shopper: Tabloid	34.41		
Advertising to Total Newspaper	55.57	55.88	54.21
Space: Shopper	79.23	79.19	79.28
Adv. Rev./Col. In. Per Newspaper	.40	.42	.37
Thou. Pd. Circ.: Shopper	.28	.28	.24

Courtesy of the National Newspaper Foundation.
(All Newspapers by Source of Printing, 1978)

OPERATING RATIOS

The cost study contains operating ratios which can be used to determine where your business deviates substantially from the newspaper averages in the study.

Circulation penetration shown is total paid circulation divided by households in the county of publication. The revenue-to-retail-sales ratio is total retail revenue expressed as a percentage of total county retail sales.

Advertising revenue per page is simply the total advertising revenue divided by the number of pages printed. Advertising to total space is the percentage of total space occupied by advertising. Advertising revenue per column inch per thousand paid circulation is advertising revenue (less preprinted inserts) divided by the product of column inches of paid advertising multiplied by paid circulation (in thousands).

IDPA SERVES DAILIES

Widely known for its cost and revenue studies for daily newspapers is the Inland Daily Press Association in Chicago. More than 350 dailies participate in IDPA's studies. Circulations of the participants range from 3,100 to more than 500,000.

Participants fill out a report form (see Fig. 17–7). After the data are compiled, each participant receives complete data on all newspapers in his circulation group and the groups immediately above and below it, with average figures for each group, a summary of averages for all circulation groups, a table of industry norms, and a supplement showing the norms in graphic form. IDPA supplements the project with cost and revenue seminars.

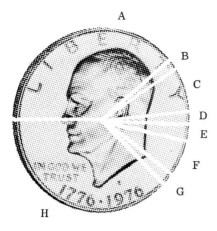

A	Local advertising	38.79%
B	National advertising	1.04%
C	Classified advertising	8.29%
D	Legal notices	1.47%
E	Printed inserts	3.36%
	Total advertising	52.95%
F	Circulation	7.20%
G	Miscellaneous	2.03%
H	Commercial printing	37.83%

FIGURE 17–1 Sources of weekly newspaper income and the proportion of the total income dollar produced by each source for newspapers that print on their own presses. Figures based on 1979 National Newspaper Foundation Cost Study.

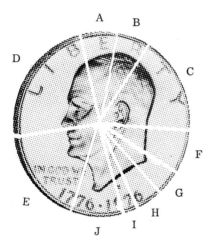

A	News payroll	6.60%
B	Advertising payroll	6.13%
C	Production payroll	16.17%
D	Printing costs	22.39%
E	Operating costs	19.73%
F	Administative payroll	7.59%
G	Other compensation costs . .	4.15%
H	Depreciation, lease payments	5.44%
I	Miscellaneous	2.60%
J	Profit before taxes	9.21%

FIGURE 17–2 Division of the revenue dollar among various expense categories by weekly newspapers that print on their own presses. Figures based on 1979 National Newspaper Foundation Cost Study.

A	Local advertising	59.00%
B	National advertising	2.82%
C	Classified advertising	8.72%
D	Legal advertising	2.96%
E	Preprinted inserts	2.81%
	Total advertising	76.33%
F	Circulation	12.05%
G	Commercial printing	8.70%
H	All other income	·2.91%

FIGURE 17–3 Sources of weekly newspaper income and the proportion of the total income dollar produced by each source for newspapers that purchase printing from others. Figures based on 1979 National Newspaper Foundation Cost Study.

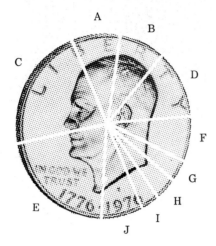

A	News payroll	8.77%
B	Advertising payroll	8.85%
C	Printing costs	21.37%
D	Production payroll	12.77%
E	Operating expenses	20.40%
F	Administrative payroll	8.60%
G	Other compensation	3.78%
H	Depreciation, lease payments	4.33%
I	Miscellaneous	3.59%
J	Profit before taxes	7.55%

FIGURE 17–4 Division of the revenue dollar among various expense categories for weekly newspapers that purchase press work from others. Figures based on 1979 National Newspaper Foundation Cost Study.

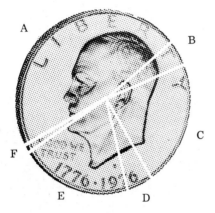

A	Retail Advertising	46.9%
B	National advertising	5.3%
C	Classified advertising	22.6%
D	Circulars/Inserts	4.0%
	Total advertising	78.8%
E	Circulation	20.7%
F	Other	.5%

FIGURE 17–5 Sources of daily newspaper income and the proportion produced by each source for a newspaper with 260,000 circulation. Chart based on an analysis prepared by Scott D. Timmerman of Newspaper Analysis Services, Cincinnati, that appeared in *Editor & Publisher,* March 29, 1980. *Reprinted by permission.*

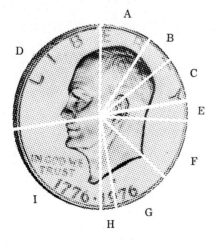

A	Editorial	8.7%
B	Advertising	5.4%
C	Mechanical	9.4%
D	Newsprint and ink	28.0%
	Total direct	51.5%
E	Building	2.4%
F	Circulation and distribution	10.9%
G	Administration	9.7%
	Total indirect	23.0%
H	Deductions	3.5%
I	Profit before taxes	22.0%
		100.0%

FIGURE 17–6 Division of the revenue dollar among various expense categories for same newspaper. Based on an analysis prepared by Scott D. Timmerman for *Editor & Publisher,* March 29, 1980. *Reprinted by permission.*

If you find that you cannot supply some of the information called for, please attach a note to that effect so that you will not be troubled with follow-up requests for that information.

If further correspondence is necessary it will be addressed to the executive named on the front of this slip. If you would prefer to have these inquiries addressed to someone else, please give his **name**.

COMPOSING ROOM SCALE

Effective Date **January 1**

Journeyman's Day Rate ____ per hour
____ per hour

NEWSPAPER MECHANICAL MANHOURS WORKED

Total Composing Room Manhours Worked . . . ____
All Other Mechanical Manhours Worked . . . ____
Total Mechanical Manhours Worked ____

Newsprint waste ____ %

Expense Breakdown by Departments—Report Nearest Dollar—Omit Cents

EXPENSE ACCOUNTS BY NUMBER	News-Editorial 100	Advertising 200	Circulation 300	Distribution 400	Composing 500	All Other Mechanical 600	Building 700	Business Office 800	All Other Newspaper 900	Non-Newspaper Shopper 1000	Commercial Printing 1100	All Other Non Nsp.	TOTALS
01. Departmental Salaries													
02. Car, Truck & Travel													
03. Features, Art, Mat & Proof Serv.													
04. Telephone & Telegraph													
05. Wire Services													
06. Services of Outsiders													
07. Promotion													
08. Miscellaneous													
09. Supplies													
10. Photo & Dark Room													
11. Representatives' Commissions													
12. Postage													
13. Repairs													
14. Carriers' Salaries													
15. Rent													
16. Engravings Purchased													
17. Depreciation													
18. Insurance													
19. Taxes													
20. Heat, Light & Power													
21. Newsprint & Handling													
22. Ink													
23. Dues & Memberships													
24. Donations													
25. Readyprint Comics													
26. Other Readyprint													
27. Trust Funds, Employe Benefits													
28. Bad Debts													
29.													
30. TOTAL EXPENSE													Total Expense

Columns (left): Extra Study | Extra Supp. | Perm. No. | Number Employes: Full Time / Part Time

FIGURE 17–7 One section of a work sheet used by the Inland Daily Press Association as a basis for its cost and revenue reports. *Reprinted by permission of IDPA.*

Rules for
Problem Spotting

A number of rules of thumb are generally accepted to provide a quick way to spot problems in a newspaper operation. Some of those suggested by Thomas D. Jones, executive vice president and general manager of East Bay Newspapers, Inc., Walnut Creek, California, are:

- The growth rate of a newspaper can't be sustained beyond its return on investment without outside financing. Return on investment is net profit divided by tangible net worth (not including intangible assets such as good will, patents, etc.).

- Current assets should be double current liabilities. This is a measure of a company's ability to meet its current debt. The form of such assets is also important, as in most cases cash is more desirable than inventory.

- Debt should not exceed net worth. If the creditor's investment exceeds the owner's, the business is generally considered undercapitalized. This makes securing loans unfavorable.

- Net sales should be four times net worth. A very high ratio may indicate undercapitalization or overtrading.

Chapter 18

Marketing the Newspaper

by George W. Trotter

The Importance of Circulation

Circulation development is one of the most important functions in the operation of a newspaper.

Take any newspaper and analyze its history, its present operation, and its chances for future growth. It soon becomes apparent that much of the success of any newspaper depends on its circulation development

News development remains the key to circulation growth, but even with a superior news product, unless a newspaper reaches its circulation marketing potential, it may not attract advertisers.

For too long, circulation management has been a stepchild in the newspaper field. It was dragged out of a closet occasionally, but generally it was left unattended or largely left to chance.

Today, circulation management must have top priority if paid circulation newspapers are to compete successfully with voluntary-pay publications, shoppers, and free-distribution newspapers.

REVENUE VERSUS COSTS

Generally speaking, circulation revenue should provide from 10 to 20 percent of a newspaper's income.

Costs of obtaining this circulation will vary, depending on the newspaper and the type of local market. Country weeklies with no print competition may be able to expect as much as a 25 percent margin on circulation revenue. Larger papers located under the umbrella of a metro and with shopper and other print competition, may do well if circulation revenues cover costs of sales and distribution.

RELATIONSHIP TO NEWS AND ADVERTISING

Every publisher wants to get his newspaper into the hands of as many people as possible, to achieve the greatest possible household penetration. This makes it easier for the advertising department to sell the linage required to support the space devoted to news.

High priority must be given to circulation development in the trade area. This is generally defined as the

GEORGE W. TROTTER

The author is general manager and editor of the Bardstown *Kentucky Standard* and former executive editor and circulation director of Landmark Community Newspapers.

"The advertising, news, and circulation departments of every newspaper must coordinate their efforts to serve the reader. . . . The view that limited marketing to the mere distribution and sale of goods is obsolete."

geographical area from which people come to do their major shopping.

The newspaper that has more circulation outside its market area, including out-of-state, than in the home trade area, is in trouble. This type of circulation is worthless to advertisers, who are ultimately responsible for the success or failure of many newspapers. A good blend of circulation development and marketing is essential for the successful newspaper.

The Marketing Concept

The advertising, news, and circulation departments of every newspaper must coordinate their efforts to serve the reader.

This is the modern view of the marketing concept. The view that limited marketing to the mere distribution and sale of goods is obsolete.

Formerly, each of the newspaper's departments—news, advertising, production, and circulation—went its own way, as independent operations. This prevented the unified effort needed for a marketing program that would not only meet the customer's needs but also earn a profit.

Realizing that newspapers must serve both readers and advertisers has produced rethinking among newspapers, both big and small.

Larger newspapers, with their tightly knit pyramidal structure by departments, have had more difficulty in adapting to the modern marketing concept. That is because, on some larger newspapers, department heads act as though they were operating independent businesses.

That situation should not exist in the more loosely structured nondaily newspaper. For the weekly editor, it is hardly a problem, because he or she is not just the supervisor but a working participant in all departments.

The main benefit of the modern marketing concept is that every department is working for—and should be an active participant in—its market. For most newspapers this is the "primary marketing area," a multicounty coverage measurement. This means working together as a team, with news, advertising, and circulation personnel sharing ideas and planning together.

This concept promotes cooperation among departments and enables the newspaper more effectively to anticipate and respond to change. It preserves the freedom of the news department and improves harmony and communication within the newspaper.

THE MARKETING FUNCTION OF CIRCULATION

In evaluating the circulation and marketing function of the newspaper, these questions should be asked:

- What is the objective for circulation promotion?

- Why do nonsubscribers refuse to subscribe?

- What is the percentage of circulation to households or postal families in the trade area?

- What is the rate of subscriber losses? What is the basic cause?

- What are the areas of strong and weak readership in the local trade area?

- Is the reader number one in the newsroom?

Managing the Circulation Department
BASIC OBJECTIVES

Whether a newspaper is a "one-man band" operation, in which the editor also functions as advertising salesman and circulation manager, or a heavily staffed organization, there are several basic circulation objectives that affect each equally. These are:

- To increase yearly the sale of the newspaper, thereby achieving higher penetration of the households in the circulation area.

- To provide a maximum number of single-copy outlets and a complaint-free delivery service.

- To collect in full for all copies sold.

The goal should be to accomplish these tasks in such a way as to maximize revenue and minimize cost, thus increasing circulation's contribution to profit. This contribution can be in-

creased by emphasizing and concentrating on selling the paper in its most profitable area—its retail trade area. Likewise, unprofitable circulation should be decreased or made profitable. Subscription prices should be adjusted so they will provide a profit on the product.

ORGANIZATION OF THE CIRCULATION DEPARTMENT

Even the smallest newspaper should have one person other than the editor or advertising manager who oversees circulation and its promotion. On a very small newspaper, this person may be a front-office employee or a back-shop supervisor. Larger newspapers can designate one person to supervise circulation sales through all distribution phases, maintain mailing lists, and conduct promotions and campaigns.

Before examining the various types of circulation service, let us take a look at the importance of the role the newspaper product has in building circulation.

There is no substitute for local news and sports excellence. The steady circulation growth of the country's hometown newspapers can be attributed largely to a concentrated year-round sales program and a stronger emphasis on local news. Successful newspapers are merchandising their strong news points—features, columns, reader-involvement pieces.

If a newspaper is to achieve steady circulation growth, the question that must continually be asked is: How can this newspaper better serve this community? It can only do so with a product that will be useful to all readers.

Single Copy Sales

There are several methods of newspaper distribution and each has advantages and disadvantages.

For the community newspaper that distributes most of its copies by mail, single copy sales are one of the basics on which to build the circulation development program. Papers sold on counters and through honor racks and vending machines provide good circulation revenue. Single copy sales may even rival the in-county or trade area mail distribution. This can be unstable circulation, however, and you may want to convert these readers to the subscription list.

One of the best ways is through the use of subscription insert cards in newsstand copies every three months. This method, with a money back guarantee promotion, has been used successfully by large dailies and magazines. Basically readers are asked to try the paper for six months or a year. If, after six weeks, they report they are not satisfied, their money will be refunded.

A weekly paper may offer options of 13, 26, 52, or 104 issues rather than three months, six months, or one year. Semiweeklies should use the option of 26, 52, or 104 issues. The card should show the savings of a subscription over single copies and list the cost per issue.

Vending machines and counter sales should be at high-volume, late-hour retail establishments in city and at the best locations in all rural communities in the primary circulation area. These are usually grocery and drug stores. Ideally, vending machines should be scattered in all areas of town, but the average community newspaper cannot afford this luxury. The alternative is to establish as many counter sales points as possible. This is the ideal distribution medium for single copies. Many retailers, especially convenience stores, want papers inside to generate store traffic. Managers should be asked to display the paper on checkout lanes near cash registers. Honor racks should be used only as a last resort. Places that attract people and traffic are the best outlets.

The newspaper should constantly improve the outlets; there is no limit on locations. The newspaper should be available at hospitals, rest homes, hotels, motels, stores, airports, restaurants, supermarkets, bus stations. Motels will sometimes buy every week at bulk rate for distribution to patrons. Every crossroads store is an excellent outlet.

Another method to increase single copy sales is to contract with a local service station to accept forty or fifty copies as soon as they are off the press and offer them free to the first persons who fill their gasoline tanks. An in-paper advertisement featuring the station owner holding a copy of the paper can be an effective way of announcing the promotion.

The circulation manager should check returns weekly, evaluate vendors, and adjust the number of papers for each outlet to the average number of sales. Try to hold to a 10 percent return maximum. The number of coin-operated vending machines should be increased where feasible. Armored-housing type machines with the paper's logotype imprinted on both fronts and sides of the machines are best.

Twenty-cent newspapers should specify coin mechanisms on face plates on each machine. You might consider machines that will accept a quarter in the nickel slot, with no change; many patrons without proper change will pay a quarter for a good hometown newspaper.

Generally, the maximum profit to the dealer on counter sales should be five cents, whether the purchase price is fifteen or forty cents.

Depending on the volume of papers sold, newspapers that have a relatively large number of small dealers who use honor racks and receive discounts should consider replacing such dealers with vending machines, thus recovering the discount.

The ideal in single copy sales is to collect from stores and dealers for single copies a week in advance. If this cannot be done, a close check of the returns is necessary to keep wastage to a minimum.

Keep newsstand sales honest by having different people delivering and collecting.

News dealers and rack locations may be publicized by use of a window decal, such as

"If you are looking for
LOCAL NEWS
You'll find it HERE!"

Mail Distribution

Most of the 7,530 nondaily newspapers in the United States depend on the U.S. Postal Service to deliver their newspapers. This is especially true in rural areas.

With a second-class mailing permit and a friendly postmaster, the newspaper has the most dependable, practical, and inexpensive delivery system available. A friendly relationship with the postmaster and postal workers can be helpful in expediting newspaper handling.

Despite continuing increases in second-class mail rates, this method remains the best circulation distribution system for the average community newspaper.

Operating a community newspaper with a second-class mail permit has many advantages, but rules are strict, and penalties for violation of second-class mailing requirements are severe and becoming more so.

There is no better way to avoid trouble with the Postal Service than to read and reread part three of the National Newspaper Association manual *Federal Laws Affecting Newspapers, Postal Laws and Regulations.* It is free to NNA members.

Also, the regional post office has public relations and second-class mail experts with whom you can discuss your goals and objectives.

THIRD CLASS

Even though second class is the best method of mail distribution for newspapers, there are other ways to mail. Third-class bulk mail is used by many community newspapers just getting started. In this manner they can build a list of paid subscribers and apply for a second-class mail permit when 50 percent or more of their circulation is paid.

Home Delivery

For small dailies and some large weekly newspapers, home delivery by the newspaper boy or girl can provide the best combination of sales and service at the least cost.

For some newspapers, a combination of carrier delivery in town and mail delivery on rural routes has worked best. Sufficient population density is a necessity for a carrier system to work. The advantages of door-to-door delivery must be weighed against the higher administrative costs and headaches of carrier turnover. It will also work better for the newspaper that has no competition for carriers from a larger afternoon daily—they will manage to get the best of the carriers.

The country editor can operate just about any other phase of this circulation marketing program by himself, but a carrier system is too time-consuming for one person to handle.

Advantages of carrier delivery include same-day delivery, built-in circulation crews, ability to build a 100 percent home-delivery system, fewer problems and less expense with inserts, and better opportunities to increase publication frequency and distribute a shopper to nonsubscribers.

Disadvantages are that it has a higher cost than mail, greater carrier turnover, higher administrative expenses, and more delivery complaints.

NEWSPAPER-OWNED TUBE SYSTEMS

When delivering two or more publications a week, or the density of homes is at least four and preferably six per mile, it is often wise to purchase your own tubes, have them installed, and thereby establish your own motor route system. It makes it easier for the insert business, it will reduce the cost compared to third-class and controlled-circulation rates, and it will provide the immediate flexibility of total market coverage without redesigning the publication. The best design is to follow the postal route with the tubes and mount them on the same pole as the mailbox or within eighteen inches to the left of the mailbox, especially in the northern climates where snowplows cause a great deal of damage. In some instances, weekly newspapers can share the same pole with the daily newspaper. The newspaper may also seek out other publications for delivery in the same area to reduce the cost.

Population density, competitive aspects, accessibility, and signs of growth in a community are factors that help determine the best distribution method.

VOLUNTARY PAY

Many suburban newspapers across the country praise the voluntary pay distribution plan. Simply, what they do is distribute to all households by carrier and collect for as many papers as they can.

Some have managed, through incentive plans and contests, to reach 50 percent paid circulation and apply for a second-class mailing permit. Others, to give the total market coverage sought by most large advertisers, have continued to blanket the trade area, making up for circulation revenue by charging relatively higher ad rates.

The quality of the news product often is the deciding factor in whether or not a paper should switch to voluntary pay. If a newspaper has a paid circulation of only 30 to 40 percent, voluntary pay may be a good idea.

However, if the newspaper is giving its readers the quality product that will produce 80 to 90 percent penetration in the trade area with paid circulation, voluntary pay offers no benefits. This is because the second-class newspaper is able to keep its ad rates down by producing a healthy circulation revenue profit.

A Look at the Product

The hometown newspaper provides a unique product offered by no out-of-town newspaper: local news. This is the biggest marketing tool. No other newspaper can compete on equal terms for circulation if a newspaper emphasizes local news, and does it effectively, regardless of its current price or the competitor's price.

Successful merchandising of the newspaper is easy if it offers all the ingredients. These include agriculture, area news, books, business news, com-

munity calendar, gardening, government (what it means to readers), hobbies, horoscope, letters from readers, living features, obituaries, opinion, public record, religion, rural news, school news (what it means to readers), sports, and weather.

It has been said that before a newspaper conducts a circulation campaign it should examine its news product, improve it where necessary, then plan a subscription drive. This is true because the news product must be reader-oriented.

Sampling: Soliciting New Subscribers

Newspapers with second-class mail permits should take full advantage of the 10 percent bulk sample privilege offered by the Postal Service.

SAMPLING RURAL ROUTES

Selective sampling of rural-route families in the county and trade area is one of the best—and least expensive—methods of developing paid circulation.

A sampling program for both in-city and rural-route residents is easy to develop. The important thing to remember is give prospective patrons a long enough look at the paper. In all sampling, at least four weeks' issues should be sent.

Here is how to set up a selective sampling program on a route-by-route basis:

First, a list should be prepared of all families on each rural route from the latest figures provided by local post offices. Use "family" counts, not "box-holders." There is a difference. Both figures are available, but there will al-

FIGURE 18–1 This simple form can be used to keep track of a newspaper's sampling program.

SAMPLE USAGE, SECOND CLASS BULK MAIL

_____
Name of Newspaper

1. Total estimated weight of copies mailed previous year _____

2. 10% of the total estimated weight   _____

3. Number of pages printed during previous year   _____

COMPUTATION, SAMPLES

Date of Mailing	Sample Copies, Number	Pounds	Aggregate Total, Pounds
_____	_____	_____	
_____	_____	_____	_____
_____	_____	_____	_____
_____	_____	_____	_____
_____	_____	_____	_____
_____	_____	_____	_____
_____	_____	_____	_____
_____	_____	_____	_____
_____	_____	_____	_____
_____	_____	_____	_____
_____	_____	_____	_____
_____	_____	_____	_____

ways be a few more families than box-holders on a route, because more than one family unit sometimes get mail at a single box. It is important to get the latest figures. These are updated constantly and are readily available from local post offices.

Sampling should concentrate first on one or two rural routes—no more—where the newspaper has its weakest penetration. Send a minimum of four weeks' issues to each prospect. Include the subscription insert card used for converting newsstand patrons to subscription rolls. An in-paper promotion advertisement in the sample issues may be helpful.

REGULATIONS ON SAMPLING

The Postal Service provides that newspapers with second-class mailing permits may mail sample copies "at any time during a calendar year to the extent of 10 percent of the total estimated weight of copies to be mailed to subscribers during the calendar year." Not 10 percent of the copies, but 10 percent of total *weight* of copies mailed.

The circulation manager can keep track of his newspaper's sampling program with a simple form that includes the date, number of sample copies mailed, their weight, and an aggregate postal column. (See Fig. 18–1.)

Since the newspaper will not know until the end of the year the total weight of mailed copies for that calendar year, some guesswork is involved. Total weight of copies mailed during the previous year provides a good guide. This total is available from postmasters. Circulators may take 10 percent of this total as a guide and begin the route-sampling program, keeping track as it progresses.

Postal regulations require that sample copies be labeled as such. Replating on press can be avoided by setting the words "Sample Copy" in the nameplate area and giving the pressman instructions to run the specified number of samples. Then he may stop the press, remove the inscription with an abrasive retouching eraser, and complete the press run.

For instance, the newspaper may

sample Route 1, Centerville, which the postmaster says has 750 postal families. The newspaper has 256 subscribers on that route. The 494 nonsubscribers on that route represent the audience the newspaper wants to attract.

Selective sampling of rural routes using the 10 percent second-class sample bulk mailing privilege is one of the easiest and least expensive methods of getting a newspaper into the hands of nonsubscribers.

The secret is giving these prospects enough sample copies of the community paper to allow them not only to evaluate it but to create a desire for them to read the newspaper regularly.

A subscription insert card included in every sample will make it easy for prospective patrons to accept the newspaper's money-back guarantee offer. As an alternative, the newspaper can insert a first-class business reply envelope in each sample, soliciting subscriptions with introductory offers.

A newspaper that does not take advantage of its 10 percent second-class sample privilege is missing one of the best ways to add new subscribers economically.

IN-CITY SAMPLING

Soliciting new subscribers in cities where there are street addresses and carriers is another matter. The newspaper must adjust its program for this facet of the audience.

The secret of in-city sampling lies in tying this program in with telephone solicitation. Using a combination of in-city sampling and telephone follow-up, the country weekly, along with weeklies, semiweeklies, triweeklies, and small daily papers, can build a circulation development program that is both effective and economical.

It is easy for newspapers with second-class mailing permits to sample rural routes, using the paper's 10 percent bulk sample privilege. Sending samples in-city is another matter. A list of nonsubscribers is needed for in-city sampling; at least a list of street addresses. A newspaper just cannot blanket a city carrier route as it can in rural-route sampling.

One way to solve this problem is to prepare a nonserved list, using the community's telephone book. By comparing names in the telephone book with the paper's mailing list, a fairly accurate list of the people who are not subscribers to the paper can be compiled.

Or, if the publisher or editor is on good terms with the manager of the local electric utility or water company, it may be possible to obtain the utility company's list of patrons and build a nonserved list from this.

With the list of names and street addresses prepared for the in-city sampling, the newspaper can make the program more elaborate and effective by utilizing telephone sales.

After a list of nonsubscribers is compiled, the newspaper can begin sending sample copies. Small papers should send ten or fifteen samples weekly. Larger ones may want to send as many as fifty.

The in-city selective sampling program may be supplemented with an introductory letter, subscription insert cards as in other sampling, and a follow-up by telephone to get subscriptions.

Three to five days before the first sample is sent, a letter should be sent to each prospective patron. It should quote no rates but simply inform prospects they will receive four weeks of sample copies. This letter describes the reasons the prospects should be subscribing to the paper and tells them that each sample copy will contain a special introductory offer.

Newspapers should begin the telephone sales program after the arrival of the second sample copy. By the time four samples have been sent, prospects will have had time to evaluate the newspaper and will be ready for a sales presentation.

A regular staff member may be used for the telephone sales effort, or part-time workers can work from their homes. The newspaper sales presentation provides answers to questions that may be asked and objections that may be voiced.

By mixing sample copies with regular mailings, these sample totals may be part of the 10 percent bulk sample privilege.

A payment system that works well for the average newspaper is the minimum wage plus a 20 percent commission for each new subscriber. Telephone solicitors usually find it best to make calls between 5:30 and 9 P.M. when most people are at home.

OTHER PROSPECTS

New subscriptions can be obtained with Welcome Wagon participation. Utility company records also may be used to get newcomer lists. A four-week free subscription to newcomers is recommended. Other potential subscribers include newlyweds and parents of each new baby. Letters should be sent to each group three to five days before sending the first sample, with a subscription insert card in all samples.

Many community newspapers depend on mail and single copy sales for the bulk of their paid circulation. For these papers, selective sampling of rural routes, plus in-city sampling with telephone follow-up, can pay big dividends in subscription sales.

The newspaper that sends sample copies to nonsubscribers on rural routes and in city-carrier areas will soon use up its 10 percent second-class bulk sample privilege. That is why it is important to keep a running tally on the sample usage chart.

In the past, oversampling was a costly affair. The billing, at second-class transient rates, was ten cents for the first two ounces and four cents for each additional ounce. New transient rates allow a newspaper to sample less expensively than in the past.

Small dailies estimate a new start is worth about fifteen dollars. Metropolitan newspapers put the value much higher.

Using a well-planned sampling program, the newspaper can add starts for half its local subscription price or less.

House-to-House Circulation Drives

Selling subscriptions through door-to-door campaigns provides a good means of increasing circulation. High school groups, community organizations, senior citizens, and the newspaper's staff provide the best solicitors. Outside solicitors should not be used unless their references are checked carefully.

Pay scales vary for solicitors according to subscription rates, but the general trend is to pay the minimum wage, plus a 20 percent commission on new subscriptions.

Renewals

Many community editors remember the days when the newspaper's subscription renewal program consisted exclusively of four different colored envelopes, with as many different letter appeals. First-class postage was three cents. Newspapers were moved free in-county. Subscriptions rarely exceeded two dollars a year.

A coordinated renewal solicitation program is just as important now as it was then. Only the guidelines are different.

MONEY-BACK GUARANTEE

The money-back guarantee theme and the stop-saver program are among the newest and best additions to the circulation promotion. Both can play an important role in a newspaper's circulation management program.

Saving stops is the newspaper's first concern. The term originated with large dailies, where circulation has been a number one priority longer than in the community field. Basically, it is a plan to keep subscribers on the rolls.

The job of the circulation department is to sell new subscriptions, but it is up to the news department to keep them. Newspeople "sell" renewals.

STOP-SAVER PROGRAM

Here is one way the newspaper can use the stop-saver program.

A postage-paid business reply subscription renewal envelope is mailed four to six weeks before the expiration date. It contains a genuine sales appeal in the copy, not just a "you owe us, please send x" ultimatum.

Readers being asked to pay ten to thirty dollars for a year's subscription to a community newspaper deserve the early notice so they can plan to set aside the cash before their subscriptions expire.

Many patrons (up to 70 percent) will respond before the third week of the expiration month. At that time the newspaper should telephone local patrons whose renewals have not been received. That effort generally brings them in.

At the end of the expiration month, all expired subscriptions should be removed from the mailing list. As soon as some subscribers miss an issue, they renew.

During the second week after expiration, the newspaper should follow with phone calls to in-county subscribers and letters to out-of-county expirations, using the appeal "We are sorry we have lost you as a subscriber." The newspaper should also seek reasons for stops. This last effort always prevents a few stops.

The well-planned renewal solicitation program is a must for the community newspaper. It is just as important as promoting single copy sales, sampling and soliciting new subscribers, or any other phase of the circulation development program.

Record Keeping and Revenue Planning

Record keeping and revenue planning are among the most vital elements in a successful circulation development program. Whether it is a 2,000-circulation country weekly or a 10,000-circulation suburban newspaper, the ability to plan and organize this phase of circulation development will not only pay off in new starts but will also keep costs down. With newsprint selling at record prices, and production and wages fol-

6 Week
Money-Back Guarantee

We make this money-back guarantee to you because we are confident you will find offers you more for your money.

YOU RECEIVE ALL THE NEWS . . . in _____ . Local news is our lifeblood. Each week we tell our readers what's happening in _____ . Our news concerns local community activities, schools, churches, social affairs, sports, business and government. We do a better job of reporting _____ than anyone else. All of us at the News are dedicated to producing the best newspaper possible.

YOUR SUBSCRIPTION WILL COST YOU NOTHING . . . if you clip the ad coupons that appear each week in _____ . Our local ads inform you of the best buys in food, clothing, household goods, whatever you may need. The ad coupons you clip from _____ during your introductory offer will more than pay for the cost of your subscription.

If you don't like the paper, you'll get your money back. If you do take the paper, you can save hundreds of dollars a year through store coupons and buying bargains.

Money-Back GUARANTEE

If, after having _____ delivered to your home for a period of six weeks you are not satisfied with the product or delivery service, your full subscription price will be refunded upon presentation of your written statement explaining the reason for cancellation. Requests for refund must be received by Circulation Department within six weeks of order date.

Clip This Order Form And Mail, With Remittance To

MONEY-BACK GUARANTEE ORDER FORM

Yes, I'll accept your Money-Back Guarantee. Start my subscription immediately.

[Select the subscription option of your choice.]

26 issues $ ☐   52 issues $ ☐   104 issues $ Save $ ☐

Please include check or money order. (This offer good only for residents of _____ .)

Name _____

Address _____

City _____ Date _____

Mail to

lowing close behind, accurate record keeping and revenue planning are more important than ever before.

Here are guidelines to consider in keeping those costs down.

- Maintain adequate records for accurate circulation development. Analyze postal reporting forms.

- Provide adequate supervision to ensure accuracy.

- Provide safety features: Duplicate mailing lists, two "on-off" card files (A–Z, Jan.–Dec.); count mail-subscription cards every three months.

- Limit unpaid circulation.

- Reduce variance in net paid and press runs.

ABC

The best-known circulation record-keeping system available for the community newspaper is that used by the Audit Bureau of Circulation (ABC). Their *Weekly Newspaper Record Keeping Aid* is available by writing to: Audit Bureau of Circulation, Education Department, 123 North Wacker Drive, Chicago, Illinois 60606.

Having your circulation audited could help you attract national or co-op advertising.

DESIGNING YOUR OWN FORMS

Newspapers that are not members of the ABC can design their own circulation record-keeping forms, tailored to their individual needs. Whatever system the circulation manager uses, it will take only about five minutes a week to complete a circulation report that will give a good look at the news-

FIGURE 18–2 This form can be used for a money-back guarantee theme, a popular addition to circulation promotion.

paper's performance during the past week in all phases of circulation development. Here regular efforts can be made to keep wastage to a minimum.

Circulation reporting systems should be monitored constantly. The same goes for postal reporting forms, which should be double-checked by the newspaper to make sure correct computations have been made by postal officials.

SAFETY FEATURES

Several safety features should also be provided.

Newspapers should always have an extra set of address labels. A list should be kept in a fireproof file and replaced every six months.

Maintain two "on-off" files, separate from the subscription card system. Arrange one by month of expiration, the other alphabetically by subscriber name. Unpaid circulation should be included as a separate group.

The "on-off" cards should include name, address, date of renewal, plus changes of address as they occur. They constitute a valuable circulation history that will save the newspaper time and trouble in its record-keeping program.

As an additional safety feature, a newspaper's mail subscription cards should be counted every three months. Good dates to do this are March 31, June 30, September 30, and December 31. Circulation reports can be reconciled on these dates also.

PACKAGE LABELS

Use adhesive package labels. These labels are available free from post offices and will eliminate "header cards" used to separate mailing destinations and wasted papers. Packages must be limited to six or more copies for the same destination.

UNPAID CIRCULATION

Each newspaper should constantly

monitor its unpaid circulation and papers used for the office and files. Variance between net paid and press runs should never total more than 10 percent. Unpaid circulation should be limited to exchanges, copies to press associations, and voucher copies to advertisers who have an ad appearing in each issue. Tear sheets or single copies should be sent to those who advertise on an irregular basis. Every newspaper should control complimentary copies sent to advertisers, favored friends, and employees' relatives. However, sending "comps" to the local postmaster and local carriers is a move that can pay big dividends. A newspaper cannot have a better friend than a postmaster. Exchanges with other papers should be limited only to those from which the paper's staff can learn something in the way of content, design, or layout.

Circulation Promotion

Regardless of the size of the newspaper's budget, it can have a successful promotion program.

"Win-a-Bike Contest" is a good spring and summer promotion for either the weekly or daily newspaper. In a two-month contest, boys and girls are offered a new three-speed bike for new orders (number of orders to be determined on individual-paper basis). Prizes of radios and watches can be given for fewer orders. Children with not enough orders will get a dollar per order.

Newspapers may have a unique premium offer for new subscriptions: the work of a talented local artist. Scenes of local historical interest, printed on good stock, provide an extraordinarily fine subscription premium at a moderately low cost.

Newspaper bingo is one of the more popular and productive circulation and advertising games on the market. Readers can win up to one hundred dollars in "Bingo Bucks" from local advertisers each week of this thirteen week promotion.

Newspapers should use every member of their staffs to sell subscriptions to the people they meet as they sell advertising and gather the news. Modest commissions should be paid for new subscriptions only.

NEWSPAPER-IN-EDUCATION PROGRAM

The Newspaper-in-Education program requires careful planning and involves more than just dropping a bundle of papers at a school and hoping they find their way to the classroom. If developed correctly this program can add concrete circulation and public service benefits to a newspaper.

Papers used in this program should be sold at a 50-percent discount or some other special rate for a number of weeks. They should not be distributed free. If half the regular price is charged, these papers may be counted as paid circulation.

To be successful, the Newspaper-in-Education program must be both diverse and comprehensive—diverse because it must offer selected teacher and student aids in broad curriculum areas and comprehensive because, in combination with the newspaper, it provides a timely alternative to the standard textbook approach.

IN-PAPER PROMOTION

Promote yourself. The newspaper should follow the same advice given to advertisers by running advertising for itself. But it should not attempt to develop circulation on a helter-skelter basis. Coordinate it with a plan for promoting subscriptions.

Use a series of in-paper ads with the money-back guarantee theme, inviting nonsubscribers to clip the coupon portion of the ad.

Advertising yourself should also include discounts to senior citizens and promotion of gift subscriptions, especially at Christmas. And as a final touch to the in-paper promotion, periodically publish a list of newsstands and dealers.

Promote the concept of the newspaper as an instrument instead of an expense, as an inflation fighter rather than an inflation feeder, and as a product that will not cost the purchaser a cent if he reads the ads for bargains and clips the store coupons. Logically and effectively convince readers and prospects alike that they cannot afford *not* to buy your newspaper.

OTHER PROMOTIONS

Getting the newspaper's subscription sales message to nonsubscribers economically is a problem. Direct mail may be prohibitive for the average community newspaper. One way newspapers have found to tell their circulation story to prospective patrons is via the local radio station. Through a trade agreement, you can feature spots on the local radio station that reinforce your money-back guarantee and savings-through-store-coupons themes.

Billboards may also be used to good advantage to announce a new feature or a special circulation promotion. Television is valuable if it is affordable.

Drastic cut-rate offers and elaborate giveaways should be avoided. Neither works very well. Cut-rate offers establish hard-to-break patterns with the people in the community. If such offers are used regularly, subscribers will begin following the pattern, letting their subscriptions expire and then getting back on as new subscribers when they are offered a special deal. Remember, if the newspaper is distributed by second-class mail, the price cannot be reduced more than 50 percent—and this must include the value of premiums. Big promotions add subscribers, but keeping these people is another matter.

In summary: Planning and organizing are the keys to a successful circulation program.

Rates
SINGLE COPY PRICES

A newspaper's location, in regard to competition, has much to do with the price put on single copies of the newspaper.

Although the days of the ten-cent paper are long gone, there are several factors that must be taken into consideration in providing single copy revenue.

Community newspapers in noncompetitive situations are in a position to charge a higher price for their single copies than those with competition. If the competition is a large daily, however, the hometown newspaper should not hesitate to charge a nickel more than it does. The community newspaper is and will continue to be one of the best bargains available to the buying public.

SUBSCRIPTION RATES

Like other commodities, quality newspapers can demand higher prices. Annual mail-subscription rates for the trade area should reflect a substantial savings over single copy prices if the newspaper intends to concentrate on building a strong mailing list rather than single copy sales.

If, however, the newspaper wants to depend mainly on single copy sales as the prime source of circulation revenue, then trade area mail rates should vary only slightly from the paper's cumulative single copy price.

The newspaper's local trade area is generally considered the county in which the newspaper is published and parts of those surrounding it. It is this area in which advertisers are most vitally interested. Out-of-state circulation is no value to them. The cost of sending papers to areas beyond postal zones one and two makes it imperative that the community newspaper get a premium price for these subscriptions. Ordinarily, the weekly paper should charge three to five dollars more for a subscription outside its trade area.

Total Market Coverage

Advertisers are interested in having their message delivered to as many households as possible in a newspaper's trade area. If the newspaper cannot provide this high penetration coverage (at least 80 percent), the advertiser will look elsewhere—third class or door-to-door delivery, for example. One hundred percent coverage is no more possible for the hometown newspaper than is perfection of any other kind, so there must be other ways of providing the circulation demanded for total market coverage. This is discussed in detail in Chapter 19.

The Post Office

Knowing what is required of the newspaper from the U.S. Postal Service is one of the most important aspects of circulation management. The local postmaster may not have all the answers, but the rate and classification official at the sectional center facility is a potential friend. His job is to provide up-to-date information and consultation on second-class postal matters. Both he and the local postmaster can smooth the way through the regulations concerning mailing.

To keep up with changes in postal regulations, order *Memo to Mailers,* a monthly publication of the Public and Employee Communications Department, U.S. Postal Service, P.O. Box 1600, La Plata, Maryland 20646. There is no charge.

Trends in Newspaper Circulation

- We can expect more emphasis to be placed in the future on total marketing of newspapers.

- Hopefully, more colleges and universities will realize the growing need to include community journalism sequences and courses in their curricula.

- The growing importance of the circulation department will place the post of circulation manager on a level with that formerly shared by the news editor and the advertising manager. Quality as well as quantity will become more important in the circulation

departments of all newspapers.

- Increased postal rates may force many smaller newspapers to carrier distribution, especially in town and city areas.

- A bigger push is also seen for single copy sales, with vending machines taking the place of honor racks.

- As advertising supplement business continues to grow, newspapers will move strongly toward motor routes and mailing tubes to distribute supplementary shoppers and other free newspapers.

- Credit cards are being used more widely in renewals of both carrier and mail subscriptions. Newspapers can obtain machines for processing credit cards. They obtain authorization from subscribers on a special form to renew subscriptions automatically. When a subscription expires, the carrier submits the subscriber's name and card number to the circulation department and renewal is automatic.

Circulation Suggestions

- Be sure all the newspaper's employees are subscribers. By charging 50 percent of the regular rate, these "new subscribers" can be added to the paid list. (You can, of course, offer complimentary subscriptions as a company benefit.)

- Tests have proven that a twenty-cent newspaper is actually easier to sell than a fifteen-cent newspaper.

- Keep newsstand sales honest by having different people delivering and collecting. Losses should not exceed 10 percent on honor racks. Rotate employees on rack sales.

- Most often, dealers that sell fewer than twenty-five copies of each issue should be eliminated.

- Watch returns—10 percent or less is the ideal.

- Maximum profit to the dealer on counter sales should be five cents on a newspaper.

- A doorknob hanger featuring the money-back guarantee theme is a good supplemental promotion. It should contain a tear-off reply card.

- Send each money-back guarantee subscriber an acknowledgment letter that will reinforce advantages of newspaper reading.

- Average costs for weekly newspaper telephone-sales starts should not exceed a dollar fifty.

- The best season for phone solicitation is fall and winter.

- Fall is the best time of year to promote rural circulation.

- Eighty percent penetration of postal families in city and county should be a minimum goal for any newspaper.

- The telephone manners of office personnel are an important public relations tool.

- No newspaper should distribute more than fifty copies free.

- October is the best time to raise subscription rates.

- Don't be afraid to charge what the product is worth!

- Circulation is a marketing product—the better the product, the easier it will be to sell.

Finally, and perhaps most importantly, there is simply no substitute for good planning and marketing. One major campaign and perhaps two to four minor campaigns annually are a must.

Chapter 19

WILLIAM E. BRANEN

The author is publisher of the Burlington (Wisconsin) *Standard Press,* owner of several other newspapers including shoppers, and past president of the National Newspaper Association.

"Today few speak about shoppers as not being effective. One once heard about the great number of shopper publications in wastebaskets of post offices where they had been thrown by patrons. The implication was that no one read shoppers. Few say that today."

The Shopper— Friend or Foe?

by WILLIAM E. BRANEN

If advertising is news, the so-called "shopper" is a newspaper—but for more than fifty years the bona fide newspaper as defined by postal authorities and state legislators would never accept the shopper into the newspaper fraternity. As the shopper became accepted by the public, which occurred more and more in the 1960s than ever before, many daily and community newspapers in the country began studying the shopper phenomenon.

They started to set up separate publications or to combine an advertising product with their main news product to attain saturation coverage of the area.

Many of the shopper publishers dislike the term "shopper" as a definition of their product. They maintain the shopper is the person who reads the publication and uses it to plan their shopping.

Probably the most difficult task today is defining the shopper and determining whether it is synonymous with a newspaper, which is a statutory term used in many states.

The inclusion of a free newspaper and shopping guide within the definition of a newspaper for most purposes would go a long way in solving many of these problems. Laws vary from state to state, making a broad definition difficult.

A shopper is a newspaper containing principally advertising which is distributed free, door-to-door and without request, as defined in the case *Union Leader Corporation* v. *Newspapers of New England, Inc.* in 1961. It could be noted that many also are placed in mailboxes, since about half the shoppers are distributed by the U.S. Postal Service.

A handbill is a loose printed sheet to be distributed by hand for advertising purposes. This definition came from a Mississippi case in 1943. It had been previously defined in a Kentucky case as a written or printed notice displayed to inform those concerned of something that will happen. Handbills and leaflets date back to the early founding of this nation and are usually announcements for one firm or individual.

This is in contrast to a newspaper, which is a publication, usually in sheet form, intended for general circulation. It is published regularly at short intervals and contains intelligence of current events and news of general interest. The U.S. Postal Service interpretation states that it must have at least 50 percent plus one paid circulation, whether it be delivered through the mail, by carrier, or at news racks or stands. Some states require a much higher percentage of paid circulation to qualify as a legal publication.

Born During the Depression

Shoppers began in earnest during the Great Depression of the 1930s, when merchants in concentrated areas found it necessary to try to reduce their advertising budgets by uniting to form "cooperatives" which would publish for limited urban neighborhoods. The circulars they produced were primarily advertisements for several stores in one area, in the form of a downtown shopping news or a neighborhood shopping guide.

These publications flourished in larger cities. Then, because of higher costs and better concentration by the paid newspapers plus the emergence of World War II, their popularity waned.

After World War II, shoppers began to spring up in certain states and in the 1960s and early 1970s, new ones emerged in all parts of the country. Estimates in 1979 indicated there were close to 10,000 shoppers of one type or another published in the United States. Their national organization (National Association of Advertising Publishers) has about 20 percent of that total listed in its directory. The headquarters are located in Madison, Wisconsin.

THE LATEST BOOM

In the 1960s and 1970s, a new shopper craze swept most sections of this country, going by a variety of names: penny saver, circular, free sheet, throwaway. The wise newspaper publisher started some type of free publication of his own or at least had a plan to introduce one in case he faced competition in his community.

If the newspaper publisher was first in his market, he was most likely to escape antitrust action by a shopper publisher. If he waited too long and moved in after the competition was entrenched, he often found a letter addressed to him from the competitor's lawyer, and costly antitrust action ensued. Following the leader is a dangerous game in shopper–newspaper relationships.

Actually the shopper craze has been caused by the invasion of large retail chain stores into selected markets. The size of the community is not the criterion as to whether or not a shopper will commence. It depends on the type of retailers who move into the community. Chain stores have insisted on saturation coverage and after some reluctance to recognize the insistence, paid-circulation newspapers have begun to accept these wishes and provide new publications which give near 100 percent area coverage.

During the late 1960s and early 1970s, many publishers found readership dwindling. People did not have enough time to read the full content of their newspapers. These same people, however, were still interested in bargains. They began reading the advertising shoppers laid at their doorsteps or delivered by mail instead of subscribing to the daily community newspaper. Weekly newspapers did not feel the pinch as much as the large or medium-sized metropolitan papers, but cities with two or three newspapers suddenly found themselves with just one.

Why Shoppers Work

The shopper escapes most of the hazards encountered in publishing a newspaper. It does not have sharp editorials criticizing local governments; it does not print court cases involving local merchants; it does not carry editorials praising or questioning the actions of a congressman from a particular party; and it does not carry stories on ecology and consumerism which actually level attacks upon some of the merchants. The shopper, avoiding all editorial content, comes out with page after page of bargains for the consumer, without an ill word about anyone.

Newspaper audits show good circulation figures in most cases, with claims of anywhere from 60 to 90 percent coverage. When a shopper begins, it claims 100 percent coverage for its advertisers. In most cases today, a shopper will have a two-to-one circulation advantage over a paid newspaper. For instance, if the newspaper has 5,000 circulation, the shopper very often will have about 10,000.

Shoppers have gained great notoriety for exclusiveness with coupons, and during the past two decades more large retail chains and grocers began using them in their advertisements. The shopper, delivered free to everyone, showed very high percentages of coupon redemption.

The emergence of the web press also gave shoppers a new life. Press time became available in a hungry jobber's plant or in a central printing plant and that printer or publisher looked for prospective customers. The best type of customer to assign to a contract was one who was starting a shopper in a community near that printer's plant.

Large chain stores have financed new shopper publications so that their messages could receive 100 percent coverage. Others were launched when disgruntled newspaper employees, usually in advertising sales, thought they could do a better job of merchandising or advertising than the paid publication.

It should be pointed out that shoppers also are successful because of association. When one advertiser places an ad in a shopper and it happens to be a large and respected advertiser, other businesses will follow. One grocery store is followed by others. It's the old "monkey see, monkey do" concept with some economic realities added; businesses want to reach each potential customer and to get their message across whenever and wherever their competition does. Shoppers concentrate on areas most sensitive to the ad market—classified, grocery, and entertainment. In rural areas, auction advertisements are especially susceptible.

Shoppers do not have to fight underhanded. Their punch is hard enough. Most established shoppers became successful because someone else was complacent, stubborn, or inattentive when the shopper invasion began.

It took the newspapers more than a dozen years to catch on to techniques to bring that margin of advantage down.

Newspapers Strike Back

As shoppers became tough competitors, the only way newspapers found to defeat them was to offer what the merchants wanted, but what most newspaper publishers previously refused to accept: total market coverage (TMC), nonduplicating coverage (NDC), or target coverage. The paid newspaper publisher found that merchants wanted saturation, and the only way the newspaper could give 100 percent coverage—an impossibility with a paid newspaper—was to enter the TMC or NDC fray.

Many newspapers have had to accept this 100-percent distribution concept, which at first seems costly, hard to manage, and difficult to initiate.

The three methods use different means to obtain saturation coverage. The author coined the term *nonduplicating coverage* in the early 1960s. Merchants like slogans, initials, and gimmicks, so it was decided to use initials for this concept as well. Nonduplicating coverage actually means delivering some product, usually a remake of the newspaper into a shopper, once or even twice a week. Ads can be sold at combination rates and delivered to each home not receiving the paid product. The rates must bring a profit to the newspaper or again antitrust action is feasible.

Nonduplicating coverage is an insurance by the newspaper that every household in the immediate circulation area receives some type of publication on a nonduplicated basis. NDC may be delivered by mail or with complete tube, claim, or hook setup. If households do not get the ads in paid-circulation newspapers, they will get them in a free shopper or NDC. If a publisher from one town does not have an ad in his newspaper, he will cooperate with the adjoining towns' publications, either weeklies or dailies, and make sure the ad runs in the total trade area.

NDC means rejecting the claims of most newspapers, for they must admit that 10, 20, 30, even more than 50 percent of the residents in their trade area do not subscribe to their publications.

Total market coverage means that a chain store or some regional advertiser decides an entire market must be covered by the newspaper. This can be accomplished in the central city by nonduplicating coverage and can be extended to total coverage of every household in certain suburban areas where the newspaper may not have good numbers because of competitive media coming in from other directions.

Meanwhile, target coverage is aiming extra coverage at a particular area not totally served by the paid newspaper, but needing saturation because of instability in circulation or because a certain advertiser thinks his business needs it.

With strong indications that people are reading less editorial matter, it becomes apparent that newspapers must find new and better ways of reaching these people at least with advertisements. If a paid-circulation newspaper finds that many households in its circulation area are not subscribing to the newspaper, the newspaper should be able to go to every household, either through some common effort among newspapers or with direct circulation such as NDC, TMC, or target coverage.

HOW TO FIGHT SHOPPERS

It has been said that the best way to combat shoppers is put out an exciting newspaper. That is always a good remedy, but it is not enough.

There are several ways for newspapers to combat shoppers or to gain shopper exclusivity in their particular areas:

- The newspaper can buy out the competitor. This will cost the paid newspaper anywhere from one half to three quarters of the competitor's gross.

- Newspapers can establish shoppers of their own, but that could lead to antitrust action and could be a very expensive move.

- They could publish controlled-circulation newspapers which are established at a lower rate by the U.S. Postal Service, providing the controlled-circulation papers contain 25 percent news and meet other regulatory requirements.

- They could embark on an NDC, TMC, or Target Coverage program.

- The publishers could join with fellow publishers in the area and start a common section.

- They also could join with their friends and print a common shopper.

Newspapers can, of course, allow matters to remain as they are, as many throughout the country have done, but to do this may place their very survival in jeopardy.

For the last several years, items about shoppers have appeared in state press association bulletins. State press association managers have worried about their threat. One Midwest manager said shoppers are very successfully competing with newspapers for advertising, so successfully in fact that they are forcing a reassessment of some long-held positions in the paid newspaper fraternity.

Many local shoppers, carrying no burden of public service are heartily disliked by the newspaper publishers who have to compete with them. There seems to be little question that to compete with local shoppers, a newspaper must publish something that gives saturation, too—ideally giving more coverage for a lower rate but still making a profit.

The big problem is not only local community shoppers, but also the well organized regional shoppers. These regionals are growing rapidly, seemingly expanding all the time.

Shoppers Are Effective

Today, few speak about shoppers as not being effective. One once heard about the great number of shopper publications in wastebaskets of post offices where they had been thrown by patrons. The implication was that no one read shoppers. Few people say that today.

If a publisher prints his own shopper, he generally has good things to say about it as an advertising medium. Some publishers say they dislike being involved with shoppers, and that they are only doing it because they have to fight fire with fire. If the truth were known, these publishers make more money and make it much more easily with their shopper or NDC or TMC than they do with the paid newspaper. This is true because there are no editorial costs. The greatest expenses for shoppers are distribution and printing.

Why are shoppers successful? It would seem because they provide a good advertising service. That has to be the case. As J. Lyle Crowder, publisher of the Charles City (Iowa) *Press,* said at a Wisconsin Newspaper Association meeting, "There's always sufficient room for any shopper to get a toehold in a community if the newspaper itself doesn't provide 100 percent circulation." He ought to know because he operated a shopper for years in competition with the daily he later managed.

The regional shoppers are particularly difficult to deal with, especially for the small daily or the larger weekly. They come in and say, "Look, this whole region is in fact one shopping area. Do you think your town and its immediate area—the postal routes, for example—really represent the shopping area of your community? Do you think the people in your town won't go down the road thirty, forty, or fifty miles to buy what they need?

"Do you think a farmer who wants to buy a tractor won't get in his pickup truck and drive a hundred miles to take a look at a tractor if it's advertised accurately and cleverly? Sure he will!"

The shopping area is in no way confined to one community under the regional shopper concept. It covers a region of ten to twelve communities served by ten to twelve individual weekly newspapers, with maybe two or three dailies interspersed.

"Now what we do is put our shopper into *every* person's hands in this great, big, common, natural shopping region," the regional shopper sales

FIGURE 19–1 The *Peach* was the first common supplement started in the United States. It is now circulated in eight newspapers in southeastern Wisconsin. *The Leader* is a shopper distributed in Evansville, Wisconsin, and surrounding areas.

person says. "And we do it for a lot less than if you advertised in every one of the newspapers in this region on its own terms."

Common Supplements

The ten or twelve newspapers have perhaps a $14-per-inch rate when added up collectively. The regional shopper may have a $6 to $7 rate, half the total for the group. In such cases it has been advocated that newspapers join in what would be called a *common supplement,* a common section distributed in each of the paid newspapers in the group.

The first such section, the *Peach,* was started in southeastern Wisconsin in 1962. Since then, hundreds have started in all parts of the country. The common section has become extremely successful. In fact, some dailies and weeklies have worked together to turn out a section which appears in all involved newspapers with a single supplement heading.

The common sections are the least likely to invite antitrust action if they are in a competitive area, because the common section is going to the regular paid subscribers under a regular formula of pricing.

The common section also is the least expensive way of getting numbers into circulation without involving expensive distribution costs, and merchants love numbers. True, with a common section you do not get 100 percent circulation, but you do obtain quantity, which satisfies demanding merchants, especially chains.

A publisher can print extra common sections and distribute them to nonsubscribers as an aid in combating shoppers or to help keep them out altogether. However, he must follow certain postal regulations when he uses this extra free circulation, and he must be sure to make a profit on the additional coverage.

Common sections have some flaws:

- There is some duplication of circulation among contiguous towns.

- Some competitive irritations surface among members involved.

- Households of nonsubscribers are ignored unless extra supplements are printed.

One also has immediate requirements when establishing a common supplement:

- You need a printing plant. It does not have to be your own because you can subcontract.

- One of the publishers must bill for the advertising inches involved, and someone has to direct page layout, no matter how minimal.

- You have to obtain cooperation on deadlines and understanding in case of errors. Since your associates are all in the same situation, all should be willing and able to help one another without too much friction.

Classifieds and Promotions Help Sales

Classifieds are the strongest selling ally for a shopper. Occasionally they are offered free or at exceptionally low rates. If one has a newspaper and can use an NDC, common section or one's own shopper, the publisher should try in some way to compete for those classifieds. They are very important to the growth and strength of newspapers.

Experts in the field maintain that free classified ads are illegal and subject to legal action against the perpetrator. However, publishers should do everything possible to sell classified columns, even at cut-rate, to monitor those in competitors' products, and try to obtain as many as possible through special gimmicks. Classified selection and promotion is weak in many paid-circulation newspapers, especially in smaller communities. The publishers ignore classifieds because they think they do not have the manpower to obtain them in any quantity.

Exciting Newspaper Needed

Another way of combating shoppers

is to publish an exciting newspaper. Even this does not guarantee that everyone will subscribe—that is an impossibility. But an exciting product brings more subscriptions and increases the potential to discourage competitors.

Publishers often sorely neglect finding out what their readers and nonreaders really would like from their newspaper. This invites competition from shoppers. Properly conducted surveys can help improve a product.

Advertising representatives often neglect the promotion of their ads. They will sell a well-balanced, attractive ad but fail to merchandise that ad through such actions as posting tear sheets in a retailer's business or putting up signs or reminders in store windows. Merchandising will give the advertiser a feeling that he is dealing with professionals.

The newspaper industry may have to examine its whole philosophy on paid circulation. Shoppers in the 1960s and 1970s were telling publishers something very important: there is no substitute for total market coverage. Either the newspaper provides it, or someone else will.

Of course, all the suggestions about NDC, TMC, and target coverage create problems for the publisher, because he is told that, if undue competitive action is taken against a shopper or some other type of publication, he might be subject to legal action.

Antitrust*

What about antitrust? This topic creates an atmosphere that is ambiguous and indecisive. There are no definite answers. Here are some suggestions and observations for someone starting or contemplating a shopper or NDC, TMC, or target publication.

It is now rather firmly established that a newspaper can usually show it has a reasonable business purpose in starting an adjunct shopper quite apart from any general or specific intent to injure competitors. In other words,

---

* See Chapter 25 for a detailed discussion of antitrust.

whether competitors were present or not, merchants would be demanding more distribution coverage.

However, a newspaper should first make a fair assessment of its relative economic power in its geographic market area. This will have some relevance to the degree of flexibility it will have in implementing the plan. If it concludes that, as a practical matter, it has the power to control the advertising market in the area in which it operates, it must recognize it is subject to closer scrutiny by a competitor and his legal staff; the newspaper must, in this case, abide by stricter rules than it otherwise might. Without sophisticated market studies, the assessment may be made by asking the following questions:

Would merchants have any effective means of shifting over to other media for communicating with their customers if we raised our rates or warned them we wouldn't do business with them if they did business with any of our competitors? Are they at our mercy or not?

If a newspaper has the practical power to raise rates or exclude competitors in a given area, then it has monopoly power. That doesn't mean it can't take reasonable commercial action to develop new products or expand its business; but this action might raise the presumption it is doing so for an illegal purpose.

If a newspaper doesn't have that power, it has more flexibility, but that flexibility still doesn't mean it can enter into actions which have no economic justification or which can be explained in no way other than as an attempt to achieve monopoly status.

Keeping this in mind, the focus shifts to the economic justification for initiation of the new shopper publication by the paid newspaper as a separate operation.

COMBINATION RATE LIKELY

For example, it is most likely that a combination advertising rate will be established for the newspaper and the shopper. It may be that the additional rate for space in the shopper will be a pickup rate over the space rates in the newspaper. It is essential that the combination rate plan be voluntary for the merchant, at least insofar as it relates to his decision on whether or not to use the shopper. (It may be legal to require that a merchant use the newspaper if he uses the shopper—a situation called "reverse tying." That question has not been tested legally.)

The point is that the pickup rate goes into the accounting system for the shopper entity.

A newspaper will have to cost-account its shopper publishing venture, and it is advisable not to manipulate this accounting system. It should attribute in a fair manner all costs directly involved in the publication, and if the initial projections are that the shopper should be profitable immediately, a newspaper might stretch a bit and apportion some costs to it which it might think questionable. The reason is that if litigation ensues, a competitive shopper publication will attempt to show that the newspaper started its adjunct solely for the purpose of excluding competition as demonstrated by the fact that it has no economic justification in itself. The newspaper will try to show it has a sound business basis. If it is obvious that the newspaper is not making a fair distribution of costs, it will raise doubt as to its motivation.

Any preliminary analysis and preplanning for the venture should be directed solely toward the business considerations vis-à-vis merchants and the economic justification for the new publication. It should not under any circumstances include anticompetitive statements or comparisons of proposed rates with those charged by competitors; the latter could be found to express an intent to exclude competition.

SET GROUND RULES

There should be a clear understanding among the entire staff, and particularly among the advertising sales people, of the ground rules to be followed. Situations have occurred in which management had a clear understanding of its limitations, but sales people engaged in questionable selling tactics which implicated the company as a whole.

Advertising and promotion activities must adhere strictly to the facts, particularly if any comparison is made between itself and its competitors. In one case, it was contended that the newspaper engaged in illegal practice by showing on the masthead of the shopper a figure which would have led one to believe it was the distribution figure for the shopper when in fact it was the combined circulation-distribution figure for the newspaper and shopper. This dangerous approach is seen quite frequently.

There are a few clearly prohibited activities which are so anticompetitive in nature that no business competitor should ever consider using them. They include:

- Refusal to accept advertising from any advertiser if he also advertises with a competitor.

- Granting secret discriminatory concessions and rates to certain advertisers, particularly if the rates and concessions are given in return for promises not to utilize another competitive publication.

- Attempting to induce advertisers to group together to boycott a competitor.

Pinning Down Nonsubscribers*

There are certain suggestions for meeting competition, and one is to obtain a list of nonsubscribers.

For the daily or the weekly—although weeklies are less likely to start motor routes—not using the U.S. Postal Service, it is wise to place a tube in front of every home. Mark the nonsubscriber drops with a colored adhesive tape and deliver NDCs or TMCs to those households once or twice a week. The distribution costs are then minimal if the newspaper is already delivering the paid product.

Or, the publisher may use the mail for the nonsubscribers. He can ob-

---

* See Chapter 18 for additional information on distribution relating primarily to subscribers and sampling.

tain a nonsubscriber list by crossing off subscribers' names when a new telephone directory is issued or through an assessor's household list, a utility company's route list or a plat book listing. Some telephone companies issue a cross-reference listing booklet which can be very valuable.

The publisher must know where the nonsubscribers live. This can be accomplished through those various methods, all time-consuming but at least 90 percent accurate.

One also can follow a foot mailman in the city or a rural route postal delivery person in the country and list all non-newspaper drops in sequence. Or the publisher can have his own carriers list nondrops by address and apartment number. It might be wise to send a second person along on the day or days this project is planned to assure more speed and accuracy.

In areas where coverage is extremely weak, the publisher might choose the 100 percent shopper-type coverage, which is called target coverage, giving some duplication, but a much better and less complicated delivery system.

If the stand sales (counter or street sales) are heavy, the publisher might try some type of survey to ascertain where the buyers of newspapers live. A survey card inserted in that newspaper might give some results, or a plan might be devised where the merchant who sells the newspaper does the survey at the checkout counter. The merchant would be told that the results will eliminate duplicate coverage and tend to keep his linage price down.

For distribution, one could use third-class mail or deliver by carrier who tosses the papers on driveways or places them on hooks or springs attached to rural route mailbox posts or on individual rods. In a metropolitan area, even though the post office may be used for paid circulation coverage, the publisher might find it economically sound to deliver nonpaid remakes of the newspaper by independent carriers. The price is less than third class. Here the publisher must be careful not to hire persons too young and not to abuse the Little Merchant Law for delivery of nonpaid products. (The Little Merchant Law allows twelve- and thirteen-year-olds to deliver and collect for paid newspapers. Other publications are not covered, and employing boys and girls of that age seems to be in violation.)

THE "50 PERCENT PLUS ONE" RULE

When planning new coverage using the paid-circulation product as a base, the publisher always should remember there is a postal regulation called the "50 percent plus one" rule which must be met in order to obtain free circulation privileges.

First, map out the circulation area. Then block out the outlying areas in which circulation is spotty and place mass-coverage tubes there. Into such spotty areas, one can legally deliver a complete paper or a remake of a newspaper or even a section of that newspaper to any number of households up to 50 percent minus one of the number of paid-circulation households without jeopardizing second-class mailing privileges. This advantageous circulation builder was unavailable until 1976. In 1977, Darwin Sharp, then director of the Office of Mail Classification, U.S. Postal Service, Washington, D.C., was asked to explain just what the 50 percent plus one rule meant.

Sharp explained that, if a publisher has copies of a second-class newspaper containing two twelve-page sections, a "reasonable" number of copies of one of these sections may be mailed at third-class rates to nonsubscribers, and doing so will not be in violation of Section 132.41 of the Postal Service Manual. (This same section also says that incomplete copies of a second-class newspaper which are put in the mail are subject to applicable third- or fourth-class rates.) But, Sharp said, the number of partial copies distributed should not be large enough to give the section "independent status," thereby precluding its being part of a newspaper or other second-class publication. The publisher can legally mail this publication by third or fourth class; he can leave stacks in a local supermarket; or he can place them in tubes in concentrated areas as outlined above.

However, any publication that exceeds the circulation of its paid second-class newspaper may not legally be delivered to more than 49.99 percent of the total circulation of that particular publication or section.

To be safe, the publisher should calculate about 48 or 49 percent. If challenged and postal inspectors make a thorough audit, a slight shortfall in actual paid circulation could spell disaster. Remember: a publisher is safe as long as 50 percent plus one of his total circulation is *paid* circulation.

The Future of Shoppers

Before the shopper boom, most newspapers felt they had a monopoly because they were the only newspaper in town. The publisher felt that residents had to have his newspaper because it was the only one with news. However, much has happened since then. The late news has become a regular and popular feature on TV and radio, and both beat the newspaper with most late-breaking stories. Also, advertising rates of newspapers, especially dailies, became too high. This has encouraged shopper competition.

Shoppers are probably here to stay. They claim to offer the best results and above all, they say they offer service. This service is something many newspapers have forgotten to render. They are now finding it an important word in their competitive negotiations.

TEN TIPS FOR SUCCESS

Higher cost of distribution may slow down shoppers in the years ahead, but it will have a devastating effect on newspapers as well. It appears that many consultants will be hired to guide newspapers through this critical stage. One such man giving advice to newspapers in what he calls "Tips for a Successful Shopper" is Gary Chappell, publisher of the Fremont (Nebraska) *Tribune*. His tips:

- Don't call your product a shopper. A shopper is one who makes a business of buying goods. Sell it as a weekly. A weekly that is distributed to all nonsubscribers, on a given day, in a given circulation area.

- Format the weekly (shopper) as a regular paid publication. Design the flag to resemble the daily (or paid weekly) newspaper. Never put an ad on the front page of the weekly. Make it a competitor of the daily newspaper.

- The name of the weekly (shopper) is important. A name like the *Times Weekly* would be a good start. Names to avoid are *Shopper, Shopping News, Shopper's Guide,* and *Shopper Saver.* Other words to avoid putting in the flag are *bargain, free,* and *penny saver.* After the name is selected, the flag should be designed with the same type and style as that of the regular newspaper. The two publications should look as much alike as possible.

- When selecting additional coverage, don't just add numbers as most shoppers do. Research the distribution area with the larger advertisers and select only the circulation numbers that will return the most business for this extra expenditure. It is desirable to have 100 percent nonduplicating coverage in the city zone. Add the extra coverage to the retail zone that will best suit the advertisers. Moving out of the retail trading zone with weekly contracted delivery will prove to be very expensive. Set up a foolproof monitoring system to be sure the weekly (shopper) is being delivered according to the contract outside the retail trading zone.

- Don't be bashful when setting up a commission program for the sales staff. Also remember the carriers and motor route distributors when crossing palms with silver incentives. Pay them well and the sales and delivery system will become one of the least problems. The more they make, the more the company will make.

- Keep the column inch rate as low as possible. Don't try to get rich the first year of publication. "Massage" the product until it is established and then go for the increase in revenue. Keep the rate card simple. The easiest is a flat pickup rate per column inch for all advertising. All ad rates, including those for preprints, should have the same per-thousand rate as the main newspaper.

- Don't let an advertisement run only in the weekly (shopper). Make the combination price attractive to keep the ad running in both publications. To avoid classified makeover, establish a combination pickup rate on the private party ads from the daily to the weekly (shopper) on the combination publishing day. If you do not wish to have a forced rate, give the private party ads a free ride in the weekly and massage the rate card for the necessary increased revenue.

  Some say this is not legal, but there is no definite proof as of this time. (See Chapter 25 for a discussion of this.)

- The circulation department must establish a delivery check system on the carriers and motor routes to insure that the weekly (shopper) is being delivered according to specifications. Any carrier or motor route driver caught dumping or not delivering the weekly will be terminated on the spot. Pass the word through the carrier grapevine.

- Make sure that the front page of the weekly contains good county and local news. The newsroom should save the best stories from that day's paper and the preceding day's paper for the front page news. Tease the reader. If the daily is running a six-part series on a local, state, or national issue, pop that day's column in the weekly. At the bottom of the article, tell the readers that this is a six-part daily feature and that if they subscribed to the daily, they would have been able to read all six parts.

- If you are starting a weekly to go against an existing shopper or to prevent one that is rumored to start, it will be wise to consult an antitrust lawyer and an accountant before setting rates. This is especially true for those in the large metropolitan areas.

Conclusion

From all indications, shoppers will be a part of the American print medium scene for years to come. Advertising notices have appeared in various forms, sizes, and shapes for hundreds of years and they will continue to be an important means of informing interested persons of shopping buys, notices, and classifieds in the future. There is a certain group of people that will not pay for this type of publication, and if merchants and publishers are going to team up to make sure that these people do receive the information from their stores through a cooperative printed version, the shopper is a primary vehicle for that dissemination.

Higher prices of newsprint and distribution costs possibly will curtail some of these publications, but that seems to be far in the future. Meanwhile, more and more community newspapers and larger dailies, especially the groups, will establish their own supplement-type publications. It also appears that more legal action will be taken against the larger publications for trying to monopolize.

Free newspapers have a cost factor that will keep their numbers limited. It takes great amounts of capital to maintain an editorial staff with competent photographers and other professionals. In rare cases the free newspapers will survive, but their numbers will be few. It seems possible that some news stories and features may appear in most shoppers, primarily for fill, but even that small amount of usage is expensive to maintain.

Chapter 20

CANDI VAN METER

The author is human resources director of the *Philadelphia Bulletin,* former director of human resources of the Camden (New Jersey) *Courier-Post,* and former personnel director of the Salem (Oregon) *Statesman-Journal.*

"Changes in labor force mix present new challenges to personnel managers who must consider not only the efficiency of the operations but also the changing needs of personnel."

Managing Personnel

by Candi Van Meter

Newspaper personnel management consists of managing a newspaper's human assets and resources to create organizations that are effective and efficient.

In the newspaper industry, large daily newspapers have assigned the major responsibility for human resources management to personnel departments which have become an integral part of their organizational design. Smaller dailies and weeklies often delegate management of human resources to department heads, editors, or advertising managers. Regardless of organizational design, all managers share in the responsibility for human resources

management.

Changes in our society in recent years have made the job of managing human resources increasingly difficult. These changes have prompted many newspapers to formalize their personnel programs either by appointing personnel managers or by delegating responsibility for personnel programs to an individual who may have other responsibilities.

Among the changes which have forced increased attention to the personnel function are:

- Changing demands of government

- Changing mix of the work force

- Changing values of the work force

- Changing demands of the employer

Changing Demands of Government

Perhaps the most significant of these changes is the growing body of legislation, both federal and state, which regulates the procurement, compensation, integration, and safety of employees. A few of the major pieces of federal legislation discussed in the National Newspaper Associations's *Federal Laws Affecting Newspapers* and brief descriptions of their application to newspapers follow.

CIVIL RIGHTS ACT OF 1964

The governing piece of legislation on equal employment opportunity, this law prohibits hiring, discharging, or otherwise discriminating against employees with regard to the terms and conditions of employment on the basis of race, color, religion, nationality, or sex. The law applies to all employers with more than fifteen employees. Covered employers must post an equal employment opportunity poster where notices to employees and applicants are customarily posted, and employers with more than one hundred employees must file annually with the federal government an EEO-1 report showing the numbers of employees by race and sex in various job categories.

EQUAL EMPLOYMENT OPPORTUNITY ACT OF 1972

This act empowered the Equal Employment Opportunity Commission to prevent unlawful employment practices by undertaking direct court action. Offending employers may be sued for violations, and federal courts have authority to order affirmative relief in the form of injunctions, orders to hire, orders for back pay, orders to reinstate or promote, and orders to pay employee or applicant attorney's fees.

AGE DISCRIMINATION ACT OF 1967

This law prohibits discrimination against workers between the ages of forty and seventy solely on the basis of age. The act, which applies to all employers with more than twenty employees, requires posting of a notice pertaining to the applicability of the act. The act is enforced by the Wage and Hour Division of the Department of Labor. This agency may bring suit in federal court for noncompliance, and relief may be ordered in the form of employment, reinstatement or promotion, or awards of back pay. The Age Discrimination Act does not preempt state laws which are more protective of employees.

FAIR LABOR STANDARDS ACT

This act concerns itself with a minimum wage and the requirement that time-and-a-half be paid for all hours over forty worked by an employee in a workweek. The federal laws do not concern themselves with how many hours an employee works in a day.

A special exemption is in the federal laws for daily and weekly newspapers with less than 4,000 circulation. This exemption will not excuse them under state law unless the state law so provides. Any employee of an under-4,000-circulation newspaper who spends more than 50 percent of his working time during any workweek on commercial job work is not exempt from minimum wage and overtime requirements for that week. For purposes of the "under 4,000 circulation" exemption, the total number of copies distributed governs, not the number of paid subscribers.

For newspapers coming under the law there are certain "white collar" exemptions covering executive, administrative, professional, and outside sales positions. "Whether an employee is exempt," says the Wage and Hour Division, "depends on his duties, responsibilities, and salary."

While newspapers ordinarily class their help in news, advertising, and circulation as professionals, seldom does the Wage and Hour Division agree. In order to be free from any possibility of violating government regulations, many newspapers put their entire work force under the Wage and Hour provisions, paying them on an hourly basis, with time-and-a-half for time over forty hours.

Youngsters fourteen- and fifteen-years-old may, under the federal law, be employed in office work, janitorial work, or stuffing and folding newspapers *if* their place of work is separated from the manufacturing process of the newspaper. They may not be employed during school hours, nor between 7 P.M. and 7 A.M., nor more than three hours a day on school days, nor more than eighteen hours a week in school weeks, and no more than eight hours a day and forty hours a week at any time.

Sixteen- and seventeen-year-olds may be employed, under federal law, in the back shop as well as in the occupations outlined above for fourteen- and fifteen-year-olds. They cannot, however, work on and around platen presses or paper cutters. State child labor laws should always be checked.

The newspaper-delivery exemption applies to *all* newspapers: Any employee, regardless of age, who is engaged *exclusively* in delivery of newspapers to the consumer is exempted from the minimum wage, overtime, and child labor provisions of the federal law.

EQUAL PAY ACT OF 1963

This act, which is administered by the Wage and Hour Division of the Department of Labor, requires employers to provide equal pay for male and female employees who perform the same work with substantially equal skills, effort, and responsibility. Newspapers with under 4,000 circulation are not governed by provisions of this law. Where an employer is found in violation of the law, the Wage and Hour Division may file suit and the courts may award damages.

EMPLOYEE RETIREMENT INCOME SECURITY ACT OF 1974

This act protects the rights of workers and their beneficiaries who are members of pension, profit sharing, and welfare plans. The act was passed to ensure that employees will actually receive something at retirement; it requires that pension plans be insured in the event of bankruptcy. The plan also establishes vesting requirements and regulates eligibility and funding of welfare plans.

OCCUPATIONAL SAFETY AND HEALTH ACT OF 1970

This act sets specific standards for minimum allowable exposure to certain health hazards, provides government policing of employer practices and workplaces, and provides enforcement through citations, fines, and other penalties determined by the Occupational Safety and Health Administration. The act applies to employers engaging in interstate commerce having one or more employees.

In addition to these federal laws, many states also have legislation that applies to personnel programs. With this emphasis on legalizing the protection and enhancement of human resources, the responsibility for monitoring compliance with the laws places an additional burden on those who administer personnel programs.

Changes in the Work Force

Among the major changes in the mix of personnel entering the work force are (1) increased numbers of minority members entering occupations requiring greater skills, (2) increasing levels of education for the entire work force, (3) more female employees, (4) more married female employees, (5) more working mothers, and (6) a steadily increasing majority of white-collar employees in place of the blue-collar employees.

Some of these changes in labor force mix have resulted from legislation prohibiting discrimination and requiring positive action to redress imbalances in the work force. Many employers are finding it difficult to fill entry-level positions, and the incidence of the "overqualified" or "overeducated" applicant is increasing.

Changes in labor force mix present new challenges to personnel managers who must consider not only the efficiency of the operations but also the changing needs of personnel.

The mix of the work force is not all that has changed; there is growing evidence that the work ethic is changing. The new work ethic places more emphasis on the individual and the fulfillment of individual needs and less on the organization than in the past.

Changing Demands of the Employer

Technological change and growing au-

tomation present special problems in the area of human resource and personnel management. In the newspaper industry, development of and conversion to electronic production systems has had a dramatic impact on the nature of the work performed and the skills required for newspaper employees. Many of the routine jobs, such as Teletypesetting and proofreading, have been eliminated. In their place, new jobs requiring more technical skills and knowledge have been created. With changes in the nature of the work being performed, there is also a need to restructure compensation plans so that pay levels correspond to the value of the work being performed.

The adjustment to technological changes in the newspaper industry will be more difficult for some than for others. The challenge in terms of personnel management is to anticipate the problems and to plan for these changes in order to minimize their adverse effects.

The Scope of Personnel Programs

For many years, personnel duties were very narrowly defined and limited to such things as selecting and placing employees, record keeping, data gathering, and administering wage and benefit plans. These traditional personnel responsibilities consisted of the ongoing activities that were required for the continued operation of the newspaper. While traditional personnel activities still form the base, new programs, such as communications, job evaluation, performance evaluation, affirmative action, and training and development, have been added to the scope of personnel management.

Selecting and Placing Employees

In recent years, enrollment in journal-

ism schools has soared. Many attribute the increase in part to the uncovering of the Watergate scandals in the early 1970s by Washington *Post* reporters Bob Woodward and Carl Bernstein. Young people apparently saw journalism as a way to change the world. While the cause for the increased enrollment in journalism schools may be subject to speculation, newspapers are faced with an ever-increasing number of qualified applicants for job openings in news and editorial operations.

Government regulations have forced newspapers and other employers to review carefully their selection procedures to preclude any discrimination. Employment applications, where they are used to gain factual information about an applicant, are an obvious target for review. Application forms should include no inquiries that may tend disproportionately to reject protected class members. Questions that are not directly job-related, such as sex, age, marital and family status, maiden name, credit ratings, and arrest records, must be eliminated from application forms. Studies have shown that information on applications is not always factual, particularly information on previous employment. It is advisable to verify the information filled in by the applicant. In all cases, applications should bear the signature of the applicant along with a release authorizing the newspaper to seek job-related information from former employers or schools.

Procedures for accepting applications vary. Some newspapers accept applications at any time, while others restrict the acceptance of applications to certain days of the week or to those times when actual staff vacancies exist. Applicants planning to submit applications should contact the newspaper where application will be made to determine what policies are observed.

Few companies would consider hiring anyone without an interview. Interviewing, while probably the most widely used selection method, is also the most subjective. Studies have shown that interviewing is more productive if it is structured and if interviewers receive some interview training. The following practical techniques for improving interviewing skills may be helpful for those who have interviewing responsibilities:

- Do your homework prior to the interview on job content.

- Avoid overgeneralization about the job and the company.

- Review your own prejudices—don't let them cloud your judgment.

- Be receptive—talk *and* listen.

- Avoid questions that may be interpreted as an attempt to obtain legally impermissible information.

- Never overquestion.

- Use silence—it is hard to do so, but let the applicant be first to break a silence.

- Keep the interview private.

- Keep the initiative.

- Keep your opinion to yourself.

- Shun the role of the amateur psychologist.

- Keep an eye on what you want to accomplish.

- Maintain a steady pace.

- Don't be misled by the appearance of the applicant.

- Don't shy away from either asking or answering hard questions.

- At the end of the interview evaluate carefully the information you have obtained—interpret the facts, weigh them carefully, and determine a course of action.

In determining what questions should be asked in an interview, the same rules that apply to application forms govern interview inquiries. Inquiries should be limited to information that is directly related to the position for which the applicant has applied. Some applicants will volunteer information; when the volunteered information relates to race, sex, national origin, color, or religion, the critical issue is how that information is used in the selection decision.

Federal regulations also govern job requirements and standards. In the past, arbitrary education or experience requirements screened out many capable applicants. These requirements are now being expressed in terms of spe-

cific skills, knowledges, and abilities. Under federal statute, only those requirements that an organization can clearly demonstrate as being necessary to successful performance of a given job will be considered bona fide employment qualifications.

Newspaper managers often use these selection factors in hiring news personnel:

- A degree in journalism

- Familiarity with the locale of the newspaper

- Previous writing experience

- Writing skills demonstrated by samples accompanying the résumé or application

- Curiosity demonstrated during employment interview

- Applicant's knowledge of the newspaper where application is being made

- Appearance and punctuality during interview

- Favorable references

They may also consider secondary interests, such as educational background, which could be applied to specialized reporting. With these selection factors in mind, the following suggestions may be useful to applicants for editorial positions:

- Research the newspaper where application is being made. The results of the research may be useful in preparing a letter of inquiry and may be helpful during an interview.

- Prepare a personal letter to the publisher, executive editor, or personnel manager of the newspaper. Duplicated letters are a sure sign to the individual who receives a letter that the applicant has sent dozens of letters to other papers. Frequently, mass-produced letters receive no attention and no reply.

- Letters of inquiry should show a combination of writing skill and personal style, and they should stress what the applicant can contribute to the newspaper.

Applicants who are unable to write a letter of inquiry will probably find it difficult to survive in a newsroom. Letters of inquiry should also be neat and free of spelling or grammatical errors.

- Applicants seeking an interview should contact the individual who will be interviewing to make an appointment. Dropping in unannounced presumes the interviewer has time for interviews at any time, and that is seldom true.

- Applicants should follow up an interview with a letter to the person who conducted the interview expressing thanks for the opportunity to discuss employment opportunities and restating what the applicant thinks he or she has to offer the newspaper.

- Applicants should organize clips or writing samples in a file and bring these for the interviewer to review during the interview.

John E. Blitz, former executive editor of Stromberg Publications, Ellicott City, Maryland and now publisher of the *Howard County Journal* there, was for several years responsible for recruiting personnel for twelve to fifteen weeklies in the Baltimore area. His views may be typical of those who handle personnel on smaller newspapers:

While I was executive director, I received at least two hundred job applications a year and had usually only four or five positions to fill.

In self-defense, editors or small newspaper publishers usually assign a staff member to filter job applications. And quite often little attention is paid to even the best application until a need arises.

The assigned staff member will use criteria established by the hiring executive, such as education, work experience, and a potpourri of the editor's favorite idiosyncrasies: spelling, grammar, brevity, etc.

Editors pride themselves on industry and self-sacrifice, usually demand it of their staff, and look for it in applicants.

If you reach the interview, consider yourself among the finalists. Almost every editor will ask you why you want the job. Be concise, honest and, if possible, creative in your reply. Remember, he feels strongly about his work.

No applicants have ever done this, but if they did, they would get a job with me: Research your potential newspaper. Look for possible news stories or news features. When the timing is right, suggest how you would like to work on the story when you started on the paper. Don't make it an exposé—and if it has human interest, your chances improve. The idea will show your maturity and the ability to think of your own assignments.

String books with twenty to thirty of your stories pasted up are overrated. Better just to pick the best news story you have done and the best feature. Let them represent you. Imagine a photographer showing every frame of film he exposed. He'd never get hired. Put only your best foot forward. And don't be afraid to explain why you chose the story and what abilities it demonstrates.

Other Traditional Personnel Programs

After an employee is selected, files and records must be established, a salary must be assigned, and appropriate benefits must be determined. All of these activities fall within the category of traditional personnel programs.

Employee records are kept in individual employee personnel files. These files may include any materials related to original hiring, such as letters of inquiry or application forms, letters of reference, payroll records, performance appraisals, reports of disciplinary action, records pertaining to demotion and promotion, written commendations, and certificates of completion of job-related training. Information of a personal nature not directly related to an employee's job should not be included in a personnel file.

Employee access to files is currently a matter of management prerogative. In the case of some employee records, such as performance appraisals, and reports of disciplinary action or demotion, employees should receive a copy of the information being placed in their personnel files. Whenever possible, these documents should be signed by the employee as an indication that the employee has read the document, not as an indication that the employee agrees with the document. Where newspapers allow employees to review their files, it is suggested that a management representative be present to interpret information contained in the file. Privacy legislation in the future may have an impact on company policies related to access to files and use of the information contained in these files.

COMPENSATION AND SALARY ADMINISTRATION

One of the most difficult functions of personnel management is that of determining rates of compensation. George Veon, personnel director for Lee Enterprises, Inc., suggests a three-part process for the development of compensation plans:

- Develop a plan that provides internal equity in compensation based on the duties being performed in various jobs.

- Compare compensation levels to the local job market and to other newspapers, both regionally and nationally.

- Pay at a level targeted by comparison to other companies and newspapers.

A plan providing internal equity should begin with a position description by all employees. This should include a description of special skills required for the job, important working relationships, and a listing of duties performed. A sample position description form is shown in Fig. 20–1.

Position descriptions should be agreed upon by employees and management. In all cases, descriptions should reflect what the employee actually does and not what he or she should be doing.

Once descriptions have been reviewed and the relative value of various positions in the organization have been determined, salary ranges can be established. These salary ranges may then be compared to ranges for similar positions in other organizations.

Many jobs are unique to the newspaper industry, and comparisons to jobs in private industry are difficult. For these positions, state, regional, and national newspaper association salary surveys may be useful in determining the appropriateness of salary levels.

Salary ranges for positions that are not unique to the newspaper industry, such as clerical, secretarial, and maintenance positions, should be compared to ranges paid for similar positions in the local job market. State employment departments usually conduct salary surveys for the most common job classifications. Many newspaper classifications will be found on these surveys.

The third step Veon outlines in developing and implementing a compensation plan is to determine a target for salaries. Some newspapers may set a target which is near the average, while others will prefer to be either above or below average. The financial position of the newspaper will bear heavily on the decision about where to set salary levels in relation to other newspapers and employers.

Compensation plans differ in their design. Some plans set minimum salaries and outline step-up salary increases based on predetermined frequencies of review. Commonly, these plan designs require an increase after six months and annual increases thereafter. Under these compensation plans, all employees with similar experience levels are paid at the same rate.

Other plan designs set minimum and maximum salaries for various job classifications and may set some guidelines for frequency of review. These plan designs allow managers and supervisors the freedom to reward employees based on individual job performance. Under such plans, it is possible for two employees with the same experience to be paid different rates based on performance. While these plans provide greater freedom in salary administration, they also place a greater bur-

FIGURE 20–1 A special form can help both management and employees understand and agree on position descriptions. *Reprinted courtesy of the Salem (Oregon)* Statesman-Journal.

STATESMAN-JOURNAL NEWSPAPERS

POSITION DESCRIPTION

POSITION TITLE _____ EMPLOYEE _____

DEPARTMENT _____ DATE _____

A. BASIC PURPOSE OF POSITION: Indicate the purpose for which your position exists (if possible, in a brief statement or sentence).

B. KEY WORKING RELATIONSHIPS:

Internal — Identify your most important working relationships with people inside the company. Indicate who they are and the nature, frequency, and reasons for the contacts.

External — Identify your most important working relationships with people outside the company. Indicate who they are and the nature, frequency, and reasons for the contacts. Include subscribers, advertisers, vendors, sources, associations and groups when a working relationship is involved.

Statesman Journal Newspapers

C. EDUCATION, EXPERIENCE, AND SKILL REQUIREMENTS: Define the talent required to be minimally qualified to perform the work of this position. (i.e. what would be required in recruiting a new employee).

1. Formal Education:

2. Prior Experience:

3. Special Skills or Abilities:

D. PRINCIPAL DUTIES: Describe the tasks or duties you perform regularly. List them in their order of importance to accomplishment of the basic purpose stated in Section A. Also try to indicate an approximate percentage of time devoted to each activity.

den on the supervisor to document performance in order to justify the differences in salary.

A good compensation plan should, as Veon suggests, provide internal equity. It is important to remember that the true test of the success of a compensation plan is the plan's effectiveness in attracting and keeping personnel in the organization. Ideally, it should motivate employees to higher levels of performance.

EMPLOYEE BENEFITS: NONTAXABLE COMPENSATION

Employee benefits may include all expenditures designed to benefit employees over and above regular wages and direct monetary incentives related to work output. Since World War II, the growth of benefit plans has been rampant. During that period, wages were tightly controlled and labor unions were willing to accept nonwage compensation in lieu of higher wages. Another factor which has contributed to the growth of benefit plans has been the new attitude of paternalism that has led many to believe that the employer has a moral responsibility for the lives of employees.

Fringe benefits may represent from 25 to 35 percent of employee salaries. Indications are that these benefits will continue to be an important and growing part of employee compensation.

The return to the company for this investment can come in various forms, including (1) more effective recruitment, (2) improved morale and loyalty, (3) lower turnover and absenteeism, (4) good public relations, (5) reduced influence of unions, and (6) reduced threat of further government intervention.

There are several principles that apply to employee benefit plans. Among these principles are the following:

- The employee benefit should satisfy a real need.

- Benefits should be confined to ac-

tivities in which the group is more efficient than the individual.

- The benefit should be extended on as broad a basis as possible.

- The costs of the benefit should be calculable, and provision should be made for sound financing of the benefit.

These principles may be used as a guide when reviewing and selecting benefits in an organization.

Benefit plans common to newspapers are group medical plans, group life insurance plans, group accidental death plans, long-term disability plans, vacation plans, sick leave plans, paid holidays, workers' compensation plans, federal and state unemployment plans, profit sharing, retirement plans, and stock purchase plans. Many of these plans are designed to protect employees from catastrophic financial losses if major hazards occur.

Benefits need not be limited to protective benefits. Benefit plans may also include such things as provision of an employee lunch room or lounge, credit unions, recreational programs, subsidies for professional memberships, educational subsidies for job-related course-work, and discounts for advertising and newspaper subscriptions.

Given the rising cost and increasing popularity of employee benefit plans, an important aspect of an overall personnel program is the monitoring of benefit plans to insure that maximum value is being derived from the expenditures for these benefits.

New Concerns in Personnel Management

Because of the limitations of staff size and a lack of interest in expanding personnel programs, newspapers have limited personnel activities in the past to the traditional programs we have discussed.

However, there is a growing interest in expanding overall personnel

programs to include such things as communications, performance appraisal, job evaluation, affirmative action, and training and development. The following section will describe some of these new concerns and their value to the total newspaper operation.

COMMUNICATION

Mark Twain on the weather: "Everybody talks about it, but nobody does anything about it."

Twain's comment applies to communication on some modern newspapers. Although newspapers are a part of the communications industry, some have neglected their own programs for internal communication.

The organizational design of newspapers frequently requires getting things done through others, and, therefore, an effective plan for disseminating information upward, downward, and laterally is essential if efficiency and high levels of productivity are to be achieved.

Poor communication is costly and can lead to mistakes from misunderstandings, duplication of effort, and projects or assignments left undone. The highest cost of poor communication is low morale. Poor communication is almost certain to lead to low morale.

Experts in the communications field say that an effective communication program requires a maximum of information be held in common among personnel required to work together toward a common goal. Openness, trust, honesty, and candor are necessary if a communication program is to work on a two-way basis.

Methods of upward communication include (1) personal interviews, (2) group supervisory meetings, (3) formal meetings where employees are invited to speak up on issues of importance to them, (4) suggestion boxes, (5) employee surveys, (6) exit interviews, (7) formal employee counseling programs, and (8) labor unions.

Upward communication tends to be formal in order to preserve order and unity of command. Provisions for such formal channels are necessary to discover clashes of interest, to reconcile conflicts, and to coordinate efforts.

Many of the upward methods of communication may also be used for downward communication. In addition, downward channels may include (1) posters and bulletin boards, (2) a company newsletter, (3) letters to employees, (4) public address systems, (5) annual reports, (6) paycheck inserts, (7) information racks or centers, (8) employee orientation programs, and (9) employee handbooks.

Since the publication of employee handbooks is becoming increasingly common, handbook content will be discussed in greater detail later in the chapter.

Perhaps the most critical factor in the success of any communication program is the climate that is created to facilitate communication. Employees must feel that their opinions are valued or they will not participate in the communication flow. Immediate feedback to employee suggestions, ideas, or concerns is one way to reinforce a company's position that employee input is valued.

Any discussion of communication should include the informal communication in an organization, the grapevine. When the emloyee grapevine is more active than the formal communication programs, it may be an indication that employees are not getting enough information about the organization. Most studies show that a more effective formal communication program will decrease the activity of the employee grapevine.

which may be included.

TABLE 20–1: TABLE OF CONTENTS

Introduction—Letter from the Publisher

I. **Getting Acquainted with the Newspaper**
Organization chart, biographies of key managers, history of newspaper, map of physical plant
II. **Our Departments**
Brief description of each of the newspaper's departments
III. **General Information**
Building information, safety and fire prevention, accident procedures, description of services such as cafeteria operation
IV. **Company Responsibilities**
Policies related to drugs and alcohol in the plant, handling of confidential information, dress, overtime, accepting favors from advertisers, and other pertinent subjects
V. **Benefits**
Descriptions of all company benefits
VI. **Other Information**
May include descriptions of suggestion boxes; outline procedures for promotion and transfer, completion of timecards, paycheck distribution, employee rating programs, grounds for dismissal, salary administration, and other pertinent data

---

EMPLOYEE HANDBOOKS

Employee handbooks contain an accumulation of information about the newspaper which is necessary in order for new employees to adjust to their new surroundings. Handbooks are also a handy reference for other employees who may have questions about the company.

Each newspaper must determine individually what information should be included in an employee handbook. The sample table of contents gives examples of the kind of information

PERFORMANCE APPRAISAL

It is inevitable that the performance of an employee will be evaluated at some time. The extent to which this process has been formalized in the news department of newspapers has been a matter of controversy for newspapers of all sizes. News executives disagree on the applicability of written performance appraisals for professional journalists because of the creative nature of the work journalists perform. Some executives point to the inability to quantify such attributes as

initiative, rhythm in language use, etc., as major obstacles to the using of written performance appraisal systems in news departments.

There are numerous types of appraisal forms being used by newspapers. The format for appraisals fall basically in four categories:

- *Comparative Techniques.* The employee is ranked against others in the same department or job classification.

- *Absolute Standards.* The employee is rated against standards determined by company policy and written on appraisal forms.

- *Goal Setting.* The employee is rated according to the degree to which he or she has attained predetermined job goals (such as management-by-objective systems).

- *Direct Indices.* The employee is rated on the basis of predetermined categories of performance, such as productivity, punctuality, initiative, etc.

Some newspapers have experimented with employee self-appraisal. Under this system, the employee and the supervisor rate the employee's performance independently of one another. These ratings are then compared, and differences are discussed during the appraisal interview which follows.

The initial task in the development of a performance appraisal system is the selection of an appraisal form and method.

The effectiveness of an appraisal system will be determined less by the form used than by the quality of the rater. Generally, the rater is the employee's immediate supervisor. When the responsibility for performance appraisals is given to supervisors, it is essential that they understand the system and that they are trained to avoid common rating errors.

Following pages:

FIGURE 20–2 (pages 178–179) A New York *Times* evaluation program for reporters places emphasis on seven standards. *Reprinted with permission.*

FIGURE 20–3 (pages 180–181) The evaluation sheet at a smaller paper can serve all departments. *Courtesy of John E. Blitz.*

REPORTER JOB STANDARDS
FROM NEW YORK TIMES APPRAISAL SYSTEM

The standards set by the Times are:

1. Accuracy - "A reporter should consistently be able to report accurately. A record of inaccuracy on facts that could be checked by normal reporting techniques is not acceptable."

2. Lucid, Grammatical and Intelligent Writing - "Reporters should be able to write stories in readily understandable and grammatical English, capturing both any subtleties and profundities in the event being reported."

3. Write Under Deadline Pressure - "Reporters should be able to write accurate and lucid copy under pressure of early deadline and also consistently meet normal deadline requirements."

4. News Sense - "Reporters should have a clear ability to determine what the most important elements of a story are, know what generally constitutes a story that will be printed by the Times and be able to assess the significance of the events they are covering."

5. Quantity - "Reporters should be capable of covering and writing spot news stories that develop on a daily basis; of writing feature stories that require interviews, investigation and research; and of writing major and lengthy stories on complex subjects. The length of time required to complete an assignment is assumed to be one day unless the reporter and an editor agree on a different time period. Stories should be handed in within the deadline and require only minor revisions after review with an editor."

6. Initiative and Perseverence - "Reporters should regularly demonstrate their vision, imagination and depth of understanding of news events. They should regularly recommend possible story ideas, demonstrate intellectual curiosity and resourcefulness in gathering the news."

7. Reporting Techniques - "Reporters should know, and utilize all the basic techniques for gathering and presenting the news. Finished stories should be complete, necessitating a minimum of queries for additional information, sourcing, clarification and organization. While some editing is considered normal and reasonable, a constant need for heavy editing, frequent major revision or major reorganization of pieces will be considered a deficiency in reporting technique."

NEW YORK TIMES APPRAISAL SYSTEM

Supervisors are asked to rate the reporter in each of the categories listed on the previous page. The ratings are:

1. excellent performance
2. acceptable performance
3. improvement needed

In addition to these ratings, the supervisor is also asked to rate the employee's present overall job effectiveness "as they see it." There are four boxes, one of which is to be checked.

Job Performance Needs Considerable Improvement - "Overall performance is unsatisfactory. Is weak in most of the requirements of the job. Work is frequently unacceptable."

Generally OK, But Needs Some Improvement To Meet Normal Requirements - "Areas for necessary improvements exist which are not counterbalanced by outstanding strong points. Work is sometimes less than acceptable."

Satisfactorily Meets Normal Requirements of the Job - "Overall performance is adequate in all respects. Does good work most of the time. Slightly below average performance in some respects is clearly outweighed by demonstrated strengths in other areas. Meets the full requirements of the job."

Better Than Most - "Overall performance is excellent in many respects and never less than satisfactory."

The supervisors are asked to support these ratings with additional information if necessary. Supervisors discuss ratings with the employee who may add comments if he/she feels it is necessary. Employees are also asked to identify career goals and to express views on whether or not their talents being put to good use.

PERFORMANCE EVALUATION

Employee: Department:

1. How well does employee understand requirements of job to which assigned?

_____Thoroughly understands all aspects of job.
_____Has sufficient knowledge to do job.
_____Insufficient knowledge of some phases.
_____Continually needs instruction.

2. Does employee work harmoniously and effectively with co-workers and supervisors?

_____Exceptionally willing and successful as a team worker.
_____Gets along well enough, no problems.
_____Cooperation must be solicited, seldom volunteers.
_____Tends to be a troublemaker.

3. How does this employee accept all responsibilities of the job?

_____Accepts all responsibilities fully and meets emergencies.
_____Conscientiously tries to fulfill job responsibilities.
_____Accepts but does not seek responsibilities.
_____Does some assigned tasks reluctantly.
_____Indifferent - avoids responsibility.

4. How well does the employee begin an assignment without direction and recognize the best way of doing it?

_____Self starter - makes practical suggestions.
_____Proceeds on assigned work without prompting; readily accepts suggestions.
_____Relies on others; needs help getting started.
_____Must usually be told exactly what to do.

5. How much satisfactory work is consistently turned out by employee?

_____Maintains high output of neat, accurate work; seldom needs correction.
_____Does sufficient amount of acceptable work.
_____Inclined to be slow and is occasionally careless.
_____Inadequate turn out of work that is inaccurate.

6. How punctual is this employee in reporting to work?

_____Always reports on time.
_____Generally punctual.
_____Often reports late.
_____Continually late.

PERFORMANCE EVALUATION

Summary

Evaluated by:_____

               Supervisor

        or Department Head   Date

Comments:

Discussed with employee by:_____

                   Interviewer   Date

Employee Comments?:

Reviewed by:_____

           Personnel Manager   Date

Effective performance appraisal systems provide both necessary feedback to employees and information to management which may be important in decision making. They can constitute a workable and useful tool in developing greater efficiency and better morale.

AFFIRMATIVE ACTION

All personnel programs and activities require continual review to ensure compliance with civil rights laws and federally established affirmative action policies. Affirmative action represents positive steps taken by an organization to provide equal employment opportunity.

In many cases, federal courts have ordered major corporations to comply with federal antidiscrimination laws through mandated affirmative action programs. With the exception of a few larger newspapers, most newspapers have not been subjected to court review of their employment practices. Contrary to the beliefs of some in the industry, however, it is clear that newspapers are not immune from these laws.

A 1978 research project sponsored by the American Society of Newspaper Editors showed that 17 percent of the U.S. population was nonwhite but that only 4 percent of professional newsroom employees were nonwhite. Two thirds of the daily newspapers in the United States were reported by the research to have no nonwhite professional employees. The report also revealed that only 1 percent of American newspaper management is nonwhite.

The newspaper's continuing responsibility in the area of equal employment opportunity was summarized by John C. Quinn, senior vice president of Gannett Newspapers. Quinn said, "In the matter of hiring minorities, of covering minorities, we have found a lot of excuses to do something else. We must find a way to recreate the feeling that there is a moral reason to do the right thing—to get ourselves fired up to right a wrong we have uncovered at city hall."

Training

The major values of training are increased productivity, a reduced need for supervision, improved morale, increased organizational stability, and, from the editor's point of view, better news stories.

There are many methods of training, the most common of which is on-the-job training. This method has the advantage of allowing employees to learn in their assigned work location, and it places the burden for training results on the supervisor.

Starting with writing skills as a base, there are some additional skills and knowledge which are often acquired through on-the-job training. These may include (1) operation of video display terminals, (2) interviewing skills, (3) learning where to get information on a specific beat, (4) learning how to deal with barriers to gathering information, (5) learning to meet and cope with deadlines, and (6) learning how to determine what kinds of stories to look for on a specific beat. On-the-job training for journalists may also include reviewing copy for omissions or errors and for clarity and completeness.

In addition to on-the-job training, employee training may be provided by seminars and conferences which focus on specific aspects of a journalist's job. These seminars provide an opportunity for the employee to learn from the seminar leaders as well as other participants.

Conclusion

Not all newspapers have centralized the personnel function, but it should be clear that all newspapers have personnel programs and personnel concerns whether they are small weeklies or large dailies.

It is likely that the trends toward increased government regulation and changing employee demands will continue. It is also likely that the makeup and nature of the work force will continue to change.

A carefully planned personnel program will enhance the newspaper operation by contributing to employee productivity, efficiency, and morale and will have a major impact on the success or failure of the organization.

Chapter 21

CAROLYN A. STROMAN

Dr. Stroman is research assistant/assistant professor at the Institute for Urban Affairs, Howard University. She formerly taught African and Afro-American Studies at the University of North Carolina, Chapel Hill, and has also taught at Atlanta, Syracuse, and Oregon Universities. She is also the author of articles relating to minorities and the mass media.

PAULA M. POINDEXTER

Dr. Poindexter is a member of the journalism and mass communication faculty at the University of Georgia. She has been a research consultant to daily newspapers, an associate of the Communications Research Center and ANPA News Research Center at Syracuse University, and author of articles on newspaper readership.

"Without a doubt, editors and publishers of black newspapers have been faced with some of the same problems as those faced by the editors and publishers of the general press. They also have problems . . . unique to the minority publisher."

The Minority Press

by Carolyn A. Stroman and Paula M. Poindexter

The minority press in America has a long, rich history. Examples of early American minority newspapers include the earliest Spanish-language newspaper, *El Misisipí*, founded in New Orleans in 1808; *Freedom's Jour-* *nal*, the first black newspaper, published in New York in 1827; the *Cherokee Phoenix*, the first Native American newspaper which was printed in both Cherokee and English and appeared in New Echota, Georgia, in 1828; and *Jīn Shān Xīn Wén*, the first Chinese-language newspaper, published in San Francisco in 1854.

Although the first minority newspapers had a common purpose for their foundings—to provide information not provided in the general press—they also had unique functions to fill. While early Spanish-language newspapers championed the rights of Mexican–Americans, early Native American papers played the roles of teacher, watchdog, and advocate. The Native American press told of the white man's exploitation of the Indian in addition to his civilization and accomplishments. The early Chinese-language newspapers served as mouthpieces for the different political and ideological factions. The first black newspapers' major objective was to protest racial discrimination in America and especially the institution of slavery.

Thousands of minority newspapers have followed in the traditions begun by the early ones. Although their functions have changed over the years, and they have gone through periods of growth and decline, minority newspapers continue to flourish and serve minority communities.

The minority press can be defined as any weekly, biweekly, or daily newspaper which is owned and managed by members of a racial or ethnic minority group and which serves the needs of a particular racial or ethnic minority.

This chapter will focus on the

current status of newspapers which fit this definition. Since the black press is the minority press that has been researched most, it will be used as the prototype of the minority press. Thus, the chapter focuses heavily on black newspapers, although available facts regarding other minority newspapers will be included when applicable.

The Minority Press Today

From the outset, it should be clearly understood that minority newspapers run the gamut in terms of physical layout, editorial stance, styles of writing, and content. This is most apparent if one compares, for example, the Syracuse *Gazette*, a fairly recent addition to the black press, to the older, more established Houston *Forward Times*, or the *Costilla County Free Press*, a small Spanish-language paper, with one of the largest Spanish-language papers, *El Diario-La Prensa*.

Minority newspapers may be found in many sections of the United States; four states, however, dominate: California, Florida, Texas, and New York. The 1979 *Editor & Publisher International Year Book* lists 21 Spanish-language newspapers, 11 Chinese-language newspapers, and 184 black newspapers in the U.S. Undoubtedly, there are other minority newspapers not contained in this listing.

Minority newspapers vary in their circulation. The Washington *Informer*, a black weekly, reports a circulation of 55,000; more typical would be the *Carolina Times*, 6,000; the Minneapolis *Spokesman and Recorder*, 13,000; and the New York *Recorder*, 29,400. The majority of Chinese-language newspapers have a circulation of less than 10,000; *Young China*'s 7,300 circulation and *Chinese World*'s 3,311 circulation are typical. Spanish-language newspapers generally have higher circulations than the others: *El Mañana*'s 56,429 circulation is a representative figure.

Table 21–1 lists minority newspapers with circulations of 30,000 or more. Except where indicated, the fig-

ures are based on publishers' statements rather than auditors' records.

Local News Favored

The vast majority of the 184 black newspapers listed in the *International Year Book* are community newspapers. Published weekly, these newspapers strive to give black people an additional

viewpoint on issues and events in addition to presenting a positive image of blacks.

The essence of black community newspapers is reflected in their content: news of the local black community predominates. Generally, the front page of a black newspaper is devoted to the activities of the local school board, the local branch of the National Association for the Advancement of Colored People, local educational institutions, and local personalities, especially political figures.

TABLE 21–1: LARGEST CIRCULATING MINORITY NEWSPAPERS, 1979

Name	Circulation	Place of Publication
Chinese-Language Newspapers		
World Journal	35,000	New York
Spanish-Language Newspapers		
El Sol De Texas	100,000	Dallas
El Diario-La Prensa	68,979 ABC*	New York
El Mañana	56,429	Chicago
La Nacion Americana/La Tribuna	55,000	Franklin Park, New Jersey
Diario Las Americas	54,913	Miami
The Voice	53,277	Miami
La Opinion	30,497 ABC	Los Angeles
La Tribuna de North Jersey	30,000	Newark
Black Newspapers		
Bilalian News	150,000	Chicago
Daily Challenge	89,067	Brooklyn, N.Y.
New York Voice	83,000	Queens, N.Y.
New York Amsterdam News	80,000 ABC	New York
South End Citizen	66,309	Chicago
Southwest Wave	65,250	Los Angeles
Metropolitan Gazette	61,000	Compton, California
Tribune	60,000 ABC	Philadelphia
Informer	55,000	Washington, D.C.
Oakland Post	54,000	Oakland
Cleveland Metro	50,000	Bedford Heights, Ohio
Southwest News	44,335	Los Angeles
Michigan Chronicle	40,000 ABC	Detroit
Dallas Weekly	40,000	Dallas
Sacramento Observer	39,500	Sacramento
St. Louis Metro Sentinel	36,000	St. Louis
Birmingham Times	36,000	Birmingham
Reporter	35,000	Akron
Atlanta Voice	35,000	Atlanta
Buffalo Challenger	35,000	Buffalo
Sentinel	34,000 ABC	Los Angeles
Weekly Challenger	33,000	St. Petersburg
Atlanta Inquirer	32,000	Atlanta
Forward Times	31,166 ABC	Houston
Southside Journal	31,115	Los Angeles
Southwest Sun	30,025	Los Angeles
Precinct Reporter	30,000	San Bernadino
Sentinel-Bulletin	30,000	Tampa
Omaha Star	30,000	Omaha

Source: *Editor & Publisher International Year Book,* 1979.
* Member Audit Bureau of Circulation.

The activities of local social organizations, especially fraternities and sororities, command a great deal of attention in black newspapers, as does religious news. Generally, a page or more is filled with news of the various local churches. In addition, large sections are sometimes devoted to obituaries and funerals.

Sports news of black athletes, especially college athletes, appears frequently in black newspapers. An entertainment section is usually included as well, covering movies, theater performances, art shows, etc.

Editorials in black newspapers usually provide guidance on local and national topics. Recent issues have contained editorials on such diverse subjects as youth unemployment, the local transit system, foreign affairs, and local minority businesses.

In explaining how he decides on editorial content for each issue, Ernie Johnston, Jr., managing editor of the *New York Amsterdam News,* reports that he examines what is happening on both the New York and national scenes and from this decides which issues to discuss in editorials. Similarly, Ernest Pitt, editor of the Winston-Salem *Chronicle,* reports that he surveys the significant issues in the Winston-Salem community and then makes recommendations about these issues, being as positive as possible.

Columnists are both local and national. Vernon Jordan's "To Be Equal" is carried in many black newspapers, as is a column by one of the members of the Black Congressional Caucus.

Advertising forms a significant portion of the content of black newspapers. Much of the advertising is done by local black-owned businesses. However, it is not uncommon to see Kool cigarettes, Sears, and other national advertisers featured, since national advertising is obtained through Amalgamated Publishers, Inc.

Who Reads the Minority Press?

One of the most difficult problems in

analyzing the black press is trying to determine its readers, since readership studies of individual black newspapers are seriously lacking. Ernest Pitt, whose readership is currently being examined, was able to provide this information on his readers. The typical person reading the Winston-Salem *Chronicle* is between the ages of 24 and 44, female, nonprofessional, head of household, with an annual income range of $7,000 to $12,500.

Special devices, aimed at attracting and retaining readers, are utilized by some black newspapers. One such device, "Super Scholar," was run in issues of the Charlotte *Post* and the *Carolina Peacemaker.* Designed to attract young readers, the series provided sample competency exam material, black history information, puzzles, and cartoons. The *New York Amsterdam News,* from time to time, will try to attract readers through promotional ads on radio.

Black newspapers are usually delivered to their subscribers through the mail or by a carrier. Unlike urban area carriers, "the carriers at the Winston-Salem *Chronicle* experience no difficulties in delivering the papers," according to Ernest Pitt.

The *New York Amsterdam News,* like other black newspapers that are published in large urban areas, is available on newsstands.

Who Writes It?

In general, black newspapers have small staffs, frequently comprised of fewer than ten persons. The Grand Rapids *Times,* a weekly tabloid of circulation 12,000, has a staff of three—one full-time and two part-time employees. The Philadelphia *New Observer* employs seven persons. Staff members possess varying degrees of training and education. The editor of the *Carolina Times,* for example, Mrs. Vivian Edmonds, has no formal training. At the Winston-Salem *Chronicle,* however, the editor and all five of the reporters (three full-time, two part-time) hold B. A. degrees in journalism.

By definition, the community

which it serves is usually a community newspaper's chief source of news. Consequently, most of the news is written by staff reporters or special correspondents. In the case of Chinese-language newspapers, reporters are few, and most local news is brought to the office by interested persons, reports Paul Slater in his article "San Francisco's Chinese Newspapers: A Lingering Institution."

For news outside of the community, particularly national news, minority newspapers generally rely on UPI. Each minority press also utilizes specialized news services. The Chicago *Challenge,* a black daily, and the Wilmington *Journal,* a black weekly, use Community News Service. *Diario Las Americas* uses Agence France-Presse. In 1969, Paul Slater reported that Chinese newspapers use the wire services, correspondents in the Far East, and the Chinese Information Service as their three main sources of foreign news.

Unique Problems

Without a doubt, the editors and publishers of black newspapers have been faced with some of the same problems as those faced by the editors and publishers of the general press. They also have problems which are unique to the minority publisher.

Steve Davis, executive director of the National Newspaper Publishers Association, says major problems among black newspapers include circulation, readership, and distribution. Other major problems identified by publishers include advertising and attracting and retaining qualified personnel. The latter is a particularly unique problem among black publishers.

Since most black newspapers are small business operations, they are generally unable to pay competitive salaries. As a result, inexperienced journalists will normally accept lower pay in return for a chance to obtain experience. Once that experience is obtained, however, they move on to better-paying jobs.

Of course, this is not a problem

that is unique to blacks; it holds for other minority publishers as well. The difficulty of recruiting writers and printers was identified as perhaps the greatest threat to the existence of the Chinese press in America. Paul Slater wrote: "Young Chinese journalists today are attracted to the better-paying and more prestigious English-language dailies." Apparently, the desire of the general press to have at least one minority on its staff has hampered the recruitment efforts of the minority press.

The need for advertising revenues is a problem that has plagued the black press for many years. Once almost nonexistent, advertising has slowly increased in black newspapers, but it is still not anywhere near adequate. Raymond Garrison, associate editor of the Philadelphia *New Observer,* cites local advertising as his biggest problem. As an example, he says that a major communications firm patronizes small white newspapers in the area but refuses to place ads in the *New Observer.*

At the 1979 midwinter meeting of the National Newspaper Publishers Association (NNPA), advertising revenue was one of the major priorities. At this meeting, it was reported that black publishers "receive less than ½ of 1 percent of the money spent nationally on newspaper advertising."

Since many black newspapers are understaffed, often no one person can devote full time to obtaining advertising. It is not uncommon for the person who is in charge of advertising also to serve as reporter, layout person, copy editor, etc.

The problems identified above have an effect on other problems. Apparently, there is a hard-to-penetrate cycle at work here. Lack of sufficient advertising revenues leads to inadequate salaries, which leads to inexperienced personnel, which affects the quality of the newspaper, which decreases readership and circulation, which in turn diminishes advertisers' desires to advertise in a newspaper which doesn't command a certain readership level.

As is true of the general press, competition for readers and advertisers is a major problem. Chief among black newspapers' competitors are black magazines and black-oriented radio stations. Spanish-language radio and other Spanish media, which are reported to be growing very rapidly, also pose a threat to Spanish-language newspapers. Of course, a common competitor of all minority newspapers would be the general media, especially television.

Recognizing the unique problem that black publishers and editors face, several organizations have been formed to provide services to the black press. One of the oldest is the Washington-based National Newspaper Publishers Association; founded in 1940, it provides a forum in which black publishers and editors can attempt to identify solutions to their unique problems.

Two other organizations which provide important services for the black press are Amalgamated Publishers, Inc., and Black Media, Inc. Both obtain national advertising for black newspapers.

A fairly new organization, the Southeastern Black Press Institute (SBPI), was formed in 1977 with the express goal of "creating a service mechanism which supports the black press in its traditional role as a vehicle for community education and development." Funded through a Rockefeller Foundation grant, SBPI was initially a project of the Curriculum in African and Afro-American Studies at the University of North Carolina. Presently, it is housed on the campus of North Carolina Central University. While located at the UNC campus, SBPI sponsored summer journalism workshops which were designed to interest high school students in careers with the black press, and it also provided college students with internships at black newspapers.

Efforts by black colleges to increase the number of college-educated minority journalists—and thereby increasing the pool of potential employees for the black press—must not be overlooked. Presently, twenty black colleges offer a B.A. degree in journalism.

The Role of the Minority Press

Having examined the current status and unique problems of the black press, the next question is, what is the present-day purpose or role of the black press? A recent article by the authors, "The Black Press and the Bakke Case: An Analysis of Coverage," posed a similar question. The conclusion reached was that the strong protest function long associated with the black press has been replaced, and that one of the major roles of the black press today is to chronicle important black issues and events.

The black press serves several functions; reporting news of the local black community is the general overall function. Others that we have identified are (1) recording black history, black achievements, and black progress; (2) giving recognition to black community workers and leaders; (3) stimulating black community thinking on important issues and problems; (4) providing entertainment from a black perspective; and (5) serving as a unifying force for the black community.

In essence, the black newspaper's greatest value is its ability to do what the general press does not do: to chronicle, in-depth, the "happenings" in the black community. According to Pitt, the black newspaper brings to the attention of blacks information that they would not otherwise be exposed to. Indeed, he sees his paper, the *Chronicle,* as a unifying factor in the Winston-Salem black community.

Other minority community newspapers have similar functions. One purpose of each minority-group newspaper is to present the viewpoint of that particular group.

Emile Bocian, editor of *The Chinese Post,* identified one function that is perhaps unique to foreign language newspapers. In Elliot Parker's "Chinese Newspapers in the United States," Bocian says that "one of the functions of the Chinese press is to help newly arrived immigrants become assimilated into the local culture and life."

The Future

What will be the future role of the minority press? Will there be a need for the minority press in the future? These and other questions have been posed about minority newspapers for many years.

The origin of concern over the future of the minority press may lie in the demise of some portions of the foreign-language press. However, since we have indicated that other components of the foreign-language press, namely the Spanish-language press and the Chinese-language press, have not suffered any fatal setbacks, the fear that minority newspapers will follow the course of German, Polish, and Yiddish newspapers is perhaps unfounded.

Minority newspapers came into existence because of the inability or unwillingness of the general press to portray minority communities adequately; undoubtedly they will continue to exist for the same reason. In spite of the 1968 Kerner Commission Report, which severely criticized the white media for its failure to portray minorities, white newspapers, by and large, have yet to obtain a level of minority coverage that minorities deem adequate.

Because they are, for the most part, community newspapers, minority newspapers seem destined to survive. Indeed, there are those who believe that the survival of the newspaper as an institution lies with community newspapers. It is not surprising, then, that much of the growth in the black press has been in the number of new community organs that sprang up in the 1960s rather than in increased circulation of the older, national black papers. Roland E. Wolseley, in *The Black Press U.S.A.*, reports that as many as thirty new, small newspapers were founded during the second half of the 1960s.

Although Henry La Brie, in "The Disappearing Black Press," reports a decline in the number of black newspapers, black community newspapers continue to be founded. A recent University of North Carolina master's thesis by Allen H. Johnson, "The *Chapel Hill Journal:* A Blueprint for Journalistic Activism," outlines in great detail concrete plans for still another black community newspaper.

The relatively frequent founding of black community newspapers indicates a continuing need for such publications. That there is a need for black community newspapers was documented in a study done by Amalgamated Publishers, Inc.; the findings, which were reported in the *Editor & Publisher* article, "Study Finds Blacks Need Own Papers," indicated that black newspaper readers show an increasing desire and need for their own community newspaper.

Dean Lionel Barrow of Howard University's Communication School says that in his opinion, the need for the black press continues. In "Role of the Black Press in the Liberation Struggle," Barrow says, "We need a vigilant fighting press, sure in its blackness, concerned and knowledgeable about the facts and images needed by its community."

Perhaps James Williams best summarized the need for black community newspapers when he wrote in *The Black Press and the First Amendment,* "Blacks continue to need a press that speaks to their needs, their concerns, and is under their control. They need a press that will report their births, triumphs, failures, deaths and all the other events that shape and make up their lives. They need a press which is directly responsible to them and which serves their needs—a press to which they have access and whose existence guarantees that their voice will be heard."

The above needs will not go unfulfilled; there appears to be a continuous desire on the part of some individuals to fulfill these needs. An interesting point to note here is the desire of some editors of black newspapers to speak to these needs more frequently. Ernest Pitt and Raymond Garrison both spoke of their plans to publish daily newspapers. When asked about the future of his newspaper, Pitt replied that the future of the Winston-Salem *Chronicle* was limited only by his vision.

The bright picture painted for the future of black community newspapers applies to other minority newspapers as well. "The Chinese press," writes Elliott Parker, "in attempting to answer the unique informational and social needs of its readership, seems destined to remain, as it has for hundreds of years, an important, evolving, and expanding institution of the Chinese community."

The future of the minority community press and the black press in particular will depend on its ability to meet the challenges presented by a changing society, a changing role of the press in general, and the changing needs of the reader in particular. In addition to adapting to these changes, the black press must also concentrate on improving itself. La Brie says improvements in the black press are needed in both the business and editorial departments.

On the business side, there needs to be a coordinated advertising campaign to persuade major corporations that the buying power of Black America is rapidly increasing. To aid this campaign, black newspapers need to conduct scientific readership studies and have their circulations audited. Readership studies and audited circulations would be persuasive tools when trying to attract and retain advertisers.

On the editorial side, newspapers need competent journalists. Furthermore, La Brie, in *The Black Press Handbook,* points out there should be a strong, responsible black news service which the community papers could subscribe to. Also, the editorial page needs to be upgraded and promoted.

In "The Black Press Assessed," Roland Wolseley, professor emeritus of journalism at Syracuse University, adds that the quality of reproduction in the newspapers needs to be improved. The newspapers need to get rid of the large quantities of free publicity of questionable merit. Finally, Wolseley says, more vigorous stances in opposing social injustices for all minorities are needed.

In summation, the minority community newspapers are largely a result of deeply entrenched discriminatory practices. If such practices continue to push America toward three societies (white, black, and Hispanic) or more, the need for minority community newspapers—newspapers which report and interpret events from a minority perspective—will continue.

Chapter 22

JOHN B. JASKE

The author is vice president for labor relations and assistant general counsel of the Gannett Co., Inc. His chapter presents a management view of newspaper labor relations problems and management strategies for coping effectively with them.

"A commitment must be made at all levels of management to find out what employees are thinking, why they are thinking it, and how to make the best possible response."

Labor Relations in the Newspaper Industry

by John B. Jaske

The Newspaper Unions

Most newspaper managers have been exposed to an outline of the history of organized labor in this country. Names of organizations like the Knights of Labor and of individuals such as Samuel Gompers and John L. Lewis are not unfamiliar. Nor is a general knowledge of the American Federation of Labor and the Congress of Industrial Organizations, not to mention the historic merger of those two organizations.

However, newspaper people in general and newspaper management in particular often have little knowledge of the history of unions which represent employees in this industry. While the International Brotherhood of Electrical Workers, the International Association of Machinists, the Communications Workers of America, and even the Longshoremen have newspaper members, a few unions represent the bulk of organized newspaper employees today, particularly in small and medium-sized newspapers. The two most prevalent are the International Typographical Union (ITU) and the International Printing and Graphic Communications Union, known as the IP&GCU or, more commonly, the Pressmen. To a lesser extent, mailroom employees are also represented by the International Mailer's Union (IMU) and editorial, advertising, circulation, and business office employees by the Newspaper Guild. The following brief history of each of these unions may be useful to those who must deal with one or more of these organizations.

THE ITU

The Typographical Union claims to be, and probably is, the oldest international union in the country. It was initially formed under the name National Typographical Union in 1852, and its Washington local traces its existence to the year 1815. At that time there was nothing like the jurisdictional differentiation between departments and workers' skills that exists even in the small newspaper today. The printer was often one of the most educated men in his community, able to read and write as well as operate the simple printing equipment of the time. Benjamin Franklin was this type of printer, and it seems that no historical drama can be complete without the scene of a shirt-sleeved printer operating a hand press.

The organization was renamed the International Typographical Union in 1869. Like most unions of the day, its structure was loose and it had no full-time officers until 1884, functioning through largely autonomous locals.

Press operators or "pressmen"

had joined the union from its inception. They were printers and were encouraged to be members. The ITU sought to represent all other publishing industry workers including stereotypers, electrotypers, photoengravers, bookbinders, and mailers. The only group that remained, however, at least in part, with the mother union, was the mailers. Early in its existence, the ITU adopted a constitution, and to this day it adheres to a written constitution, bylaws, and general laws. These three documents are published annually by ITU headquarters in Colorado Springs, Colorado, and are required reading for any newspaper manager.

Although it was an early member of the AFL, the ITU was expelled by that organization in 1939. (It later affiliated with the AFL-CIO.) By that time the union had consolidated its power over composing room and mailroom work. It controlled these areas, particularly the composing room, with such an iron fist that for a time it could defy national labor laws passed in the 1940s which outlawed closed shop agreements. Its journeyman membership reached an all-time high of more than 94,000 in 1961, largely in composing and mailrooms.

This narrow base made the union vulnerable to automation. While an extensive apprenticeship program and a continued emphasis on training for journeyman employees allowed it to weather the advent of the linotype and teletypesetter with some success, it has been no match for computerized typesetting, which expanded rapidly during the 1970s. As a result, its membership has declined dramatically.

Early in this century, the ITU sought to organize and represent news writers. But craft printers and journalists were not compatible. The attempt failed. Recently, in an effort to stem the decrease in its membership, the union has sought to organize journalists again and form an alliance with the union that represents news and other front-office employees, the Newspaper Guild.

THE NEWSPAPER GUILD

This union was formed in 1933 by a famous columnist of the day, Heywood Broun. He envisaged the organization as an elite group of journalists well above the level of organized labor of the day. Indeed, the word *union* appears nowhere in the Guild's name, although it is affiliated with the AFL-CIO.

The Guild's success was almost instantaneous. It organized many large newspapers almost as soon as Broun announced he would form a union. However, because it was conceived as an exclusive organization, it intentionally attracted only a few members. Except in a few locations such as the San Joaquin Valley outside San Francisco, it has had little success in organizing small and medium-sized newspapers. Indeed, while its strongest local is in New York City, there are a large number of newspapers surrounding that city which do not have and never have had the Guild.

The union moved to broaden its appeal in 1937 by voting to include advertising, circulation, and other employees as members. However, this decision had a negative side. Journalists who regarded the Guild as their private domain were disenchanted by the thought that it would have nonjournalist members. This tension hindered the union's growth. In addition, a constant problem for the Guild over the years has been a lack of money. This is not only a result of its limited membership, but also the fact that there is a substantial number of journalists who are represented by the Guild but pay no dues. Periodic strikes have repeatedly depleted the Guild's financial resources, and it has never been able to sustain a financial base from which to broaden its organizing efforts. Membership in 1977 stood at 33,000.

Perhaps the Guild's greatest problem has been the fact that it attempts to organize the unorganizable. Journalists are by disposition and training naturally skeptical of anyone who seeks to limit their freedom or group them together. In addition, many traditional trade union concepts—seniority, wage scales, regulated hours, working conditions—do not readily transfer into the fluid atmosphere of the newsroom. In recent years, Guild leadership has formulated a model contract, which it insists its locals propose to management. Many of the provisions in the model contract are not only extremely objectionable to management, but have not particularly caught on with rank and file Guild members. Collective bargaining has become a slow, expensive process for a union that cannot afford it.

For a number of years, the Guild has attempted to merge with another union. Unions with which it would have a natural professional affinity, such as the Screen Writers Guild or the American Federation of Television and Radio Artists, have apparently shown no interest. Thus, the Guild moved toward a merger with the ITU. The ITU is stronger, both in terms of members and money. Guild leadership is apprehensive over the future of the union if it is merged into a larger union which has historically represented production employees. There is also animosity between locals of each union, particularly since, in the past, one has not supported the other during strikes.

THE PRESSMEN

What is now known as the IP&GCU was an offshoot of the ITU. In the 1880s, large power printing presses were put into operation, and the operators of this equipment were clearly separated in skill and function from the compositors. Pressmen also felt that they were not given equal treatment by the ITU. In 1889 the International Printing Pressmen's Union of North America was formed by thirteen press locals. Eight years later the union changed its name to International Printing Pressmen and Assistants' Union of North America. Much more recently it changed its name to the International Printing and Graphic Communications Union.

In bargaining, as early as the 1890s the Pressmen endeavored to follow the view that management's interests were its own interests. It recognized that management could only afford to increase pay to its employees if the business prospered, and it counseled its bargainers to educate themselves towards helping in these aims.

One of the chief complaints of the Pressmen at the turn of the century was the practice of placing a compositor in charge of the pressroom. Whether this dispute was a result of their feeling that the compositor was not sufficiently knowledgeable on pressroom practices or simply a continuing objection to being directed by a member of the union with which they had severed their alliance, the Pressmen succeeded in 1892 in pushing a bill through Congress which created the position of foreman of presswork at the Government Printing Office with equal authority to the foreman of printing. At one time virtually all press union contracts contained a provision stipulating that the foreman must be a journeyman pressman.

By the 1940s the primary issue for the Pressmen was the "manning" of presses, the number of workers hired to operate the equipment. Many newspapers had installed high-speed presses, and press crews had been reduced. The union obviously desired to curtail this trend, since a reduction in press crew sizes meant fewer dues-paying union members. Accordingly, a resolution was passed instructing local negotiating committees to attempt to increase the number of men per press wherever possible. Efforts by management in recent years to remove "manning tables" from press contracts have caused a number of newspaper strikes.

The union also hotly contested provisions of the Taft-Hartley Act of 1947, which outlawed closed shops and excluded from representation supervisory foremen. It had previously broadened its arbitration agreements with management associations. These "terminal" or "interest" arbitration agreements exist in many press contracts today. They provide that, rather than strike or lock out, the terms of a new agreement may be determined by arbitration. In recent years, management has sought to remove these provisions where it has achieved substantial bargaining strength. The courts have supported this effort by ruling that these clauses are not "mandatory bargaining subjects;" that is, the union cannot insist that they be maintained in a contract.

THE MAILERS

The International Mailers Union is the youngest of the four main newspaper unions, having been formed in 1943. Like the Pressmen decades before it, it was an offshoot of the ITU. However, unlike the Pressmen, a large number of mailroom employees remained affiliated with the ITU. Today, they are represented by the ITU either as part of what is, generally, a composing room collective-bargaining contract or under a separate agreement applicable only to the mailroom. The IMU broke away from the ITU mainly as a result of internal union disputes, particularly involving the selection of international officers. Only one vice president of the ITU had been designated to be a Mailer, a practice that continues to this day.

When it broke away from the ITU, the IMU took with it some small and medium-sized newspaper mailrooms. In many cases, these locals have not been able to achieve what ITU mailrooms have gained in wages and benefits. This is not only due to the fact that the IMU is a much smaller union, but it also does not benefit from the bargaining strength the ITU obtains when it speaks for both a composing room and a mailroom in the same newspaper. As a result, the IMU and ITU have recently merged at the national level, leaving locals free to combine or remain separate. It is not anticipated that many old IMU locals will soon merge with an ITU local. Thus these Mailers will remain a separate bargaining entity for years to come.

OTHER UNIONS

Emphasis on the four main unions in the newspaper industry should not divert attention from the fact that a number of other labor organizations have, from time to time, shown interest in representing newspaper employees. The International Brotherhood of Teamsters is active, particularly in and around large metropolitan areas where they have a source of strength. Their efforts have reached every area of the newspaper although their main point of success has been in circulation departments.

In addition, unions such as the Communications Workers of America have shown increasing interest in representing newspaper employees. The Graphic Arts International Union, formed out of the merger of three smaller unions, the Photoengravers, the Lithographers, and the Bookbinders, also represents a share of employees in photoengraving and camera rooms.

What Is a Union?

Listing the major labor organizations in this country and outlining their history is useful to any newspaper manager. However, it is well to explain what a union is to understand how to deal with it effectively.

There are a number of legal definitions of what constitutes a labor organization. The most practical description is that a union is a group of employees performing the same or similar tasks who have banded together in the belief that they can achieve more as a group than they can achieve alone.

The key to this definition is the employee's perception of his own status and his relationship to his employer. Not even the most optimistic union organizer can readily state that simply forming a union guarantees any employee higher pay or better benefits and working conditions. Nationwide statistics support this fact. In 1977 there were approximately 19 million unionized employees in this country. This is only about 3 million more employees than were unionized in 1955. Unions now represent less than one out of every four nonfarm workers, a decline from one third of the work force in 1955.

Recognizing that an employee's decision of whether or not to join a union is an indication of how he perceives himself and his relationship to his employer answers the question, Why not have a union? For, if a group of employees decides that their relationship with their employer is so uncertain or unfair that they must seek the assistance of an outside party to help them deal with "the boss," this is a clear indication that management has failed. Around 40 to 50 percent of a newspaper's expenses go to pay the wages and benefits received by its employees. With this substantial reliance on manpower, a newspaper publisher or department head who fails to show his or her employees that they are being fairly and properly treated has failed to meet the responsibilities of a good manager.

The decision by an employee to join a union might best be equated to the decision by any person to seek legal representation. If the employees believe that their situation is so difficult, uncertain, or unfair that they cannot properly handle it alone, they, like the potential litigant who seeks the advice of an attorney, may turn toward a union for advice and representation. Thus, the key to obtaining and maintaining nonunion status in a newspaper plant is for management to commit itself to doing anything and everything possible to make employees feel that they are being fairly and properly treated. Again, the emphasis is on the employee's perception. It may be that you pay quite well or even better for skills in a particular department than any other employer in the area. However, if your employees do not know this or, worse, believe that they are underpaid, management has failed just as surely as if it paid no more than minimum wage. The same applies to every aspect of the employer-employee relationship.

Maintaining Nonunion Status

The small or medium-size newspaper generally does not have the resources, either in money or manpower, to establish and properly run a full-fledged personnel department. Thus, the important task of properly and fairly handling the needs of employees is often left to department or subdepartment heads who have many other responsibilities besides personnel management. The ideal for any newspaper—or any business—is to establish a trained personnel department. Where this is not possible, there are many things that management can do to achieve the goal of making employees feel that they are well-treated.

COMMUNICATION IS THE KEY

The primary goal is communication. Nothing will turn an employee to a union faster than being taken for granted. Professional labor negotiators can readily cite instances in which, in sitting down to negotiate a first contract after a union has organized a group of employees, management hears for the first time some of the complaints which had led employees to unionize. Sometimes these complaints are valid; often they are not. Usually, employees simply did not fully understand their situation and, as a normal human reaction, assumed they were getting a bad deal.

Since most small and medium-size newspapers have no professional personnel counselors, a commitment must be made at all levels of management to find out what employees are thinking, why they are thinking it, and how to make the best possible response. The methods of finding out what employees are thinking are as broad as management's imagination and practical circumstances will allow. Individual employee interviews conducted in a frank and open manner, with the assurance given to the employee at the outset that the interviewer is interested in learning what the employee thinks about his or her job, is perhaps the best way to begin a process of communication. Such interviews should *not* be held at the time the employee is being considered for or granted a pay increase. The raise tends to divert the employee from what should be the main purpose of the discussion.

The problem with individual interviews, again because of the size of the organization, is that they cannot be conducted on a regular basis and thus often become annual matters taken for granted by both the employees and management. A lot can happen the other 364 days of the year.

Small group or department meetings held on a regular basis provide a more routine vehicle by which managers can learn what their employees are thinking. These meetings can be particularly productive if they are regularly called to seek the employee's input into a management decision: a redistricting for the circulation department, a format change in the news department, a rate increase in the advertising department. The manager who, before making a final decision, seeks input from his own employees reaps double benefits. First, he is dealing with those who will most often have to implement the decision. They may immediately spot flaws in the theory which did not occur to those who conceived the change. Secondly, it becomes virtually impossible for the employee to criticize the decision once it has been made, having already been offered the opportunity to comment in the early stages of discussion.

Employees unionize against management. If they have been made part of management's decisions, they are part of management, and it becomes much less likely that they will, in effect, organize against themselves.

FIRST-LINE SUPERVISION

No one spot in the organization is of more importance in obtaining or maintaining nonunion status than the immediate supervision over rank and file employees. Every effort should be made to impress upon supervisors that they are responsible for knowing what their employees are thinking and why. A union-organizing campaign in a department is an indictment of the supervision of that department.

Much of the difficulty with first-line supervision occurs because supervisors view themselves as authoritarian figures. They feel responsible only to carry out management pronouncements received from their superiors, without any two-way communication with the employees who report to them. This is often a product of the fact that first-line supervision is dealt with, itself, in an authoritarian fashion. A foreman is called into a meeting with the production director and is informed of a change in policy. He is expected to carry out the new policy without being asked his view of its effectiveness and without having any input into the policy change. His natural reaction is to deal with rank and file employees in the same manner.

If, instead of dealing in a completely authoritarian manner, supervisors are counseled to view themselves not only as managers but also as representatives of the employees who report to them, a much different atmosphere is created. First, in order to represent those employees effectively, the supervisor must naturally seek their views. This creates the positive result of the supervisor's learning what his or her employees really think about their jobs. Second, the employees perceive that their views are being heard by management.

Newspaper management which has successfully counseled first-line supervisors to represent rather than dictate to employees has taken an argument away from the union organizer—that with a union they will have a say in their future.

WAGES AND BENEFITS

The points discussed above—developing and maintaining an openness in communication, especially between employees and first-line supervisors—cost virtually nothing. They may in fact reap benefits to management in that good, intelligent employees and first-line supervisors may be encouraged to remain with the company and improve their performance rather than become discouraged and seek opportunities elsewhere. Moreover, giving employees and first-line supervisors a voice in management decisions can prevent costly decisions which, over time, must naturally occur when decision making is left in the hands of a few without any input from those who must implement those decisions.

While unionization of employees may result in an employer's being forced to pay higher wages and benefits, the same can be said if an employer pays low wages or grants few benefits in comparison to similar size newspapers. There is a natural pressure on management to improve wages and broaden the benefit package. This often comes as much from middle managers as from the employees themselves, since the managers must deal with the day-to-day unhappiness that such a situation creates with the employees they supervise.

The effect of unionization can, today, sometimes be insignificant. In fact,

in some newspapers which have moved rapidly to remedy a history of low wages or poor benefits, unionization by the employees will sometimes dampen management's desire to continue this pattern of improvement. Often, when employees go from nonunion to union status, benefits which had previously been liberally granted "at the discretion of management" become severely limited. An example of this is sick leave, which is normally extended in a nonunion situation to all but the most flagrant violators. In union situations, it is not unusual for even a first contract to have a limitation placed on sick leave, such as a certain number of days per year or a one- or two-day waiting period before sick pay begins. Unionized newspapers normally pay higher wages and benefits than nonunionized newspapers because unions are more heavily represented in big city newspapers which would pay more anyway. No union organizer can candidly promise employees in a small midwestern newspaper that they will get, through unionization, the same wage-benefit package that is paid to their counterparts in large newspapers in New York, Chicago, or San Francisco.

What function, then, do wages and benefits play in the employee's desire to unionize? The answer again is the employee's perception. If they believe they are being unfairly treated in relation to their peers at the newspaper, elsewhere in the newspaper industry, or in similar jobs in the community, they will tend to press for higher wages and benefits. If this pressure is met by a flat rejection without explanation by management, employees will be likely to turn to a union in an effort to enforce their demands.

There are two keys to this problem. The first is to be sure that all employees understand the nature and extent of all benefits extended to them. An employee handbook is good; an employee handbook supplemented by periodic meetings to discuss and analyze benefits with employees is better. Further, there should be one individual at the newspaper who has a working knowledge of all benefits, particularly benefits granted under health insurance plans. Every employee should know that he or she has the right to go to this individual and receive an answer to a question about his or her benefits.

Does the medical plan pay for allergy shots for a college-age son? Does the funeral leave policy take into account that an ailing mother lives three thousand miles away and the employee is the executor of her estate? Answers must be readily available.

The experienced labor negotiator is familiar with many situations in which, in negotiating a first contract, newly unionized employees actually ask for a benefit which they already receive. This is the tragic result of management's failure to tell its employees what they have.

A second key to handling wages and benefits is that, in discussing them with the individual employee, management should be fully prepared to answer the simple question, "Why aren't I paid more and why aren't my benefits better?" There is a world of difference between the answer, "We have studied your job and its salary potential and feel we are paying fairly in relationship to what other employers in this community pay" or "You know we publish this newspaper 365 days a year and we can't grant as many holidays as other companies in town" and the answer, "You are paid what you are worth."

While no amount of openness and candor will completely solve a situation in which management is paying grossly less than what other newspapers or employers are paying for the same skills, candid communication with employees about wages and benefits can be a great help. It is natural for employees to assume that they are not being paid what they are worth. It is a mistake not to meet this natural human tendency with candor.

COMBATING APPREHENSIONS

As management strives for greater productivity and product quality, it must be constantly sensitive to the fact that changes it proposes are usually viewed by employees not in terms of effects on the company, but in terms of the effects on their own lives. Again, it is not unusual for employees to assume that new programs, new goals, and a general change in their working conditions will be bad. This is particularly true where the change has been made without any prior notice to employees or input from them.

Management must recognize that employees below supervisory level often are not interested in the frequency of on-time press starts, market penetration, circulation gains, and the host of other problems in running a newspaper that fill a manager's day.

Rather, most employees ask themselves, Will management's new policies make it easier or harder to do my job? Will I be paid more? Will I have more or less free time? Managers should consider that their employees may have an adverse reaction to a policy change because they don't understand the reason for the change, and lack of understanding breeds resentment. Not only does this resentment lessen the probability of success for the new policy, but it also fosters a general resentment toward management.

When, on the contrary, management seeks to enlist employees in the decision-making process and explains why changes are being made—stressing that even changes which appear to make things more difficult for the employee are necessary to assure the overall success of the newspaper, thereby securing the employee's job—a positive relationship can be created. Ignorance breeds insecurity. And employees' insecurity about their job situation, whether real or perceived, is the factor most likely to drive them to a union.

PROBLEMS OF PARTIAL UNIONIZATION

As the ITU and IP&GCU did not aggressively seek to broaden their membership, the situation often exists in small and medium-sized newspapers in which areas of the production department, particularly the composing room and pressroom, are unionized, while other areas—circulation, advertising and the newsroom—remain unorganized. However, with the decline in their memberships in recent years, these unions have begun actively to organize other employees. Newspapers have been faced with the challenge of dealing with union organizers who are

full-time employees in their own plants.

In addition to the open, communicative atmosphere discussed previously, there are other steps that management can take to keep employees in nonunion departments a part of the management team. The best rule for achieving this is not to allow union negotiations to set wages and benefits for the *entire* newspaper. When management has followed a policy of first negotiating a benefit change with the union and then granting it to its unorganized employees or, worse, giving it only to the unionized department, the union organizer has a perfect argument to tempt the unorganized: "We in the union get bigger and better benefits than you do, so sign up with us."

On the other hand, if management grants wage and benefit increases to unorganized departments before the unionized departments negotiate for the improvements, it takes away the organizer's argument and replaces it with: "Look how much better you, in the unorganized departments, are doing dealing directly with management than the departments that pay dues to union officials are doing."

Management is forbidden by law from instituting policies aimed at defeating a union. However, where proper business reasons exist, sick leave policies, vacation policies, holiday benefits, even pensions and health insurance can be better in unorganized departments, particularly since management retains discretion in their administration. It must be understood that there is absolutely nothing illegal or improper in dealing with union and nonunion departments separately. Contrary to what some unions would lead management to believe, management has no obligation to grant benefit increases plant-wide and can limit the increases to nonunion departments and make the union departments bargain for them.

It must be also remembered, however, that this policy can only apply department to department, not individual to individual. It *is* illegal to grant benefit increases to some individuals within a particular department and withhold them from others on the basis that one group is pro-union or pays union dues and another segment of the department does not belong to

the union or support it. Discrimination on the basis of an employee's union affiliation is illegal. Granting benefit increases to nonunion departments or withholding them from union departments is not if there are lawful reasons for the distinction. For example, management's reluctance to incur the cost of extending a new benefit to a large union department is a proper lawful reason.

In the event that management determines that a benefit increase should, for reasons of policy or convenience, be granted to a union department, it is often wise to offer the benefit to the union unilaterally without waiting for the union committee to demand it at the bargaining table. The reason for this is clear: Even if management has already decided to grant the benefit increase, the union can still take credit for obtaining the benefit for its members if it gets the benefit through the bargaining process, thereby solidifying its position at the newspaper. If, however, management offers the benefit to the union unilaterally without being asked for it, it tends to establish with the employees that they obtain only what management offers irrespective of the union's bargaining strength. It must be understood that benefit changes, even benefit improvements, cannot be made without the union's agreement. How then does one offer a unilateral benefit increase as suggested?

The method is simple. Suppose management decides to improve the company pension plan which covers all departments, including unionized departments. Management can offer the benefit to union employees by addressing a letter to a proper union official. The letter should read, in substance, "Management has decided to increase the company pension plan. We feel that it is in the best interest of all our employees, including the employees represented by your union, that they enjoy this benefit. Unless you object, we will put this benefit improvement into effect for the employees you represent in the very near future."

Such a letter places the union on the horns of a dilemma. On the one hand, it does not want to give management the obvious credit for giving employees they represent a benefit increase; it wants the credit itself. On the other hand, it does not want to be criticized by its members for standing in the way of a benefit improvement. The response normally followed by a union in this situation is to respond that it does not object to the benefit improvement but thinks it should have been granted a lot sooner, and the union will expect to ask for even greater improvements in a future contract bargaining. However, this response does little to lessen the impact of granting the benefit to the employees. They should recognize that it came solely as a result of a management decision on their behalf. Management can tell employees that this is the case. In doing so, however, management should be careful not to imply that this is in furtherance of any policy to undermine the union's strength. In fact, it is not. It is proper for management to react, not to the outside influences of a union, but to the desires and needs of its own employees.

Of course, such benefit increases should not be granted if management clearly feels that it can obtain a better bargaining position by withholding the benefit until the union contract expires. It may well be that management feels that it will inevitably have to grant the benefit increase since it wishes to make the benefit uniform throughout the plant. However, even though this may be the case, the benefit is desirable to the employees and a price can often be exacted for it. If management has only given the benefit in exchange for being granted something from the

union in return, this again has a long-term effect on management's relationship with its unorganized employees.

The "in-house organizer" may go to the unorganized department and use the argument, "You have the same benefits we in the union got and we weren't even representing you. Imagine how well we can do for you if we do represent you." Management's response to this can be, "Yes, they have the same benefits, but do you realize that in the year they got the last benefit increase, they gave up something to get it? You gave up nothing." Such a situation obviously makes union membership much less desirable to the unorganized.

Responding to a Union Organizing Campaign

Most of the unions in the newspaper industry endeavor to organize new employees in essentially the same way. Each union has a number of international employees generally called representatives. Each is assigned to a particular geographic area. Sometimes they will work out of a particular local as an employee of a newspaper. More often, they are full-time union employees paid with union funds. They are responsible for assisting already established locals with grievances, arbitra-

tion, and contract bargaining, as well as internal union problems. They also are strongly encouraged to find and bring in new groups of employees for organization, either in plants where the union is already established or in a newspaper where the union does not yet have a foothold.

HOW A UNION ORGANIZES

The decision to attempt to organize a particular newspaper is made along very pragmatic lines. The organizer must consider first what the chances are for organization. Have there been prior attempts to organize the newspaper and, if so, why have they failed? He must also consider what the chances are of obtaining a contract are and whether he can get a sufficient number of dues paying members to justify the expense and trouble of the organizing campaign.

It is not unusual for employees to seek out the union first, and many successful union campaigns have started from such employee-to-union contact rather than the reverse. The reason for this is obvious. The organizer has very little knowledge of a particular nonunion paper or nonunion department in a paper. He may have some familiarity with the newspaper, since most union representatives are long-time members of the newspaper industry. However, the specific information that he needs to organize, such as pay rates, benefits, the number and classification of employees, and the nature and quality of supervision, are often not available to him. Even if he has an idea that the newspaper might be ripe for organization, an overt approach such as a mass mailing or an invitation to a union meeting to all employees has several obvious drawbacks. Such overt conduct becomes immediately known to management, and management can move to counter the effort. More importantly, such overt appeals are often resented by employees and have little impact.

Management should remember that the union organizer is no magician. Very often he is a long-time newspaper employee who, after many years

Figure 22–1. Sample Authorization Card

Authorization

Name _____   Phone _____

Address _____   City _____

Name of Company _____   Location _____

Department _____   Shift hours _____

I hereby designate and authorize the XYZ Union, AFL-CIO, as my collective bargaining representative in respect to rates of pay, wages, hours of employment, and other terms and conditions of employment. I also hereby authorize said union to request recognition from my employer as my bargaining agent for said purposes.

Date _____   Signature _____

of working in a particular plant, got a job with the international union. The quality of these individuals varies greatly. But it is fair to say, and they would admit, that few if any of them have the ability to convince employees who have been treated properly that they have not been treated properly or tell employees who are paid well that they are paid poorly. In short, management almost always brings unionization on itself. The newspaper unions of today have little ability to force unionization on employees or on a company.

Once the union organizer has determined, through contacts initiated by him or by the employees, that there is a potential for a sufficiently large bargaining unit to justify the time and expense of organizing, he will take steps to solidify his position. He will endeavor to establish a small group of employees as a "steering committee" or "organizing committee" to serve both as a nucleus for convincing additional employees and as a source of information about the company which is his target.

Organizing usually proceeds with meetings at employees' homes and informal social occasions such as picnics. The purpose of these efforts is to obtain the support of as many employees as possible before management finds out about the organizing campaign. During the organizing process, pragmatism again governs the organizer's activities. He knows that the legal rules that govern unions are that they can only represent "an appropriate bargaining unit." While the rules for determining what constitutes an appropriate bargaining unit are many and varied, the organizer generally attempts to organize along the lines of a newspaper's department. Therefore, if he finds strong support for the union, but this support is diversified over a number of departments and he judges that he will never obtain a strong majority in any one department, he may abandon the effort. Also, if he determines that strong support exists in one department which is so small in relation to the rest of the newspaper that he cannot hope to bargain a favorable contract or, more importantly, get enough members to justify organizing and bargaining, he may also move on.

Decisions of this type may be dif-ferent from one union to another. For example, the Newspaper Guild has historically avoided attempting to organize newsrooms in small newspapers. They apparently believe that there is not sufficient potential for dues-paying members in newsrooms of less than one hundred to justify the effort. In several locations, the Typographical Union, in need of new members to offset recent declines in membership, has stepped in and organized these departments. The ITU apparently feels that its need to diversify out of composing rooms, which have been heavily hit by automation, offsets the risk of expending funds without a return of dues-paying members.

If the organizer determines that there is a sufficient number of employees in an "appropriate bargaining unit" to justify his continued efforts, he will try to get as many employees as possible to sign authorization cards. With minor variation these cards normally read as in Fig. 22–1.

The cards are legally binding documents. They authorize the union to seek an election or, in certain circumstances, to represent the employees without an election. They do not, however, obligate the employee to vote for the union in a Labor Board election. While a union is legally prohibited from obtaining employees' signatures on these cards through outright deception, it is not unusual for the cards to be solicited on the basis that they will simply be utilized to obtain more information. In fact, the cards are sometimes included with a document similar to a questionnaire asking what the employee is paid, whether he thinks he is paid enough, whether he thinks he has enough holidays, and similar inquiries. However, the authorization card is separately utilized by the organizer to support his organizing effort.

Misrepresentation seldom goes beyond this. Again, the reason is obvious: Most union organizing efforts end up in a vote. If the employees find out either on their own or with the help of management that they have been deceived into signing an authorization card, the likelihood of their voting for the union diminishes. Rather, the organizer will tend to talk about "job security," the certainty of having things down "in black and white," and the benefits of other unionized newspapers in an effort to sign up employees.

Having obtained a sufficient number of authorization cards, the organizer will generally file a petition with the local office of the National Labor Relations Board asking that an election be scheduled. The organizer can also utilize these cards to demand recognition from the employer. While this does not often happen in this industry, the organizer can simply come in to the newspaper, ask to see the publisher, present a set of signed authorization cards, and demand that the publisher bargain for a contract. Needless to say, this can be a disconcerting moment for any publisher.

However, in the event this occurs, management has no obligation to accept the union as the bargaining representative for its employees, even if all employees have signed authorization cards. The reason for this is that the possibility exists that the cards could have been obtained by deception, could have been forged, could be stale (that is, signed many months previously and thus not representative of current employee sentiments), or could otherwise be found not to represent the wishes of a majority of the employees. Also, there are questions as to whether the employees form an appropriate bargaining unit within the legal guidelines laid down by the Labor Board. For all these reasons, the publisher when confronted by a union organizer armed with a pack of authorization cards should simply respond that he has "a good-faith doubt that the authorization cards represent the sentiments of an appropriate unit of employees."

Sometimes the organizer is not so easily put off and will attempt to insist that the cards be inspected by the publisher or that they be submitted to an impartial third party such as a public official or a clergyman for an independent inspection. Again, management has no obligation to respond to such a request and may simply offer the authorization cards back to the organizer and courteously dismiss him from the office. In the event that the organizer will not take the authorization cards back, it is perfectly proper for management simply to take the authorization cards and, without reviewing them, place them in an envelope and, in the presence of a witness such as the publisher's secretary, address the envelope to union headquarters or some other known union official. The cards can then be mailed back to the union; usually, however, the organizer, not wishing to risk having the cards lost in the mail and seeing that the strategy has failed, will quickly take them back and leave.

If, as is usually the case, the union seeks an election through a National Labor Relations Board petition, it may legally do so with cards signed by only 30 percent of an appropriate bargaining unit. Since the union organizer knows that in a Labor Board–sponsored election he must obtain the favorable votes of a majority of the employees, seldom are election petitions filed with less than 60 to 75 percent of the employees having signed authorization cards. The organizer knows that during the interim between the filing of the petition and the election, a number of employees may well realize that they have made a mistake in signing an authorization card and will ultimately not vote for the union.

ANSWERING THE UNION

Once the union petitions for an election, it is advisable for the publisher to seek professional legal counsel. As noted above, there are many rules concerning who can and cannot be a part of a bargaining unit. Often extensive litigation takes place after the union has filed its petition to determine which employees are properly part of an "appropriate unit," whether certain employees are supervisors, management employees, or confidential employees and thereby legally prohibited from being in a union, and other legal issues. Hopefully management will learn of the organizing effort before the petition is filed. There are certain guidelines that should govern management's response. If management responds quickly and correctly, the petition may never be filed.

If, as should be the case if there is a good rapport between supervision and rank and file employees, management learns of the union's organizing efforts at an early stage, management can take steps to determine why the

organizing campaign is under way. Often management will feel that they are somehow legally prohibited from taking any position with respect to unionization. This is foolish. It is not unheard of for employees to organize simply because management says nothing about the matter, and employees assume that management is in favor of the union when quite the contrary was true.

Management can say that it does not want unionization, that it wants to continue to deal with employees on a personal basis without the intervention of a third party who is only interested in getting as many dues-paying members as possible. Management may also take steps to try to find out why its employees are considering unionization.

It is advisable to have professional counsel at this stage. However, the general rules concerning what an employer can and cannot do are set forth here so that the publisher, when faced with an organizing campaign, will have an idea how to respond while he is considering whether to use outside counsel.

The general rules for dealing with employees who are thinking of unionizing provide that an employer may not discriminate for or against employees because of their union sympathies. That is, an employer cannot fire or discipline or threaten to do these things because a particular employee or employees are supporting the union. Nor can he grant pay increases, improve working conditions, or promise to do so in exchange for a commitment by his employees that they will not support the union. The employer is also legally prohibited from interrogating his employees specifically about their union sympathies. While there are many subtleties to these broad rules for which the wise employer will seek legal counsel, they generally govern the conduct of any employer in a union campaign.

There is one crucial difference which applies after a union has filed an election petition with the National Labor Relations Board but does not apply before this event takes place. Before the petition a newspaper may, with a substantial degree of freedom, change terms and conditions of employment. That is, it can increase wages, shorten

hours, grant additional holidays, improve other fringe benefits, and generally take affirmative action to make things better. The company cannot, however, discriminate. Improvements must be made without regard for the union sympathies of those who receive them. Nor can the changes be made to counteract union activity. If the changes are perceived *only* as a reaction to the union campaign, they are generally illegal. If there is a proper business reason for them, they are normally permissible.

This situation does not exist after the petition has been filed. The Labor Board has a fairly firm rule that, unless a change had been specifically planned and announced before the petition was filed, an employer cannot improve benefits during this so-called "critical period" between the election petition and the election. The Labor Board will generally assume that such a change is an effort, in effect, to bribe employees to vote against the union and may well rule that it is unlawful. Such a ruling can, in certain cases, result in the employer's being required to recognize and bargain with the union without even being afforded an opportunity to go to an election.

Thus, special care must be taken during this "critical period" between the petition and the election. The same reasoning applies to a refusal to grant planned benefit or wage changes after the petition is filed. If the employer had announced that it was going to improve a fringe benefit or had a regular policy of granting wage increases at certain intervals and then refuses to make the change or grant the increases after a union petition is filed, the Labor Board will assume that this refusal is a design to punish employees for supporting the union effort. Unless the employer can show a proper business justification for its conduct, it may well be found to have violated the law and could be required to bargain without an election.

Within these rules, the employer is certainly entitled to discuss the good points of his company with his employees. He is also entitled, being careful not to specifically interrogate employees about whether they favor or do not favor the union, to discuss their problems and concerns with management. Such questions will very often draw out the reasons that the employees are considering unionization. Employees, even those who are initially strongly in favor of the union, are often apprehensive about the possibility of moving from a nonunion to a union environment and are generally willing to discuss the matter with management. If, upon generating this exchange of information, the employer finds that employees are thinking of unionization because of misunderstandings about benefits, wages, or their relationship with the company, the employer may certainly tell them the true facts, either before or after the petition.

Communication between management, particularly first-line supervision, and employees is especially important when a union movement is active. Supervisors have a tendency to think that they should say nothing about the union movement. This is a serious mistake, since first-line supervision, as at any other time, can have an important impact on the employee's likelihood of ultimately voting the union in. When properly advised about what they can and cannot say, supervisors should be encouraged to talk about the matter with their employees. After all, the decision to unionize a particular department has perhaps its greatest effect on first-line supervisors who will have to deal in a new environment if the union comes in. They are prohibited only from discriminating or indicating they intend to discriminate on the basis of the employee's union sympathies.

It is also proper for management to point out the facts about the particular union involved. The union's strike record, its bargaining success or lack of it either in other areas of the paper or in other newspapers, are all relevant information for employees to know before they decide whether to vote the union in or out. Management should take the tack of giving the employees *all* the facts, not just deflating the promises they may have received from a union organizer, and then letting them make up their own minds. Financial information concerning both the international unions and a particular local union can be obtained from the Department of Labor in Washington. All international unions and local unions are required to file annual disclosure statements about their financial

status, the dues and initiation fees they charge, the salaries they pay their officers and employees, and other pertinent financial data on forms called LM-2 or LM-3. Any form on file may be obtained from the Department of Labor in Washington for a nominal copying charge. Other information about a particular union may be obtained from newspaper organizations, other trade organizations, or other employers.

All these facts can and should be given to the employees, who can then make an intelligent decision. While certain matters are often best set forth in written form—a list of union strikes, an outline of a union's financial situation, a graphic description of current company benefits—a most effective method of dealing with employees who are considering unionization is on a face-to-face basis, either in small groups or one-on-one. Campaigning of this type can take place on company premises and company time or outside the company, at a planned social event or simply over a drink after work. Almost any type of contact is advisable, except that the employer, unlike the union organizer, is legally prohibited from visiting employees at their own homes. Also, a supervisor should avoid calling employees into his office for such discussions since the surroundings may be deemed coercive.

Management's approach should not focus on whether the newspaper is the best newspaper it can be—any organization has room for improvement—or whether, philosophically, unions are good or bad. The issue in any union election is whether this particular union is right for this particular group of employees at this time. Whether in a political campaign or a union election, experience has shown that many voters do not vote *for* a particular candidate, but *against* one. It is a naive employer who believes that his employees will give him a vote of confidence any time he asks for it. As mentioned earlier, employees naturally feel they are not paid what they are worth. Add this basic fact to the problems that any newspaper management, no matter how conscientious, fair, and open, creates for itself, and management is unlikely to win a pure "vote of confidence."

On the other hand, the employer should try to show that the union the employees are considering has not effectively represented employees elsewhere, that where there is the appearance of a good contract it is in fact not the result of union pressure on a particular newspaper, but simply the high cost of living that forces a large newspaper in a large city to pay more than small or medium-sized newspapers can pay. Employees should understand that collective bargaining is often a long difficult process and that, legally, benefits and working conditions can become less desirable as a result of collective bargaining. Contrary to what many employees and some employers believe, employees do not start with all their benefits and conditions intact and then, through the union, obtain greater benefits. It is not, for example, unheard of for the union, seeking a union security clause which would require all employees, as a condition of employment, to pay union dues, to agree to a restriction or reduction of certain employee benefits employees had enjoyed. In short, collective bargaining is a two-way street, and benefits can be bargained up as well as down.

All these things should be made known to employees before they decide to unionize. However, the key to success will lie in whether the employees can feel secure in continuing to deal with management without having to employ a union to deal for them. The extent to which management has established an openness, a fairness, and a willingness to respond intelligently and positively to employee problems will have a great impact on the outcome of the election.

Collective Bargaining

In the event that the company is unsuccessful in its efforts to dissuade employees and the union is voted in, the union will have to begin bargaining for a contract. To the same extent, in those papers which have been organized for many years, the employer will periodically be faced with the task of renegotiating the long-standing collective bargaining agreement. In either case there are certain procedures that can change what might otherwise be an intimidating and chancy exercise into a predictable and ultimately successful undertaking.

STRIKE PREPARATION

The first thing the management of a newspaper should do prior to any other action in preparation for collective bargaining is to prepare for a strike. This may seem contradictory; however, it must be remembered that the only weapon the union has to force management to agree to any proposal is the threat or actuality of a strike. Taking away this threat puts management in an excellent bargaining position. Of course, the threat can never be totally removed, since the decision to strike lies ultimately in the hands of the employees. However, preparing to publish and distribute the newspaper no matter what actions are taken by employees makes it less likely that the employees with whom management is negotiating will actually walk out.

Some newspaper executives believe that strike preparations will increase the possibility of a strike by "inflaming the situation;" employees will undoubtedly find out about the preparations and tend to retaliate.

This has generally proved not to be the case. Management has an obligation to its other employees, subscribers, advertisers, and the general public to see that the newspaper is printed and distributed on schedule no matter what. Once this explanation is clearly and forcefully made, most unions will not press an objection to strike preparation. In fact, there is nothing a union can do legally to prevent strike preparations any more than the company can prevent the union from striking.

Strike preparation centers around the question, What would we do if the employees with whom we are negotiating walked out? How would we print and distribute the paper? Answering this question obviously depends on the size and complexity of the group of employees with which management is bargaining. Management should assume that all union employees, even those not directly involved, will cease work if any group strikes. For a unit

of three or four transportation department mechanics, it may only be necessary to consider how supervisory employees would be deployed to replace these employees or be sure that other sources of trained mechanics are available.

When dealing with a much larger unit, for example, a hundred or more composing room employees or a large pressroom operation, it may be necessary for management to engage in lengthy and complicated strike preparations, including the training of potential replacement employees, taking advance security measures, and stocking additional supplies; in sum, doing everything and anything possible to insure that publication will continue. Management should be careful not to leave to the last minute matters which can be prepared in advance. Experience has shown that when a walkout occurs, many unexpected problems occur, so everything that can be done ahead of time should be.

The publisher should generally train his or her own employees for strike duty, whether or not an outside source of help is available. They have a stake in the newspaper's continuing production. Only when in-house help is clearly insufficient should arrangements be made either to bring in outsiders or to farm some work out.

The value and sensitivity of equipment in even the smallest paper make security of paramount importance when a strike is threatened. Professional security firms are very expensive—but so is a computer.

PREPARING BARGAINING OBJECTIVES

At least sixty to ninety days in advance of negotiations, management and department heads involved should meet to consider the objective of negotiations, from management's point of view. First-line supervision should be consulted in this matter, since they may be aware of problems which are unknown to the publisher. If the company is bargaining for a first contract with a newly certified union, consideration should be given to the delineation of management's rights in appropriate

clauses of the first contract as well as an appropriate no-strike clause. When bargaining for a renewal contract, management should review the old document to see not only what present problems are involved but also what latent defects there are in the contract. For example, in recent years, provisions in press contracts which provide for arbitration in the event management and the union do not reach agreement have been ruled to be nonmandatory subjects of bargaining. That is, management cannot be pushed to renew such provisions if it does not want to, and the union cannot strike to force a renewal of such a clause.

Counsel to the newspapers should be consulted with respect to the current contract and his or her assistance enlisted in drafting the actual language of the contract. In the event that qualified labor counsel is not available to the local in the newspaper's community, the ANPA or another trade association can render assistance.

PREPARATION OF PROPOSALS

Once bargaining objectives have been determined, actual proposals should be prepared in writing. Management should avoid bargaining on oral proposals as this causes confusion. Care should be taken in drafting the proposals so that their meaning and intent is clearly understandable both to management and to the union. This will avoid unnecessary grievances and arbitrations over the meaning of poorly drafted proposals in the future.

THE BARGAINING TEAM

It is generally advisable to have a management bargaining team of two to four individuals, as it is important that perceptions and input be obtained from several sources as bargaining proceeds. The bargaining team should generally be made up of those management representatives who are both the most articulate and knowledgeable about the objectives to be attained and also have the strength of character to function in a situation which can be at times quite testing.

LOCATION

Contrary to what many employers believe, there is no obligation on the part of management to provide a place for negotiations. Most professional negotiators believe that, particularly when they are dealing with a complicated and time-consuming set of negotiations, it is best to have the negotiations take place away from the newspaper premises. A neutral site is generally more conducive to progress. Moreover, it generally makes a bad impression on unorganized employees to see union representatives trouping into the plant at regular intervals and meeting with management representatives.

Nor need management schedule meetings only to the convenience of the bargaining committee or pay members of the committee. Management may insist that bargaining sessions take place only at times when union committee members are off work. However, this rule cannot be used to thwart negotiations altogether—for example, by insisting that bargaining sessions take place only at times when it is impractical for the union to meet.

THE NECESSITY OF CANDOR

The bargaining process should begin with an exchange of proposals, the union making its proposals for a new contract first. Care should be taken to comply with any provision in an expiring contract which calls for notice of proposals a specific amount of time, usually thirty or sixty days, in advance of the expiration of the old agreement. After written proposals are exchanged, time should be taken before actual discussions and negotiations begin. This will allow management time to assess and agree on a response to union proposals, particularly those which are not of an economic nature.

Management should be fully pre-pared, capable of explaining its proposals and objections candidly and completely. This, like clearly written proposals, will prevent unnecessary future grievances. To the extent that management finds it necessary to modify or redraft its proposals, such modifications can sometimes be done orally to facilitate progress in the negotiations. However, when oral proposals are made it is best to confirm them in writing as soon as possible, at least by the next bargaining session.

The frequency of bargaining sessions depends on the desires of the individual parties and the complexity of the issues involved. The only legal obligation is to meet at "reasonable" intervals and bargain in good faith. Bargaining in good faith does not mean that either side must agree to any proposal. However, there is an obligation to consider the other side's point of view.

MINUTES OF BARGAINING MEETINGS

One member of management's bargaining team should be designated to take minutes. These need not be a verbatim transcript but should accurately summarize the progress of each bargaining session. Proposals exchanged can be attached to the minutes of each session.

Minutes of bargaining sessions serve two purposes. First, they can help the bargaining team, in drawn-out negotiations, to review where they have been and can pin down previous positions taken by both management and the union. Second, minutes should be kept so that explanations of written proposals will be available should a grievance over a clause be filed at some later date. Arbitrators give attention to "bargaining history," and, to the extent that this history is memorialized by written notes, it can carry great weight with an arbitrator.

There is no necessity that the union agree to the minutes, nor that an official transcript be kept. In fact, this is generally believed to be a counterproductive process since the parties will tend to "make speeches for the record," and disputes can develop over what was actually said at the bargaining session. The fact that the union has not officially agreed to management's minutes does not significantly detract from their effectiveness in a subsequent arbitration.

GENERAL TIPS

The wise negotiator does not make regressive proposals—proposals which are more onerous or restrictive than prior proposals. This has a generally confusing and negative effect on negotiations and, in extreme circumstances, can be found to be illegal bargaining by the Labor Board. Negotiations should progress with the parties either modifying and clarifying proposals or standing on a proposal based on previously explained needs. Only in unusual cases should proposals be modified to make them more restrictive and then only with a clear explanation as to the reason for the change, such as a failure of an initial proposal to state management's intent correctly or a reaction and trade-off to a proposal by the other side. Management should also be quick to challenge any attempt by the union to make regressive proposals.

The successful negotiator couples both patience and aggressiveness. There is usually a stage during collective bargaining negotiations when sufficient time should be allowed for explanation and consideration of the positions of both parties. The time may be anything from a few hours to many sessions. However, when management finds itself repeating its arguments over and over, the time has come to challenge the union aggressively to accept the proposal as drafted. By the same token, a time will come when management must review its proposals and discard those which are of limited value. Often proposals will be made initially and, upon discussion with the union, it will be found that there is no real dispute and that the present contract language adequately covers the imagined problem. These decisions should be summarized in the minutes.

A good negotiator never "bargains against himself." This means that if management makes a proposal, it should insist that the union make a counterproposal, not simply reject its proposal and have management make another. This puts pressure on the union to make concessions of its own and prevents management from making all its concessions without getting any counterconcessions from the union's side.

A method to test the water concerning the union's position on a number of proposals is to make a "package proposal": management makes a proposal modifying some of its initial positions but makes the new offer conditional on the union's accepting other management proposals. For example, at the start of bargaining, management proposes a management's rights clause, a no-strike clause, and a time limitation of fifteen days for a union to file any grievance it might have over the contract. Later, management might offer a package proposal offering to extend the time limit on filing of grievances from fifteen to thirty days if the union will accept the management's rights and no-strike clauses. In the event that the union does not accept this "package," management states that it has the right to withdraw from all or any part of it. This gives management the option of going back to the fifteen-day proposal and still puts pressure on the union to make some concession or at least indicate its true position concerning each of the three clauses. This process can be done with any number of clauses and any variation of proposals.

It is generally in management's best interests to save economic items for last. These are generally union proposals concerning increased wages and benefits. Often unions will agree to negotiate noneconomic items, which are generally management proposals, first. Technically, management does not have the right to refuse to discuss economic items before all noneconomic items are dealt with. However, management can take the position that its economic proposal is "No wage or benefit increases unless our noneconomic proposals are dealt with." Management is not refusing to discuss the economic proposals, it is simply rejecting them. This is a significant difference, since, as stated above, neither side has a legal obligation to accept any proposal.

If international union representatives or even local union negotiators attempt to negotiate by intimidation—

aggressive behavior, shouting obscenities, and the like—the response to this will depend on the makeup of the particular management team. If its members think they can give as good as they receive, so be it. They may decide simply to ignore the attempted intimidator, ridicule him as childish, or walk out and resume negotiations later. The important thing to remember is not to be intimidated or act rashly.

When about to discuss economic items, it is advisable for management—particularly when a union international rep is across the table—to educate the union bargainers about the ultimate direction in which management wishes to take the negotiations. Often the rep has no interest in provoking a confrontation between management and the union, particularly over economic items. He may be quite willing to assist in obtaining a settlement if he is given the ammunition to do so. Sometimes this can be done in off-the-record discussions between management and the representative involved. The effectiveness of such discussions varies from representative to representative. Many appreciate such talks and will treat them with strictest confidence. Other union bargainers are, frankly, less reliable. When dealing with a union international representative, it is wise to find out either from other newspapers where he has negotiated or from professional negotiators in the newspaper industry about the representative and his trustworthiness.

Even if side discussions are not possible, other signals of management intent can be given. A common method of doing this when dealing in wage negotiations is to "bracket" the figure that management has decided will be its final economic position. This means that if, for example, the company has decided that its final wage increase figure for a particular year of the contract will be a fifteen-dollar-a-week increase, its proposals should progress towards this figure at the same rate as the union's proposal, if possible. Thus, if the union's last proposal is twenty dollars, management might propose ten; when the union comes to nineteen, management can move to eleven. If the union drops to seventeen fifty, management might raise to twelve fifty. Experienced union negotiators will soon see

the pattern and will be able to predict to other less experienced members of the union bargaining team that he believes management's final offer will be fifteen dollars. When this proves to be true, this not only makes the union bargainer look good, but also enables him to pave the way for a smooth settlement.

When management, supported by good strike preparation, carefully prepared written proposals, and a firm but candid bargaining approach, has reached a tentative agreement with the local union bargaining team, the normal procedure is for the bargaining committee to take the tentative agreement to the membership for ratification. When the parties are on the verge of a settlement, it is advisable for management to do two things. First, as part of its acceptance of the union's last proposal, management should make acceptance conditional on the union bargaining team's recommending the contract to the membership. This will place at least a moral obligation on the union bargaining team to work for ratification, making it more likely that the proposed contract will be ratified. Second, management should make it clear that the tentative agreement also represents management's best offer on each and every aspect of the proposed contract.

In the event the local union turns down the tentative agreement, management will not soften its position to buy ratification. This may seem like a dangerous posture and, indeed, it is not for the faint of heart. However, the alternative can be that the local union will repeatedly send its bargainers back to the table following rejection votes to get more and more concessions from management. Sometimes management makes the mistake of continually making more and more concessions and ends up with a contract much worse than the tentative agreement which, had management been firm, probably would have been ratified. In today's newspaper industry, the unions which management faces in small and medium-sized newspapers are unlikely to risk a confrontation, particularly if management has been firm and fair at the bargaining table and has prepared adequately for a possible work stoppage.

Administering the Labor Contract

Once negotiations have resulted in a collective bargaining agreement, management and the employees must work under its terms. Often, of course, disputes arise as to the interpretation or application of a particular contract clause. In these instances, management will wish to resort either to its bargaining notes or to a past practice which, though not specifically set forth in the contract, can be of assistance to it in establishing a correct interpretation. A past practice exists when one party or the other to the collective bargaining agreement has allowed, without objection, a particular practice to continue for a period of time. Past practices can work for or against management. Thus, management should be careful not to allow a past practice to be created, thereby weakening its position should a dispute arise. If management does not particularly mind that a particular practice occurs for a period of time, but does not want to establish a past practice which might preclude it from making a change in the future, management should handle the situation in the following manner.

Suppose, for example, the contract calls for an eight-hour shift. Neither management nor employees object to a practice by which the employees work through their lunch hour and leave when the work is done, before the end of the actual eight-hour shift. Management, however, does not wish to establish this as a permanent practice, since a change in its operations might someday require it to insist that employees take their lunch hour and work to the end of the shift.

The solution is for management to send a letter to the union indicating the specific contractual language, the practice that is in derogation of this language, and its intention to allow the practice to continue so long as its operations allow, if the union will agree that the practice can be discontinued at any time and that no "past practice" is created by allowing the condition to go on. The union will normally agree that a past practice is not created, and management may continue to operate without fear that it is restricting itself for the future.

Department heads should take care that their first-line supervisors are not creating past practices. Sometimes a foreman or supervisor allows practices to go on, ignorant of the fact that they may be creating a situation which cannot be changed in the future. Department heads should caution their foremen to check any change in working conditions with the department head.

Discipline and Discharge

A common dispute between newspaper management and a union is whether a particular employee can be disciplined or discharged for his conduct. Since it is becoming increasingly difficult to convince an arbitrator to uphold a discharge case, newspaper management should carefully follow the guidelines set forth below.

WARN FIRST. Employees should clearly be put on notice as to conduct which management will not tolerate. Such forewarning may occur through work rules clearly posted in the working area. These rules should be general enough so they will allow management some latitude in handling unanticipated problems but not so general as to be unenforceable. Many ITU contracts specifically require that office rules be posted in the composing room. Arbitration which management would otherwise have won has been lost simply because management failed to have its work rules posted for employees to see.

In the event that there are no rules posted or there can be a reasonable difference of opinion as to whether a specific rule covers an employee's conduct, the employer should give the employee a clear written warning that his or her conduct is not in conformance with the company standards before any actual punishment is meted out. The only instances in which warnings do not need to be given are those in which there is a clear and obvious violation of basic conduct. Examples include fighting, drunkenness, gross insubordination, and intentionally creating a safety hazard. This does not mean that management should not be careful to clearly establish that the employee is guilty of such an offense before discharging. Methods for doing so will be discussed below. However, once such an offense is clearly established, management can usually discharge without a prior warning.

Situations which clearly should be handled with a warning prior to any punitive action include allegations of incompetency, tardiness, absenteeism, and the like. In short, any situation in which the employee could argue with some credibility that he or she did not realize that management was unhappy with his or her conduct should be dealt with by warning.

The warning should be in writing, setting forth the specific acts or course of conduct which management believes are improper and specifically telling the employee that continuation of this conduct will lead to his or her dismissal. One copy of the warning should be given to the employee, one placed in his or her personnel file, and one given to the employee's union representative. It is important that the warning be in writing for two reasons: the employee will not be able to argue that he or she did not clearly understand what was expected by management, and management will be able to establish clearly to an arbitrator what was said and when. In those instances where oral warnings have been given to an employee and the employee's improper conduct continues, the prior oral warning should be referred to specifically in a subsequent written warning. The more detail concerning the employee's conduct included in the warning, the better.

KEEP IT RELEVANT. Generally a work rule or warning cannot concern employee conduct which does not relate to the job. Thus, for example, an employee cannot be warned, much less disciplined, because he or she is in debt, is involved in some community or personal controversy, or is even allegedly involved in criminal activity, so long as these activities do not interfere with the employee's job performance.

INVESTIGATE. It is crucial to any discipline or dismissal case that management conduct an investigation and not simply rely on first impressions or the statements of supervisors. Supervisors should clearly understand that management, in conducting this investigation, is not doubting their word or undercutting their authority. Rather, if the investigation is not conducted, management stands a substantial chance of losing subsequent arbitration.

The investigation should include interviewing both the individual charged with improper conduct, all witnesses, and anyone else with relevant knowledge. The interviews should be conducted by an appropriate management person, normally the department head, with a witness present to record in writing the information obtained during the investigation. Even when, for example, an employee has been warned about repeated absences and has been specifically told, in writing, that another unexcused absence will result in discharge, management should interview the employee if there is a subsequent absence before firing. This will preclude the employee, once discharged, from presenting the arbitrator with what sounds like a perfectly valid excuse for the final absence and then asserting that management certainly would not have acted if management had bothered to ask the reason for the absence. Of course, it is true that arbitrators do not always accept such belated excuses. The point is that management can protect itself from ever losing an arbitration on this basis; it simply takes the time to investigate even in those instances where misconduct is glaringly apparent. Union members charged with misconduct have a right to have a union representative present at any interview.

GIVE SEVERAL CHANCES. Management today is almost mandated by arbitrators to engage in "progressive discipline," which means that, except in situations where the employee's conduct is grossly improper, management

must first warn the employee several times in writing, clearly stating that the continuation of the conduct will result in his or her discharge; then suspend the employee for several days if the conduct continues; and then, only if the conduct continues after suspension, discharge the employee. Building such a case history is management's best assurance that the discharge will stick.

Under many newspaper union contracts, suspension may be specifically outlawed. In these instances, it is advisable for management, prior to discharging the employee and after several warnings, to propose to the union that it will suspend rather than discharge the employee for a subsequent offense if the union will agree to allow the suspension and waive the contractual restrictions. Sometimes the union will do this, sometimes it will not. In either instance, management will be able to assert to an arbitrator that it made every effort to rehabilitate the employee through progressive discipline before actually discharging.

BE CONSISTENT. Management should be careful to avoid being accused of discrimination in its administration of discipline. Thus, if one employee is discharged for a particular offense and another employee is not, the reason for the difference in handling should be clearly documented in management records. Often arbitrators will look to a particular employee's general work record to determine whether discharge was an appropriate penalty. Management should likewise. The employee who has a poor work record in a number of respects may often be discharged sooner and for less serious misconduct than the employee who has a long history of good work practices.

Discipline and dismissal under a union contract are often difficult subjective judgments for newspaper management. If, after clearly setting forth the conduct that is expected of employees and then giving written warnings to those who failed to abide by these standards, management can argue to an arbitrator that the employee effectively discharged himself by knowingly engaging in improper conduct, man-

agement will win many more discipline and discharge arbitrations that it loses.

The Process of Decertification

Unions are often voted out by their members at newspapers. This may be a result of union weakness and ineffectiveness and the high cost of union dues—particularly when big city strikes result in assessments for all members—coupled with increasingly enlightened management approaches to employee handling. The process by which a union is voted out is called decertification and is much like the process to vote the union in.

Management is legally prohibited from giving any assistance to employees in the decertification process. The employees, acting on their own, must obtain the signatures of at least 30 percent of the bargaining unit and file a petition with the National Labor Relations Board. About the only thing management can do if it is approached concerning a decertification is refer the employees to the local office of the Labor Board. Labor Board representatives will generally give the employees advice on the decertification procedure.

Once the decertification move is under way, management is entitled to state that it favors the decertification and otherwise campaign for it. As in any other union election, management is restricted from making any promises of specific benefits or threatening any retaliation against employees to influence the outcome of the vote.

To the extent that management has treated nonunion employees in an enlightened fashion and made them feel part of the newspaper team, and to the extent that management has bargained with the union in a manner which makes it clear to the unionized employees that they receive only what management decides to give and no more, management will have taken giant strides toward control of the newspaper's future irrespective of the newspaper unions.

Chapter 23

Public Notices, Postal Laws, and Other Legal Issues

by William A. Bray

Public Notice Advertising

Public notice advertising is an essential ingredient of our representative form of government. It is vital to the administration of many of our laws. As Thomas Barnhart says in his book *Weekly Newspaper Management,* representative government can be successful only so long as it commands the confidence of the great majority of people. People must be kept informed of what is happening to their investment and their lives and property.

The citizen has a personal interest in this "legal" advertising, although many do not understand it or even think about it. His personal interest lies in the fact that through the public notice he is enjoying his constitutional right of due process of law to be placed "on notice" when his life, rights, or property are threatened through a legal action.

Most newspaper publishers have listened to public officials complain about the time and expense of publishing a required legal notice. Unthinking readers sometimes complain because a

page in the newspaper contains a couple of columns of public notices. Some persons actually think that the main purpose of legal advertising is to provide revenue for the newspaper and do not consider its true purpose. Because it is a service performed by the newspaper and one for which the newspaper is paid, it is important for the publisher to understand it fully and to defend it.

WHAT DOES THE PUBLIC NOTICE DO?

Public notice advertising serves three basic purposes. First, the public notice safeguards the pocketbook of the taxpayer with an effectiveness that can be accomplished in no other way. Second, it furnishes the only means of fulfilling in a practical way the Constitutional guarantee of security to every citizen— the so-called "due process" of law as set out in the Fifth and Fourteenth Amendments to the Constitution. Third, it informs citizens of their duties as citizens in such matters as voting and elections, new laws and proclamations.

WILLIAM A. BRAY

The author is executive director of the Missouri Press Association and teaches courses in community newspapers and newspaper management at the University of Missouri.

"No public official will spend money like a drunken sailor if a list of his expenditures is going to be published . . . for all of his constituents to look over. . . . Newspapers need not apologize for getting paid for doing this kind of job."

KINDS OF PUBLIC NOTICE

In order to fulfill the three purposes of the public notice, we have three kinds or types of notices. The public accounting notice, the informational notice, and the warning notice.

The *public accounting notice,* or published report of the fiscal transactions or legislative work of governmental bodies, is the safeguard for the taxpayer's pocketbook. It is an aid to the individual discharging a public trust as well. The value of the public accounting notice is apparent to anyone whose attention is directed to it. It includes such notices as treasurer's reports for all units of government as well as financial proceedings on the municipal, county, state, and national level.

In an article in the *Michigan Publisher,* the executive director of the State Bar of Michigan, Henry L. Woolfenden, Jr., wrote that no public official will spend money like a drunken sailor if a list of his expenditures is going to be published at the end of the month or end of a fiscal period for all of his constituents to look over. No dealer "on the inside track" is going to sell the city, county, or any other unit of government a bill of goods at an excessive price when every competitor he has will go over the list of purchases with a fine-toothed comb the minute it is published. It discourages the unscrupulous public official from making kickbacks and other deals. It cannot be said that the published accountings required by law have completely stamped out incompetency and malfeasance in public office, but public notice advertising is the cheapest and most effective insurance the taxpayer can buy on the ability and integrity of elected officials.

If there is any fault to be found with legal advertisements of this kind, it is that there are too few of them and that they are not in detail. Who got the money? How much? What did he get it for? These are the questions the citizen asks and is entitled to know. The certified public accountant's audit may attest to the honesty of the accounts, but his audit will not determine the best buy or point out excessive expenses or salaries. Only the public can determine this.

The second type of notice, the *informational notice,* serves to notify the citizen of the many duties to which he is obligated. An example is the election notice—advising him of the time and place of the election and who is seeking office. He should be given the exact wording of any proposition he

is to vote on. Citizens cannot be expected to go to city hall, the county courthouse, or the state capitol to find election information. It must be provided in a convenient manner, and the public notice is convenient.

New laws passed which affect the citizen's property should be called to his attention. It cannot be expected that the citizen be familiar with every statute or ordinance that is passed, but he can be given basic details. Just because the citizen does not attend every open meeting of the governmental unit does not mean that he has to forfeit his right to knowledge of what is going on. Notice to bidders and contractors is essential to good government because competitive bidding helps save the taxpayers money. News that a project is under discussion or that certain items or services are needed should be made available to the public so that all who are interested may come forth.

The third general type of notice is the *warning notice.* It alerts particular parties that some action is about to be taken or of a proceeding about to be instituted which will affect their lives or their property. Such notices constitute the best guarantee the individual citizen has of the security of his property and Constitutional rights. Into this class of warning notice fall many different kinds of proceedings: probate notices, chancery sales, chancery orders for appearance, mortgage foreclosures, guardian notices, divorce notices, and certain financial reports such as those required of banks. We cannot discuss each of the hundreds of proceedings that require notice under this classification; however, we can explain the twofold purpose behind them.

First, the warning notice safeguards the defendant in any litigation by requiring the plaintiff to give him notice of the institution of suit. Of course, notice should be given personally, but often this is not possible and the substituted notice by publication must be given through a newspaper of general circulation. Second, it provides the plaintiff with the means to exercise his legal right against the defendant when the latter cannot be served personally.

A good example of the warning notice is in the case of probate. When a person dies, if he has not completely

taken care of the disposition of his property it has to go into probate court for settlement. Often the heirs are not all known or cannot all be located. The published notice helps call them forth. Also, the probate notice serves to let creditors know that someone has an estate to be settled and that they should come forth and claim their money so the matter can be closed.

PUBLIC VERSUS PRIVATE FUNDS

It is important that the newspaper publisher understand the difference between "public funds" and "private funds." Rates for public notice advertising are set by the governing body in each state. In so doing, most states distinguish between private and public funds. This means that any public notice required by law which is to be paid from public funds is paid at a rate set by the statutes. Public funds are those funds paid by the public in the form of taxes, fees, and licenses into the treasury of a public body. All notices in the first two categories—the public accounting notice and the informational notice—fall into the public fund category.

In the third category, the warning notice, payment for the notice comes from private funds. That is, the estate of the deceased must pay for the notice, or the person getting the divorce. Proceeds from a foreclosure sale pay for that notice. All of these are private funds of an individual or business, and in most cases the newspaper has the right to set the rate just as it does for any other type of advertising. There are exceptions in some states where the legislature sets the rates for all notices required by law. The publisher must understand the rate statute in his state.

An example which demonstrates the difference between a public accounting notice and a warning notice is a bank financial statement. Periodically every bank must publish a financial statement showing the location of its funds and its liabilities and assets. This is not a public accounting notice because it is paid for by the bank from its own funds. It is actually a warning notice to let the public know the financial condition of the bank in case they want to go elsewhere with their banking business.

QUALIFYING FOR PUBLICATION

Every state sets forth criteria which determine which newspapers are eligible to carry public notices. If a notice appears in a paper which does not qualify, the notice is invalid.

Eastern and southern states have only a few laws in this regard. The central and midwestern states seem almost to vie with each other in setting up requirements both for the newspaper and for all public bodies and individuals responsible and accountable to the public.

Usually, to be eligible, a newspaper must possess a second-class mailing permit, have established a certain period of regular and continuous publication, be published at least weekly, have general circulation, and have paid subscribers. Some states require a minimum number of paid subscribers, and some even have size requirements. Some midwestern states require that the newspaper be "published in whole or in part in the town in which its office of publication is located."

North Dakota has an unusual way of picking the newspapers which may run public notices. The newspapers in each county file and enter a political race like a candidate. The two newspapers in each county with the largest vote in the primary election then run in the general election. In other words, the public chooses the newspaper of record.

A few states say the newspaper eligible to run public notices shall be the newspaper with the largest circulation. About all this sort of law does is to encourage newspapers to pad the subscription list.

CHARGING THE LEGAL RATE

One or two states have modernized their legal rate structures into something reasonable for today's newspaper. Texas, for example, uses "the newspaper's lowest classified advertising rate." The state of Washington uses the newspaper's general open rate. With these exceptions, most states are badly outdated. All newspapers are grouped under one rate regardless of how large an audience they serve. This discourages the large newspapers from seeking public notice advertising. To run it is actually to lose money. It is not reasonable to pay a newspaper of 1,000 circulation the same amount as a newspaper of 250,000 circulation.

Newspapers usually charge "all the law allows" for public notices. The reason is that the rate is usually far below other rates. The care and accuracy required in public notice advertising is greater than in any other category. If a mistake is made, the newspaper may have to begin an entire series again. The newspaper is entitled to some return for having to do without such advertising for the specified period of time required for qualification. Maintaining a bona fide list of subscribers is expensive. Some states require the newspaper to have a performance bond in order to run the notices. This costs money, but the state wants to be absolutely certain of performance. Certainty of performance is also the reason for using only paid-circulation newspapers.

Not least among the reasons why newspapers should get an extra rate for public notice advertising is the fact they must supply and prepare an "affidavit of publication" on every such notice. The affidavit must be notarized and this is a further expense. The affidavit is then attached to the case or litigation dossier as proof that proper notice has been given and becomes part of the court record.

Many unusual requirements are found which bind and complicate notice publishing for qualified newspapers. If, for example, you want to run the big election ballot, election notice, or proposed amendments to the state constitution in Missouri, the newspaper must declare a political orientation or alliance. The law in this regard says that the Secretary of State shall choose two newspapers in each county, one for each of the major political parties in the last election, to carry the notice.

This is in addition to the other requirements. Generally an independent newspaper in the country is simply ruled out under this statute unless, perchance, it is the only newspaper in the county and then it gets to run these notices because they must run in every county.

PROMOTING PUBLIC NOTICES

Because it is the newspaper that gets paid for the public notice, it usually falls to the press to defend and fight for these notices. The public for the most part does not seem to care. It is simply taken for granted.

How important really is the public notice? It is as important as the difference between a secret election and an open one. It is as important as picking a public official for a job because his record is good and clean as opposed to one whose performance is not known.

Newspapers need not apologize for getting paid for doing this kind of job. There are many services and functions to be performed in our kind of society and someone must be paid. If a lawyer is entitled to a fee, if the policeman is entitled to a salary, if the merchant is entitled to a profit on the goods he sells, then the newspaper is entitled to be paid for the service it performs.

One of the aspects of public notices most often overlooked by the newspaper is their news value. An obligatory publication such as a notice of public hearing can mean a news tip. Financial statements often lead to news stories. There are countless suggestions. Some newspapers run front-page boxes of one or two lines describing current public notices running in the newspaper.

Public notices should be set in regular reading type, as easy to read as any other part of the newspaper. They should never be set in small (agate or six-point) type. The page or section should have an attractive heading. Advertisements educating the public on the value of the notices make excellent house ads.

Postal Regulations

Historically, Congress has said that dissemination of the "printed word" in the United States is an important function of government. Since the beginning of the Republic, there have been special provisions in the postal laws allowing reduced rates for newspapers.

The second-class mail category was set up solely for periodicals and is certainly the most economical method of newspaper distribution, especially for weekly and small daily newspapers.

The cost of mailing a newspaper by second class is determined by a complicated system which combines (1) number of pieces mailed, (2) percentage of advertising, (3) distance to be mailed, and (4) weight of the newspaper. The basic charge is by the pound, with a small surcharge for each piece. The lowest rate is for copies sent within the same county in which the publication is located. Newspapers with fewer than 5,000 copies going out of the county and that are not issued more frequently than once a week enjoy the lowest rates.

Pound rates for all newspapers accelerate rapidly as the distance to be mailed increases. Lower, special rates within the second-class category have been established for publications of nonprofit organizations, schools, and religious groups, as well as for certain educational, scientific, and agricultural publications.

In order to take advantage of second-class mailing privileges, the publisher must contend with a large number of regulations and requirements that concern record keeping, news and advertising content, ownership, and debt disclosure, as well as addressing, wrapping, bundling, and ZIP sorting. Because the postal regulations are so comprehensive, most states require newspapers to hold a second-class mail permit in order to be eligible for publication of public notices. Obviously, the reasoning for this requirement is that it saves many pages of detailed statutes in the state law books.

In this text it is not practical to go into the scores of postal regulations dealing with newspapers. Postal laws and regulations are subject to constant change. Newspaper publishers and other managerial personnel must keep currently informed in this area. Regulations dealing with sampling, supplements, special dispatches, addressing, etc., are too detailed to include. Only the basic aspects of second class are treated in the sections which follow.

WHO QUALIFIES FOR SECOND CLASS?

Only newspapers and other periodical publications may be mailed at second-class rates. They must be issued not less than four times a year at a stated frequency such as weekly, daily, monthly, or quarterly.

ISSUANCE AT KNOWN OFFICE. Publication must be issued and mailed at a known office or place of publication. This is a place where the business of the publication is transacted during usual business hours. The office must be in the same place (city) where the second-class mail permit is originally authorized. Publications can have more than one office location, and additional mail privileges can be authorized at other post offices.

PREPARATION. Publications must be formed of printed sheets and cannot be mimeographed, stenciled, or hectographed.

CONTENTS. Publications must be originated and published for disseminating information of a public character or devoted to literature, science, art, or some special industry. They cannot contain material violating copyright law, threats against the President, fictitious matter, fraudulent matter, libelous matter, lottery information (unless the state has legalized lotteries), treasonable matter, matter of an obscene or crime-inciting nature, or any other material that would cause them to be unmailable.

LIST OF SUBSCRIBERS. Publications must have a list of subscribers who pay or agree to pay for copies during a stated time. The rate cannot be a token rate nor can rates be reduced to lower than 50 percent of the stated rate. If publications do not carry general advertising, they may be excused from having paid subscribers.

ADVERTISING. Publications designed primarily for advertising purposes may not qualify for second class. They include (1) those having in excess of 75 percent advertising in more than one half of their issues during any twelve-month period, (2) those controlled or owned by individuals or businesses and conducted essentially for the advancement of the individual or business, (3) those that consist primarily of advertising and editorial write-ups of advertisers, (4) those that consist mainly of advertising and have a token list of subscribers and that print advertisements free for advertisers who pay for copies to be sent to a list of persons furnished by the advertisers, and (5) those published under a license from individuals or institutions and that feature other business of the licensor.

FREE CIRCULATION PUBLICATIONS. Publications designed primarily for free circulation may not qualify for second class.

Postal regulations should be checked for a complete list of advertising restrictions.

APPLYING FOR SECOND CLASS

Newspapers which qualify may apply for an original entry permit on Form 3501. After the application is made and the fee paid, the applicant must wait for approval by the director of mail classification in Washington, D.C. There is no prescribed time period and the wait for approval may be from three weeks to several months. During this period the publication must be mailed at third-class rates. The difference between the second- and third-class rate may be refunded once the second-class permit is approved, *but only if the local postmaster has kept a record of the third-class mailing on Form 3503.* No refund is made if this form is not kept or if the newspaper is mailed with postage stamps affixed.

When the second-class permit is approved, the newspaper will be given a publication number. This number must be shown on the front page of the publication and on all wrappers. In addition to the number, second-class publications must show the name of the publication on the front in a position, style, and size of type so as to distinguish it. The following information is required on one of the first five pages in each issue in a position where it can be easily located:

- Date of issue

- Frequency of publication

- Issue number (issues must be numbered consecutively)

- Subscription price

- Address of the known office of publication, including the ZIP code

- Second-class entry which reads "Second-class postage paid at (town), (state) (ZIP code). If a publication is mailed from two or more offices the entry must also state "and additional mailing offices." While second-class application is pending the notice should read "Application of mail at second-class postage rates is pending at (town), (state) (ZIP code).

A statement of mailing for each issue is required by the postmaster. He will use this form to compute the proper postage. This form must be accompanied by a "marked copy" on which is clearly indicated all advertising portions. The postmaster will advise and help fill out the form until the applicant can do it himself.

All mailings must be paid in advance. The postmaster will accept a deposit in money for as many mailings as desired and furnish receipts.

STATEMENT OF OWNERSHIP, MANAGEMENT, AND CIRCULATION

On or before October 1 of each year, the newspaper must file a statement of ownership, management, and circulation. The form is supplied by the postmaster and the contents must also be published in the newspaper in the first issue in October. Information required includes the names of the newspaper's owners, publishers, and editors; their addresses; names of known bondholders, mortgagees, and other security holders; a breakdown of circulation figures, showing methods of distribution, paid and free subscriptions, and other information.

Newspapers are supposed to be given high priority treatment by the postal service. At times there is delay, and when subscribers complain about slow delivery they should be encouraged to contact their local post office to try and determine the cause.

CONTROLLED-CIRCULATION PUBLICATIONS

Because third-class rates are much higher than second class, a special category of mail has been set up for certain publications. This special category for "controlled-circulation publications" has a rate higher than second class but lower than third class. It is intended for publications that do not have paid subscribers, but which are, in fact, newspapers distributed free and which do not otherwise qualify for second class. To qualify, such newspapers must have at least twenty-four pages in each issue (for this reason many are in tabloid format), contain at least 25 percent nonadvertising, be issued at regular intervals, and be circulated or mailed free.

In dealing with the Postal Service, the local postmaster is one of the most important persons in the world to the publisher of a newspaper. His cooperation and good will can save endless, agonizing hours of wading through postal regulations and forms. He has great authority at the local level and his decisions are seldom overridden by Washington. It is always best to try to settle postal problems at the local level; however, if this cannot be done, the publisher can turn to the USPS Mail Classification Center. The

local postmaster can supply the name, address, and telephone number. State and national press associations can also be very helpful in answering questions and solving problems.

Other Legal Issues

All business enterprises are subjected to a myriad of state, local, and federal laws and regulations. Even though newspapers have the special protection of freedom of the press under the First Amendment to the Constitution, they find they are actually faced with more restrictions than many other businesses.

Other than those laws generally affecting all businesses, newspaper management is chiefly concerned with legislation covering libel, privacy, antitrust, wage and hour, child labor, obscenity, lotteries, fraud, advertising, contempt of court, search of newsrooms, copyright, and access to news through meetings, records, and courts.

Some of these laws are discussed in greater detail in other chapters. Following is a brief explanation of a few areas not covered elsewhere.

ACCESS TO NEWS

W. Terry Maguire, vice president for legal and government affairs for the American Newspaper Publishers Association, says that gaining access to the news which a newspaper wishes to cover can be one of the most difficult of all journalistic tasks. It can be divided into three areas: access to papers, access to places, and access to people.

Access to papers or records is governed by at least two kinds of statutes in most states. On the federal level, there is a strong Freedom of Information Act which should help any publisher who wishes to obtain records from the federal government. Second, there is some provision in virtually every state governing access to state and local records. These are called open records laws or freedom of information laws. Many of them are stronger than the federal statute.

Gaining access to places is also subject to parallel federal and state regulations. The federal access question is answered in most cases by the government in the Sunshine Act. At the state level, open-meeting laws abound and govern press and public access to most meetings.

Maguire believes the best way to think about this form of access is, if the general public can enter the place, then the reporter is also free to do so. Add to that the idea that if there is a situation involving serious injury or a catastrophe, the press is usually safe in proceeding with officials to the scene (but only with official permission). At the other extreme, entering private property in order to cover a story might expose a reporter to the risk of a trespass suit.

Apart from these general rules, there are some other important things to keep in mind. A great deal of access to government institutions—including courtrooms and courthouses—is governed by regulation or rule of the court. Violating these rules may lead to prosecution for contempt of court, even if the rules were unconstitutional in the first place.

The specific question of reporter access to courtrooms has been the subject of considerable litigation. Richard W. Cardwell, general counsel of the Hoosier State Press Association, summarizes the legal status of the issue at this writing as follows: "In 1979 a majority of the U. S. Supreme Court ruled that the public has no independent sixth amendment right to attend a pretrial suppression hearing.* In 1980, the Court held that the first amendment guarantees the public, including the press, the right to attend criminal trials. Although that ruling did not address the question of access to pretrial proceedings, it is likely that the reasoning employed there will be urged as a basis for pretrial attendance rights as well."

A reporter who finds such a motion being made in a court that he or she is covering should try, if the court rules permit, to register an objection with the judge presiding over the case.

Reporters have no constitutional right to enter local, county, state, or federal jails. Access is governed by the rules and regulations of the individual institutions, and the press has no greater right than the public.

Access to people is much more difficult. Usually this involves access to newsmakers. There are few statutes on the point, but governments of all sorts have established a variety of policies with respect to issuing press passes for press conferences and related events. In addition, access to individuals is often governed by some of the same provisions that regulate access to places, such as prisons. On the purely private level, there is only a very limited amount of protection for reporters—usually none at all—in trying to gain access to individuals residing on private property.

CONTEMPT OF COURT

Contempt of court citations can arise for any number of actions that the court deems to interfere with the administration of justice. Some of these reasons are

- Disobeying a court order (such as taking pictures without permission after a judge has ordered against it)

- Refusing to testify as to news sources when subpoenaed (Some states have "shield" or "confidence" laws that allow reporters to have confidential communication)

- Publishing comment or criticism that might influence a jury while the trial is still in progress

- Publishing grossly inaccurate reports of court proceedings

LAWS REGULATING ADVERTISING

The regulation of advertising is an important part of "newspaper law." With increasing attention being turned to consumer protection, federal and state officials are spending considerable time on advertising issues. Honesty in advertising has been a goal of newspaper people for many years. The idea is that the better advertising serves, the more of it can be sold.

Almost all states have laws protecting the public from fraudulent and misleading advertising. These laws relate to false statements about price, quality, and value as well as the old "bait and switch" tactic.

A newspaper has the right to accept or reject any advertising it desires so long as it does not help create a monopoly. Many court cases have established the fact that a newspaper is a private business and can choose with whom it will do business. The only danger in refusing advertising is for the newspaper to give a reason which could indicate an antitrust violation or collusion in restraint of trade.

As previously noted, postal laws require all advertising to be marked or clearly identified as advertising.

There are federal and state laws regulating political advertising. These laws usually require such ads to indicate who has ordered and paid for them. Other laws place certain restrictions on liquor and tobacco advertising or require statements in relation to discrimination in advertising for housing, employment, lending, etc.

In most advertising, restrictions and penalties apply to the advertiser, not the newspaper. The newspaper does, however, have the moral duty to notify prospective advertisers when they know of a violation. It would be impossible for the newspaper's advertising department to have full knowledge of all laws relating to advertising in all businesses and professions.

COPYRIGHT LAW

W. Terry Maguire, ANPA vice president for legal and government affairs, recommends that newspapers of all sizes should seriously consider carrying a notice of copyright on each issue. This notice tells potential plagiarists that the publisher of the newspaper recognizes that he or she has produced

---

* Mr. Cardwell defines a suppression hearing as "one in which the defense attorney attempts to secure a court ruling that evidence possessed by the prosecution should not be admitted at the trial . . . The basis for 'supression' of such evidence usually is improper conduct by the authorities in securing it."

a literary work and intends to protect his or her right to the exclusive use of that material.

The form of the notice is open to some variation but the safest method is to use the word "Copyright" followed by the year of publication and then the name of the owner of the copyright. That name should be the corporate name of the publisher, but if there is no separate corporate name, the name of the newspaper or the publisher will suffice. The notice should appear on the first page, preferably just below the nameplate.

In order to comply with the copyright statute, a publisher should send two copies of each issue of the newspaper to the Library of Congress, Washington, D.C. 20559 within three months of publication. These copies may be sent via second-class mail and no note need accompany them.

If a publisher feels that he or she wants to protect the newspaper more fully, then an additional step is probably necessary—registration. This requires the filing of a form with the Copyright Office and the payment of a fee for each issue. In the event that a publisher feels that litigation might occur in the future, Maguire suggests it is best to consult with a lawyer who knows copyright law before deciding to proceed with registration.

On the other side of the copyright issue is the reporter or advertising manager who wants to use something that had been copyrighted. The reporter is probably safe if quotes from copyrighted material are kept to a bare minimum and are credited. The mention that a work is copyrighted offers no additional protection. For the advertising director, life is a bit more complicated, and any advertising which appears in a publication carrying a copyright notice or an ad which itself is copyrighted should not be reused in anyway except on advice of counsel.

An excellent publication, *Law and Regulations Affecting Newspapers as Employers,* published by the National Newspaper Association can answer most questions involving newspapers.

Chapter 24

Libel and Invasion of Privacy

by David L. Hill

The mere possibility of lawsuits involving libel places a great burden on newspapers today. In an earlier era, a plaintiff might have felt bold to seek a judgment of $5,000. Now the amount may be closer to $500,000 or even $5 million.

Larger dailies must maintain legal counsel to screen hazardous news material. They must ask often, how much of a risk should we take in our efforts to keep the public informed? Although we know the information is true, how much is *provable* truth? Even winning libel suits involves great expense for the newspaper and takes up valuable time of editorial staff members.

The fact that states interpret and apply U. S. Supreme Court rulings differently also adds to the libel hazard. In Oklahoma, which is regarded as one of the high-risk states, managing editor Jim Standard of the *Daily Oklahoman* reported that his newspaper faced libel suits totaling $122 million at one time, even though the paper has never had to pay a libel judgment.

The matter of expensive litigation over libel and privacy actions may seem remote to the community newspaper, which usually does not have either the resources of the metropolitan daily or the inclination to engage in investigative reporting or exposés of misconduct that often give rise to libel actions. Yet in other ways the smaller newspaper may be even more vulnerable to actions based on libel and privacy invasion. Just one such action can cripple such a newspaper.

Much tort litigation stems from careless and inaccurate reporting of news. Some staff members are fresh from journalism schools, and some even have no formal journalism training. They may never have heard of limitations the law places on the publication of information, especially about private individuals.

Smaller newspapers lack the legal resources of larger newspapers. This is true in the evaluation of the libel hazard before publication and in defending against actions for defamation if they arise after publication. Even judges in isolated communities may have little understanding of a newspaper's rights or of what is meant by such terms as "public figures" or "privilege."

All of these factors make it important for news personnel—and especially management—to understand not only the definitions related to libel and privacy, but also the key court decisions that have shaped and modified these definitions.

This chapter reviews briefly the development of the law of defamation that includes libel and slander and the related tort, invasion of privacy. It examines several areas of potential liability and suggests several ways of avoid-

DAVID L. HILL

The author is a partner in a Washington, D.C., law firm specializing in communications law. He has conducted seminars for newspapers in the Capitol area.

". . . The most effective way for a newspaper to avoid liability is still a firm commitment to accurate and fair reporting."

ing, or at least minimizing, your exposure to lawsuits.

Newspapers face three basic areas of potential tort liability in the everyday conduct of their business:

- Liability for false statements

- Liability for invasion of privacy, even though the material is true

- Liability for defamatory comment, criticism, or opinion

What Is Defamation?

Defamation may best be defined as "the unconsented and unprivileged communication (printed or broadcast) to a third party of a false statement which injures or tends to injure one's reputation by lowering the community's estimation of that person by causing that person to be shunned or avoided, or by exposing him to hatred, contempt, or ridicule." The necessary elements of a *prima facie* case of defamation are

- Communication to a third party (publication)

- of a false statement

- which injures or tends to injure reputation.

The law of defamation includes the torts of libel and slander. Generally, most oral publications are actionable as slander. Publication by more permanent means, such as writing or film, is actionable as libel. Originally, the distinction between libel and slander was based upon which court might try the action, rather than whether the statement was written or oral. The primary effect today is in the proof of damages. As newspaper publishers and writers, your actions, at least official actions, will be in permanent form, and your concerns will be with the law of libel.

Libel

Libel may be defined as any defamation published in writing, or in some cases by other forms of publication (such as broadcasting), where the potential for harm is significant. A statement actionable as libel which is defamatory on its face is classified as libel *per se*. Historically, words classified as libel *per se* have been so injurious to another's reputation that damages were pre-

sumed by the courts. It has been declared libel *per se* to refer falsely to an individual as a quack, fraud, communist, queer, crook, or fascist. A newspaper story that erroneously identifies a person as being arrested on a criminal charge is an example of libel *per se.*

If the statement complained of is libelous only by reference to extrinsic facts, it is classified as libel *per quod*. In such instances, a news story may seem innocent on its face, but there may be extrinsic facts or meanings that make it defamatory. Such actions often arise from careless reporting—wrong addresses, wrong names, even wrong middle initials or other such errors. Some states require that in libel *per quod* actions that the plaintiff must plead and prove actual pecuniary loss to maintain his case.

WHO IS LIABLE?

Common law imposed strict liability on everyone involved in the publication of a libelous statement—including publishers, owners, editors, and reporters—even if publication was innocent. Even typesetters, printers, and newsboys who knowingly distribute a libelous article could be held liable under common law. As a practical matter today, however, few lawsuits are brought against individual employees whose connection with the libel is incidental.

Strict liability attaches not only to editorials and articles written by the newspaper's own staff, but also to defamatory matter in articles, photographs, and advertisements acquired from others such as a news service, letters to the editor, or even in copy furnished by an advertiser. The newspaper that republishes the material can be held liable for any libelous statements contained therein.

DEFENSES TO LIBEL ACTION

Four possible affirmative defenses will completely defeat an action for defa-

mation. These defenses are (1) truth, (2) consent, (3) privilege, and (4) fair comment.

TRUTH. Under common law, provable truth is a complete defense to a civil defamation action, and it still is the rule in many states. Other states require that the newspaper prove "truth with good motives" or "truth for justifiable ends."

One raising the defense of truth used to be required to prove the literal truth of each and every detail of the statement in question. The trend now is to lessen this burden, and in some jurisdictions the defendant may be required only to show that the essential facts are substantially true.

CONSENT. If a person consents to the publication of what may be a defamatory statement, that consent is a complete defense to any subsequent libel action. The question of whether there is consent is a factual one, and without a written document, consent may be difficult to prove at trial. Yet written consent, for all practical purposes, is unavailable in the day-to-day business of news gathering. Thus, the publisher, without specific written consent, should assume that he does not have any consent and proceed accordingly.

PRIVILEGE. Privilege may be more easily understood if it is considered as an immunity rather than a right. Privilege permits a newspaper to cover *fairly* and *accurately* governmental and, in some instances, other public records and proceedings without risk of liability for the reproduction of any libelous statements made in the records or at the covered proceedings. However, those who participate in judicial proceedings or members of legislative bodies, for example, are protected by absolute privilege in statements made in the course of these official functions. The law thus provides a conditional privilege to newspapers to report on these matters of public importance.

Conditional privilege is premised upon the interest of society that communications in certain vital areas should not be hampered by fear of lawsuits. These privileges, which are of particular interest to the newspaper, relate to the privilege to report, which includes reports of official documents and proceedings, including those of the judicial branch, and the privilege of fair comment, which permits comments on matters of public interest. The reporter should remember that this limited opportunity to publish defamatory material is contingent upon the fairness and accuracy of the reporter's account.

FAIR COMMENT. The right of fair comment has long been an important defense against libel actions. Newspapers have been privileged to comment upon or criticize matters of public interest, such as current newsworthy events, public figures, public officials, candidates, and matters affecting the public welfare. This right of comment also extends to matters such as artistic and literary endeavors, entertainment, and even sports activities.

The reporter should remember that in general, any *factual* assertions about matters commented on must be true in order to avoid liability. The fair comment defense applies only to the defamatory *implications* in statements of opinion about these matters of public interest. The reporter is thus granted broad leeway in expressing opinions on matters of public interest, provided those opinions are "fair"— that is, without malice—and that the statements on which the opinions are based are true.

CONSTITUTIONAL PRIVILEGE

Since 1964, the U.S. Supreme Court has rendered a series of opinions which have restructured in a most dramatic fashion the law of libel in the United States. If a student or a newspaper employee is to have an understanding of libel and its defenses, it is important to understand the issues in these cases.

NEW YORK TIMES v. SULLIVAN. In the 1964 landmark decision of *New York Times* v. *Sullivan,* the common law privilege of fair comment was radically changed. The court was required to consider to what extent the constitu-

tional protection of free speech and free press limits a state's power to award damages in a libel suit instituted by a "public official" for criticism of his official conduct.

On March 29, 1960, the *New York Times* had printed an "editorial" advertisement, entitled "Heed Their Rising Voices," which sought financial support for the Negro right-to-vote movement. The advertisement had been paid for by the Committee to Defend Martin Luther King and the Struggle for Freedom in the South.

Specific reference was made to the fact that students in Montgomery, Alabama, having sung "My Country 'Tis of Thee" on the state capitol steps, were expelled from school. It was further reported that "...truckloads of police armed with shotguns and tear gas ringed the Alabama State College campus and that when the entire student body protested to state authorities by refusing to re-register, their dining hall was padlocked in an attempt to starve them into submission." Furthermore, it was stated that "Southern violators" in response to Dr. King's peaceful protest, had "repeatedly answered...with intimidation and violence" and that they had "bombed his home, almost killing his wife and child...and assaulted his person." The advertisement also referred to Dr. King's having been arrested seven times.

In response to this advertisement, the plaintiff, Sullivan, who had been elected public affairs commissioner of Montgomery, Alabama, claimed that even though his name was not mentioned in the advertisement, the events reported inaccurately therein had libeled him in that his official duties included supervision of Montgomery's police department. He claimed that, by reporting in such fashion upon the activities of the city's police force, the *New York Times* was attributing such conduct to his discretion as the official so responsible. He asserted that in light of the fact that police officers are understood by most in society as those obligated to conduct arrests, the article would be understood by readers as equating "Southern violators" with the Montgomery police department.

Unquestionably, the article contained factually erroneous commentary. Only nine students had been ex-

pelled, and the reason for such expulsion had been their demand for service at a lunch counter on a day other than that on which the demonstration on the state capitol steps had taken place. Only a portion of the student body had protested against the expulsion. The protest had taken the form of a boycott of classes on a single day, rather than a refusal to register. The dining hall had not been padlocked, and the only students barred from admission were those who had failed to sign a preregistration application and request temporary meal tickets. While police had been deployed, they did not "ring the campus." Finally, Dr. King had been arrested four rather than seven times.

In response to the claims made and the inaccuracies noted, the Court enunciated a new standard of proof which public officials would henceforth be compelled to bear if they were to succeed in an action brought for defamation. The Court held that the Constitutional protections of free speech and free press require a rule which prohibits a public official from recovering damages for a defamatory falsehood relating to his official conduct unless he proves that the statement in question was made with *actual malice*. The Court defined actual malice as either knowledge that the statement was false or reckless disregard of whether it was false.

The Court, therefore, recognized that erroneous statements are inevitable in the conduct of free debate, and that such debate must be protected if free speech is to be preserved. There is a national commitment to the principle that debate on public issues should be uninhibited and robust and that it may often encompass caustic and unpleasant attacks upon public officials. Any rule compelling a critic of official conduct first to guarantee that the factual assertions which he makes be true or else face the certainty of an adverse libel judgment for a virtually unlimited amount in damages, would result in the imposition of self-censorship. The First Amendment was designed to avoid such a "chilling effect" upon speech.

CURTIS PUBLISHING CO. v. BUTTS. In 1967, the Supreme Court, in *Curtis Publishing Co.* v.

Butts, extended the *New York Times* v. *Sullivan* standard of proof of actual malice to plaintiffs who had willingly become involved in matters of justifiable and important public interest. (In *Curtis Publishing Co.,* the Court was reviewing the consolidated cases of *Associated Press* v. *Walker* and *Curtis Publishing Co.* v. *Butts.*)

With respect to the *Butts* case, the *Saturday Evening Post* had published an article entitled "The Story of a College Football Fix," which accused Wallace Butts, athletic director of the University of Georgia, of conspiring to fix a football game between that university and the University of Alabama. The article charged that Butts had disclosed, during a telephone conversation with Paul Bryant, coach of the Alabama team, both offensive plays and defensive deployments which would be used by the Georgia squad. The article stated that "[t]he Georgia players, their moves analyzed and forecast like those of rats in a maze, took a frightful physical beating," and further declared that the players and other persons who observed the contest, were aware that "the Alabama team was privy to Georgia's secrets."

Associated Press v. *Walker* concerned a news dispatch reporting a massive riot which had erupted over federal efforts to enforce a Court decree ordering the enrollment of a Negro, James Meredith, as a student at the University of Mississippi. The article claimed that the respondent, General Edwin Walker, an individual acutely interested in federal intervention, was regarded as a man of significant political prominence in that region of the country and had amassed a following calling themselves "Friends of Walker."

The article stated that Walker had taken command of the violent crowd on the campus of the University of Mississippi and had personally led a charge against federal marshals sent there to preserve order. The dispatch described Walker as encouraging rioters to use violence and as offering technical advice on combating the effects of tear gas.

Having considered the facts presented in both cases, the Supreme Court announced the standard which would henceforth be followed in such instances.

...[A] public figure who is not a public official may also recover damages for a defamatory falsehood whose substance makes substantial danger to reputation apparent, on a showing of highly unreasonable conduct constituting an extreme departure from the standards of investigation and reporting ordinarily adhered to by responsible publishers.

Employing the standard, the Court said that "an extreme departure from the standards of investigation and reporting ordinarily adhered to by responsible publishers" had taken place in the *Butts* case. The story was in no sense "hot news." Elementary professional precautions had been ignored despite the fact that the publishers had recognized the need for a thorough investigation of the serious charges. Despite the questionable reputation of the informant in that case, the story was published without substantial support independent of the affidavit of that informant. The informant's notes had never been reviewed by any of the magazine's personnel prior to publication of the subject article.

In addition, no attempt had been made to screen the films of the football contest to see if the informant's information had been accurate, nor had any attempt been made to determine whether the University of Alabama football team adjusted its plans following the alleged divulgence of information. Furthermore, the writer assigned to the story was not considered to be a football expert, nor was an attempt made to check his story with someone knowledgeable in the sport. Experts who testified at the trial had stated that the information alleged to have been exchanged was totally valueless. In light of these factors, the recovery which Butts had been awarded in the lower court was upheld.

In the *Walker* case, however, the evidence produced was insufficient to support more than a finding of ordinary negligence. The AP report in question was most definitely "hot news" and required immediate dissemination to the reading public. The author of the dispatch had been present during the riot. The only discrepancy noted concerned the difference between the oral account given by the reporter to his office and the later written dispatch. That discrepancy related solely

to whether or not Walker had spoken to his followers before or after approaching the federal marshals.

In the light of all of the facts, Walker and Butts became the first individuals to be ruled "public figures" for purposes of libel law. As such, both were required to prove actual malice. Since Walker had not done so, he was denied recovery.

GERTZ v. WELCH. *Gertz* v. *Welch,* in 1974, represented the Supreme Court's third pronouncement of whether private figures claiming they had been defamed for their activities in matters of general public concern would have to prove actual malice. *Gertz* involved the case of a Chicago policeman named Nuccio, who had shot and killed a youth named Nelson. Nuccio was subsequently convicted for second-degree murder. The family of the deceased thereupon instituted a civil action against that officer, Nuccio, and retained Elmer Gertz as their attorney in that civil litigation. Gertz had in no way been involved with the criminal suit brought against Nuccio.

With respect to that criminal trial, the John Birch Society, publisher of the monthly periodical *American Opinion,* had for years maintained that a nationwide conspiracy had been organized to discredit local enforcement agencies and create in their place a national police force capable of supporting a communistic dictatorship. The managing editor of *American Opinion* believed that the Nuccio trial was evidence of that conspiracy and commissioned an article to be written on that case entitled "Frame-Up: Richard Nuccio and the War on Police."

Despite the fact that Gertz had played no part in the criminal proceeding against Nuccio, the subject magazine article portrayed him as an architect of the "frame-up." The article claimed that the police file on Gertz took a "big, Irish cop to lift." The article further maintained that the petitioner had been an official of the "Marxist League for Industrial Democracy, originally known as the Intercollegiate Socialist Society, which has advocated the violent seizure of our government." It declared that Gertz was a "Leninist" and a "communist fronter." It stated that Gertz had been an officer of the National Lawyers

Guild and claimed that this communist organization "probably did more than any other outfit to plan the communist attack on the Chicago police during the 1968 Democratic Convention."

The article was inaccurate. Gertz had been a member and officer of the National Lawyers Guild, but that was fifteen years earlier. There was no evidence that he or that organization had taken any part in planning the 1968 demonstrations in Chicago. Neither was Gertz a "Leninist" nor a "communist fronter." He had never been a member of the "Marxist League for Industrial Democracy" or the "Intercollegiate Socialist Society." Furthermore, the managing editor of *American Opinion* had made no effort to verify or substantiate the charges against Gertz. He had included a photograph of Gertz under which appeared the caption "Elmer Gertz of the Red Guild Harrasses Nuccio."

The Court of Appeals had applied the *New York Times* v. *Sullivan* malice standard to the case and had held that Gertz had failed to prove knowledge of falsity or reckless disregard for the falsity of the matter. The Supreme Court reversed this decision in Gertz's favor and said:

A publisher or broadcaster of defamatory falsehoods about an individual who is neither a public official nor a public figure may not claim the New York Times *protection against liability for defamation on the ground that the defamatory statement concerned an issue of public or general interest.*

It held that Gertz was a private individual and as such need not prove actual malice on the part of the publisher. The fact that he became an attorney in a widely publicized case did not automatically make him a public figure.

The Court maintained that private individuals characteristically have less effective opportunities to rebut charges made against them than do public officials and public figures. Private individuals are therefore more vulnerable to injurious effects from defamation. The burden of proof imposed upon private individuals should be less severe than that expected of public officials and public figures, since private individuals do not voluntarily expose themselves to increased risk of injury

from defamatory falsehoods. Accordingly, the Court, in balancing the public's interest to obtain news against a private individual's interest in preserving his or her reputation, held that the individual's interest in preserving a reputation must prevail.

Furthermore, the Court maintained that private individuals may not recover damages for libel unless they can show fault on the part of the newspaper. But states were given the right to decide for themselves which standards of fault would be appropriate. Some states have since opted for a simple "negligence" standard, while others have adopted stricter standards. In addition, the court ruled that the states may not permit recovery of presumed or punitive damages unless the plaintiff proves knowledge of falsity or reckless disregard to the falsity of the statement made. This has given newspapers greater protection in libel *per se* actions.

TIME, INC. v. FIRESTONE. There have been numerous libel cases before the Supreme Court since *Gertz.* Perhaps the most notable is the 1976 case, *Time Inc.* v. *Firestone.* In a libel action growing out of a widely publicized divorce case, the Court held that Mrs. Firestone, a socially prominent member of society, could sue a national news magazine as a private individual rather than as a public figure. In upholding *Gertz,* the Court said that Mrs. Firestone was not a national public figure. She did not thrust herself to the forefront of any particular public controversy. Rather, she was compelled to go to court by the state in order to obtain legal release from the bonds of matrimony.

Thus, it appears that the *New York Times* v. *Sullivan* malice standard will continue to apply only to public officials and to willing public figures. Private individuals who are forced to become involved in matters of general or public concern may be held to a lesser standard of proof, namely a publisher's negligence in printing a defamatory story. In *Wolston* v. *Reader's Digest Association, Inc.,* decided in 1979, the Court continued this trend, which has narrowed the public-figure libel standards, making it easier for "public" figures to bring actions as "private" individuals.

Invasion of Privacy

Closely related to the tort of defamation is the rapidly emerging body of law which has come to be referred to as invasion of privacy. Invasion of privacy may be defined as an unconsented, unprivileged, and unreasonable intrusion into an individual's life. It covers the right to protection against interference with one's solitude as well as the right to protection of an individual's personality. As the law has evolved in this area, the concept of invasion of privacy includes not one but four distinct torts:

- Public disclosure of private facts about an individual

- Appropriation of one's name or likeness for commercial purposes

- Publication of facts about a person which places that individual in a false light in the public's eye

- Intrusion into an individual's private affairs or seclusion

PUBLIC DISCLOSURE OF PRIVATE FACTS ABOUT AN INDIVIDUAL. Newspapers have been found liable in numerous instances for public disclosure of private facts of an objectionable nature about an individual. For the plaintiff's action to prevail, the disclosure in question must be viewed as offensive to the sensibilities of the reasonable person. The facts disclosed must also be those not already a matter of public record. Accordingly, while a reporter is privileged to report correctly the names in the transcript of a criminal court proceeding, he ordinarily would not be privileged to publish names of juvenile offenders which he had obtained from the records of a juvenile court, since such documents are not normally available for public inspection in most jurisdictions.

The final element required is that the disclosure be made to the public at large and not merely to a third party or to a limited number of persons. Public disclosure in the invasion of privacy sense is distinguishable from publication in the defamation sense. In the latter, a statement written by A to B

The Most Common Libel Hazards for Editors and Reporters . . . and How to Avoid Them

by Larry Worrall
President, Media/Professional Insurance, Inc.

A study of several thousand libel cases involving community newspapers shows the following factors to be the most frequent causes of such litigation. They are arranged from one to ten in descending order of frequency of each particular factor.

While the list applies basically to smaller newspapers, the same factors seem to be true for the publishing industry in general.

1. Most lawsuits against newspapers can be traced to negligence and carelessness in reports of arrest, ongoing investigations, and judicial and legislative proceedings. These matters must be summarized and interpreted accurately. Inexperience with legal terminology is no excuse; if you do not understand complicated legal proceedings, consult a lawyer or the prosecutor for clarification.

2. Never sacrifice accuracy for a "hot news" item. The newspaper will lose credibility and may be faced with a libel or invasion of privacy suit. Any story of an embarrassing or intimate nature should be tested. Ask yourself, if I'm wrong, or the single source is wrong, is it worth a lawsuit? Is the story a matter of real interest to a substantial or meaningful number of readers?

   Watch those photographs, too. A photograph, innocent in itself, can become the basis for a libel or false-light privacy claim if it seems to illustrate something that does not in fact accurately describe the subject of the photographer; for example, a photograph of a teenager drinking beer in a public park accompanying a story on "pot-smoking" and "beer-drinking" in the park.

3. Handle stories based upon "nondisclosable" sources with extreme care. You must consider the following:

   - Does the source have a valid reason for requiring a promise of confidentiality?

   - What is in it for the source? Does the source have a motive to libel the person named?

   - Is the source in a position to have obtained the information by virtue of his job, title, or position or through his or her relationship to the person named?

   - If the source cannot be identified and his or her information cannot be corroborated, should you proceed? Is the story important enough or newsworthy enough to warrant an expensive lawsuit with the possibility

that defenses may be stricken and the person you are attempting to expose not only vindicated but rewarded with a large verdict?

4. Be especially prudent when putting together investigative stories concerning law enforcement personnel or anyone in the teaching profession. Persons from these two professions account for more than 25 percent of libel and invasion of privacy suits. Take care also when persons from either of these two groups are the primary sources of the story alleging malfeasance or misfeasance of another member of the group or profession. It is essential to obtain signed or recorded statements from such a source or sources so that in the event of litigation they will neither deny authorship nor deny that they were quoted accurately.

5. Extreme care should be taken in reporting comments or statements made by policemen, detectives, and the lower echelon of law enforcement officers in general unless those statements have also been incorporated in a public record. Do not publish "off-the-record remarks" concerning the guilt, innocence, or involvement of a person in a felony investigation. However, remarks made by law enforcement personnel over a citizens' band radio are *not* privileged.

6. Watch letters to the editor! These letters constitute a frequent source of libel suits disproportionate to their importance to the newspaper. The liability of the publisher for publishing a defamatory letter to the editor is the same as if the newspaper had originated the letter in question.

7. Be careful when reporting town meetings or school meetings involving controversial persons or matters—in the confusion, reporters often misquote or misunderstand what was said and by whom, and libel suits frequently arise out of the chaos.

8. Do not mix up *misstatements of fact* with opinion. Make certain of basic facts and state them clearly and accurately before taking a strong editorial position in the form of opinion or criticism of someone based upon those facts. Usually, pure opinion is something that cannot be proved to be either true or false.

9. There may be times when editorial policy is best served by saying, "We are sorry." Any inaccuracy or mistake should be corrected when discovered. If a negligent misstatement is libelous in content to a private individual, a nominal settlement, expeditiously arranged, will not foster new claims or show weakness on part of newspaper. Conversely, a jury award to a private individual does foster new claims and suits because of media publicity given to the judgment.

10. Be selective in "*X* Years Ago" columns. Do not resurrect embarrassing crime stories from years past if the subject of the story is alive and living in community served by newspaper. Society loves a "reformed sinner" and a "reborn Christian." In such a case, let bygones be bygones.

regarding C may be found libelous even in the absence of further parties' being notified of the nature of such statement. By contrast, public disclosure contemplates that the revealing of private facts about the plaintiff which would offend the sensibilities of a reasonable person will be made to numerous individuals.

It is important to note that liability for public disclosure of private facts can be found even if the facts as reported are true. Hence, while truth constitutes a solid defense to a claim of defamation, a similar defense will not succeed for invasion of privacy.

One of the earliest opinions concerning the public disclosure tort was

rendered by a California court in the 1931 case of *Melvin* v. *Reid*. The case involved a former prostitute who had been acquitted of murder in a trial which had received great notoriety. Following the acquittal, the woman in question sought to lead an exemplary life, married, and moved to a new community whose residents knew nothing of her past indiscretions until her entire story was revealed in a subsequent movie wherein her name appeared. The plaintiff was permitted to recover for the publication of those true but extremely embarrassing personal facts about her past life.

All newspaper reporters should familiarize themselves completely with the nature and implications of the tort of public disclosure, because newspapers may be held liable not only for publication of the written word, but for publication of photographs as well. Specifically, the courts have allowed recovery for the public disclosure of medical photographs of a person's more intimate anatomy. In addition, they may be held liable for the disclosure of one's significant and delinquent debts which he refuses to pay. By the same token, an article revealing the masculine characteristics of a particular woman or the feminine characteristics of an identified male may cause a newspaper to be held liable.

The tort of public disclosure was refined by the U.S. Supreme Court in 1975 in *Cox Broadcasting Corp.* v. *Cohn.* A reporter employed by the defendant, Cox Broadcasting, had, during the course of a television news report, broadcast the name of a deceased rape victim which that reporter had obtained from indictments constituting public records available for inspection. The victim's father instituted an action for damages and relied upon a Georgia statute which declared it a misdemeanor to broadcast a rape victim's name. The father of the deceased claimed that his right of privacy had been invaded by the broadcast of his daughter's name. On appeal, the Supreme Court held that it is not permissible for the state, consistent with the First and Fourteenth Amendments, to

. . . *impose sanctions on the accurate publication of the name of a rape victim obtained from public records—more specifically, from judicial records which are maintained in connection with a public prosecution and which themselves are open to public inspection.*

Since the reporter in question based his television presentation upon notes taken during the course of open court proceedings and obtained the victim's name from official court documents open to public inspection, the protection of freedom of the press provided by the First and Fourteenth Amendments would bar the state of Georgia from enforcing a statute making the broadcast of a rape victim's name the basis of an action for invasion of privacy that penalizes pure expression. The Georgia statute was therefore ruled unconstitutional.

Reporters should be aware, however, that the decision in *Cox* was limited merely to the very narrow issue of whether a state could legitimately impose sanctions on the accurate publication of the name of a rape victim obtained from open public records. The decision should not be read as holding that a publisher cannot under any circumstances be held liable for invasion of privacy for accurate reporting of factual information. As previously stated, regardless of the truth and validity of the facts reported, if such data have been obtained from records not legally available for public scrutiny, an action for invasion of privacy predicated on public disclosure may be sustained, if such invasion is found to be offensive to the reasonable person.

For an action to be sustained on the grounds of public disclosure of private facts about the plaintiff's life, it will be necessary for that party to prove by a preponderance of the evidence that the facts reported, though true, offend the sensibilities of the reasonable person and that the matters in the subject article lack newsworthiness and are not of legitimate concern to the public.

APPROPRIATION OF ONE'S NAME OR LIKENESS FOR COMMERCIAL PURPOSES.
A second form of invasion of privacy is the use by a defendant, for his own benefit or advantage, of the plaintiff's name or likeness. This tort is called appropriation.

In appropriation, it is the plaintiff's name as a symbol of his identity rather than as merely a name which is involved. It is only when the defendant seeks to make use of the name "to pirate the plaintiff's identity for some advantage of his own" that he becomes liable. Accordingly, liability will not be found where in the course of a novel a name is merely used which is similar to that of the plaintiff's unless the context or circumstances would indicate that the name was intended to reflect the plaintiff. By the same token, publication of a picture of the plaintiff's automobile, house, hand, or foot, in the absence of further factors which would serve to distinguish to whom they apply, will not result in the imposition of liability for appropriation.

Court decisions serve to recognize or create an exclusive right in the individual plaintiff to a species of trade name, his own, and a kind of trademark in his likeness, and that both the name and the likeness are proprietary in nature.

PUBLICATION OF FACTS THAT PLACE AN INDIVIDUAL IN A FALSE LIGHT.
The act of placing one in a false light in the public's eye may attribute to that individual views he or she does not hold or claim that such person has committed actions which he or she did not in fact perform. The plaintiff's burden of proof in sustaining an action of this nature is threefold. First, he must prove that there has been a publication of the false facts to a third party. Second, the facts so published must prove offensive to the sensibilities of a reasonable person. Third, the plaintiff must prove the defendant's actual malice, defined in *New York Times* v. *Sullivan* as knowledge of falsity or reckless disregard of whether or not the facts reported are false.

A newspaper could be found liable, for example, for publishing, in connection with an article on negligence in the care of small children, the picture of a mother who in fact has been most attentive and responsive to her children's needs. While the picture, when considered in light of the article, would not necessarily be defamatory, an action could be brought for invasion of privacy based upon facts tending to place the plaintiff in a false light.

INTRUSION INTO AN INDIVIDUAL'S AFFAIRS OR SECLUSION.
The tort of intrusion requires proof of prying or intruding into a plaintiff's solitude or seclusion which would be objectionable to the reasonable person. The subject matter of the intrusion must be deemed a private thing; that is, one within the plaintiff's private domain. Accordingly, an

action for intrusion based upon the defendant's prying into the plaintiff's bank account will in all likelihood be sustained, as would a claim that the plaintiff's bedroom and the privacy he expects therein has been invaded by the defendant's microphones. A plaintiff will not be permitted to prevail, however, on a complaint that his pretrial testimony was recorded by the defendant, or that the police, acting within their statutory powers, have taken the plaintiff's photograph, fingerprints, or measurements. Similarly, a complaint will not be sustained where there is inspection and public disclosure of corporate records which the plaintiff was required by law to keep and make available.

While it may, in fact, be an intrusion upon the plaintiff's privacy to photograph him while he is standing within the walls of his home, it is not an invasion of his privacy to take his photograph while he is standing in a public place "since this amounts to nothing more than making a record of a public site which anyone would be free to see."

PUBLIC FIGURES AND THE INVASION OF PRIVACY

The preceding point was basically concerned with the private figure who, because of momentous events occurring around him, is suddenly thrust into the public spotlight. Such an individual should be distinguished from the public figure who, by virtue of his accomplishments, fame, manner of living, or profession, has given the public a legitimate interest in his affairs and character and has become a "public personage," that is, a celebrity. These public figures are viewed as having lost, at least to some extent, their right of privacy. Traditionally, three reasons have been given to support this position:

- The public figure has sought publicity and has consented to it and therefore cannot later complain when he or she receives it

- When a person's personality and affairs have become public, they

can no longer be regarded as that person's own private business

- The press has a privilege, guaranteed by the Constitution, to inform the public about those individuals who have become legitimate matters of public interest

Accordingly, the courts have found that there is no liability when a public figure is given additional publicity as to matters legitimately within the scope of the public interest they have aroused. Nevertheless, such public stature must already exist before the privilege will apply. By contrast, a newspaper, by directing attention to an individual previously obscure and unknown, cannot by its action create a public figure with respect to whom it would be privileged to report certain private facts.

DEFENSES TO AN ACTION FOR INVASION OF PRIVACY

As previously stated, while truth will serve as an absolute defense to an action for libel or slander, it is by no means a defense to a claim of invasion of privacy—except in false-light cases. By contrast, consent constitutes a defense to invasion of privacy just as it does to claims of defamation. Keep in mind, however, the evidentiary problems relating to proof of consent mentioned in the discussion on libel.

The absolute and conditional privileges mentioned in the area of libel would seem to apply to the invasion of privacy cases based upon publication of facts placing the plaintiff in a false light and public disclosure of private facts about a plaintiff. For example, if provable facts were disclosed in a legislative proceeding, and a newspaper published a fair and accurate report of the events at the proceeding, qualified privilege to report should provide immunity.

Mistake, even if reasonable, inadvertence, good faith, or lack of malice will not generally constitute good defenses to complaints of invasion of privacy.

How to Avoid Liability

Notwithstanding the ebbs and flows of the Constitutional protections extended by the First Amendment, the most effective way for a newspaper to avoid liability is still a firm commitment to accurate and fair reporting. This commitment must be shared by the publisher as well as every reporter on the staff. This commitment should not be left to chance. Methods and procedures should be designed to encourage accuracy and fairness. These procedures should be followed with great care.

Each newspaper, of course, has to develop its procedures based upon its own particular circumstances. Nonetheless, the following suggestions are representative of the types of procedures and precautions that should be taken.

CAREFUL USE OF PHOTOGRAPHS

Guidelines for the use of photographs should be developed to ensure accuracy. The photographer should identify the person and place photographed, and this information should appear on the back of photograph itself.

Photographs of the victims of accidents and other disasters and catastrophes should be used carefully. The degree of protection that will generally be afforded the newspaper will relate directly to the degree of newsworthiness of the event.

SPECIAL STORIES AND INVESTIGATIVE REPORTING

Special procedures should be devised for handling particularly sensitive stories and all investigative reporting. At a minimum, the procedures should require that no changes be made in the copy without the approval of the editor responsible. This rule should be strictly enforced. It is also recommended that articles under this classification be reviewed by legal counsel before publication.

Development and use of such procedures should permit the production of news in a manner least likely to result in lawsuits, while still permiting the publisher, editor, and reporters the flexibility and freedom they need to meet the newspaper's obligation to keep its readers informed.

LIBEL INSURANCE

Notwithstanding Constitutional developments and efforts to ensure accuracy, the newspaper must consider libel insurance. The trends and court decisions relating to libel and privacy have caused a growth in the libel insurance business. Protection given to private individuals, as a result of *Gertz* and other decisions, makes newspapers more vulnerable to libel actions. They now risk judgments that could easily pass the million dollar mark. Rare is the small newspaper with the resources to pay such a judgment, as well as the costs of defense. Libel insurance is expensive, but it should be considered as a necessary cost of doing business. However, the libel insurance policy, while another tool available to help the newspaper meet its obligations to its readers, certainly should not serve as a substitute for accurate reporting.

Conclusion

Sensitivity to the principles and problems inherent in the laws of libel and privacy, along with a firm commitment to proper journalistic practices, will help the newspaper strike a reasonable accommodation between the law and the freedoms of speech and press protected by the First Amendment.

Chapter 25

ROBERT L. BALLOW

The author is a founding partner in the law firm of King & Ballow and a consultant and lecturer on antitrust laws affecting the newspaper industry. The law firm and its partners are general counsel to the International Circulation Managers' Association and several regional trade associations, and special counsel for labor and antitrust to the National Newspaper Association.

"As newspaper antitrust suits become increasingly common, existing business practices and future plans should be examined carefully with the antitrust laws in mind."

which have broad public exposure, and newspapers have become one of the most popular targets. There are no indications that this trend will change in the foreseeable future. It is thus imperative that newspapers examine their existing business practices and future business plans in light of the federal antitrust laws.

A newspaper publisher will be wise to have a sound notion of how these federal laws operate, when they apply, and which elements must combine before a violation of each law can be found to exist.

In addition to the federal antitrust laws discussed below, many states have their own antitrust statutes. Although a thorough treatment of all state antitrust laws is beyond the scope of this chapter, state laws should not be overlooked as a possible source of antitrust liability.

Antitrust Law and the Newspaper Industry

by Robert L. Ballow

Ten years prior to the turn of the century, it became apparent to Congress that some form of protective legislation was needed to ensure the healthy existence and growth of the free market system. This concern was made manifest in the Sherman Antitrust Act, a measure which served not only to protect this nation's competitive economy, but also to penalize severely those who would disregard this goal.

In 1914, Congress enacted two additional antitrust statutes, the Clayton Antitrust Act and the Federal Trade Commission Act, and the strength and scope of federal antitrust regulation grew to combat the effects of anticompetitive business practices which were never addressed by the Sherman Act.

The last of the major federal antitrust laws, the Robinson-Patman Act, followed in 1936, amending one of the Clayton Act provisions and prohibiting price discrimination in interstate commerce. Each of these statutes represents a potential source of federal antitrust liability.

In recent years, costly antitrust suits based upon one or more of these statutes have been brought with increasing frequency against businesses

Federal Antitrust Laws

THE SHERMAN ANTITRUST ACT

The Sherman Antitrust Act represents the federal government's first attempt to regulate business conduct via antitrust legislation. Enacted by Congress in 1890, the Sherman Act was intended to serve as a means by which the federal government could encourage and protect free and open competition in the business community, and thereby ensure the continuing vitality of the American free enterprise system. Although a variety of other, more specialized forms of antitrust legislation have since become law, the Sherman Act remains as the core of American antitrust law.

The Sherman Act is composed of two principal sections. *Section 1* is a broadly worded provision which prohibits restraints on trade. Reduced to its basic elements, the provision prohibits a given business practice only if three requirements are met:

- There must be a contract, combination, or conspiracy

- It must be in restraint of interstate or foreign trade or commerce

- The restraint must be unreasonable

Clearly, some form of concerted activity by two or more persons is required before there can be a Section 1 violation. Independent activity on the part of a single individual can never result in a Section 1 violation, for an individual cannot contract, combine, or conspire with himself.

Courts commonly use the terms *horizontal* and *vertical* to describe two basic types of business conduct in antitrust cases. Where the parties involved are competitors or where they are on the same level in a distribution system, they are said to be in a *horizontal* relationship. Where the parties are in a buyer-seller relationship, their relationship is described as being *vertical*. Courts generally view anticompetitive horizontal agreements with greater disfavor because there is little justification for agreements between actual competitors. Vertical agreements, on the other hand, are justifiable in some circumstances even where they are shown to have some anticompetitive effects.

Even if a given business practice meets the "contract, combination, or conspiracy" requirement, there can be no violation of Section 1 unless that business practice results in a restraint of interstate or foreign trade or commerce. While foreign trade is usually relatively easy to recognize, the task of determining which business activities are in interstate commerce has proved to be a more difficult matter. Over the years, the term interstate commerce has been held to include all of the following:

- The actual movement of goods across state boundaries

- Any activity which happens "in the flow of commerce," even if it occurs wholly within one state

- Any activity which affects interstate commerce, regardless of where it occurs

MOST NEWSPAPERS INCLUDED.

Given this broad definition, the operation of a newspaper which utilizes a national wire service, publishes national advertising, purchases newsprint and ink from out-of-state sources, or transports its product across state lines will probably fall within the meaning of the term "interstate commerce" for Sherman Act purposes. In *Lorain Journal Co.* v. *United States,* for example, the Supreme Court held that an Ohio daily newspaper which sent only 165 of its over 20,000 daily circulation out of Ohio, but which published quantities of state, national, and international news and national advertising, was engaged in interstate commerce. The Court stated:

There can be little doubt today that the immediate dissemination of news gathered from throughout the nation or the world by agencies especially organized for that purpose is a part of interstate commerce. The same is true of national advertising originating throughout the nation and offering products for sale on a national scale. The local dissemination of such news and advertising requires continuous interstate transmission of materials and payments, to say nothing of the interstate commerce involved in the sale and delivery of products sold. . . .

Section 1 of the Sherman Act prohibits only those concerted business practices which have an *unreasonable* restraint on interstate or foreign commerce. Such unreasonable restraints of trade fall within two basic categories. The first category includes those business activities which by their very nature are deemed to restrict trade unreasonably. These are the so-called *per se* violations of Section 1. In general, restraints presumed to be unlawful *per se* are those whose purpose is solely to control the price in, or access to, the marketplace. Thus, horizontal agreements to fix prices, divide territories, and engage in collective refusals

to deal are all *per se* violations of Section 1. Vertical agreements to fix prices, boycott third parties, and make the sale or purchase of one product conditional on the sale or purchase of another product are also *per se* illegal under Section 1.

Restraints of trade which do not fall within the category of *per se* violations will violate Section 1 only if they are found to be unreasonable restraints based upon an examination of their purpose and effect under what has been called the *rule of reason* standard. Under this standard, a person accused of engaging in an anticompetitive business practice is afforded an opportunity to justify his conduct; that is, to show that such conduct is reasonable in light of existing business conditions in the marketplace.

Section 2 of the Sherman Act sets forth three separate offenses which may bring about either civil or criminal penalties or both. These three offenses are

- Monopolization

- Attempts to monopolize

- Combinations or conspiracies to monopolize

In order to commit the offense of monopolization, one must possess "monopoly power" in the marketplace. Monopoly power is generally thought of as the ability to control prices in or to exclude competition from the marketplace. The market in which such power is measured is defined both in terms of a relevant product market and a relevant geographic market. In general, a product's relevant product market will consist of those items with which the product is reasonably interchangeable from the customer's point of view. The relevant geographic market consists of the area or areas in which a particular firm actually competes or operates, and includes all other firms in the same area which sell the same or similar goods or services.

Courts usually define the relevant market of a daily newspaper as including only the daily newspapers within a specified geographic area. Although newspapers clearly compete with radio and TV stations for advertising accounts, courts have been very reluctant to include radio and TV stations in a newspaper's relevant market.

The fact that a firm possesses monopoly power is not in and of itself illegal. Monopoly power can be innocently acquired, for example, if only one firm out of several has survived a competitive struggle by virtue of its superior skill, foresight, and industry. In order to violate Section 2, it must also be shown that the firm in question intended to obtain its monopoly power via unfair or illegal business practices. If a firm has not engaged in such practices, a Section 2 violation will not exist, unless it is further shown that the firm possessed a general intent to obtain or expand its position or dominance in the relevant market.

As mentioned earlier, Section 2 of the Sherman Act also prohibits attempts to monopolize. Generally, if a firm engages in anticompetitive conduct with the intent to acquire monopoly power, and if there exists a dangerous probability that such conduct will result in the acquisition of monopoly power, then that firm will be guilty of an attempt to monopolize. A firm need not actually achieve monopoly power to be found guilty—all that is required is a dangerous probability that a monopoly will be achieved. Furthermore, a firm may fail in its efforts to achieve a monopoly and still be guilty of an attempt to monopolize.

The offense of conspiracy to monopolize is quite similar to the attempt to monopolize offense discussed above. One important difference, however, is that to prove the existence of a conspiracy to monopolize, one must prove a common scheme to achieve or maintain a monopoly in which alleged conspirators knowingly participated.

THE CLAYTON ACT

In an effort to supplement the provisions of the Sherman Act and to prohibit certain anticompetitive business practices which had developed since the passage of that act, Congress, in 1914, enacted the Clayton Act. While the Sherman Act served to prohibit conduct which had an *actual* anticompetitive effect in the marketplace, the Clayton Act went so far as to prohibit conduct which *might lead to* an anti-

competitive effect. The Clayton Act thus brought about a tremendous expansion in the application of the federal antitrust laws to anticompetitive business practices.

The most significant substantive provisions of the Clayton Act are Sections 2 and 3.

Section 2 of the Clayton Act was the first federal price-discrimination legislation. Its primary purpose was to prohibit price discrimination by sellers which injured other sellers. In 1936, Congress enacted the Robinson-Patman Act as an amendment to the Clayton Act. As Kintner has pointed out in his treatise, *A Robinson-Patman Primer,* the primary objectives of the Robinson-Patman Act were

- To prevent unscrupulous sellers from attempting to gain an unfair advantage over their competitors by discriminating among buyers

- To prevent unscrupulous buyers from using their economic power to exact discriminatory prices from sellers to the disadvantage of less powerful buyers

Section 2 of the Robinson-Patman Act completely replaced Section 2 of the Clayton Act and is now the core of federal price-discrimination law.

For business conduct to violate Section 2(a) of the Robinson-Patman Act, several elements must be shown to exist. First, the person, such as a newspaper, charged with price discrimination must be "engaged in commerce." Next, it must be established that: Two or more consummated sales were made (one of which crossed state lines)

- which were reasonably close in time;

- the sales being of commodities

- of like grade and quality

- with a difference in price;

- by the same seller

- to two or more different purchasers

- for use, consumption, or resale within the United States or a foreign nation

- where the result of such sale may involve a competitive injury to one of the purchasers or to a third party.

Each of these requirements must be established before business conduct can be found violative of Section 2(a). It should also be noted that under the provisions of Section 3 of the Robinson-Patman Act, persons guilty of price discrimination may be subject to criminal liability.

Section 3 of the Clayton Act prohibits, among other things, that which is commonly referred to as a "tying arrangement." The term *tying arrangement* was defined by the Supreme Court in *Northern Pacific Railroad Co.* v. *United States* as follows:

For our purposes a tying arrangement may be defined as an agreement by a party to sell one product (tying product) but only on the condition that the buyer also purchase a different (or tied) product.

One form of tying arrangement in the newspaper industry is when a newspaper refuses to sell its newspaper to a distributor unless the distributor also purchases poly bags or rubber bands from the newspaper.

The anticompetitive effect of tying arrangements has led courts to conclude that such arrangements are *per se* illegal in certain circumstances. Under Section 3, there are two basic requirements that must be met before a business practice will constitute a *per se* illegal tying arrangement. The first of these is the separate products requirement. An illegal tying arrangement will exist only where the business practice in question involves both a tying product and a separate tied product, and where one may not be purchased unless the other is also purchased.

In addition to separate products, a *per se* illegal tying arrangement will be found to exist only where it is shown that (1) the tying product possesses sufficient economic power to restrain free competition in the tied product, or (2) the tying arrangement forecloses more than an insubstantial amount of interstate commerce.

In short, Section 3 of the Clayton Act prohibits tying arrangements in which (1) two separate products are involved, and (2) *either* the defendant has sufficient economic power to restrain competition *or* more than an insubstantial amount of commerce is affected.

Exclusive dealing arrangements are also regulated under Section 3 of the Clayton Act. An exclusive dealing arrangement is one whereby a buyer agrees to purchase a product exclusively from one seller. In the newspaper business, for example, an exclusive dealing arrangement might take the form of an agreement between the newspaper and a distributor whereby the distributor agrees that it will not purchase or sell any other publications for a given period of time.

Unlike tying arrangements, exclusive dealing agreements may have procompetitive effects and are usually motivated by other than anticompetitive desires. Consequently, they are not *per se* unlawful.

THE FEDERAL TRADE COMMISSION ACT

In 1914, the Federal Trade Commission Act established a federal administrative agency, the Federal Trade Commission (FTC), designed to enforce some of the federal antitrust laws. The act also expanded federal regulation over certain unfair methods of competition which had developed in the American business community. To this end, Section 5 of the act declared that "unfair methods of competition in commerce" would be illegal and that the FTC could prohibit such business conduct.

From its inception, the phrase "unfair methods of competition" has caused a great deal of difficulty in interpretation for the FTC and federal courts. Generally speaking, any conduct which results in anticompetitive effects may be regulated under Section 5.

Given the broad language in Section 5, it appears that the FTC will be able to proceed against any methods of competition which

- Violate one of the federal antitrust laws

- Violate the basic policies of the federal antitrust laws

- Violate consumer interests independent of possible or actual effects on competition

Metro Expansion

Many community newspapers have experienced a loss in circulation as a result of expanding metropolitan dailies. The number of zoned editions published by metropolitan dailies has increased significantly over the past few years. Community newspaper publishers often ask whether the antitrust laws provide a solution to the problems which these new zoned editions are causing. The answer to this question is generally "no" in the absence of some specific instance of anticompetitive conduct on the part of the metropolitan daily. In terms of the antitrust laws, there is really nothing a daily or weekly community newspaper can do to curtail its loss of subscribers and to prevent the expansion of a metropolitan daily's circulation as long as the metropolitan daily is competing fairly.

What community newspaper publishers should do is attempt to determine, from a business standpoint, the reasons for the success of metropolitan papers in their community. By determining the cause of the subscriber shift, a community paper may be able to isolate those areas in which it can perhaps change its product to improve service to its local subscribers, the end result being a stronger competitive position with respect to the metropolitan daily.

Community newspapers should also attempt to determine whether the subscription rate charged by the metropolitan daily in the metropolitan area is the same as that which is charged in suburban communities. If the metropolitan paper is charging a lower subscription rate in outlying areas than it charges in the metropolitan area, this may constitute at least some evidence

of predatory intent on the part of the metropolitan paper. Further investigation would then be required in order to determine whether or not it would be appropriate to file an antitrust complaint.

THE ANTITRUST SPECIALIST

To whom should a community newspaper publisher turn if he believes his newspaper has been injured by anticompetitive conduct on the part of a metropolitan daily or any other competitor? Generally speaking, it would be advisable to contact an antitrust specialist from the outset. While there are some local attorneys who are capable of providing sound antitrust advice, there are others who are not because of their lack of knowledge, training, or experience in the complexities of antitrust law. Of course, if a publisher knows that the newspaper's local attorney is experienced in antitrust matters, the local attorney should be called upon first, since the local attorney will have the advantage of being familiar with the newspaper's operation.

If, on the other hand, a local attorney is contacted first and it turns out that he has little or no experience in antitrust matters, the local attorney may simply refer the publisher to an antitrust specialist or consult an antitrust specialist himself and work on the case in conjunction with that specialist. In either case, the publisher probably would have been better off, in terms of time and money expended, if he had contacted an antitrust specialist at the outset. If the publisher does not know of a reliable antitrust specialist, an inquiry can always be made to one of the newspaper trade organizations.

It would probably not be a good idea to go directly to the state or federal antitrust authorities. First, there is always the chance that anticompetitive practices within the publisher's own operation may come to light in the course of a government investigation. Few, if any, newspapers can be 100 percent sure that their own operation is free of antitrust violations. Second, there is no guarantee that government antitrust authorities will take action against the person who has allegedly violated the antitrust laws.

Because of the limited economic resources available to most government antitrust agencies, not all antitrust complaints can be followed up. Unless the alleged anticompetitive conduct falls within an area in which the government authorities are particularly interested, or unless the alleged antitrust violation involves a significant economic injury to the public in general, government antitrust authorities may simply decide not to get involved in the matter. Thus, it would probably be advisable simply to contact an antitrust specialist and leave it up to him to decide whether or not it would be beneficial to call upon the federal or state antitrust authorities.

Shoppers

Publishing a shopper may give rise to a number of serious problems under the federal antitrust laws, the most common of which have their basis in Section 2 of the Sherman Act and Section 3 of the Clayton Act. These two sections, as indicated earlier, prohibit monopolization (including attempts to monopolize and conspiracies to monopolize) and tying arrangements, respectively. Given the antitrust liability which publishing a shopper can bring about, it is crucial for newspaper management to have at least some general notion of how to avoid costly mistakes in this area.

The problems which publishing a shopper may create begin with the newspaper's initial decision to publish one. If a newspaper decides to publish a shopper solely as a response to a competing shopper in the same market, and if the goal in mind is to drive the competing shopper out of business through the use of anticompetitive business practices, then this will likely result in charges that the newspaper is guilty of monopolization or an attempt to monopolize.

In order to guard against future antitrust problems when starting up a shopper, careful planning and the exercise of good business sense are imperative. Certain steps should be taken to protect against claims that your shopper was initiated for anticompetitive purposes. Once you decide to begin publishing a shopper, this decision and its motivations should be fully documented in your corporate minutes or in an official memo of some sort, even if there are no other shoppers in your market area at the time. This will be especially important if, for example, another shopper should appear in the same market before your shopper plans are put into effect. Once you have the reasons for initiating your shopper down in black and white, it will be that much more difficult for someone to prove later that you began publishing your shopper simply to drive another out of business.

What other factors will be viewed by a court in determining whether a newspaper is simply trying to compete fairly for advertising revenues or whether there are predatory motivations behind the publication of its shopper? One factor often viewed by the courts in this regard is whether the shopper is operating at a profit or a loss. If a newspaper continues to publish a shopper in spite of the fact that the shopper has been losing money over an extended period of time, a court may infer the existence of an anticompetitive motive.

The reasoning which underlies such an inference goes something like this. First, it is assumed that making a profit is the common goal of every business. From this, it follows that a business generally will not continue along a given course of action for an extended period of time when that particular course of action consistently produces a loss, except where that business believes that by absorbing losses over a certain period of time, it can succeed in driving its competition out of business. Then it will not only recover its past losses, but make monopolistic profits as well.

Thus, courts will often conclude that the only reason a newspaper would continue publishing a shopper at a loss over an extended period of time is that the newspaper intends to drive competing shoppers out of business.

A CASE IN POINT

In *Greenville Publishing Company* v. *Daily Reflector, Inc.,* the Greenville (North Carolina) *Daily Reflector,* the only daily newspaper in its particular market, made plans in 1970 to expand its operation and publish a weekly shopper. At approximately the same time, an independent shopper company, the Greenville Publishing Company, was organized to publish a weekly shopper. Both shoppers were introduced on the same day. Both shoppers operated at a loss during their first year. After that, a reduction in the page size of the daily newspaper's shopper resulted in lower costs, more revenue, and a profit. The independent shopper, however, continued to operate at a loss, and by the end of 1972, had sustained a $70,000 operating loss.

In 1973, the independent shopper brought suit against the daily newspaper alleging violations of Sections 1 and 2 of the Sherman Antitrust Act. The specific allegations were that the daily newspaper had deliberately set its shopper's advertising rates below cost in an attempt to eliminate any competition from the independent shopper. Reversing the lower court's decision in favor of the daily newspaper, the Court in 1974 noted that:

Although [deliberate below-cost pricing] may not be illegal in itself, it can furnish evidence of either the specific intent required to prove an illegal attempt to monopolize or the general intent which, accompanied by monopoly power, constitutes the offense of monopolization.

The Court went on to indicate that proof that the daily newspaper's shopper was not paying its own way would support an inference that the daily newspaper's pricing policies were designed to drive the independent shopper out of the market. Thus, the Court appeared to adopt the rule that a shopper must make a profit in order to lawfully compete for the advertiser's dollar.

It should be emphasized, however, that a shopper does not have to turn a profit from the very outset. It is entirely reasonable and understandable that a new shopper may suffer losses during the initial phase of publication. Nevertheless, a shopper's advertising rate structure should always be set up with making a profit in mind; that is, a profit should be projected after some reasonable introductory period has elapsed.

HOW TO DETERMINE PROFIT-MAKING STATUS

With the profit-making status of a shopper being as important as it is from a legal standpoint, many questions have been raised with respect to how a newspaper determines whether or not its shopper is making a profit. While this might sound like a simple matter, courts have had some difficulty in this area.

Based upon rudimentary economic concepts, one can say that a newspaper is making a profit on its shopper if the revenues earned by the shopper exceed the newspaper's costs of producing the shopper. The amount of revenue created by a free distribution shopper is relatively easy to ascertain, for it is simply the sum of all advertising revenues attributable to the shopper.

One thing that should be kept in mind, however, is that all revenues which are attributed to a shopper for in-house ads should actually be paid to the shopper by the newspaper, and not simply counted as shopper revenue without ever actually being paid. Assuming that one can easily arrive at a shopper's total revenues, the major problem in determining a shopper's profitability lies in the calculation of the shopper's production costs. There are a number of ways to measure production costs, and depending upon the method utilized, the profit or loss created by a given shopper could vary significantly.

Some antitrust plaintiffs have argued that in calculating shopper production costs a newspaper must take into account the *total cost* of producing the shopper—not only the cost of the materials and labor directly used to produce the shopper, but also a proportional part of the newspaper's fixed

costs, such as management expenses, depreciation on equipment, and property taxes or rent. Others have argued that a shopper's production costs need only take into account those *variable costs* associated with the production of the shopper—the cost of materials, energy, and labor actually used to produce the shopper. A third possible measure of production cost is *marginal cost*.

While the law is not settled as concerns the proper method for calculating the costs of a shopper, the current trend seems to indicate that the minimum cost figure a newspaper should use to determine shopper profitability is marginal or average variable cost. Marginal cost is the extra cost created by the production of one additional unit of output.

As a practical matter, newspapers generally do not maintain the type of economic records which would be required for calculating a shopper's marginal cost. Average variable cost is determined by dividing total variable costs by the number of units produced. This is probably the best available measure for determining shopper production costs. It should be noted, however, that a newspaper would be on much firmer ground legally if it could demonstrate that the profit figures for its shopper took into account the *total costs* of the shopper, both total variable and total fixed costs.

"TYING" IS A HAZARD

Antitrust problems may also accrue to a newspaper which publishes a shopper and requires that advertisers place an ad in the newspaper before they are allowed to place an ad in the shopper. This sort of advertising policy should be avoided at all costs, for it could be characterized as an illegal tying arrangement under Section 1 of the Sherman Act.

A newspaper should always allow advertisers to purchase ad linage in its regular newspaper or in its shopper separately if they so desire. This is not to say that there is anything inherently wrong with a discount combination rate. Combination rates are en-

tirely acceptable as long as the amount of discount involved reasonably reflects the cost savings realized from running repeat advertising in the shopper.

It may be a violation of Section 2(a) of the Robinson–Patman Act for a newspaper to give preferential ad rate treatment to some, but not all, of the advertisers who advertise in its shopper. Furthermore, the Robinson–Patman Act may prohibit other forms of preferential treatment, such as offering rebates or bonuses to a select group of shopper advertisers which would be unavailable to other advertisers.

It has often been argued that Section 2(a) of the Robinson–Patman Act does not apply to sales of newspaper advertising because such advertising is a service rather than a commodity. Despite a number of court decisions which have supported this interpretation, the FTC continues to view advertising as a commodity. Thus, it appears that a newspaper could still encounter Robinson–Patman Act problems for selling ads to large volume advertisers at lower rates.

PUBLISHERS OVERLY CAUTIOUS

To summarize, the most common allegation made against a newspaper which publishes a shopper is that the newspaper is engaging in some sort of predatory activity in order to attain or maintain a monopoly. The predatory acts which a newspaper is most often charged with are publishing a shopper at a loss over an extended period of time or making the sale of advertising in the shopper conditional upon purchase of advertising space in the newspaper. Price discrimination among shopper advertisers may also present significant legal problems for a shopper publication. Thus, any plans to publish a shopper should take into account these areas of potential antitrust liability.

Many publishers appear to be overly cautious about starting a shopper because of the antitrust problems which they fear may arise. This is unfortunate, for there is clearly nothing wrong with attempting to increase your advertising revenues by starting a shopper. Likewise, there is nothing wrong with starting a shopper so as to compete with existing shoppers for advertising revenues. After all, it is the basic goal of antitrust law to promote such competition. The law simply requires that you compete fairly.

Joint Operating Agreements

THE ANTITRUST EXEMPTION

In its decision in *Citizen Publishing Company* v. *United States,* the Supreme Court held that two newspapers located in the same geographic area violated the Sherman Act by entering into joint operating agreements under which they combined their printing, advertising, and circulation departments, the effect being to eliminate competition between them in those areas. At the time of the *Citizen Publishing Company* decision, similar joint operating agreements were in effect in twenty-two other cities.

In response to this Supreme Court decision, and out of its concern to preserve the existence of newspapers which had entered into joint operating arrangements so as to avert economic distress, Congress, in July of 1970, enacted the Newspaper Preservation Act, a measure which created an antitrust exemption for certain joint operating arrangements so as to prevent the destruction of editorial and reportorial competition and independence in the nation's cities.

The key provisions of the Newspaper Preservation Act are as follows:

(a) It shall not be unlawful under any antitrust law for any person to perform, enforce, renew, or amend any joint newspaper operating arrangement entered into prior to July 24, 1970, if at the time at which such arrangement was first entered into, regardless of ownership or affiliations, not more than one of the newspaper publications involved in the performance of such arrangement

was likely to remain or become a financially sound publication: Provided, *that the terms of a renewal or amendment to a joint operating arrangement must be filed with the Department of Justice and that the amendment does not add a newspaper publication or newspaper publications to such arrangement.*

(b) It shall be unlawful for any person to enter into, perform, or enforce a joint operating arrangement not already in effect, except with the prior written consent of the Attorney General of the United States. Prior to granting such approval, the Attorney General shall determine that not more than one of the newspaper publications involved in the arrangement is a publication other than a failing newspaper, and that approval of such arrangement would effectuate the policy and purpose of this chapter.

(c) Nothing contained in the chapter shall be construed to exempt from any antitrust law any predatory pricing, any predatory practice, or any other conduct in the otherwise lawful operations of a joint newspaper operating arrangement which would be unlawful under any antitrust law if engaged in by a single entity. Except as provided in this chapter, no joint newspaper operating arrangement or any party thereto shall be exempt from any antitrust law.

In addition to the act's filing and application procedures, there are two major substantive requirements which must be met in order for newspapers to qualify for the act's antitrust exemption. First, both newspapers must be "newspaper publications." This term is defined as a publication produced on newsprint paper that is printed and distributed at least once a week and in which a substantial portion of the content is devoted to the dissemination of news and editorial opinion. Thus, a weekly news magazine published on slick paper is excluded from the exemption created by the Newspaper Preservation Act. Also excluded are shoppers devoted primarily to advertising and any monthly or bimonthly publication.

The second major substantive requirement is that at least one of the newspapers in the arrangement must be a "failing newspaper," defined in the act as "a newspaper publication

which, regardless of its ownership or affiliation, is in probable danger of financial failure."

THE CINCINNATI CASE

As of this writing, there have been only two attempts to obtain the Attorney General's consent to a joint operating arrangement since the passage of the Newspaper Preservation Act in 1970. The first involved two newspapers in Anchorage, Alaska. Their application was approved without a hearing in 1974.

The second attempt involved two Cincinnati newspapers and was followed closely by members of the newspaper industry since it provided valuable insight into the procedure for obtaining the federal government's approval of a joint operating arrangement. On September 28, 1977, the Cincinnati *Enquirer,* Inc., and the Cincinnati *Post,* published by E. W. Scripps Co., Inc., submitted a proposed joint operating agreement to the Justice Department and applied for the Attorney General's approval of the agreement. The agreement provided for the combination of their production, circulation, business, and advertising departments. The application alleged that the Cincinnati *Post* was a "failing newspaper" within the meaning of the Newspaper Preservation Act.

On December 28, 1977, the Assistant Attorney General in charge of the Antitrust Division, in accordance with the regulations discussed above, issued a report recommending that a hearing be held with respect to the application of the *Post* and the *Enquirer.* The Assistant Attorney General found that there was an issue of material fact as to whether the *Post* was a "failing newspaper" within the meaning of the act. In his report, he also stated that the test to be applied to determine whether or not a newspaper is a "failing newspaper" is a more stringent test for *proposed* joint operating agreements than it is for such agreements in effect when the act was passed. For the latter type of agreement to qualify for the exemption, it is sufficient to show that one of the newspapers was unlikely "to remain or become a financially sound publication." For a proposed agreement, however, it must be shown that one of the newspapers is in "probable danger of financial failure." The Assistant Attorney General also found that applications for a joint operating agreement have the burden of showing that the failing newspaper could not operate at a profit under new ownership or management.

After conducting an extensive hearing on the two Cincinnati newspapers' application for approval of their joint operating agreement, administrative law judge Donald R. Moore, on May 1, 1979, recommended that the Attorney General approve the agreement. An order approving the proposed joint operating agreement was subsequently issued by Attorney General Benjamin R. Civiletti, effective December 6, 1979.

The order stated that, after having reviewed the hearing record, the recommendation of Judge Donald R. Moore, and the exceptions and responses to Judge Moore's recommendation, the Attorney General adopted all undisputed findings of fact made by the judge and all but a few disputed findings of fact.

Three conclusions of law were set forth in support of the approval decision, those being that:

- The Cincinnati *Post,* considered regardless of its ownership or affiliations, is in probable danger of financial failure

- The Cincinnati *Post* is a failing newspaper

- Approval of the joint operating agreement will effectuate the policy and purpose of the Newspaper Preservation Act.

Circulation

CARRIER STATUS

In many respects, a newspaper's antitrust exposure will vary in scope depending upon the type of circulation system it utilizes. The status of a newspaper's carriers, whether they be independent contractors or employees, will be of the greatest significance in Section 1 Sherman Act cases.

If an *employee* carrier force is utilized, a newspaper will be able to engage in retail price maintenance or impose territorial route restrictions without violating Section 1, for a company and its employees are treated as a single person for antitrust purposes and a single person cannot contract, combine, or conspire with itself. If, on the other hand, an *independent* contractor distributor or delivery agent system is utilized, each distributor and delivery agent will be viewed as a separate legal entity with which the newspaper can contract, combine, and conspire.

Under an independent contractor-distributor system where the distributor purchases newspapers from the publisher and resells to subscribers, the newspaper will be subject to the full force of Section 1 and must be careful in structuring its business relationship with its distributors so as to avoid any arrangements which could be construed as illegal concerted activity. If independent contractor delivery agents are utilized, however, certain additional restraints may be imposed by the newspaper without violating Section 1. For example, the newspaper can set the retail price charged to subscribers under a delivery agent system. Although the delivery agents are independent contractors, there will be no Section 1 violation for price fixing because there is no sale-resale relationship between the newspaper and the delivery agent. Rather than purchasing newspapers at wholesale and reselling at retail, the delivery agent merely delivers newspapers which have been sold to subscribers by the newspaper.

It should be noted at this point that the Section 1 "contract, combination, or conspiracy" requirement does not serve as much of an obstacle for courts once they detect the presence of anticompetitive conduct on the part of the newspaper. For example, in *Albrecht* v. *The Herald Company,* the Supreme Court demonstrated just how far a court may venture to find a combination when it feels that competition has been restrained. In *Albrecht,* the newspaper gave its distributors exclusive territories subject to termination if the resale price exceeded the maximum established by the newspaper. Al-

brecht, a distributor, unilaterally raised his resale price beyond the maximum. Instead of terminating him, the newspaper attempted to force him to lower the price. The newspaper advised his customers by mail that it would deliver papers to those persons who desired a newspaper at a lower price. The newspaper also hired a circulation sales company to solicit subscribers in Albrecht's territory. These measures resulted in Albrecht's losing 314 of his 1,200 subscribers. Yet, Albrecht still refused to lower his price, so the newspaper terminated him and gave his route to another distributor.

At the trial, the newspaper defended its illegal conduct by claiming that it had acted unilaterally. Justice William O. Douglas, writing for the Supreme Court, disagreed with this assertion. He found that five separate combinations were present:

- Between the newspaper and the circulation sales company

- Between the newspaper and the distributor who replaced Albrecht

- Between the newspaper and Albrecht himself (at least during the time he complied with the maximum resale price

- Between the newspaper and all other distributors who acquiesced in the maximum price

- Between the newspaper and Albrecht's customers who sought to pay only the maximum price

In light of these findings, it appears that courts will not allow the contract, combination, or conspiracy requirement of Section 1 to be much of an obstacle to a finding of illegality—at least in situations where the court perceives that a newspaper has engaged in anticompetitive conduct.

PRICE CONTROLS

Agreements to fix prices, both horizontal and vertical, have long been condemned under Section 1 as being *per se* unlawful. Not only are express price-fixing agreements deemed unlawful, but indirect agreements or concerted conduct to raise, lower, or stabilize prices are also illegal. Resale price maintenance agreements are one form of indirect price fixing. Thus, they are *per se* illegal regardless of whether it is a maximum or minimum resale price that is being set.

In newspaper circulation, price-fixing problems often arise from the terms of the contract between the independent contractor-distributor and the newspaper. Any attempt by the newspaper to control an independent contractor-distributor's resale price to subscribers will lead to antitrust liability. This does not mean that a newspaper cannot suggest the resale price it wishes the distributor to utilize, but any attempt to force compliance on an unwilling distributor will lead to antitrust problems.

TERRITORIAL ROUTE RESTRICTIONS

A common feature of many newspaper circulation systems is that the distributor is confined to a specified geographic territory or route. Such territorial restrictions, whether imposed vertically or horizontally, may create antitrust problems for newspapers under the Sherman Act.

For many years it has been clear that any scheme of market division among competitors, any horizontal territorial allocation, is illegal *per se* under Section 1. For example, if a newspaper's distributors agree among themselves to divide the market area and establish exclusive areas for each distributor, Section 1 would be violated. As stated by the Supreme Court in *United States* v. *Topco Associates, Inc.:*

One of the classic examples of a per se *violation of §1 is an agreement between competitors at the same level of the market structure to allocate territories in order to minimize competition.*

The law concerning vertical territorial restrictions, however, has been subject to fluctuation in recent years. In *United States* v. *Arnold Schwinn & Company,* the Supreme Court held that a manufacturer committed a *per se* vio-

lation of Section 1 of the Sherman Antitrust Act whenever it attempted to place territorial restrictions on a distributor's ability to market the products which the distributor had purchased from the manufacturer. In practical terms, the application of the "Schwinn doctrine" to newspaper circulation absolutely prohibited newspapers from placing territorial restrictions upon their distributors.

In *Continental TV, Inc.* v. *GTE Sylvania, Inc.,* the Supreme Court ruled that vertical territorial restrictions should not be viewed as *per se* violations, but should instead be evaluated under a "rule of reason" standard. According to the Court, restrictions on competition between distributors of the same brand of product could be outweighed by more effective competition between brands which vertically imposed territories can promote.

As a practical matter, the *GTE Sylvania* decision may open the door for newspapers to reimpose reasonable territorial restrictions upon distributors. If these restrictions are challenged, newspapers will at least have a chance to defend them as being a means of providing for effective and profitable circulation. However, the *GTE Sylvania* decision leaves open the question of the legality of territorial restrictions where there is only one "brand" of newspaper in a given geographic area. It must also be emphasized that the *GTE Sylvania* decision does not stand for the proposition that every newspaper's territorial restrictions will be legal, but it does mean that the legality of a particular newspaper's territorial restraints on newspaper distributors will now be determined through an application of the "rule of reason" standard on a case-by-case basis.

TIE-INS AND REFUSALS TO DEAL

As mentioned previously, a *tie-in* or tying arrangement generally may be defined as an arrangement whereby a seller makes the sale of a product or service (the tied product) conditional upon a buyer's purchasing a separate product or service (the tying product).

In the newspaper circulation field, a tying arrangement will most likely be found in an agreement between newspaper and distributor or newspaper and subscriber. Arrangements between newspaper and distributor whereby the newspaper agrees to sell its morning newspaper to the distributor only if the distributor also purchases the afternoon paper, or where the sale of a weekday newspaper is conditional upon the purchase of the Sunday newspaper, may be viewed as illegal tying arrangements. Agreements between the newspaper and a subscriber to the same effect are also subject to challenge under the federal antitrust laws.

The reason for prohibiting tie-ins is a general belief that such arrangements deny competitors free access to the tied product market, not because the party imposing the arrangement has a superior product, but because of the leverage created by the tying product. For example, in the newspaper circulation area, it is feared that a newspaper company with a strong morning newspaper but a weak afternoon newspaper will force a distributor to deliver the afternoon newspaper, thus depriving a competing afternoon paper of the distributor's services. This same reasoning applies where a newspaper forces subscribers to purchase both newspapers, thus depriving another afternoon newspaper of a potential subscriber.

It should be remembered, however, that before this type of arrangement with either a distributor or a subscriber may be declared *per se* illegal, at least two elements must be shown to exist: First, the arrangement must involve two distinct products and provide that one may not be purchased unless the other is also purchased. Second, there must be *either* (1) a sufficient economic power in the market area for the tying product, *or* (2) more than an insubstantial amount of commerce foreclosed by the arrangement.

While past cases have not established any all-encompassing rules with respect to whether or not the morning-afternoon or weekday-weekend editions of a newspaper are separate products, they do offer some insight into the controlling legal principles. In *Times-Picayune Publishing Company* v. *United States,* the Supreme Court held that a newspaper did not violate the antitrust laws by requiring that advertising space be purchased in both the morning and afternoon newspapers published by the newspaper. The basis of the Court's view was the fact that the morning and afternoon newspapers were not separate products.

In *Kansas City Star Company* v. *United States,* the government's contention was that the morning paper (the *Times*) and the evening paper (the *Star*), although both owned by the *Star,* were two separate products. The newspaper's contention was that they were simply different issues of a single product. The jury ultimately found that the morning and afternoon papers were separate newspapers but this did not change the Court's belief that separate editions of the *same* paper were not separate products for antitrust purposes.

In *Paul* v. *Pulitzer Publishing Company,* a newspaper was charged with illegally tying the purchase of a Saturday edition to the purchase of Monday-through-Friday editions. The court found, however, that the Saturday edition was not a separate product.

These cases thus seem to indicate that separate editions of the same newspaper are a single product for antitrust purposes. This may not prove to be true in every instance, however, since courts decide on a case-by-case basis.

Another type of restraint that often appears in the newspaper circulation area is the unilateral refusal to deal. In *United States* v. *Colgate,* the Supreme Court announced the rule that a businessman is free, in the absence of monopolistic purposes, to refuse to deal with any present or potential supplier or customer.

Notwithstanding this general principle, the Supreme Court has made it clear that there are important limitations imposed on this right. Specifically, a refusal to deal will be treated as a violation if it involves concerted conduct or if it is undertaken in furtherance of a scheme that constitutes a prohibited restraint of trade. In other words, if a newspaper refuses to deal with a distributor because the distributor will not comply with maximum price restraints, the refusal will constitute a separate violation of Section 1. Nevertheless, a newspaper remains free to refuse to deal with a distributor in the absence of concerted conduct, a monopoly claim, or some demonstration that the refusal will further an unlawful agreement.

Conclusion

It is safe to assume that the number of antitrust suits brought against newspapers will increase in the course of the next few years. The broad public exposure which is essential for financial success in the newspaper industry also places newspapers among the most popular targets for antitrust plaintiffs. As newspaper antitrust suits become increasingly common, existing business practices and future plans should be examined carefully with the antitrust laws in mind.

Chapter 26

Evaluating Newspaper Properties

by Gerald L. Grotta

Evaluating a newspaper property used to be a fairly simple process. The potential buyer could use a few rules of thumb, average the results, enter into negotiations with the owner of the newspaper, and, if agreement was reached, purchase the newspaper. However, the situation has changed dramatically in the past few years.

Perhaps the most significant change is that opportunities for an individual to buy a weekly or small daily newspaper have become severely limited. Newspaper groups have moved into the community newspaper field in growing numbers, and there are no indications that this will change in the future.

For example, in its annual roundup of newspaper sales reported during 1978, *Editor & Publisher* pointed out that of 53 daily newspaper transactions during the year, 47 were purchased by groups. This included 42 previously independently owned newspapers. The newspapers acquired by groups ranged in circulation from less than 5,000 to 350,000. The majority of the dailies sold were small to medium-sized papers—12 had circulations of 5,000 or less, 15 had between 5,000 and 10,000, 16 between 10,000 and 50,000, 3 between 50,000 to 100,000, and 4 over 100,000 circulation.

Metros Buy Weeklies

Editor & Publisher also reported the sale of 175 weekly newspapers and shoppers, including "a large number of acquisitions by publishers of daily newspapers." Some of the groups buying weekly newspapers and shoppers during 1978 included the Minneapolis *Star & Tribune,* Scripps-Howard, the New York *Times,* the Des Moines *Register & Tribune,* Ottaway Newspapers (Dow Jones Co.), Thompson Newspapers, and Cox Enterprises. These large groups purchased weekly newspapers as small as 2,200 circulation. Other media companies with large holdings in the weekly newspaper field include Donrey, Harte-Hanks, and Panax.

Clearly, acquisitions of weekly newspapers by groups are increasing. This limits the prospects for an individual to buy even a smaller weekly newspaper. At the start of 1979, efforts were continuing on many fronts to restrict the growth of newspaper groups. As *Editor & Publisher* reported in January 1979, "With 42 more independently owned daily newspapers passing into groups in 1978, the lobby for adoption of the Independent Local Newspaper

GERALD L. GROTTA

Dr. Grotta is a member of the journalism faculty at Texas Christian University and vice president of RMH Research, Inc. He was a reporter and editor for more than ten years and has served as a research consultant to more than one hundred newspapers.

". . . Buying a newspaper is not a promising prospect for an individual, unless that individual has enough money (preferably several million dollars) and expertise to compete with some of the biggest money and best minds in the business."

Act will be busy in Washington." One bill, HR 9484, introduced by Representative Morris K. Udall (Democrat, Arizona), would change tax laws which now encourage owners of independent newspapers to sell to groups rather than to individuals. These tax advantages for groups include tax-free stock transfers which enable the newspaper's owner to reduce the tax load to the seller, and high estate taxes for heirs, which often make it impossible to retain ownership of the newspaper. In addition, Udall mentioned "the huge financial offers of the big chains."

When a good newspaper property comes onto the market today, ten or more groups will be bidding for it, according to Richard Clester, for five years senior corporate marketing director for Harte-Hanks Communications, Inc. This has had a profound effect on determining a "fair" price for a newspaper. And some choice newspaper properties really never "come onto the market." The general manager of one small group told of trying for ten years to convince a publisher to sell, and in early 1979 the efforts were still in progress.

Complicating the effects of ten or more groups bidding on a newspaper, each group may have a different set of goals for the property. For instance, one group might be looking for immediate revenue and profit, another for a long-term investment in a market, and a third a place to spend current profits to avoid paying taxes. Each group would come up with a different "fair" price, depending on how well the newspaper meets its goals.

Old Guidelines

In 1965, Marion Krehbiel, president of Krehbiel-Bolitho Newspaper Service, Inc., a major newspaper brokerage firm, wrote that the answers to four key questions would give a rough idea of the value of any weekly or small daily newspaper. These questions were

- What is the newspaper's last annual gross income?

- What is the size of the community?

- What is the newspaper's paid circulation?

- Is the newspaper making any money and if so, how much?

For each of the four questions, Krehbiel had several guidelines, based on having handled the sale of 119 weekly and 36 daily newspapers at that time. For example, the first guideline was the newspaper's *last* annual gross income figure—"the most reliable 'yardstick' for a starting point in negotiations between buyer and seller of the average, normal newspaper." The other guidelines in 1965 were:

- Population: an average of $20 a head

- Circulation: an average of $25 per paid subscriber

- Net Profit: about ten years' net profit should pay the purchase price

Krehbiel states that determining a price with each of the four guidelines, adding up the total, and dividing by four would give a good estimate of the value of the "stripped" weekly newspaper, with normal and average inventories and equipment, free and clear of any indebtedness, without cash and receivables, and without real assets. Any or all of these additional factors would then have to be taken into account in order to determine a fair price.

The Rules Change

Not only have these rules of thumb changed dramatically in recent years; Krehbiel said in January 1979 that they continue to change each year. What might be a good guideline today may be meaningless tomorrow.

In 1980, Krehbiel updated the guidelines for the four rules of thumb. By then, he had handled 329 newspaper transactions in the United States, Canada, and Costa Rica. Here are his revised guidelines for weekly newspapers:

- Gross Income: 105 percent of gross annual income with no

plant, 130 percent with an up-to-date plant

- City Population: $40 a head

- Circulation: $45 per paid subscriber

- Net Profit: twelve years' net profit

The "fair" price of a weekly newspaper had obviously increased substantially in the fifteen years between 1965 and 1980.

DAILIES DIFFER

For daily newspapers (small- to medium-circulation, not the big metropolitan papers), the rules of thumb are substantially different. To determine the value of 100 percent of the capital stock of the corporation, including net current assets, land, and building, less any long-term indebtedness, Krehbiel cited the following as average figures in 1978:

- Gross Income: 210 percent of last year's gross

- City Population: $110 per person

- Circulation: $155 per paid subscriber

- Net Profit: twenty-five years' net profit (after taxes)

Krehbiel said in early 1979, "The 'four-formulae' thing has been an effort to help publishers get a ballpark figure. You'd be surprised how many value their holdings too low—almost as many as value them too high!"

Other Factors Change Values

However, he pointed out that, "Putting a value on any publication is a tough job," and "values can be affected materially by just one of a hundred factors" in addition to the four guidelines.

These "plus or minus factors" can change the value of a newspaper by 25 to 50 percent or more. Here are Krehbiel's "plus or minus factors":

Competition: *Another newspaper or free sheet in town? Does it carry more than half as much advertising as yours? Another local job shop? Radio competition? TV time sold locally? Outside dailies bearing down on the field? Are you at least fifteen miles from any other larger or comparable newspaper? Are you suburban, semisuburban or "out in the country"?*

Vigor of Field and Market: *Appearance of town and stores. Are retail stocks complete and prices right? How many national dealerships? How many heavy chain store advertisers? Food advertisers? Good or poor schools, parks, municipal plants, hospital, paving? Is it a college town or is there one near? Good recreational facilities? Any dominant racial, religious, or foreign groups in the field? Are most principal churches represented? Are you on a federal interstate highway? Near a commercial airport? County seat or best town in county?*

Economy of Field and Market: *Population going up or down? Bank and S&L deposits above or below national average of $2,500 per capita of town population? Banks progressive or ultraconservative? How does town compare on total retail sales? Purchasing power, per capita income? If an agricultural field, is it one-crop or diversified, dryland or irrigated? Is area economy booming or stable? Healthy growth? Any local industrial payroll as buffer for agricultural lows? How do property taxes compare? Is labor union-scale or open? Lease available on building? How does rent compare? What's the paper's best and poorest earning record in recent years—stable? How many times has paper changed hands in recent years? Does [profit-and-loss statement] show any unavoidably large expenses peculiar to the field? Is your town under 1,500 population? Is your county population exceptionally small? Is all your volume in one newspaper or in several separate newspapers? Water? Power? Labor supply? Newsprint supply?*

Opportunities for Expansion and Growth: *Could the man who might buy you out gross and net more than you? Is your circulation up to the average*

of 85 percent of town population if a weekly, 65 percent if daily? Is more than 30 percent of your volume in 'farm-out' and commercial printing? If so, it's lopsided and will be valued downward. Is your weekly gross $30–$40–$50 per capita of your town population? ($35 is average for weekly, $50 for daily.) Is it obvious that the town is progressing, or is it slipping in relation to other nearby towns?

An extensive list of factors which can materially change the "ballpark" figure from the "four-formulae" results!

Krehbiel summed up the complexity of valuing a community newspaper this way:

In the final analysis, you [would] have had to sell more than three hundred [newspapers] to get the feel of what they really might be worth. It's sort of a judgment call.

At the beginning of 1979, Harte-Hanks' Clester said that *two to four times* one year's gross income is a good "starting point" for determining the value of a community newspaper. And even the higher number is often "violated." Two daily newspapers in Texas, with a combined circulation of less than 30,000, were sold in late 1978 for *five and one half* times one year's gross.

On the circulation side, *Publisher's Auxiliary* reported selling prices for daily newspapers in 1978 ranging from $57 per subscriber to *$500 per subscriber*. Clearly, no simple rules of thumb can cover such a wide range of prices.

Market Very Important

Clester listed several considerations used by Harte-Hanks in determining a "fair" price as a starting point for negotiations. The market itself is as important as the newspaper (even more so in many cases).

An important consideration, also cited by Krehbiel, is the competitive

nature of the market. The less competition, both for audience and for advertising, the more desirable a newspaper property becomes; the price goes up accordingly.

Circulation is a critical factor, but not just *total* circulation. What is the newspaper's *penetration* of the market; that is, how many paid subscribers does the newspaper have *per household* in the market? If the newspaper has less than 50 percent penetration, Clester said he would take a very close look at the situation to determine why it is so low. This translates as the strength of the newspaper in its market—its "franchise." The stronger the franchise, the more the newspaper is worth.

Pricing of circulation also is a key factor. What does the newspaper charge for a subscription or for a single copy? If it is priced below other similar newspapers in the area, this becomes a plus in the value of the paper—particularly if it has a strong hold on the market with 65 or 70 percent penetration. In this situation, said Clester, a new management could raise subscription or single copy price or both without risking the franchise, and thus increase revenues substantially.

Retailing in the market also is a major factor in evaluating a newspaper property. Clester said he looks at how many big accounts the newspaper currently has, and the potential for new ones to come into the market—either major stores or new shopping centers. In other words, what is the potential for significant growth in retailing and, hence, advertising revenue in the market?

In addition to looking closely at past and current circulation pricing, Clester said he makes a careful analysis of the newspaper's advertising rate card. Again, is there potential for growth in revenue from current advertisers? This analysis is complex and involves, among other factors, a comparison of the newspaper's rates with similar newspapers in the area or state. If the newspaper is underpriced in its advertising rates in comparison with similar newspapers, this indicates a potential for raising rates and increasing revenues. On the other hand, if the newspaper has gone through a recent series of large rate increases, the potential for further increases may be limited.

New Products Possible

Is there potential for introducing new products into the market? If there are no shoppers in the market, or no television programming guide, etc., the new management of the newspaper could generate additional revenues in the market by introducing new products. Even the number of issues published during the year is a consideration. If the current management of a daily does not publish several days a year—Thanksgiving Day, the Fourth of July, etc.—it might be because the present owner just doesn't want to work those days. If there is potential for publishing additional days during the year, this also could increase revenue, said Clester.

Of course, the potential for additional revenues through new products or new editions depends in large part on the retailing situation in the market. Would the present retail base (or potential new retailers) be able to support new products?

The total market situation obviously is an essential consideration. Is the market growing, in terms of population, retailing, industry, etc., or is it stagnant (or even declining)? If the population is growing, where is the growth—in younger, higher-income people or in older, lower-income and retired people? If industry is moving into the market, is it a diversified industrial base, or is the growth concentrated in one or two industries? The more the market is dependent upon one or two industries, the more vulnerable it will be if those industries suffer a downturn.

Even the current management of the newspaper is a vital concern. Clester pointed out that a newspaper in a good market might not have strong revenues and profits because of weak management. In that case, a new owner could significantly increase revenues and profits simply through more aggressive marketing and more efficient management of costs.

All Factors Vital

Obviously, no single factor, or even a combination of a few factors, can provide a reliable guide to the value of a newspaper property. The past revenues and profit levels could be very misleading if a potential buyer does not carefully analyze *all* factors affecting the newspaper and its market. As Krehbiel pointed out, a newspaper could have attained high revenues and profits by neglecting to maintain and to update the plant. The buyer "will not want to be hooked by a publisher who buys a newspaper, puts nothing into the plant, inflates gross by special promotions, and sells him Potemkin Village," Krehbiel wrote.

Clester of Harte-Hanks related a recent example which he encountered. A newspaper which was on the market would have been priced at $4 million on the basis of four times gross. However, Clester said an analysis of the newspaper's plant showed that another $1½ million would have to be invested in a run-down plant, which would have made the "real" price of the newspaper to a new owner $5½ million instead of $4 million.

Clester summed up the basic process of evaluating the worth of a newspaper property by citing a *pro forma* analysis of the property. After carefully investigating all of the factors mentioned above (and more), the financial future of the property can be simulated. (This could involve the use of complex computer analysis.) If the *pro forma* analysis indicates that the newspaper should provide adequate revenues and profits in future years, a "starting point" price can be arrived at and negotiations can begin.

If this seems like a very complicated process, the stakes justify it. For example, the two small daily newspapers cited earlier (less than 30,000 combined circulation) sold for a reported $33 million! Even small weekly newspapers in good markets sometimes sell for well into the millions of dollars, and few papers sell for less than six figures.

Check Loyalty toward the Newspaper

Actually, the factors outlined so far do not even cover the range of possibilities in evaluating a newspaper property. Something as intangible as attitudes of the people in the market—especially those of community leaders and major advertisers—can become a major factor in determining the worth of a newspaper.

For example, how loyal are people in the market toward the newspaper? Even if the newspaper has a high penetration in the market and a seemingly strong franchise, if the people in the market do not like the newspaper, or are indifferent toward it (would not miss it very much if they could no longer read it), this would be a warning sign that someone else might be able to move into the market. Some new publishers have been faced with tough new competition before they could get established in the market. If there are weak loyalties toward the newspaper, the market is ripe for competition from a new newspaper or, more likely, a zoned edition of a nearby metropolitan daily newspaper aggressively marketed in the community.

If major advertisers are basically negative toward the newspaper, someone else might move into the market with a shopper and take away a big share of the newspaper's advertising revenue. In some markets, major advertisers have been so strongly against the local newspaper that they actually encouraged someone else to come into the market with an alternative advertising medium—usually a shopper. When this competing publication comes into the market, the community newspaper loses the accounts of its dissatisfied advertisers, thereby losing much of the revenue it counts on. Sometimes the new owner of a newspaper isn't even aware of the problem until the new shopper appears and his advertising revenue disappears.

This is why some groups conduct major market research surveys in a community as part of their evaluation of the newspaper. Anonymous surveys of community leaders and major advertisers are quite common. If such a survey indicates a major potential problem in the market, then the potential buyer must determine whether the situation can be reversed quickly, before someone else can move into the market.

Look for Potential Growth

Underlying all of the evaluation factors, in summary, is the potential for growth. Clester of Harte-Hanks said he looks for growth—in population, retailing, and other areas—which is *above* state and national averages. In other words, far beyond just buying a newspaper, be looking for a market with a future for growth and expansion.

The complexity of the analysis involved in evaluating newspaper properties explains the great variations in selling prices for newspapers. One newspaper can sell for several times the price of another newspaper with the same circulation, depending on all the other factors affecting the newspaper and its market.

And an individual, considering a "good" newspaper in a "good" market, probably will be competing against several newspaper groups, each with corporate staffs of experts in all aspects of newspaper operations, financing, and pricing.

In the past, an alternative for the individual was to find a market with potential and start a new paper. However, even this avenue to newspaper ownership is limited today. With their acquisition staffs actively seeking new properties and with fewer and fewer good newspapers for sale, newspaper groups also look for markets where *they* can start new products—newspapers, shoppers, whatever the market will bear.

It Could Take Millions

Summarizing the current situation, then, buying a newspaper is not a promising prospect for an individual, unless that individual has enough money (preferably several million dollars) and expertise to compete with some of the biggest money and best minds in the business.

If an individual discovers a "great buy" in a newspaper, it just *might* be a rare find, but the odds are much greater that one or more groups have looked at the property and rejected it at the selling price. If it really were a "great buy," or even a reasonably good buy, it would not still be on the market.

Clearly, buying a newspaper today is not a task for an inexperienced person eager to own a newspaper. The best advice for a newcomer to the field would be to use the services of a good newspaper appraiser or consultant before proceeding.

The best bet for an individual today is to find a publisher who does not want to sell to a group, who will try to find another individual to take over the newspaper. For example, a recent classified advertisement in *Editor & Publisher* read:

Retiring Washington Publisher seeks intrepid Ad-selling co-partner who can soon inherit the whole thing. No outlay capital required. Box. . . .

Such opportunities are rare, however, and an individual considering such an opportunity should check it out as carefully as a potential purchase. Perhaps the publisher just wants some "cheap" help; perhaps the property isn't worth inheriting anyway.

Get Expert Help

What if an individual does overcome all of the obstacles to finding a "good buy" in a newspaper and arrives at a "fair price" with the current owner? This brings up an entire new set of problems—financing the purchase price, paying off the loans, the transition of ownership, etc.

Of course, these considerations should have been pretty well settled long before the final stages of the negotiations, and they can be as complex as evaluating the worth of the newspaper property. As with determining the price, these problems are not for the amateur to handle. In addition to the advice of a good newspaper broker, the potential buyer of a newspaper will want the advice of financial consultants at this stage of the process.

If the newspaper property really is a good investment, the potential buyer should be able to find help in financing—from a bank or other source. However, the buyer should not proceed without a substantial amount of cash for the down payment. Otherwise, the interest and payments could become too much of a burden and leave the new owner with serious cash flow problems.

The closing stages of buying a newspaper, however, become so complex that the potential buyer should not attempt to handle all of the details. Not only will the advice of newspaper brokers and financial consultants become necessary; attorneys and tax experts also should be used.

All things considered, the newspaper field is no longer a business which a young person with a lot of enthusiasm can enter easily, without money and expertise to back up the enthusiasm.

Chapter 27

IRVAN J. KUMMERFELDT

Dr. Kummerfeldt is executive secretary of the International Society of Weekly Newspaper Editors and a member of the Department of Journalism faculty at Northern Illinois University.

". . . The newspaper associations collect and disseminate information to and about members, usually conduct a program of legislative relations, provide in-service training for professionals, and encourage and assist student journalists in a variety of ways."

The Newspaper Associations

by Irvan J. Kummerfeldt

Sociologists will tell you that humans naturally tend to associate. Popular belief is that Americans are joiners. A guide to American groups will list some 14,000 associations in its next edition.

Newspapers are made up of people who tend to gather together. If you don't believe that, drop in at the bars or press clubs in New York, Chicago, Denver, or any other major city. Check the Main Street café at midmorning in small towns.

Newspaper associations simply are organizations of people with similar interests and goals. In that, newspaper groups are like the local stamp club or the American Medical Association. The subject of the interests and goals is what makes newspaper associations unique.

There are state-wide associations in almost every state, some vigorous and a very few almost dormant. There are regional associations and there are many national and international organizations.

The *Editor & Publisher International Year Book* lists 180 newspaper associations, ranging from the American Agricultural Editors' Association to the United States Basketball Writers Association. That's only in the section covering national and international groups. Those based on geography—the state, regional and city groups—double that number.

For the student, the working newspaper person, the scholar, and the others interested in the press, this plethora of associations has significance. To put it simply, there is a newspaper association near you. Furthermore, although not as geographically widespread, there is a newspaper association to match your specific interests. You're a photojournalist? Contact the National Press Photographers Association in Durham, North Carolina. You want to join a burgeoning writing field in this age of technology? Ask the Council for the Advancement of Science Writing in Oak Park, Illinois.

If your interests are broader, then the "giants" of the newspaper associations can help. These include the American Newspaper Publishers Association (ANPA) and the National Newspaper Association (NNA), both in Washington, D.C.

Canadian residents will find counterparts to these groups in the Canadian Daily Newspaper Publishers Association (CDNPA) and the Canadian Community Newspapers Association (CCNA), both in Toronto.

Those interested in the community journalism field will find the NNA in the United States and the CCNA in Canada the best sources of information and assistance.

Most associations function to serve the interests of their members; newspaper groups present no startling change from this pattern. At state, regional, and national levels, the newspaper associations collect and disseminate information to and about members, usually conduct a program of legislative relations, provide in-service training for professionals, and encourage and assist student journalists in a variety of ways.

Community dailies and weeklies are the dominant members of state press associations and most national organizations. Latest data on U.S. newspapers lists more than 1,700 daily newspapers and 7,600 of less than daily frequency (predominantly weeklies).

In at least two states—New York and Utah—the *only* members of state press associations are weekly newspapers. The dailies in these states have their own organizations.

This should not be surprising, based on the nature and functions of press associations. A major reason for the existence of any association is to bring the benefits of size to a large group of smaller members. Newspaper associations do this.

A national group, such as the National Newspaper Association, can speak with one voice to Congress on behalf of members, whether the issue is access to information or a postal regulation affecting circulation. State newspaper associations can do the same in state capitals.

A spokesman for the South Carolina Press Association summed it up: "The biggest benefit of the Association is to smaller papers. They can do things cooperatively that they couldn't do individually." A representative of the Oregon Newspaper Publishers Association said it shorter: "The Association provides collective clout."

State Press Associations

State press associations serve a variety of functions for their membership. In addition to legislative relations on a full- or part-time basis, the associations hold one or, more often, two conventions or conferences each year, publish some form of newsletter, sponsor or encourage seminars on all aspects of the newspaper business, and serve as a clearinghouse for newspaper-related information in their states.

Conducting legislative relations is both a lobbying and information effort. Most state associations monitor pending bills which could affect newspapers and pass the information to members.

But the legislative role for state associations usually is more active. Like other interest groups, newspapers see a need to initiate legislation on behalf of their readers or for business reasons. For example, a check at this time shows that the Alabama Press Association is involved in strengthening its state open meetings law, while the Arizona Newspapers Association feels its state "has one of the best open meetings law." In Arizona, the emphasis is on passing a bill banning search warrants for newspaper offices and substituting use of subpoenas.

Business interests are the focus in Arkansas, where the battle is against an attempt to tax advertising, and the Colorado Press Association is concerned about legislation regarding legal publications. In Minnesota, the issue is a definition of "legal newspaper," related to free-distribution publications.

The staff used for this legislative effort ranges from all-volunteers in some states to the state press association manager plus volunteers to a paid lobbyist or use of a law firm on retainer basis. In at least one state, a retired publisher shoulders the load in the legislative halls.

Conventions by the state associations serve to bring legislative and other problems to the membership. The meetings, which usually combine business and social aspects, are actually

FIGURE 27-1 Education and training of members has become an important function of state press associations. In this Minnesota Newspaper Association seminar, participants are shown how to make effective advertising presentations. More than one hundred newspaper employees have completed the seminar. *Reprinted with permission of Minnesota Newspaper Association.*

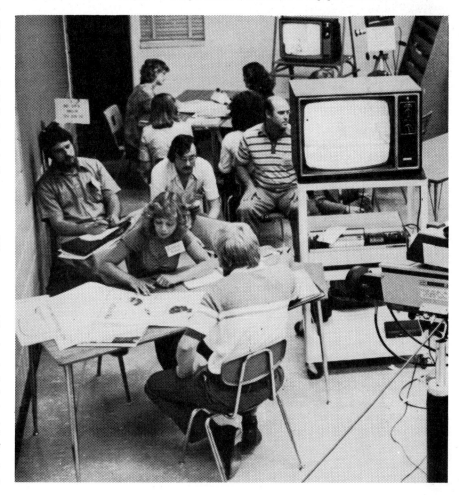

FIGURE 27–2 This seminar, entitled "Improving Your Small Newspaper," was one of twelve held at the Pennsylvania Newspaper Press Association Press Center by the PNPA Foundation. Others dealt with circulation, advertising, reporting, and postal problems. *Reprinted with permission of PNPA Foundation.*

a primary communication device for the associations. Here the association, as a united interest group, lays its plans for its activities, conducts some in-service programs on topics ranging from newspaper design to circulation campaigns, perhaps decides its target issue or issues for an upcoming legislative session, and sets its efforts to assist education.

In addition to seminars and workshops for members, the state press associations generally feel responsibility for prospective members of the profession. This is more than a general feeling that journalism education should be helped; the associations take direct action on specific assistance programs.

More than half of the state groups funnel scholarship support to journalism schools or departments. More than half also have some type of arrangement to provide working professionals as guest lecturers or workshop participants in journalism classrooms.

The state associations—again more than 50 percent of them—provide educational materials to journalism programs as well as to active members. To assist both members and journalism graduates, approximately 90 percent of the state associations operate some type of job service, either formally or informally.

The one area of educational support which ranks low among the state associations is internship programs.

Only about 20 percent of the state groups handle internships through the association office. This may be explained by a tendency for newspapers to handle their own internships or to cooperate in a national program, such as those arranged through the Newspaper Fund.

State press associations can be seen as a whole group through these general observations of functions and activities. However, exploring the operations of four such associations in more detail would provide a better "feel" for the groups. In addition to those which follow, the reader should talk to representatives of his or her own state press association.

OKLAHOMA PRESS ASSOCIATION

Founded in 1888 as the Indian Territory Press Association, this organization serves 51 daily newspapers and 193 weeklies. One of the most active press groups in the nation, OPA is owned and controlled by its newspaper membership through a board of directors and has a full-time staff of twenty.

The OPA assists journalism education through the Oklahoma Newspaper Foundation, established in 1964. The Foundation's main job is to improve journalism education at both college and high school levels. Scholarship aid has assisted students seeking

advanced college degrees, while the ONF also has provided equipment for journalism programs. The OPA itself provides filmstrips on news, advertising, circulation, and printing careers to high schools and colleges and fills speaker requests for school Career Days.

Member services include monthly or more frequent bulletins on a variety of topics, from new rulings and interpretations of state and federal law to placement service notices. The *Oklahoma Publisher,* a tabloid-size newspaper, has been printed monthly since 1930 as a trade journal for the state's newspapers.

In addition, the OPA conducts a heavy schedule of meetings designed to improve newspapers. Two conventions each year are supplemented by a News Clinic each spring, an Advertising Clinic each fall and a Circulation Clinic in early winter. Short courses are offered in news writing, advertising copy, layout, and selling. Workshops are held on editorial writing, photography, classified advertising, newspaper bookkeeping, newspaper design, and supervisory skills.

Another OPA program is the Capitol News Bureau, a cooperative venture covering state government. University journalism students work with experienced newspersons to cover politics and government. The OPA executive vice president and manager also writes a weekly column, "Capitol Spotlight," during legislative sessions. Capitol News Bureau stories go to all members, and the manager's column also is available. For sixteen years the OPA has compiled a legislative directory and for twenty-six years has conducted a monthly column-writing and editorial contest. Its annual Better Newspaper Contest dates back to 1928.

Through its affiliate, the Oklahoma Press Service, advertising sales and services are provided, as are a variety of public relations activities, including news release mailing and the state's only clipping service.

The OPA's set of bylaws sums up the reason for the group's existence: "The purposes of this Association shall be educational and to safeguard and advance the newspaper profession in the State of Oklahoma, so that both the profession and the public may benefit."

A similar purpose is repeated, either directly or by implication, in the work of all newspaper associations, state, regional, and national.

MAINE PRESS ASSOCIATION

Based at the University of Maine at Orono, the Maine Press Association has 38 members—7 daily newspapers and 31 weeklies. Its membership includes all but nine of Maine's newspapers.

Although one of the smaller state newspaper associations, the Maine organization's three full-time staff members provide a typical range of services.

Included among these is an ethics committee which investigates allegations of unethical practices by members. An example within the membership involved the alleged use of a photograph by a daily which a weekly paper claimed as its property.

The MPA maintains a legislative relations program, communicating information on bills through the *MPA Bulletin,* the association's monthly publication. The *Bulletin* also provides communication on placement for members.

Other services include an annual Better Newspaper Contest, a scholarship fund, and two meetings per year.

Membership requirements in the organization are in two classes. (Most state press associations have two or more categories for membership.) Voting memberships, carrying the privilege of holding office, are usually reserved for what the MPA calls *active members.* In Maine, active members are those newspapers which hold a second-class mailing permit, are qualified to accept legal advertising, and charge a subscription price. As in most other states, active membership dues to the MPA are based on total circulation and advertising rates. *Associate members,* including individuals and firms furnishing materials and equipment to Maine newspapers, pay flat annual dues.

OHIO NEWSPAPER ASSOCIATION

In 1933, Ohio's daily and weekly newspapers joined together to form the Ohio Newspaper Association, which now represents 294 members out of the state's total 347 papers—94 dailies and 200 weeklies.

William J. Oertel, ONA executive director and secretary, has thirty-seven years' experience in association management. His views on newspaper associations come close to summing up the varied services and functions. Oertel says, "My view is that education is a key project area for most associations. Most of what we do is to educate someone in some way to know more through newspapers, about newspa-

---

Founding Dates of Press Associations

by George Speers, General Manager, New England Press Association, Boston

Alabama Press Association	1871	Michigan Press Association	1867
Allied Daily Newspapers (Washington State)	1935	Minnesota Newspaper Association	1867
American Newspaper Publishers Association	1887	Mississippi Press Association	1866
American Newspaper Representatives	1952	Missouri Press Association	1867
Arizona Newspapers Association	1930	Montana Press Association	1885
Arkansas Press Association	1873	National Newspaper Association	1885
California Newspaper Publishers Association	1972	National Newspaper Publishers Association	1940
Canadian Community Newspaper Publishers Association	1919	Nebraska Press Association	1873
Canadian Daily Newspaper Publishers Association	1920	Nevada State Press Association	1924
Colorado Press Association	1878	New England Press Association	1930
Florida Press Association	1879	New Jersey Press Association	1857
Georgia Press Association	1887	New Mexico Press Association	1908
Hoosier State Press Association	1933	New York Press Association	1853
Idaho Newspaper Association	1890	New York State Publishers Association	1921
Illinois Press Association	1866	North Carolina Press Association	1873
Inland Daily Press Association	1885	North Dakota Press Association	1886
Iowa Press Association	1915	Ohio Newspaper Association	1933
Kansas Press Association	1865	Oklahoma Press Association	1888
Kentucky Press Association	1869	Oregon Newspaper Publishers Association	1937
Louisiana Press Association	1880	Pennsylvania Newspaper Publishers Association	1925
Maine Press Association	1864	Publishers Bureau of New Jersey	1941
Maryland–Delaware–D.C. Press Association	1909	South Carolina Press Association	1875
Massachusetts Newspaper Publishers Association	1973	South Dakota Press Association	1882
Massachusetts Press Association	1869	Southern Newspaper Publishers Association	1903
		Suburban Newspapers of America	1971
		Tennessee Press Association	1869
		Texas Press Association	1880
		Utah Press Association	1897
		Virginia Press Association	1881
		Wisconsin Press Association	1853
		Washington Newspaper Publishers Association	1887
		West Virginia Press Association	1953

Compiled in 1980 from information obtained from association managers and other officials.

pers, or to be helped by newspapers."

In its summary of services, the ONA provides its members with a comprehensive list of activities. These include a general bulletin, special publications on legislation, surveys, and research, and a monthly *Bulletin of Business Research*. The ONA works to encourage use of newspapers in classrooms, operates a placement service, aids journalists at the high school and college levels, publishes a directory of Ohio newspapers, and publishes supplements to the *Ohio Newspaper and Publications Law* it originally published in 1954.

The association operates with six full-time staff members to provide this range of services. Oertel notes that the ONA has pioneered some programs, including a National Essay Contest on the topic "What the First Amendment Means to Me." It also conducted a series of Free Press/Free Enterprise Workshops for high school and college students and adults.

NEW YORK PRESS ASSOCIATION

It was 1853 and the linotype wouldn't cast its first slug for about thirty years. In Elmira, a meeting of thirty-two New York publishers formed the Western New York Typographical Association. By 1865 membership was state-wide and the name became the New York Press Association.

Then in 1921, the state's daily newspapers decided to form their own press association. The NYPA devoted itself exclusively to community journalism.

The association's three full-time staff members serve 220 newspapers in the state, performing a variety of functions. The NYPA publishes a biweekly bulletin, which includes free classifieds for placement and for new or used equipment, plus newspaper-related facts and issues. Its central office monitors the state legislature in Albany, alerts members, and prepares memoranda in support of or in opposition to specific bills. It may also initiate letter, telephone, or telegram campaigns to support or oppose legislation. In ad-

dition, the association arranges graphic arts supplies, purchasing discounts, and low-cost insurance programs for members and sponsors a collection service for delinquent accounts.

As with many state press groups, the NYPA's affiliated New York Press Service offers advertisers an easy one-bill, one-check service for access to the pages of members. Also like some other state associations, the NYPA is affiliated with American Newspaper Representatives, the ad sales arm of the National Newspaper Association.

National Associations and Others

The number of newspaper organizations is large. Many are based on some comparatively narrow special interests, ranging from music (Music Critics Association) to travel (Society of American Travel Writers). The following associations were selected for brief description because of their general nature and their relationship with hometown newspapers in the United States.

NATIONAL NEWSPAPER ASSOCIATION

This organization is one of the largest press groups in the nation with direct ties to community newspapers. A large number of the state press associations are affiliated with the NNA, either through a voluntary state and national dues arrangement or through American Newspaper Representatives, the NNA national advertising organization, or both.

The NNA approach is "grassroots" in nature. The association's base is a membership of more than 6,000 weekly and daily newspapers. The weeklies predominate.

The association publishes the widely read *Publishers' Auxiliary,* with circulation reaching beyond membership to government representatives, national advertisers, journalism educa-

tors, students, and the general public. NNA services also include an active government relations program, including representation before Congress and federal departments and agencies. The association has also sponsored government affairs conferences, bringing together government leaders and community press representatives. It also organizes an annual convention and trade show, an annual contest aimed at improving community newspapers, information files on newspaper topics, research and publications on federal laws and regulations related to newspapers, and cooperation with other newspaper organizations.

The NNA is committed to education through its National Newspaper Foundation, which conducts a variety of programs, including the sponsorship of this book.

AMERICAN NEWSPAPER PUBLISHERS ASSOCIATION

This organization carries on a broad range of activities to serve the newspaper business and its members.

In the past, the ANPA has focused on research into newspaper readership habits and how to help editors apply this research to regular editing. It has joined with the NNA to monitor U.S. Postal Service actions.

The ANPA is continually active in domestic and international protection of press freedoms, monitoring government and private business actions related to newspapers and providing information to members and the public through a variety of publications.

The association's concern for education can be seen in its efforts through the ANPA Foundation. In addition to seeking to develop informed, intelligent readers and strengthen public understanding of the press, the Foundation aims to advance the professionalism of the press.

One of the newest additions to the ANPA list of functions and services is the monthly magazine, *presstime.* The publication's contents range across the newspaper spectrum, from postal affairs to computerizing newspaper libraries.

INLAND DAILY PRESS ASSOCIATION

Located in Chicago, the IDPA is the oldest and largest regional daily press association in the nation, with 570 members in twenty states and Canada. It was founded in 1885.

The IDPA is known most widely for its costs and revenue studies, wage and salary surveys, and educational programs for management. Other projects include an educational foundation to sponsor mid-career training programs, advertising comparison reports, personnel services, and information bulletins.

SOUTHERN NEWSPAPER PUBLISHERS ASSOCIATION, INC.

The SNPA is an organization of daily newspapers in fourteen states from the Midwest to the East Coast. Organized in 1903, it has more than 450 members and more than seventy associate members. Headquarters are in Atlanta.

The SNPA's basic function is to provide information to its newspaper members, largely through its widely circulated *SNPA Bulletin.* The organization holds meetings that cover a wide range of subjects, but it is probably best known for its work in personnel and labor relations. The SNPA Foundation also conducts seminars for news and editorial personnel. Almost half of the SNPA's members have circulations of less than 15,000, and a third of them less than 10,000.

NATIONAL NEWSPAPER PUBLISHERS ASSOCIATION

Founded in 1940, the NNPA was created to serve black publishers and editors. It devotes much of its efforts to problems relating to circulation, advertising, readership, and personnel. The NNPA is discussed further in Chapter 21, "The Minority Press."

INTERNATIONAL SOCIETY OF WEEKLY NEWSPAPER EDITORS

Amid the giants of the newspaper association field, the ISWNE is a smaller group dedicated solely to the improvement of editorial content and editorial pages in the community press. Founded in 1954, the society's programs include an annual conference designed to confront major issues which could be suitable community-press editorial-page topics. The conference also involves a dedicated group of editors in a detailed critique of their own editorial pages. The ISWNE publishes a quarterly magazine, *Grassroots Editor,* designed for the weekly press. The society also publishes a monthly newsletter. Membership comprises newspaper professionals in the United States, Canada, and many overseas nations. Each year the ISWNE brings a young editor from Great Britain to its conference and sponsors a young American editor as well. The group also conducts the annual (since 1961) Golden Quill Award contest, in recognition of outstanding editorial and opinion writing, and the Eugene Cervi Award (since 1976), honoring an editor for a career of public service in community journalism.

Conclusions

These are the newspaper associations. Their geographical locations are widespread, but their goals and their reasons for existence are similar. In one form or another and with varying levels of activity, each of the associations seeks to:

- Make newspaper professionals more effective by having them work together toward common goals

- Provide channels for communication for information and education to improve the profession

- Lend assistance to the prospective journalist through aid to students and teachers in colleges and schools

- Give the profession a "one voice" effect, larger than possible by individuals or single newspapers, in dealing with all levels of government and with the public

Newspaper associations were created to serve functions common to many other organizations in the United States. The associations communicate, give continuing education to members, provide career information and educational assistance to future professionals, and strive to improve their profession.

Any one of these functions would be reason enough to join one or more associations in journalism. Taken together, these functions and goals make newspaper association membership by students and working newspaper persons an individual and a professional obligation.

Chapter 28

D. EARL NEWSOM

D. Earl Newsom has been associated with seven newspapers—from small weeklies to metropolitan dailies—as reporter, copy editor, editor, manager, and advertising manager. He was professor of journalism at the University of Maryland for twenty years. He has designed and directed many training courses for newspaper associations and has served many individual newspapers on a consulting basis. His column, "Ideas for Publishers," appears in *Publishers' Auxiliary.*

"It may be that by the turn of the twenty-first century, we will not recognize the industry as we now know it, but underneath the new exterior will be this thread of continuity, exemplified by the same exciting way of life and the special breed that wants no other way."

Things to Remember— for Today and Tomorrow

by D. Earl Newsom

The preceding chapters probably contain the most information about the newspaper business ever put together in a single volume. The importance of each of these chapters illustrates how complex newspaper life has become, whether on large dailies or small weeklies.

Dailies are caught in the throes of change in technology, labor relations, the encroachment of competition from other media, decisions on whether to publish morning or afternoon editions or both, and how to build readership.

In bygone days, the hardened metropolitan-daily journalist could look forward to the dream of eventually "relaxing on a country weekly." There is little hope of that today. Few community publishers spend their time in quiet relaxation. Instead, they, too, are in the midst of a struggle to stay abreast in technology, promotion, circulation, and learning about laws relating to antitrust, libel, and even labor relations. It is difficult in the newspaper world today to find a place where an individual may rest, reflect, or meditate for any length of time.

Of the material presented by the authors in this text that can help solve some of these problems, certain ideas and facts are more basic than others and should be noted by students and experienced professionals alike. They represent areas that have sometimes been misunderstood or neglected. The publisher may find that if basic functions are handled well and fundamentals of the business are kept in mind, some of the more complex problems may never arise. A number of these are detailed here.

Clear Writing Is Still Vital

News is still the primary commodity of a newspaper. The quality of the content lifts the newspaper to a level above the shoppers, throwaways, even the electronic media. The success of all departments may depend on how well the newsroom does its job. But editorial content of the highest quality may lose its relevance if the message or story cannot be grasped quickly by the audience. There is a need for clarity in writing in all newspapers, large and small. A buried lead or an unclear story often results in a dull headline. This in turn can result in low readership of the story, and all resources invested in the effort are wasted.

Even experienced reporters and editors will profit by reviewing Chapters 3 and 4 on writing and news headlines. If scientific reader surveys reveal news or editorial readership problems, the publisher should be aware that ponderous or poorly organized writing may be a major cause.

Market Data Needed

The dramatic social, economic, and technological changes have had great impact on the advertising operations of both dailies and weeklies. Today, metropolitan dailies, television stations, radio stations, magazines, shoppers, and other media claim the market that was once the almost exclusive territory of the isolated small-town newspaper. There is severe competition for national and co-op dollars that once came routinely to the small paper. The local retailer's file may be crammed with market data showing how each of these media can reach this market with advertising. Often the one item missing from the file is the market data from the local newspaper, for many have not gathered valid information to challenge that of the "intruders."

Today even the small newspapers must become systematic and scientific in gathering market information and in keeping it up-to-date. The presentation of this material can be elaborate or simple, but it should be in a form easily understood by potential advertisers. From this information, the newspaper advertising staff and publisher should consider effective promotion campaigns. Chapters 11 and 13 offer guidance on how to gather information and how to use it in promotion.

Many newspapers are losing co-op advertising revenue largely through default. Each newspaper should have a system for checking local advertising accounts for co-op potential and for follow-through on each account.

Selling Becomes Sophisticated

The above factors have made the selling of newspaper local retail advertising much more sophisticated than in the past. Advertising representatives must organize their work and their time. They must plan sales calls carefully and be armed with suggested layouts, market data, readership information, or any other material that will bring about a sale. Each must show convincingly why his newspaper is the most effective medium in the market. Each must be able to help clients in preparing copy that will sell and in designing effective layouts.

At least as important as these factors is the need for an advertising representative to be able to counsel clients on how and when to invest their advertising funds. It has been estimated that as much as 80 percent of advertising funds may be wasted because of inadequate copy, lack of proper budgeting, or poor timing. Chapter 10 can be of great help to advertising people as they show retailers how much they should invest in advertising and how to allocate these funds by department and by monthly periods. The copy fundamentals in Chapter 15 can improve the content of your ads.

Departments Must Coordinate

In the midst of changes occurring in the media, circulation development must have high management priority if the newspaper is to compete with those that seek to move into its territory—the shopper publications, voluntary-pay newspapers, free-distribution newspapers, and even electronic media.

The newspaper must succeed in developing circulation primarily in its trade area. To achieve this, the advertising, news, and circulation departments of every newspaper must coordinate their efforts to serve the reader. Circulation success may depend on the news content, and advertising success will depend on how well circulation is covering the immediate trade area. Only a coordinated effort accompanied by adequate promotion can bring success. How well the newspaper covers the area with local news, features, and pictures plays an important role in this effort.

Management Faces Problems

In addition to directing and sometimes handling the preceding functions, newspaper management today must be concerned with many other facets of the business that require specialized knowledge.

Every newspaper needs a record-keeping system that permits management to pinpoint accurately income, expenses, profit or loss, return on investment, depreciation, and net worth. Management should have at its fingertips comparative figures for this year and previous years or the current month's income and expenses versus the previous month. An accountant who specializes in newspaper accounting is highly desirable. The system should also permit management to compare its costs and revenues with those of similar newspapers.

Management today must have some familiarity with laws dealing with personnel, postal problems, antitrust, libel, and labor relations.

In personnel, there are federal laws and sometimes state laws that affect everything from job interviewing to firing people. The personnel matter has become so complex that even smaller newspapers have set up personnel departments or at least have one individual assigned to personnel functions. Urgent attention is being given to planned programs to communicate with personnel. Failure to employ enlightened personnel practices can result in complex labor relations problems.

A newspaper publisher may face competition from a shopper, or he may decide to start a shopper. In either case, a knowledge of antitrust laws has become very important.

Libel laws have become more confusing, especially with the uncertainty over the definition of "public figure." It is not unusual for libel actions to involve millions of dollars. Management may find its best safeguard is fair and accurate reporting, with special procedures instituted to handle investigative stories.

An area in which newspapers are improving but still lacking is in local editorials and editorial pages. Many smaller newspapers have none at all. Others have editorial pages, some of them very attractive, but no local editorials. Readers place a high value on local editorials and expect them. As Paul Greenberg, author of Chapter 5, says, "A newspaper without editorials is like a day without sunshine. . . . Editorials give a newspaper a character of its own apart from the news it reports." Larger dailies should analyze the readability of their editorials.

Management must stay abreast of technology. Changes are so rapid that equipment may become obsolete between the time it is ordered and the time it is installed. Yet the newspaper that fails to keep abreast may fall behind in production and quality. Should I change? What should I buy? When should I buy it? These and other questions will be problems for management for many years.

Newspaper Careers Are Rewarding

All of these problems and challenges may give the impression that the newspaper is not an attractive place for a career or business venture, but such is not the case. Yet questions must surely arise: How can one cope with all the problems? Can one enjoy life in the midst of such pressures and changes?

Actually, newspapers have thrived on complexities and changes. Evidence of this are the net profit figures discussed in Chapter 17 and the value of newspaper properties discussed in Chapter 26. Some metro dailies have looked enviously at community newspapers and have sought to diversify by investing in them. The opportunities in community journalism have attracted men and women of outstanding business ability to management positions. This in turn has resulted in better equipment, better methods, and high-quality personnel.

Life on small newspapers has become more difficult for those who have been slow to adapt to modern methods and marketing techniques, but for the most part, the small-town newspaper is a coveted business.

Newspaper people have found answers to many of their problems by attacking them mutually through their associations. As Irvan J. Kummerfeldt states in Chapter 27, newspaper people are a gregarious lot. They flock to conventions of their state press associations, regional associations, and national associations such as the NNA and the ANPA. The associations have responded well to the challenges and are rendering great service to their members in technology, marketing, industry, and news presentation. The dedicated newspaper person may also be a dedicated association person. More often than not, the most successful newspaper managers are also leaders in the newspaper associations.

Apart from the help they render in technology and business, the associations also provide activities that offer relief from the tensions and pressures of daily life. They provide entertainment programs, travel abroad, social gatherings and other types of activities for members and their families. Newspaper management people generally seem happy with their choice of a life's work.

FREEDOM FROM BOREDOM

Newspapers also have attractions for news and advertising people. One factor that attracts people to newspaper work is the freedom from the boredom that prevails in some occupations. This is as true on a small daily or weekly as on a larger newspaper. Each day may begin as any other day, but few days end the same, and rarely are any two days alike. The unforeseen and the unpredictable one encounters daily have a great appeal to this particular breed, a greater appeal to many even than financial rewards. Newspaper employees with long periods of service often have difficulty adjusting to other types of work because of this factor.

The community newspaper will have a special appeal for many beginners. Salaries have improved, and

newspaper people can live for less in the nonmetropolitan areas. The small-town atmosphere, lower costs, and reduced traffic appeal to many.

Newspaper Ownership Difficult

At the same time, opportunities for ownership of newspapers have greatly diminished. It is virtually impossible at this writing for a young journalist to bid successfully against a chain or metropolitan daily for purchase of an established newspaper in an established market. The costs are astronomical. Perhaps the most disturbing trend in the community field is the acquisition of newspapers by chains and the resultant absentee ownership, although this trend has created opportunities in newspaper management and advertising for those who have the ability and interest.

Some enterprising individuals have become publishers through finding a market not fully developed and hanging on with a marginal publication until the market became adequate to support the newspaper. Advances in technology have made it possible for them to do their own production and take camera-ready pages to a central plant. Others have sought entry into the publishing field by starting a free publication and challenging an existing newspaper. This is difficult because it requires considerable financial reserves just to survive. Since these publications are business ventures rather than journalistic publications, they have little appeal to university graduates who want to be reporters and editors.

How to Meet Tomorrow's Challenges

There are predictions galore about the future of the newspaper—of plateless presses, voice-activated typesetting machines, new uses of computers and lasers, marvels *ad infinitum.* Many of these may well materialize, along with others still not on the drawing board.

William C. Rogers, Sr., publisher of the Swainsboro (Ga.) *Forest Blade,* and 1979–80 president of the National Newspaper Association, believes that along with the starry-eyed predictions in technology are earthly problems that will face newspapers in the last two decades of the twentieth century. He sees the following as major issues for newspapers:

- Competition from new types of electronic media, especially cable television with its potential for competing for local news and local advertising, heretofore the exclusive turf of the local newspaper

- Continuing attacks on the protections afforded to all citizens by the First Amendment by the courts, the police, and legislators, coupled with a lack of public understanding and appreciation of the importance of these guarantees to each person

- The decreasing number of reading Americans who value the printed word and rely on traditional print media for news, information, and entertainment

- The constant financial problems of matching revenues to expenses for salaries and fringe benefits, equipment purchases, fuel, newsprint, and all other escalating costs associated with the publishing, printing, and distribution of newspapers and with finding and keeping dedicated, high-quality people

- Availability of materials at any price, as government regulations and costs of production impinge even further on those who produce newsprint, inks, and fuels.

Even in the face of all of these problems, however, Rogers maintains a basic optimism about the future of newspapers. He predicts that with effective management, dedicated news coverage, and creative advertising, newspapers will be able to meet successfully the coming challenges.

Some Things Won't Change

In view of the changes predicted for the future, one may ask whether so much information about the newspaper business as is included in this volume can remain relevant over a period of time.

The author recalls more than forty years ago a stern lecture from a judge who was described after an interview as "gray-heeled" instead of "gray-haired." In answering the question about his courtroom staff, he was quoted as saying that working for him was a "pretty dim" proposition. Who at age sixteen should be expected to have heard of such words as *per diem*?

"Age is no excuse for errors," the judge said. "Reporters ought to double-check everything they write and then someone else ought to check it, too. If they don't know what a word means, they ought to ask someone who does. Every error you print can hurt somebody and embarrass your newspaper."

Then mellowing somewhat, he picked a dusty book from a shelf and added, "I can see you are determined to be a newspaperman, so let me show you this as something to guide you." In an 1804 court decision, he had underlined the words, "truth published with good motives and for justifiable ends."

Comments similar to those of forty years ago appear in this book today, as does the quotation about truth. They will probably be relevant forty years hence.

Those who were in the newspaper business forty years ago can read the Rogers outlook for the future and realize that these problems were in the future for that era, too. And if someone forty years hence dares to undertake a volume of this magnitude, that individual may find the newspaper people of that generation, the news and advertising they create, and the problems they face strikingly similar to those of today. The information herein may well be highly relevant, for in spite of changes in technology, there is a certain consistency in some of the more important aspects of newspaper life and the people who are dedicated to it.

It may be that by the turn of the twenty-first century, we will not recognize the industry as we have known it, but underneath the new exterior will probably be this thread of continuity, exemplified by the same exciting way of life and the special breed that wants no other way. In this respect, perhaps more than any other, the past is indeed prologue for the newspaper.

Glossary

ABC. Audit Bureau of Circulation. A firm that audits and certifies newspaper circulations.

AGATE. The agate line is one column wide and approximately five and one half points deep. It is often used for classified pages and is the unit of measurement advertising agencies use to order newspaper space.

AIR. A colloquial expression used to describe white space around type or other elements.

ASCENDER. That part of a lowercase letter which projects into the top of the body of the type.

ATTRIBUTION. The source of statements in news copy. All quotations should be attributed to someone.

ART. Any illustration that accompanies printed material.

BALANCE SHEET. Financial statement that shows a firm's assets, liabilities, and net worth.

BANNER. A large headline, usually extending across the top of page one.

BENDAY. A shading medium often used to provide background on line artwork.

BLEED. An illustration that extends to the edge of a page.

BODY TYPE. Type used to set masses of copy. In newspapers, body type is usually 8-point or 9-point size.

BOX. News story or other printed material enclosed in rules.

BULLETS. Dots used as typographical ornaments, usually to give emphasis to items in advertising or news copy.

C&lc. Used in printing markup on copy, headlines, and proofs to specify that the first letter of each word is to be set in capital letters.

CAPTION. In newspapers, this word usually refers to cutlines, or text under pictures. It is also sometimes used to describe display lines above art.

CATCHLINE. Display line between cut and cutlines.

COLUMN INCH. One column wide and one inch deep. Often used to designate newspaper advertisement dimensions.

COLUMN RULE. Thin vertical rule between columns of news. Most newspapers have eliminated them.

COMMON SUPPLEMENT. Also called common section. One newspaper section included in a group of newspapers, making possible a lower advertising rate than if each participating newspaper printed the section separately.

CONTROLLED CIRCULATION. A special postal rate class for publications that do not qualify for second-class permits. Usually, these are publications going to members of an organization or specialized group. Subscriptions may be free or paid. Most newspapers would not be eligible for this class, although some shoppers could find it advantageous.

CO-OP ADVERTISING. Retailers share with manufacturers or distributors the cost of advertising a product in media.

COPY. Written material to be reproduced: news copy, ad copy, etc.

COPY EDITOR. Person who checks, corrects, and marks copy to be printed.

CREDIT LINE. Name of photographer or source, usually placed under newspaper pictures or at the end of cutlines.

CROP. Marking photographs to get rid of unwanted areas when they are reproduced for publication.

CUT. Used loosely to refer to any art, line or halftone, that appears in printed material.

CUTLINES. Text under a picture.

DATELINE. A line at the beginning of a news story indicating where it originated and sometimes the date.

DESCENDER. That part of a lower case letter which descends below the baseline.

DOWNSTYLE. In headlines, capitalizing only the first word and proper nouns. In news style, a tendency to capitalize fewer words.

DUMMY. A guide prepared by editors showing where to place headlines, news stories, pictures, and other elements on the printed page.

EAR. Printed matter or art placed on either side of the nameplate in a newspaper.

EM, EN. Printing measurements. An em is a square of the type size being used. A 10-point em, for instance, is 10 points wide and 10 points deep. An en is half as wide as an em. Paragraphs are often indented one en.

EYEBROW. See Kicker.

FLAG. Nameplate.

FLAT. Page-size sheet on which art and type are pasted to make a camera-ready page.

FOG. A term used to describe excess verbiage or ponderous wording of news copy that makes it hard to understand.

FOLIO. In newspaper terminology, a line, usually at the top of each page, that states the date of issue, page number, and name of publication.

FORMAT. Usually designates the style or size of a publication: 8-column format, tabloid format, etc.

F.Y.I For your information.

GUTTER. The inside margin of a page at the binding.

HALFTONE. A printing plate made of a photograph or other continuous-tone art in which a special screen with crisscrossing lines is placed between the art and the film. The photograph that appears in print is thus broken up into small dots.

HAMMER. Large one-line head placed over a smaller head.

HEADLINE SCHEDULE. A printed sheet or paste-up of a newspaper's headlines from smallest to largest size, showing per-column count of each size.

INVERTED PYRAMID. News writing style in which major facts are given first to summarize the story, and minor facts are placed near the end.

ITALIC. Type that slants to the right.

JIM DASH. A dash used between decks of a headline. Most newspapers have eliminated jim dashes.

JUMP. To continue a news story from one page to another. The continued portion is also referred to as a jump.

JUSTIFY. To space out a line to make it flush at the right margin. Unjustified (uneven) lines are called "ragged."

KICKER. Smaller one-line head above and to the left of a main headline. Also called "eyebrow" or "overline."

KILL. To destroy news or advertising matter so that it will not be used.

LEAD. (Pronounced "leed.") Usually refers to the first paragraph of a news story. Sometimes used to refer to a news tip.

LEADING. (Pronounced "ledding.") White space between the lines of type. Once done manually by inserting thin metal strips between lines, most leading is now done automatically. Also called "line-spacing."

LEGIBILITY. The degree to which printed characters can be recognized with ease.

LETTERPRESS. Printing from a raised surface such as a piece of metal type. Newspapers used the letterpress process with hot metal typesetting machines until the switch to offset in recent years.

LINE CUT. Printing plate consisting of only black or white areas reproduced without the use of a halftone screen. Line art from which the plate is made may be pen and ink drawings, charcoal drawing, or type.

LOWERCASE. Small letters of the alphabet, as opposed to capitals.

MAKEUP. Arrangement of headlines, text, art, and other elements on the page.

MORTISE. To cut out part of a picture, either on the inside or on the edge, in order to insert type or other art.

NAMEPLATE. The name of a newspaper, usually a logotype, as it appears on page one.

NATIONAL ADVERTISING. Usually for a product that has national or regional distribution, on which an advertising agency commission may be paid.

NONPAREIL. 6-point type or spacing.

OCR. Optical character reader. See Scanner.

OFFSET. A printing process in which an image is transferred from the plate cylinder to a second cylinder and then onto the paper. An outgrowth of lithography, offset prints from a flat plate as opposed to the raised surface of letterpress printing.

OP-ED. The page opposite the editorial page.

OPERATING STATEMENT. Shows income, expenses, and profit or loss for a given period. Also called profit-and-loss statement.

OVERLINE. See Kicker.

OVERSET. News copy set in type but not used.

PAD. To include extraneous or superfluous words in a news story just to make it longer.

PARTIAL QUOTE. A few words but less than a complete sentence in quotation marks.

PENNY SAVER. A free publication; a shopper, containing largely advertising.

PHOTOCOMPOSITION. High-speed typesetting process in which letters are photographed, rather than typed directly on the paper or set in metal type as in letterpress.

PICA. A printing measurement, 12 points in size.

PMT. Art reproduced through a photomechanical transfer process without use of a negative. In newspaper production, the process is used to produce screened positive prints that can be pasted up on flats with line copy, and to reproduce line art for advertising illustrations. (See Chapter 9).

POINT. The basic unit of measurement in printing. There are 72 points to an inch. Type sizes are specified in points.

PROCESS COLOR. Use of a halftone screen and filters to reproduce color artwork with continuous tone, such as color photos or paintings.

PROFIT-AND-LOSS STATEMENT. See Operating Statement.

RACE. Broadest classification of type into romans, sans serifs, square serifs, etc.

RAGGED RIGHT (OR LEFT). Lines of type set unevenly; that is, not aligned one under the other at the margin.

READABILITY. The degree to which copy can be read with ease.

REGISTER. Aligning plates properly on the press so the image is imprinted in the proper place on the printed sheet.

REPRO-PROOF. A high-quality proof suitable for use in the reproduction of a printed page.

REVERSE. Type reproduced so as to show white on black rather than black on white.

ROMAN. Used to specify type set "up-and-down" or regularly, as opposed to having it set in italics.

ROMAN. A class of type whose letters have serifs at the ends of the strokes. Roman typefaces include Bodoni, Garamond, Caslon, Century, and many others.

ROP. Run-of-paper. Advertising material in a newspaper that does not have preferred position. ROP color refers to color other than black applied to newsprint during the normal press run.

RUNAROUND. Type set at varying line lengths to fit around an illustration.

SANS SERIF. Type without serifs. A geometric type usually with heavy elements. Sometimes called gothic. Type families in the sans serif race include Tempo, Optima, Futura, Spartan, and Helvetica.

SCANNER. Also called an optical character reader. A machine that "reads" typewritten copy and transmits it to either a computer or a tape which is used to activate the typesetting machine.

SECOND-CLASS MAIL. A special rate lower than first or third class for publications of paid general circulation, including newspapers, made available in the interest of the public's right to be informed.

SHOPPER. A free publication whose primary purpose is the dissemination of advertising rather than news.

SLUG. Usually two or three words at the top of each page of a news story that tell the subject of the story.

SPEC LAYOUT. A suggested or sample advertising layout usually prepared as part of a sales presentation to an advertiser.

SPOT COLOR. The use of a color without blending it with other colors. A simple example would be printing a headline or a box in red.

SQUARE SERIF. A classification of type that resembles the sans serifs but with large rectangular serifs on the ends of the elements. Also called Egyptian types, block serifs, slab serifs.

STRAIGHT MATTER. Small type set in quantity, usually body type.

THUMBNAIL. A small picture, usually a half column wide.

TOMBSTONE. Headlines of the same size and type placed side by side.

UPPERCASE. Capital letter.

VDT. Video display terminal. Also called CRT or cathode-ray tube. Typesetting device in which the news story appears on a television-like screen as it is typed by the reporter on a keyboard below. Copy can be transmitted directly into a computer.

VOLUNTARY PAY. A circulation method in which newspapers are delivered to homes and the recipients may pay or not. Used mostly in suburban areas.

WIDOW. A short line at the end of a printed paragraph, sometimes only one word.

x-HEIGHT. The height of lower case letters without ascenders or descenders. Named for small x.

Bibliography

Chapter 1

American Newspaper Publishers Association. *Facts About Newspapers 1978.* Washington: May 1978.

Harvard Business School. "Note on the Newspaper Industry—Condensed." Cambridge, Mass.: Intercollegiate Case Clearing House, 1976.

SHAW, EUGENE F. "Newspaper Reading in Small Towns," address at University of Tennessee, Knoxville, June 9, 1978.

"Survey: What Happens to Results . . . It's Up to Newspapers!" *Nebraska Newspaper,* June 1978, pp. 1–3.

WHITE, WILLIAM ALLEN. Editorial, Emporia (Kansas) *Gazette,* July 27, 1922.

Chapter 2

BYERLY, KENNETH R. *Community Journalism.* Radnor, Pa.: Chilton, 1961.

DURKIN, MARY. Letter to author, July 1978.

MARTIN, HAROLD H. "He Works in God's Pastures." *Saturday Evening Post,* Dec. 13, 1958.

SMITH, DON J. Interview with author, July 1978.

Chapter 3

FOWLER, HENRY W. *A Dictionary of Modern English Usage,* 2nd ed. rev. (London: Oxford University Press, 1965.

HILLS, LEE. "Does Editorial Quality Make a Difference?" Speech, Atlanta, Ga., April 1974.

SPENCER, HERBERT. *A Philosophy of Style.* New York: D. Appleton and Company, 1972.

STRUNK, WILLIAM, JR., and E. B. WHITE. *The Elements of Style,* 3rd ed. New York: Macmillan, 1979.

Chapter 4

Associated Press Managing Editors. *Report on News Credibility.* New York: 1969, 1970.

Gannett Co., Inc. *Editorially Speaking,* Vol. 30, No. 11. Rochester: 1974.

Chapter 5

HOBBES, THOMAS. *Leviathan.* 1651.

LEHMAN, CHARLES. "Average Readership of Editorials Equals That of All Non-Ad Items," *News Research for Better Newspapers,* Vol. 7. Washington: American Newspaper Publishers Association, 1975.

MENCKEN, HENRY L. "Transcript of Remarks to the First Meeting of the National Conference of Editorial Writers." *The Masthead,* Spring 1968. Washington, D.C.

Pine Bluff (Ark.) *Commercial,* Nov. 23, 1978; Dec. 7, 1978; Dec. 21, 1978.

WHITE, ROBERT M., II. Letter to D. Earl Newsom, September 26, 1978.

Chapter 6

ARNOLD, EDMUND C. *Modern Newspaper Design.* New York: Harper & Row, Pub., 1969.

FOX, RODNEY, and ROBERT KERNS. *Creative News Photography.* Ames: Iowa State University Press, 1961.

KALISH, STANLEY E., and CLIFTON C. EDOM. *Picture Editing.* New York: Rhinehart, 1951.

KENNEDY, BRUCE M. *Community Journalism.* Ames: Iowa State University Press, 1974.

Time-Life Publications. *Photojournalism.* New York, 1972.

WEST, RANDY. Editorial, Corydon (Indiana) *Democrat,* May 14, 1971.

Chapter 7

American Newspaper Publishers Association. *ANPA News Research Report* No. 2 (1967) and No. 3 (1976). Washington.

Association for Education in Journalism. *Journalism Quarterly,* Spring 1977. Minneapolis.

———. *Newspaper Research Journal.* Minneapolis.

BUSH, CHILTON R., and others. *The Newspaper and Its Public.* Stanford (Calif.): Stanford University Institute for Communication Research, 1957.

McCOMBS, MAXWELL, and LEE BECKER. *Using Mass Communication Theory.* Englewood Cliffs, N.J.: Prentice-Hall, Inc., 1979.

McCOMBS, MAXWELL, DONALD SHAW, and DAVID GREY. *Handbook of Reporting Methods.* Boston: Houghton Mifflin, 1976.

VAN FLEET, ROBERT S. "The Reader Surveys of Ottaway Newspapers, Inc." Campbell Hill, N.Y.: Ottaway Newspapers, 1978.

Chapter 8

American Press Institute Design Seminar. Hayward Blake, Richard A. Curtis, Harold Evans, Gus Hartoonian, Peter Masters, and Louis Silverstein. Washington, D.C., 1978.

ARNOLD, EDMUND C. *Modern Newspaper Design.* New York: Harper & Row, Pub., 1969.

BONDURANT, BILL, TRUEMAN FARRIS, and MIKE FINNEY. "Map Making: A Must for Today's Newspaper." *Associated Press Managing Editors Report, 1978.* New York.

CLICK, J. W., and GUIDO STEMPEL, III. "Reader Response to Modern and Traditional Front Page Makeup." American Newspaper Publishers Association News Research Center study delivered at Ohio University, Athens, Ohio, June 1974.

REHE, ROLF F. *Typography: How to Make It Most Legible.* Carmel, Ind.: Design Research International, 1974.

———. "Is Unjustified Typesetting Justified?" *Technical Communication,* First Quarter, 1978. Washington, D.C.

Chapter 12

PIPER, MORLEY L. *Positive Impressions.* Salem, Mass: New England Newspaper Advertising Bureau, 1976.

Chapter 15

BURTON, PHILIP WARD. *Advertising Copywriting* 4th ed. Columbus, Ohio: Grid Publishing, Inc., 1978.

CAPLES, JOHN. *Tested Advertising Methods* 4th ed. Englewood Cliffs, N.J.: Prentice-Hall, Inc., Reward Paperbacks, 1980.

EDWARDS, BETTY. *Drawing on the Right Side of the Brain: A Course in Enhancing Creativity and Artistic Confidence.* Los Angeles: J. P. Tarcher, Inc., 1979.

HAFER, W. KEITH, and GORDON E. WHITE. *Advertising Writing.* St. Paul: West Publishing Co., 1977.

MALICKSON, DAVID L., and JOHN W. NASON. *Advertising: How to Write the Kind That Works.* New York: Scribner's, 1977.

NELSON, ROY PAUL. *The Design of Advertising* 4th ed. Dubuque, Ia.: Wm. C. Brown Co., 1981.

NEWSOM, D. EARL. "Pay Close Attention to Ad's Copy," *Publisher's Auxiliary,* Aug. 15, 1977.

OGILVY, DAVID. *Confessions of an Advertising Man.* New York: Ballantine Books, 1963.

Chapter 16

Advertising Age. How It Was In Advertising—1776–1976. Chicago: Crain Books, 1976.

Council of Better Business Bureaus. *Tips On Work-At-Home Schemes.* Washington: 1975.

Encyclopedia Britannica Vol. I. William Benton, Publisher. Chicago: 1972.

Federal Trade Commission. *Guides Against Deceptive Advertising of Guarantees.* Washington: 1960.

HODGINS, ARTHUR G. "Budget and Control," *Principles and Practices of Classified Advertising.* Association of Newspaper

Classified Advertising Managers. Danville, Ill.: 1975.

LEHMAN, CARL R. "Promotion," *Principles and Practices of Classified Advertising.* Danville, Illinois: 1975

Macmillan Educational Corporation. *Collier's Encyclopedia,* Vol. 1. London and New York: P. F. Collier, Inc., 1978.

New Caxton Encyclopedia, The. London: Thames Publishing Co., 1969.

New Encyclopedia Americana—International Edition, The. Danbury, Connecticut: Americana Corporation, 1980.

Chapter 17

Inland Daily Press Association. *Accounting Manual for Daily Newspapers.* Chicago: 1978.

JONES, THOMAS D. Special research and materials prepared for this publication, 1978.

National Newspaper Foundation. *Annual Weekly Newspaper Cost and Revenue Survey, 1979.* Washington: 1979.

TIMMERMAN, SCOTT D. "Ad Revenues Product 78.8% of Total Income," *Editor & Publisher,* March 29, 1980, p. 18.

Chapter 18

Audit Bureau of Circulation. *Weekly Newspaper Record Keeping Aid.* Chicago: 1979.

Editor & Publisher Co., Inc., *Editor & Publisher Market Guide, 1979.* New York: 1979.

National Newspaper Association. "Postal Laws and Regulations," *Federal Laws Affecting Newspapers.* Washington: 1975.

Sales & Marketing Management Magazine. *S&MM Survey of Buying Power.* New York: 1979.

Chapter 19

BERRY, JACKSON V. 11 So. 2d 439 (Miss. 1943); accord, People v. Davis, 238 N.W.S. 2d 981 (City Ct. 1963).

BRANEN, WILLIAM E. *Shoppers and the Newspaper.* Delavan and Burlington, Wis.: Central Printing Corp., 1979.

CHAPPELL, GARY. "Tips for a Successful Shopper." Speech, International Newspaper Advertising Executives, San Francisco, July, 1977.

Kelly v. Board of Trustees, 172 S. W. 1047, 1048 (Ky. App. 1915).

SHARP, DARWIN. Interviews. 1977.

Chapter 20

BLITZ, JOHN E. Special statement prepared for this publication. 1978.

FLIPPO, EDWIN B. *Principles of Personnel Management* 3rd ed. New York: McGraw-Hill, 1971.

HARRIS, J. Research project on minority journalists conducted for the American Society of Newspaper Editors, 1978.

National Newspaper Association. *Federal Laws Affecting Newspapers.* Washington: 1975.

PROCHNOW, HERBERT V. *Speaker's Handbook of Epigrams and Witticisms.* New York: Harper & Row, Pub., 1955.

QUINN, JOHN C. Address to editors of Gannett Company, Inc., Washington, 1978.

VEON, GEORGE. Interview, November 1978.

Chapter 21

BARROW, LIONEL C., JR. "Role of the Black Press in the Liberation Struggle," *Black Press Handbook.* Washington: National Newspaper Publishers Association, 1977.

DAVIS, STEVE. Interview with Paula Poindexter, Feb. 15, 1980.

Editor & Publisher Co., Inc. *Editor & Publisher International Yearbook, 1979.* New York: 1979.

GARRISON, RAYMOND. Interview with Carolyn Stroman, March, 1980

GROSS, BELLA. "Freedom's Journal and the Rights of All." *Journal of Negro History,* 17 (July 1932):241–86.

GUTIERREZ, FELIX. "Spanish-Language Media in America: Background, Resources, History." *Journalism History,* 4 (Summer 1977):34–41, 65–67.

JOHNSON, ALLEN H. "The *Chapel Hill Journal:* A Blueprint for Journalistic Activism." Unpublished M.A. thesis, University of North Carolina—Chapel Hill, 1979.

JOHNSON, THOMAS A. "Despite Decline in Number of Black Papers, Publishers Predict Era of Strong Growth." *New York Times,* Jan. 21, 1979, p. 20.

LA BRIE, HENRY. "The Disappearing Black Press." *Editor & Publisher,* Mar. 17, 1979, p. 53.

———. "2027: Bi-Centennial of the Black Press and the Challenges Publishers Must Meet," *Black Press Handbook.* Washington: National Newspaper Publishers Association, 1977.

MURPHY, SHARON. *Other Voices: Black, Chicano, and American Indian Press.* Dayton: Pflaum/Standard, 1974.

PARKER, ELLIOTT S. "Chinese Newspapers in the United States: Background Notes and Descriptive Analysis." Paper presented to the Association for Education in Journalism, Seattle, 1978.

POINDEXTER, PAULA M., and STROMAN, CAROLYN A. "The Black Press and the Bakke Case: An Analysis of Coverage." *Journalism Quarterly,* in press.

RILEY, SAM G. "The *Cherokee Phoenix:* The Short, Unhappy Life of the First American Indian Newspaper." Journalism Quarterly, 53 (Winter 1976):666–71.

SLATER, PAUL. "San Francisco's Chinese Newspapers: A Lingering Institution." Journalism Quarterly, 46 (Autumn 1969): 606–10.

"Study Finds Blacks Need Own Papers." Editor & Publisher, May 3, 1975, p. 26.

WILLIAMS, JAMES D. *The Black Press and the First Amendment.* New York: National Urban League, 1976.

WOLSELEY, ROLAND E. "The Black Press Assessed," *Black Press Handbook.* Washington: National Newspaper Publishers Association, 1977.

———. *The Black Press, U.S.A.* Ames: Iowa State University Press, 1971.

Chapter 23

BARNHART, THOMAS L. *Weekly Newspaper Management.* New York: Ap-
pleton-Century-Crofts, 1952.

CARDWELL, RICHARD W. Interviews, August 1980.

Editors of the *Harvard Post. How to Produce a Small Newspaper.* Harvard, Mass.: Harvard Common Press, 1978.

MAGUIRE, W. TERRY. Special research and materials prepared for this publication, 1980.

National Newspaper Association. *Federal Laws Affecting Newspapers.* Washington: 1975.

WILLIAMS, HERBERT LEE. *Newspaper Organization and Management* 5th ed. Ames: Iowa State University Press, 1978.

Chapter 24

Associated Press v. *Walker.* See *Curtis Publishing* v. *Butts.*

Cox Broadcasting Co. *v.* Cohn, 420 U.S. 469 (1975).

Curtis Publishing Co. *v.* Butts, 388 U.S. 130 (1967).

Gertz *v.* Robert Welch, Inc., 418 U.S. 323 (1974).

Melvin *v.* Reid, 112 Cal. App. 285, 297 p. 91 (1935).

New York Times *v.* Sullivan, 376 U.S. 254 (1964).

Rosenbloom *v.* Metromedia, Inc., 403 U.S. 29 (1971).

Time, Inc. *v.* Firestone, 424 U.S. 448 (1976).

Wolston *v.* Reader's Digest Association, Inc., - U.S. - (5 Med. L. Rpter. 1273) (1979).

Chapter 25

Albrecht *v.* The Herald Company, 390 U.S. 145 (1968).

American Bar Association. *Antitrust Law Developments.* Chicago: 1975.

BALLOW, ROBERT L. *ICMA Legal Manual.* Reston, Va.: International Circulation Managers Association, 1978.

Citizen Publishing Company *v.* United States, 394 U.S. 131 (1969).

Commerce Clearing House, Inc. *Trade Regulation Reporter.* Chicago.

Continental T.V., Inc. *v.* GTE Sylvania, Inc. 433 U.S. 36 (1977).

Greenville Publishing Co. *v.* Daily Reflector, Inc., 496 F.2d 391 (4th Cir. 1974).

The Kansas City Star Company *v.* United States, 240 F.2d 643 (8th Cir. 1957), cert. denied, 354 U.S. 923 (1957).

Kintner. *An Antitrust Primer.* New York: Macmillan, 1973.

———. *A Robinson-Patman Primer.* New York: Macmillan, 1970.

Lorain Journal Co. *v.* United States, 342 U.S. 143 (1951).

Northern Pacific Railroad Co. *v.* United States, 356 U.S. 1 (1958).

Paul *v.* Pulitzer Publishing Company, 1974 CCH Trade Cases, ¶75, 116 (E.D. Mo. 1974).

Report of the Assistant Attorney General in Charge of the Antitrust Division In the Matter of: Application by the Cincinnati Enquirer, Inc., and E. W. Scripps Company for Approval by the Attorney General of a Joint Operating Agreement Pursuant to the Newspaper Preservation Act (1977).

Sullivan, Lawrence A. *Handbook on the Law of Antitrust.* St. Paul: West Publishing Company, 1977.

Times-Picayune Publishing Company *v.* United States, 345 U.S. 594 (1953).

Unites States *v.* Arnold, Schwinn & Co., 388 U.S. 365 (1967).

United States *v.* Colgate, 250 U.S. 300 (1919).

United States *v.* Topco Associates, Inc., 405 U.S. 596 (1972).

Chapter 26

CLESTER, RICHARD. Interviews, Nov. 1978 and Jan. 1979.

Editor & Publisher, Dec. 30, 1978, p. 57; Jan. 6, 1979, p. 47–50

KREHBIEL, MARION R. Interview, Dec. 1978.

———. Letter to author, Dec. 1978.

———. Additional information sent to editor, May 1980.

The Publisher's Auxiliary, Nov. 6, 1978, p. 5.

Chapter 27

BOYKIN, BILL. Interview, Dec. 1979.

Editor & Publisher International Year Book. New York: 1979.

Inland Daily Press Association. *Membership Directory*. Chicago: 1979.

KUHN, RUTH. Letter, March 18, 1980.

MULLEN, WILLIAM G. Interview, Jan. 1980.

National Newspaper Publishers Association. *Brief History of NNPA*. Dec. 27, 1977.

SARRATT, REED. Letter, Jan. 8, 1980.

SHAW, ROBERT M. Letter, April 1, 1980.

SPEERS, GEORGE. "Founding Dates of Press Associations." Boston: 1980.

State Press Association Managers. Telephone interviews, Nov. and Dec. 1979.

Index

Abstract writing, 17–18
Acquisitions of newspapers, 229
Adverbs, use of, 16
Advertisers. *See also* Advertising.
  and circulation, 151
  and editorial policy, 2, 3
  loyalty of, 232–33
  motives of, 3
  and shoppers published by community
    newspapers, 224
  and total market coverage, 160–61
Advertising. *See also* Advertising gimmicks
    and promotions; Advertising sales;
    Display advertisements; Public no-
    tice advertising; Retail advertising;
    Shoppers.
  in black newspapers, 185
  laws regulating, 208
  and minority press, 186
  pictures in, 42
  placement of, 70
  and postal regulations, 206
  and record-keeping, 144–45
  role in income-producing, 145–46
  in weekly newspaper, 2
Advertising agencies, classified ads and,
    133–34, 137
Advertising clichés, 126
Advertising gimmicks and promotions,
    108–15
  bonus plans for salespeople, 111, 113
  contests, 111
  employee promotions, 113, 115
  ideas for, 113
  and inserts, 113
  motivations for, 109
  and shopping centers, 115
  spare-time, 110
Advertising sales, 100–107, 241. *See also*
    Cooperative advertising.
  approaches, 102
  closing techniques, 103–5
  criteria for success, 100–101
  handling objections, 105–6
  market data and, 95–99
  news and, 151–52
  planning, 101–2
  presentation, 103, 104
  promotional material for, 99
  and seeking new business, 102
  service and, 106–7
  setting goals, 84–85, 91
  tools needed for, 102–3
Advertising salespeople:
  qualifications needed by, 107
  and shoppers, 167
Advertising shoppers. *See* Shoppers.
Advertising supplements, 161
Affirmative action, and personnel manage-
    ment, 182

Age Discrimination Act of 1967, 171
Albrecht v. *The Herald Company,* 226
American Newspaper Publishers Associa-
    tion (ANPA), 2, 3, 238
American Newspaper Representatives, Inc.
    (ANR), 122
Anniversary pictures, 39
Annual breakfast or luncheon, 113
Antitrust laws. *See* Federal antitrust laws.
Antitrust specialist, 222–23
Appropriation tort, 216
Audience. *See* Readership research.
Audit Bureau of Circulation (ABC), 159
Automotive advertising, 134

Balloon race, 113
Black community newspapers. *See* Minor-
    ity press.
Bonus promotions, 111, 113
Bookkeeping system for newspaper, 143–
    45
Boxed head, 63
Boxes and rules, 64
Budget reserves, 86
Bureaucratese, simplification of, 18
Business management. *See* Newspaper
    management.
Business news, 10
Buying patterns, 80–81

Cable television, 243
Canada, newspaper associations in, 234
Capitol News Bureau, 236
Captions, in page design, 62. *See also* Cut-
    lines.
Carrier delivery, 78, 153–54
Carrier status, and federal antitrust laws,
    226
Cartoons, on editorial page, 31
Catchlines, 38
Chinese newspapers, 185
Cincinnati *Enquirer,* Inc., 225–26
Cincinnati *Post,* 225–26
Circulation, 151–61
  and advertising sales, 103
  and antitrust laws, 226–28
  development of, 241
  and evaluation of newspaper property,
    231
  and home delivery, 153–54
  house-to-house drives, 157
  in-paper promotion, 160
  and mail distribution, 153
  management of, 152
  and marketing concept, 152
  of minority newspapers, 184
  Newspaper-in-Education program, 160
  and nonduplicating coverage, 164

Circulation *(Continued)*
  and nonsubscriber lists, 168
  and postal regulations, 161
  promotion, 159–60
  and rates, 160
  and record keeping and revenue plan-
    ning, 157, 159
  revenue from, 145–46, 151
  and sampling, 154–57
  of shoppers, 163
  and single copy sales, 152–53
  and subscription renewals, 157
  tips for growth of, 161
  and total market coverage, 160–61
  trends in, 161
  unpaid, 159
Citizen Publishing Company v. *United
    States,* 225
Civil Rights Act of 1964, 170–71
Classified advertising, 133–42
  copywriting, 141–42
  headlines for, 141–42
  historic background, 133
  national, 133–34
  role of, 142
  and shoppers, 166
  sources of information on, 142
  standards of acceptance, 139–40
Classified advertising sales:
  budgets for, 139
  contracts for, 137
  creative selling, 140–41
  organization of, 134–35
  phone rooms for, 134–35
  and promotion, 137–39
  rates for, 135–37
  training for, 135
Classified rate card, 135, 136
Clayton Antitrust Act, 219, 221–22
"Cold type" systems, 72–73. *See also* Com-
    puter typesetting revolution.
Collective bargaining, 197–200
Colonial journalists, 5
Color, 64, 66
  and display ads, 131–32
Color photography, 64
Color tissue overlay, for advertising sales,
    103
Column rule, 64
Column width, 61
Combination advertising rate, for newspa-
    per and shopper, 166–67
Common supplements, 165–66
Communication:
  and maintaining nonunion status, 191
  and personnel management, 176–77
Community journalists, and courage, 4
Community newspapers. *See also* Minority
    press; Shoppers.
  and access to news, 207–8
  and advertising. *See* Retail advertising.
  as business. *See* Newspaper manage-
    ment.
  business news coverage, 10
  changes in, 240
  compared with suburban newspapers, 8
  crime news reporting, 11–12

Community newspapers *(Continued)*
  editorial page, 27–32
  evaluation for purchase. *See* Evaluation of newspaper property.
  farm news, 13
  feature stories, 13
  future challenges to, 242–43
  health news, 13
  and invasion of privacy issues, 214, 216–18
  and labor relations. *See* Labor relations.
  legal issues affecting, 207–9
  and libel. *See* Libel.
  as majority of American press, 1–2
  news reporting for, 7–14
  obituaries, 13–14
  and offset, 4–5
  personal items, 12–13
  pictures, 13
  publication of shoppers by, 223–25
  religious news, 10–11
  role of, 14
  school news, 9–10
  and sports news, 12
  statistics on, 2
  women's page, 12
Compensation plans. *See* Salaries.
Competition, from new types of media, 243
Comprehensive, for display ads, 127
Computer typesetting revolution, 71
Conditional privilege, 211–12
Consent, as defense to civil defamation action, 211
Conspiracy to monopolize, 221
Contempt of court, 208
Content characteristics, 48
Contests, and advertising promotion, 111
Continental TV, Inc. v. *GTE Sylvania, Inc.,* 227
Controlled circulation publications, postal regulations, 207
Convicted persons, publishing names of, 11
Cooperative advertising, 82, 116–22, 241
  disadvantages of, 120–21
  funding based on sales of, 117
  legislative control of, 121
  and manufacturers, 117, 120
  mechanics of, 117
  method, 116–17
  requirements for qualifying for, 118–19
  retailers and, 120
  and small retailers, 121–22
Copy block:
  sizes, 61–62
  and white space, 64
Copyright law, 208–9
Copywriters, guidelines for, 124–26, 141–42
Corrections, 12
Correspondents, and news pictures, 43
Cost study, and newspaper management, 145–49
County commissioners' meetings, 8
Courage, and community journalists, 4
Court news, 11–12
Courtrooms, reporter access to, 208
Cox Broadcasting Corp. v. *Cohn,* 216

"Create-an-Ad" contest, 124
Credit cards, and subscriptions, 161
Credit lines, 38
Crime news, 11–12
  headlines and, 25
Criminals, glorifying, 12
Cropping, 36, 57
Curtis Publishing Co. v. *Butts,* 212–13
Cutlines, 13, 38
  and newspaper page design, 58

Dardanell Publications, 108–15
Decertification, 202
Decks, 63
Defamation, defined, 211
Delivery, preparations for, 78
Demographic analysis of newspaper readership, 48–49
Departmental and merchandise-line budget, 82
Discharge, 201–2
Discipline, 201–2
Dismissal. *See* Discharge.
Display advertisements:
  and clichés, 126
  and color, 131–32
  creating, 123–32
  design principles, 127–29
  guidelines for copywriters, 124–26
  headlines for, 126
  illustrations for, 131
  layout, 127
  length of copy, 125–26
  placement of, 129
  production techniques, 132
  purposes, 124
  stock art for, 131
  theme of, 124
  typesetting tips, 130–31
  typography for, 129–30
  and visualization of ad, 126–27
Downstyle headlines, 63
Drawings, for display ads, 131
Dummies, 75
Duotones, 64

Editing:
  of editorials, 30
  electronic, 73
  news pictures, 36–38
Editorializing, in headlines, 23
Editorial page, 27–32, 242. *See also* Editorial writing.
  contents of, 31–32
  pictures, 42
  recommended reading on, 32
  role of, 27
Editorial policy:
  and advertisers, 2, 3
  on news pictures, 35–36
Editorial tear sheets, for advertising sales, 103
Editorial writing, 29–31
  in black newspapers, 185
  sources of ideas for, 29

Editorial writing *(Continued)*
  style of, 31
  subjects for, 27–28
  tone of, 28–29
Editor-photographer relationship, 33–34, 35
Election campaigns, local, 9
Employee benefits. *See* Fringe benefits.
Employee handbooks, 177
Employees. *See* Personnel management.
Employee training, 182
Employment interview, 172–74
Employment Retirement Income Security Act of 1974, 171
Equal Employment Opportunity Act of 1972, 171. *See also* Affirmative action.
Equal Pay Act of 1963, 171
Evaluation of newspaper property, 230–33
  guidelines for, 230–31
  market factors, 231
  and market loyalty, 232–34
  and potential for new products, 232
  and potential growth, 233

Fact graphics, 58
Fair comment, as defense against libel actions, 212
Fair Labor Standards Act, 171
Fairness in reporting, 11
False light tort, 216
Family news pages, pictures on, 39
Farm news, 13
Feature graphics. *See* Flavor graphics.
Feature writing, 13
  and avoidance of liability, 217–18
  in shoppers, 169
Federal antitrust laws, 219–28
  and carrier status, 226
  Clayton Act, 221–22
  and expansion of metropolitan dailies, 222–23
  Federal Trade Commission Act, 222
  historic background, 219
  and joint operating agreements, 225–26
  and price controls, 226–27
  Sherman Antitrust Act, 219–21
  and shopper published by community newspaper, 223–25
  and shoppers, 166–67
  and territorial route restrictions, 227
  and tying arrangements or refusals to deal, 227–28
Federal Trade Commission Act, 219, 222
Firing. *See* Discharge.
First Amendment. *See also* Invasion of privacy; Libel.
  attacks against, 243
  and Constitutional privilege, 212–14
Flat, 76
Flavor graphics, 58
Format characteristics, 48. *See also* Newspaper page design.
"Fragmentation of the market," 80
Free circulation publications, and postal regulations, 206. *See also* Shoppers.

Freedom of Information Act, 207–8
Freedom of speech, 4. *See also* First Amendment.
Fringe benefits, 176
    and maintaining nonunion status, 192
Front page, 55, 56

Gertz v. *Welch*, 213–14
Glossary, 245–46
Grand Tour concept, 113
Graphics, and newspaper page design, 58–59
Greenville Publishing Company v. *Daily Reflector, Inc.*, 223–24
Group ownership, 5

Hammers, 63
Headlines. *See also* News headline writing.
    for classified ads, 141–42
    in color, 64
    for display advertisements, 126
    for editorial page, 31
    in page design, 62–63
    and readership research, 49, 50, 51
    size of type for, 63
"Headlinese," 24
Health news, 13
"Hen and chicks" approach, 39
Hiring, 172–74
Home delivery:
    and circulation, 153–54
    and newspaper-owned tube systems, 154
Hood. *See* Boxed head.
Horizontal agreements, 220

Informational notice, 204
Initials, in headlines, 23
Inland Daily Press Association (IDPA), 239
    cost and revenue studies, 146, 149
In-paper promotion, 160
Inquirer-Sun (Columbus, Georgia), 4
Inserts, 78. *See also* Subscription insert cards.
    for advertising sales, 113
International Brotherhood of Teamsters, 190
International Mailer's Union (IMU), 188, 190
International Printing and Graphic Communications Union, (IP&GCU), 188, 189–90
International Society of Weekly Newspaper Editors (ISWNE), 239
International Typographical Union (ITU), 188–89
Internship programs of state press associations, 236
Intrusion tort, 216–17
Invasion of privacy, 214, 216–18
    and appropriation of one's name or likeness for commercial purposes, 216
    defenses to action for, 217

Invasion of privacy *(Continued)*
    and intrusion into an individual's affairs or seclusion, 216–17
    and publication of facts that place individual in false light, 216
    and public disclosure of private facts about an individual, 214–16
    and public figures, 217
Investigative reporting, and avoidance of liability, 217–18
Italic type, 60

Jails, reporter access to, 208
Job application, 175
Joint operating agreements, 225–26
    Cincinnati case, 225–26
Journalism education:
    growth of, 5–6
    and state press associations, 236
    total newspaper concept, 6
Journalistic ethics, 3
Juvenile lawbreakers, publishing names of, 12

Kansas City Star Company v. *United States*, 228
Key words in headlines, 24–25
Kickers, 63
Ku Klux Klan, 4

Labeling, 68–69
Labor contracts, administration of, 201
Labor relations, 188–202. *See also* Newspaper unions.
    and administering labor contracts, 201
    and decertification, 202
    and discipline and discharge, 201–2
    and maintaining nonunion status, 191–94
    and problems of partial unionization, 193–94
    and strike preparation, 198
    and union organizing campaign, 194–97
Laws. *See* Federal antitrust laws; Invasion of privacy; Legislation; Libel.
Layout. *See also* Newspaper page design.
    of display advertisements, 127
    of news pictures, 38–39
    of picture pages, 39
Leads, 20
Legal notices. *See* Public notice advertising.
Legislation:
    and access to news, 207–8
    and acquisition of weekly newspapers, 229–30
    on classified advertisements, 140
    and personnel management, 170–72
    and state press associations, 235–36
Letters column, 32
Libel, 210–14
    avoidance of, 217–18
    and Constitutional privilege, 212–14
    and crime stories, 11

Libel *(Continued)*
    and defamation, 211
    defenses to, 211–12
    defined, 211
    hazards for editors and reporters, 215
    headlines and, 25
Libel insurance, 218
Libel laws, 241
Lighting, for posed pictures, 35
Linage figures, for advertising sales, 103
Line drawings, 76
Line length, 60–61
    for advertising copy, 130
Linotype machines, 71–72
Local government, news coverage of, 8–9
Lorain Journal Co. v. *United States*, 220

Mail distribution, 78, 153
Maine Press Association (MPA), 237
Market. *See also* Market research; Readership research.
    penetration of. *See* Penetration of market.
    relevant, legal definition of, 220–21
Marketing. *See* Circulation.
Marketing representative, role of, 95
Market research:
    and advertising sales, 95–99
    and circulation, 152
    data requirements, 96
    and evaluation of newspaper property, 232–33
    importance of, 241
    sources of information, 96–98
    use of data, 98–99
Melvin v. *Reid*, 215–16
Memo billing, in co-op advertising, 117
Merchandising trade-out, in co-op advertising, 117
Metropolitan dailies:
    antitrust actions by community newspapers against, 222–23
    audiences for, 2
    compared with hometown newspapers, 3
Minority journalists, 186
Minority press, 183–87
    circulation of, 184
    defined, 183
    future of, 186–87
    historic background, 183
    news coverage in, 184–85
    readership of, 185
    role of, 186
    staffs, 185
    unique problems of, 185–86
Minutes of collective bargaining meetings, 199
Mistakes, in obituaries, 14
Modifiers:
    in headlines, 23
    placement of, 19
Modular design, 55
Money-back guarantee, and circulation, 157, 158

Monopolization. *See* Federal antitrust laws.
Municipal council meetings, 8

National Newspaper Association (NNA), 238
National newspaper concept, 1
National Newspaper Foundation, cost study by, 145–46
National Newspaper Publishers Association (NNPA), 186, 239
New York Press Association (NYPA), 238
New York Press Service, 238
New York Times, 2
New York Times Appraisal System, 178–81
New York Times v. *Sullivan,* 212
News, access to, 207–8
News (Davis, Oklahoma), 4
News headline writing, 22–26
  basic rules, 23–24
  counting method, 25
  and "headlinese," 24
  key word principle, 24–25
  and libel, 25
  and misleading qualifiers, 22
  staff involvement in, 25–26
  time and space problems, 23
Newspaper advertising. *See* Advertising.
Newspaper Advertising Bureau (NAB), 122
Newspaper antitrust suits. *See* Federal antitrust laws.
Newspaper associations, 234–39, 242
  national and international, 238–39
  reasons for joining, 239
  role of, 234–36
  state press associations, 235–38
Newspaper careers, 242
Newspaper groups, acquisition of weeklies by, 229–30
Newspaper Guild, 188, 189
Newspaper industry, and antitrust laws. *See* Federal antitrust laws.
Newspaper-in-Education program, 160
Newspaper management, 143–50
  and cost study, 145–49
  and maintaining nonunion status, 191–92
  problems of, 241
  and record keeping, 143–45
  rules for problem spotting, 150
Newspaper ownership, difficulties of, 242
Newspaper page design, 55–70
  and boxes and rules, 64
  and captions and headlines, 62–63
  and color, 64, 66
  and controversial devices, 63
  and copy block sizes, 61–62
  and cutlines, 58
  functions of, 55
  goals of, 70
  and graphics, 58–59
  and justified vs. unjustified lines, 61
  and labeling, 68–69

Newspaper page design *(Continued)*
  and packaging elements, 66–68
  and photographs, 55–58
  and readership research, 66
  and tabloids, 66
  and TNP planning, 69–70
  and typeface, 59–61
  and white space, 64
Newspaper personnel. *See* Personnel management.
Newspaper Preservation Act (1970), 225–26
Newspaper production, 71–78
  centralization of, 72
  and display ads, 132
  and dummy pages, 75
  and electronic editing, 73
  getting pictures onto pages, 77
  and offset platemaking, 77
  and offset printing, 78
  and pasteup, 75–76
  and preparation for delivery, 78
  and preparation of presses, 77–78
  and processing pictures, 76
  and proofreading, 74–75
  technology and, 71–72
  and typesetting, 72–74
Newspapers. *See also* Community newspapers; Newspaper management; Newspaper production.
  eligibility for carrying public notices, 205
  headlines and credibility of, 22
  research on characteristics, 48
  response to shoppers, 164
  sales in 1978 of, 229
  value of. *See* Evaluation of newspaper property.
Newspaper unions, 188–90
  and collective bargaining, 197–200
  and community newspapers, 5
  and decertification, 202
  defined, 190–91
  historic background, 188
  response to organizing campaign, 194–97
News pictures, 33–43
  cutlines, 38
  editing, 36–38
  on editorial pages, 42
  and editor-photographer relationships, 33–34, 35
  good, 33
  layout of, 38–39
  and picture pages, 39
  policy on, 35–36
  posed, 34–35
  in sections, 39, 42
  in small newspapers, 42–43
News Reporter (Whiteville, North Carolina), 4
Newsstand sales, 152–53
News writing, 240. *See also* News writing basics.
  and advertising sales, 151–52
  on local government, 8–9
  in shoppers, 169

News writing basics, 15–21
  avoidance of wordiness, 15–19
  leads, 20
  use of neutral words, 20–21
  use of verbs, 19
"No-interest ad dollars," 82
Nonduplicating coverage, 164, 166
Nonsubscribers, lists of, 167–68

Obituaries, 13–14
Occupational Safety and Health Act of 1970, 171
OCR, 73
Offset printing, 77, 78
  and pictures, 13
  preparation of presses, 77–78
Ohio Newspaper Association (ONA), 237–38
Oklahoma Newspaper Foundation, 236
Oklahoma Press Association (OPA), 236–37
Operating statement of newspaper, 143–45

Packaging, 66–68
Page design. *See* Newspaper page design.
Page dummies, 69
Page negatives, 77
Pasteup, for display ads, 127
Pasteup artist, 75–76
Paul v. *Pulitzer Publishing Company,* 228
Penetration of market, and evaluation of newspaper property, 231
"Penny saver," 5
Performance appraisal, 177
  forms for, 178–81
Personal items, 12–13
  in suburban newspapers, 8–9
Personnel management, 170–82, 241. *See also* Labor relations.
  and affirmative action, 182
  changes in, 172
  and changes in work force, 172
  and changing demands of employers, 172
  and changing demands of government, 170–72
  and communication, 176–77
  and compensation plans, 174, 176
  and employee handbooks, 177
  and employee records, 174
  and employee training, 182
  and fringe benefits, 176
  new concerns in, 176–82
  and performance appraisal, 177–81
  and selection and placement of employees, 172–74
Photographs, 59
  and avoidance of liability, 217
  for display ads, 126–27, 131
  and invasion of privacy, 216–17
  and newspaper page design, 55–58
  processing, 76
Photojournalism. *See* News pictures.

Phrases, simplification of, 16–17
Picture essay, 39
Picture group, 39
Picture morgue, 42
Picture pages, 39
Pictures, 13. *See also* News pictures; Photographs.
    in ads, 42
    and page makeup, 77
Picture story, 39
Pioneer journalists, 5–6
Political journalism, early, 5–6
Posed pictures, 34–35
Postal regulations, 206–7
    and circulation, 161
    and controlled circulation publications, 207
    "50 percent plus one" rule, 168
    and statement of ownership, management, and circulation, 207
Prepositions, use of, 16
"Prepublication sense," 2
Press associations. *See* Newspaper associations.
Pressroom, 78
Price-fixing agreements, 226–27
Primary data, 96
Probate notice, 204
Production. *See* Newspaper production.
Project budget, 82
Promotion:
    of advertising sales, 99
    of circulation, 159–60
    of classified advertising sales, 137–39
    of minority press, 185
    of public notices, 205
Proofreading, 74–75
    on pages, 76
Proof sheets, 36
Props, for posed pictures, 35
Public accounting notice, 204
Public disclosure torts, 214–16
Public figures:
    and invasion of privacy, 217
    and libel, 212–14
Public notice advertising, 203–5
Public records, publication of material from, 216
Public relations budget, 82
Pulitzer Prize, 3, 4

Qualifiers, in headlines, 22
Quotes:
    accuracy in, 11–12
    in headlines, 23
    paraphrasing, 17

Readability, and line length, 60–61
Readership. *See also* Readership research.
    loyalty, evaluation of newspaper property and, 232
    minority press, 185
    predictors of, 49–50
    of weekly newspaper, 2–3

Readership research, 44–54. *See also* Market research.
    and attitudes and behavior, 50–51
    benefits of, 45
    on design, 55
    on entire newspaper, 46–47
    focus of, 45–47
    goals of, 47
    on newspaper advertising, 108
    and newspaper characteristics, 48
    and newspaper page design, 66
    organizing, 48–53
    on packaging, 66
    and personal characteristics of newspaper audience, 47
    and placement of photographs, 57
    and previous research, 52–53
    and readership factors, 49–50
    on responses to newspaper, 47–48
    response to, 45
    and scientific sampling, 44–45
    on sections, 46
    and selection of researcher, 53
    on specific items, 46
    on typeface, 59–60
    using, 51–52
Record keeping:
    and circulation development, 157, 159
    and newspaper management, 143–45
    in personnel management, 174
Refusal to deal, 228
Religious news, 10–11
Retail advertising. *See also* Retail advertising budget.
    media selection, 79–80
    reasons for, 79
    and sales trends, 81
    and setting sales goals, 84–85, 91
    and timing for biggest market, 80–81
Retail advertising budget:
    and allocation of space, 86–87
    and development of schedule, 87–88
    forms for, 91–93
    methods, 82–88
    reasons for, 81–82
    and typical sales patterns, 88–90, 94
Retailer sales patterns, typical, 88–90, 94
Reverse type, 60
Robinson-Patman Act (1936), 121, 221
Rough layout, for display ads, 127
Rule of reason standard, 220
Rumor, in crime news, 11

Salaries, 174, 176
    and maintaining nonunion status, 192
    on minority newspapers, 185–86
Sampling, 154–57
    in-city, 156–57
    regulations on, 156
    of rural routes, 154, 156
    second-class bulk mail form, 155
Sans serif type, 59
    and advertising, 130

Scanners, and proofreading, 74–75
School news, 9–10
"Screened PMTs," 77
Second-class mail permit, 153, 155
    applying for, 206–7
    and "50 percent plus one" rule, 168
    postal regulations on, 206
Secondary data, 96
Sections, readership research on, 46
Semibold type, 60
Sentences, length of, 18–19, 125
Serif type, 59
Sherman Antitrust Act, 219–21
    and joint operating agreements, 225
    and shoppers published by community newspapers, 223–24
    and tying arrangements, 224
Shoppers, 162–69
    and antitrust laws, 166–67, 223–25
    and classified advertisements, 166
    and common supplements, 165–66
    effectiveness of, 164–65
    future of, 168–69
    historic background, 162–63
    and list of nonsubscribers, 167–68
    and Newspaper Preservation Act, 225
    and newspaper subscriptions, 164
    profit-making status of, 223–24
    reasons for success of, 163
Shopping centers, and newspaper advertising, 115
Side head, 64
Single copy price, 160
    and evaluation of newspaper property, 231
Single copy sales, 152–53
Sizing, 36, 38, 57
Small newspapers. *See* Community newspapers.
Southeastern Black Press Institute (SBPI), 186
Southern Newspaper Publishers Association, Inc. (SNPA), 239
Spanish-language newspapers. *See* Minority press.
Specialization, 1
Special pages, readership research on, 46
Special task budget, 82
"Spec" layouts for advertising sales, 102–3
Sports news, 12
    in black newspapers, 185
Sports pages, readership research on, 46
Sports pictures, 39, 42
Sports writers, 19
Statement of ownership, management, and circulation, 207
State press associations, 235–38
    founding dates of, 237
Stock art, for display ads, 131
Strike, preparation for, 198
Subheads, 62
Subscribers lists, and second-class rates, 206

Subscription insert cards, 153
Subscription rates, 160
   and evaluation of newspaper property, 231
Subscription renewals, and circulation, 157
Subscriptions, and credit cards, 161
Suburban newspapers:
   classified advertising staff, 135
   compared with community newspapers, 8
   news reporting for, 7–9

Tabloids, and newspaper page design, 66
Target coverage, 164
Tear sheets, for advertising sales, 103
Technology:
   changes in future in, 242
   and news pictures, 33
   and personnel management, 172
   small newspapers and, 5
Territorial route restrictions, and federal antitrust laws, 227
Testimonial letters, for advertising sales, 103
Third-class bulk mail, 153, 207
Thumbnail, for display ads, 127
Time, Inc. v. *Firestone,* 214
Time management, for newspaper advertising salespeople, 101–2
Time-Picayune Publishing Company v. *United States,* 227–28

Timing, and advertising effectiveness, 80–81
Tint blocks and rules, 64
To an Anxious Friend (White), 4
Total market coverage (TMC), 164
Total newspaper concept, 1
   and offset, 4–5, 6
Total newspaper product (TNP) planning, 69–70
Truth:
   as defense to civil defamation action, 211
   and public disclosure torts, 215–16
Tube systems, 154
Tying arrangements, 221–22, 227–28
   and shoppers owned by community newspapers, 224
Typesetting, 73–74
Typography, 59–61
   and copy block size, 61–62
   for display ads, 129–30
   for headlines, 62–63
   in journalism education, 5–6
   length of line, 60–61
   x-height of, 59–60

United States v. *Arnold Schwinn & Company,* 227
United States v. *Colgate,* 228
United States v. *Topco Associates, Inc.,* 227
Unjustified typesetting, 61
Upward communication, 176–77

Verbs, use of, 19
Vertical agreements, 220
Video display tube (VDT), 6, 73
   and headline counting, 25
   and proofreading, 74–75
Visuals, for advertising sales, 103

Want ad pages. *See* Classified advertising.
Warning notice, 204
Web-fed rotary press, 78
Wedding pictures, 39
Weekly newspaper. *See* Community newspapers.
White space, 64
"Window," 77
Women's page, 12
Wordiness, avoidance of, 15–19
Words:
   neutral, 20–21
   short, for headlines, 24
Writing. *See* News writing basics.

x-height, 59–60

Yellow pages, and prospective newspaper advertisers, 102

Zero-base budget, 82